Prevention and Intervention in Childhood and Adolescence 20

Special Research Unit 227 – Prevention and Intervention in Childhood and Adolescence
An interdisciplinary project of the University of Bielefeld

conducted by *Prof. Dr. Günter Albrecht, Prof. Dr. Otto Backes, Prof. Dr. Michael Brambring, Prof. Dr. Detlev Frehsee, Prof. Dr. Wilhelm Heitmeyer, Prof. Dr. Klaus Hurrelmann (Coordinator), Prof. Dr. Franz-Xaver Kaufmann, Prof. Dr. Hans-Uwe Otto, Prof. Dr. Helmut Skowronek*

Early Childhood Intervention

Theory, Evaluation, and Practice

Edited by
Michael Brambring
Hellgard Rauh
Andreas Beelmann

Walter de Gruyter · Berlin · New York 1996

Prof. Dr. Michael Brambring,
Department of Psychology, Research Center 227, University of Bielefeld, Germany

Prof. Dr. Hellgard Rauh, Institute of Psychology, Department of Philosophy 2,
University of Potsdam, Germany

Dr. Andreas Beelmann
Institute of Psychology, University of Erlangen-Nürnberg, Germany

With 57 figures and 71 tables

♾ Printed on acid-free paper which falls within the guidelines of the
ANSI to ensure permanence and durability.

Library of Congress — Cataloging-in-Publication Data

Early childhood intervention. : theory, evaluation, and practice / edi-
ted by Michael Brambring, Hellgard Rauh, Andreas Beelmann.
XII, 514 p. 17 × 24 cm. — (Prevention and intervention in
childhood and adolescence : 20)
"Special Research Unit 227 — Prevention and Intervention in
Childhood and Adolescence" — P. facing t.p.
Revised and edited versions of the papers presented at a sym-
posium held in 1993.
Includes index.
ISBN 3-11-015410-2 (alk. paper)
1. Handicapped children — Services for.   I. Brambring,
Michael, 1943-   .   II. Rauh, Hellgard.   III. Beelmann,
Andreas.   IV. Sonderforschungsbereich 227 — Prävention und
Intervention im Kindes- und Jugendalter.   V. Series.
HV888.E14   1996
362.7 — dc20
96-30392
CIP

Die Deutsche Bibliothek — Cataloging-in-Publication Data

Early childhood intervention : theory, evaluation, and practice ;
[with 71 tables] / ed. by Michael Brambring ... —
Berlin ; New York : de Gruyter, 1996
(Prevention and intervention in childhood and adolescence ; 20)
ISBN 3-11-015410-2
NE: Brambring, Michael [Hrsg.]; GT

Printing: WB-Druck, Rieden am Forggensee. — Binding: Mikolai GmbH, Berlin. — Cover
Design: Hansbernd Lindemann, Berlin. — Photo: Jan Lukas, Hamburg.
Printed in Germany.

Preface

The symposium "Early Childhood Intervention: Theory, Evaluation, and Practice" was held in Bielefeld (Germany) at the end of 1993 by the Special Research Unit "Prevention and Intervention in Childhood and Adolescence." The Special Research Unit consists of 10 projects from the disciplines of educational science, law, psychology, sociology, and sports science that are studying issues aimed at improving the living conditions of children and adolescents. The meeting in 1993 was the 10th international symposium held by the Special Research Unit. The Special Research Unit has been in existence since 1986 and is funded by the German Research Association (DFG).

The 10th international symposium tackled the topic of early intervention for children with impairment or at-risk. About 40 guests and speakers were invited from Germany, the Netherlands, Russia, Sweden, Switzerland, and the USA. They presented papers on their research, their ideas, and the practice of early intervention in their own countries.

This book contains revised and edited versions of the papers presented at the symposium and covers numerous aspects of the multidisciplinary, multimethod field of early intervention.

The proceedings are divided into five sections. The first section presents an overview of the early intervention systems in Germany, Russia, Sweden, and the USA. The four papers emphasize common trends and paradigms, but also clear differences in practical implementation and in the legal and financial frameworks of early intervention in the individual countries.

The second section deals with not only assessment but also developmental trajectories in children with impairment or at-risk. One focus of the papers is on the analysis of the interaction between biological and psychological risk factors and their impact on childhood development.

The third section addresses the core of early intervention: the family system. The topics covered by the individual papers include which family characteristics promote the development of children with impairments, the effects of the birth of a handicapped child on family structure and family living conditions, and how formal and informal social support networks can support the efforts of the family.

The fourth section deals with issues in the planning and evaluation of early intervention. The papers tackle the way research is carried out on early intervention, the quality of the planning and implementation of early intervention, and the effects of implemented early intervention measures on childhood development. Evaluation research no longer focuses on whether early intervention has any effect at all, but on which type of early intervention at which time and how intensive is most effective for which type of child and which families.

The fifth section not only reports concrete research findings from intervention studies of children with impairments or at-risk, but also describes methods of intervention that may promote childhood development. The final paper looks forward to the 21st century and deals with the training of early intervention personnel in the near and distant future.

The expert discussions during the symposium were stimulating and cast light on shared features but also differences in early intervention in the various countries. From both a scientific and a practical perspective, early intervention presents a continuous challenge to provide assistance to families with children with impairment or at-risk.

The editors wish to thank all participants for their valuable contributions to the symposium. We also wish to thank those persons who helped to compile this book: *Jonathan Harrow*, who tackled the translation of texts into English and text corrections; *Peter Sonneck*, who set up the text, tables, and figures; *Gertrud Immelmann*, who was responsible for the final corrections; and *Irene Stieglitz*, *Manuela Twisden-Peareth*, and *Petra Udelhoven*, who were responsible for typing the numerous manuscripts.

Bielefeld, Potsdam, and Erlangen-Nuremberg, March 1996

Michael Brambring
Hellgard Rauh
Andreas Beelmann

Contributors

Bailey, Don, Ph.D.,
Frank Porter Graham Child Development Center, CB #8180, University of North Carolina 27599, USA, e-mail: bailey.fpg@mhs. unc.edu

Beckman, Paula, Ph.D.,
Professor Special Education, Department of Special Education, 1380 Benjamin Building, University of Maryland, College Park, Maryland, USA, e-mail: Paula J Beckman@ un-mail.umd.edu

Beelmann, Andreas, Dr.,
Institut für Psychologie, Universität Erlangen-Nürnberg, Bismarckstr. 1, D-91054 Erlangen, Germany

Brack, Udo B., Professor Dr.,
Humboldt-Universität zu Berlin, Institut für Rehabilitationswissenschaften, Abteilung Interventionsmethoden, Georgenstr. 36, Unter den Linden 6, D-10099 Berlin, Germany

Brambring, Michael, Professor Dr.,
Abteilung für Psychologie, Sonderforschungsbereich Prävention und Intervention, Universität Bielefeld, Postfach 10 01 31, D-33501 Bielefeld, Germany, e-mail: m. brambring@hrz.uni-bielefeld.de

Bricker, Diane, Ph.D.,
Early Intervention Program, 5253 University of Oregon, Eugene, Oregon 97403-5253, USA, e-mail: Diane Bricker@ccmail.uoregon.edu

Chatelanat, Gisela, Dr.,
9, rte de Drize, FAPSE, Université de Genève, CH-1227 Carouge, Switzerland, e-mail: chatelan@ibm. unige.ch

Dijkxhoorn, Yvette, Dr.,
Rijks Universiteit Leiden, Valegroep Orthopedagogick, Wassenaarseweg 52, P. O. Box 955, NL-2300 Leiden, Netherlands

Dunst, Carl J., Ph.D.,
Senior Research Scientist, Child and Family Studies Program, Allegheny Singer Research Institute, 320 E. North Avenue, Pittsburgh, PA 15212, USA, e-mail: dunst@ asri.edu

Esser, Günter, Professor Dr.,
Institut für Psychologie, Philosophische Fakultät II, Lehrstuhl Klinische Psychologie, Universität Potsdam, Postfach 60 15 53, D-14415 Potsdam, Germany

Fewell, Rebecca R., Ph.D.,
The Debbie Institute, University of Miami School of Medicine, P. O. Box 014621, Miami, FL 33101, USA

Janson, Ulf, Professor Dr.,
University of Stockholm Department for Education, S-10691 Stockholm, Sweden, e-mail: janson@ped.su.se

Klein, Gerhard, Professor Dr.,
Fakultät für Sonderpädagogik der
Pädagogischen Hochschule
Ludwigsburg, Außenstelle
Reutlingen, Postfach 23 44,
D-72713 Reutlingen, Germany

Largo, Remo H., Prof. Dr. med.,
Universitäts-Kinderklinik, Steinwie-
senstr. 75, CH-8032 Zürich,
Switzerland, e-mail: Largo@kispi.
unizh.ch

Neuhäuser, Gerhard, Prof. Dr. med.,
Director, Abteilung Neuropädiatrie
und Sozialpädiatrie, Zentrum für
Kinderheilkunde der Justus-Liebig-
Universität, Feulgenstr. 12,
D-35385 Gießen, Germany

Odom, Samuel L., Ph.D.,
Box 328, Peabody College,
Vanderbilt University, Nashville,
TN 27203, USA, e-mail: odom@
uansv5.vanderbilt.edu

Oerter, Rolf, Professor Dr.,
Ludwig-Maximilians-Universität
München, Lehrstuhl Entwicklungspsychologie und Pädagogische Psychologie, Leopoldstr. 13, D-80802
München, Germany, e-mail:
oerter@mip.paed.uni-muenchen.de

Ottenbacher, Kenneth J., Ph.D.,
Office of the Dean, School of Allied Health Sciences, University of
Texas Medical Branch, 11th & Me-
chanic Streets, Galveston, TX
77555-1028, USA, e-mail:
kottenba%sahs@mhost.utmb.edu

Peterander, Franz, PD Dr.,
Ludwig-Maximilians-Universität
München, Forschungsgruppe "Sy-
stemanalyse Frühförderung", Leopoldstr. 13, D-80802 München,
Germany, e-mail: peterander@lrz.
uni-muenchen.de

Rauh, Hellgard, Professor Dr.,
Institut für Psychologie, Philosophi-
scheFakultät II, Universität
Potsdam, Am Neuen Palais 2, Postfach 60 15 53, D-14469 Potsdam,
Germany, e-mail: rauh@fub-46.
zedat.fu-berlin.de

Sarimski, Klaus, Dr.,
Kinderzentrum München, Heigl-
hofstr. 63, D-81377 München,
Germany

Schlack, Hans G., Prof. Dr. med.,
Director, Kinderneurologisches
Zentrum, Waldenburger Ring 46,
D-53119 Bonn, Germany

Sheehan, Robert, Ph.D.,
Director, Student Assessment &
Program Review, Office of the Vice
Provost for Strategic Planning,
Cleveland State University,
Cleveland, OH 44115, USA,
e-mail: r.sheehan@csu-e.csuohio.
edu

Simeonsson, Rune, Ph.D.,
School of Education & Frank Porter
Graham Child Development Center,
University of North Carolina,
Chapel Hill, NC 27599-8180, USA,
e-mail: simeonsr.fpgsm@mhs.unc.
edu

Trivette, Carol M., Ph.D.,
Director, Family, Infant and Pre-
school Center for Family Studies,
Western Carolina Center, 300 Enola
Road, Morganton, NC 28655, USA

Usanova, Olga, Professor Dr.,
Scientific-Practical Center
"Correction", The Institute of Psychology and Pedagogy, Bochkova
5#129, Moscow 129085, Russia

Contents

Part Three
Family and the Early Intervention Process

Part Four
Planning and Evaluation of Early Intervention

Part Five
Practice of Early Intervention

M. Brambring, H. Rauh, and A. Beelmann (Eds.). (1996). *Early childhood intervention: Theory, evaluation, and practice* (pp. 1-8). Berlin, New York: de Gruyter.

Introduction

Michael Brambring

In the West, and increasingly in Eastern Europe as well, early intervention for impaired and at-risk children is viewed as a public obligation that calls for the mandatory provision of personnel and material resources. Services cover medical, educational, psychological, and financial support to the families concerned when their children are neonates, infants, and preschoolers. However, countries vary greatly in the legal and financial framing of provisions, in the criteria for eligibility of families to such programs, in the type and extent of assistance available, and in the amount of scientific research carried out in the field.

In simple terms, the early intervention system can be depicted as a triangle figure with the points representing three major components (see Figure 1).

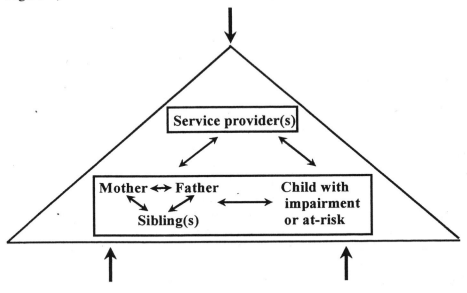

Figure 1. The triangle-model of early intervention.

The first component refers to the impaired or at-risk child for whom an early intervention is indicated. The second component refers to the rest of the family - the parents and eventual siblings - whose social living conditions are affected by the impaired child. Although both components can be separated for the purpose of analysis, they represent a single unit that has to be viewed as a complete family system in practice. The third component refers to the service providers that offer support to the family system.

The simplification in Figure 1 is that the interactions between the components are represented as being weighted equally, and the dynamic process, that is, the temporal changes in the interactions, is not visible. For example, one can assume that the effects of the impaired child on the emotional well-being of the family are more severe at the announcement of the diagnosis than during the further course of the child's development. One can also anticipate that the parents' well-being is once more subject to strong fluctuations during critical life phases such as the child's enrollment in preschool or school. The type of service provision can also be assumed to lead to differences in the weighting and in the temporal course of early intervention. Both the impact on the family and parental involvement will be much greater in a home-based early intervention program than in outpatient care within the framework of a physiotherapeutic treatment. Furthermore, it is evident that early intervention is not static, but subject to dynamic changes, that is, the contents of early intervention change greatly as a function of the child's biological or developmental age. As yet, little is known about the weighting and the temporal changes of these intra- and extrafamilial interactions.

The papers in this book can be classified, though not always unequivocally, to the three components in Figure 1.

The overviews in the first part of the book describe the entire systems of early intervention in individual countries - *Carl J. Dunst* (USA), *Gerhard Klein* (Germany), *Ulf Janson* (Sweden), and *Olga Usanova* (Russia). The papers describe their historical development and their current state, and point out desirable improvements in the early intervention systems in each country. They provide the reader with a good insight into the common features, but also the differences, in the early intervention systems of the four countries involved.

The papers on evaluation research, particularly those of *Robert Sheehan* and *Scott Snyder*; *Kenneth J. Ottenbacher,* and *Andreas Beelmann* can also be viewed as overviews on analyzing the entire early intervention system. These papers address the scientific analysis of the ways in which early intervention can be effective. Not only the effects on childhood development and childhood behavior but also, to an increasing extent, the effects on the family system are taken into account. These effects are conceived as being multidimensional, calling for a multiple assessment of both child and family characteristics. Alongside impact evaluation, evaluation research focuses increasingly on program-process evaluation. This concerns the structure of the services provided and their specific impact on the child and the family.

Evaluation research is far from being able to provide satisfactory answers to all the questions that arise. This is due to the difficulties in confirming effectiveness statistically because sample sizes are generally so small; the specific procedures to control outcome because of the heterogeneity of types of impairment; the confounding of many layers of child and family characteristics that makes it harder to confirm effectiveness; and the difficulty in assessing the complex interactions resulting from the multiplicity and variety of services provided.

Currently, early intervention is understood as the provision of support to families with impaired or at-risk children. This change from a more child-centered to an increasingly family-centered paradigm is strongest in the USA where an Individualized Family Service Plan (IFSP) has to be compiled at the beginning of each early intervention. The family takes a decisive role in compiling this plan, and it has to take account of their central wishes and individual needs. The goal of family-centered, socioecological early intervention is to improve the socioemotional living conditions of families, to overcome the parents' uncertainties about how to bring up an impaired child, and to strengthen parental competencies and resources.

Early intervention focuses on a family system that has generally become strongly imbalanced as a result of the child's impairment or risk of impairment. The central task of research and practice is to ascertain which intra- and extrafamilial variables contribute to a stabilization of family structure and the well-being of all family members.

Figure 2 lists some of these variables that relate to and interrelate with the aspired goals.

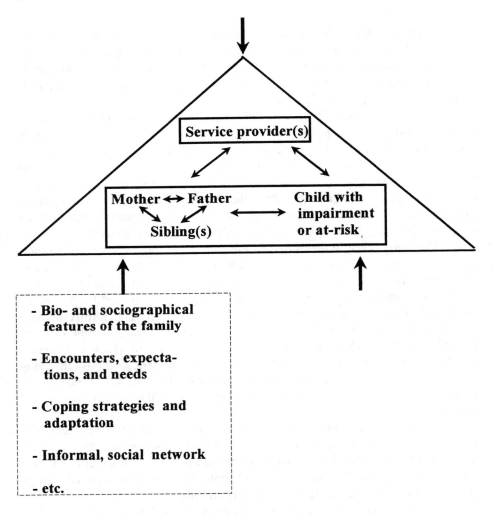

Figure 2. The triangle-model of early intervention including family
          variables.

These family variables are dealt with in detail in the papers of *Gerhard
Neuhäuser*; *Klaus Sarimski*; *Rune J. Simeonsson,* and *Carol M. Trivette,
Carl J. Dunst,* and *Deborah Hamby.* These and other variables listed are
interrelated and impact on the dynamic process by which the family
members process the impairment or risk to development of their child and
try to stabilize their family system. Research has only recently begun to
explain the complex structure of these variables, and the papers mentioned
above present major findings on these issues.

Figure 3 displays the central variables that impact on the development of the impaired or at-risk child. The psychosocial variables are linked closely to the family variables mentioned above.

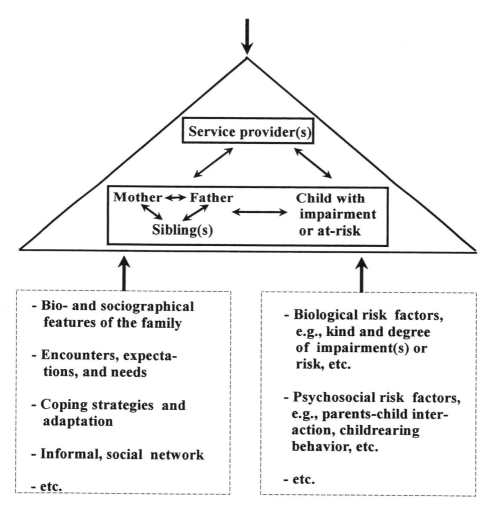

Figure 3. The triangle-model of early intervention including family and child variables.

The papers of *Günter Esser, Manfred Laucht,* and *Martin H. Schmidt* as well as *Remo H. Largo* and *Kurt von Siebenthal* analyze how biological and psychosocial risk factors interact in child development. One outcome of this increasingly large body of research is that psychosocial factors carry more weight than biological ones, though under the constraint that this finding can be ascertained only after the infant phase and seems to apply only to children without profound multiple impairments.

The development and intervention studies of *Michael Brambring*; *Yvette M. Dijkxhoorn*, *I. A. van Berckelaer-Onnes*, and *D. van der Ploeg*; *Rebecca R. Fewell*, and *Hellgard Rauh*, *B. Schellhas*, *S. Goeggerle*, and *B. Müller* emphasize the particular developmental conditions of impaired and at-risk children. These empirical studies do not focus on comparisons with nonimpaired children, but on presenting the specific development of blind, autistic, low-birthweight, and Down's syndrome children.

Figure 4 presents the complete triangle-model of early intervention that also includes the expert-related variables.

The central question in this problem area refers to the impact of the service system through the service providers on what happens during early intervention. On the one hand, this concerns the organizational and internal structure of the early intervention system, but, on the other hand, it also concerns an explanation of how far service providers are affected by the training and working conditions within the early intervention system, and how these structural framing conditions impact on their expectations, values, and competencies with regard to an early intervention that supports the child and the family.

The papers of *Don Bailey*; *Paula J. Beckmann*; *Gisela Chatelanat*, and *Franz Peterander* and *Otto Speck* tackle such problems in the service system. Topics include the integration of impaired children into regular institutions, analyses of the structures of the early intervention system for providing services to the families involved, institutional factors that inhibit or promote professional work, as well as the adequate and future-oriented training of professionals to meet the demands of a family-centered, community-oriented, and interdisciplinary early intervention.

The mostly implicit expectations and values that professionals have toward their work are assigned a great importance for early intervention work. Incongruities between the expectations and values of parents and those of professionals can lead to far-reaching tensions in the practical work of early intervention.

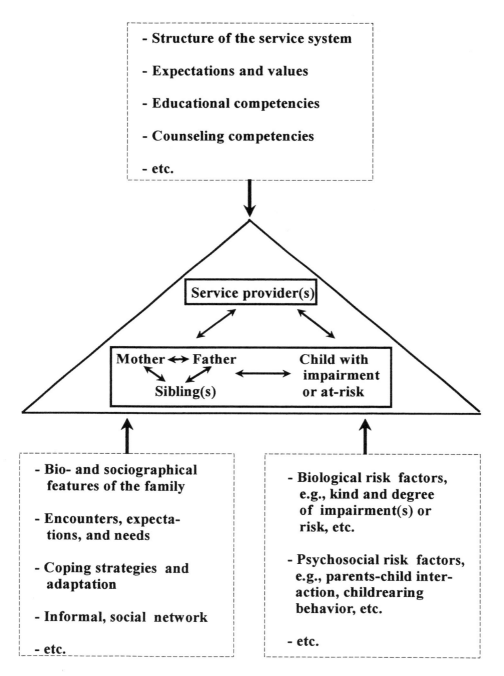

Figure 4. The triangle-model of early intervention including family, child, and expert-related variables.

Educational competencies refer to the child-related skills of the professionals. Counseling competencies cover the family-oriented abilities of the professionals to provide appropriate emotional and educational support. Of central importance to early intervention are the diagnostic, interventional, and evaluative skills of the professionals in their dealings with the child and the entire family. The papers of *Udo Brack*; *Diane Bricker*; *Samuel L. Odom* and *Scott R. McConnell*; *Rolf Oerter,* and *Hans Schlack, B. Ohrt, R. H. Largo, R. Michaelis,* and *G. Neuhäuser* address these multilayered issues of adequate methods for planning, carrying out, and evaluating early intervention.

The complete triangle-model of early intervention reveals the complex structure and various variables that can be effective within the total early intervention work. Research is still a long way from a complete assessment of the structure of early intervention in all its interactions and temporal changes. However, by using multivariate designs, an attempt is being made to perform a more precise and differentiated assessment of the complex structure of early intervention in order to allow the best possible service to meet the individual needs of families with children facing specific impairments and risks.

Part One

International Perspectives:

Models, Systems, and Practices of Early Intervention

M. Brambring, H. Rauh, and A. Beelmann (Eds.). (1996). *Early childhood intervention: Theory, evaluation, and practice* (pp. 11-52). Berlin, New York: de Gruyter.

Early Intervention in the USA: Programs, Models, and Practices

Carl J. Dunst

1 Introduction

The term *early intervention* is used broadly in this chapter to refer to a wide array of experiences and supports provided to children, parents, and families during the pregnancy, infancy, and/or early childhood periods of development. This definition is deliberately inclusive so as to encompass a range of programs, initiatives, and entitlements provided by public and private agencies and organizations throughout the USA to pregnant women and families of preschool-aged children.

The kinds of programs now operating in the USA that legitimately may be considered early intervention are described in a subsequent section of the chapter. Although many of the programs have common underpinnings and also share similar assumptions and tenets, they differ in a number of respects with regard to the theories and models that guide practice. The purpose of this chapter is to describe the state-of-practice in early intervention in the USA with particular emphasis on the theoretical bases, conceptual models, and interventive practices that underscore these programs.

The chapter is divided into three sections. The first includes a historical overview of the evolution of early intervention in the USA. The second includes brief descriptions of contemporary early intervention programs and practices. An analysis of a number of features of 12 major kinds of early intervention programs is presented in the third section of the chapter.

2 Historical Spheres of Influence

The roots of current early intervention practices in the USA as well as the rationale for such practices have been attributed to a myriad of sources by a number of scholars (see Caldwell, 1970; Condry, 1983; Halpern, 1990; Richmond & Ayoub, 1993; Shonkoff & Meisels, 1990). These underpinnings can be conveniently organized into five nonmutually exclusive "spheres of influence": Early Childhood Education, Theories of Child Behavior and Development, Experimental Effects of Environmental Interventions, Governmental Initiatives, and Grass Roots Initiatives. Developments and advances in each of these spheres at different times during the past century have coalesced repeatedly, and progressively built a stronger and stronger case for early intervention. This is not to say that early intervention has not been without its critics at almost every juncture in its evolution (e.g., Bartz & Bartz, 1970; Ferry, 1981; Holt, 1987; McNemar, 1940; Pinneau, 1955). Proponents of early intervention, however, far outnumber critics; to a larger degree, based on the kinds of milestones and evidence described next.

2.1 Early Childhood Education

The first sphere of influences can be traced to several different kinds of early childhood education program. The "idea" that early education could serve as a means to influence behavior and development originated in Europe. The kindergarten programs established by Froebel (1782-1852) in Germany (Froebel, 1904), and the nursery schools begun by Montessori (1912) in Italy and McMillan (1919) in England, are often cited as important developments emphasizing the value of early education. Although these contrasting early childhood "movements" differed in terms of their goals, instructional practices, and expected outcomes, both nonetheless emphasized the importance of preschool experiences as a factor contributing to child growth and development.

The first public kindergarten in the USA was established in St. Louis in 1872 (Peterson, 1987). By the turn of the century, there were more than 5,000 of these programs in the USA (Osborn, 1980). To this day, kindergartens are considered as an important early experience preparing children for academic-oriented schooling.

Nursery schools in the USA became increasingly common in the 1920s, and by the early 1930s, there were more than 200 of these programs scattered throughout the country. "Over half were associated with colleges and universities (that) housed some of the most productive child development laboratories of the time; the other half were run as private schools or were sponsored by child welfare agencies" (Richmond & Ayoub, 1993, p. 3). The majority of these programs emphasized the use of nurturing experiences to facilitate social-emotional development, in contrast to school readiness, which was fundamental to most kindergarten programs.

There was a proliferation in the number of nursery schools in the 1930s and 1940s as a result of two federally funded initiatives: The Work Projects Administration (WPA) and the Landam Act. The WPA established nursery schools during the Great Depression for 2- to 6-year-old children to insure employment opportunities for unemployed teachers and to support the well-being of children of unemployed parents. The Landam Act nursery schools were established during World War II to provide childcare to women working on behalf of the war effort. Both programs differed from other nursery programs in one major, significant way. "Neither program has as its primary goal meeting the needs of children, but rather assisting adults to work outside the home in times of economic and national crisis" (Richmond & Ayoub, 1993, p. 4). Not surprisingly, therefore, the two programs were terminated at the end of the depression and war, respectively. Nonetheless, they have significantly influenced the course of early childhood education since their inception (Osborn, 1980).

2.2 Theories of Child Behavior and Development

The assertion that experiences early in a child's life influence behavior and development, especially during the infancy and preschool periods, is a cornerstone of the rationale for early intervention. A number of human development and psychological theories that emphasize the view that behavior is influenced by environmental circumstances have proven instrumental in building a case for early intervention. These theories repeatedly challenged the strongly held contention that intelligence and development are principally genetically predetermined (e.g., Burt et al., 1934; Galton, 1869; Jensen, 1969). Successive "generations" of theory have built a stronger and stronger case that the kinds of experiences encountered early in life indeed shape the course of child behavior and development.

Theoretical advances during the past century reveal numerous instances of conceptual formulations that "pushed" the scientific community to at least consider, if not acknowledge, the role the environment plays in shaping behavior and development, including "early intervention." For example, early work by John Dewey (Dewey & Dewey, 1915) and John B. Watson (1928) among others (see Hunt, 1961) built a foundation that stands today as central to the idea of the importance of early learning opportunities.

Three books published between 1949 and 1964 added substantially to the argument that early experiences made a difference in a child's life. The first was Hebb's (1949) *The Organization of Behavior*. Among other valuable contributions, Hebb noted the importance of early perceptual (primary) learning as a foundation for later learning, especially of the kind that prepared children for cognitively mediated instruction. The second was Hunt's (1961) *Intelligence and Experience*. In this most influential book, Hunt built a convincing case for the plasticity of intelligence, and how environmental enrichment and deprivation can, respectively, have positive and negative effects on child behavior and development. The third was Bloom's (1964) *Stability and Change in Human Characteristics* in which he concluded that environmental influences on child behavior and development are greatest during the preschool years. Collectively, these three scholarly books described theories that bolstered the belief that experiences early in a child's life could have either positive or negative effects on behavior and development.

At least two other theoretical orientations captured the attention of scholars interested in the effects of environmental influences on child behavior and development. One was Piaget's (1952) theory of infant development with its emphasis on child-environmental transactions as a determinant of behavioral competence. The other was infant operant learning theory (Lipsitt, 1969; Watson, 1966) and the contention that the environmental (reinforcing) consequences of child behavior significantly influenced a child's learning capacity. Despite the fact that these two theories are derived from different worldviews (Reese & Overton, 1970), Piaget's theory and infant learning theory played central roles as part of building a case for early intervention; and both have been used for guiding the development of early intervention practices (e.g., Dunst, 1981; Lancioni, 1980).

In the intervening years since the above theories were formulated and tested empirically, several other theoretical and conceptual frameworks have emerged for explaining the complex influences environmental experiences have on child behavioral and developmental outcomes. They include Bronfenbrenner's (1979) ecological model of human development, Sameroff and Chandler's (1975) model of transactional development, and a host of environmental risk-protection-opportunity models of behavior and development (see Dunst, 1993; Dunst & Trivette, 1994, for reviews of such models). These as well as other theories and models of early behavior and development (see, especially, Meisels & Shonkoff, 1990) significantly expanded our understanding of the *ecology* of early intervention.

The evolution of early intervention in the USA has mirrored advances in child development theories during the past century. On the one hand, theories emphasizing the importance of early development, and environmental influences as a determinant of this development, have built a convincing case for the potential benefits of early intervention. On the other hand, recent advances have provided the kinds of frameworks that have significantly expanded the manner in which early intervention has been conceptualized and implemented (e.g., Dunst, 1985; Zigler & Berman, 1983).

2.3 Experimental Effects of Environmental Interventions

A number of early studies specifically aimed at overcoming the detrimental effects of adverse environmental conditions are a third sphere of influence building a case for early intervention. The first include a series of studies conducted by Skeels and his colleagues (Skeels, 1966; Skeels & Dye, 1939; Skeels et al., 1938) who investigated the effects of several different kinds of experience on the mental status of institutionalized children. The results, taken together, yielded evidence indicating that children receiving supplemental stimulation and those participating in an environmental enrichment program outperformed control subjects on a number of immediate and long-term outcome measures.

Several studies conducted by Spitz (1945; Spitz & Wolf, 1946) with institutionalized children found that a sample of infants reared in a nursery in which incarcerated mothers had the opportunity to interact with their infants on a daily basis demonstrated significantly better outcomes compared to infants reared in an unstimulating founding home. In several experimental investigations conducted by Kirk (1950; Kirk & Johnson, 1951), an educational intervention program implemented with preschoolers with disabilities was found to have advantageous effects in comparison to a control group not having the same educational opportunity. The findings from the Spitz and Kirk studies as well as the results from the Skeels' investigations proved extremely important in the evolution of early intervention.

The more contemporary roots of early intervention are the experimental early intervention programs with children from poor backgrounds initiated in the early 1960s. These included the Perry Preschool Project (Weikart et al., 1978), the Early Training Project (Gray & Klaus, 1970; Klaus & Gray, 1968), and the Institute for Developmental Studies Early Enrichment Project (Deutsch et al., 1983) among others (see, especially, Bronfenbrenner 1975; Lazar et al., 1982; Moss et al., 1982). The majority of these experimental projects are perhaps best represented by the Consortium for Longitudinal Studies (1983), a group of 11 early intervention projects serving environmentally at-risk children and their families. The consortium was formed to answer questions about the immediate and long-term effectiveness of early education programs specifically aimed at promoting the behavior and development of children from low-income families. Collectively, the findings from these studies produced "convincing evidence that high-quality preschool education programs had positive, long-term effects on the subsequent school experiences of participating children" (Condry, 1983, p. 28).

A new generation of experimental early intervention programs was initiated in the 1970s and 1980s, both building upon previous efforts and significantly expanding the scope and types of intervention provided to the participant children and their families. Among the best known are the Carolina Abecedarian Project (Ramey & Campbell, 1987), Project Care (Wasik et al., 1990), the Parent-Child Development Centers Project (Andrews et al., 1982), the Infant Health and Development Program (1990; Ramey et al., 1992; Spiker et al., 1991), the Yale Child Welfare Project (Provence & Naylor, 1983; Trickett et al., 1982), the Prenatal/Early Infancy Project (Olds et al., 1986), and the Brookline Early Education Project (Hauser-Cram et al., 1991) (see Campbell, 1983; Farran, 1990; Schorr & Schorr, 1988; Sonenstein et al., 1991; Upshur, 1990; for reviews of other important projects and programs). These investigations were significant because they either included different groups of children and families as the focus of intervention (e.g., low-birthweight children, teenage mothers); and/or demonstrated the added benefits of different kinds of interventions, and in particular, those that had an ecological orientation and focus (Bronfenbrenner, 1975).

In addition to the types of programs and investigations described above, a host of early intervention studies of children with identifiable disabilities were conducted throughout the 1970s and 1980s that produced encouraging results (see Bricker et al., 1984; Dunst, 1986; Dunst & Rheingrover, 1981; Dunst, Snyder, & Mankinen, 1988, for reviews). Despite the fact that many of these studies have methodological problems, they nonetheless yielded evidence indicating that children with disabilities were able to achieve levels of development and acquire behavioral capabilities that, less than 25 years ago, were considered unattainable by these youngsters.

Evidence demonstrating the environmental effects of early education and intervention on the behavior and development of infants and preschoolers has proven particularly important as part of building a case for, and shaping the direction of, early intervention in the USA. The results from these studies produced the kinds of data needed to support the contention that environmental experiences afforded prospective parents and young children and their families could be used effectively to influence the course of child development.

2.4 Governmental Initiatives

A fourth sphere of influence has been a host of federal initiatives. For almost 100 years, the US government has played a significant role in emphasizing the importance of different kinds of early intervention services, despite periods of retrenchment (Shonkoff & Meisels, 1990). Early initiatives included the establishment of a Children's Bureau in 1912 and the enactment of Title V of the Social Security Act in 1935. Among the activities of the Children's Bureau were federal grants to establish health care services to promote the health and development of the nation's most vulnerable children and to decrease infant mortality. The Title V initiative authorized the establishment of three programs – Maternal and Child Health Services, Services for Crippled Children, and Child Welfare Services – to develop health-related and protective services for children living in economically depressed areas of the USA and for children experiencing crippling diseases.

A number of federal initiatives begun during the 1960s contributed to the development of early intervention services in the USA. One of these included the Social Security Act Medicaid provisions of 1965, which established the Early and Periodic Screening, Diagnosis and Treatment Program (EPSDT). This program not only promoted increased attention to the health care needs of children living in poverty, but also emphasized the importance of the provision of early intervention (broadly conceived) as part of an "overall plan of care."

The Economic Opportunity Act of 1964 was the springboard for the most far-reaching experiment of the 1960s – Project Head Start. From its beginning, Head Start emphasized the development and delivery of a comprehensive system of compensatory education, health services, nutritional services, social and psychological services, and parent and family involvement. Head Start was envisioned as a program that would lead children from poor backgrounds on a path out of poverty (Zigler & Valentine, 1979). Head Start, like other early intervention programs for environmentally at-risk children, has not been without its critics (see Condry, 1983). The legacy, impact, and contributions of the program, however, are undeniable; and recent legislative increases in funding for the program attest to the fact that Head Start is now deeply woven into the fabric of early intervention in the USA.

During the 1960s, 1970s, and 1980s, several landmark pieces of legislation were enacted that significantly advanced the development of early intervention services for children with disabilities and those at-risk for poor

developmental outcomes (see especially Hebbeler et al., 1991). Public Law
(PL) 90-538 established the Handicapped Children's Early Education
Assistance Act of 1968 (subsequently renamed Early Education Programs
for Children with Disabilities) to promote the development, validation, and
dissemination of model-demonstration programs for infants, toddlers, and
preschoolers in need of early intervention. The passage of PL 94-142
(Education for All Handicapped Children Act of 1975) included provisions
that provided states with incentives to establish special education and related
services for 3- to 5-year-old preschoolers. By far the most important piece
of legislation ever enacted on behalf of children birth to 3 years of age was
the Part H Infant and Toddler Program established as part of PL 99-457
(Education for All Handicapped Children Act Amendments of 1986) and
reauthorized as part of PL 102-119 (Individuals with Disabilities Act
Amendments of 1991). The Part H program has enabled states to plan,
develop, and implement statewide systems of comprehensive, coordinated,
multidisciplinary, and interagency early intervention programs for infants
and toddlers with disabilities and those deemed developmentally delayed.
States, at their discretion, also can serve children considered at-risk for poor
developmental outcomes. The cornerstones of the infant and toddler program
is the Individualized Family Service Plan (IFSP), the significant role given
to families with regard to the selection of services that are provided to
eligible children and their parents, and the manner in which these services
are delivered.

When placed in historical context, the role the US government has
played in the evolution of early intervention has been sometimes reactive
and sometimes proactive. Regardless of the motivations for federal
involvement, the well-being of our very youngest citizens and the betterment
of their lives and the lives of their families has been a central feature of
early intervention-related public policy for nearly a century. Several recent
federal initiatives that broaden the meaning of early intervention even more
are described in the next section of the chapter.

2.5 Grass Roots Initiatives

A fifth sphere of influence building a foundation for current early
intervention practices was a number of grass roots initiatives that
emphasized the important role parents, families, and communities play in
supporting the optimal development of children and protecting children from
harm (Halpern, 1990; Kagan & Shelley, 1987; Weiss & Halpern, 1991;
Weissbourd, 1987). Chief of these were the establishment of settlement

houses intended to "strengthen the capacity of the family for self-direction and growth" (Weissbourd, 1987, p. 44). Hull House, established in the 1890s in Chicago by Jane Addams (1935), is perhaps the best known example of this kind of grass roots effort. As noted by Weiss and Halpern (1991):

> Many components of [the] settlement workers' community foreshadowed the community-action strategies of the 1960s, and can still be found in today's parent support and education programs... . Settlement [house] workers conducted parent education to immigrants [and] provided practical assistance with child care, housing, legal and other problems. (p. 12)

Another 1890s effort that shaped the provision of advice and guidance to families from poor backgrounds around issues of child-rearing was the emergence of "Friendly visiting." "Friendly visiting involved home visits to poor families by well-to-do women who provided a mixture of support, scrutiny, and advice" (Weiss & Halpern, 1991, p. 12). According to Boyer (1978), friendly visiting was seen as a way to alleviate problems associated with living in poverty, and many of the assumptions and strategies of this approach can be found in the home-visiting programs of the 1960s, 1970s, and 1980s.

A long-standing interest in the importance of parent education and the transmission of childrearing advice by grass roots organizations has had an enduring influence on contemporary early intervention practices. The establishment of both the National Congress of Parents and Teachers in 1897 (which later became the Parent-Teacher Association) and the National Council of Parent Education (Brim, 1959) are examples of these kinds of efforts. Although these efforts were typically directed at the parenting and childrearing practices of middle-class families, they indirectly influenced parents from less advantaged and poor backgrounds by member parents and professionals who engaged in community work with families of children who today would be considered "at-risk" (Weiss & Halpern, 1991).

Another grass roots influence on contemporary early intervention practices is the self-help and mutual support group movement (Weissbourd, 1987). Among these are the many parent-to-parent support groups that have been formed over the past 25 years. Collectively, these groups "share a common belief in mutual support and action, [in which] parents can effectively confront and reduce feelings of helplessness and isolation to better protect and nurture their children" (Pizzo, 1987, p. 228).

    The combined effect of the above kinds of grass roots movement was
the development of community-based early intervention (Halpern, 1990) and
family support and education programs (Weissbourd & Kagan, 1989; Zigler
& Black, 1989) that emphasized the empowerment and self-determination
of program participants and the important role informal supports play in
promoting the flow of community resources to strengthen family functioning
and parenting abilities. These programs, at least until recently, emphasized
primarily the support available by indigenous community members as
primary sources of support for meeting family needs (see, especially,
Halpern, 1990). Grass roots family support and education programs started
to appear in more frequent numbers in the early and middle 1970s, and by
the late 1980s, there were between 3,000 and 4,000 of these programs
scattered throughout the USA and Canada.
    The contemporary interest in community-based family support programs
as a particular kind of early intervention was a major factor leading to the
establishment of the Family Resource Coalition (FRC) in 1981 (Weissbourd,
1987). This organization is a national federation of individuals and
organizations furthering the development of prevention- and promotion-
oriented, community-based programs to strengthen families. The members
represent diverse and heterogeneous kinds of programs working with
pregnant teenagers, teen moms, older pregnant women, incarcerated parents,
substance- abusing parents, families from poor and culturally diverse
backgrounds, migrant families, and so forth, as well as parents simply
interested in childrearing and other kinds of parenting advice and
information. The FRC and its diverse activities and initiatives has played in
the past and continues to play an important role in shaping current thinking,
policy, and practice in the early intervention field (see, e.g., Powell, 1988).

2.6 Summary

Contemporary early intervention in the USA is deeply rooted in a broad
range of activities and events unfolding over the past 100 years.
Collectively, the five spheres of influence described here have frequently
interfaced and often fed one another as wellsprings of information and
evidence about the value and importance of early intervention. The paths
that early intervention took sometimes proved misguided, but the impact and
legacy of past efforts are collectively undeniable. The kinds of programs the
spheres of influence birthed are examined next.

3   The Contemporary Landscape of Early Intervention

The state-of-practice of contemporary early intervention in the USA now encompasses a number of different kinds of programs and initiatives. Early intervention efforts having the greatest impact, and those that hold particular promise are briefly described in this section. An overview of the type presented here will necessarily be incomplete. The reader is referred to Meisels and Shonkoff (1990), Schorr and Schorr (1988), and Sonenstein et al. (1991) for descriptions of additional kinds of early intervention programs and practices.

As noted in the introduction, current early intervention practice in the USA, defined broadly, is quite diverse despite having common historical roots and conceptual underpinnings. Such practices include a variety of federal, state, community, and grass roots initiatives. Early intervention is now provided to children with disabilities, developmental delays, and those at risk for poor outcomes for environmental, medical, and systemic reasons. Many of these programs serve pregnant women, teenage mothers, as well as working parents, incarcerated parents, single parents, foster and adoptive families, and families from culturally diverse backgrounds.

The landscape of contemporary early intervention programs has become expansive. The child him or herself is now rarely the sole focus of early intervention programs or practices. Rather, the child and his or her family, and sometimes the communities in which they reside, are now the emphasis of intervention. Additionally, many of these programs are now guided by conceptual frameworks that emphasize an ecological, social systems approach to building support and resource networks for children and families (Garbarino & Abramowitz, 1992). Still further, a large number of programs have adopted consumer-driven practices in which families play significant roles in identifying their needs and choosing resources that best fit their families' unique life-styles. A number of these programs are described next as a panorama of the landscape. Table 1 summarizes a number of key characteristics of these programs.

3.1 US Department of Education Initiatives

Part H Infant and Toddler Program. The PL 99-457 Part H early intervention program for infants and toddlers birth to 3 years of age and their families provides states funds to develop statewide, comprehensive systems of early intervention.

Table 1. *Major Kinds of Contemporary Early Intervention Programs in the USA*

Organization/Program	Child Characteristics					Program focus
	Age[a]	Type[b]		Family SES[c]		
		Primary	Secondary	Primary	Secondary	
US Department of Education						
Part H Early Intervention Program	B-3	CD,DD	AR	L,M,H		Provides multidisciplinary developmental and therapeutic services to eligible children, service coordination to the children and their families, interagency coordination, transportation services, and individualized family support services.
Part B Preschool Program	3-5	CD	DD	L,M,H		Provides free appropriate public education (FAPE) and related services to eligible children, including special education and child therapy, and the provision of such services in the least restrictive and inclusive environments.
Even Start	B-7	AR,DD	CD	L	M,H	Provides early childhood education services to eligible children, and adult literacy and parent training and education services to adult family members.
US Department of Health and Human Services						
Head Start	3-5	AR,DD	CD	L	M,H	Provides educational, nutritional, health, and other developmental services to eligible children; parent education, social and psychological services to families; and assistance with obtaining other community services and resources.
Parent and Child Centers	B-3	AR,DD	CD	L	M,H	Provides health and social services to participant parents and their children, parent education and support, and educational services to eligible children.
Comprehensive Child Development Program	P-6	AR,DD	CD	L		Provides early intervention, early childhood development services, child care, parent education and training, case management, and health care to eligible children and other family members.

(table continues)

Table 1. *(continued)*

Organization/Program	Child Characteristics			Family SES[c]		Program focus
	Age[a]	Type[b] Primary	Secondary	Primary	Secondary	
Maternal and Child Health Bureau EI Program	P-S	CD,DD, AR		L,M,H		Provides assistance to states for implementing the medical/health component of the Part H early intervention program, creates interdisciplinary and interagency partnerships necessary for continuity in the delivery of early intervention services, and facilitates the development of community-based systems of care.
Family Preservation and Support Program	P-S	AR,DD	CD	L,M,H		Provides family support and preservation services, aftercare and respite care services to eligible families, parent education and support, information and referral services, and other kinds of assistance in obtaining community services and resources.
State Government Initiatives						
State Parent Education Programs	B-5	AR,DD	CD	L	M,H	Provides parent training and education, related services, and assistance with referrals to other community services.
State Family Support Programs	B-5	AR,DD	CD	L	M,H	Provides parent education and support; social, psychological, and referral services; advocacy and community building; and adult literacy opportunities.
Grass Roots Initiatives						
Community-Based EI programs	P-5	AR,DD	CD	L		Provides early child education and development services, parenting advice and guidance, assistance in obtaining community resources and services, and emotional support to parents.
Family Resource Programs	P-S	AR,DD	CD	L,M	H	Provides parent education and support, parent support groups, family-to-family support, respite care and drop-in services, health care and counseling, child and parent advocacy, information and referral services, and various other kinds of family support.

[a] B = birth, P = pregnancy, S = school age, and P-S = pregnancy period to school age. [b] CD = children with disabilities, DD = developmentally delayed, and AR = at-risk.
[c] L = low socioeconomic (SES) background, M = middle SES, and H = high SES.

The Part H program requires states to serve children with disabilities and developmental delays; and, at a state'discretion, children considered at risk for poor outcomes are also eligible to receive services.

The Infant and Toddler Program was begun in 1986. The governor in each state was required to name a "lead agency" to administer the development and implementation of the Part H program. At present, departments of education are the lead agencies in about one third of the states; departments of health are the lead agencies in approximately one third of the states; and, in the remaining one third, state departments of human resources, mental retardation/developmental disabilities, and mental health are the lead agencies. Federal funds available to states were made contingent upon each state meeting 14 requirements and achieving specific implementation milestones (e.g., developing an operational definition of developmental delay, providing comprehensive multidisciplinary evaluations of child needs and family concerns, child find and referral services, and procedural safeguards). All 50 states presently participate in the Part H program, although they differ considerably with respect to the point at which implementation has occurred.

In addition to selecting a lead agency, each governor was required to appoint an Interagency Coordinating Council (ICC) to assist with the development of policies for delivery of early intervention services in the 14 required components as well as assist with the development of recommendations with regard to policy implementation. As noted by Harbin and McNulty (1990), state ICCs have played an instrumental role in shaping the content and direction of the Part H programs.

As noted previously, the hallmark of the Part H program is the Individualized Family Service Plan (IFSP) that must be developed by a multidisciplinary team with a parent or guardian participating as a functioning team member. The IFSP must include outcome statements (goals) for the child and family; the specification of services, resources, and supports for achieving these outcomes; and criteria and methods for measuring success. The IFSP must also name a service coordinator to assist the family in procuring the services, resources, and supports specified in the plan.

The Part H Infant and Toddler Program holds the greatest promise for reaching and serving the largest number of children with disabilities and developmental delays and their families in the USA. State implementation, however, has been hampered by a number of problems either not foreseen or underestimated (see, e.g., Richmond & Ayoub, 1993). Thus, the ultimate success of the program has yet to be determined.

Part B Preschool Program. PL 94-142 enacted in 1975 provided state departments of education incentive funds to serve 3- to 5-year-old children with disabilities. PL 99-457 made continued participation in the Part B program contingent upon states mandating special education and related services to all eligible children ages 3 to 5. Within the first few years of this decade, all states had enacted such a mandate. As part of the PL 102-119 reauthorization of the Part B program, states, at their discretion, were for the first time permitted to include developmental delay as a legitimate eligibility category in addition to those originally included in PL 94-142.

The Part B program was originally intended to be an extension down of PL 94-142 that requires states to provide a free and appropriate public education (FAPE) and related services to all eligible children. The particular services a child receives are described as part of the development of a child-focused Individualized Education Plan (IEP). The utility of IEPs, and the manner in which they have been developed and implemented, however, has been criticized repeatedly (e.g., Billingsley, 1984; Brinckerhoff & Vincent, 1986). The failure of IEPs to deliver on their promise, in part, was a major factor leading to a proposal for a different kind of plan as part of the Part B Infant and Toddler Program described above.

The extension downward of a school-based model to preschoolers with disabilities has, from its beginning, generated considerable controversy. This controversy was addressed directly as part of PL 99-457 and its reauthorization, PL 102-119. States may now, at their discretion, employ the Part H Infant and Toddler Program IFSP requirements and methods of service delivery for serving preschoolers with disabilities rather than use the PL 94-142 IEP requirements.

Even Start. Even Start was enacted by PL 100-297 as a program of the Elementary and Secondary Education Act School Improvement Amendments of 1988 and amended by PL 102-73 (National Family Literacy Act of 1991). The federal government awards funds to state departments of education who, in turn, provide support to local educational agencies (LEAs) to establish Even Start programs.

There are more than 200 Even Start programs operated in 49 states. The program serves children birth to 7 years of age and their parents, who reside in an elementary school attendance area designated as Chapter 1 eligible (meaning that 60% of the children in that school area are from low socioeconomic backgrounds). The program serves primarily children considered at risk for subsequent school failure.

The purpose of Even Start is to provide family-oriented services to help parents become full partners in the education of their children, assist eligible children in reaching their full potential as learners, and provide literacy training for their parents. The law authorizing the program includes three components: early childhood education services for the children and adult literacy and parent training for the children's parents. Program participation requires parent and family involvement in all three components, thus making the services prescriptive rather than tailored to the individual needs of the children and their parents.

3.2 US Department of Health and Human Services Initiatives

Head Start. As previously noted, Head Start was established in 1965 as a community-based, multicomponent education and social services program with a strong emphasis on parental involvement as a key to its success. As noted by Richmond and Ayoub (1993), "Head Start pioneered the practice of intervention aimed at both the child and family" (p. 7).

Head Start serves children 3 to 5 years of age from poor socioeconomic backgrounds and their families. Federal legislation, however, requires that at least 10% of all children enrolled in a Head Start program have identifiable disabilities. There are more than 1,900 Head Start programs located throughout the USA. Most of these are operated by community action organizations rather than publicly funded programs and agencies, which gives them a decidedly community-based orientation.

As originally envisioned, and as practiced today, Head Start addresses the educational needs of both children and their parents, the nutritional and health-related needs of the children, and promotes the use of social and psychological services by program participants by referrals to other programs and agencies. Although it is now well-recognized that the initial goals of Head Start were not likely to be realized from the program design, improvements in the program over the past 25 years have made the expectations for Head Start programs more realistic and attainable. According to Zigler, Head Start is America's most successful educational experiment (Zigler & Muenchow, 1992).

Parent and Child Centers. Parent and Child Centers (PCCs), begun in 1967, serve children birth to age 3 and their families. PCCs were established as an extension down of Head Start programs. As noted by Weiss and Halpern (1991), these programs were "Initially envisioned as a nationwide network of multipurpose family centers, providing parent education, health, and social services to low-income parents with infants from birth to three years of age" (p. 16). There are more than 100 PCCs in operation across the USA.

PCCs serve primarily children and families from poor socioeconomic backgrounds, although many also serve children with disabilities. They are decidedly preventive in focus and orientation, community-based, and responsive to the broad-based needs of both children and their families.

Comprehensive Child Development Programs. The Comprehensive Child Development Program (CCDP), authorized by PL 100-297 (Comprehensive Child Development Act), provided funds to establish child and family support programs to serve families with an unborn child or child under one year of age. There are now 37 of these programs scattered across the USA in 28 states. The programs are designed to provide integrated, comprehensive, and continuous support services to children from low-income families from birth to age 6 and their parents and other household members (Hubbell et al., 1991). The goals of the CCDPs are to prevent the subsequent educational failure of the target children, decrease the likelihood that the children will be caught in a cycle of poverty, and prevent welfare dependency and promote family self-sufficiency and educational achievement.

Each of the 37 CCDPs is mandated to provide the following core services to all participating children and families: early intervention, early childhood development, child care, parent education and training, case management, and health care to children and adults. The programs either provide these services directly or help families become linked with existing services in their communities.

Maternal and Child Health Bureau Early Intervention for Children with Special Health Care Needs Program. The Maternal and Child Health (MCH) Bureau provides assistance to states for ensuring that the medical/health component of the PL 99-457 Infant and Toddler Program is in place for young children with special health care needs and their families by creating interdisciplinary and interagency partnerships necessary to ensure continuity of early intervention services. These goals are accomplished by facilitating the development of community-based systems of early intervention that are comprehensive, family-centered, and fully coordinated (Brewer et al., 1989).

The MCH early intervention initiative is supported by the Maternal and Child Health Services Block Grant to states, which is authorized as Title V of the Social Security Act. The MCH program includes the following major components: (a) leadership, technical assistance, and funding to ensure that necessary health services are available to, and utilized by, young children with special needs and their families; (b) activities that promote collaboration between human service agencies rendering services to young children with special health care needs; (c) collaboration between human services practitioners and the families of these children; and (d) development of community-based systems of care. The MCH Bureau has played an instrumental and important role in shaping the course of early intervention for children with special health care needs as part of a number of capacity-building projects and activities (see, e.g., Johnson, 1990; Shelton et al., 1987).

Family Preservation and Support Program. A new federal initiative just begun provides assistance to states to plan and develop programs to strengthen families and their children. This program will fund a variety of family support, preservation, aftercare, and respite care services. This initiative was made possible by the passage of the PL 103-66 (Family Preservation and Support Services Act of 1993).

PL 103-66 encourages states to develop two types of programs: Family preservation services to prevent imminent foster-care placement and family break-up, and family support services to promote and enhance healthy family development. The latter kind of programs may include any combination of parent education, child development/preschool programs, job counseling, preventive health care, and resources and referral services necessary to link families with other human, health, and social services programs.

The enabling legislation for family preservation and family support programs provides funds to state child welfare agencies to expand existing programs or begin new ones. Family preservation programs will most likely operate within the context of existing community child protection and social services programs, whereas family support programs are expected to operate in local community centers or as home-visiting programs. States, however, have considerable latitude in deciding who is funded, where programs reside, and what are the specific foci of the programs.

Both types of programs will serve families with children of varying ages, although the family support programs will have a decidedly early intervention orientation. The goal of these programs is to increase the capacities of families to nurture their children by making available supports and resources that give families the time and energy, and knowledge and skills, to carry out childrearing responsibilities in a competent and empowering manner. The programs will be preventive and promotive in orientation, be universally available to families in the community in which they are located, and therefore not be targeted to any particular kind of family based on means-tested eligibility criteria. Although the ultimate success of these kinds of family support programs is obviously yet to be determined, the likelihood that they will be successful seems especially great given their broad-based, social systems approach to intervening with young children and their families.

3.3 State Government Initiatives

Family Support and Parent Education Programs. Although the US federal government has played in the past and continues to play an instrumental role in developing early intervention programs, individual states have, on their own, taken the initiative to begin preventive programs to strengthen families (see, especially, Harvard Family Research Project, 1992a,b; Weiss, 1989; Weiss & Halpern, 1991). The pioneering initiatives include the Minnesota Early Childhood Family Education Program begun jointly in 1975 by the State Departments of Education and Community Education, the Missouri Parents as Teachers Program started in 1981 by the State Department of Elementary and Secondary Education, the Connecticut Parent Education and Support Centers Program begun in 1986 by the State Department of Children and Youth Services, and the Maryland Family Support Centers Program started in 1986 by the State Department of Human Resources. Collectively, these programs generally broke with public tradition in which services were rendered only to those children and families deemed poor or at increased risk for poor outcomes.

In the short time since the above pioneer programs were begun, a number of other states have started similar kinds of programs (Arkansas, Kentucky, North Carolina), and several other states are contemplating the development of such initiatives (North Dakota, California, Wisconsin, Alaska, Massachusetts, New Mexico, Illinois). North Carolina, for example, has just embarked upon a bold, innovative program called Smart Start. The authorizing legislation for this program states that:

> (1) Parents have the primary duty to raise, educate, and transmit values to young preschool children, (2) the state can assist parents in their role as the primary caregivers and educators of young preschool children, and (3) there is a need to explore innovative approaches and strategies for aiding parents and families in the education and development of young preschool children. (North Carolina, 1993, p. 192)

This early childhood initiative gives local communities maximum flexibility and discretion in determining the approaches that will be used to improve the: (a) quality and quantity of child care services and early childhood education programs, (b) support services to families, and (c) the coordination of services from public and private sources aimed at strengthening community and family capacity to nurture child development. Programs like Smart Start are predictably the "next" generation of the kinds of early intervention programs that will probably become the *status quo* in the USA in this and the next decade.

Close examination of state government initiatives finds that they are of two different kinds: State Parent Education Programs that place primary emphasis on promoting parenting knowledge and skills that are directed at enhancing child behavior and development (Minnesota, Missouri, Arkansas, Kentucky) and State Family Support Programs that address the broad-based needs of families, including, but not limited to, those pertaining to parenting capabilities (Connecticut, Maryland, North Carolina). As noted below, the differences in the philosophies and methods of the two types of program result in quite different kinds of initiatives despite apparent similarities.

3.4 Grass Roots Initiatives

Two kinds of grass roots programs provide early intervention to young children and their families: (a) community-based early intervention initiatives for children birth to 3 years of age in specific populations of low-income families (Halpern, 1990) and (b) family resources and support programs for parents and young children differing considerably in family backgrounds and living conditions (see, especially, Kagan et al., 1987; Weiss & Jacobs, 1988). Whereas the former tend to focus primarily on parent education and childrearing issues, the latter tend to be much more broader-based in terms of their interventive focus.

Community-based early intervention. According to Halpern (1990), "community-based early intervention programs (are) those in which neighborhood-based agencies employ lay family workers, sometimes in concert with professionals, to provide sustained goal-oriented support to low-income families during pregnancy and/or infancy" (p. 470). Lay workers typically provide parenting advice and guidance; assist families in obtaining community supports, resources, and services; offer encouragement and emotional support; and, of particular importance, "identify and activate latent helping resources in low-income communities" (Halpern, 1990, p. 470). In contrast to community-based family resource programs described next, community-based early intervention programs tend to be more narrowly focused and limited in scope. They differ from the other kinds of early intervention programs described above principally in terms of: (a) their use of lay family workers as the primary agents of service delivery and (b) the grass roots, neighborhood agency affiliation of the programs. The interested reader is referred to Halpern (1990) for an excellent description of this particular kind of early intervention initiative.

Family resource programs. There and now between 3,000 and 4,000 family support programs located throughout the USA (and Canada) that have evolved as grass roots, community-based, and culturally and socially responsive endeavors. These community-based, family support programs aim to significantly alter the ways in which services and resources are delivered to families (see, especially, Kagan et al., 1987; Powell, 1988; Weiss & Halpern, 1991; Weiss & Jacobs, 1988). These kinds of programs are especially diverse and tend to be shaped by the families served by the programs and the ecology of the communities in which they operate. The participants include expectant parents, teen moms, incarcerated parents, adoptive and step parents, families of children considered at risk for any number of socioenvironmental reasons, working parents, parents of children with special needs, families from culturally diverse backgrounds, families of children at risk for or victims of maltreatment, grandparents, and so forth. The programs serving these families offer a variety of services, among which are parent education and support, parent support groups, family-to-family support, respite care and drop-in centers, health care and counseling, child and parent advocacy, information and referral services, and assistance in linking families with other community resources.

Community-based, grass roots family support programs take different forms in different communities, and therefore their diversity defies simple description. They do, however, tend to share common features. According to the Family Resource Coalition (1993), the relationship between program and family is one of equality and respect; participants are viewed as having existing strengths and capabilities, and as a vital resource to themselves, the program, and the broader community; the programs serve as a bridge between the families and other resources outside the scope of the program; parent education, information about human development, and skill building for parents are considered essential elements of the programs; and seeking support and information is viewed as a sign of a family strength and not a weakness. The interested reader is referred to Kagan et al. (1987) and Weiss and Jacobs (1988) for descriptions of the diverse kinds of family resources programs operating throughout the USA.

3.5 Other Early Intervention Programs and Initiatives

The above represent the major kinds of contemporary early intervention programs in the USA. In addition, there are many other programs and initiatives that provide or promote the development of early intervention to young children and their families. A number of these are described briefly here to fill in the details of the landscape of early intervention in the USA. The interested reader is referred to a joint US Departments of Education and Health and Human Services (1989) report to Congress, and Levine (1988), Sonenstein et al. (1991), and Weiss and Halpern (1991) for descriptions of other public and private initiatives.

US Department of Education. The Elementary and Secondary Act of 1988 (PL 100-297) funds two kinds of early intervention programs and service. Part A of the Act provides Local Education Agencies (LEAs) monies to serve children birth to school age from poor backgrounds and their parents. Part D funds grants to states to provide early intervention, special education, and related services to children with disabilities, including those birth to age 5, served by state-operated or supported facilities and programs. Part D funded programs serving children birth to age 3 are required to adhere to the PL 99-457 Part H requirements, whereas programs serving children 3 to 5 years of age must adhere to the PL 99-457 Part B requirements.

US Department of Health and Human Services. This federal department operates a host of programs that assist states and local programs and organizations to provide a wide array of health and social services to children birth to 5 years of age. The Social Security Act, which funds Medicaid to provide services to low-income persons, includes the Early Periodic Screening, Diagnostic and Treatment (EPSDT) Program. EPSDT provides comprehensive and preventive health services to screen children for physical and mental disabilities and to provide treatment for conditions found through the diagnostic services. Medicaid also provides inpatient and outpatient health-related services, including physical, occupational, speech, and developmental therapy to eligible children, and parent and family counseling and support services. At a state's discretion, a Women and Children Program may be established to provide medical services to pregnant women and children birth through age 5 for persons whose family income does not exceed 100% of the poverty level.

The Social Security Act also provides federal assistance to state public welfare agencies to render an array of services to protect and promote the welfare of all children, including those who are of preschool age. The services provided by states include, but are not limited to, child day care and respite care, family counseling, case management, foster and adoptive home placements, and child abuse and neglect treatment services.

The Public Health Services Act funds the establishment and operation of Community Health Care Centers to provide primary child medical services and health care to medically underserved populations, including pregnant women. The Act also funds mental health services that may be directed at pregnant women, parents of young children, and preschool-aged children with mental-health-related problems and needs.

Other federal programs that include services to pregnant women and infants, toddlers, and older preschoolers are described in a Select Committee on Children, Youth and Families (1984) report and a joint US Departments of Education and Health and Human Services (1989) report to Congress.

US Department of Agriculture. This federal department provides assistance to states to operate the Special Supplemental Food Program for Women, Infants and Children (WIC), which includes nutritional screening and counseling, and provision of food supplements, to income-eligible pregnant women and mothers and their children up to 5 years of age. This program is generally an underutilized early intervention service, despite the fact that staff from these programs offer have a wealth of information, skills, and resources that might prove beneficial to young children and their families.

Private foundations. An increasing number of private foundations have begun initiatives that specifically aim to support and strengthen family functioning and enhance and optimize child development. These include, but are not limited to, the Annie E. Casey Foundation Child Welfare Reform Initiative and the Pew Charitable Trusts Children's Initiative. These kinds of efforts are primarily systems change and capacity building programs in which funds are made available to states and community agencies and organizations to alter the ways in which services are rendered to pregnant woman and young children and their families. For example, the specific aim of the Pew Children's Initiative is to "improve children's health and development on a broad scale through a *reorientation and reconfiguration* of the formal systems that serve (the children) and their families" (Leiderman et al., 1991, p. i, italics added). The Annie E. Casey and Pew Charitable Trusts initiatives are but two examples of an increasing number of public-private sector partnerships being forged in the USA to improve the delivery of resources and services to young children and their families, especially children at risk for poor outcomes associated with economic and social disadvantages.

3.6 Summary and Conclusion

The brief overview presented here of the broad range of early intervention programs in the USA illustrates that early intervention is a diverse enterprise. On the one hand, all the different kinds of early intervention initiatives share the belief that early experiences can alter the course of development of young children and their families, and that without these opportunities, negative outcomes will accrue. On the other hand, the various initiatives differ considerably in the assumptions and approaches that constitute "best practices" for accomplishing program goals. An analysis of selected aspects of the 12 major kinds of early intervention initiatives described above is presented next to better detail the landscape of early intervention programs and practices in the USA.

4   Analysis of Early Intervention Models and Practices

The purpose of this section is to analyze early intervention programs and practices in terms of three shifts that have been noted increasingly by scholars in both the early intervention and related fields (Bond, 1984; Bronfenbrenner, 1974, 1975; Powell, 1989; Rappaport, 1981; Richmond & Ayoub, 1993; Seeman, 1989; Zigler & Berman, 1983; Zigler & Black, 1989). The shifts that are the focus of the analysis here include: (a) increased recognition of the social ecology of early intervention, (b) the replacement of child- and professionally centered approaches to early intervention with family-centered models, and (c) the movement beyond the use of treatment and even prevention methods toward promotion approaches to early intervention. It should be made explicit at the outset that the analyses performed for this chapter were assessments of how programs are described and not how programs operate in practice. The latter would be expected to vary considerably within and across the major kinds of early intervention initiatives. An analysis of program descriptions is nonetheless instructive for at least two reasons: First, it provides an objective way of ascertaining both similarities and differences in the major kinds of early intervention initiatives. Second, and perhaps more importantly, it provides a foundation for understanding which theoretical frameworks, assumptions, and so forth policymakers and program builders have used either implicitly or explicitly in developing program designs.

4.1 Evaluative Dimensions

The three evaluative dimensions chosen for assessing the extent to which the different early intervention initiatives have been sensitive to the call for shifts toward ecologically oriented, family-centered, and promotive approaches to early intervention are described next. Each dimension includes three evaluative "items" designed to capture a number of key aspects of theory, models, and practice. The nine items were individually rated on 5-point scales as a basis for assessing the extent to which the program descriptions were consistent with operationally defined criteria. The sum of the ratings were used to rank-order the early intervention initiatives on a continuum varying from most to least sensitive to the shifts noted above. Interrater reliability found exact agreements on 89% of the 108 ratings and 100% agreement on ratings for contiguous scores. No ratings were found to differ more than a single point for the two independent codings of the nine items.

Social ecology of early intervention. Bronfenbrenner's (1975) ecological analysis of early intervention programs and his subsequent descriptions of the ecology of human development (1977, 1979) have shaped the thinking of a number of early intervention scholars and enthusiasts (Dunst, 1985; Garbarino & Long, 1992; Powell, 1989; Zigler & Black, 1989; Zigler & Freedman, 1987; Zigler & Weiss, 1985). A social ecology orientation toward early intervention recognizes the fact that a child and family are embedded within the context of broader-based social systems and units, and that the people, agencies, organizations, and programs (including early intervention), as well as other community settings (and people within settings) that a family comes into contact with either directly or indirectly influence child, parent, and family functioning (Cochran & Brassard, 1979). For example, Bronfenbrenner (1979) noted that:

> Whether parents can perform effectively in their childrearing roles within the family depends on role demands, stresses, and supports emanating from other settings ... . Parent's evaluations of their own capacity to function, as well as their view of their child, are related to such external factors as flexibility of job schedules, adequacy of child care arrangements, the presence of friends and neighbors who an help out in large and small emergencies, the quality of health and social services, and neighborhood safety. (p. 7)

As noted by Zigler and Freedman (1987), the ecological orientation espoused by Bronfenbrenner "has changed the focus of many intervention programs from single individuals toward the relations among family members and between the family as a whole and the community at large" (p. 57). This translates into program activities that include both the provision of a host of services to children and their families and the mobilization of supports and resources from members of a family's informal and formal community support network. Such an approach includes interventions directed at the child him or herself, the child's parents and other family members, and the communities in which families reside.

The analysis of the social ecology of the early intervention initiatives described in this chapter focused on three aspects of the programs:

1. Theoretical orientation. This item measured the extent to which the program developers either implicitly or explicitly employed an ecological framework or model for conceptualizing the overall design of the program. The item was scored on a continuum varying from *a nonecologically-based model* (1), to *an implicitly adopted ecological framework* (3), to *an explicitly adopted ecological theory or framework* (5).

2. Unit of intervention. This item measured the extent to which interventions are directed at the family as a whole. The item was scored on a continuum varying from *the child being the principal unit of intervention* (1), to *the parents as the unit of intervention but only in terms of family needs related to child development* (3), to *the broad-based needs of families as the unit of intervention* (5).

3. Resource-based practices. This item measured the extent to which solutions to meeting child and family needs are defined in terms of a broad range of informal and formal community supports and resources. The item was scored on a continuum varying from solutions to meeting child and family needs being *defined solely in terms of program-specific professional services* (1), to solutions *defined in terms of professional services from different programs and agencies* (3), to solutions *defined in terms of a broad range of formal (professional) and informal community supports, resources, and services* (5).

Family-centered early intervention practices. An increasing number of proponents of early intervention have called for a shift away from solely child-centered toward family-oriented approaches to service delivery (Dunst et al., 1991; Johnson, 1990; Shelton et al., 1987; Thurman, 1993; Weissbourd & Kagan, 1989; Zigler & Berman, 1983). Not all family-oriented early intervention practices, however, are necessarily family-centered. Dunst et al. (1991) differentiate between four classes of human services practices that all focus on the family as the unit of intervention, but which differ in terms of their "degree-of-family-orientedness." The models are: professionally-centered, family-allied, family-focused, and family-centered.

Proponents of *professionally-centered models* view professionals as experts who determine the needs of families from their own as opposed to the family's perspective. In *family-allied models*, families are seen as the agents-of-professionals, and are enlisted to implement interventions that professionals deem important and necessary for the benefit of the family.

Advocates of *family-focused models* view families as consumers of professional services, and assist families in choosing among options that professionals believe will best meet family needs. Proponents of *family-centered models* view professionals as the agents and instruments of families in obtaining resources, supports, and services in an individualized, flexible, and responsive manner. Professionals who employ family-centered practices provide families with the information necessary to make informed decisions and choices, create opportunities that strengthen family functioning as well as enhance acquisition of new competencies, intervene in ways that are culturally sensitive and socially relevant, and treat families both as equals and with dignity and respect.

The three aspects of family-centeredness against which the major kinds of early intervention programs were judged were as follows:

1. Theoretical orientation. This item measured the extent to which program developers implicitly or explicitly adopted a particular family-oriented model for conceptualizing the design of the program. The item was scored on a continuum varying from *family-allied* (1), to *family-focused* (3), to *family-centered* (5). (Insofar as none of the early intervention programs were judged to be solely professionally centered, this program paradigm was not included in the evaluative criterion.)

2. Needs-based practices. This item measured the extent to which the focus of intervention practices is based on family-identified needs rather than professionally identified needs. The item was scored on a continuum varying from *professionally identified needs* primarily guiding intervention practices (1), to a *combination of professionally and family-identified needs* guiding practices (3), to *family-identified needs* primarily guiding the major aspects of practice (5).

3. Responsive intervention practices. This item measured the extent to which program supports and services are made available to families in ways that are flexible, individualized, and responsive to the family's life-styles and cultural beliefs and values. The item was scored on a continuum varying from *highly rigid/nonresponsive* intervention practices (1), to *implicitly responsive* practices (3), to *explicit and highly flexible/culturally responsive* practices (5).

Promotion and enhancement approaches to early intervention. A call for adoption of promotion and competency-enhancement human services practices in general, and early intervention programs specifically, has been voiced increasingly during the past decade (Bond, 1984; Danish & D'Augelli, 1978; Dunst, 1985; Dunst et al., 1990; Rappaport, 1981, 1987; Seeman, 1989; Stanley & Maddux, 1986; Zautra & Sandler, 1983). Promotive approaches to intervention are seen as conceptually and procedurally distinct from either prevention or treatment models (see Dunst et al., 1990).

As used here, *treatment* is defined as the management and provision of care (assistance, help, etc.) in order to eliminate or minimize the negative effects of a disorder, problem, or disease. Interventions focus on the remediation or amelioration of an aberration or its consequences. Primary emphasis is typically placed on the reduction of negative effects associated with an identifiable problem or disability. *Prevention* is defined as the deterrence or hindrance of a problem, disorder, or disease. Interventions occur prior to the onset of negative functioning in order to reduce the incidence or prevalence of negative outcomes. The primary orientation of the prevention model is protection against either actual or perceived events that are likely to result in negative reactions or outcomes. Major emphasis is placed on the deterrence or forestalling of otherwise negative consequences (Cowen, 1985).

In contrast to treatment and prevention models that are both problem-oriented, *promotion* is defined as the enhancement and optimization of positive functioning. Interventions focus on the acquisition of competence and capabilities that strengthen functioning and adaptive capacities. The promotion model is best characterized as having a mastery and optimization orientation. Major emphasis is placed on the development, enhancement, and elaboration of a person's competencies and capabilities (Bond, 1984), particularly those that increase a sense of control over important aspects of one's life (Rappaport, 1981). Cowen (1985) called this approach proactive, because it gives primacy to actions that support and strengthen functioning. Promotion efforts are strengths-based because they assume all people have existing strengths as well as the capacity to become competent (Rappaport, 1981). Moreover, by building on strengths rather than rectifying deficits, people become more adaptive in not only dealing with difficult life events but in setting growth-oriented goals and achieving personal aspirations.

The three aspects of the early intervention programs that were assessed with respect to a promotive orientation were as follows:

1. Theoretical orientation. This item measured the extent to which program developers implicitly or explicitly adopted a conceptual framework that had promotion and enhancement underpinnings. The item was scored on a continuum varying from primarily a *treatment orientation* (1), to primarily a *prevention orientation* (3), to primarily a *promotion orientation* (5).

2. Strengths-based practices. This item measured the extent to which families are viewed as having existing strengths as well as the capacity to become more competent. The item was scored on a continuum varying from beliefs/practices that viewed families as *having deficits and weaknesses that needed to be corrected* (1), to families being primarily *weak and needing to be protected by professionals* (3), to families *having existing strengths* as well as the capacity to become more competent by building on strengths as the focus of intervention practices (5).

3. Empowerment/enhancement practices. This item measured the extent to which a primary focus of program activities was the empowerment of families in ways that support and strengthen family functioning. The item was scored on a continuum varying from practices that were primarily *paternalistic and usurpating* (1), to practices that created *opportunities for families to acquire information and skills that professionals deemed important* (3), to practices that were *competency-enhancing in ways that would promote families' sense of control* over a variety of life events and experiences.

4.2 Results

The individual ratings on the nine evaluative items as well as the overall rank ordering of the major kinds of early intervention programs are shown in Table 2. In general, early intervention programs that were more systems-oriented and broader-based in their focus tended to be ranked the highest, and programs that were more parent-education-oriented tended to be ranked the lowest. To a large degree, this was the case because the former kinds of programs tend to be based upon premises that attempt to reorient policy and practice about the best ways to support and strengthen families (Weissbourd, 1990), whereas the latter tend to place primary emphasis on educating and training parents so that they can become better "teachers" of their children.

Interprogram findings. Inspection of the sum of scores for the nine separate ratings shows that they range from 15 (Part B Preschool Program) to 43 (Grass Roots Family Resource Programs), with the highest score being almost triple that of the program ranked the lowest. This in and of itself attests to the variability in the programs in terms of the extent to which the initiatives have been sensitive and responsive to the three shifts that are the focus of the analyses described here.

Further analysis of the total scores for each initiative using 9-point ranges for ascertaining the degree to which program designs are collectively underscored by ecologically oriented, family-centered, and promotion-based theory, models, and practices finds three programs showing strong adoption (37-45), four programs showing moderate adoption (28-36), and two programs showing weak adoption (19-27), with two programs evaluated

Table 2.   Results of the Analysis of the Major Kinds of Early Intervention Program

Programs	Social ecology			Family-centered			Promotion			Program measures	
	Theory	Unit of Intervention	Resource-based	Theory	Needs-based	Culturally responsive	Theory	Strengths-based	Empowerment	Total Overall Score	Overall rank
Family Resources Programs	5	5	5	5	4	5	4	5	5	43	1
Family Support Program[a]	4	5	5	4	4	5	5	5	5	42	2
Head Start	4	4	5	4	4	4	4	4	4	37	3
Parent & Child Centers	4	4	4	4	4	4	4	4	4	36	4
Maternal & Child Health EI Program	3	4	3	5	4	5	4	4	3	35	5
State Family Support Programs[b]	3	4	4	4	3	3	4	3	3	31	6
Part H EI Program	3	3	3	3	4	3	2	4	3	28	7
Community-Based EI Programs	3	4	4	2	3	2	3	3	3	27	8
State Parent Education Programs[c]	2	3	3	3	2	3	3	3	3	25	9
Comprehensive Child Develop. Programs	3	4	4	2	2	2	3	2	2	24	10
Even Start	2	3	2	1	2	1	3	2	2	18	11
Part B Preschool Program	2	2	1	1	2	2	1	2	2	15	12

[a] The evaluations made here are for the family support component only of PL-103-66 (see text). [b] Combined ratings for Connecticut, Maryland, and North Carolina. [c] Combined ratings for Minnesota, Missouri, Arkansas, and Kentucky.

almost entirely nonresponsive to the shifts described above (9-18). Taken together, these data indicate considerable diversity among the 12 early intervention programs with regard to the implicit and explicit adoption of the three particular philosophical and conceptual dimensions examined here.

Intraprogram findings. Examination of the variability in the individual scores within initiatives sheds additional light on the nature of program diversity. Inspection of the pattern of scores for the different early intervention initiatives shows that 95% of the intraprogram ratings are but one point different for all pairwise contrasts. On the one hand, this finding indicates that individual programs were likely to be rated in a similar fashion regardless of the particular dimension assessed. On the other hand, the results indicate that there is considerable internal consistency in the ratings. This was confirmed by a series of Spearman rank-order correlations between the nine separate ratings. The average correlation was .74 ($SD = .13$), with all but two of the 36 correlation coefficients significant beyond the .05 level.

Descriptive characteristics. Inspection of the pattern of ratings for individual programs yielded additional insights into the similarities and differences among the early intervention initiatives. These are described next in terms of the particular characteristics that made individual initiatives unique or groups of programs much alike.

First, the Grass Roots Family Resource Programs, the PL 103-66 Family Support Program, Head Start, and the Parent and Child Center Program each received high ratings on all nine items, indicating generally explicit adoption of the philosophical and program practices on which they were evaluated. This was not surprising, given the fact that these particular initiatives have been shaped by similar kinds of thinking and also share a common heritage (see, especially, Weissbourd & Kagan, 1989; Zigler & Black, 1989). Collectively, these programs are broad-based in their orientation, emphasize the use of both formal and informal sources of supports and resources for meeting child and family needs, place families in pivotal roles in all aspects of program operations, and aim to promote and enhance the capabilities of both children and families by building on strengths rather than correcting weaknesses.

Second, the Maternal and Child Health (MCH) Bureau Early Intervention Program received generally high ratings on both the family-oriented and promotion-based items, but somewhat lower ratings on the social ecology items. The high ratings on the family-centered items were not surprising, given the fact that MCH has explicitly advanced family-centered care as an essential feature of a comprehensive, coordinated system of community-based early intervention (Brewer et al., 1989). Likewise, the high ratings on the promotion-based items reflects MCH's increased commitment to both the prevention of health-related problems and the promotion of healthy functioning (Surgeon General, 1979) as primary goals of agency-related activities. The lower ratings on the social ecology items were due, in part, to the limited recognition and emphasis on informal community resources as sources of support for meeting child and family needs (see Trivette, Dunst, Allen, & Wall, 1993).

Third, both the State Family Support Programs and PL 99-457 Part B Early Intervention Program received predominantly moderate ratings on all nine items. But the similarities between these two programs end there. Whereas the State Family Support Programs tend to focus on the broad-based needs of children and families and the use of informal sources of support for meeting these needs, the Part H Program focuses primarily on family needs as they relate to child development and the use of professionals as primary sources of support for meeting needs. In contrast, the Part H Program tends to place a great deal of emphasis on family-identified needs as the focus of intervention as well as the identification of family strengths as part of assessment practices, whereas the State Family Support Programs tend to base intervention practices more on professionally identified needs and the recognition of family strengths, but not necessarily on the use of these competencies for strengthening family functioning. The major difference between the two programs, however, is related primarily to the fact that the State Family Support Programs show a presumption toward adoption of promotion-based intervention strategies, whereas the Part H Programs employ predominantly treatment models for structuring intervention practices.

Fourth, both the Community-Based Early Intervention Programs and Comprehensive Child Development Programs received moderate to high ratings on the social ecology measures, but low to moderate ratings on the family-centered and promotion-based items. Whereas both initiatives generally recognized the broader-based systems context of early intervention, recommended practices do not seem to match this orientation. For example, both kinds of programs tend to place primary emphasis on professionally identified rather than family-identified needs as the focus of intervention. Overall, both programs tend to employ family-allied models for addressing child and family needs, and the Comprehensive Child Development Program, in particular, tends to emphasize the correction of child and family weaknesses as interventive foci.

Fifth, the State Parent Education Programs received low to moderate ratings on all evaluative items. As a whole, these programs tend to employ primarily a program-specific rather than a broad-based systems perspective of early intervention, and specifically emphasize the involvement of families as agents-of-professionals implementing education-related activities that professionals deem necessary for parents to learn to become better teachers of their children.

Sixth, both the Even Start and PL 94-142 Part B Preschool Program received mostly low ratings on all the evaluative items. Both programs are almost entirely family-allied in their orientation, emphasize the correction of child or family weaknesses as a primary focus of intervention, and tend to consider program-specific services as the principle sources of resources for meeting child and family needs that professionals rather than families have identified.

Summary. Collectively, the results from the various quantitative and descriptive analyses reported in this section indicate that the major kinds of contemporary intervention programs can generally be classified as to whether they are broad-based in their orientation or more narrowly focused. The former tend to be programs that emphasize the provision and mobilization of supports and resources to meet the broad-based needs of children and families, whereas the latter tend to be programs that emphasize meeting family needs only as they relate to child development and childrearing matters.

Second, the different early intervention programs tend to differ according to whether they are family-centered (or show a presumption toward being family-centered) or family-allied (and to a lesser degree family-focused). Family-centered programs are ones that base intervention goals on family-identified needs and, to a large degree, are responsive to the desires and priorities of families. In contrast, family-allied programs place primary emphasis on teaching parents (and sometimes other family members) to carry out interventions directed primarily at influencing child behavior and development.

Third, the programs are found to differ in terms of whether they place primary emphasis on enhancing positive aspects of human functioning as a way of strengthening behavior and development or emphasize primarily prevention of poor outcomes or treatment of real or perceived problems. The different kinds of early intervention programs are also found to differ regarding whether they build upon child and family strengths as a primary focus of intervention practices or correct weaknesses and deficits as a major program goal. Whereas the former generally are guided by an empowerment philosophy (Rappaport 1981), the latter are mostly paternalistic in orientation (see Swift, 1984).

5 Conclusion

The threefold purpose of this chapter was to: (a) present a historical overview of the evolution of early intervention in the USA, (b) describe the different kinds of contemporary early intervention programs and initiatives in the USA, and (c) ascertain the extent to which the program designs of these initiatives have been sensitive to the call for shifts toward ecologically oriented, family-centered, and promotion-based approaches to early intervention. Examination of the historical roots of early intervention found five spheres of influence shaping the belief that early experiences could be used to influence child behavior and development. The kinds of contemporary early intervention programs operating in the USA were found to be numerous and diverse, and included federal government, state government, grass roots, and private foundation initiatives.

The analyses of the diverse kinds of early intervention programs produced evidence indicating that they differed from each other despite their common heritage and apparent similarities. The various kinds of early intervention programs were found to differ considerably in their program designs, and these differences were underscored to a large degree by variations in the assumptions and beliefs that guided the translation of theory into models and practices. Whether or not the differences are associated with differential outcomes has not been directly tested empirically. However, such comparative studies are needed, and seem especially warranted, in light of the call for "second-generation" research on the efficacy of early intervention that includes, among other things, evaluations of the contributions of program features to child, parent, and family outcomes (Guralnick, 1991, 1993). Findings from available research would lead one to hypothesize that early intervention programs that are based upon different beliefs and assumptions about the best ways to influence child and family functioning would indeed result in different kinds of effects (see, e.g., Dunst et al., 1990), and both cross-sectional and case study research conducted by my colleagues and myself on the characteristics and consequences of contrasting kinds of intervention practices strengthen such predictions (Dunst et al., 1989; Dunst, & Trivette, 1988; Dunst et al., 1993a, 1993b, 1994; Trivette & Dunst, 1993; Trivette, Dunst, LaPointe, & Hamby, 1993).

In conclusion, early intervention in the USA has become deeply embedded in the fabric of human services programs. Early intervention now encompasses a broad range of models and activities directed at very young children and their families. Despite similarities, early intervention as a whole is a diverse enterprise, with different kinds of programs differing considerably in their philosophies and practices. When placed in historical perspective, early intervention has changed considerably during the past 50 years, and all signs point to further advances as we move toward the 21st century.

6   Postscript

A number of changes have occurred in the landscape of early intervention in the USA since this chapter was completed, among which are the following. First, Part D of the U.S. Department of Education Elementary and Secondary Act of 1988 (PL 100-297) has been folded into Parts B and H of the Individuals with Disabilities Education Act of 1991 (PL 102-119). Second, the U.S. Department of Health and Human Services Comprehensive Child Developmental Program (Human Services Amendments of 1994, PL 103-252), providing funds to continue the CCDPs and expand these kinds of programs in other communities. Third, the Pew Charitable Trusts Children's Initiative has been terminated, whereas a number of other private foundations are now funding a variety of early intervention initiatives for young children and their families. Fourth, the U.S. Department of Health and Human Services, National Center on Child Abuse and Neglect, is now funding the development of Community-Based Family Resource Programs as part of efforts to promote activities that prevent child maltreatment, including during the preschool years. Collectively, the changes that have occurred are to a large degree internally consistent with the shifts toward ecologically oriented, family-centered, and promotive approaches that increasingly are becoming characteristics of early intervention programs, policies, and practices in the USA.

Note

Special thanks and acknowledgement is extended to Mary E. Brown for typing various versions of the chapter and to Carol A. Berardelli for feedback on the paper and assistance in preparing the reference material.

References

Addams, J. (1935). *Forty years at Hull House*. New York: MacMillan.

Andrews, S., Blumnthal, J., Johnson, D., Kahn, A., Ferguson, C., Lasater, T., Malone, P., & Wallace, D. (1982). The skills of mothering: A study of Parent Child Development Centers. *Monographs of the Society for Research in Child Development*, *47*, (6, Serial No. 198).

Bartz, S., & Bartz, J. (1970). Early childhood intervention: The social sciences base of institutional racism. *Harvard Educational Review*, *40*, 29-50.

Billingsley, F. (1984). Where are the generalized outcomes? An examination of instructional objectives. *Journal for Persons with Severe Handicaps*, *9*, 186-192.

Bloom, B.S. (1964). *Stability and change in human characteristics*. New York: Wiley.

Bond, L. (1984). From prevention to promotion: Optimizing infant development. In L. Bond & L. Joffee (Eds.), *Facilitating infant and early childhood development* (pp. 5-39). Hanover, NH: University Press of New England.

Boyer, P. (1978). *Urban masses and moral order in America*. Cambridge, MA: Harvard University Press.

Brewer, E., McPherson, M., Magrab, P., & Hutchins, V. (1989). Family-centered, community-based, coordinated care for children with special health care needs. *Pediatrics*, *83*, 1055-1060.

Bricker, D., Bailey, E., & Bruder, M. B. (1984). The efficacy of early intervention and the handicapped infant: A wise or wasted resource. In M. Wolraich & D. Routh (Eds.), *Advances in developmental and behavioral pediatrics* (Vol. 5, pp. 373-423). Greenwich, CN: JAI Press.

Brim, O. (1959). *Education for childrearing*. New York: Free Press.

Brinckerhoff, J., & Vincent, L. (1986). Increasing parental decision making at the individualized educational program meeting. *Journal of The Division for Early Childhood*, *11*, 46-58.

Bronfenbrenner, U. (1974). Developmental research, public policy, and the ecology of childhood. *Child Development*, *45*, 1-5.

Bronfenbrenner, U. (1975). Is early intervention effective? In M. Guttentag & E. Struening (Eds.), *Handbook of evaluation research* (Vol. 2., pp. 519-603). Newbury Park, CA: Sage.

Bronfenbrenner, U. (1977). Toward an experimental ecology of human development. *American Psychologist*, *32*, 513-531.

Bronfenbrenner, U. (1979). *The ecology of human development*. Cambridge, MA: Harvard University Press.

Burt, C., Jones, E., Miller, E., & Moodie, W. (1934). *How the mind works*. New York: Appleton-Century-Crofts.

Caldwell, B. (1970). The rationale for early intervention. *Exceptional Children*, *36*, 717-726.

Campbell, S. (1983). Effects of developmental interventions in the special care nursery. In M. Wolraich & D. Routh (Eds.), *Advances in developmental and behavioral pediatrics* (Vol. 4, pp. 165-179). Greenwich, CN: JAI Press.

Cochran, M., & Brassard, J. (1979). Child development and personal social networks. *Child Development*, *50*, 601-616.

Condry, S. (1983). Historical background of preschool intervention programs and the Consortium for Longitudinal Studies. In Consortium for Longitudinal Studies (Ed.), *As the twig is bent: Lasting effects of preschool programs* (pp. 1-31). Hillsdale, NJ: Erlbaum.

Consortium for Longitudinal Studies (Ed.). (1983). *As the twig is bent: Lasting effects of preschool programs*. Hillsdale, NJ: Erlbaum.

Cowen, E. L. (1985). Person-centered approaches to primary prevention in mental health: Situation-focused and competence-enhancement. *American Journal of Community Psychology, 13*, 31-48.

Danish, S. J., & D'Augelli, A. R. (1978). Promoting competence and enhancing development through life development intervention. In L. Bond & J. Rosen (Eds.), *Primary prevention of psychopathology* (Vol. 4, pp. 104-129). Hanover, NH: University Press of New England.

Deutsch, M., Deutsch, C., Jordon, T., & Grallo, R. (1983). The IDS Program: An experiment in early and sustained enrichment. In Consortium for Longitinal Studies (Ed.), *As the twig is bent: Lasting effects of preschool programs* (pp. 377-410). Hillsdale, NJ: Erlbaum.

Dewey, J., & Dewey, E. (1915). *Schools of tomorrow*. New York: Dutton.

Dunst, C. J. (1981). *Infant learning*. Allen, TX: DLM Publishers.

Dunst, C. J. (1985). Rethinking early intervention. *Analysis and Intervention in Developmental Disabilities, 5*, 165-201.

Dunst, C. J. (1986). Overview of the efficacy of early intervention programs: Methodological and conceptual considerations. In L. Bickman & D. Weatherford (Eds.), *Evaluating early intervention programs for severely handicapped children and their families* (pp. 79-147). Austin, TX: PRO-ED.

Dunst, C. J. (1993). Implications of risk and opportunity factors for assessment and intervention practices. *Topics in Early Childhood Special Education, 13*, 143-153.

Dunst, C. J., Johanson, C., Trivette, C. M., & Hamby, D. (1991). Family-oriented early intervention policies and practices: Family-centered or not? *Exceptional Children, 58*, 115-126.

Dunst, C. J., & Rheingrover, R. (1981). An analysis of the efficacy of infant intervention programs with organically handicapped children. *Evaluation and Program Planning, 4*, 287-323.

Dunst, C. J., Snyder, S., & Mankinen, M. (1989). Efficacy of early intervention. In M. Wang, M. Reynolds, & H. Walberg (Eds.), *Handbook of special education (Vol. 3): Low incidence conditions* (pp. 259-294). Oxford, England: Pergamon Press.

Dunst, C. J., & Trivette, C. M. (1994). Methodological considerations and strategies for studying the long-term follow-up of early intervention. In S. Friedman & H. C. Haywood (Eds.), *Developmental follow-up: Concepts, domains and methods* (pp. 277-313). New York: Academic Press.

Dunst, C. J., Trivette, C. M., Boyd, K., & Brookfield, J. (1994). Helpgiving practices and the self-efficacy appraisals of parents. In C. J. Dunst, C. M. Trivette, & A. G. Deal (Eds.), *Supporting and strengthening families (Vol. 1): Methods, strategies and practices* (212-220). Cambridge, MA: Brookline Books.

Dunst, C. J., Trivette, C. M., Davis, M., & Cornwell, J. (1988). Enabling and empowering families of children with health impairments. *Children's Health Care, 17*, 71-81.

Dunst, C. J., Trivette, C. M., Gordon, N., & Starnes, A. L. (1993a). Family-centered case management practices: Characteristics and consequences. In G. Singer & L. Powers (Eds.), *Families, disabilities, and empowerment* (pp. 89-118). Baltimore, MD: Paul Brookes.

Dunst, C. J., Trivette, C. M., Starnes, L., Hamby, D., & Gordon, N. (1993b). *Building and evaluating family support initiatives*. Baltimore, MD: Paul Brookes.

Dunst, C. J., Trivette, C. M., & Thompson, R. (1990). Supporting and strengthening family functioning: Toward a congruence between principles and practice. *Prevention in Human Services*, *9*(1), 19-43.

Family Resource Coalition (1993). *The principles of family support*. Chicago: Author.

Farran, D. (1990). Effects of intervention with disadvantaged and disabled children: A decade review. In S. Meisels & J. Shonkoff (Eds.), *Handbook of early childhood intervention* (pp. 501-539). New York: Cambridge University Press.

Ferry, P. (1981). On growing new neurons: Are early intervention programs effective? *Pediatrics*, *67*, 38-41.

Froebel, F. (1904). *Pedagogies of the kindergarten*. New York: Appleton.

Galton, F. (1869). *Hereditary genius: An inquiry into its laws and consequences*. London: MacMillian.

Garbarino, J., & Abramowitz, R. (1992). The ecology of human development. In J. Garbarino (Ed.), *Children and families in the social environment* (2nd ed., pp. 11-33). New York: Aldine de Gruyter.

Garbarino, J., & Long, F. (1992). Developmental issues in human services. In J. Garbarino (Ed.), *Children and families in the social environment* (2nd ed., pp. 231-270). New York: Aldine de Gruyter.

Gray, S., & Klaus, R. (1970). The Early Training Project: A seventh year report. *Child Development*, *41*, 909-924.

Guralnick, M. J. (1991). The next decade of research on the effectiveness of early intervention. *Exceptional Children*, *58*, 174-183.

Guralnick, M. J. (1993). Second generation research on the effectiveness of early intervention. *Early Education and Development*, *4*, 366-378.

Halpern, R. (1990). Community-based early intervention. In S. Meisels & J. Shonkoff (Eds.), *Handbook of early childhood intervention* (pp. 469-498). New York: Cambridge University Press.

Harbin, G., & McNulty, B. (1990). Policy implementation: Perspectives on service coordination and interagency coordination. In S. Meisels & J. Shonkoff (Eds.), *Handbook of early childhood intervention* (pp. 700-721). New York: Cambridge University Press.

Harvard Family Research Project (1992a). *Pioneering states: Innovative family support and education programs* (2nd ed.). Cambridge, MA: Harvard Graduate School of Education.

Harvard Family Research Project (1992b). *Innovative states: Emerging family support and education programs* (2nd ed.) Cambridge, MA: Harvard Graduate School of Education.

Hauser-Cram, P., Pierson, D., Walker, D., & Tivnan, T. (1991). *Early education in the public schools*. San Francisco: Jossey-Bass.

Hebb, D. O. (1949). *The organization of behavior*. New York: Wiley.

Hebbeler, K., Smith, B., & Black, T. (1991). Federal early childhood special education policy: A model for the improvement of services for children with disabilities. *Exceptional Children*, *58*, 104-112.

Holt, L. (1987). *The diseases of infancy and childhood*. New York: Appleton.

Hubbell, R. et al. (1991). *Comprehensive Child Development Program: A national family support demonstration*. Washington, DC: CSR Incorporated.

Hunt, J. McV. (1961). *Intelligence and experience*. New York: Ronald Press.

Infant Health and Development Program. (1990). Enhancing the outcomes of low-birth-weight premature infants. *Journal of the American Medical Association*, *263*, 3035-3042.

Jensen, A. (1969). How much can we boost IQ and scholastic achievement? *Harvard Educational Review*, *39*, 1-123.

Johnson, B. H. (1990). The changing role of families in health care. *Children's Health Care*, *19*, 234-241.

Kagan, S., Powell, D., Weissbourd, B., & Zigler, E. (Eds.). (1987). *America's family support programs*. New Haven, CT: Yale University Press.

Kagan, S., & Shelley, A. (1987). The promise and problems of family support programs. In S. Kagan, D. Powell, B. Weissbourd, & E. Zigler (Eds.), *America's family support programs* (pp. 3-18). New Haven, CT: Yale University Press.

Kirk, S. (1950). A project for pre-school mentally handicapped. *American Journal of Mental Deficiency*, *55*, 305-310.

Kirk, S., & Johnson, G. (1951). *Educating the retarded child*. Cambridge, MA: Riverside Press.

Klaus, R., & Gray, S. (1968). The Early Training Project for disadvantaged children. *Monographs of the Society for Research in Child Development*, *33* (Serial No. 120).

Lancioni, G. (1980). Infant operant conditioning and its implications for early intervention. *Psychological Bulletin*, *83*, 516-534.

Lazar, I., Darlington, R., Murray, H., Royce, J., & Snipper, A. (1982). Lasting effects of early education: A report from the Consortium for Longitudinal Studies. *Monograph of the Society for Research in Child Development*, *47* (Serial No. 195).

Leiderman, S., Reveal, E., Rosewater, A., Stephens, S., & Wolf, W. (1991). *The Children's Initiative: Making the system work*. Bala Cynwyd, PA: Center for Assessment and Policy Development.

Levine, C. (Ed.). (1988). *Programs to strengthen families: A resource guide* (Rev. ed.). Chicago, IL: Family Resource Coalition.

Lipsitt, L. (1969). Learning capabilities of the human infant. In R. Robinson (Ed.), *Brain and early development* (pp. 227-249). New York: Academic Press.

McMillan, M. (1919). *The nursery school*. London: Dent.

McNemar, Q. (1940). A critical examination of the University of Iowa studies of environmental influences upon the IQ. *Psychological Bulletin*, *37*, 63-92.

Meisels, S., & Shonkoff, J. (Eds.). (1990) *Handbook of early childhood intervention*. New York: Cambridge University Press.

Montessori, M. (1912). *The Montessori method* (Trans. 1964). New York: Schochen Books.

Moss, H., Hess, R., & Swift, C. (Eds.). (1982). Early intervention programs for infants. *Prevention in Human Services*, *1*(4).

North Carolina (1993). *Early childhood education and development initiatives.* Senate Bill 27, Sec. 254 (State General Statutes, Article 3, Chapter 143B).

Olds, D., Henderson, C., Chamberlin, R., & Tatelbaum, R. (1986). The prevention of child abuse and neglect: A controlled trial of nurse home visitation. *Pediatrics, 78,* 65-78.

Osborn, D. (1980). *Early childhood education in historical perspective.* Athens, GA: Education Associates.

Peterson, N. (1987). *Early intervention for handicapped and at-risk children.* Denver, CO: Love Publishing Co.

Piaget, J. (1952). *The origins of intelligence.* New York: International Universities Press.

Pinneau, S. (1955). The infantile disorders of hospitalism and anaclitic depression. *Psychological Bulletin, 52,* 429-459.

Pizzo, P. (1987). Parent-to-parent support groups: Advocates for social change. In S. Kagan, D. Powell, B. Weissbourd, & E. Zigler (Eds.), *America's family support programs* (pp. 228-242). New Haven, CT: Yale University Press.

Powell, D. (Ed.). (1988). *Parent education as early childhood intervention.* Norwood, NJ: Ablex.

Powell, D. (1989). Families and early childhood programs. *Research Monograph of the National Association for the Education of Young Children, 3*(142).

Provence, S., & Naylor, A. (1983). *Working with disadvantaged parents and their children.* New Haven, CT: Yale University Press.

Ramey, C., Bryant, D., Wasik, B., Sparling, J., Fendt, K., & LaVange, L. (1992). Infant Health and Development Program for low birth weight, premature infants: Program elements, family participation, and child intelligence. *Pediatrics, 3,* 454-465.

Ramey, C., & Campbell, F. (1987). The Carolina Abecedarian Project: An educational experiment concerning human malleability. In J. Gallagher & C. Ramey (Eds.), *The malleability of children* (pp. 127-139). Baltimore, MD: Paul Brookes.

Rappaport, J. (1981). In praise of paradox: A social policy of empowerment over prevention. *American Journal of Community Psychology, 9,* 1-25.

Rappaport, J. (1987). Terms of empowerment/exemplars of prevention: Toward a theory for community psychology. *American Journal of Community Psychology, 15,* 121-148.

Reese, H., & Overton, W. (1970). Models of development and theories of development. In L. Goulet & P. Baltes (Eds.), *Life-span developmental psychology: Research and theory* (pp. 115-145). New York: Academic Press.

Richmond, J., & Ayoub, C. (1993). Evolution of the early intervention philosophy. In D. Bryant & M. Graham (Eds.), *Implementing early intervention* (pp. 1-17). New York: Guilford Press.

Sameroff, A., & Chandler, M. (1975). Reproductive risk and the continuum of caretaking causality. In F. Horowitz, M. Hetherington, S. Scarr-Salapatek, & G. Siegal (Eds.), *Review of child development research* (pp. 187-244). Chicago, IL: University of Chicago Press.

Schorr, L., & Schorr, D. (1988). *Within our reach.* New York: Doubleday.

Seeman, J. (1989). Toward a model of positive health. *American Psychologist, 44,* 1099-1109.

Select Committee on Children, Youth and Families (1984). *Federal programs affecting children.* Washington, DC: U.S. Government Printing Office.

Shelton, T., Jeppson, E., & Johnson, B. (1987). *Family-centered care for children with special health care needs.* Bethesda, MD: Association for the Care of Children's Health.

Shonkoff, J., & Meisels, S. (1990). Early childhood intervention: The evolution of a concept. In S. Meisels & J. Shonkoff (Eds.), *Handbook of early childhood intervention* (pp. 3-31). New York: Cambridge University Press.

Skeels, H. (1966). Adult status of children with contrasting life experiences: A follow-up study. *Monograph of the Society for Research in Child Development, 31* (Serial No. 3).

Skeels, H., & Dye, H. (1939). A study of the effects of differential stimulation on mentally retarded children. *Proceedings and Addresses of the American Association on Mental Deficiency, 44*, 114-136.

Skeels, H., Updegraff, R., Wellman, B., & Williams, H. (1938). A study of environmental stimulation: An orphanage preschool project. *University of Iowa Studies in Child Welfare, 15*(4).

Sonenstein, F., Ku, L., Juffras, J., & Cohen, B. (1991). *Promising prevention programs for children.* Alexandria, VA: United Way of America, United Way Strategic Institute.

Spiker, D., Kraemer, H., Scott, D., & Gross, R. (1991). Design issues in a randomized clinical trial of a behavioral intervention: Insights from the Infant Health and Development Program. *Developmental and Behavioral Pediatrics, 12*, 386-393.

Spitz, R. (1945). Hospitalism: An inquiry into the genesis of psychiatric conditions in early childhood: Part I. *Psychoanalytic Study of the Child, 1*, 53-74.

Spitz, R., & Wolf, K. (1946). The smiling response: A contribution to the ontogenesis of social relations. *Genetic Psychology Monographs, 34*, 57-125.

Stanley, M. A., & Maddux, J. E. (1986). Cognitive processes in health enhancement: Investigation of a combined protection motivation and self-efficacy model. *Basic and Applied Social Psychology, 7*, 101-113.

Surgeon General. (1979). *Healthy people: The Surgeon General's report on health promotion and disease prevention.* Washington, DC: U.S. Department of Health, Education, and Welfare.

Swift, C. (1984). Empowerment: An antidote for folly. *Prevention in Human Services, 3*(2/3), xi-xv.

Thurman, S. K. (1993). Some perspectives on the continuing challenges in early intervention. In W. Brown, S. K. Thurman, & L. Pearl (Eds.), *Family-centered early intervention with infants and toddlers* (pp. 303-316). Baltimore, MD: Paul Brookes.

Trickett, P., Apfel, N., Rosenbaum, L., & Zigler, E. (1982). A five-year follow-up of participants in the Yale Child Welfare Research Project. In E. Zigler & E. Gordon (Eds.), *Day care: Scientific and social policy issues* (pp. 200-222). Boston, MA: Auburn.

Trivette, C. M., & Dunst, C. J. (1993). *Characteristics and consequences of helpgiving practices in human services programs.* Paper submitted for publication.

Trivette, C. M., Dunst, C. J., Allen, S., & Wall, L. (1993). Family-centeredness of the Children's Health Care Journal. *Children's Health Care, 22*, 241-256.

Trivette, C. M., Dunst, C. J., LaPointe, N., & Hamby, D. (1993). *Relationship between key elements of the empowerment construct.* Paper submitted for publication.

Upshur, C. (1990). Early intervention as preventive intervention. In S. Meisels & J. Shonkoff (Eds.), *Handbook of early childhood intervention* (pp. 633-650). New York: Cambridge University Press.

U.S. Departments of Education and Health and Human Services (1989). *Meeting the needs of infants and toddlers with handicaps.* Washington, DC: Authors.

Wasik, B., Ramey, C., Bryant, D., & Sparling, J. (1990). A longitudinal study of two early intervention strategies: Project CARE. *Child Development, 61,* 1682-1692.

Watson, J. B. (1928). *Psychological care of infant and child.* New York: Norton.

Watson, J. B. (1966). The development and generalization of contingency awareness in early infancy: Some hypotheses. *Merrill-Palmer Quarterly, 12,* 123-136.

Weikart, D., Bond, J., & McNeil, J. (Eds.). (1978). The Ypsilanti Perry Preschool Project: Preschool years and longitudinal results through fourth grade. *Monographs of the High/Scope Educational Research Foundation* (No. 3).

Weiss, H. (1989). State family support and education programs: Lessons from the pioneers. *American Journal of Orthopsychiatry, 59,* 32-48.

Weiss, H., & Halpern, R. (1991). *Community-based family support and education programs: Something old or something new?* New York: Columbia University, National Center for Children in Poverty.

Weiss, H., & Jacobs, F. (Eds.). (1988). *Evaluating family programs.* New York: Aldine de Gruyter.

Weissbourd, B. (1987). A brief history of family support programs. In S. Kagan, D. Powell, B. Weissbourd, & E. Zigler (Eds.), *America's family support programs* (pp. 38-56). New Haven, CT: Yale University Press.

Weissbourd, B. (1990). Family resource and support programs: Changes and challenges in human services. *Prevention in Human Services, 9*(1), 69-85.

Weissbourd, B., & Kagan, S. (1989). Family support programs: Catalysts for change. *American Journal of Orthopsychiatry, 59,* 20-31.

Zautra, A., & Sandler, I. (1983). Life event needs assessment: Two models for measuring preventable mental health problems. In A. Zautra, K. Bachrach, & R. Hess (Eds.), *Strategies for needs assessment in prevention* (pp. 35-58). New York: Haworth Press.

Zigler, E., & Berman, W. (1983). Discerning the future of early childhood intervention. *American Psychologist, 38,* 894-906.

Zigler, E., & Black, K. (1989). America's family support movement: Strengths and limitations. *American Journal of Orthopsychiatry, 59,* 6-19.

Zigler, E., & Freedman, J. (1987). Head Start: A pioneer of family support. In S. Kagan, D. Powell, B. Weissbourd, & E. Zigler (Eds.), *America's family support programs* (pp. 57-76). New Haven, CT: Yale University Press.

Zigler, E., & Muenchow, S. (1992). *Head Start: The inside story of America's most successful educational experiment.* New York: Basic Books.

Zigler, E., & Valentine, J. (Eds.). (1979). *Project Head Start: A legacy of the war on poverty.* New York: Free Press.

Zigler, E., & Weiss, H. (1985). Family support systems: An ecological approach to child development. In R. Rapoport (Ed.), *Children, youth, and families* (pp. 166-205). Cambridge, MA: Cambridge University Press.

M. Brambring, H. Rauh, and A. Beelmann (Eds.). (1996). *Early childhood intervention: Theory, evaluation, and practice* (pp. 53-71). Berlin, New York: de Gruyter.

Early Intervention in Germany

Gerhard Klein

1 Introduction

In Germany, the term "early intervention" (*Frühförderung*) covers all services of early assessment, early therapy, early education, and parent counseling. It is provided for disabled and developmentally at-risk children from birth to the age of 6 years. Sometimes, early intervention is subdivided into services for infants and children from birth to 3 years and services for children between 3 and 6 years. Services up to the age of 3 years are usually delivered exclusively at home by itinerant teachers, whereas, after the age of 3, disabled children additionally attend regular or special preschools. About 20 years ago, the major impetus for the establishment of early intervention services in Germany was given by the recommendations of the Advisory Council on Education regarding the "education of children and youth with disabilities and/or exposed to developmental risk" (Deutscher Bildungsrat, 1973).

2 The System of Early Intervention

It is certainly speculative to talk about a "system" of early intervention. Any kind of generalized system of early intervention clearly does not exist in Germany. Each of the now 16 federal states has developed its own unique and specific system involving cooperation between different subsystems. When compared with each other, the existing institutions of early intervention and the agencies responsible for them differ just as much as their funding systems, the composition of their teams, and the ways in which different professionals cooperate in providing early intervention services. The new East German states are now beginning to develop their own models of service delivery on the basis of Western models. Speck (1989, p. 149) refers to a term from the natural sciences when he reflects on whether this system could be considered "chaotic."

In the following (see Table 1), I shall outline some of the most significant components and subsystems of early intervention that appear to be comparable across the different federal states. I shall focus on comparing the organizational structure of early intervention services in four states: Baden-Wuerttemberg, Bavaria, Hesse, and the Rhineland-Palatinate. Wide variations and differences in the patterns of service delivery can be found.

Table 1. *Early Intervention in Four German Federal States*

	Baden-Wuerttemberg	Bavaria	Hesse	Rhineland-Palatinate
State				
Area (in 1,000 km^2)	35.7	70.6	21.1	19.8
Population (in millions)	10.1	11.7	5.9	3.9
Type of Institute				
Early intervention centers	261	114	54	-
Preschools or special preschools	176	287	276	85
Sociopediatric centers	14	9	7	8 (36)
Disabilities covered (% of institutes)				
No differentiation	8.0	70.1	69.0	100.0
Blind/visually impaired	3.5	5.3	7.1	8 Socio-pediatric centers with 36 branch offices
Hearing-impaired	3.8	5.3	4.3	
Speech-impaired	38.7	19.3	1.3	
Physically handicapped	6.9		16.4	
Mentally retarded	29.0		Autistic	
Educable mentally retarded	10.0		children (1.3)	
Personnel (%)				
Physicians	only consulting	only consulting	3	10
Medical therapists	7	30	30	54
Educators	7	50	53	36
Special educators	85	10	7	-
Psychologists	1	10	7	-
Funding (%)				
Health insurers	4	30	30	50
Local welfare agencies	10	60	40	37
Ministry of Social Welfare	10		28.5	13
Ministry of Education	70	10		
State Welfare	6		1.5	1.5

Note. Several figures are taken from Trost (1991). *Frühförderung in Baden-Württemberg*, Hessisches Sozialministerium et al. (no year); and Landestag Rheinland-Pfalz (no year). 12. Wahlperiode, Drucksache 12/5013. The percentages are estimated values.

Table 1 shows that the four states have very different structures. In the Rhineland- Palatinate, there are eight sociopediatric centers (with 36 branches) that are responsible for the care of all disabled children (stationary and ambulant). For long-term care between the ages of 3 and 6 years, preschools and special preschools are available. In contrast to the Rhineland-Palatinate, care during the first 3 years of life in the other three states is predominantly the responsibility of regional early intervention centers; after the age of 3, preschools and special preschools are additionally available.

2.1 Institutions

A particular organizational feature of German social services is covered by the term *freie Träger* (voluntary, private providers of services). This is a legal construct meaning that the state fully subsidizes private institutions that take over state responsibilities. The state finances private nonprofit organizations that carry out functions of public concern such as early intervention or preschool. The major nonprofit organizations of this kind in Germany are:

1. The *Bundesvereinigung Lebenshilfe e.V.* (a parent organization of mentally retarded children).
2. Diakonie (the social welfare organization of the protestant church).
3. Caritas (the social welfare organization of the catholic church).
4. Arbeiterwohlfahrt (a social welfare organization that has grown out of the social democratic movement).

Apart from these nonprofit welfare organizations that function under public law, early intervention centers are also affiliated with special education schools and/or pediatric clinics. Other agencies responsible for early intervention centers can be local and district councils.

2.2 Regional Early Intervention

Regional early intervention centers concentrate on educational support and counseling. They also offer services for disabled and developmentally delayed children, their parents, and their families. They may cooperate with preschools and daycare centers. Their task profile is characterized by three major aspects: (a) social support of parents and families; (b) assessment of children and the development of individualized education plans; and (c) the practical implementation and coordination of education and rehabilitation.

Their regional organization enables early intervention centers to bring their services to families if indicated, thus providing early education in two modes: ambulant and in the parental home. Ambulant services include treatment and counseling. Home services are provided by itinerant early intervention specialists.

Most early intervention centers contain specialists with different professional backgrounds who work together. Peterander and Speck (1993) have found that the number of specialists working in Bavarian centers may range from 1 to 30. Large centers with mixed teams not only serve children with all kinds of disabilities but also deliver services to larger geographic areas. Very small centers may limit their services to a single category of disability. In some states, for example, there are many early intervention centers that limit their services to children with speech impairments. Early intervention centers for children with impaired vision or hearing are a special case: As a rule, these are specialized centers with organizational links to special schools that deliver services within larger geographic areas. While there are a few centers that specialize in autism, the majority provide services for mentally and physically handicapped children. The comparison between the four states nonetheless reveals wide differences in distribution and organizational structure (see Table 1).

2.3 Special Preschools and Preschools

Disabled and developmentally delayed 3- to 6-year-olds attend special preschools in small groups of 4 to 10 children. Special preschools are organized along categorical lines. Whereas some of the educators have additional special training, most receive regular assistance from special teachers. Physiotherapists and speech therapists also provide regular services. The mainstreaming movement has led to more handicapped children attending regular preschools or daycare centers. Mainstreaming is usually supported by an additional educator and smaller groups with a maximum of 20 children.

2.4 Sociopediatric Centers

Sociopediatric centers serve children who cannot be served adequately by general practitioners or early intervention centers because of the kind, severity, or extent of their disorder. They are run by interdisciplinary teams under medical direction and are fitted out with extensive equipment including modern neurodiagnostic facilities. The teams consist of specialized physicians, psychologists, and specialists from different medical treatment fields (physiotherapists, occupational therapists, speech therapists). They are frequently affiliated with pediatric clinics providing services for larger geographic areas.

In 1991, the Federal Ministry for Labor and Social Affairs published a pamphlet listing all early intervention centers in the old German states. This revealed that there are about 700 early intervention centers and 35 sociopediatric centers. However, their general distribution is rather imbalanced: 375 of the early intervention centers are located in Baden-Wuerttemberg and Bavaria. In the Rhineland-Palatinate, there are eight sociopediatric centers with 36 branch offices, but not one early intervention center.

2.5 Responsibility for the Institutions According to Type of Impairment

Table 1 shows that services for various types of impairment are differentiated in different ways across the individual states. Only the Rhineland-Palatinate does not differentiate but treats all disabled children in sociopediatric centers. The most differentiated services are provided by Baden-Wuerttemberg.

2.6 Professions

Early intervention tasks are dealt with by different professions working in a variety of institutional settings. The major professional fields involved are education and medicine. Table 1 shows that early intervention has a strong medical orientation in the Rhineland-Palatinate and a strong educational orientation in Baden-Wuerttemberg. The other two states take an intermediate position. The medical field is characterized by cooperation between general practitioners, pediatricians, child and youth psychiatrists, physiotherapists, speech therapists, and occupational therapists. In the educational and psychological field, special teachers, social workers, educators, and psychologists work together in early intervention centers, special preschools, and special education centers. Although there is widespread agreement on the need for interdisciplinary cooperation, practical problems in attaining this goal are inherent to the system.

2.7 Funding

The costs of medical diagnosis, medical treatment, and medically prescribed therapy are carried by health insurers. Health insurance is obligatory in Germany. Local welfare agencies pay for educational, psychological, and social support services. Federal social welfare laws specify that disabled and at-risk persons have the right to measures and arrangements that support their integration into society. One paragraph defines integration aids for preschool children as special education measures. Further funding may be provided by the social welfare ministries in each individual state. When early intervention centers are associated with special education schools, personnel costs for these special teachers are funded by the state education departments. Finally, state welfare agencies can also cover some of the costs of early intervention. However, it has to be concluded that funding for early intervention differs from state to state (see Table 1). In many cases, securing funding is a permanent process of negotiation with health insurers, nonprofit private organizations, local welfare agencies, state departments, and others.

3   Early Assessment

Early assessment of disabilities and developmental risk is a necessary precondition for any early intervention service. It can be performed at different times by different professionals. Leaving aside modern possibilities of prenatal diagnosis, the first early assessment is immediately after birth. Germany has a set of nine routine pediatric examinations (U1 to U9) from birth up to the age of 6 years (see Table 2). Since 1971, these have been provided free of charge for all children. They are paid for by the obligatory health insurers.

Table 2 shows that the focus of early diagnosis for disabled and diseased children is during the first year of life. Only one pediatric examination is carried out per year at ages 3, 4, and 5 to diagnose developmental delays and abnormalities. Hence, children with developmental delays are only detected and treated when they reach these ages.

Table 2. *Free Pediatric Examinations of Children During Infancy and Early Childhood*

Examination	Time frame (Age)
U 1	Immediately after birth
U 2	3 to 10 days
U 3	4 to 6 weeks
U 4	3 to 4 months
U 5	6 to 7 months
U 6	10 to 12 months
U 7	20 to 27 months
U 8	43 to 50 months
U 9	58 to 66 months

Criteria for inclusion in early pediatric examinations are defined by law (§ 25, section 3, SGB V). They are:

1. The disease has to be curable.
2. Prestages and early stages of the disease must be accessible to medical diagnosis.
3. The symptoms assessed have to be defined sufficiently in technical and medical terms.
4. Sufficient physicians and medical institutions have to be available to diagnose and treat the assessed cases of the disease.

Overall participation in these nine routine examinations is approximately 100% during the first year of life. About 90% of children are assessed in the seventh examination at the age of 2 years. The rate declines to about 80% for the eighth examination at age 4. Parents with low socioeconomic status show a higher dropout rate with increasing age compared to middle-class parents. These nine early examinations can be viewed as a screening procedure. They are carried out by physicians in private practice, mainly pediatricians, or at children's clinics.

Early educational and psychological assessment does not have any similar, standardized procedure. Such assessment generally follows on from a medical diagnosis of abnormality or risk, or observations by somebody in the child's environment. Frequently, parents are advised by preschool teachers to consult an early intervention center. It is rare for parents to do this on their own initiative.

Disabilities and developmental risks that are not highly visible are still, and too frequently, recognized rather late. For example, about 40% of all deaf infants are identified only after they have reached the age of 1 year. The situation is similar for children with visual impairments. The early assessment of children with emotional deficits and children with delayed cognitive development is still most unsatisfactory. In particular, the detrimental effects on child development of social risks, caused by deprived life conditions, are frequently disregarded or underestimated. Early assessment efforts for these children should focus on the socioeconomic conditions under which these children grow up (Klein, 1993). The long-range negative effects of social risks on child development are demonstrated clearly in some of the contributions to this book.

4   Early Intervention in the Former German Democratic Republic

An overview of early intervention in the former German Democratic Republic (GDR) has been published by Baronjan (1993). This section sketches the main points in this work.

4.1 Early Assessment

Before unification with the Federal Republic of Germany (FRG), the GDR possessed a broad network of childcare counseling centers for mothers. Attending prenatal care and mother counseling was a precondition for the payment of the state birth assistance of 1,000 Marks (app. $500). Regular examinations were carried out in state-run crèches and preschools. This system ensured an almost complete and very early identification of disabled and at-risk children. This system of early assessment provided a much better access to children from socially marginalized families than that in the old FRG.

4.2 Forms of Organization

Mobile early intervention in the form of early education in the parental home did not exist in the GDR. Ambulant early intervention services were available at counseling centers for the speech-, language-, and hearing-impaired. A comprehensive network of special preschools provided early intervention for developmentally abnormal, retarded, and disabled 3- to 6-year-olds. However, waiting lists had to be introduced because there were not always sufficient places.

For infants and the under-3s, early intervention was rather inadequate. Parents were assigned a lay person´s role in all intervention measures, although they were relieved from the everyday care of their children by crèches and preschools.

4.3 Professional Personnel

The professional personnel in the special crèches for disabled children were child nurses and crèche educators. There was a lack of opportunities for further education and inservice training. Medical and therapeutic staff were available in only small numbers. However, there were mostly hardly any problems in the cooperation between the different professions. Nonetheless, the interaction between child and adult was determined by the principle of the "leading role of the educator."

5   Programs and Concepts in the Old German States

In the early 1970s, early intervention was still conceived as a function-oriented therapy that was oriented toward medical concepts of treatment. For example, Pechstein (1975) has written:

> It has to be ascertained that early therapy is not just the necessary application of surgical, dietary, or medicinal treatment but predominantly early learning therapy ... . Learning therapy should be conceived here as the medically indicated, purposeful initiation of learning processes in specific functional areas of childhood development while taking account of a differentiated diagnosis of the neuropsychological level of development. (p. 28, translated)

Hellbrügge (1978) has described this procedure in the following way:

> This makes the developmental diagnosis not only the indispensable basis for the therapy, but, as a scale of normal development, it also simultaneously contains the goals of therapy or the rough stages of therapy ... . The design of developmental therapy in the individual

areas follows the guidelines of the set developmental scale. (p. 178, translated)

In this therapy concept, physiotherapy, occupational therapy, and speech therapy are essential measures for the promotion of disabled and developmentally delayed children. These measures are the easiest to implement because they can be prescribed by a physician and are paid for by health insurers. As treatment occurs generally only once a week, parents are trained as cotherapists so that exercises can be continued in daily life.

Several early intervention programs were developed on the basis of such concepts and are comparable with the Portage Program of Shearer and Shearer (1972).

For example, Kiphard (1975) developed the *Sensomotorische Entwicklungsgitter*, an instrument for diagnosing sensorimotor development, on the basis of numerous scientific studies and many years of personal experience. The developmental profile obtained with this instrument served as a starting point for training programs. Individual items were not just used to check development, but also as a "purposeful exercise program for the systematic promotion of children with developmental delays" (p. 14, translated).

Ohlmeyer (1979) adopted this idea and formulated the individual items from Kiphard´s instrument into exercise tasks that were published as an early intervention program for disabled children. Straßmeier (1981) developed a similar promotion program with 260 exercises in daily living skills based on a screening test. He has commented that the tasks tested by the developmental test also have to be seen as goals that can be striven toward when the child is still unable to master the skill. The promotion program was based on Quick and Campbell´s (1976) "Lesson Plans for Enhancing Preschool Development Progress." However, Straßmeier (1981) has stressed that the program should be viewed only as an aid and stimulation and not as a set action guide or "recipe." The special needs of the individual child have to be perceived through observation and empathy. The early educator must pay attention to ". . . what does the child tell me about what he or she wants to learn?" (p. 13, translated), and create experiential scopes for the child.

Many practitioners have found these and similar programs helpful and have been happy to apply them. Not only did the basic concept initially seem to be clear and plausible, but also these programs provided clear action guidelines and thus confidence in their work for therapists. It was particularly educators who had been assigned the task of early intervention without any special training or experience who demanded such confidence in their work. However, the programs were not subjected to any systematic evaluation.

In the practice of early intervention by therapists, several problems arose: The role of cotherapist proved to be difficult and stressful for parents (Speck, 1983). Many therapists were confronted with the dilemma that, on the one hand, they wanted to respond to the situational and individual interests and needs of the child, whereas, on the other hand, they were forced to carry out the set exercises in the limited time available.

Professionals themselves questioned the specific effectiveness of physiotherapy with the indication that given an assumed success rate of 75%, 60% could be assigned to the personal application, loving acceptance, and motivational style of the therapist; a further 10% to nonspecific stimulation of perception and movement; and only the last 5% to special physiotherapy (Hoehne, 1980, p. 4). In particular, there was a strong call to limit the indication for physiotherapy (Michaelis et al., 1989), and the mental stress accompanying Vojta therapy in particular was pointed out (Michaelis, 1982, 1983; Moini et al., 1982). The frequent refusal of children to cooperate also raised doubts about the appropriateness of this therapy.

Even educators who kept strictly to the intervention programs soon found that it was increasingly difficult to motivate their clients, and that some children did not just express their lack of interest but even refused to cooperate (Kautter, 1982; Klein, 1982). Alongside these practical experiences, there were also theoretical criticisms of the concept underlying early intervention.

Speck (1981) criticized the approach known as developmental therapy or learning therapy by questioning the orientation toward a normative model of development as a basis for the curriculum. He particularly criticized the postulated invariance of the individual stages of development. This paid insufficient attention to the individual courses of development and the differences in learning and socialization conditions. The interactional character of educational activity, which encourages open, unplanned, and situation-related experiences, was being replaced by a "manipulative therapy." The curricular model of development left little scope for the "construction of reality through one´s own active confrontation with the environment" (p. 503, translated) in the sense of Piaget.

I have performed a critical analysis of the practice of equating early intervention with therapy in the medical sense (Klein, 1982). When early intervention is conceived as a therapy in this sense, the primary purpose of the diagnosis is to ascertain deficits, losses, and developmental delays. The goal of therapy is then to compensate the deficits through directed exercises and thus bring performance on individual functions up the standard developmental level for that age. Such a deficit-oriented training of functions not only presupposes the invariance of developmental stages criticized by Speck (1981) but also assumes that the missing developmental steps can be stimulated and completed through sequences of exercises to which children can be introduced from outside. This procedure and its implicit assumptions are problematic in several ways:

1. Insufficient attention is paid to the child as a person with his or her own biography; his or her own hopes, wishes, and fears.
2. No attention is paid to the findings in developmental psychology indicating that the major developmental steps that a child makes are carried out through his or her own active confrontation with the environment. Instead, an attempt is made to guide childhood activity by providing set action plans and goals.
3. Through the orientation toward developmental norms, therapists generally know very precisely what children have to do next, and they direct all their efforts to motivating the child to perform the desired activity.
4. When children announce their own interests, this tends to be disruptive and is not evaluated as a sign of self-initiated exploration of the world.

Within a long-term research project, we have learned to respect the child as the agent of his or her development (Kautter et al., 1988). Adults can provide the child with a "secure basis" (Bowlby), a "prepared environment" (Montessori), and each child must take his or her own steps into the next "zone of proximal development" (Leont'ev).

From a medical perspective, Schlack (1989a) has described the change in the approach to early intervention as a change in paradigms. The thinking in linear causal chains that characterizes natural science and medicine is not suitable for explaining the complex process of childhood development. Studies on interaction between children and reference persons have shown the great importance of an optimal balance in the reciprocal influence between child and adult. "The adult must be willing and able to pay attention to the child's signals. To do this, the adult must also take the child seriously and view the child as an equal partner" (Schlack, 1989a, p. 15, translated). The adult has to respond to the child, that is, he or she must coordinate his or her reactions with the child. This requires "responsiveness", an attitude "that allows the child space and time for his or her own activities, but is prepared to respond to the child's activities in a supportive and guiding way" (p. 15, translated).

In summary, Schlack (1989a) determines:

> . . . an impaired child does not simply require a large amount of additional stimulation; it is far more the case that, just like a healthy child, he or she needs the opportunity to test the effects of his or her own initiative, to practice his or her own remaining abilities, to gain experience and self-confidence through this, and use it as a basis for expanding his or her own repertoire of actions, understanding, and social skills. (p. 16, translated)

This sensitive balance of interaction between child and adult is susceptible to disruption in many ways. Among adults, the child's reduced activity triggers a trend toward more activities, to dominance, guidance, and control. Among parents, there arises an increased need for therapeutic activity and the desire to change something. And, finally, this interaction is always also determined by the subjective perceptions of the child and the parents. Schlack (1989a, p. 17) summarizes the premises of this new paradigm in five points:

1. A disability is a state that sets some limits on the possibility of change toward normalcy.
2. Therefore, the goal cannot be to follow normal development more or less completely, but to try to promote the competence of the child. This means to bring out hidden abilities as well as possible; to extend the child's action repertoire, understanding, and social abilities; and to strengthen the child's self-awareness.
3. The subjective experience and well-being of the child is an important guideline for the design of early intervention, that is, it is important to take seriously and understand the signals that the child gives out in this area. This avoids failures due to overtaxing the child, lack of motivation, or defensive reactions.
4. The parent's role and the therapist's role should be kept as separate as possible. The competence of the parents has to be respected and strengthened. It is not a lesser competence than that of professionals but a different one.
5. A systematic outlook that takes account of many reciprocal dependencies and influences is viewed as correct and necessary. This also includes an awareness among professionals that their intervention forces them, whether they want to or not, into becoming a part of this system of relationships. They may

strengthen the compensatory power of this system, or they may well disturb or handicap it unwittingly and despite their good intentions.

However, it cannot be assumed that this understanding of early intervention has permeated all areas of practice. It is far more the case that a strong tendency can be seen to persist in the medical and natural science concept. There are several reasons for this:

1. As mentioned above, programs with clear action guidelines also provide therapists with confidence in their practical work.
2. Medical therapeutic professionals such as speech therapists, ergotherapists, and physiotherapists, are oriented more toward the classical understanding of therapy through their training and their professional self-image.
3. It is much easier to obtain funding from health insurers for such medically prescribed therapy than for educational early intervention that is directed toward open interaction.
4. Finally, being able to state clearly what one has to do with the child, and, thus, that one can do something, is much more in line with the hopes and wishes of parents.

5.1 Analyses and Principles

As mentioned above, very few studies in Germany have dealt explicitly with the effectiveness of individual early intervention programs. What has been studied, in contrast, is the system of early intervention with its complex conditions, the forms of interaction among the persons involved, and the course of individual intervention measures.

Research activities can be broken down roughly into the following areas:

1. Organizational and structural conditions of early intervention in individual federal states.
2. Interaction with disabled children.
3. Families (parents and siblings) of disabled infants.
4. Infants with Down's syndrome.
5. Blind and visually impaired children.
6. Psychosocial risks in early child development.

For the first field, studies have been performed on Berlin, Baden-Wuerttemberg, and Bavaria. Vogel et al. (1990) have studied the field of practice of early intervention in West Berlin. Their main findings were that (a) far fewer children than the expected 5% actually receive early intervention; (b) there is a one-sided emphasis on children whose disabilities are physically recognizable; and (c) the demarcation of responsibilities impairs practical work.

Interdisciplinary cooperation between different professional groups is impaired by the various types of training and the heterogeneous ways in which people enter the professional field of early intervention.

Trost (1991) has studied organizational and personnel-related aspects of early intervention in the state of Baden-Wuerttemberg and compared it with early intervention in Bavaria, Hesse, and the Rhineland-Palatinate. The study provides an overview of early intervention institutes in Baden-Wuerttemberg and the children they help. He has used five points to summarize weaknesses that need to be overcome in the future:

1. The lack of an interdisciplinary orientation.
2. Insufficient coordination and cooperation within the existing assistance system.
3. Unfavorable framing conditions in special education counseling centers.
4. Regional deficits in quantitative and qualitative service delivery.
5. A lack of opportunities for further training of early intervention personnel.

Peterander and Speck (1993) have subjected the early intervention system in Bavaria to a very differentiated examination aimed toward increasing the transparency of organizational conditions and the educational and therapeutic activity of personnel. This is reported in the present volume.

The topic of interaction between disabled infants and their parents has been addressed in a series of studies that point to possible disruptive elements in interaction, confirm the importance of "responsiveness" in reference persons, and emphasize infants' and toddlers' active involvement in shaping interaction (Papousek, 1994; Sarimski, 1986; Schlack, 1989b).

There is a range of different studies on the area of families, parents, and siblings. Much space is taken by studies on the cooperation between parents and professionals in early intervention. This concerns the roles of parents and professionals. The discomfort of parents becomes clear in many fields, just like the difficulty in linking together everyday life with special intervention measures. The major conclusion derived from this work has been that parents have to be taken seriously and respected as competent partners in early intervention. Other studies have dealt with how siblings cope with having a disabled brother or sister. Another field of study is how it is broken to parents that they have a disabled child. Results reveal how unsatisfactory the current solutions to this problem are (Dittmann & Klatte-Reiber, 1993; Hackenberg, 1983; Hinze, 1991; Seifert, 1989; Speck & Warnke, 1983; Walthes et al., 1994; Weiß, 1989).

The most recent work on this topic will be presented briefly. As part of a large research project on the role of mobility training in early childhood for the blind and visually impaired, Renate Walthes et al. (1994) have performed a study of the situation of families with blind, multiply handicapped, or visually impaired children. They interviewed 31 parents of 1- to 9-year-old children. The goal was to assess the everyday situation of the family and the concrete ways in which parents and children treated each other. Particular emphasis was placed on experiences with physicians, experiences with the institutions of preschool and school, and cooperation between parents and professionals. It is not possible to give a detailed report on the methods used and the many qualitative and quantitative findings here. A few findings will be mentioned briefly: Most parents rated their experiences with hospitals and physicians negatively,

> . . . so that the impression arose that this study has stumbled on a disaster area in social communication . . . most parents felt not only misunderstood but thoroughly ignored by physicians, and that their parental responsibilities and rights were taken away from them by the high-handed activity of physicians (p. 180, translated)

Analyses of interviews asking how parents found out about different therapy provisions reveal the following picture.

Physiotherapy was prescribed in more than 90% of cases. In 12 children, there were indications of motor and cerebral problems. For 9 children, physiotherapy was prescribed because of premature birth. In 13 children, there were indications of neuromotor impairments (p. 306). Parents did not obtain information on provisions for early intervention for blind and partially sighted children from hospitals or anywhere else, although they have been available for decades in the early counseling centers of schools for the blind. Parents were mostly left to cope by themselves. (p. 307).

The analysis of the cooperation between parents and professionals also revealed the problems with the role of co-therapist mentioned above and confirmed the need for cooperation. Although early intervention through special education was perceived to be helpful, there were frequent complaints about a divergence between the expectations regarding specific early intervention and the lack of experience and competence in the early intervention personnel.

The authors concluded that parents should be encouraged to openly confront professionals and that more attention should be paid to the communication situation between the two groups.

Comprehensive and very differentiated longitudinal studies have been carried out on the clearly demarcated and relatively small groups of infants with Down's syndrome as well as on blind and visually impaired children. These are reported in detail by Hellgard Rauh and Michael Brambring in this book.

A series of studies have been presented on the problem of psychosocial risks as causal factors in disability. These confirm that the negative effects of psychosocial risks on childhood development are more severe than the biological ones (Laucht et al., 1992; Meyer-Probst & Teichmann, 1984; Neuhäuser, 1987; Rauh, 1984). This is dealt with in detail in Esser's chapter in this book.

References

Baronjan, Ch. (1993). Die Situation der Früherkennung und Frühförderung in den neuen Bundesländern. In Vereinigung für Interdisziplinäre Frühförderung e.V. München (Eds.), *Früherkennung von Entwicklungsrisiken: Dokumentation des 7. Symposiums Frühförderung Tübingen 1993* (pp. 143-149). Basel: E. Reinhardt.

Deutscher Bildungsrat (1973). *Empfehlungen der Bildungskommission. Zur pädagogischen Förderung behinderter und von Behinderung bedrohter Kinder und Jugendlicher.* Stuttgart: Klett.

Dittmann, W., & Klatte-Reiber, M. (1993). Zur veränderten Lebenssituation von Familien nach der Geburt eines Kindes mit Down-Syndrom. *Frühförderung interdisziplinär, 12,* 165-175.

Hackenberg, W. (1983). *Die psycho-soziale Situation von Geschwistern behinderter Kinder.* Heidelberg: Schindele.

Hellbrügge, Th. (1978). *Münchener funktionelle Entwicklungsdiagnostik. Fortschritte der Sozialpädiatrie* (Vol. 4). München: Urban & Schwarzenberg.

Hessisches Sozialministerium, Landeswohlfahrtsverband Hessen, Projektgruppe Frühförderung (no year). *Information über Frühförderangebote in Hessen.* Wiesbaden: Author.

Hinze, D. (1991). *Väter und Mütter behinderter Kinder.* Heidelberg: Schindele.

Hoehne, R. (1980). Frühe Krankengymnastik - überschätzte Therapie, überforderte Therapeuten. *Frühförderung interdisziplinär, 3,* 1-6.

Kautter, H. (1982). Ganzheit und Selbstgestaltung in der Frühförderung: Eine Fallstudie. In G. Klein, A. Möckel, & M. Thalhammer (Eds.), *Heilpädagogische Perspektiven in Erziehungsfeldern* (pp. 59-62). Heidelberg: Schindele.

Kautter, H., Klein, G., Laupheimer, W., & Wiegand, H. S. (1988). *Das Kind als Akteur seiner Entwicklung. Idee und Praxis der Selbstgestaltung in der Frühförderung entwicklungsverzögerter und entwicklungsgefährdeter Kinder.* Heidelberg: Schindele.

Kiphard, E. J. (1975). *Wie weit ist ein Kind entwickelt?* Dortmund: modernes lernen.

Klein, G. (1982). Pädagogische Frühförderung ist mehr als Therapie. In G. Klein, A. Möckel, & M. Thalhammer (Eds.), *Heilpädagogische Perspektiven in Erziehungsfeldern* (pp. 55-59). Heidelberg: Schindele.

Klein, G. (1993). Ökologische und interaktionale Aspekte pädagogischer Früherkennung. In *Beiträge zur Frühförderung interdisziplinär (Bd. 3): Früherkennung von Entwicklungsrisiken.* München: Reinhardt.

Landestag Rheinland-Pfalz (no year). *Drucksache 12/5013, Anlage 1.* Mainz: Author.

Laucht, M., Esser, G., Schmidt, M. H., Ihle, W., Löffler, W., Stöhr, R.-M., Weindrich, D., & Weinel, H. (1992). "Risikokinder": Zur Bedeutung biologischer und psychosozialer Risiken für die kindliche Entwicklung in den beiden ersten Lebensjahren. *Kinderpsychiatrie, 41,* 274-285.

Meyer-Probst, B., & Teichmann, H. (1984). *Risiken für die Persönlichkeitsentwicklung im Kindesalter.* Leipzig: Volk und Wissen.

Michaelis, R. (1982). Die Belastung der Eltern-Kind-Beziehung durch therapeutische Maßnahmen. *Pädiatrische Praxis, 27,* 629-634.

Michaelis, R., Niemann, G., & Krägeloh-Mann, I. (1989). Theorie und Praxis krankengymnastischer Methoden auf neurophysiologischer Grundlage. In D. Karch, R. Michaelis, B. Renner-Allhoff, & H. G. Schlack (Eds.), *Normale und gestörte Entwicklung* (pp. 105-115). Berlin: Springer.

Moini, A. R., Schlack, H.-G., & Ebert, D. (1982). Frühbetreuung entwicklungsgestörter Kinder. Verhaltensstörungen bei Säuglingen und Kleinkindern durch inadäquate krankengymnastische Behandlung. *Pädiatrische Praxis, 27,* 635-640.

Neuhäuser, G. (1982). Über notwendige und mögliche Kooperation bei der Frühförderung behinderter Kinder. *Frühförderung interdisziplinär, 1,* 4-10.

Neuhäuser, G. (1987). Entwicklungsneurologie und psychosoziale Bedingungen. *Pädiatrische Praxis, 36,* 207-213.

Ohlmeyer, G. (1979). *Frühförderungsprogramme für behinderte Kinder (0-6), 980 Übungsanweisungen mit Materialangaben.* Dortmund: modernes lernen.

Papousek, M. (1994). *Vom ersten Schrei zum ersten Wort: Anfänge der Sprachentwicklung in der vorsprachlichen Kommunikation.* Bern: Huber.

Pechstein, J. (1975). Sozialpädiatrische Zentren für behinderte und entwicklungsgefährdete Kinder. In Deutscher Bildungsrat (Ed.), *Gutachten und Studien der Bildungskommission. Sonderpädagogik, 6.* Stuttgart: Klett.

Peterander, F., & Speck, O. (1993). *Strukturelle und inhaltliche Bedingungen der Frühförderung.* München, Ludwig-Maximilians-Universität.

Quick, A. D., & Campbell, A. (1976). *Lesson plans for enhancing preschool developmental progress: Project Memphis.* Dubuque, IA: University of Dubuque.

Rauh, H., (1984). Frühgeborene Kinder. In H.-Ch. Steinhausen (Ed.), *Risikokinder* (pp. 11-35). Stuttgart: Kohlhammer.

Sarimski, K. (1986). *Interaktion mit behinderten Kindern. Entwicklung und Störung früher Interaktionsprozesse.* München: Reinhardt.

Schlack, H. G. (1989a). Paradigmawechsel in der Frühförderung. *Frühförderung interdisziplinär, 8,* 13-18

Schlack, H. G. (1989b). Psychosoziale Einflüsse auf die Entwicklung. In D. Karch, R. Michaelis, B. Rennen-Allhoff, & H. G. Schlack (Eds.), *Normale und gestörte Entwicklung* (pp. 41-59). Berlin: Springer.

Seifert, M. (1989). *Geschwister in Familien mit geistigbehinderten Kindern.* Bad Heilbrunn: Klinkhardt.

Shearer M., & Shearer, D. (1972). The Portage project: A model for early childhood education. *Exceptional Children, 39*, 210-217.

Speck, O. (1981). Das normative Entwicklungsmodell als curriculare Basis für die pädagogische Förderung geistigbehinderter Kinder. *Zeitschrift für Heilpädagogik, 32*, 494-504.

Speck, O. (1983). Das gewandelte Verhältnis zwischen Eltern und Fachleuten in der Frühförderung. In O. Speck & A. Warnke (Eds.), *Frühförderung mit den Eltern* (pp. 13-21). München: Reinhardt.

Speck, O., & Warnke, A. (Eds.).(1983). *Frühförderung mit den Eltern.* München: Reinhardt.

Speck, O. (1989). Frühförderung als System. *Frühförderung interdisziplinär, 8*, 148-156.

Straßmeier, W. (1981). *Frühförderung konkret. 260 lebenspraktische Übungen für entwicklungsverzögerte und behinderte Kinder.* München: Reinhardt.

Trost, R. (1991). *Frühförderung in Baden-Württemberg. Bestandsaufnahme und Perspektiven der Weiterentwicklung.* Stuttgart: Ministerium für Arbeit, Gesundheit, Familie und Frauen.

Vogel, D., Rauh, H., & Jordan, S. (1990). *Therapieangebote für behinderte Kinder* Berlin: Marhold.

Walthes, R., Cachay, K., Gabler, H., & Klaes, R. (1994). *Gehen, Gehen, Schritt für Schritt ... Zur Situation von Familien mit blinden, mehrfachbehinderten oder sehbehinderten Kindern.* Frankfurt: Campus.

Weiß, H. (1989). *Familie und Frühförderung. Analysen und Perspektiven der Zusammenarbeit mit Eltern entwicklungsgefährdeter Kinder.* München: Reinhardt.

M. Brambring, H. Rauh, and A. Beelmann (Eds.). (1996). *Early childhood intervention: Theory, evaluation, and practice* (pp. 72-91). Berlin, New York: de Gruyter.

Early Intervention in Sweden

Ulf Janson

1 Introduction: Children in Need of Special Support in Sweden

In Swedish legislation and practices, there is no term equivalent to "early intervention." Professionals sometimes use an expression with the meaning of "early initiatives" rather than "early intervention." Since there is no direct reference to the concept of "early intervention," the guiding concepts for this account will be "children at risk" and "children in need of special support."

Dunst et al. (1989, p. 24) define children at risk in terms of four "nonmutually exclusive" groups: "those at risk due to environmental factors (e.g., poor conditions of rearing), those at risk due to biological factors (e.g., Down's syndrome), those at risk due to medically-related factors (e.g., prematurity), and those at risk due to family or systemic factors (e.g., parental alcohol and drug abuse)." The Swedish National Board of Health and Welfare, in its preliminary work for the parliamentary committee on psychiatric services, defines children at risk as "some groups of children whose situation definitely necessitates attention and societal support" (Socialstyrelsen, 1991a, p. 28, my translation). These groups are specified as: (a) children with functional impairments (in the report called "children with handicaps"); (b) children with minimal brain dysfunction (MBD/DAMP); (c) physically, psychologically, and/or sexually abused children; (d) children in immigrant, especially refugee families; (e) adopted children; and (f) children with divorced parents. The present account will focus mainly on children with functional impairments (intellectual, motor, sensory), that is, the biological risk group according to Dunst et al.'s classification.

The term "children in need of special support" has been used for some time in Sweden, mainly in connection with preschool and day care services in which these children constitute a priority group. The concept was introduced by the committee on child care, resulting in the Child Care Act of 1977, later on incorporated into the Social Services Act of 1982. There is no clear definition or delineation of the group. The child care committee defines the group as children with ". . . difficulties due to physical, psychological, social, or emotional injury or due to deficits in rearing conditions" (SOU 1972:26, p. 122, my translation). The Social Services Act, in the sections on "care of children and young persons," mentions "children who, for physical, mental, or other reasons, need special support for the sake of their development" (Social Services Act, Section 15, Ministry of Health and Social Affairs, International Secretariat, 1990). The term is used in the same broad and vague sense in prescriptions and recommendations from the National Board of Health and Welfare on preschool and child care services (Socialstyrelsen 1987:3, 1991a:1). Roughly speaking, the terms "at risk" and "in need of special support" can be said to identify the same group of children, though the first term primarily underlines what characterizes their actual situation; the second term, what kind of services they are entitled to.

How large is the number of "at-risk" or "special needs" children? It is rather characteristic that there is no completely reliable and up-to-date account of prevalences. The reasons for uncertainty in these respects are, among others, vagueness in concepts and definitions, difficulties in identification of the actual risk population, and changes in the population due to political decisions, economy and market situations, and so forth. However, at least some figures can be presented for at least some subgroups.

According to the National Board of Health and Welfare, in 1984 there were 16,900 children and young persons (0-19 years) with intellectual impairments or mental retardation. In a total population of about 1.8 million in the corresponding age group, this means roughly 1% (Socialstyrelsen, 1985). Another, quite diverging figure from the same period of time and for the same age groups is reported by Daun (1987). This is based on national statistics: 0.08% persons with profound mental retardation and 0.14% with mild and moderate impairments.

Prevalences for different motor impairments and related handicaps are reported for different periods of time. The prevalence of cerebral palsy was 2.3 per 1,000 in the mid-1950s. It decreased during the 1960s, but returned to the level of the 1950s in the 1970s and the 1980s due to decreased mortality in premature children (Sanner, 1992). Spina bifida has a reported prevalence of 0.3 to 0.5 per 1,000, and 80% of these children also have hydrocephalus (Arvidsson, 1992). For children with MBD/DAMP, there is one population-based study from the Gothenburg region reporting a prevalence of roughly 6% at the age of 6 to 7 years. Of these, one fifth take a severe form (Gillberg, 1981).

Visual impairments among children and adolescents aged between 0 and 19 years amounted to 0.2% in 1984 (Socialstyrelsen, 1985). Of these, roughly 40% were diagnosed as intellectually impaired or mentally retarded. According to consultants' records in the national agency for handicapped children in preschools and schools (SIH), about 0.2 to 0.3 children per

10,000 are functionally blind from birth, of whom almost two thirds have additional impairments (Janson & Gustafsson, in press). In total, this agency registered 933 preschool-aged children with visual impairments in 1988, equivalent to 0.14% of the entire child population in the corresponding age range (0-6 years; Svensson & Enqvist, 1989). Finally, the National Board of Health and Welfare reports that 0.2% of children and adolescents aged between 0 and 19 years are hearing impaired, among whom half have severe impairments and 15% have additional impairments like mental retardation (Socialstyrelsen, 1985). The incidence of hearing impairments, motivating special educational intervention to promote satisfactory language development, is estimated at 150 to 200 children per year (Blücher, 1987).

2   Ambitions and Objectives in Social Policy and Legislation

During the last three to four decades, there has been a characteristic shift in welfare policy and social services. While laws and decrees in the 1940s and 1950s were very specific in terms of target groups, aims, and recommended outcomes, legislation for groups with special needs from the 1960s onward has gradually been integrated into general welfare legislation. Parallel to this development in legislation, public services in the corresponding period of time have tended toward generalization and globalization. Aims and objectives have gradually tended to embrace larger proportions of the population and larger sectors of the life of the individual. Goals and recommendations for education, health care, and social services tend to be derived more and more from what is politically and ideologically motivated, rather than from the services' traditional tasks and competencies (Lagerberg et al., 1990).

This tendency toward generalization and globalization of services, which previously concentrated their efforts on very specific tasks or very limited segments of the population, can be seen as an aspect of a trend toward including all community members within a general welfare program. This trend is quite obvious when it concerns services to persons with disabilities and functional impairments. Legislation and practices formed during the 1980s have stressed repeatedly that all services, as well as all aspects of community life, should be made available to the disabled. Two kinds of legislation complement each other with the aim of fulfilling this objective: general laws on social and medical service, education, national insurance, and so forth; and so called "plus" laws, regulating the rights of persons in need of special support.

Basic and general services, relevant for the topic of this presentation, are guaranteed through three acts: the Social Services Act (1980), the Health and Medical Services Act (1982), and the National Insurance Act (1962). According to the Social Services Act, municipal authorities are obliged to provide for the basic welfare and security of the individual. The ambitions, according to the first section of this act, are set very high:

> Public social services are to be established on a basis of democracy and solidarity, with a view to promoting economic and social security, equality of living conditions, and active participation in the life of the community. With due consideration for the responsibility of individuals for their own social situation and that of others, social services are to be aimed at liberating and developing the innate resources of individuals and groups. Social service activities are to be based on respect for the self-determination and privacy of the individual. (Social Services Act, Section 1, Ministry of Health and Social Affairs, 1990)

According to Section 21 of this act, the social welfare committee in the municipality "shall endeavor to ensure that persons who for physical, mental, or other reasons encounter difficulties in their everyday lives are enabled to participate in the life of the community and to live on equal terms with others." More specifically, this means that they are entitled to financial assistance, transport services, home-help services, and preschool and leisure center places (Ministry of Health and Social Affairs, 1986).

Under the Health and Medical Services Act, which is administrated by county councils, disabled persons are entitled to health and medical care on the same terms as the rest of the general public, as well as special health care services needed because of their impairment. The national insurance system includes benefits of different kinds for disabled and functionally impaired persons. Of special relevance in this context is the child care allowance, paid to parents taking care of their disabled and functionally impaired children. The aim of this allowance is to facilitate developmentally stimulating caring conditions for the child.

Laws on services specifically designed for persons with disabilities or other kinds of special needs have, as mentioned above, the character of "plus" laws. This means that they do not replace but supplement general welfare legislation with the aim of making normalization, integration, and participation in societal life a reality. Also stressed are principles of self-determination and respect for the individual. In service delivery to children with functional impairments, this means that parents should be actively involved in identification of needs and objectives, in planning, and in implementation. Of equal importance are services aimed at short-term relief for parents. The closing down of institutions has meant not only opening up society to the disabled person but also heavy responsibilities for parents of disabled children. Parents' right to relief is consequently acknowledged in the plus laws.

The most relevant plus law in this context is the Special Services for Intellectually Handicapped Persons Act (1986). The basic aim of this legislation is ". . . the phasing out of institutional care such as special hospitals and residential homes" (Ministry of Health and Social Affairs, 1986, p. 3). As a consequence, services include measures to facilitate daily living. Of specific relevance to children and their families is the right to counseling and other forms of personal support, short-term stays away from home, mainly in order to ". . . relieve next of kin of the tasks of care and supervision" (Ministry of Health and Social Affairs, 1986, p. 6), and accomodation in family homes or boarding homes for those children and young persons who need to live away from their parental homes. Service provision should be based on joint planning with the recipient of services. This means that services should be requested by individuals or their representatives; they are not delivered automatically. This, in turn, is dependent on the fact that persons are no longer registered by the authorities responsible for the service provision. The abolishment of such registration, mandatory before the 1986 legislation, has been an important principal question of democracy, equality, and respect for the individual.

The special services in the 1986 legislation are further extended in a new act, entering into force on January 1st, 1994 (Act Concerning Support and Service for Persons with Certain Functional Impairments, see Ministry of Health and Social Affairs, 1993). Services relevant for functionally impaired children and their families in this legislation are:

1. advice and other personal support that requires special knowledge about problems and conditions governing the life of a person with major and permanent functional impairments;
2. help from a personal assistant or financial support for reasonable costs for such help;
3. escort service;
4. help from a personal contact;
5. relief service in the home;
6. short stay away from the home;
7. arrangements for living in family or in residential homes for those children who need to live outside their parental home.

3   Organization of Services and Provision Practices

Service practices designed to realize the objectives and decrees mentioned in the preceding section form a quite extensive, complicated, and sometimes, as it seems, inconsequent system. In part, this is due to the fact that traditional forms of service delivery encounter new demands, and that professionals trained in old roles have to adapt to new ones. I shall try to give a comprehensive view of service deliveries by identifying three aspects of this system:

1.   organizational level (state, county, municipality);
2.   category of special need (in this account, focusing on intellectually and developmentally impaired, motor impaired, visually impaired, and hearing impaired children and their families);
3.   target of intervention, immediate recipient of service (individual child, parent or family, preschool).

In general, the system of public services in Sweden is organized on municipality (local responsibility) and county (regional responsibility) levels. As inclusion, integration, and participation in ordinary life are the guiding principles in policy making, the basic rule is that this general system also provides services to disabled persons and, in the case of disabled children, to their families.

Municipalities have the basic responsibility for day care, schools, and social security (economic aid and psychosocial support). Counties administer health and medical services as well as certain special services to functionally impaired and handicapped persons. The latter include special schools and, in certain cases, preschools. As part of the integration and inclusion philosophy, special schools are mostly integrated locally in ordinary schools. The same is true for special preschools. The general rule, however, is that preschool children in need of special support attend ordinary preschool groups. A vast majority of intellectually impaired children, of children with motor, visual, and hearing impairments, as well as children at risk for psychosocial reasons are individually placed in such preschools. According to statistics from the year 1987, 75% of the entire population of preschool children with the four above-mentioned impairments attend ordinary preschools, as compared to 48% for the total child population in preschool ages (Socialstyrelsen, 1991a). Exceptions to this rule can be found among severely and multiply impaired children, children with autism and other psychotic disturbances, and deaf and hearing impaired children. However, even among these latter groups, many children attend ordinary preschools either individually or integrated in groups.

For special-needs children in ordinary preschools, the municipality has the basic responsibility for everyday care, whereas the county, and in some cases the state, provides for special services like motor training, adaption to daily life (ADL), speech and communication training, occupational therapy, and so forth as an integrated part of preschool activities.

In addition to municipality and county resources, the state (nationwide responsibility) is in charge of certain specialized tasks. A special state agency is responsible for the development of technical aids. Another agency organizes consultant teams for hearing, motor, and visually impaired children and is also in charge of developing special education equipment. The state is furthermore the principal for some residential schools and former residential schools, now working and resource centers, responsible for assessments, courses for parents, assistants and preschool teachers, and so forth.

4. Service Provisions for Different Kinds of Special Needs

In this section, I shall specifically account for services in connection with different kinds of functional impairments. Services will further be distinguished in terms of target, that is, services to the child as a specific recipient, to the family, and to preschools.

4.1 Children With Intellectual and Motor Impairments and Their Families

Since the service systems for intellectually and motor impaired children in many ways parallel each other, they will be treated jointly in this account. Basic service provisioners to these groups are the municipality and the county. Provisions for daily life, including personal assistants, escort service, help from personal contacts, and different kinds of relief services, are duties of the municipality; whereas professional support and training specifically related to the impairment should be provided for by the county. Such professional support is organized in specialized teams for care of the intellectually impaired and in rehabilitation teams working with motor impaired children. Many counties have coordinated services for intellectually and motor impaired children in what are called "joint rehabilitation teams." The main reason for such coordination is the high prevalence of multiple impairments. It is hoped that coordinated services will bring down the total number of professionals involved with the family.

Service to the individual child. Rehabilitation is conceptualized as a process (Bille, 1992) involving (a) diagnosis of the child's impairments and functional assessment of possible development; (b) information to parents about the impairment and crisis treatment to parents when needed; (c) problem identification and goal formulation in collaboration with parents; (d) joint implementation of measures and services; and (e) regular outcome assessments. Active cooperation with families in goal setting and service implementation is considered to be of crucial importance if lasting effects are to be accomplished. The basic agency for all these activities is the rehabilitation team. The team structure is multidisciplinary representing educational, medical, physiotherapeutic, psychological, social work, speech therapeutic, and technical competencies.

Service to the family. It is repeatedly stressed that parents and families are an important part of the rehabilitation process. Besides being active partners in the planning and implementation of Individualized Family Service Plans (IFSPs, in Swedish ISP, Individual Service Program), parents are acknowledged as service recipients themselves. Such services include personal psychological support, relief service, and financial support. Psychological support is a task for the rehabilitation team, whereas relief service is a municipality responsibility. Financial support is given by the state (extra care allowance for parents with disabled children). Financial support can also be given by the municipality for adapting living conditions in the home and in the physical surroundings to the special needs of the child.

Preschool services. A vast majority of intellectually and developmentally impaired children (90%) and children with motor impairments are individually mainstreamed in ordinary preschools. These children usually have a personal assistant with a specific responsibility to serve as a kind of tutor for the child. There is a risk, discussed in some research, that the assistant, rather than facilitating social integration, actually could prevent it by becoming too strongly attached to the child. Consequently, assistants are usually instructed to work as a resource in the entire group of children, but to pay particular attention to the special-needs child. Children who are not individually integrated usually attend groups that are housed in the same premises as ordinary preschools (group integration, local integration). Some counties also have special preschools within the rehabilitation organization. Children attending these preschools usually have severe and multiple impairments. However, many severely impaired children also attend the ordinary preschool group. For disabled children in ordinary preschools, the municipality is responsible for everyday care and activities, whereas the county provides for certain specialized services like motor training, ADL, speech and communication training, and occupational therapy within these activities. Such services are given by trained specialists (physiotherapists, speech therapists, occupational therapists) who regularly visit the preschool as consultants.

Lekotek. A special form of service is given by the *lekoteks*, that is, toy libraries. A register from 1993 reports a total of 73 *lekoteks* in the whole country. The majority are connected to the rehabilitation agencies in the different counties, specialized in services for motor and intellectually impaired children. The service is based on a conception of play as essential for cognitive, motor, and social development and given by a "lekotekarian," who usually is a preschool teacher with special education training. Services include lending out toys and play equipment free of charge and giving advice on suitable occupations for children at different ages and at different stages in mental development.

4.2 Blind and Visually Impaired Children

Within this group, three subgroups can be distinguished: children with multiple impairments, blind children with no additional impairments, and low-vision children with no additional impairments. The first group is entitled to the special services given by the rehabilitation team and will not be dealt with further in this section. Blind and visually impaired children with no additional impairments are not automatically entitled to rehabilitation and other services directed to intellectually and motor-impaired children. Instead, there is a specialized service organization for these children as a plus resource to the basic social and medical services. These specialized services are state, not county, responsibilities.

Service to the individual child. All medical service, including specialized ophtalmological work, is given within the county organization for health and medical service. When diagnosed as visually impaired, a child is referred to a county agency (*syncentral*) responsible for testing and prescription of optical and technical aids, like glasses, magnifying devices, and so forth. If agreed on by parents, the child is at the same time referred to a state agency (SIH) responsible for services to preschools and schools that mainstream visually impaired children. This agency provides the child with a consultant trained in special education for visual impairments. The consultant regularly visits the child's home and preschool and gives advice about general and visual development, play and play materials, social relations, peer interaction, and so forth. In early childhood, the consultant pays special attention to motor, communication, and language development.

If judged necessary, the child can also be referred to a physiotherapist, a speech therapist, or other relevant specialists. Almost every child and his or her family is referred to the national resource center for visually impaired and blind children (TRC) or the resource center for visually impaired, multiply handicapped children (ERC). These centers assist in specialized assessments of general and visual development, social relations, language and communication, and so forth. Usually, two such visits are made during the preschool years. The second visit is specifically designed as a school entrance preparation, when, among other things, advice is given concerning reading media.

Service to the family. The SIH consultant has a central role, especially in early years, in informing parents about general development in the visually impaired or blind child, in giving technical and pedagogical advice, but also in strengthening parents' confidence in themselves as able caregivers to their child. In general, the strategy can be characterized as "interactive" rather than "direct" (see Cole et al., 1993), because it emphasizes the importance of attachment and mutual interaction in the relation between parent and child rather than the training of specific competencies and abilities. Families are also referred to "parent courses" at the national resource centers. Parents are entitled to extra care allowance.

Preschool services. Most visually impaired children attend ordinary preschools (90% of legally blind children aged between 3 and 6 years). Usually, blind and severely visually impaired children are accompanied by personal assistants, working as a resource for the entire preschool group, but with specific responsibility for the visually impaired child. Preschool staff are invited to the national resource centers for courses and in-service training. Such courses are sponsored by the municipality. Preschools with visually impaired children are also visited regularly by SIH consultants who give advice about physical surroundings, play material, activities, how to promote peer relations, and so forth.

In some cases, the situation for visually impaired children is rather confusing in terms of what kinds of services the child is entitled to. The reason is that visually impaired children are not automatically entitled to rehabilitation services provided by the rehabilitation teams like *lekotek*, physiotherapists, and speech therapists. To get access to such services, the child needs to be multiply impaired. However, multiple impairments in blind or severely visually impaired children are not always easy to assess. Congenital blindness is often combined with delayed or deviant development in motor, communicative, and social areas. Observations of such lags and delays may be judged as indicative for rehabilitation services in one county; whereas in another county, they are not. Under specific circumstances, such deviances are signs of additional impairments (Janson, 1993), but there are no general rules regulating the child's entitlement to rehabilitation services.

4.3 Deaf and Hearing Impaired Children

Like the visually impaired, hearing impaired children without additional impairments are not entitled to county rehabilitation services. The incidence of multiple impairments in hearing impaired children is considerably lower than among the visually impaired. There are certain parallels in the service organization for the two groups, with the notable exception that deaf and hearing impaired children go to special schools and, to a certain extent, to special preschools.

Service to the individual child. Medical service is given by audiological clinics within the county-administered health and medical service system. When a hearing impairment is discovered, the child is referred to a special unit within the audiological clinic (*hörcentral*) that coordinates medical, technical, educational, and social work. Technical aids, like hearing aids or acoustic and optical signals, are prescribed and delivered free of charge. Educational services are provided for by a special educator. As with visually impaired children, specially trained SIH consultants are involved in the educational support of the child, though only at school, not at preschool, level. School-age deaf and hearing impaired children go to special schools, a total of five in the whole country, or to special units within the ordinary school system. For hearing impaired students with additional impairments, there are two special schools, one for students with behavior and communicative disturbances, and one for students with intellectual and developmental impairments. These seven schools, the only special schools in Sweden, all have the state as principal.

Service to the family. The special unit at the audiological clinic gives support to parents, like advice on the child's general development, communication, and language. Some counties also give psychological support, like crisis treatment in parent groups. Parents are entitled to extra care allowance.

Preschool services. Like all other disabled children, the deaf and hearing impaired are a priority group in the preschool system. It is a duty for the municipality to arrange for such placements. However, hearing impaired children are mainstreamed in ordinary preschools to a lesser extent than other groups of disabled children (estimated at 65% to 70% of a total of 800 children, Ellström, 1993). Half of this mainstreamed group is individually integrated and half in groups (Ellström, 1993). Besides these ordinary preschools, there are so-called integrated preschools, at which about one fourth of the children are hearing impaired; the remainder being without impairments. There are also a few preschools with exclusively deaf or hearing impaired children. It is considered important for the hearing impaired or deaf child to meet other children with the same disability in order to develop communication skills and self-confidence (Blücher, 1987).

5   Evidence of Service Outcomes and Effects

This section focuses on the outcomes of educational, developmental, and psychosocial services. Medical services will not be treated. Reference is made to research and evaluations based on observations and assessments of children, and also to reports from parents and service providers.

In general, scientific evidence on the efficacy of early service deliveries to children and families is sparse. Most research is concentrated on the integration and mainstreaming of functionally impaired children in the preschool system. Relatively few studies focus on service provision to families. Also, studies involving assessments of children in different areas of development are few.

Outcomes and effects of preschool mainstreaming are discussed comprehensively in a report by Daun, summarizing studies carried out during the 1970s and the first half of the 1980s (Daun, 1987). On the whole, the picture drawn in this report is a negative and pessimistic one. According to legislation, as well as service administrators and practioners, the most important goal in mainstreaming is social integration and the development of social skills and cooperation (Socialstyrelsen, 1991b). Though individual planning and adaptation of services to the needs of the child is emphasized repeatedly in laws and decrees (Socialstyrelsen, 1987), preschool staff and teachers often suppose beneficial effects of mainstreaming to emerge spontaneously as a result of children simply being together (Daun, 1987). Hill and Rabe (1987) report from studies on the mainstreaming of intellectually impaired children that even consultants and specialists advice preschool staff "not to do anything in particular," that is, to treat the intellectually impaired child just like any child. According to 86% of teachers in their study, mainstreaming has not resulted in any change in daily work and methods. This attitude may reflect a sympathetic ambition not to segregate and stigmatize the impaired child, but the effect may be the opposite. In further studies, using sociometric and observation techniques, Hill and Rabe report intellectually impaired children to be socially isolated and at risk for negative development. Children are ascribed low social status, and are not accepted, at best tolerated, by their nondisabled peers (Hill & Rabe, 1991, 1993). According to these authors, mainstreaming policy is based on oversimplified ideas about the conditions for positive social processes between disabled and nondisabled preschoolers.

On the whole, intellectually and developmentally disabled children are the most extensively studied group in preschool mainstreaming. Hill and Rabe (1987, 1991, 1993) analyzed mainstreaming from educational, psychological, and social points of view. According to teachers, a majority of children made developmental gains, especially in cognition and language. Few teachers, however, were specific about individual goals, and in most schools, mainstreaming did not seem to affect daily routines. Social integration, judged as particularly important, was not obtained. Peer choice interviews revealed negative attitudes in half of the nondisabled group. Direct observations gave even more negative results. About 80% of the disabled child's interactions were adult-directed. Very similar observations are reported by Ekholm and Hedin (1984), who compared mainstreaming of intellectually disabled and emotionally/behaviorally disturbed children. They found that intellectually impaired children were mostly alone and isolated. Social contacts, when they occurred, were 80% adult-directed.

Studies of children with motor impairments either observe social behavior in mainstreamed preschools (Marsk et al., 1984) or compare integrated and special preschool groups (Dvoretsky, 1980; Miller, 1989). According to Marsk et al., impaired children in mainstreamed preschools act more like observers than participants. Dvoretsky reports that teachers in mainstreamed preschools judged social interaction between disabled and nondisabled children to be very satisfying. However, this was only partly true. Children with severe disabilities elicited strong emotional reactions in the nondisabled. On tests of intellectual and general development, more children in specialized than in integrated groups demonstrated significant improvements. Miller found that benefits from integrated settings were related to degree of impairment. Mildly and moderately impaired children gained socially from the integrated group, while severely disabled did not. On the other hand, the more intensive treatment and motor training in the special preschool was beneficial for the severely impaired, while of less importance for the mildly and moderately impaired.

Studies of visually impaired and blind children in preschool are few. Palmer (1987) and Preisler (1991) report a high degree of social isolation and few social initiatives in the blind. The child's need for information and assistance was satisfied by adults. Janson and Merényi (1992; Janson, 1992) studied play interactions between blind and sighted children and found more adult dependency in the blind child than in the sighted, but also a substantial degree of peer-directed initiations from blind children, and a marked tendency in sighted children to respond to needs for information and assistance. However, there was considerable asymmetry in blind-sighted interaction, with sighted children taking a predominantly active, initiating role, whereas blind children acted more dependently and reactively. Further studies have implemented systematic teacher interventions in order to facilitate interaction. Preliminary results seem to indicate decreased asymmetry and decreased adult dependency in blind children and the adoption of more efficient social techniques (Janson & Merényi, 1993). In a study of the so-called "morning circle," Gustafsson (1991) has demonstrated that blind children increase their degree of participation and activity in socially structured situations and in situations with a limited number of participants.

As mentioned above, deaf and hearing impaired children attend mainstreamed preschool services to a lesser extent than other groups of disabled children. Deaf children, in Swedish publications, are generally characterized as not being at risk, provided training in communication skills and sign languages is given. If placed in mainstreamed preschools without such support, however, these children are in a vulnerable position (Nordén & Preisler, 1981). According to Ellström (1985), teachers found group integration in ordinary preschools to be preferable for hearing impaired children, whereas for the deaf, segregated alternatives generally were preferred. In free and structured play with nonimpaired peers, Ellström (1990) reports no substantial differences between hearing impaired children and children without impairments. Analyzing peer preferences, Ellström found that hearing impaired children played with nondisabled peers to a greater extent than the deaf. The more pronounced communication difficulties in deaf children prevented such interactions. However, in her final conclusions, Ellström found that the preschools studied were unsuccessful in achieving social integration. She concludes that "merely placing hearing-impaired and deaf children together with nonimpaired children does not in itself lead to social integration. Thus, being on the same premises may be seen as a necessary but insufficient condition for achieving social integration" (Ellström, 1993, p. 229).

If studies of the preschool system and services are few in number, even fewer have addressed direct services to children and families. Some studies highlight the psychosocial situation of the family and the sometimes extreme amount of stress experienced by parents (Brodin & Lindberg, 1990; Esscher et al., 1989; Hellström et al., 1987; Janson & Lagerberg, 1989). A report from the National Board of Health and Welfare concludes that families, including siblings, are subject to considerable psychological and social stress, and that public as well as private support seldom is sufficient (Socialstyrelsen, 1991a). To what extent, then, has service and support succeeded in satisfying existing needs?

Brodin and Lindberg (1990) interviewed 30 families with intellectually and multiply impaired children in five counties. They concluded that parental needs for relief services are great and unsatisfied. In a study specifically addressing the issue of relief services in 278 of the 284 municipalities in Sweden, the same authors point to the vital importance of this service, but also to its lack of efficiency (Brodin & Lindberg, 1988). Furthermore, parents are insufficiently informed about existing support and aids, services are insufficiently coordinated, and collaboration between parents and professionals does not work in a satisfactory way (Brodin & Lindberg, 1990). A majority of parents in the study were not actively involved in the planning of intervention and support. Obviously, according to this study, the intention of the plus laws is not fulfilled to an acceptable degree.

Janson and Lagerberg (1989; Lagerberg & Janson, 1990) studied families' perceptions of rehabilitation services in a suburb of the city of Uppsala. They found unsatisfied needs when relief services and psychological and social support were considered. Another part of the study focused on cooperation between different agencies in rehabilitation, health care, and social services. The authors report inadequate cooperation and collaboration, and a lack of competence among staff working in close contact with child and family in identifying needs and giving advice and support.

Granlund (1991) points to a tendency among professionals to explain incomplete implementation of services in terms of a lack of motivation among parents. He further reports that in a group of 46 families with multiply disabled children, 61% had not received the amount of service and support they needed. Only 44% of families had been involved in goal setting when planning interventions. This is in accord with the repeatedly stressed importance of actively involving families in service planning and implementation. The services provided were found to be insufficiently adapted to the families' perceptions of their needs. When families and professionals systematically cooperate in assessing the needs and abilities of the child, in setting goals, and in implementing intervention, outcomes are markedly positive, both in terms of families' perceptions and rated child behavior (Granlund et al., 1990).

6   Conclusion

Though highly incomplete in the coverage of the total service field, the reported studies in several respects point in the same direction. Though resources are relatively extensive, consumer satisfaction is not very evident, either in families or among personnel who receive consultant services from specialists.

It is of some interest to compare this picture of service delivery in Sweden to the characteristics of effective service delivery programs as discussed by Bruder in a recent article (Bruder, 1993). According to this author, an effective program has eight salient characteristics: It should have a program philosophy for inclusive early childhood services; a consistent and ongoing system for family involvement; a system of team planning and program implementation; a system of collaboration with other service providing agencies; well-constructed IFSPs; integrated delivery of educational and related services; a system for training and staff development; and a comprehensive system for program evaluation.

Though evidence from Swedish practice is incomplete, it seems justified to conclude that these practices do not meet such standards. There is a generally accepted philosophy of inclusive services; there is a belief, in principle, in family involvement, in collaboration between agencies, in integration of educational and related services, and in the importance of in-service training and staff development. In practice, however, family involvement is insufficient, collaboration is lacking, and when it is implemented, it frequently causes conflicts between agencies and different professionals (Janson et al., 1990). Systematic individualized educational and family service planning is not a rule. In addition, follow-up and evaluation of services are often incomplete or absent, and, when carried through, they are in most cases subjective and unreliable.

Peterson and McConnell (1993) characterize impact as a product of effectiveness and likelihood of implementation. At least in the case of preschool inclusion, Swedish practices seem neither to rely on proved effectiveness in choosing working models nor to systematically examine and test intervention integrity, that is, the degree to which an intervention is delivered as planned. In the case of service delivery to families, the principles of active family involvement are widely accepted but seldom put into practice according to studies by Brodin and Lindberg (1990) and Granlund (1991).

This state of affairs has implications not only for service delivery but also for research. With some notable exceptions, present research in Sweden focuses too much on the "status quo," that is, on existing practices in service delivery and preschool inclusion, which, according to all experience, are not optimally designed. Such research is necessary in identifying targets for further development, but it is not useful in guiding service delivery or in forming a basis for political decisions. Recommendations for the future are that service agencies and researchers should engage jointly in projects designed to test systematically planned and implemented service and intervention models. If this does not occur, research may come to play a destructive role by reinforcing disappointed and pessimistic attitudes in a field in which creativity, development, and enthusiasm should be the landmarks.

References

Arvidsson, J. (1992). Ryggmärgen. In B. Bille & I. Olow (Eds.), *Barnhabilitering* (pp. 102-109). Stockholm: Almqvist & Wiksell.

Bille, B. (1992). Habiliteringsteamet. In B. Bille & I. Olow (Eds.), *Barnhabilitering* (pp. 102-109). Stockholm: Almqvist & Wiksell.

Blücher, G. (1987). Barn med hörselhandikapp. In N. Ericsson (Ed.), *Att möta barn med behov av särskilt stöd* (pp. 134-144). Stockholm: Esselte Studium.

Brodin, J., & Lindberg, M. (1988). *Avlösarservice - en rättighet eller ett privilegium.* Stenhamra: WRP (Women Researchers in Play and Disability) International.

Brodin, J., & Lindberg, M. (1990). *Utvecklingsstörda i habiliteringen.* Stockholm: Riksförbundet FUB.

Bruder, M. B. (1993). The provision of early intervention and early childhood special education within community early childhood programs: Characteristics of effective service delivery. *Topics in Early Childhood Special Education, 13*, 19-37.

Cole, K. N., Dale, P. S., Mills, P. E., & Jenkins, J. R. (1993). Interaction between early intervention curricula and student characteristics. *Exceptional Children, 60*, 17-28.

Daun, H. (1987). *Förskolan och integrering av barn med behov av särskilt stöd för sin utveckling.* Stockholm: Gotab.

Dunst, C. J., Snyder, S. W., & Mankinen, M. (1989). Efficacy of early intervention. In M. C. Wang, M. C. Reynolds, & H. J. Walberg, (Eds.), *Handbook of special education: Research and practice. Vol. 3. Low incidence conditions* (pp. 259-264). Oxford: Pergamon Press.

Dvoretsky, B. (1980). *Beskrivning och analys av rörelsehindrade barns situation i förskola och årskurs 1 i grundskola.* Göteborgs Universitet: Institutionen för praktisk pedagogik.

Ekholm, B., & Hedin, A. (1984). *Förtursbarn och "vanliga" barn på tolv daghem.* Linköpings universitet: Pedagogiska Institutionen.

Ellström, E. (1985). *Gruppintegration av hörselskadade och döva barn i förskolan.* Universitetet i Linköping: Institutionen för pedagogik och psykologi.

Ellström, E. (1990). *Hörselskadade och döva barns lek i integrerad förskoleverksamhet.* Universitetet i Linköping: Institutionen för pedagogik och psykologi.

Ellström, E. (1993). Integration i institutionaliserad verksamhet. En studie av gruppintegration av hörselskadade och döva barn i förskolan. *Linköping Studies in Education and Psychology, 39.* Linköpings Universitet. [With an English summary]

Esscher, E., Nordgren, I., & Lindqvist, A. (1989). Att vara förälder till ett barn med handikapp. Intervjuer med 100 barns föräldrar. *SoS-rapport 1989:9.* Stockholm: Socialstyrelsen.

Gillberg, C. (1981). *Neuropsychiatric aspects of perceptual, motor and attention deficits in seven-year old Swedish children.* Unpublished manuscript, Uppsala University.

Granlund, M. (1991, October). *Intervention with the multiply impaired child in an integrated setting. Variables effecting the collaborative process between families and consultants.* Paper presented at the workshop on rehabilitation and early intervention with multiimpaired children. Finnish Academy of Sciences, Helsinki.

Granlund, M., Olsson, C., Dardel, T. von, & Andersson, M. (1990). Parents, group home staff and school staff working together around children with profound multiple disabilities. *British Journal of Mental Subnormality, 36,* 37-52.

Gustafsson, B (1991). *Gravt synskadade förskolebarn i kommunal förskola. En studie av samlingen.* Gruppen för handikappforskning, Rapport 1. Stockholms Universitet: Pedagogiska Inst.

Hellström, B., Jalling, B., Kempe, P., & Rubarth, M. (1987). Habilitering av rörelsehindrade barn i Stockholm. Familjesituationen pressad trots stödinsatser. *Läkartidningen, 32.*

Hill, A., & Rabe, T. (1987). Psykiskt utvecklingsstörda barn i kommunal förskola. Integrering belyst ur ett socialpsykologiskt perspektiv. *ACTA, Göteborg Studies of Educational Sciences, 61.* Göteborgs Universitet.

Hill, A., & Rabe, T. (1991). Får vi vara med och leka? Om socialisation av attityder och värderingar hos barn. In *Människa, Handikapp, Livsvillkor. Socialförvaltningen, Rapport 9.* Örebro Läns Landsting.

Hill, A., & Rabe, T. (1993). Socialisation av attityder och värderingar hos förskolebarn. In *Människa, Handikapp, Livsvillkor. Social-och omsorgsförvaltningen, Rapport 18.* Örebro Läns Landsting,

Janson, U. (1992, August). *Preschool integration of handicapped children in Sweden: Review of and proposals for research.* Paper presented at the 9th World Congress of the IASSMD, Gold Coast, Australia.

Janson, U. (1993). Normal and deviant behavior in blind children with ROP. *Acta Ophthalmologica, suppl. 210,* 20-26.

Janson, U., & Gustafsson, B. (in press). *SIH:s konsulentverksamhet för barn med synskador. Insatser och utvecklingsbehov.* Stockholm: National Swedish Agency for Special Education.

Janson, U., Hagelin, E., & Hermodsson, A. (1990). Ju mer vi är tillsammans... Om samverkan i tjänstesektorn. In D. Lagerberg & C. Sundelin (Eds.), *Barnfamiljerna och samhällets ambitioner* (pp. 59-87). Stockholm: Liber Förlag.

Janson, U., & Lagerberg, D. (1989). *Samhällsservice till familjer med handikappade barn.* Rapport 25 från projektet Barnfamiljerna och samhällets service. Uppsala Universitet: Pediatriska Institutionen.

Janson, U., & Merényi, A. C. (1992, August). *Social play between blind and sighted preschool children.* Paper presented at the ICEVH Early Childhood Conference, Bangkok, Thailand.

Janson, U., & Merényi, A. C. (1993). Vuxenpåverkan på samspelet mellan blinda och seende förskolebarn. In *Människa, Handikapp, Livsvillkor. Social- och omsorgsförvaltningen, Rapport 18.* Örebro Läns Landsting.

Lagerberg, D., & Janson, U. (1990). Samhällsservice till familjer med handikappade barn inskrivna vid barnhabiliteringen. In D. Lagerberg & C. Sundelin (Eds.), *Barnfamiljerna och samhällets ambitioner* (pp. 208-223). Stockholm: Liber Förlag.

Lagerberg, D., Janson, U., Sundelin, C., & Larsson, G, (1990). Services to families with children. A study of community work in Uppsala. *Scandinavian Journal of Social Medicine, 18,* 31-37.

Marsk, E., Paulsson, K., & Gustavsson, S. (1984). *Rörelsehindrade barn i förskolan. En studie av 17 barns situation på vanliga daghem.* Handikappforskningsgruppen. Stockholm: Karolinska Institutet.

Miller, K. (1989). *Habiliteringsenhet eller kommunal förskola för rörelsehindrade barn?* Stockholms Universitet: Psykologiska Institutionen.

Ministry of Health and Social Affairs (1986). *Special Services for Intellectually Handicapped Persons Act and Act Concerning Implementation of Special Services for Intellectually Handicapped Persons Act.* Stockholm: International Secretariat.

Ministry of Health and Social Affairs (1990). *Social Services Act and Care of Young Persons (Special Provisions) Act/LVU.* Stockholm: International Secretariat.

Ministry of Health and Social Affairs (1993). *Act Concerning Support and Service for Persons with Certain Functional Impairments and The Assistance Benefit Act.* Stockholm: International Secretariat.

Nordén, K., & Preisler, G. (1981). Personlighetsutveckling hos döva barn. In G. Strachal (Ed.), *Man kan om man får. Forskning-handikapp-samhälle.* Stockholm: Liber Förlag.

Palmer, C. (1987). *Gravt synskadade barn i integrerad förskoleverksamhet. En sammanfattning av fem fallstudier.* Stockholms Universitet: Psykologiska Institutionen.

Peterson, C. A., & McConnell, S. R. (1993). Factors affecting the impact of social interaction skills interventions in early childhood special education. *Topics in Early Childhood Special Education, 13,* 38-56.

Preisler, G. (1991). *En studie om blinda barn i integrerad förskoleverksamhet.* Stockholms Universitet: Psykologiska Institutionen.

Sanner, G. (1992). Cerebral pares. In B. Bille & I. Olow (Eds.), *Barnhabilitering* (pp. 61-84). Stockholm: Almqvist & Wiksell.

Socialstyrelsen (1985). *Barn och ungdomar med handikapp. Socialtjänsten. Allmänna råd från socialstyrelsen, 1985:9.* Stockholm: Socialstyrelsen.

Socialstyrelsen (1987). *Pedagogiskt program för förskolan. Allmänna råd från socialstyrelsen 1987:3.* Stockholm: Socialstyrelsen.

Socialstyrelsen (1991a). *Barnomsorgen är för alla barn. Förskole- och fritidshemsverksamhet för barn som behöver särskilt stöd. Allmänna råd från socialstyrelsen 1991:1.* Stockholm: Gotab.

Socialstyrelsen (1991b). *Barn och ungdomar med behov av särskilt stöd. Underlag till psykiatriutredningen.* Mimeograph.

SOU 1972:26. *Förskolan, del 1. Betänkande avgivet av 1968 års barnstugeutredning.* Stockholm: Liber Förlag.

Swedish Institute (1993). *Support for the disabled. Fact sheets on Sweden.* Stockholm: Swedish Institute.

Svensson, H., & Enqvist, J. (1989). *Några statistiska uppgifter om 933 synskadade förskolebarn i Sverige.* Stockholm: TRC.

M. Brambring, H. Rauh, and A. Beelmann (Eds.). (1996). *Early childhood intervention: Theory, evaluation, and practice* (pp. 92-98). Berlin, New York: de Gruyter.

Early Intervention in Russia

Olga Usanova

1 Introduction

For many years, the problems of early intervention for children with developmental disorders in Russia have been addressed by research in the field of developmental pathology and related sciences. In addition, the cumulative historical and international experience in organizing special education has been applied while taking account of society's requirements.

First, it is necessary to explain the meaning of the term "early intervention" in Russia. It is applied to three groups of children: (a) 0- to 1-year-olds, (b) 1- to 3-year-olds, and (c) 3- to 6-year-olds. The organization and content of early intervention are better developed for the two older age groups.

2 Incidence

The number of children with deviations in health status and mental development is tending to increase in Russia. A special epidemiological survey has been carried out in different regions in order to ascertain the incidence of developmental disorders and provide a basis for planning early intervention and organizing special education. The findings on North-West Russia (Vologda, Tcherepovetz, etc.) provide a good example of the results of the survey. The main results were:

1. The relative incidence of developmental disorders remains unchanged: First place is still taken by cardiovascular disorders followed by muscular and skeletal anomalies and disorders of the central nervous system.

2. There is a trend toward an increase in the overall rate of developmental disorders. The number of children with developmental disorders in Vologda has increased from 2.3% in 1990 to 3.1% in 1991 and 3.6% in 1992; in Tcherepovetz, from 2.74% in 1990 to 2.89% in 1991 and 3.13% in 1992.

3   Institutions

Assistance to children with developmental disorders is provided by a network of specialized children's institutions (different kinds of daycare, residential facilities, and counseling services staffed by psychologists, physicians, and special educators).

Each family receives consultations on special education for children with developmental disorders. If necessary, the children receive assistance from special education personnel and specially trained nurses. They develop the child's orientation and mobility and cognitive abilities, and they train parents so that they can continue this work at home. In all cases, the children are examined two or three times a week by specialists.

Infants from the age of 0 to 1 year receive counseling services and treatment in polyclinics, hospitals, and special education centers. One- to 3-year-olds use the same institutions, but may also attend special daycare centers or residential centers. Children with no parents live in special residential homes until the age of 3 when they transfer to preschool residential homes.

Residential homes in which orphans are treated provide speech therapies up to preschool age.

Three- to 6-year-olds can receive care and treatment in all kinds of counseling and medical centers. They may also attend a network of specialized preschool residential homes.

4   Diagnostic Groups

The large heterogeneity in the neuropsychological development of 2- to 3-year olds attending preschool institutions has made it necessary to study the specific features of mental development in different groups of children in order to improve the organization of the care system for children with developmental disorders. Developmental delays were ascertained through a comparative study of neuropsychological development in groups of children with different case histories. The smallest number of children with developmental delays was found in the group with a favorable case history (40%) and the largest in the group with unfavorable social and biological case histories.

The investigations were made by using methods elaborated by specialists of the school of A. Luria. Medical and psychological investigation methods were used to identify children's psychological development and health status. In cases of delayed psychological development, detailed neuropsychological investigations of children were undertaken.

Dr. T. Zalevsky (Moscow, 1986, 1990) has isolated the group of children with the greatest risk to neuropsychological development. This group had a marked complex of predispositions to risk in their social and biological case histories. Certain spheres and phases of development proved to be most at risk. These were active speech and sensory development and the age of 1 year and 9 months.

Special attention has also been paid to the dynamics of development between the ages of 2 and 3 years. Investigations showed that the number of children with normal, age-appropriate development decreases between the ages of 15 and 21 months and then rises gradually up to the age of 3 years. On the one hand, this shows a sensitivity to risk factors during certain age periods; on the other hand, it shows the significant compensatory abilities of the child's organism.

At present, active investigations are being carried out to establish a comprehensive system of early intervention for children with developmental disorders in Russia. Some of the problems being considered are early diagnosis, organization of interventions, integrating children with developmental delays into their social context, and personnel training.

Early diagnosis is one of the most important issues. A group of scientists headed by Dr. E. Mastjukova has developed a comprehensive approach to diagnosis and treatment for psychomotor disorders in young children. It is known that a child's psychomotor development is based on a genetic program that develops under permanently changing mediation factors and on the developing relationships between mother and child. The heterochronic maturation of different functional systems, which is particularly distinct at an early age, determines the complex character of the evaluation and diagnosis of levels and patterns of impairment during the first years of life. Diagnosis is particularly difficult under the age of 1 year. Dr. Mastjukova has introduced a special idea for diagnosing age-related development during this period: a norm that is determined by the genotype of the organism and its reactions to environmental factors during the ante- and postnatal periods. This approach involves the selection of so-called benign or nonspecific and specific deviations in development. Nonspecific, benign developmental delay is caused by delayed maturation of the brain's structures and their functions in the absence of qualitative changes in the central nervous system. Specific delay is connected to impairment of the brain's structures and their functions. The approach is now being investigated in detail and the results will be published soon.

Within the comprehensive approach to early intervention, much attention is paid to developing psychological and educational diagnostic methods. Most of the methods applied are of observational nature. Tests are used for children over the age of 5 years. Recently, good results have been obtained with a system of psychological tests for preschool-age children (Usanova, 1989, 1990, 1992). These successfully apply a neuropsychologoical approach based on the work of A. Luria. This approach permits a syndrome analysis of a disorder, the selection of a disturbed mechanism of development, and a qualitative analysis of this disturbance. It makes it possible to identify insufficiencies in the dynamic organization of mental functions (disturbed tonus, poor balance, impaired mobility), partial insufficiencies in separate brain functions (gnosis, praxis, speech), and insufficiencies in the processes for regulating the initiation, programming, and monitoring of movement. Comparisons of data obtained during different stages of investigation permit an identification of the main disturbance of mental development in the child, its classification, and a determination of the causal relationship between primary and secondary disorders. All these factors then provide a basis for predicting the tempo, time, and pattern of mental development as well as indicating interventions.

5 Special Education

Russian specialists in the field of developmental pathology are trying to develop an integrated system of preschool special education. Current theoretical and empirical work stresses the need to solve problems connected to multilateral individual development in children. A strong emphasis is placed on collecting and summarizing data and reaching sound conclusions.

An integral part of preschool education for children with developmental disorders is so-called correction training. This training is designed to help overcome some of the difficulties resulting from biological disturbances. It is used as a basis for promoting the personality of a preschool child with developmental impairments.

The focus of the system of prevention and correction work is a differential approach to education and training. This includes a wide range of activities, for example, parent education, training parents to apply educational interventions, child education, and home consultations. The system is designed to encourage creative interaction between child, parents, and specialists. One important factor is the age principle. Different systems of developmental exercises are used for children of different age groups.

Treatment outcome effectiveness is controlled by monitoring child development. The criteria are positive dynamics in psychomotor and personality development, increased activity of the child, improved cognitive abilities, continued contacts between parents and specialists, improvements in family relationships, and improvements in the child's status within the family.

6   Family Relationship

A number of special investigations have been carried out on relationships within families with a developmentally impaired child. Clinical specialists at the Institute of Correction Pedagogics have studied emotional status and mother-child relations. They have found that the pattern of mother-child relations depends on the mother's physical and mental constitution and her emotional status. The latter is influenced by the following emotional factors: (a) the birth of a severely handicapped child and (b) characteristics of the family's psychological environment.

A depressive reaction in the mother to the birth of a disabled child impairs bonding. The mother is also influenced strongly by the quality of her marriage and relationships within the family.

6.1 Attitudes

Social attitudes toward children with developmental disorders seem to be changing. We hope that the idea of social integration can become reality. In this respect, we have carried out several studies on parents' attitudes toward the problems related to the child with a developmental impairment. We found two different attitudes that we labeled adequate and inadequate.

In a family with an adequate attitude, the child is accepted as healthy but with some particular problems that have to be taken into account in childrearing. This child feels included in family life.

There are several types of inadequate attitude: The first type is that the child and his or her impairment are accepted by parents, but the child is viewed as a victim who needs to be cared for and protected. This leads to overprotection. In a second type, the impairment is accepted, but not the child. The child is not treated adequately and suffers from a lack of warm physical contact and poor emotional relationships. In a third type, the impairment is not accepted although the parents accept their child. Parents fail to pay attention to the impairment and do not take the child's specific needs into account. A final type is when the parents accept neither the child nor the impairment. Such children have to live apart from their parents in special institutions. In this framework, early intervention involves counseling parents and helping them to develop an adequate attitude toward their child.

6.2 Mother-Child Relations

A group of Russian scientists have looked for trends and regularities in the relationship between mothers and children with developmental disorders. They studied 50 children with severe psychomotor disorders and their mothers as well as a control group of 50 normal children and their mothers. Relationships between these children and their mothers and different kinds of adults were observed in different situations such as play, training, treatment, feeding, and medical examination.

The results provided a more profound understanding of the psychological mechanisms underlying normal interaction and permitted the formulation of a model of situational interaction between mother and child during early stages of ontogenesis.

Using the model of situational interaction, Dr. N. Shkolnikova has developed a new system for psychological and educational work with children suffering from severe developmental disorders and their mothers. This system is based on the nonspecific activation of self-regulation mechanisms in the behavior of both child and mother. This creates conditions that increase the efficiency of special methods designed to overcome different mental disturbances.

7   Conclusion

The theoretical and empirical investigations carried out up to now in medicine, education, and rehabilitation psychology have allowed us to ascertain some multistructural and interrelated disturbances in sensorimotor, emotional, psychological, cognitive, and social spheres. At early stages, developmental abnormalities are mainly multilateral. This is why it is necessary to use an integrated, comprehensive approach to the study of the child and his or her education.

The main task of specialists is to promote harmonious development in the child and his or her complete social integration. Specialists performing early intervention with parents and child require comprehensive knowledge on the different types of disturbance in psychological and physical development. This is why training is so important. Specialist training is part of university courses on education. These courses contain the following components: clinical aspects of basic developmental pathology, child psychology and rehabilitation psychology, psychodiagnostics, psychology of communication, psychology of parent-child relations, corrective special education.

It is important for specialists dealing with children suffering from developmental impairments to interact with other specialists who assist the family and the child, and to use all psychological, medical, and educational measures to make educational technology more effective. We are applying this approach in the educational and practical work at our institute.

References

Bragina, V. D. (1993). *Correction of some negative traits in elder pre-scholars.* Paper presented at the First International Congress on Precautions, early identification and correction of developmental impairments in children. Moscow.

Mastjukova E. M. (1993). *Current approaches to psychomotor development disorders in infants.* Paper presented at the First International Congress on Precautions, early identification and correction of developmental impairments in children. Moscow.

Shkolnikova N. N. (1993). *Psychological model of interaction between mothers and children with severe developmental disturbances.* Paper presented at the First International Congress on Precautions, early identification and correction of developmental impairments in children. Moscow.

Tjulu Z. A. (1993). *Identification of handicaps in Cherepovets and Vologda region in 1990-1992.* Paper presented at the First International Congress on Precautions, early identification and correction of developmental impairments in children. Moscow.

Usanova O. N. (1993). *Neuropsychological approach in study of children with speech disorders at brain damage.* Paper presented at the First International Congress on Precautions, early identification and correction of developmental impairments in children. Moscow.

Usanova O. N. (1990). *Special psychology. System of psychological investigations of children with special needs.* Moscow.

Semenova K. A. (1972). *Clinic and rehabilitation therapy of infantile cerebral paralyses.* Moscow.

Part Two

Developmental Assessment, Risk Factors, and Outcomes

M. Brambring, H. Rauh, and A. Beelmann (Eds.). (1996). *Early childhood intervention: Theory, evaluation, and practice* (pp. 101-117). Berlin, New York: de Gruyter.

Prognostic Significance of Risk Factors, Neonatal Imaging Findings, and Early Neurodevelopmental Assessments

Remo H. Largo and Kurt von Siebenthal

1 Introduction

Parents and all professionals dealing with handicapped and at-risk children want to know whether a developmentally disturbed infant or young child will function in the normal, mildly, or moderately to severely impaired range at school age. Therefore, the reliability and predictive validity of risk scores, imaging findings, and developmental assessments carried out in infancy and early childhood are of major clinical importance. This chapter summarizes recent research on this subject and discusses its practical relevance. The data presented are based on the literature and the results of the Zurich longitudinal studies (Largo, 1990; Largo et al., 1989).

2 Risk Factors

Most previous studies have reported no significant relationships between prenatal risk factors and neurological or intellectual outcome (Largo et al., 1989). Stanley and English (1986), using cerebral palsy as an endpoint, observed that its prevalence showed little variation with high-risk factors operating during pregnancy. Others also have failed to show a significant correlation between pregnancy risk factors and neurodevelopmental outcome (Kitchen et al., 1983; Köhler et al., 1979; Shennan et al., 1985). Nelson and Ellenberg (1985) noted that only rare maternal conditions, such as maternal mental retardation, seizure disorders, or hyperthyroidism before pregnancy, were associated significantly with cerebral palsy. With respect to intellectual development, Naeye and Peters (1987) found that low IQ values correlated with some antenatal disorders (e.g., maternal anemia or hypotension).

A great deal of research has emphasized the importance of perinatal risk factors such as hypoxia, acidosis, and respiratory distress. However, a large number of often severe perinatal complications appear to have only a minor influence on postnatal development (e.g., Drillien et al., 1980; Kitchen et al.,

1982; Largo et al., 1989). Nelson and Ellenberg (1986) reported that the events at birth and in the neonatal period accounted for only a slightly higher proportion of cerebral palsy than was accounted for when consideration was limited to factors identified before participation. Kitchen et al. (1982), in a follow-up of three cohorts of low-birthweight infants, claimed that prevention of cerebral palsy by selective treatment in the delivery room or in the nursery was not feasible, since it was not possible to predict this condition from perinatal risk factors. Drillien et al. (1980) were unable to identify specific neonatal complications as being related to impairment at school age in low-birthweight children. In another study (Drillien & Drummond, 1983), perinatal risk factors were considered definitely responsible in only 5%, and possibly responsible in a further 8%, of children with handicaps. With respect to intellectual development alone, several authors were unable to correlate events occurring during parturition, delivery, and the neonatal period with subsequent IQ values (Cohen & Parmelee, 1983; Francis-Williams & Davies, 1974; Naeye & Peters, 1987).

The only perinatal variables of prognostic significance are birthweight, and, more specifically, gestational age. Both variables are consistently correlated positively with neurological, intellectual, and language development. With respect to neurological impairment, an exponential increase in the prevalence of cerebral palsy can be observed with decreasing gestational age (see Figure 1).

This finding cannot be explained by the relationship between birthweight, gestational age, and perinatal risk factors (the smaller and younger the infant, the more frequent and severe the perinatal complications). When prenatal and perinatal risk factors are partialled out, gestational age and birthweight continued to have a correlation of the same magnitude with developmental outcome (Largo et al., 1989). Thus, there are additional prenatal and/or perinatal factors related to gestational age and birthweight that must play a role. One major factor is immaturity leading to vulnerability of most organs, in particular the central nervous system, with decreasing gestational age. Before 40 weeks of gestation, there may also be postnatal factors (e.g., of metabolic origin) that could have a negative impact on early extrauterine brain development (Largo et al., 1986).

The lack of significant correlations between perinatal risk factors and outcome could lead one to conclude that perinatal complications play no role in future development, but these results more likely reflect the improved management of the preterm infant in the delivery room and in the nursery, thus diminishing the effects of perinatal complications on longterm outcome.

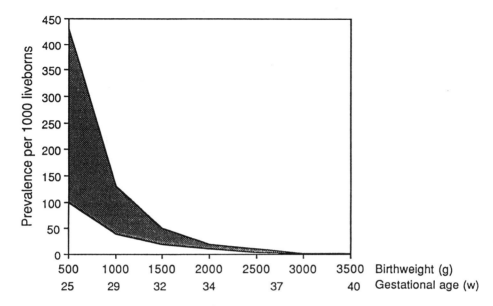

Figure 1.   Prevalence of cerebral palsy as function of birthweight and gestational age (Largo et al., 1990a, 1990b; Stanley & Albermann, 1984; Stewart, 1989).

There is a general agreement that postnatal factors such as socioeconomic status (SES) and psychosocial conditions are of major importance in neuropsychological development (e.g., Calame et al., 1976; Cohen & Parmelee, 1983; Dunn, 1986). In a longitudinal study of low-birthweight infants at 6 1/2 years of age (Drillien & Drummond; 1983), social grade emerged as one of the most significant predictors of the overall index of impairment. This has also been observed by many other authors (Calame et al., 1976; Cohen & Parmelee, 1983; Dunn, 1986; Naeye & Peters, 1987; Vohr & Garcia Coll, 1985). The Zurich longitudinal and cross-sectional studies revealed a significant correlation between SES and intellectual outcome, more specifically with verbal and psycholinguistic scores (Largo et al., 1989).

The influence of parental SES on mental performance is age-dependent: The correlations are modest between 18 and 24 months, but increase between 3 and 5 years (for reviews, see Golden & Birns, 1976; McCall et al., 1972). An additional finding is that SES correlates better with verbal scores than with performance scores (Largo, 1990). Of interest also is the observation that the impact of SES is related to the level of mental

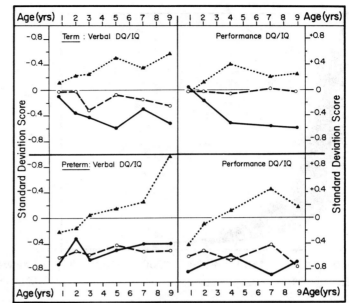

Figure 2.   Mean *SD* scores of DQ and IQ as function of social class in full-
             term   and   preterm   children.   Social   class: ●——● lowest,
             O- -O middle, ▲·-▲ highest (Largo, 1990).

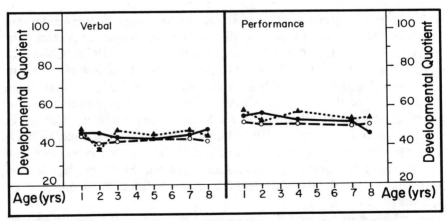

Figure 3.   Mean DQ as function of social class in retarded children. Social
             class: ●——● lowest, O- -O middle, ▲·-▲ highest (Largo,
             1990).

In the past, SES has been regarded as a measure of the environment in which the children live. Recent research, in particular adoption studies, strongly suggests that SES effects relate to genetic endowment as well as to the environment parents provide for their children (e.g., Scarr & McCartney, 1983). SES may have less effect on the development of retarded children, because they are less responsive to environmental stimuli, and/or because genetic endowment is overridden by organic impairment.

3   Imaging Techniques

Recent studies indicate that findings provided by ultrasound scanning, computerized tomography, and nuclear magnetic resonance have greater predictive significance than any risk concepts used previously. The predictive value of ultrasound scanning is demonstrated by the study of Graham et al. (1987) summarized in Table 1. The findings of cerebral

Table 1. *Prediction of Neurodevelopmental Outcome at 18 Months Based on Ultrasound-Detected Abnormalities (Graham et al., 1987)*

		Peri-ventricular hemorrhage	Prolonged flare	Cysts
		%	%	%
Accuracy	True Positives + True Negatives	54	79	94
Sensitivity	$\dfrac{\text{True Positives}}{\text{True Positives} + \text{False Negatives}}$	67	17	67
Specificity	$\dfrac{\text{True Negatives}}{\text{True Negatives} + \text{False Positives}}$	53	85	96
Positive pre-dictive value	$\dfrac{\text{True Positives}}{\text{True Positives} + \text{False Positives}}$	11	9	62
Negative pre-dictive value	$\dfrac{\text{True Negatives}}{\text{True Negatives} + \text{False Negatives}}$	95	92	97

ultrasound scanning during the neonatal period were related to presence or absence of cerebral palsy at 18 months. A consistently normal scan predicted normal outcome in more than 90% of cases. While specificity was also quite satisfactory, sensitivity was, at best, 67%. The positive predictive value varied between 9% and 62% depending on the type of lesion observed.

Computerized tomography and magnetic resonance imaging provide more detailed information on brain structures than ultrasound scanning. However, their clinical significance is similar to that of ultrasound technique: Brain lesions indicate neurodevelopmental impairment without specifying type and severity of retardation. In most infants with normal findings in computerized tomography and nuclear magnetic resonance, normal development can be expected. However, there is a small, but clinically important group of impaired children that cannot be identified by imaging techniques in the neonatal period.

4   Developmental Assessment

In 1905, Binet and Simon introduced the first mental scale, their main object being the detection of mental deficiency in school-age children. Subsequently, other infant tests were developed (Bayley, 1933a; Bühler & Hetzer, 1935; Cattel, 1940; Gesell, 1926), and scientific interest shifted from the study of mental retardation to the detection of individual differences in mental functioning and to the evaluation of mental development in normal children. In attempts to relate infant testing to later outcome, a number of longitudinal studies of normal populations were undertaken (Anderson, 1939; Bayley, 1933b, 1940; Birns & Golden, 1972; Cattell, 1940; Escalona & Moriarty, 1961; Goffney et al., 1971; Hindley, 1965; Honzik et al., 1948; Klackenberg-Larsson & Stensson, 1968; McCall et al., 1973; Moore, 1967; Werner et al., 1968). After summarizing nearly 50 years of data collection and analysis, McCall concluded in 1979 that scores for mental performance assessed during the first 18 months of life do not predict later IQ to any practical extent.

As well as this research on essentially normal children, studies have also been carried out to detect mental retardation in developmentally disturbed children (e.g., Drillien, 1964; Hunt & Bayley, 1971; Illingworth, 1961; Illingworth & Birch, 1959; Knobloch & Pasamanick, 1960, 1963, 1967; Stechler, 1964, Werner et al., 1968). The general conclusion from these studies was that prediction of future test performance tended to be better for children classified as retarded or neurologically impaired than for "normal" children.

In most studies, prediction of intellectual development from developmental testing has been based primarily on correctional analysis (for reviews, see Honzik, 1976; McCall, 1979). Of both theoretical and clinical significance is the observation that the stability of individual differences depends on the level of mental performance, being lowest in the normal children, moderate in the at-risk children, and highest in the retarded children (Largo, 1990). Greater stability in the test scores of low-scoring babies has been reported by several authors (Honzik, 1976; MacRae, 1955; Knobloch & Pasamanick, 1960). Hunt and Bayley (1971) argued that prediction of consistency in mental, emotional, and social development presupposes constancy of environment and/or genetic traits with effects persisting over time. Assuming that variability in the environment and in genetic traits is similar in normal, at-risk, and retarded children, stability in mental ability of these children is likely to be a function of brain integrity. Cerebral impairment appears to increase the stability of mental functions by limiting the variability in development over time.

For developmental psychologists studying the stability of interindividual differences in mental functioning, correlation analysis still remains the preferred mode of investigation. Clinicians are more interested in the integrity of the brain, and therefore in the stability of the level of mental performance. They want to know whether a developmentally disturbed infant or young child will function in the normal, mildly, or moderately to severely impaired range at school age. Stability of mental performance may not be depicted by correlation coefficients, which depend essentially on the stability of rank order and not on the stability of mean level of mental performance. The importance of differentiating stability of individual differences from the level of mental performance was depicted nicely by McCall (1979, p. 727), when he wrote: "Relying solely on the individual difference orientation is rather like asking why one giant sequoia tree is 30 feet taller than another, while ignoring how both came to be over 300 feet tall in the first place."

From a clinical point of view, categorizing children according to their level of mental performance is a more appropriate method of studying prediction than correlation analysis (Largo et al., 1990a). The results of the Zurich longitudinal studies demonstrate that the predictive validity of developmental testing at 9 to 24 months is reliable for normal and retarded children. A child performing in the normal range at 9 to 24 months is very likely to develop normally, while a child with a low DQ at 9 to 24 months most likely will be retarded at school age (Figures 4 & 5). Other authors have also shown that developmental testing of severely retarded children has a high predictive value, even before 9 months (e.g., Drillien, 1964). Prediction is less accurate for children with borderline performance (DQs between 70 and 90 during the first 2 years of life), and further testing between 2 and 5 years is necessary to predict the level of mental functioning at school age.

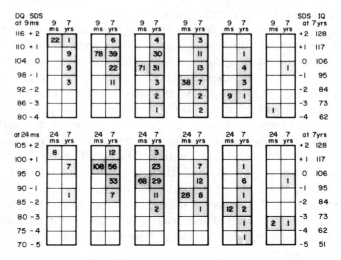

Figure 4.   Prediction of IQ at 7 years from DQ at 9 months (top) and 24 months (bottom) for full-term and preterm children combined. Children were grouped by *SD* scores on Griffiths test (C,D,E) at 9 and 24 months, then each group was categorized by *SD* scores on WIPPSI at 7 years (Largo, 1990).

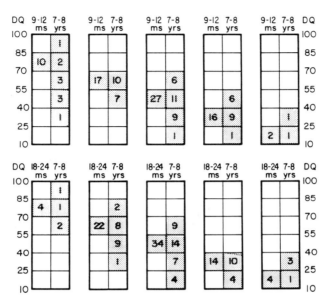

Figure 5.   Prediction of DQ at 7 years from DQ at 9 months (top) and 24 months (bottom) for retarded children. Children were grouped by DQ on Griffiths test (C,D,E) at 9 and 24 months, then each group was categorized by DQ of developmental assessment at 7 years (Largo, 1990).

Subscores and specific clusters of items have been found to predict IQ as well as, or better than, total test scores (Anderson, 1939; Fillmore, 1936; McCall, 1977; McCall et al., 1972). Vocalization by girls by 9 months had a moderate predictive value, while above-average language development during the first 2 years of life was judged a good indicator of superior, or at least average, cognitive functioning at school age (Cameron et al., 1967; McCall et al., 1972; Moore, 1967). In the Zurich studies, among the five subscores of the Griffiths test, the performance score (D, E), language score (C), and combination of C, D, and E were the best predictors of mental functioning. They had a higher predictive validity than any other subscores, combination of subscores, or the total score (A to E; Largo, 1990).

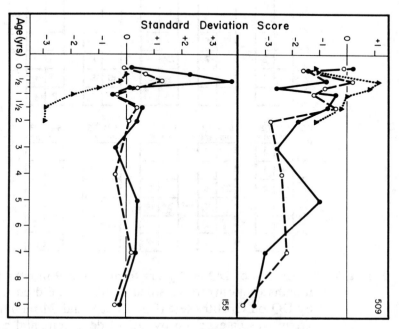

Figure 6. Deviant development of early locomotion. Top: advanced
development in a preterm girl, mildly retarded at school age;
bottom: delay in a preterm girl with subsequent normal
intellectual development. ● verbal score, O performance score,
▲ locomotion score (Largo, 1990).

There is a tendency to rely on gross motor achievements in judgments of an
infant's development, but, of all developmental subscores, the locomotor
score has the lowest correlation with intellectual outcome. It has no
predictive value for normal children and is only a weak indicator of future
intellectual functioning in retarded children. The influence of the level of
mental performance on prediction might explain why the predictive value

of locomotion has been controversial for many years (e.g., Capute et al., 1985; Illingworth, 1958; Silva et al., 1982). For most children, locomotor development reflects general development fairly well, but prediction for some children is hampered by major deviations in gross motor development. Figure 6 illustrates the extent to which locomotor development can be delayed in comparison with other areas of development, and how advanced motor development may lead to an overoptimistic view of later intellectual functioning.

Some previous studies have found that infant tests predicted later IQ better for girls than for boys (Goffeney et al., 1971; Hindley, 1965; McCall et al., 1972; Moore, 1967). We found no consistent sex differences in the Zurich studies, which is in agreement with other authors (Klackenberg-Larsson & Stensson, 1968; Werner et al., 1968).

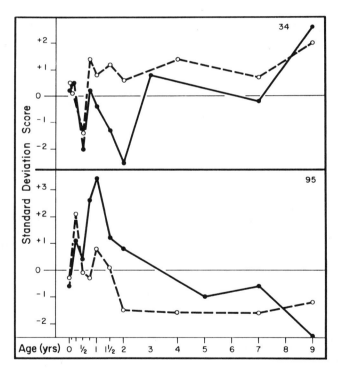

Figure 7.   Dissociation of early language development. Top: delay in a healthy full-term girl with excellent SES and psychosocial background; bottom: advancement in a preterm boy with subsequent general developmental delay. ● verbal score, O performance score (Largo, 1990).

Many causes may lead to unsatisfactory prediction in the individual child. A major cause is dissociated development, the most important being temporary delay in language development during the second and third year of life (Figure 7). Illingworth (1958) has also emphasized that isolated delay in expressive language of an otherwise normally developing child can lead to a wrong prediction. Dissociations between verbal and performance scores also occur between early childhood and school age and affect prediction to a considerable extent. Separate evaluation of performance, verbal, and locomotor scores seems to be essential for reliable prediction in the individual child. Prediction might also be improved by scoring receptive and expressive language separately, which is not possible at present with any of the developmental tests.

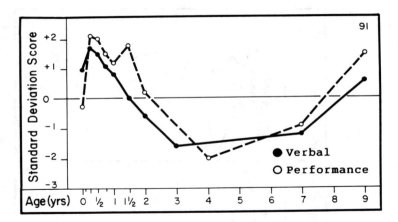

Figure 8.   A full-term boy whose parents divorced when he was 18-months-old. About 2 years later his mother developed cancer and died when he was about 6. Between 3 and 6 years, he was cared for by several foster parents; at 7 years he was adopted by relatives and his situation improved (Largo, 1990).

Children's deviations in development may be caused by organic impairment and/or major life events. The diagnosis of an etiological entity such as Down's syndrome (Gibson, 1978; Pueschel, 1984) or fragile-X syndrome (Largo & Schinzel, 1985) enables a more concrete prognosis to be made. Major life events such as severe illness, admission to hospital, and separation from the family have a considerable effect on some children's development (see Figure 8). Other family factors may influence development (McCall, 1983): For example, twins may demonstrate delay in the preschool period, particularly in language development (see Figure 9).

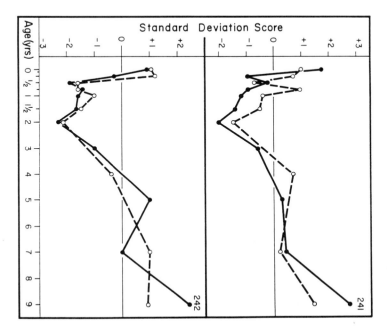

Figure 9.   Second-born monozygotic twins with a developmental delay during the first 3 years of life and above-average performance at school age. ● verbal score, ○ performance score (Largo, 1990).

5 Conclusion

In conclusion, predicting mental performance at school age from early developmental testing is reliable for normal and retarded children, but less reliable for children with borderline performance. Predictions can be hampered by dissociations in development, poor socioeconomic conditions, organic impairment, and major life events. Prediction for an individual child becomes more reliable if it is based on a detailed evaluation of various areas of development, rather than on a global judgment, and if the type and severity of cerebral impairment and environmental factors are taken into account.

Note

This work was supported by the Swiss National Science Foundation (32-30164.90) and La Fondation Suisse pour l'Encouragement de la Recherche Scientifique sur l'Arrièration Mentale.

References

Anderson, J. E. (1939). The limitations of infant and preschool tests in the measurement of intelligence. *Journal Psychology, 8*, 351-379.

Bayley, N. (1933a). *The California First Year Mental Scale.* Berkeley, CA: University of California Press.

Bayley, N. (1933b). Mental growth during the first three years. *Genetic Psychology Monographs, 14*, 1-92.

Bayley, N. (1940). Mental growth in young children. In *Intelligence: Its Nature and Nurture. Thirty-ninth Year Book of the National Society for the Study of Education. Part II: Original Studies and Experiments.* Bloomington, IA: Public School Publishing.

Binet, A., & Simon, T. (1905). Methodes nouvelles pour le diagnostic du niveau intellectuel des anormeaux. *L'Année Psychologique, 11*, 191-244.

Birns, B., & Golden, M. (1972). Prediction of intellectual performance at 3 years from infant tests and personality measures. *Merrill-Palmer Quarterly, 18*, 53-58.

Bühler, C., & Hetzer, H. (1935). *Testing children's development from birth to school age.* New York: Farrar & Rinehart.

Calame, A., Reymond-Goni, I., Maherzi, M., Roulet, M., Marchand, C., & Prod'hom, L. S. (1976). Psychological and neurodevelopmental outcome of high risk newborn infants. *Helvetica Paediatrica Acta, 31*, 287-297.

Cameron, J., Livson, N., & Bayley, N. (1967). Infant vocalisations and their relationship to mature intelligence. *Science, 157*, 331-333.

Capute, A. J., Shapiro, B. K., Palmer, F. B., Ross, A., & Wachtel, R. C. (1985). Cognitive-motor interactions. *Clinical Pediatrics, 24*, 671-675.

Cattell, P. (1940). *The measurement of intelligence in infants and young children.* New York: Psychological Corporation. (Reprinted 1967; New York: Johnson Reprint Corporation)

Cohen, S. E., & Parmelee, A. H. (1983). Prediction of five-year Stanford-Binet scores in preterm infants. *Child Development, 54*, 1242-1253.

Drillien, C. M. (1964). *The growth and development of the prematurely born infant.* Edinburgh: Churchill Livingstone; Baltimore, MD: Williams & Wilkins.

Drillien, C., & Drummond, M. (1983). Development screening and the child with special needs. A population study of 5000 children. *Clinics in Developmental Medicine, No. 86.* London: S.I.M.P. with Heinemann Medical; Philadelphia, PA: Lippincott.

Drillien, C. M., Thomson, A. J. M., & Burgoyne, K. (1980). Low-birthweight children at early school-age: A longitudinal study. *Developmental Medicine and Child Neurology, 22*, 26-47.

Dunn, H. G. (Ed.). (1986). Sequelae of low birthweight: The Vancouver study. *Clinics in Developmental Medicine, Nos. 95/96.* London: MacKeith Press with Blackwell Scientific; Philadelphia, PA: Lippincott.

Escalona, S. K., & Moriatry, A. (1961). Prediction of school-age intelligence from infant tests. *Child Development, 32,* 597-605.

Francis-Williams, J., & Davies, P. A. (1974). Very low birthweight and later intelligence. *Developmental Medicine and Child Neurology, 16,* 709-728.

Fillmore, E. A. (1936). Iowa tests for young children. *University of Iowa Studies in Child Welfare, 11,* 1-58.

Gesell, A. (1926). *Mental growth of the preschool child.* New York: Macmillan.

Gibson, D. (1978). *Down's syndrome: The psychology of mongolism.* Cambridge: Cambridge University Press.

Goffeney, B., Henderson, N. B., & Butler, B. V. (1971). Negro-white, male-female eight months developmental scores compared with seven-year WISC and Bender test scores. *Child Development, 42,* 595-604.

Golden, M., & Birns, B. (1976). Social class and infant intelligence. In M. Lewis (Ed.), *Origins of intelligence* (pp. 299-351). New York: Plenum Press

Graham, M., Levine M. I., & Trounce J. Q. (1987, September 12). Prediction of cerebral palsy in very low birthweight infants: Prospective ultrasound study. *Lancet,* pp. 593-587.

Hindley, C. B. (1965). Stability and change in abilities up to five years: Group trends. *Journal of Child Psychology and Psychiatry, 6,* 85-99.

Honzik, M. P. (1976). Value and limitations of infant tests: An overview. In M. Lewis (Ed.), *The origins of intelligence* (pp. 59-95). New York: Plenum Press.

Honzik, M. P., Macfarlane, J. W., & Allen, L. (1948). The stability of mental test performance between two and eighteen years. *Journal of Experimental Education, 18,* 309-324.

Hunt, J. V., & Bayley, N. (1971). Explorations into patterns of mental development and prediction from the Bayley scales of infant development. In J. P. Hill (Ed.), *Minnesota Symposia on Child Psychology* (pp. 52-71). Minneapolis, MA: University of Minnesota Press.

Illingworth, R. S. (1958). Dissociation as a guide to developmental assessment. *Archives of Disease in Childhood, 33,* 118-122.

Illingworth, R. S. (1961). The predictive value of developmental tests in the first year with special reference to the diagnosis of mental subnormality. *Journal of Child Psychology and Psychiatry, 2,* 210-215.

Illingworth, R. S., & Birch, L. B. (1959). The diagnosis of mental retardation in infancy: A follow-up study. *Archives of Disease in Childhood, 34,* 269-273.

Kitchen, W. H., Ryan, M. M., & Rickards, A. (1982). Changing outcome over 13 years of very low birthweight infants. *Seminars in Perinatology, 6,* 373-389.

Kitchen, W., Yu, V. Y. H., Orgill, A. A., Ford, G., Rickards, A., Astbury, A., Lissenden, J. V., & Bajuk, B. (1983). Collaborative study of very low birthweight infants: Correlation of handicap with risk factors. *American Journal of Diseases of Children, 137,* 555-559.

Klackenberg-Larsson, I., & Stensson, J. (1968). The development of children in a Swedish urban community. IV: Data on mental development during the first five years. *Acta Paediatrica Scandinavica, Supplement 187,* 67-93.

Knobloch, H., & Pasamanick, B. (1960). An evaluation of the consistency and predictive value of the 40-week Gesell developmental schedule. *Psychiatric Research Reports of the American Psychiatric Association, 13*, 10-13.

Knobloch, H., & Pasamanick, B. (1963). Predicting intellectual potential in infancy. *American Journal of Diseases of Children, 106*, 43-51.

Knobloch, H., & Pasamanick, B. (1967). Prediction from the assessment of neuromotor and intellectual status in infancy. In J. Zubin, & G. A. Jervis (Eds), *Psychopathology of mental development* (pp. 387-400). New York: Grune & Stratton.

Köhler, L., Svenningsen, N. W., & Lindquist, B. (1979). Early detection of preschool health problems - role of perinatal risk factors. *Acta Paediatrica Scandinavica, 68*, 229-237.

Largo, R. H. (1990). Predicting developmental outcome at school age from infant tests of normal, at-risk and retarded infants. *Developmental Medicine and Child Neurology, 32*, 30-45.

Largo, R. H., Molinari, L., Comenale-Pinto, L., Weber, M., & Duc, G. (1986). Language development of term and preterm children during the first five years of life. *Developmental Medicine and Child Neurology, 28*, 333-350.

Largo, R. H., Molinari, L., Kundu, S., Hunziker, U., & Duc, G. (1990a). Neurological outcome at schoolage of high risk AGA-preterm children. *European Journal of Pediatrics, 149*, 835-844.

Largo, R. H., Molinari, L., Kundu, S., Lipp, A., & Duc, G. (1990b). Intellectual outcome, speech and school performance in high risk AGA-preterm children. *European Journal of Pediatrics, 149*, 845-850.

Largo, R. H., Pfister, D., Molinari, L., Kundu, S., Lipp, A., & Duc, G. (1989). Significance of prenatal, perinatal and postnatal factors in the development of AGA preterm infants at five to seven years. *Developmental Medicine and Child Neurology, 31*, 440-456.

Largo, R. H., & Schinzel, A. (1985). Developmental and behavioral disturbances in 13 boys with fragile X syndrome. *European Journal of Pediatrics, 143*, 269-275.

MacRae, J. M. (1955). Retests of children given mental tests as infants. *Journal of Genetic Psychology, 87*, 111-155.

McCall, R. B. (1977). Challenges to a science of developmental psychology. *Child Development, 48*, 333-344.

McCall, R. B. (1979). The development of intelligence functioning in infancy and prediction of later IQ. In J. Osofsky (Ed.), *Handbook of infant development.* New York: John Wiley.

McCall, R. B. (1983). Environmental effects on intelligence. The forgotten realm of discontinuous non-shared within-family factors. *Child Development, 54*, 408-415.

McCall, R. B., Appelbaum, M. I., & Hogarty, P. S. (1973). Developmental changes in mental performance. *Monographs of the Society for Research in Child Development, 38*, 1-84.

McCall, R. B., Hogarty, P. S., & Hurlburt, N. (1972). Transitions in infant sensorimotor development and the prediction of childhood IQ. *American Psychologist, 27*, 728-748.

Moore, T. (1967). Language and intelligence: A longitudinal study of the first eight years. Part I: Patterns of development in boys and girls. *Human Development, 10*, 88-106.

Naeye, R. L., & Peters, E. C. (1987). Antenatal hypoxia and low IQ values. *American Journal of Disease of Children*, *141*, 50-54.

Nelson, K. B., & Ellenberg, J. H. (1985). Antecedents of cerebral palsy. 1: Univariate analysis of risks. *American Journal of Disease of Children*, *139*, 1031-1038.

Nelson, K. B., & Ellenberg, J. H. (1986). Antecedents of cerebral palsy: Multivariate analysis of risk. *New England Journal of Medicine*, *315*, 81-86.

Pueschel, S. M. (1984). *A study of the young child with Down syndrome*. New York: Human Science Press.

Scarr, S., & McCartney. K. (1983). How people make their own environment: A theory of genotyp > environment effects. *Child Development*, *54*, 424-435.

Shennan, A. T., Milligan, J. E., & Hoskins, E. M. (1985). Perinatal factors associated with death or handicap in very low birthweight infants. *American Journal of Obstetrics and Gynecology*, *15*, 231-238.

Silva, P., McGree, R., & Williams, S. (1982). The predictive significance of slow walking and slow talking: A report from the Dunedin Multidisciplinary Child Development Study. *British Journal of Disorders of Communication*, *17*, 134-139.

Stanley, F., & Albermann, E. (1984). Birthweight, gestational age and the cerebral palsies. In F. Stanley & E. Albermann (Eds.), The epidemiology of the cerebral palsies. *Clinics in Developmental Medicine*, *87*, 57- 67.

Stanley, F. J., & English, D. R. (1986). Prevalence of and risk factors for cerebral palsy in a total population cohort of low-birthweight (<2000g) infants. *Developmental Medicine and Child Neurology*, *28*, 559-568.

Stechler, G. (1964). A longitudinal follow-up neonatal apnea. *Child Development*, *35*, 333-348.

Stewart, A. L. (1989). Outcome. In D. Harvey, R. W. I. Cooke, & G. A. Levitt (Eds.), *The baby under 1000 g.* (pp. 331-348). London: Wright.

Vohr, B. R., & Garcia Coll, C. T. (1985). Neurodevelopmental and school performance of very low-birthweight infants: A seven year longitudinal study. *Pediatrics*, *76*, 345-350.

Werner, E. E., Honzik, M. P., & Smith R. S. (1968). Prediction of intelligence and achievement at 10 years from 20 months pediatric and psychological examinations. *Child Development*, *39*, 1063-1075.

M. Brambring, H. Rauh, and A. Beelmann (Eds.). (1996). *Early childhood intervention: Theory, evaluation, and practice* (pp. 118-127). Berlin, New York: de Gruyter.

A Developmental Screening Questionnaire for Five-Year-Olds

Hans G. Schlack, B. Ohrt, R. H. Largo, R. Michaelis, and G. Neuhäuser

1 Introduction

Screening is a necessary but often methodologically unsatisfactory procedure for detecting children with developmental problems. At preschool age, developmental screening focuses mainly on minor neurological dysfunctions and on problems of adaptation and behavior that may be relevant for school. In contrast, major disabilities have probably been detected already in earlier childhood.

Not all pediatricians are equipped to assess minor developmental dysfunctions in preschool-age children, and there is strong need for a reliable screening instrument for the practicing pediatrician. A differentiated assessment including neurological examination and psychological tests cannot be used as a screening. Such a comprehensive assessment and the interpretation of its results requires both special knowledge and experience as well as a large amount of time. Generally, these conditions are not met in a pediatrician´s practice. Nonetheless, it is important for the pediatrician to obtain the best possible impression of a child´s development.

Why a questionnaire? Several investigations have shown a satisfactory correlation between the results of developmental tests and information about a child´s development and abilities provided by parents, provided that the parents were given structured criteria. A sufficient validity in parental questioning with a low amount of false-positive and false-negative results has been found when questionnaires are oriented toward standardized developmental tests (e.g., Gesell Test: Knobloch et al., 1979; Griffiths Test: Sonnander, 1987). Coplan (1982), Hickson et al. (1983), and Glascoe et al. (1989) have reported similar results. However, the questionnaire based on the Denver Developmental Screening Test has proved to be less valid. The authors have concluded that this questionnaire is appropriate only for parents with higher academic training (see Frankenburg et al., 1976).

In summary, it can be assumed that parents usually are able to judge their children´s development, also in comparison to peers, and to articulate their worries and concerns accurately. Hence, it may be postulated that a standardized questioning of parents may provide valid results, and probably better ones than an inadequate examination of the child. Compared to other types of screening, questioning parents has disadvantages as well as advantages: On the one hand, parents´ reports are dependent on their perception and judgment, and it is rather difficult to operationalize items precisely in relation to this. On the other hand, parental reports are more or less independent of the actual situation and the child´s willingness to cooperate, and the method of questioning is easy to learn.

We decided that it would be worthwhile to construct a questionnaire for developmental screening in 5-year-olds containing items on motor, cognitive-language, and socioemotional abilities in order to detect problems that possibly require intervention before school enrollment (Ohrt et al., 1993-1994). To the best of our knowledge, no similar screening instrument is available, at least in German-speaking countries. We have been able to test our questionnaire on about 5,000 children within the Bavarian Longitudinal Study.

2   The Construction of the Questionnaire

We applied the following criteria for item selection:
1. The questions had to refer to age-appropriate abilities, dependent on development and culture.
2. The abilities surveyed had to relate to the child´s daily life.
3. The questions had to be easy to understand, and the ability or behavior concerned had to be easy to observe.

All five authors, who have worked in the field of developmental neurology for many years, finally agreed unanimously on a selection of 18 items. These items can be classified into three categories: (1) gross- and fine-motor abilities (4 items), (2) cognitive and language items (6 items), and (3) social competence (8 items) (see Table 1).

Motor abilities. Gross- and fine-motor abilities relate to neurological functions. For example, riding a bicycle makes great demands on balance control and requires fluent, rhythmic movements as well as the ability to perform anticipatory acts; catching a ball requires good visuomotor coordination.

Cognitive and language abilities. Most of the "cognitive " items refer to language, because parents are probably most familiar with their child´s language abilities. In addition, parents are asked how well their child can draw a human figure. This requires not only fine-motor but also cognitive capacities such as imagination, perception of details, concept of body, shape, proportions, and reproduction.

Social competence. These items concern more complex abilities. Even though they depend on a multitude of factors and are difficult to define, they are thought to reflect important criteria of social and emotional development, self-esteem, and increasing autonomy.

We considered that these three categories covered basic abilities that most 5-year-olds should be able to master. We limited the questionnaire to 18 items for practical reasons. Each item had to be rated on a 4-point scale. To increase the reliability of the answers, a short and precise definition was given of each point on the rating scale, indicating an ascending competence in the ability to cope with the function in question. Parents were asked to mark the description that corresponded best to the child´s current level of competence. Great care was taken to ensure that the questions were phrased in such a way that parents could answer them freely. Negatively phrased questions or questions implying a suspicion of developmental delay had to be avoided. We cannot expect parents to give correct answers to questions that provoke anxiety or at least ambivalent feelings.

Table 1. *Items and Scaling in the Developmental Screening for Five-Year-Olds*

Motor abilities

---

1. Riding a bicycle
- Not yet possible
- Possible with stabilizers
- Possible for short periods without stabilizers
- Without stabilizers for more than six months

2. Catching a ball
(a 10 to 15 cm diameter ball thrown from a distance of 3 to 4 meters)
- Cannot catch ball
- Can catch ball only sometimes and with difficulty
- Generally catches the ball with both hands
- Catches the ball confidently and with good coordination

3. Running
- Cannot run
- Makes rather slow and jerky movements that seem to be poorly coordinated
- Runs quite well, but jerkily
- Runs rapidly with good coordination

(table continues)

Table 1. *(continued)*

4. Unbuttoning item of daily clothing
 - Cannot undo buttons
 - Can undo buttons when helped
 - Ability acquired during the past few weeks
 - Has been undoing buttons alone for quite a long time

Cognitive abilities

5. Draw a person
 - No recognizable figure at all
 - Only head and legs
 - Figure with head, trunk, limbs
 - Figure with additional details like hair, ears, fingers
6. Concept of time
 - No time words used at all
 - Time of day (morning, afternoon, evening) understood and used
 - Yesterday, today, tomorrow understood and used
 - Concept of time understood and expressed reliably for longer periods
   (weeks, months)
7. Language expressiveness
 - Insufficient and distinctly retarded
 - Slightly retarded
 - Not retarded or even better
 - Distinctly better than peers
8. Reporting of experiences and retelling of stories
 - No report possible at all
 - Report only fragmentary
 - Report mostly in logical and temporal order
 - Clear and understandable report with logical and temporal structure
9. Articulation of spontaneous language
 - Not understandable
 - Partially understandable
 - Incorrect formation of several sounds
 - Clear and correct articulation
10. Sentence construction
 - Grammatical structure either unrecognizable or only slightly recognizable
 - Many mistakes in sentence construction
 - Slight and infrequent mistakes
 - Sentence construction always correct

(table continues)

Table 1. *(continued)*

Social competence

11. Separation from mother or other reference person
- Not tolerated
- Tolerated only for short time
- Occasional difficulties
- No problems over several hours

12. Comprehension and observance of game rules
- Neither understood nor kept
- Kept for a short time, then broken
- Occasional problems in keeping to rules and accepting losing
- Rules are accepted and losing can be tolerated

13. Acceptance in peer group
- Not accepted
- Accepted at times with considerable reservations
- Mostly accepted, but with occasional reservations
- Full acceptance

14. Friends
- No friends
- Only occasional, short-term friendships (child disinterested or breaks off quickly)
- Interested in friendships but unable to maintain them
- Stable friendships with mutual invitations

15. Role play
- No participation
- Unwilling participation
- Enjoys role play, but only age-inappropriate roles
- Plays different roles, changing in line with play situations and playmates

16. Comprehension of emotional expressions
- No comprehension
- Considerable difficulties in perceiving and reacting adequately
- Perceives and comprehends, but often reacts inadequately
- Comprehends and acts adequately (e.g., comforts, shares toys, verbal comments)

17. Getting dressed
- Unable to get dressed, even within extended time
- Needs help and an increased amount of time
- Needs little help
- Gets dressed completely and independently

18. Toilet training
- Still wets over the day
- Not yet reliably dry and clean, needs help
- Dry and clean, if sent to toilet or reminded to go
- Completely independent in use of toilet

3   Standardization and Application

We were able to standardize the questionnaire by using it in the Bavarian Longitudinal Study. This study is evaluating the development of 4,855 children born in 1985. These children have all been subject to different risks during the perinatal period and early infancy. There is also a control group of 757 children with no perinatal or postnatal risks.

Data from the study were used to select a representative sample of the population of Southern Bavaria in terms of socioeconomic status, residential area (urban vs. rural), gender, and gestational age. This representative sample consisted of 431 children (224 girls and 207 boys).

Although all parents in the Bavarian Longitudinal Study completed the questionnaire in order to test its practicability, the standardization was based on the representative sample. All children were aged 4 years and 8 months at this time. After being given the questionnaire, parents were asked to answer all 18 items on the basis of the current developmental state of their child. In general, parents reported that they had no problems in understanding or answering the questions. Additional explanations were necessary in only a few cases.

4   Results

In order to avoid classifying too many children as retarded or at risk, we decided to use a cutoff point for each item approximately at the 95th percentile. However, using a rating scale with only 4 points, it was not possible to produce a clear-cut limit by selecting the "slowest" children beyond the 95th percentile. Therefore, the actual cutoffs varied between the 88th percentile (catching a ball, unbuttoning clothes) and the 99th percentile (getting dressed).

For practical purposes, it is possible to draw a "cutoff line" (90 - 95 % of 4,;8-year-old children) in order to perform a quick evaluation of the questionnaire. All scores to the left of the line indicate a function that is probably retarded. Such scores may led to further assessment, depending on the total number of "suspect" scores and other conditions. According to the cutoff points, the parental reports shown in Table 2 should be regarded as warning signals at the end of the 5th year of life. The copy of the questionnaire with a dividing line, as demonstrated here, is meant for examiner's use only. The copy handed out to the parents has a uniform light background in order not to influence their answers.

Table 2. *Cutoff Points for 5-Year-Olds With Developmental Risks*

Gross- and fine-motor abilities

1	Riding a bicycle	Not yet possible	Possible with stabilizers	Possible for short periods without stabilizers	Without stabilizers for more than six months
2	Catching a ball (a 10 to 15 cm diameter ball thrown from a distance of 3 to 4 meters)	Cannot catch ball	Can catch ball only sometimes and with difficulty	Generally catches the ball with both hands	Catches the ball confidently and with good coordination
3	Running	Cannot run	Makes rather slow and jerky movements that seem to be poorly coordinated	Runs quite well, but jerkily	Runs rapidly with good coordination
4	Unbottoning item of daily clothing	Cannot undo buttons	Can undo buttons when helped	Ability acquired during the past few weeks	Has been undoing buttons alone for quite a long time

Cognitive abilities

5	Draw a person	No recognizable figure at all	Only head and legs	Figure with head, trunk, limbs	Figure with additional details like hair, ears, fingers
6	Concept of time	No time words used at all	Time of day (morning, afternoon, evening) understood and used	Yesterday, today, tomorrow understood and used	Concept of time understood and expressed reliably for longer periods (weeks, months)
7	Language expressiveness	Insufficient and distinctly retarded	Slightly retarded	Not retarded or even better	Distinctly better than peers
8	Reporting of experiences and retelling of stories	No report possible at all	Report only fragmentary	Report mostly in logical and temporal order	Clear and understandable report with logical and temporal structure
9	Articulation of spontaneous language	Not understandable	Partially understandable	Incorrect formation of several sounds	Clear and correct articulation
10	Sentence construction	Grammatical structure either unrecognizable or only slightly recognizable	Many mistakes in sentence construction	Slight and infrequent mistakes	Sentence construction always correct

(table continues)

Table 2. *(continued)*

Social competence

11	Separation from mother or other reference person	Not tolerated	Tolerated only for short time	Occasional difficulties	No problems over several hours
12	Comprehension and observance of game rules	Neither understood nor kept	Kept for a short time, then broken	Occasional problems in keeping to rules and accepting losing	Rules are accepted and losing can be tolerated
13	Acceptance in peer group	Not accepted	Accepted at times with considerable reservations	Mostly accepted, but with occasional reservations	Full acceptance
14	Friends	No friends	Only occasional, short-term friendships (child disinterested or breaks off quickly)	Interested in friendships but unable to maintain them	Stable friendships with mutual invitations
15	Role play	No participation	Unwilling participation	Enjoys role play, but only age-inappropriate roles	Plays different roles, changing in line with play situations and playmates
16	Comprehension of emotional expressions	No comprehension	Considerable difficulties in perceiving and reacting adequately	Perceives and comprehends, but often reacts inadequately	Comprehends and acts adequately (e.g., comforts, shares toys, verbal comments)
17	Getting dressed	Unable to get dressed, even within extended time	Needs help and an increased amount of time	Needs little help	Gets dressed completely and independently
18	Toilet training	Still wets over the day	Not yet reliably dry and clean, needs help	Dry and clean, if sent to toilet or reminded to go	Completely independent in use of toilet

4.1 An Initial Test of Validity

An initial attempt to test the validity of the questionnaire was carried out by comparing the control group (n = 431) with the group of children with a very low gestational age (< 32 weeks; n = 247). The number of children beyond the cutoff line was compared for each item. Differences were significant for 17 items, 16 in favor of the controls (Table 3).

Table 3. *Number and Relative Frequency of Children With Retarded Individual Functions According to Parent's Reports*

	Skill	Preterms n = 247		Control Sample n = 431		
		n	%	n	%	
1.	Riding a bicycle	34	13.8	25	5.8	***
2.	Catching a ball	68	27.5	54	12.6	***
3.	Running	19	7.7	16	3.6	*
4.	Unbottoning	46	18.6	52	12.0	*
5.	Draw a person	53	21.5	32	7.5	***
6.	Concept of time	42	17.0	22	5.1	***
7.	Language expressiveness	22	8.9	5	1.2	***
8.	Reporting	10	4.0	2	0.5	***
9.	Articulation	36	14.6	21	4.9	***
10.	Sentence construction	62	25.1	50	11.5	***
11.	Separation	11	4.5	38	8.9	*
12.	Game rules	29	11.7	12	2.8	***
13.	Acceptance in peer group	17	6.9	8	1.9	***
14.	Friends	46	18.6	28	6.6	***
15.	Role play	29	11.7	17	4.1	***
16.	Comprehension of emotional expressions	35	14.2	33	7.7	***
17.	Getting dressed	6	2.4	1	0.2	***
18.	Toilet training	11	4.5	15	3.5	n. s.

Note. Comparison between controls and the preterm group (gestation < 32 weeks; children with cerebral palsy and early ontogenetic disorders excluded).
    * p < .05. *** p < .001

5 Discussion

The questionnaire seems to provide a useful screening instrument for problems in development and adaptation at the end of the 5th year of life. One particular feature is the number of items addressing social competence. This is considered to be very important for academic achievement at school. Despite the complex nature of social abilities and the problems involved in operationalizing items to address them, it would seem that it is possible to obtain meaningful information through questioning parents. In general, the questionnaire results discriminate well between normal, low-risk children and children with a very low gestational age (< 32 weeks). In addition, the broad application of the questionnaire has supplied us with normative data (cutoff points near the 50th percentile are also available).

We consider that our questionnaire may be a useful aid in the pediatrician´s practice for detecting those children who are in need of additional assessment and, if necessary, intervention and assistance before they start elementary school.

References

Coplan, I. (1982). Parental estimate of child´s development in a high risk population. *American Journal of Disease in Childhood, 136*, 101-104.

Frankenburg, W. K., Doorninck, W. J. van, Liddell, T. N., & Dick, N. P. (1976). The Denver Prescreening Developmental Questionnaire. *Pediatrics, 57*, 744-753.

Glascoe, F. P., Altemeier, W. A., & MacLean, W. E. (1989). The importance of parents´ concerns about their child´s development. *American Journal of Disease in Childhood, 143*, 955-958.

Hickson, G. B., Altemeier, W. A., & O´Conner, S. (1983). Concerns of mothers seeking care in private pediatric offices: Opportunities for expanding services. *Pediatrics, 72*, 619-624.

Knobloch, H., Stevens, F., Malone, A., Ellison, P., & Risemberg, H. (1979). The validity of parental reporting of infant development. *Pediatrics, 63*, 872-878.

Ohrt, B., Schlack, H. G., Largo, R. H., Michaelis, R., & Neuhäuser, G. (1993-1994). Erfassen von Entwicklungsauffälligkeiten bei Fünfjährigen. Ein normierter Fragebogen. *Pädiatrische Praxis, 46*, 11-19.

Sonnander, K. (1987). Parental development assessment of 18-month-old children: Reliability and predictive value. *Developmental Medicine and Child Neurology, 29*, 351-362.

M. Brambring, H. Rauh, and A. Beelmann (Eds.). (1996). *Early childhood intervention: Theory, evaluation, and practice* (pp. 128-154). Berlin, New York: de Gruyter.

Diachronic Developmental Assessment of Mentally Handicapped Young Children

Hellgard Rauh, B. Schellhas, S. Goeggerle, and B. Müller

1 Introduction

Developmental tests have been used mainly either for research purposes or for assessing the developmental status of individual children, particularly children at risk or with handicaps. Whereas they have become a major tool for deciding about the timing and type of an intervention, they have been applied less frequently for evaluating interventions. There are, however, cultural differences in the popularity of developmental testing: Whereas legislation in the USA prescribes developmental testing of at-risk infants as a basis for individualized intervention plans, a general reluctance to use any tests at all prevails in many parts of Germany. Parents fear that their child may be labeled, classified, or stigmatized, or that benefits that they receive for their handicapped child may be questioned. Accordingly, in Germany, developmental tests for infants are either outdated or, at best, superficially standardized to German norms; and American norms have usually been adopted for research purposes. Except for pediatric evaluation reports, little need is felt for standardized norms; most practitioners, if they employ tests at all, use them mainly for diagnostic classification - or the test items as objectives for intervention. Whereas the usefulness of tests appears to be underrated by German practitioners and parents, their multipurpose use as recommended in the USA is also not yet validated sufficiently in relation to our limited knowledge of individual growth patterns and trajectories in both nonhandicapped and at-risk children.

Most developmental tests have been standardized for nonimpaired children, and only the most recent American tests report on assessment experience with specific groups of at-risk or handicapped children (e.g., Bayley, 1993; Reuter & Bickett, 1985). Furthermore, test norms are usually based on cross-sectional data. Hence, little can be inferred from these group data to individual patterns of development over time. Only under the premise that development proceeds at a constant rate and in a basically linear fashion, even in children with developmental problems, is it feasible to use developmental tests for evaluating intervention in relatively small samples of children of usually heterogeneous chronological and mental ages. If, however, individual developmental progression proceeds with "natural" spurts and plateaus, or even differently from child to child, then interindividual differences will not be sufficiently stable over time to serve as control measures for interventions and evaluations, even at small-group levels.

Our interest lies in these longitudinal, diachronic individual patterns of development. Few longitudinal studies, such as the Berkeley Growth Study (Bayley, 1940) and the Guidance Study (McFarlane et al., 1954), both starting in 1928, used sufficiently small time intervals of assessment, at least in early childhood, to warrant the analysis of growth curve types and of developmental changes in the factorial structure of test achievements (McCall et al., 1977; Wohlwill, 1980). Although many longitudinal studies have been started since the famous Berkeley studies, methods appropriate to analyze developmental patterns over time have rarely been applied. Except for the statistical implications of repeated measurement, chronological age has generally been used like any other differential classification variable in analyses of variance, correlations over time, multiple regression analyses, causal modeling, and even the most recent LISREL models. Wohlwill's agenda, delineated in his famous paper on "the age variable in psychological research" (Wohlwill, 1970), still awaits to be followed.

In order to study and analyze individual growth curves or diachronic patterns of development, repeated assessments at densely spaced intervals are necessary. Not only is it difficult to find subjects willing to participate in such a study, but objectivity and reliability of assessment must also be reconciled with ethical standards in research with children. In addition, test items are either unduly sensitive to learning effects through repeated testing or insensitive to minor developmental changes. The cross-sectional standardization procedure emphasizes obvious, and preferably quantitative, age differences in achievement. Important qualitative developmental changes in skill, motivation, attention, or communication may escape the scoring and will remain unrecognized.

Infants with Down's Syndrome are a particularly interesting special group of children for studying developmental phenomena that may also be of major relevance in nonhandicapped infants. In contrast to most other risks or handicaps, incidence of Down's Syndrome occurs, as an "experiment of nature," in all social strata and proves to be unrelated to SES. The population of Down's Syndrome children is therefore socioeconomically representative of the general population. Young children with Down's

Syndrome are diagnosed at birth. Although they can accumulate all kinds of minor and major additional health problems, none of them are specific to this syndrome, nor do they necessitate clearly deviant patterns of development. Nevertheless, all children with Down's Syndrome are more or less retarded from an early age; therefore their parents are usually interested in repeated developmental assessments and consultation. During infancy, they generally develop at half speed or less (Rauh et al., 1991). Testing at 3-monthly intervals would thus be equivalent to a time interval of one and a half months in a nonhandicapped infant. Provided their development is generally similar to the development of nonhandicapped children, developmental courses and developmental processes could be studied as if under a magnifying glass and with fewer learning effects caused by repeated testing. Still, some direct or indirect intervention effect can neither be denied nor dismissed in any diachronic or longitudinal assessment.

2   Subjects and Procedure

Altogether 30 infants with Down's Syndrome, born between 1986 and 1992 in Berlin, and their families are included in our research project; of these, 25 infants could be followed over 5 years and longer. Whereas we actively approached the first families, we were contacted by parents, physicians, or social workers in the following years. Accordingly, the social composition became more and more positively skewed. Only about one half of the mothers have completed higher secondary education or less, and the other half have college or university level education. Thirteen fathers in contrast to seven mothers have university training. The sample is ethnically mixed so that at least five children are growing up in a bilingual environment.

Nineteen mothers were below 35 years of age at the birth of the child, the age at which prenatal genetic examination is offered in Germany. Thirteen infants were first-born; most of them now have siblings. Of the 25 infants with long-term participation, 12 were born with less than 39 weeks gestational age. Ten infants had perinatal complications; four infants initially had severe health problems (heart failures, anus deformation, seizures). With very few exceptions, most infants suffered repeatedly from various infections, sometimes including hospitalization; the most common illnesses being bronchitis, pneumonia, tonsillitis, pseudocroup, pertussis, chicken pox, scarlet fever, and enteritis. One child was diagnosed as severely hearing impaired and had hearing aids from 4 months until 5 years of age but, after surgery and the introduction of tubes, can now hear without aids. Most children started to wear glasses from the age of 2 years.

The children entered our study cumulatively as soon after birth as they became known to us; in five cases, even within the first 5 weeks of life. Five families contacted us only after their infant's first birthday. Most infants, however, were first seen between the ages of 3 and 6 months.

Two types of developmental tests were used: individual infant tests and a parent-report questionnaire. The Bayley Scales of Infant Development (Bayley, 1969) were administered by trained psychologists in the university video studio in the presence of at least one parent at 3-monthly intervals until the children were about 4-years-old. The assessment schedule was then changed to 6-month intervals in order to reduce practice effects. When the children reached the ceiling of these scales, that is, the developmental age of 30 months (usually between the ages of 4 and 6 years), the Bayley Scales were replaced by the McCarthy Scales of Children's Abilities (McCarthy, 1972; U.S. norms) and the K-ABC (Kaufman & Kaufman 1983; German standardization by Melchers & Preuß, 1991), and, most recently, by the Bayley II (Bayley, 1993). All testings were videotaped in full.

For our research purposes, we adopted the U.S. norms but reverted to mental and motor developmental ages as measures, instead of MDI or PDI, as being more adequate for our retarded subjects (Bayley, 1993). Mental (Developmental) Age or Motor (Developmental) Age represent that chronological age at which the particular test performance equates the average achievement (MDI or PDI of 100) of the nonhandicapped standardization sample. Besides offering a direct comparison to the normative sample, Mental or Motor Age scales can be treated statistically as interval scales.

As a second measure of infant development, we used a parent-report questionnaire, the KESS (Rauh & Müller, 1989; Rauh & Peisdersky, 1985), the German experimental version of the American Kent Infant Development or KID Scale (Katoff et al., 1980; Reuter & Bickett, 1985; Reuter & Reuter, 1990). This scale uses 250 items to cover the developmental age range from 1 to 14 months. The items in this questionnaire are presented at random with respect to developmental level and subscale. Parents are asked to mark whether they have observed the described behavior in their infant during the last week, whether the infant showed this behavior previously but has outgrown it, or whether the infant has lost a previously observed behavior. Parents are not requested to perform any test-like activity with their infant. Separate developmental age norms are available for the USA for the Full Scale and for the Motor, Mental, Language, Social, and Self-help subscales. These American norms were adopted for our project. The KID Scale has been used extensively in the USA, especially with handicapped infants. Comparisons with Bayley assessments have yielded high congruence between Bayley performances and parental or caregiver KID-Scale reports (Reuter & Bickett, 1985), particularly for the motor scales in both tests. The infants' language or vocal behavior as well as their social behavior tended to receive higher scores from parents than from the psychologist who saw the infant only during the test examination.

The KESS was mailed to the parents each month. When the infants approached the ceiling of this test, usually between 18 and 25 months of age, it was replaced by the Minnesota Child Development Inventory (Ireton & Thwing, 1974). These "Minnesota Scales" cover the developmental age range from birth to 5 years, but with far fewer items; they are a cruder measure of developmental progression than the KID Scales, and were therefore completed by parents only every 3 or 6 months.

When we started the project, testers were exchanged for each session; but parents complained about these frequent changes. There are still changes of testers due to necessary adjustments to work and time schedules, but much less frequently.

In order to keep parents returning for repeated testing, they received oral interpretations of their infant's test behavior and written reports on their child's progress. These reports informed about the child's characteristic problem-solving and interactive behavior and the developmental level achieved; care was taken not to transmit individual item descriptions and their scoring to the parents. Parents were also offered a videotape copy of the test assessment. In spite of this open communication about the child's progress, we trust that parents rarely indulged in anything near to test-item training. Also, the infants themselves would usually not reinforce such parental endeavors unless they had just discovered something new and exciting at exactly their achieved level of competence. As soon as a task became only slightly too difficult for them, they sometimes even ingeniously evaded that item. The main "training" effect on the parents through both observing the tester-child interaction or completing the questionnaires probably was that they became more sensitive to even more subtle progress in their child. This, in turn, motivated them to continue in the project.

Nevertheless, some effects of repeated testing on the children's behavior could not be avoided. They became more familiar with the testing location, the testers, and the type of interaction. Sometimes, even at a very young age, they seemed to remember those items that they had found exciting at the last assessment. Familiarity of the tester with the particular child also had advantages that we tried to exploit. Knowing the child's previous test performance allowed the examiner to concentrate on items close to the child's present zone of achievement and to repeat those items from below the child's mean performance level that had not yet been mastered clearly.

In this respect, repeated testing is organized differently from initial or singular testing of an unfamiliar child. One positive consequence of our testing procedure was that total or partial test denials were rare. Repeated testing obviously reduced the disturbing effects of maladapted motivation, and, for this reason, may be more adequate to reveal these children's competencies in the sense of optimal testing. Furthermore, if infant tests were used for monitoring the development of an individual child, the situation would not be very dissimilar from our handling of the test.

3   Experiences Gained From Carrying Out Developmental Tests

The use of tests that have been standardized for nonhandicapped children in the very retarded calls for a flexible adaptation of materials and testing behavior within the limits set by the test standardization. Implementing the test too strictly according to the given guidelines can stress the children so much that they evade or refuse cooperation, whereas a too liberal interpretation of the standard conditions impairs comparability. Therefore it is essential for the testers to have a sound training in test construction and developmental psychology and for them to learn to observe both the children's and their own behavior very carefully. A useful form of training has proved to be the documentation of videotapes of tests carried out by oneself as well as other testers. The videotapes often make it possible to follow precisely how the situation becomes more stressful for the child or how misunderstandings arise between the tester and the child. At times, the children's behavioral reactions can only be understood in retrospective.

A number of adjustments to the test materials also had to be made for children with Down's syndrome. The ring provided in the test materials for assessing grasping reactions in 3- to 6-month-olds proved to be too thick for the particularly small hands of most members of this group, and therefore did not elicit grasping reactions. However, it was easy to obtain this reaction when the ring was replaced by plastic pegs sold as baby toys in all drug stores. The blocks provided in the test materials were too heavy to lift for many infants under the age of 1 year with a feeble motor system, and they were too smooth for the older children to build a tower with. As soon as they found the task strenuous, they just gave up, and it was hard to motivate them to continue. In addition, it was easier for them to grasp an elongated object that is held upright (such as a spoon) than a block (both alternatives are permitted in the test instructions). Frequently the children "rewarded" such a change of materials by behaving on a markedly higher developmental level than anticipated initially. Instead of giving the child the small doll from the test box to point to eyes, nose, hands, feet, and so forth, as well as "feeding" and "wiping its nose" in simple symbolic play, we used a larger Mickey Mouse toy whose more exaggerated body parts motivated the children more easily to give the desired answers.

In very young infants, it is necessary to pay attention not only to their alertness but also to the stabilization of their body posture. Some particularly feeble children showed no grasping reactions when lying on their backs, but did show them, and with both hands, when they could make the grasping movement with and not against the pull of gravity. Between the ages of 6 and 12 months, many infants were either unable to maintain a sitting position, or sitting demanded so much attention that they were unable to process any further stimulation. However, when their heads and backs were supported, they achieved surprising test performances that were beyond their expected capability. Testers were very resourceful in trying out and accepting the best body posture for the child. Therefore, many tasks were carried out on the floor or on the staircase rather than at a table. The older children sat at child-sized tables, but were allowed to get up by themselves at any time in order to relax themselves physically and mentally by running round the room or up and down stairs.

One particular difficulty, even for testers with experience of testing and children, was adapting to the slowness of behavior and reactions in children with Down's syndrome. Whereas an infant with normal development has be tested at a certain speed in order to maintain motivation and interest, it is necessary to proceed much more slowly with children with Down's syndrome. This applies to the speed of movements and speech just as much as to having to wait for the child to react. They respond more slowly than the temperament of most adults can tolerate. Reaction speed is additionally often slower than that laid down in the test standardization. This can lead to a major underestimation of the competence of a handicapped child and finally also to a loss of motivation. We could frequently observe that the children required a great deal of time and effort to focus their attention on a task in the way required by the instructions, and also a lot of time to implement the motor program for their action. Sometimes, children answered with a reaction to the previous task when the next task was presented. Correspondingly, they had trouble in dealing with a rapid switch in task materials and types of response. Therefore, both should be minimized as far as possible compared with the standard testing of nonhandicapped children when the goal of testing is to assess a child's competence and not his or her adaptation to a standardized environment in which he or she does not fit.

A further problem is the delay in being able to use language to communicate. Just like, after a certain stage in development, many tasks on motor development simply assume that a child can sit or walk, a series of cognitive tasks at the developmental level of approximately 2 years assume a command of language. The discrepancy between language level and cognitive level is conspicuous in children with Down's syndrome, and places particular demands on testers when they have to use a language level for children under 2 to communicate tasks that can be classified to an almost 3-year-old's cognitive level. Often, talking speed, the choice of words, and gestures decide whether a child will in any way understand what he or she is expected to do. The majority of developmental tests that end at 30 months or begin at 30 to 36 months assume too readily that the child is capable of expressive language and the comprehension of complex content. This is also an aspect in which the further development of the Bayley II (Bayley, 1993) fills a gap.

Although developmental tests predominantly assess the child's cognitive, verbal, and motor competencies, performance depends essentially on the children's motivation, their mood, and, with increasing age, their developing self-image as expressed in behavior during the test.

Two problematic behaviors could be observed particularly frequently in our children: giving up and evading; the former more frequently among young children, and the latter among the older ones.

Even when one overstimulated small babies only slightly, they would give up unexpectedly and suddenly, even at the tender age of 4 weeks in the test for new-born infants when they could hardly have had any experiences of failure. As if they could somehow sense that their physical energy reserves were no longer sufficient, they would break off attention after a minimal increase in stimulation, and their motor system would go slack. This hardly changed over the following months. In the normal process of development during the first 6 months of life, one natural and important game between adults and infant seems to be to build up a shared stimulation until the infant laughs and chortles and then to let it abate. Initially, the adult helps the infant to control this arousal curve; later, the infant's own contribution to controlling his or her arousal increases. Babies with Down's syndrome give the impression that they need much more time to build up any sort of arousal curve (Cicchetti & Sroufe, 1978), so that most adults give up too soon and thus break off the action. Or, on the other hand, adults increase the intensity and speed of their stimulation so strongly, in the anticipation of a more rapid and higher increase in arousal in the child, that the system suddenly collapses in the child, which can lead to a feeling of disappointment in both interaction partners. In general, this behavioral system, which seems to be fundamental for learning processes, appears to be far more fragile in infants with Down's syndrome than in other infants. However, here as well, sensitive empathy on the part of the adult can lead to satisfying interactions for both sides.

As the children grow older, they tend to react with evasion. Some children in our study were very ingenious in this respect. For example, when things became difficult, they would always stare at their hands intensively as if they wanted to say "I'm busy." Or instead of accepting the proposed action, they offered the previous one or another one that had been successful before, while seeming to be thoroughly aware that this was only a "substitute." Particularly popular among the children and unpopular among the testers was to throw away the test materials, which, on closer analysis, was found to always occur when the children felt overtaxed.

Anne Schäfer (1993) and Ulrike Hamer-Elvert (1993) have studied the communication behavior of two project children with a comparable speed of cognitive development in an analysis of videotapes of the Bayley Test. They compared the children on their mental levels at 4, 8, 12, 16, and 20 developmental months (equivalent to chronological ages between 6 and 36 months). Each task, beginning with the instructions to the child, served as an episode, broken down, in turn, into the phases instructions - performance - completion - pause or instructions - evasion - pause. For the comparative analysis, the number of such episodes was standardized to a total test duration of 60 minutes, and the results were converted into a percentage of episodes. Both children exhibited evasion on approximately one half of the episodes; in Child A, a girl, evasion declined from almost 70% at a developmental age of 4 months to approximately 40% at a developmental age of 20 months, whereas in Child C, a boy, its frequency remained relatively stable across age. Even when broken down according to type of task, that is, with or without an object, with direct interaction between tester and child (e.g., on some motor tasks), with demonstration, or with verbal instructions, the patterns of evasive behavior were mostly individual and revealed no clear developmental trend. These two children were in no way the champions at evasion. Evasive behavior is already a very frequently applied strategy in infants with Down's syndrome. It increases as they get older, depending on developmental level and temperament, to include aggressiveness and anger (particularly during the stubborn phase between 16 and 24 developmental months) or, particularly among older children, charm and gestures of helplessness or mischief. Wishart (1986) has already pointed out this behavior and labeled it "avoidance motivation," a motivational attitude of learned helplessness that is the opposite of achievement motivation, and although it protects the child from (purported) failure, it does not permit him or her to practice and extend the limits of his or her achievement.

In a further stage of analysis, Schäfer and Hamer-Elvert studied the communicative behavior of the two children within the subsectors or phases of the episodes. Both children exhibited their greatest communicative activity in eye contacts, vocalization, and action during the pauses between tasks, followed by the phase of task preparation. They were obviously interested in not breaking off the communication and interaction with the tester. This allows us to dismiss many testers' fears that the children "drop out" of the interaction when they exhibit evasive behavior.

Communicative eye contacts could already be observed at the developmental level of 4 months; communicative utterances and communicative actions entered the children's repertoire at roughly the 12- to 16-month developmental level. At the 12-month level, they used pointing gestures with direct touching of the object; at 16 months, they also pointed to more distant objects. At the 16-month level, both children began to react to questions by shaking or nodding their heads, to accompany their actions with utterances, and to use signals to communicate completion of a task.

However, most of these communicative behaviors are not entered in the quantitative test protocol. Particularly during the transition from prelanguage to linguistic and symbolic activity in the children, from sensorimotor to concrete and preoperational intelligence, observation of children's motivational and communicative behavior could provide important additional information on development.

4 Quantitative Results on the Developmental Courses

Figures 1 and 2 depict the course of mental and motor development in the Berlin sample of children with Down's syndrome at 3-month intervals from the age of 3 months to 5 years as revealed by their performance on the Bayley Scales (Bayley 1969). The number of children per wave is superimposed as a block diagram; it varies somewhat, because the children entered the project at different times and ages, and they also occasionally missed appointments. In all, the figure indicates a relatively continuous and almost linear course of development. Mean developmental age was about one half of chronological age (DA_{ment} = .627, CA = +.45; DA_{mot} = .452, CA = +1.67 for the first 24 months); that is, at the age of 24 months, the children had an average level of mental development of 16 months and an average level of motor development of 13.5 months; at the age of 48 months; 23.7 and 24.7 months respectively. After the age of 48 months,

some children reached the ceiling for the Bayley Test of 30 developmental
months and switched to another test. This is why the developmental curve
levels out in the higher age groups.

However, there were major interindividual differences in developmental
speed, particularly after the first year of life. At the age of 18 months, the
standard deviation on the Mental Scale was almost 3 months (SD = 2.9
months), and rose to more than 4 months (SD = 4.09) at the age of 48
months; that is, among the 4-year-olds, the mean variation range (+/- 1 SD)
was more than 8 developmental months, or, in light of the halved speed of
development, more than 16 calendar months. The increase in mean variation
was even stronger on the Motor Scale. It increased already from under 2
months (SD = 1.73) at the age of 18 months to more than 5 months (SD =
5.67) at the age of 24 months and then continued to remain on a high level.

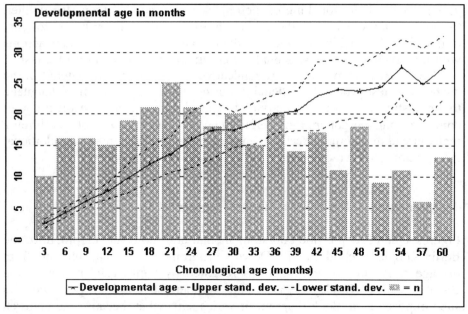

Figure 1.   Mental development of young children with Down's Syndrome
                 (Bayley Scales of Infant Development; 25 Ss, Berlin sample,
                 longitudinal assessments) (y-axis: Developmental age in
                 months, and number of Ss at each assessment age)

For the age range from 3 to 24 months, comparison data from Australia are
available for a total of 176 infants with Down's syndrome as well as more
than 500 Bayley Test protocols from Canada. Rudinger (Rauh et al., 1991)

has subjected these to a complex, longitudinal LISREL analysis. Table 1 reports findings from this analysis.

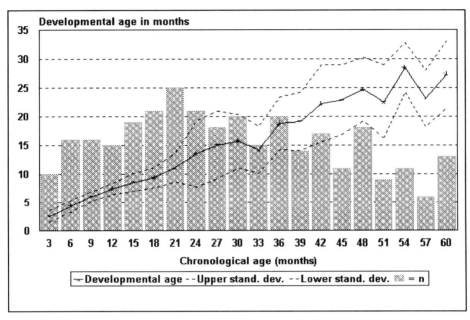

Figure 2.   Motor development of young children with Down's Syndrome (Bayley Scales of Infant Development; 25 Ss, Berlin sample, longitudinal assessments) (y-axis: Developmental age in months, and number of Ss at each assessment age)

Their main findings are as follows: The children's development during this age span (the first 24 months) can be characterized best and most simply as linear progress without any spurts or plateaus. The stability in interindividual differences was high, and rose from .50 between 6 and 12 months to .90 between 12 and 24 months on the Mental Scale; from .70 to .80 on the Motor Scale. During the first year of life, Rudinger's LISREL analysis (Rauh et al., 1991) revealed that the Mental Scale provided a better representation of the general developmental level; during the second year of life, mental and motor developmental age were equally representative.

In the international sample, the scores for mental development were higher than those for motor development. This was also confirmed in the Berlin sample. However, the means on both scales in the Berlin sample are slightly higher than those in the international sample (comparison between the "adjusted" LISREL-reconstructed means and standard deviations in the

Table 1.   *Mental and Motor Ages (in months) of Down's Syndrome Infants Between 3 and 24 Months Chronological Age*

| | Mental ages | | | | | Motor ages | | | | |
| | LISREL sample | | | Berlin sample | | LISREL sample | | | Berlin sample | |
CA	M	SD	n	M	SD	M	SD	n	M	SD
3	(2.32)	...	10	2.54	0.73	(2.58)	.....	10	2.58	0.96
6	3.77	1.56	16	4.31	0.80	3.82	1.51	16	4.42	1.04
9	5.38	2.31	16	6.20	0.82	5.06	2.03	16	6.13	0.87
12	6.99	2.99	15	7.72	1.27	6.31	2.63	15	7.46	1.04
15	8.60	3.48	19	9.84	2.35	7.55	2.91	19	8.63	1.51
18	10.21	4.00	21	12.04	2.89	8.80	3.29	21	9.43	1.73
21	11.82	4.63	25	13.58	2.86	10.04	3.76	25	11.19	2.51
24	13.43	4.96	21	16.02	4.60	11.28	4.59	21	13.51	5.68

Notes. Estimated means and standard deviations of developmental ages, reconstructed from **LISREL** modeling based on an international sample, and empirical means and standard deviations from the **Berlin** sample.

LISREL estimates: DA_{ment}= .537, CA = +.551 DA_{mot} = .415, CA = +1.332

Berlin Sample: DA_{ment}= .627, CA = +.446 DA_{mot} = .452, CA = +1.671

international sample and the original values in the Berlin sample, see Table 1). The standard deviations in the Berlin sample, particularly in the first year of life, were much lower than in the international study. It is possible that the frequent test repetitions and the children's familiarity with the testers and the test situation in Berlin prevented drops in performance. In contrast, it seems less plausible that the higher means and lower standard deviations in the Berlin sample can be traced back to better early intervention. Unlike the Canadian and Australian children, the Berlin sample did not receive any intensive psychological and educational training during the first 2 years. The usual sequence of interventions in Berlin was physiotherapy, occupational therapy, and speech training, generally without any systematic cognitive training (Vogel et al., 1990).

For a quantitative description of developmental courses in infants with Down's syndrome, it seems to be appropriate to simply halve their chronological age as an aid to orientation. However, because of the high standard deviations, this only applies to the average infant.

Results obtained from the questionnaires completed by parents (KESS or KID Scale; Müller, 1993; Müller et al., 1994) were very similar to those obtained with Bayley Tests. Figures 3 and 4 illustrate this with findings on the subscales for cognitive and motor development (means and standard deviations) for 22 of the infants with Down's syndrome based on 251 assessments (an average of 11 per infant) between the ages of 3 and 22 months. The ordinate gives the number of everyday observations that parents answered positively. The results of a longitudinal study of 41 nonhandicapped infants in Berlin are also entered in these figures (Müller, 1993). Their parents completed the questionnaire an average of four times in a period of 3 to 14 months (a total of 189 assessments). The figures show how the developmental trajectories drift apart. However, if the chronological ages of the infants with Down's syndrome are halved or those of the controls are doubled, the developmental trajectories in both groups are almost completely the same. Thus, here as well, the speed of development in infants with Down's syndrome was about one half of "normal" speed (linear regression function for cognitive development: Dev. Age = .531, CA = +1.91 months; for motor development: Dev. Age = .505, CA = +1.17 months). The stability of individual differences on the total scale was also high (r = .72, .84, and .97 for the correlations between 5 and 10, 10 and 15, and 15 and 20 months respectively).

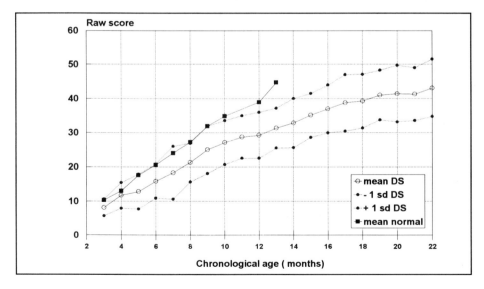

Figure 3.   Cognitive development of young children with Down's Syndrome and non-handicapped infants, longitudinally assessed via Parent Report (KID-Cognitive Subscale) (Berlin Down Syndrome sample: 22 Ss, 251 assessments; non-handicapped Berlin sample: 41 Ss, 189 assessments)

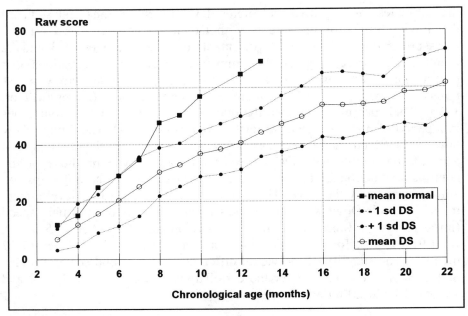

Figure 4.   Motor development of young children with Down's Syndrome and non-handicapped infants, longitudinally assessed via parent Report (KID-Cognitive Subscale) (Berlin Down Syndrome sample: 22 Ss, 251 assessments; non-handicapped Berlin sample: 41 Ss, 189 assessments)

Because the individual courses of development in the first 2 years of life corresponded to a large extent with a linear model in both the Bayley Scales and the KID Scales, a further analysis of the specific coefficients of the individual regression lines (b values as indicators for regression gradient, a values as indicators for the intercept with the y axis) were intercorrelated. Each pair of coefficients contained 8 to 22 test assessments per child. Therefore, it was not individual test results but performance curves that were correlated. In the first analysis, the test protocols were subjected to stepwise multiple and canonical correlations. Table 2 and Figures 5 and 6 present findings computed on the basis of positive slopes (b values). In the first model (first column in Table 2, Figure 5), the course data in both tests for 14 children were correlated for the almost identical period of 3 to 22 or 24 months; in the second model (second column in Table 2, Figure. 6), the computations were repeated in a sample expanded to 20 children, in which

Table 2.   *Correlations Between KID Scale (Full Scale; Cognitive and Motor Subscales) and Bayley Scales (Mental and Motor) Based on b Coefficients of Individual Growth Trajectories (Two Models)*

Variables	Model 1:		Model 2:	
	Bayley 3 - 24 months **KID 3 - 22 months**		**Bayley 3 - 36 months** **KID 3 - 22 months**	
	n = 14		**n = 20**	
Bivariate correlations				
KID Full x				
Bayley Mental	.57		.52 s	
KID Full x				
Bayley Motor	.53		.37	
KID Cognitive x				
Bayley Mental	.69 s		.49	
KID Motor x				
Bayley Motor	.43		.41	
Multiple correlations				
KID Full x				
Bayley Mental &	.64 s		.55 s	
Motor				
KID 5 Subscales x				
Bayley Mental	.77 ns		.58 ns	
KID 5 Subscales x				
Bayley Motor	.60 ns		.45 ns	
Canonical correlation				
KID Cognitive & Motor	1st factor	2nd factor	1st factor	2nd factor
Bayley Mental &	.77	.53	.55	.19
Motor				
Variance explained:				
KID	62%	38%	79%	21%
Bayley	60%	40%	68	32%

the test scores on the Bayley Test were included up to the age of 36 months, whereas the age span for the KID Scale was unchanged (up to 22 months). As in the analyses of the international sample, the Mental Scale of the Bayley Test seems to represent the general developmental trend better than the Motor Scale (simple and multiple correlations). When the canonical correlations included the subscales of the KID scale corresponding to the Bayley scales (Cognitive, Motor), there were two substantial variates: the first representing predominantly the course of motor development plus aspects of the course of mental development; the second, mostly features of mental development with only slight motor portions (see Figure 5). However, this clear picture arose only with a complete temporal correspondence between both tests. When the values entered into the regression lines in the Bayley Test were extended into the third year of life, all simple, multiple, and canonical correlations decreased. Only the first canonical variate remained substantial. It represented both cognitive and motor development in both tests; the former, somewhat more clearly. The low canonical correlation with the second variate is explained by the contrast in motor and mental development that is now visible in both tests, but more clearly in the Bayley Scales (Figure 6).

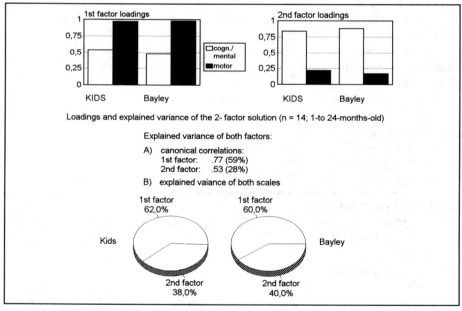

Figure 5.   Canonical factors from correlating Bayley Mental and Motor Scales with KID Cognitive and Motor Subscales, Model 1 (correlation of b-values representing individual growth trajectories of 14 Down's Syndrome infants, 3 to 22/24 months of age)

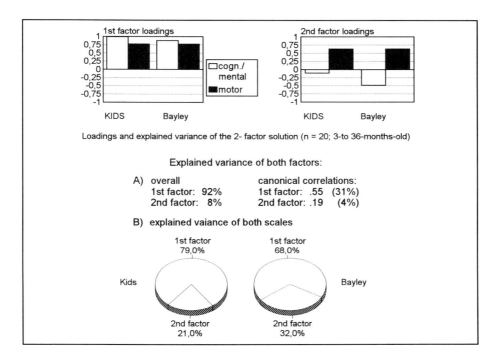

Figure 6.   Canonical factors from correlating Bayley Mental and Motor
Scales with KID Cognitive and Motor Subscales, Model 2
(correlation of b-values representing individual growth
trajectories of 20 Down's Syndrome infants, 3 to 22 months of
age in the KID Scale and 3-36 months in the Bayley Scales)

In sum, these findings indicate that (a) the features of the developmental
course in individual children correlate substantially across two different
tests, one a classical development test and the other a parent-report
instrument; (b) in the first 2 years of life, it is possible to discriminate
between the mental and motor development of infants with Down's
syndrome; and (c) much of the child's individual developmental course can
be characterized in terms of mental and motor development. Changes in the
patterns of correlations and loadings when the third year of life was
included in the Bayley Scales suggest that the developmental trajectories
change during this period.

The developmental courses of individual children revealed in the Bayley
Scales confirm the interpretations of the canonical correlations (Figure 7.1
and Figure 7.2). In most children, the courses of motor and mental

development actually do differ greatly (Rauh, 1992). Several children initially had major delays in motor development, because they required a great deal of time to learn to walk by themselves, whereas their mental development advanced continuously. They remained "stuck" on a level of motor development of 10 to 12 months for long periods of time, but then caught up so that both developmental trajectories coincided approximately by the end of the third or during the course of the fourth year of life, and this as soon as they reached a level of mental development corresponding to approximately 18 to 22 months. After this, however, it was their mental development that was delayed, essentially due to the particularly impaired development of symbolic comprehension and expressive speech. Carr (1975) has already reported a similar pattern of development, although on the basis of group data.

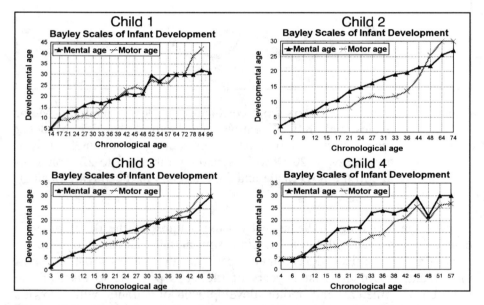

Figure 7.1 Bayley mental and motor growth patterns of individual Down's Syndrome children

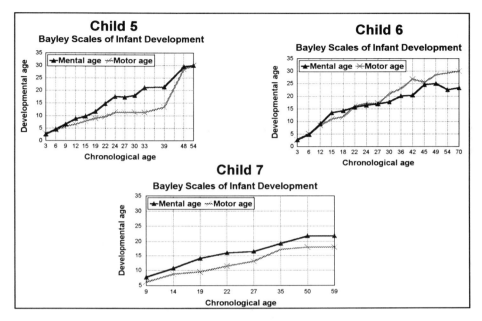

Figure 7.2   Bayley mental and motor growth patterns of individual Down's
              Syndrome children

Analyses of the milestones of motor development in the Berlin sample of
children with Down's syndrome (Lienert & Rauh, 1993) have been able to
show that they "discover" very different forms of locomotion before they
manage to walk by themselves: They roll or shuffle around while sitting
with one leg facing backwards or they crawl. The time intervals between the
different stages of development also vary very strongly: Whereas some
absolve the complete sequence or a part of it very quickly, in others, it is
particularly the transition from locomotion close to the ground to unassisted
walking that takes a very long time. However, no clear relations could be
found to the type of early motor intervention.

The children also show a variety of developmental patterns in language
development (Rauh et al., 1995). The Expressive Speech Scale in the
Minnesota Scales was used to classify the 5-year-olds into three linguistic
competence groups: (a) Those with *relatively good* language development:
They spoke in very simple sentences that were relatively easy to
comprehend (a mean level of language development of 31.4 months, 6
children). (b) Those with *intermediate* language development: They were
just about able to put together two-word sentences (a mean expressive
language level of 25 months, 12 children). (c) Those with *poor* language

development: They were still no further than single-word sentences (a mean level of language development of 17.6 months, 7 children). (For the 8 children who had not quite reached the age of 5 years, the anticipated level of language development was computed from a linear regression of the last test score, and this was used to derive group membership; see Figure 8).

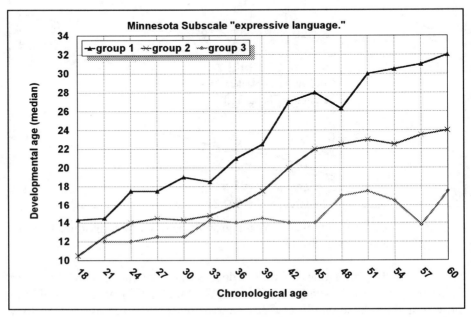

Figure 8.   Expressive language development in three subgroups of Down's Syndrome children of different language comepetence at age five (Group 1: talks in simple sentences; Group 2: two-word sentences; Group 3: not yet two-word sentences)

Although the 18-month differences in the level of prelanguage development on the KID Scales took the expected direction in these three linguistic competence groups, univariate analyses of variance revealed that they were not significant. However, the variation between groups was very large, making it impossible to predict later language development on the basis of prelanguage utterances. However, group differences became apparent between the ages of 2 and 4 (Figure 8). The data and analyses available so far suggest that there are only differences of level between children in the "good" and "intermediate" linguistic competence groups, whereas there are also qualitative differences between these two groups and the "poor" group. Children in the first two groups exhibited a clear discrepancy between cognitive and motor development in favor of cognitive development; in the third group, the course of motor development was mostly better than in the second group, and the otherwise typical discrepancy between motor and mental development was frequently missing. The sequence of milestones in language development, assessed with marker items from the Bayley Scales and the Minnesota Scales, differed in the third group compared with the other two (see Figure 9). The children with particularly slow language development (Group 3) had previously made a lot of utterances and their first two recognizable words at a developmental age of approximately 16 months like the other children. However, they were much later than the other children in repeating individual words (at 17 vs. 14 developmental months). They finally put together their first two-word utterances at a developmental age of approximately 22 months on the basis of a vocabulary of less than five words, whereas the vocabulary of at least 10 words in the children in the other groups was also already much lower than that of children with normal language development.

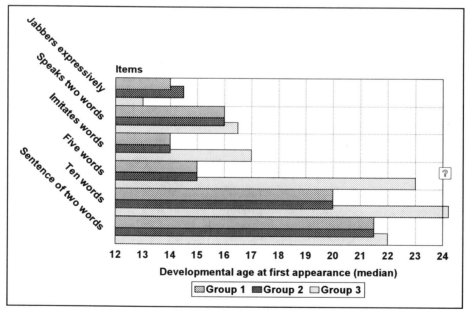

Figure 9.   Mental age at first appearance of selected expressive language milestones for three linguistic competence subgroups of Down's Syndrome children (Group 1: talks in simple sentences; Group 2: two-word sentences; Group 3: not yet two-word sentences)

To test the regularity in the sequence of developmental steps, 25 items from the Minnesota Scales, covering the aspects of speech production, speech comprehension, symbolic comprehension, and symbolic play, were subjected to a scale analysis (Mokken, 1971). A total of 306 test protocols (81 for the first group, 71 for the second group, and 145 for the third group) were entered into the analyses, which could be performed without controlling for chronological age. For the first two linguistic competence groups, the items were highly scalable ($H = .65$ and $.66$), but not for the third group ($H = .32$, even using the short form of the scale). The changed sequence in the level of difficulty of the items in the third group compared with the other two groups revealed that children with very poor language development particularly exhibited less active or spontaneous interest in all symbolic activities, be they symbolic play, looking at books, or active communication. They clearly left the initiative to others and only reacted. In addition, the developmental profile in the sequence of items in the third group differed from child to child and tended to be unstable within the individual child. Thus, whereas the developmental pattern in the first two (better) linguistic competence groups was, in principle, similar, though with time delays, the children in the third group with very slow language development revealed a deviant pattern of development.

Finally, differences in linguistic competence also impacted on the children's cooperation on the Bayley Test (Bayley, 1969). This was assessed with the "Cooperation" scale in the Infant Behavior Record (Bayley, 1969) that testers completed immediately after carrying out the Bayley Test. Up to the developmental age of 16 months, the three linguistic competence groups showed hardly any differences in their behavior. At the developmental age of 17 to 20 months, as can be expected, the willingness to accept the tasks proposed by the testers dropped (due to defiance, and negativism). This decline in cooperation was most marked in children in the group with poor language development. Even at a developmental level of 30 months, they did not regain the relatively strong willingness to cooperate that characterized the children in the other two linguistic competence groups (see Figure 10). For a long time, they were difficult to test, and their low linguistic competence may have impaired their behavior, but also their less cooperative behavior may have made it harder to assess their linguistic competence and possibly their other competencies as well.

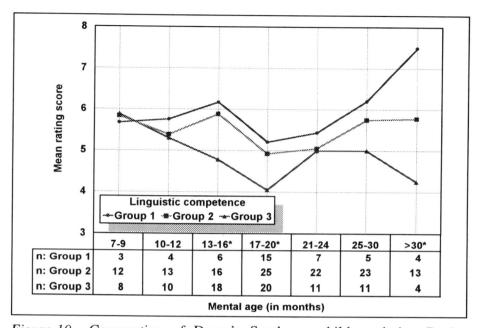

	7-9	10-12	13-16*	17-20*	21-24	25-30	>30*
n: Group 1	3	4	6	15	7	5	4
n: Group 2	12	13	16	25	22	23	13
n: Group 3	8	10	18	20	11	11	4

Mental age (in months)

Figure 10. Cooperation of Down's Syndrome children during Bayley testing development of three linguistic competence groups matched for mental age level (longitudinal assessment) (Group 1: talks in simple sentences; Group 2: two-word sentences; Group 3: not yet two-word sentences) (* group differences frall short of statistical significance acc. to one-way analyses of variances and Friedman H- tests)

5   Summary and Discussion

Developmental tests that have been developed and standardized on nonhandicapped children are applied to handicapped children for a number of purposes: for classification as well as for counseling, the development of intervention programs, and for evaluation. They require the assumption that handicapped children are addressed by the tasks in the same way as nonhandicapped children, that, in principle, they take the same path of development as the children in the standardization sample, and that the scores that are often collected in longitudinal assessments correspond to the standard scores that are mostly collected cross-sectionally.

Observations and results from a sample of children with Down's syndrome, who have gone through at times more than 20 individual test sessions from the first months of life up to school enrollment age, show, control groups. The sources of error determined by individual developmental patterns cannot be overcome through a single matching according to developmental age or chronological age, particularly not in samples that are as small as those with which one is confronted in practical terms when studying handicapped children. A better approximation is already available through diachronic assessments of developmental patterns. However, these require a lot of time and effort. Therefore, it seems appropriate to involve the parents in developmental observation by giving them questionnaires. These parent-report procedures prove to be highly valid instruments that can also, as noninvasive procedures, provide more differentiated information on emotionally and socially sensitive behaviors in the child than professionally administered developmental tests. They could therefore provide a meaningful addition to professional developmental tests through the assessment of diachronic developmental patterns.

References

Bayley, N. (1940). *Factors influencing the growth of intelligence in young children. In G. M. Whipple (Ed.), Intelligence: Its nature and nuture: Part 2. 39th Yearbook of the National Society for the Study of Education* (pp. 49-79). Bloomington, IL: Public School Publishing.

Bayley, N. (1969). *Manual for the Bayley Scales of Infant Development.* New York: Psychological Corporation.

Bayley, N. (1993). *Bayley Scales of Infant Development - Second Edition.* San Antonio, TX: The Psychological Corporation/ Harcourt Brace & Company.

Carr, J. (1975). *Young children with Down's syndrome.* London: Butterworth.

Cicchetti, D., & Sroufe. L. A. (1978). An organizational view of affect: Illustrations from the study of Down's syndrome infants. In M. Lewis & L. A. Rosenblum (Eds.), *The development of affect* (pp. 309-350). New York: Plenum.

Hamer-Elvert, U. (1993). *Kommunikative Entwicklung von Kleinstkindern mit Down-Syndrom in einer Entwicklungstestsituation* [Communicative development of young children with Down's Syndrome observed during developmental testing situations]. Unpublished master's thesis. Free University of Berlin: Institute for Psychology.

Ireton, H., & Thwing, E. (1974). *Manual for the Minnesota Child Development Inventory.* Minneapolis, MN: Behavior Science Systems Inc..

Katoff, L., Reuter, J., & Dunn, V. (1980). *The Kent Infant Development Scale Manual (First Edition).* Kent, OH: Kent Developmental Metrics.

Kaufman, A. S., & Kaufman, N. L. (1983). *K-ABC: Kaufman Assessment Battery for Children: Administation and scoring manual.* Circle Pines, MN: American Guidance Service.

Lienert, C., & Rauh, H. (1993). Entwicklung der Fortbewegung bei Kindern mit Down-Syndrom. Ergebnisse einer Längsschnittstudie [Development of locomotion in children with Down's syndrome. Results of a longitudinal study]. *Kindheit und Entwicklung*, 6, 227-238.

McCall, R. B., Eichorn, D. H., & Hogarty, P. S. (1977). Transitions in early development. *Monographs of the Society for Research in Child Development*, 42(3), Serial No. 171.

McCarthy, D. (1972). *McCarthy Scales of Children's Abilities. Manual.* Cleveland, OH: The Psychological Corporation.

McFarlane, J. W., Allen, L., & Honzik, M. P. (1954). *A developmental study of the behavior problems of normal children between 21 months and 14 years.* Berkeley, CA: University of California Press.

Melchers, P., & Preuß, U. (1991). *K-ABC: Kaufman Assessment Battery for Children. Deutschsprachige Fassung* [German Standardization]. Frankfurt: Swets & Zeitlinger.

Mokken, R. J. (1971). *A theory and procedure of scale analysis.* The Hague: Mouton.

Müller, B. (1993). *Die Erfassung des Entwicklungsstandes in der frühen Kindheit durch Elternurteil* [Developmental assessment in infancy by parental report data]. Unpublished master's thesis. Free University of Berlin: Institute for Psychology.

Müller, B., Schulz, J., & Rauh, H. (1994, June - July). *Differential developmental patterns in normal and Down's syndrome infants.* Paper presented at the XIIIth Biennal Meetings of the ISSBD, Amsterdam.

Rauh, H. (1992). Entwicklungsverläufe bei Kleinkindern mit Down-Syndrom [Developmental trajectories in infants with Down's syndrome]. In J. W. Dudenhausen (Ed.), *Down-Syndrom: Früherkennung und therapeutische Hilfen* (pp. 93-108). Frankfurt: Umwelt & Medizin.

Rauh, H., Göggerle, S., Arens, D., & Schellhas, B. (1995, September). *Entwicklung von Symbolspiel, Sprache und Verhalten bei Kleinkindern mit Down-Syndrom. Exploration von Zusammenhangsmustern* [Development of symbolic play, language, and behavior in young children with Down's Syndrome. Exploration of interpatterings]. Paper presented at the 12. Tagung der Fachgruppe Entwicklungspsychologie, Leipzig..

Rauh, H., & Müller, B. (1989). *KESS. Übersetzung der KID- Scale von Reuter & Bickett. Unveröffentlichte Experimentalversion* [KESS. Translation into German of the KID-Scale of Reuter & Bickett. Unpublished second experimental version]. Free University of Berlin: Institute for Psychology.

Rauh, H., Rudinger, G., Bowman, T., Berry, P., Gunn, P. V., & Hayes, A. (1991). The development of Down Syndrome children. In M. Lamb & H. Keller (Eds.), *Infant development: Perspectives from German speaking countries.* (pp. 329-355). Hillsdale, NJ: Erlbaum.

Rauh, H., & Peisdersky, P. (1985). *KESS. Übersetzung der KID-Scale von Reuter & Bickett. Unveröffentlichte Experimentalversion (1. Fassung)* [KESS. Translation into German of the KID-Scale of Reuter & Bickett. Unpublished first experimental version]. Free University of Berlin: Institute for Psychology.

Reuter, I., & Bickett, L. (1985). *The Kent Infant Development Scale. Manual* (2nd ed.). Kent, OH: Kent Developmental Metrics.

Reuter, L. F., & Reuter, J. M. (1990). *Addendum to the second edition of the KID scale manual. Restandardization of the Kent Infant Development (KID) Scale. The 1990 normative study.* Kent, OH: Kent Developmental Metrics.

Schäfer, A. (1993). *Kommunikative Entwicklung von Kleinstkindern mit Down-Syndrom in einer Entwicklungstestsituation* [Communicative development of young children with Down's syndrome observed during developmental testing situations].   Free University of Berlin: Institute for Psychology.

Vogel, D., Jordan, S., & Rauh, H. (1990). *Therapieangebote für behinderte Kinder*. Berlin: Edition Marhold.

Wishart, J. G. (1986). *Cognitive avoidance in infants and young children with Down's syndrome*. Paper presented at the International Down's Syndrome Congress, Brighton, England.

Wohlwill (1970). The age variable in psychological research. *Psychological Bulletin*, 77, 49-64.

Wohlwill, J. F. (1980). Cognitive development in childhood. In O. G. Brim Jr. & J. Kagan (Eds.), *Constancy and change in human development* (pp. 359-444). Cambridge, MA: Harvard University Press.

M. Brambring, H. Rauh, and A. Beelmann (Eds.). (1996). *Early childhood intervention: Theory, evaluation, and practice* (pp. 155-171). Berlin, New York: de Gruyter.

The Significance of Biological and Psychosocial Risks for Preschool-Age Behavior Problems

Günter Esser, Manfred Laucht, and Martin H. Schmidt

1   Introduction

Since the early investigations of Pasamanick, Rogers, and Lilienfeld (1956), pre- and perinatal complications have been viewed as significant risks for later development. But already in 1966, Pasamanick and Knobloch pointed out that organic risks are often contaminated with psychosocial factors, such as less appropriate preventive behavior in mothers from low socioeconomic classes.

The last 30 years have seen enormous progress in neonatal intensive care, whereby a lot of earlier risks could be countered (Largo et al., 1989; Rettwitz-Volk, 1992). As a result, many recent longitudinal studies have been able to demonstrate only a slight impact of pre- and perinatal complications (Hadders-Algra et al., 1988a; Hadders-Algra & Touwen, 1990; Lefevre et al., 1988; Lindahl et al., 1988; Lloyd et al., 1988; Portnoy et al., 1988; Stewart et al., 1988; Stewart et al., 1989; Zubrick et al., 1988). The results of these studies mainly depend upon the inclusion of handicapped children in the analysis. While about 10% of children with extreme low birthweight (under 1,000 g) show at least mild forms of mental handicaps (Daily et al., 1989; Hofmann-Williamson et al., 1990; Saigal et al., 1990a; Szatmari et al., 1990), hardly any positive correlation between learning disorders or behavior problems and pre- and perinatal complications can be found within the group of normal or subnormal children.

In the past two decades, more and more psychosocial risk factors have been taken into account: at the beginning, especially socioeconomic status; later on, also more specific factors of the parents like mental health, delinquency, low educational level, early parenthood, marital discord, or divorce. While it is true that most of these factors enhance the probability for developmental disorders, mostly they are confounded with other psychosocial factors and reveal nothing about the mechanisms of their impact on the child. Rutter (1988) therefore has stressed the differentiation of risk indicators and processes. Additionally, later conditions of socialization (e.g., chronic and acute stressors, quality of parent-child interaction) are worthy of notice (Ernst & Luckner 1985;, Esser et al.,

1993). The isolated view on the impact of single biological and psychosocial factors therefore has to be replaced by a more complex one that also takes account of the influences of later stages of development.

The Mannheimer Risikokinderstudie (Mannheim children at risk study), which is concerned with the genesis and course of neuropsychiatric disorders in children at risk during the first 8 years of life (Esser et al., 1993; Esser, Laucht, et al., 1990; Laucht et al., 1989; Laucht et al., 1992; Schmidt et al., 1992), tries to take these methodological requirements into consideration. The specific characteristics of this study are:

1. an analysis of the concurrence of biological and psychosocial risk factors for the development of the child present at birth (by eliminating their confoundation);
2. a consideration of the impact of acute and chronic stressors on further development;
3. a consideration of childrearing behavior and the quality of parent-child interaction;
4. an analysis of the course of risk factors through a microanalysis of parent-child interaction;
5. an assessment of all relevant variables of child development within a multilevel approach.

The present study focuses on behavior problems during the first 4 years of life. It thereby emphasizes the pathogenesis of behavior problems and aspects of process analysis with the help of early mother-child interaction.

2   Method

A prospective longitudinal study design was chosen, starting at birth and following the children and their families through the first 8 years of life. The two-factorial design (3 x 3) - Factor I varying the degree of organic; Factor II, the degree of psychosocial risks - allows the identification of interactive effects and raises the probability of the occurrence of disorders, because the children from five of the nine cells are suffering from at least one severe risk constellation, either biological, psychosocial, or both. A total of 362 children and their families were recruited. After the initial investigation at birth, four waves are being conducted at ages 3 months, 24 months, 4.5 years, and 8 years. Of the initial sample of 362 families, we were able to reexamine 354 at age 2 years and 352 at age 4.5 years. The study began in 1986: Over a 25-month period, the sample was collected in two gynecologic and six neonatal clinics in the Rhine-Neckar region

(Mannheim-Heidelberg). Included were all firstborn children (born or treated in one of the eight clinics) of German-speaking parents who fell into one of the nine cells of the two-factorial design but did not have physical handicaps, obvious genetic defects, or metabolic diseases. The rate of participation (recruited parents minus refusals) was 64.5%. The aim was to gather subjects consecutively until all cells were filled.

2.1 Definition of Organic Risk

In most studies, organic risks are defined either by birthweight alone or by an obstetrical optimality score like the one introduced by Prechtl (1968). Definition by birthweight has the advantage of an objective measurement, which, divided into few classes, leads to a rather good estimation of organic risks. A disadvantage of this procedure is the fact that especially within the range of low birthweight (1,500 to 2,500 g), further complications are of greater importance. Besides, the use of only one risk factor means that the recruitment of subjects is much more difficult.
Optimality scores, on the other hand, have other disadvantages:

1. Information from case reports includes variables (e.g., sufficient socioeconomic status, married mother, more than three medical controls during gestation) that are more likely to describe psychosocial than organic risks. That means, optimality scores do not permit a clear differentiation between organic and psychosocial risk.
2. Definition of many variables is not reliable because of either a lack of criteria or dependence on mother' s recall.
3. Not all variables are available in each case. Availability depends on the diagnostic procedure used in each clinic.
4. The multiple intercorrelations of the variables are unknown. They are supposed to differ considerably. This leads to an uncontrolled weighting of the variables.

Definition of organic risks in our study had to meet several methodological and practical criteria:

1. no contamination with psychosocial risks;
2. objective data;
3. availability for each subject;
4. significant differences in degree of severity between the risk groups;
5. no specific indicator of physical handicaps, chromosome defects, or metabolic diseases.

Together with the gynecologic and neonatal clinics, the following definitions were chosen:

1. *No risk:* birth weight 2,500 to 4,200 g, a gestational age of 38 to 42 weeks, no signs of asphyxia, and no operative delivery.
2. *Moderate risk:* premature birth (1,501 - 2,500 g), or signs of risk of premature birth, or EPH-gestosis.
3. *Severe risks:* birth weight < 1,500 g or clear case of asphyxia (pH < 7.1; CTG score according to Fischer < 4; lactate > 8,00 mmol/l), or complications during the first 7 days of life (sepsis, objectified by a positive blood culture; seizure; respiratory therapy). Additionally, infants in the severe risk group had to spend a minimum of 7 days on the neonatal ward. These criteria were sufficient to single out all infants with severe neonatal complications who were treated in one of the six neonatal clinics.

2.2 Definition of Psychosocial Risks

The definition of psychosocial risks was based on the Family Adversity Index (Rutter & Quinton, 1977), which has proved to be highly significant for child psychiatric disorders (Blanz et al., 1991; Voll et al., 1982). The FAI was adapted to the specific situation of young families (we included only firstborn children) and elaborated by new concepts that have become relevant in the genesis of psychiatric disorders such as social integration and support, severe chronic stress, and coping.

Eleven psychosocial risk factors were defined as follows:

1. low educational level of parents, that is, unskilled or semiskilled employment (interrater reliability: Kappa = 1.0);
2. crowded living conditions, that is, more than one person per room or not more than a total of 50 m^2 accommodation (Kappa = 1.0);
3. moderate or severe psychiatric disorders in the parents according to DSM III-R (Kappa = .98);
4. delinquency or institutional care in the history of the parents (Kappa = 1.0);
5. troubled relationship between the parents, that is, frequent and long-lasting troubles, separations, lack of emotional care (Kappa = 1.0);
6. early parenthood, that is, < 18-years-old at birth of the child, or relationship between the parents existed for less than 6 months at the time of conception (Kappa = 1.0);

7. incomplete family (Kappa = 1.0);
8. complete rejection of pregnancy (Kappa = 1.0);
9. lack of social integration and support, that is, lack of friends and
    lack of assistance from relatives (Kappa = .71);
10. severe chronic difficulties lasting more than 1 year (Kappa = .93);
11. lack of coping skills, that is, inadequate coping with stressful events
    during the last year, for example, denial of obvious problems,
    withdrawal, resignation, overdramatization (Kappa = .67).

No risk means none, moderate risk means 1 or 2, and severe risk means
that 3 or more of these 11 risk factors were present.

2.3 Assessment

Behavior problems were measured with a highly structured parent interview
(an adapted version of the Mannheimer Elterninterview; Esser et al., 1989)
and with behavioral ratings by trained raters in four standardized research
settings (home visit, EEG, neurological examination, history taking). At the
age of 3 months, behavioral problems included feeding, sleeping, and
digestive disorders as well as 13 adverse temperamental characteristics
derived from the nine temperament scales of Thomas et al. (1968). At 2
years and 4.5 years, a broad range of problem behaviors was evaluated that
included temper tantrums, hyperactivity, attentional deficits, excessive dependency, shyness and disobediance, feeding problems, sleep disturbances,
sibling rivalry, tics, stereotypes, and autistic behavior. Interrater reliability
for two raters had a mean kappa of .68 at 3 months and .83 at 2 and 4.5
years. At each of the research waves, the single symptoms of problem
behavior were summed up, leading to a theoretical range of 0 to 16 at 3
months, 0 to 23 at 2 years, and 0 to 29 at 4.5 years.
    Childrearing behavior was assessed in two ways: a direct analysis of
mother-child interaction and the Home Observation for Measurement of the
Environment Inventory (HOME; Bradley & Caldwell, 1979). Mother-child
dyads were observed and videotaped during a 10-minute semistructured
diaper and play session at 3 months. Additional 10-minute standardized play
sessions were observed at 2 and 4.5 years. The videotaped mother-child
interactions were rated with the Mannheim Rating System for Mother-
Infant-Interaction (MRS-MII, Esser, Scheven, et al., 1990). The rating
system consists of eight 5-point scales for evaluation of the mother
(emotion, physical affection, vocalization, lack of verbal restrictions,
congruency, variability of behavior, reactivity, and stimulation) and five
scales for the evaluation of the infant (emotion, vocalization, direction of

gaze, reactivity, and readiness to interact). The ratings for each scale were made every minute resulting in a total of 130 ratings per dyad. Mean interrater reliability in the 32 dyads was adequate (r_s = .88). The scales have been found to discriminate between mothers from more or less psychosocially disadvantaged backgrounds and between infants with and without severe pre- and perinatal complications. Further evaluations of mother-child interaction at ages 2 and 4.5 are currently being performed.

The Home Observation for Measurement of the Environment Inventory (HOME; Bradley & Caldwell, 1979) was used to obtain measures of the childrearing environment. It is designed to assess the quality of stimulation and support available to a child in the home environment. Information needed to score the inventory is obtained through observation and interviews in the home with the child and its primary caregiver. The infant version of the inventory contains 45 two-choice items clustered into six subscales (parental responsivity, avoidance of restriction and punishment, organization of the environment, play materials, parental involvement, and variety of stimulation). For this study, the original version was extended and adapted for German living conditions. Additionally, parental attitudes toward the child and childrearing practices in standard situations were assessed with a structured parent interview and questionnaires.

Item analysis and factor analysis were used to form a composite score of disturbed mother-infant relationship. This relied equally on observation and HOME measures at 3 months, whereas only HOME measures and parental attitudes and childrearing practices were included at 2 years and 4.5 years, because the evaluation of the videotaped interactions was not yet available.

The children's *life event schedule* was based on the Münchner Ereignisliste (MEL, Munich Life Events Schedule; Maier-Diewald et al., 1983) After completion of the MEL by the parents, onset, duration, and context of the life events were assessed with the help of a semistructured interview. Following the interview, the investigator rated the subjective and objective threat for the child on a 5-point Likert scale ranging from *no threat* (1) to *severe threat* (5). The sum of life events consisted only of those events that represented a marked to very severe (points 3-5) objective threat to the child. Whereas hospital admissions were the main life events between birth and age 3 months, the following events were considered between 3 and 24 months and between 24 and 54 months: illness of mother or father; handicaps of near relatives; pregnancy of the mother; birth of a sibling; marital discord, separation, and divorce; new partnership; changes in looking after the child; quarrels concerning the family; interference of other persons; financial difficulties; overcrowding; changes in living conditions; unemployment of parents; changes in working conditions of the parents; delinquency of the parents; and other chronic burdens.

3   Results

Effects of biological and psychosocial risks on behavior problems were evaluated with path analysis. From the 350 children who had passed all three waves of investigation, 26 with mental or motor handicaps were excluded because of their substantially different psychopathology. Thus 324 subjects were available for the analyses. The first figure (at the top) shows the most simple model in which only pre- and perinatal complications and psychosocial risks were included as predictors. The beta coefficiants underline that psychosocial factors (β = .29) are more important than biological risks (β = .11) in the genesis of behavior problems at preschool age. In total, the amount of explained variance remained low (9.2%). In a next step, behavior problems at T_1 and T_2 were added to the model. The explained variance was enhanced markedly (from 9.2% to 27%, see Figure 1 at the bottom). Pre- and perinatal complications had only a direct impact on the behavior problems at 3 months, whereas psychosocial risks showed a direct influence on behavior problems at each point of measurement. Behavior problems had no significant stability between 3 months and 2 years, but were remarkably stable between 2 and 4.5 years.

   In a third step, childrearing behavior at T_1 and T_2 as well as the changes in childrearing from T_1 to T_2 and from T_2 to T_3 were introduced into the analyses (see Figure 2). Besides those variables, the sum of life events between birth and 3 months, 3 months and 2 years, and 2 years and 4.5 years were considered. At first sight, the resulting model seemed to be rather complex. It demonstrated that behavior problems at 4.5 years depended on negative childrearing behavior at 2 (.46), changes in childrearing behavior between 2 and 4.5 (.35), and behavior problems at 2 years (.31). Psychosocial risks mainly influenced later behavior problems over negative childrearing behavior, earlier manifestations of behavior problems, and, to a slight degree, over life events. Pre-   and   perinatal complications showed only a slight impact that was mediated by early life events and behavior problems at 2 years. Psychosocial risks elicited life events in each time interval; the life events themselves were not influenced by early behavior problems of the child. A transactional process could be demonstrated in the way that behavior problems at 3 months increased the degree of negative childrearing behavior at 2 years (.40), which, in turn, increased the number of behavior problems at 4.5 years.

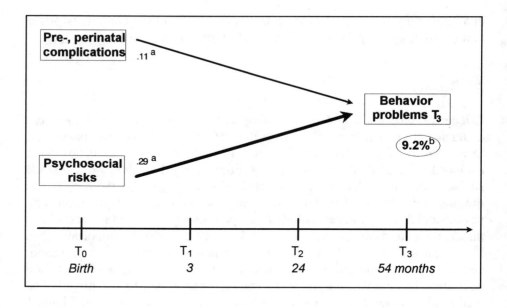

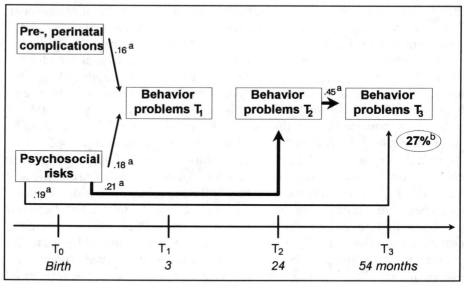

[a] significant β coefficients; [b] explained variance.

Figure 1.   Genesis of behavior problems I (above) and II (below).

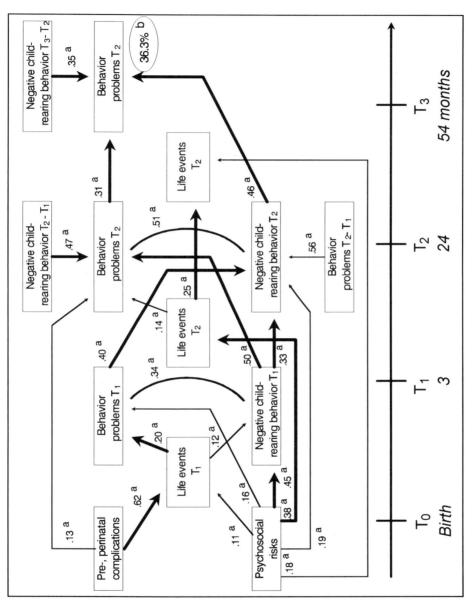

^{a} significant β coefficients; ^{b} explained variance.

Figure 2.   Genesis of behavior problems III.

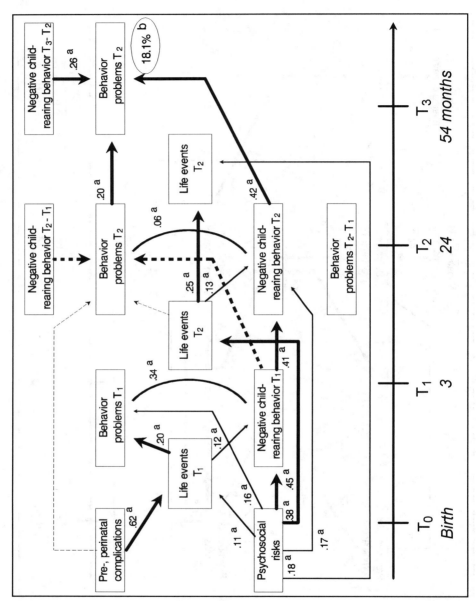

[a] significant β coefficients; [b] explained variance.

Figure 3.   Genesis of internalizing problems III.

As Figure 3 shows, the model provided a good fit only for disruptive behavior disorders (i.e., hyperactive and antisocial behavior), but not for internalizing problems - especially at 2 years. The dashed lines indicate missing significant beta coefficients that were present in the total model and the model for expansive disorders. As can be seen, internalizing problems at 2 years could not be explained by either negative childrearing behavior, pre- and perinatal complications, or life events between 3 months and 2 years. Thus no sufficient explanation for internalizing problems at 2 years could be given by the variables considered in the present model.

The kind of path models presented allow only a bird's eye view of the development of behavior problems. Going more into details, the specific role of early mother-infant interaction was analyzed.

Figure 4 reveals a remarkably high partial correlation (.42 or .31) between the quality of mother-child interaction and the development of behavior problems at ages 2 and 4.5 years. This influence is significantly higher than the stability of early behavior problems.

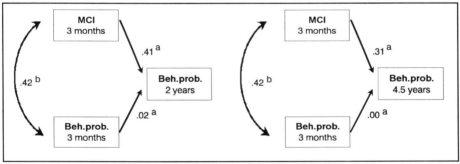

[a] partial correlation coefficient; [b] zero-order correlation; Beh.prob. = Behavior problems.

Figure 4.   Genesis of behavior Problems I.

Further analysis should clarify whether it was mainly characteristics of the mother, or of the child, or of the dyad that were responsible for later behavior problems. Therefore, disorders of mother-infant interaction were defined on the level of the dyad, global maternal behavior, and global child's behavior, as well as on the level of the single scales of the MBS-MII. The sum of the 10 ratings (1 per minute) was computed for each of the single scales. The mother's global behavior represented the sum of the eight aggregated single mother scales; and child's global behavior, the sum of the five aggregated single infant scales. The quality of the dyad was defined by the sum of the global mother behavior and the global infant behavior. Disorders were defined at each level as scores below -1 standard deviation.

Figure 5 shows the comparison between undisturbed and disturbed dyads, mothers, and infants concerning behavior problems of the child 21 months later at the age of 2 years. As can be seen, disturbances at the level of the dyad at 3 months led to 1.5 more symptoms at age 2. Disturbances at the level of the mother's global behavior were followed by an enhancement of 1.4 symptoms; at the level of the infant's global behavior, by an enhancement of 1.0. Whereas disturbances in nearly all single mother scales were followed by a significant increase in behavior problems, there were only slight effects on the side of disturbances in the infants' scales.

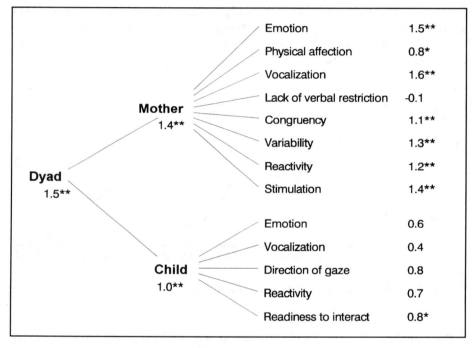

Difference in number of symptoms between children from undisturbed and disturbed interactions. * p < .05. ** p < .01 (t test).

Figure 5. Mother-infant interaction and behavior problems at 2 years.

A comparison of Figure 5 and 6 demonstrates that the long-term effects of disturbed mother-infant interactions were smaller than the short-term effects. For behavior problems at age 4.5 years, mother's interactional behavior but not that of the infant was predictive. Especially mothers who showed disturbances in emotion and vocalization had children with significantly higher symptom scores.

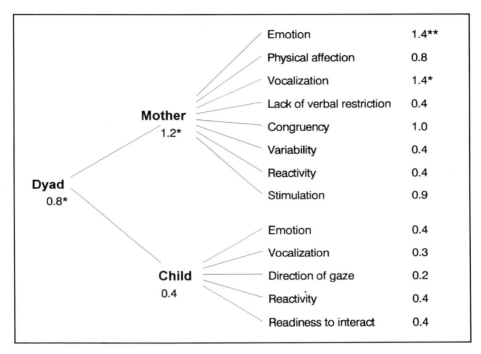

	Emotion	1.4**
	Physical affection	0.8
	Vocalization	1.4*
	Lack of verbal restriction	0.4
Mother	Congruency	1.0
1.2*	Variability	0.4
	Reactivity	0.4
	Stimulation	0.9
	Emotion	0.4
	Vocalization	0.3
Child	Direction of gaze	0.2
0.4	Reactivity	0.4
	Readiness to interact	0.4

Dyad 0.8*

Difference in number of symptoms between children from undisturbed and disturbed interactions. * $p < .05$. ** $p < .01$ (*t*-Test).

Figure 6. Mother-infant interaction and behavior problems at 4.5 years.

4   Discussion

When psychosocial and biological risks are not confounded, biological risks in total have only a slight influence on a child's behavior problems. This influence decreases with age. Psychosocial risks do not have a direct impact on behavior problems. Their influence is mediated by childrearing behavior and life events. Childrearing behavior is the most important variable. Childrearing behavior itself is influenced negatively by an infant's behavior problems. The childrearing behavior altered in this way then leads to increased behavior problems. This transactional process resembles a vicious circle and may explain the negative development of children with minor temperamental difficulties when they live under unfavorable conditions. Contradicting the findings of Thomas et al. (1968) and other authors, the correlation between early temperamental characteristics (at 3 months) and later behavior problems is very low. The main explanation for these differing findings is the different assessment of temperament. Whereas most authors (including Thomas et al.) have measured infants' temperament only by questionnaire, our judgment of infants' temperament is derived from four observational ratings and an interview with the mother. This means that while Thomas et al. have measured mainly the stability of the maternal judgment, we have tried to measure the stability of the infant's behavior. From 2 years to 4.5 years, there is a remarkable stability of behavior problems that has been confirmed by an analysis of categorized disorders (Laucht et al., 1993), which showed a persistence of 60%.

In every time interval, life events are partly caused by psychosocial risks. Even early hospital admissions (between birth and 3 months) are influenced to a certain degree by psychosocial risks. This finding underlines that early hospital admissions are not only (but mainly) caused by pre- and perinatal complications.

In general, the conclusions are valid for disruptive as well as for internalizing problems. The main difference concerns the genesis of disturbances at age 2. No significant influence can be found for internalizing problems at that time. Even childrearing behavior is not able to predict internalizing problems. This may be a consequence of the definition of a global measurement of childrearing. Further analyses will concentrate on specific patterns of childrearing behavior such as overprotection, which does not necessarily lead to a general decrease in childrearing quality. Additionally, protective factors have to be taken into account.

The quality of mother-infant interaction has a significant predictive value for later behavior problems. Although the partial correlation coefficients cannot be classified as absolutely high in comparison with other measurements of early infancy, they are of a remarkable magnitude. When discriminating between the infant's and the mother's interactional behavior, the latter is of much greater importance. This finding supports the conclusions on stability of temperament (see above). As could be expected, the long-term effect of early mother-infant interaction is lower than the short-term effect. Early mother's emotion and vocalization shows a significant association with later behavior problems. The scale emotion is defined by the facial expression of the mother ranging from depressed/angry to smiling. It can be demonstrated that the cutoff point between disturbed and nondisturbed interactional behavior identifies mothers who show very low rates of smiling during the interaction with the child. Mothers' vocalization ranges from no vocalization over adult speech to baby talk. The cutoff differentiates between mothers with and without baby talk. Thus, lack of smiling and baby talk in early mother-infant interaction can be seen as a risk process for later behavior problems in the child.

References

Blanz, B., Schmidt, M. H., & Esser, G. (1991). Familial adversities and child psychiatric disorders. *Journal of Child Psychology and Psychiatry, 32,* 939-950.

Bradley, R., & Caldwell, B. (1979). Home observation for measurement of the environment: A revision of the preschool scale. *American Journal of Mental Deficiency, 84,* 235-244.

Daily, D. K., Kilbride, H. W., & Beadle, S. (1989, September). *Patterns of neuromotor development of infants with birthweights < 800 g.* Paper presented at the 43rd annual meeting of the American Academy for Cerebral Palsy & Developmental Medicine, London.

Ernst, C., & Luckner, N. (1985). *Stellt die Frühkindheit die Weichen? Eine Kritik an der Lehre von der schicksalhaften Bedeutung erster Erlebnisse.* Stuttgart: Enke.

Esser, G., Blanz, B., Geisel, B., & Laucht, M. (1989). *Mannheimer Elterninterview.* Beltz: Weinheim.

Esser, G., Dinter, R., Jörg, M., Rose, F., Villalba, P., Laucht, M., & Schmidt, M. H. (1993). Bedeutung und Determinanten der frühen Mutter-Kind-Beziehung. *Zeitschrift für Psychosomatische Medizin und Psychoanalyse, 39*(3), 246-264.

Esser, G., Laucht, M., Schmidt, M., Löffler, W., Reiser, A., Stöhr, R.-M., Weindrich, D., & Weinel, H. (1990). Behaviour problems and developmental status of 3-month-old infants in relation to organic and psychosocial risks. *European Archives of Psychiatry and Neurological Sciences, 239,* 384-390.

Esser, G., Scheven, A., Petrova, A., Laucht, M., & Schmidt, M. H. (1990). Mannheim Rating System for mother-infant face-to-face interaction (MRS-III). *The German Journal of Psychology, 14,* 301-302.

Hadders-Algra, M., & Touwen, B. C. (1990). Body measurements, neurological and behavioural development in six-year-old children born preterm and/or small-for-gestational-age. *Early Human Development, 22,* 1, 1-13.

Hadders-Algra, M., Huisjes, H. J., & Touwen, B. C. L. (1988a). Perinatal correlates of major and minor neurological dysfunction at school age: A multivariate analysis. *Developmental Medicine and Child Neurology, 30,* 472-481.

Hadders-Algra, M., Huisjes, H. J., & Touwen, B. C. L. (1988b). Perinatal risk factors and minor neurological dysfunction: Significance for behaviour and school achievement at nine years. *Developmental Medicine and Child Neurology, 30,* 482-491.

Hofman-Williamson, M., Bernbaum, J., D'Agostino, J. A., & Farran, A. (1990, September). *Use of special education services by low birthweight school-age children.* Paper presented at the 43rd annual meeting of the American Academy for Cerebral Palsy & Developmental Medicine, London.

Largo, R. H., Pfister, D., Molinari, L., Kunda, S., Lipp, A., & Duc, G. (1989). Significance of prenatal, perinatal and postnatal factors in the development of AGA preterm infants at 5 to 7 years. *Developmental Medicine and Child Neurology*, *31*, 440-456.

Laucht, M., Esser, G., & Schmidt, M. H. (1989). Verhaltensauffälligkeiten und Entwicklungsstörungen im Säuglingsalter: Einfluß von organischen und psychosozialen Risikofaktoren. In H. M. Weinmann (Ed.), *Aktuelle Neuropädiatrie 1988*. Berlin: Springer.

Laucht, M., Esser, G., Schmidt, M. H., Ihle, W., Löffler, W., Stöhr, R.-M., Weindrich, D., & Weinel, H. (1992). Risikokinder: Zur Bedeutung biologischer und psychosozialer Risiken für die kindliche Entwicklung in den beiden ersten Lebensjahren. *Praxis der Kinderpsychologie und Kinderpsychiatrie*, *41*, 274-285.

Laucht, M., Esser, G., & Schmidt, M. H. (1993). Psychische Auffälligkeiten im Kleinkind- und Vorschulalter. *Kindheit und Entwicklung*, *2*, 143-149.

Lefevre, F., Bard, H., Veilleux, A., & Martel, Ch. (1988). Outcome at school age of children with birthweights of 1000 grams or less. *Developmental Medicine and Child Neurology*, *30*, 170-180.

Lindahl, E., Michelsson, K., Helenius, M., & Parre, M. (1988). Neonatal risk factors and later neurodevelopmental disturbances. *Developmental Medicine and Child Neurology*, *30*, 571-589.

Lloyd, B. W., Wheldall, K., & Perks, D. (1988). Controlled study of intelligence and school performance of very low-birthweight children from a defined geographical area. *Developmental Medicine and Child Neurology*, *30*, 36-42.

Maier-Diewald, W., Wittchen, H. U., Hecht, H., & Werner-Eilert, K. (1983). *Die Münchener Ereignisliste (MEL)*. München: Max Planck Institut für Psychiatrie.

Pasamanick, B., & Knobloch, H. (1966). Retrospective studies on epidemiology of reproductive causality: Old and new. *Merrill-Palmer Quarterly*, *12*, 7-26.

Pasamanick, B., Rogers, M. E., & Lilienfeld, A. M. (1956). Pregnancy experience and the development of behavior disorder in children. *American Journal of Psychiatry*, *112*, 613-618.

Portnoy, S., Callias, M., Wolke, D., & Gamsu, H. (1988). Five-year follow-up study of extremely low-birthweight infants. *Developmental Medicine and Child Neurology*, *30*, 590-598.

Prechtl, H. F. R. (1968). Neurological findings in newborn infants after pre- and perinatal complications. In J. H. P. Jonxis, H. K. A. Visser, & J. A. Troelstra (Eds.), *Aspects of prematurity and dysmaturity*. Leiden, Netherlands: Steufert Kroese.

Rettwitz-Volk, W. (1992). Epidemiologische Aspekte der Frühgeburtlichkeit. In A. Wischnik, W. Kachel, F. Melchert, & K.-H. Niessen (Eds.). *Problemsituationen in der Perinatalmedizin* (pp. 68-72). Stuttgart: Enke.

Rutter, M., & Quinton, D. (1977). Psychiatric disorder: Ecological factors and concepts of causation. In M. McGurk (Ed.), *Ecological factors in human development*. Amsterdam: North Holland.

Rutter, M. (1988). Psychological resilience and protective mechanism. In J. Rolf, A. Masten, D. Ciccetti, N. Nuechterlein, & S. Weintraub (Eds.), *Risk and protective factors in the development of psychopathology*. New York: Cambridge University Press.

Saigal, S., Szatmari, P., Rosenbaum, P., King, S., & Campbell, D. (1990a, September). *Cognitive abilities of extremely low-birthweight (ELBW) children and matched controls at school age: A regional cohort.* Paper presented at the 43rd annual meeting of the American Academy for Cerebral Palsy & Developmental Medicine, London.

Saigal, S., Szatmari, P., Rosenbaum, P., King, S., & Campbell, D. (1990b, September). *Learning disabilities and school problems in a regional cohort of extremely low-birthweight (ELBVW) children: Comparison with matched controls.* Paper presented at the 43rd annual meeting of the American Academy for Cerebral Palsy & Developmental Medicine, London.

Schmidt, M. H., Esser, G., & Laucht, M. (1992). Zur Bedeutung spezifischer perinataler Risikofaktoren für die Kindesentwicklung in Interaktion mit psychosozialen Einflüssen. In A. Wischnik, W. Kachel, F. Melchert, & K. H. Niessen (Eds.), *Problemsituationen in der Perinatalmedizin* (pp. 73-79). Stuttgart: Enke.

Stewart, A., Hope, P. L., Hamilton, P., Costello, A. M., Baudin, J., Bradford, B., Amiel-Tison, C., & Reynolds, E. O. R. (1988). Prediction in very preterm infants of satisfactory neurodevelopmental progress at 12 months. *Developmental Medicine and Child Neurology, 30*, 53-63.

Stewart, A. L., Costello, A. M., Hamilton, P. A., & Baudin, J. (1989). Relationship between neurodevelopmental status of very preterm infants at one and four years. *Developmental Medicine and Child Neurology, 31*, 756-765.

Szatmari, P., Saigal, S., Rosenbaum, P., & Campbell, D. (1990,   ). *Psychiatric disorders and impairments in adaptive functioning in a regional cohort of children with birthweights 501-1000 g and matched term controls.* Paper presented at the 43rd annual meeting of the American Academy for Cerebral Palsy & Developmental Medicine, London.

Thomas, A., Chess, S., & Birch, H. G. (1968). *Temperament and behaviour disorders in children.* New York: University Press.

Voll, R., Allehoff, W. H., Esser, G., Poustka, F., & Schmidt, M. H. (1982). Widrige familiäre und soziale Bedingungen und psychiatrische Auffälligkeiten bei Achtjährigen. *Zeitschrift für Kinder- und Jugendpsychiatrie, 10*, 100-107.

Zubrick, S. R., Macartney, H., & Stanley, F. (1988). Hidden handicap in school-age children who received neonatal intensive care. *Developmental Medicine and Child Neurology, 30*, 145-152.

Part Three

Family and the Early Intervention Process

M. Brambring, H. Rauh, and A. Beelmann (Eds.). (1996). *Early childhood intervention: Theory, evaluation, and practice* (pp. 175-195). Berlin, New York: de Gruyter.

The Service System and its Effects on Families: An Ecological Perspective

Paula J. Beckman

1 Introduction

One of the most revolutionary movements that has taken place in early intervention over the past 5 to 10 years in the United States has been a changing view of families. It is a movement that has envolved from several converging trends. Scientifically, there has been an increasing tendency both in the physical and the behavioral sciences to view the world in terms of systems and to focus on the dynamic aspects of those systems. Politically, there has been a growing recognition that there are many threats to family stability and that social systems must support this stability. Practically, there is the simple awareness of the missed opportunities and miscommunications that come in the absence of understanding the issues that confront families.

If one examines the empirical literature on families of children with disabilities, several general findings can be identified. First, some families of children with disabilities report increased stress (Beckman, 1991a; Dyson, 1991; Dyson & Fewell, 1986; Friedrich & Friedrich, 1981), depression (Breslau & Davis, 1986; Chetwynd, 1985), and isolation (Gallagher et al., 1983; Kazak & Marvin, 1984; Stagg & Catron, 1986). However, there is also evidence that not all families experience such effects (Frey et al., 1989; Gowen et al., 1989; Harris & McHale, 1989; Salisbury, 1987), and considerable effort is being made to understand the sources of this variation. In some instances, increased family stress can result in some adverse effects for children and their families. For example, extraordinary stress has been associated with more out-of-home placement (Kobe et al., 1991; Sherman & Cocozza, 1984). Other studies have found that stress is associated with subsequent patterns of mother-infant interaction (Crnic et al., 1984). Third, some correlational data suggests that social support seems to mediate effects of stressful life experiences (Beckman et al., 1986; Beckman & Pokorni, 1988; Crnic et al., 1986).

Despite these findings, there has been a general failure to examine the extent to which those service systems that are presumably designed to support the child and family are, in actuality, supportive. Consider for a moment the focus of much recent research: Studies have investigated such topics as the extent to which characteristics of the child are associated with family outcome variables such as stress, adaptation, and coping (Beckman, 1983; Beckman & Pokorni, 1988; Beckman et al., 1986; Dunst et al., 1990; Frey et al., 1989; Harris & McHale, 1989; Gowen et al., 1989). Other studies have examined the extent to which characteristics of the family (such as SES, parental resources, maternal education, etc.) are associated with family adaptation (Beckman & Pokorni, 1988; Beckman et al., 1986; Frey et al., 1989; Flynt, Wood & Scott, 1989; Heinicke, 1984; Nihira et al., 1980). The question that is often neglected is the extent to which the service system itself, and the service providers who function within it, contribute or fail to contribute to family well-being. The point here is that the implicit assumption is that the sources of stress evolve from the child or the family itself rather than from the service system. Simplistically put, the question is "when is support really support?"

The purpose of this paper is to examine the service system and the extent to which it may or may not be a source of support for families of young children with disabilities. One of the most popular and well-accepted pieces of professional wisdom that has emerged over the past decade is that social support mediates the effects of stressful life events for families of children with disabilities. Indeed, a considerable body of evidence has emerged that has shown an inverse relationship between the amount of stress reported by parents and social support (Beckman & Pokorni, 1988; Beckman et al., 1986; Bristol, 1979; Crnic et al., 1986; Dunst et al., 1986; Peterson, 1984). In examining this work, however, it is important to note that most existing evidence on this relationship is correlational. It is possible that families that are less stressed are better able to access the support network. Experimental studies are needed that demonstrate the effectiveness of various types of support for families.

It is also important to note that when studies differentiate between various sources of support, differences are frequently found in the way in which they affect families. For example, social supports are often characterized as to whether they are informal or formal. Formal support typically refers to institutionalized sources of support from service providers, agencies, and organizations that are designed to provide a service for individuals with disabilities and their families. Informal support generally refers to less institutionalized sources of support such as a spouse, friends, neighbors, or relatives. These individuals may provide both emotional and instrumental support. For the most part, informal support seems to be most consistently associated with decreased stress (Beckman, 1991a; Beckman & Pokorni, 1988; Beckman et al., 1986). The findings are less consistent when it comes to the relationship between stress and formal support. Findings from three studies conducted at the University of Maryland serve to illustrate this point.

The first is a study of 44 low-birthweight, premature infants and their families (Beckman & Pokorni, 1988). Families were followed over a 2-year period to determine if there were changes in the amount of stress and support they reported over time. Specifically, mothers were interviewed when infants were 3, 6, 12, and 24 months chronological age using a battery of interview measures. Several interesting findings emerged that are particularly relevant to the point being made here: First, concurrent correlations indicated that informal social support was significantly negatively associated with the total amount of stress mothers reported when infants were 3 months ($r = -.42$, $p < .05$); 12 months ($r = -.39$, $p < .05$); and 24 months ($r = -.42$, $p < .05$) of age. In other words, at these ages, mothers who reported more informal support reported less stress. Moreover, when the relationship between informal support at one age and the amount of stress reported at subsequent ages was examined, a similar pattern emerged. Specifically, the amount of informal support mothers received when infants were 3 months of age was significantly negatively related to the amount of stress reported at 6 months ($r = -.44$, $p < .05$), and informal support at 12 months was significantly negatively related to stress at 24 months ($r = -.41$, $p < .05$). Thus, for these data points, mothers who reported more informal support at the earlier age reported less stress at the subsequent age. However, there was *not* a significant relationship at any of the ages between formal support and stress. This was true for both concurrent data points as well as for subsequent data points.

In another study, the relationship between stress and support in mothers and fathers of 27 children with disabilities who were between 18 months and 6 years of age was examined (Beckman, 1991). Significant negative relationships were obtained between stress and informal support for both mothers ($r = -.65$, $p < .001$) and fathers ($r = -.47$, $p < .01$). However, no such relationships were obtained for either mothers or fathers when formal support was examined.

Finally, Beckman (1991b) examined the social support reported by 42 mothers of children with disabilities between 18 months and 6 years of age. Mothers were asked to rate potential sources of formal support (the infant/preschool program, private physicians, public health services, long-term respite care, private social workers, counselors/psychologists, and public social services). A summary of these findings is presented in Table 1.

Table 1. *Satisfaction With Formal Support (in Percent)*

	Not available Not helpful	Extremely helpful
Infant/preschool program	34.5	36.9
Private physican	19.0	20.9
Public health services	76.2	11.6
Respite care	78.6	9.3
Private social services	61.9	6.9
Public social services	73.8	6.9

Several findings are of interest for purposes of this paper. First, depending on the service, a fairly large percentage of parents reported that specific services were not available or not at all helpful (range was 34% to 78%). Second, only 6.9% to 36.9% (depending on the specific service) reported that a particular type of formal support was extremely helpful.

Taken together, these data suggest that formal sources of support did not always function to effectively support families. There seems to be a reluctance on the part of service providers to examine the extent to which those service systems that are presumably designed to support the child and family, in fact, function as actual supports for families. Rather, researchers tend to study such things as the extent to which characteristics of the child are associated with increased stress; the extent to which characteristics of the family (such as SES, race, maternal education, etc.) are associated with increased stress; or, the extent to which parent perceptions are associated with stress. It is rare for service providers to ask whether families actually experience various aspects of the service system as supportive or whether it contributes to the stress families experience. The major point is that, as service providers, there is a tendency to assume that the sources of stress evolve from the child or the family itself rather than from the service system.

2 Ecological Theory

One way to provide perspective on these issues is to use Bronfenbrenner's (1979) ecological framework. Bronfenbrenner describes individuals as functioning within a series of nested settings. Each setting is, itself, embedded in larger settings. In Bronfenbrenner's conceptualization, the *microsystem* is the immediate setting in which individuals spend most time. In the case of families, this is the immediate family. The *mesosystem* refers to relationships among microsystems. For families, this includes relatives, neighbors, and extended family members. The *exosystem* includes larger, relatively concrete social structures and organizations. For families, this includes the agencies, schools, hospitals, and so forth that are part of the larger, more formal system of services. Finally, the *macrosystem* includes the larger social context in which exosystem level services function. This includes the cultural context, the political and economic systems that influence the ways families operate, and so forth.

As early interventionists, we have focused historically on those immediate settings that are closest to the child and have paid less attention to the impact of more formal, organized systems. More recently, there has been a growing recognition that many of the difficulties faced by families are socially constructed, that they may derive just as much from the way the service system is constructed and implemented as from the children and families themselves. It is the responsibility of service providers to minimize the stress that is created by these systems and to maximize the support. In the remaining sections of this paper, the ways in which the families' exchanges with systems at the macro-, exo-, and meso-system levels may influence the support perceived by the family will be examined.

2.1 Macrosystem Issues

In applying an ecological model to examine the way in which the existing structures support or create stress for families of children with disabilities, it is impossible to avoid the extent to which cultural, social, and economic factors exert influence on family life. In many ways, these influences may have the most profound impact on families. These influences seem more a function of the political/social system and largely out of the control of individuals. As a result, service providers can often escape feeling responsible when influences at this level have a negative impact. Two general areas serve as illustrations of this point.

Effects of poverty. Throughout the past decade, many investigators and practitioners have been interested in biological risk (e.g., the effects of factors such as low birthweight and prematurity). But more recently, an increasing number of service providers have begun to take note of something that Sameroff and Chandler originally argued in 1975. Specifically, although biological risk certainly plays a role in long-term outcome of young children, much evidence suggests that environmental risk is a stronger predictor of adverse outcome for infants. Several factors contribute to this effect. First, children born into poverty are consistently exposed to a larger number of risks to healthy development than children from more economically advantaged families. These risks include lack of prenatal medical care, poor nutrition, high rates of adolescent pregnancy, high rates of smoking and drug use during pregnancy, homelessness, inaccessibility of timely and appropriate medical care, and so forth (Brinker et al., 1989; Shorr, 1988). Second, families in this group are likely to get into intervention later and drop out earlier than families from middle-income groups. Brinker and his colleagues cited a study of the Illinois Department of Public Health that indicated that in the poorest neighborhoods in Chicago, the infant mortality rate ranges from 21.4 - 30.6 per 1,000. Palfrey et al. (1987) found that maternal education is a significant indicator of when the educational needs of children are identified. Children of nonwhite, low-income mothers who had not completed high school generally did not have their educational needs identified until between 40 and 60 months, even when the disability was severe. Over 24% of severe disabilities in this population were not identified until 3 years of age.

In a study of infants discharged from neonatal intensive care units, Brinker et al. (1989) found that only 26% of infants from the inner city in comparison to 57% of infants from suburban settings attended at least one follow-up clinic. Moreover, these authors reported that of 105 low-income infants positively screened and referred for full developmental evaluations, only 7 infants actually received such evaluations (all 7 who were evaluated had Bayley MDIs below 75).

Brinker et al. (1989) note several possible reasons for the service system's failure to establish and maintain contact with families living in poverty. One possible explanation is that parents acknowledge the risks to their child, but do not believe that the resources to facilitate their child's development are available to them. In fact, Brinker (1992) notes that many families have relatively aversive experiences with the service system. For example, their experience with the health care system may have been primarily through the use of emergency rooms or public clinics that occupy the better part of a day. Brinker et al. (1989) also argue that mechanisms have not been in place among the various public agencies to accomplish a comprehensive system of identifying children for appropriate services. They note that, in the United States, no single agency is systematically in contact with infants and young children until the mandatory age of school attendance. Although the health care system usually has contact with young children prior to school enrollment, the system itself is decentralized and consists of many different public and private providers. As a result, it is difficult to systematically identify and maintain contact with families of young children who may be at risk.

Thus, for many families of young children living in poverty, the structure and functioning of the service system does not always provide the level of support that service providers often assume that it does. There is a need for systematic study of ways in which this system could be made more functional for the families who must access it.

Effects of culture. Another major difficulty that has been described increasingly in the literature is that there tends to be considerable cultural bias that is an integral part of most intervention programs. In the United States, these programs are dominated by a middle-class, predominately Caucasian bias. Such a bias is problematic due to changing demographics in the United States. A number of examples of these changing demographics can be found. For example, in 1987, the World Bank estimated that 17% of the population in the United States was of non-European ancestry. By the year 2000, it is estimated that 38% of children under 18 will be nonwhite, non-Anglo; by the year 2030, estimates will be over 50% (Hanson et al., 1990). Despite these changing demographic patterns, the predominately middle-class, Caucasian bias of the service system is reflected in several ways. First, most programs for young children are based on an implicit set of values (facilitating independence; parent participation). Families from different cultures may not hold the same values. For example, they may differ with respect to their beliefs about childrearing, the importance of independence, discipline, and competitiveness, views of disability, views of medicine and healing, the family, family roles, and so forth. To the extent that service providers fail to recognize those fundamental value differences, to the extent that they insist that parents conform to their values, they are likely to fail. Failure in that regard is not likely to be demonstrated on a psychometric test or in traditional outcome measures that are often used either with parents or children. It is more likely to be demonstrated when parents disappear from programs with little explanation and when they do not follow through with the programs that have been recommended. While service providers may often interpret these outcomes as evidence of some negative quality in the parents (e.g., the parent is "in denial," the parent is incompetent, the parent "neglects" the child), an equally plausible explanation is that, in many instances, the system has failed to support families in a way that is meaningful.

A second example of the way in which culture influences the way support is provided is to consider the effects of language barriers (Smith & Ryan, 1987). Lynch and Stein (1987) found that, for Latino families, one of the major barriers to participation was lack of bilingual communication and communication problems. Such factors may influence communication between parents and service providers in ways that are as basic as understanding the services being provided. For example, Lynch and Stein found that only 55% of Latino parents whose children were receiving services knew what services were listed on the Individual Education Plan (IEP).

Summary. In summary, there is substantial evidence that cultural, ethnic, and economic influences profoundly impact on the extent to which the service system is functionally supportive for families of young children who have or are at risk for disabilities. It is important that both researchers and early interventionists acknowledge that the strategies and programs traditionally developed on the basis of middle-income, Caucasian standards are not always relevant or perceived as helpful for a more diverse group of children and families. The responsibility of service providers is to respond to the diversity and allow family perceptions of their own needs to dictate the nature of the supports that are provided.

2.2 Exosystem - Service System Issues

From an ecological framework, the exosystem includes those larger, relatively concrete social structures such as the schools and the health care system in which families participate. Implicit within an ecological framework is the understanding that the exosystem is influenced by both the macrosystem and the mesosystem. When examining the issue of social support, this means that the cultural, political, and legal context influences the formal supports that function within a given system. Thus, there is likely to be considerable variation from country to country with respect to the specific exosystem influences. In this section, a number of examples of exosystem factors that may influence the effectiveness of the social support network are examined. Although these examples are from the United States, they appear to be shared in many other countries as well.

Access to services. In the United States, many cultural and political factors have converged to produce a system of services for individuals with disabilities that, in many ways, has gaping holes and, in other ways, provides unprecedented access for persons with disabilities. For example, the health care system in the United States leaves many families of children with disabilities without adequate coverage. In contrast, federal initiatives that provide intervention programs for young children with disabilities give parents unprecedented rights. Those rights are intended as a support, and in many ways function that way. For example, under current federal law, children with disabilities cannot be denied services, services are to be provided in natural environments, and services providers must increasingly collaborate with families.

But the sword is double-edged. Despite these innovations in the early intervention system, many families still report difficulty accessing the services that they view as important to their child. For example, in a study of children who were medically fragile, Thorp (1987) reported that half of the families in her sample identified specific difficulties in obtaining appropriate services. These included such difficulties as a lack of opportunity for integrated programs, the need to supplement therapy provided by the schools with private therapy, and inadequate nursing coverage. Similarly, the difficulties in identifying infants from poor, inner-city environments described above effectively prevents these families from accessing services.

Thus, even within the context of legislative mandates for early intervention, families sometimes experience difficulties accessing the services they believe their child needs. Difficulty accessing services may arise for several reasons. First, families may not be aware that needed services exist (Upshur, 1991). Second, some programs are not adequately funded, and services may be limited, based on factors such as income, disability level, and other eligibility requirements (Krauss, 1986; Upshur, 1991). In addition, there may be differences of opinion between parents and service providers (as well as between service providers themselves) about the nature and intensity of services that the child needs. For example, one service provider may feel that the child needs physical therapy on a once-per-week basis, while another recommends physical therapy three times per week. Such disagreements can become the basis of formal disputes between parents and the service providers. As a result, they may become the basis of a stressful rather than a supportive experience for families.

Moreover, it is important to recognize that families may not always perceive the implementation of new, innovative practices as positive. For example, many service providers now view the implementation of inclusive programs in natural environments as best practice. However, these program changes have implications for families. While many families may view these changes positively, it is important not to assume that all families have this perspective. Families may fear that the implementation of full inclusion is a way to take away special services. Thus, even something that service providers view as a positive innovation in service may be not experienced positively by families. It is critical that service providers who are implementing new practices take the time to consider parent concerns about such issues and to support families during the process of change.

Child care. The child care system is another exosystem factor that can have a profound influence on family adaptation. Salkever (1985) found that fewer mothers of children who are chronically ill are employed. Those who are employed tend to work fewer hours. In a study of family adaptation to children with chronic illness, Thorp (1987) reported that 50% of her sample reported stressful adjustments related to job activity; approximately one third reported having to leave their jobs. In large part, these limits on employment result from difficulty finding anyone who is qualified to care for the child or from the cost of paying such a person.

In addition, research suggests that respite care is among the most consistently reported and critical service needs of parents (Bristol & Schopler, 1983; Greig, 1993) of children with disabilities. In one study of children with autism, Bristol (1984) reported that parents of children between birth and 5 years ranked baby-sitting and respite care as two of the top five service needs they had. While the need to have a break from child care demands exists for most families (even when the child does not have a disability), the need may be particularly acute when the child is difficult to care for. Research suggests that families of children with disabilities must often cope with a number of difficult or unusual caregiving demands (Beckman, 1983). This may complicate the family's ability to obtain adequate child care while, at the same time, it magnifies the need for such services (Cohen, 1982; Deiner & Whitehead, 1988).

Moreover, although the evidence is somewhat inconsistent (Deiner & Whitehead, 1988), the availability of good respite care has been associated with many other critical issues in the lives of persons with disabilities and their families. For example, the availability of adequate child care has been associated with a number of positive outcomes including improved family functioning (Cohen, 1982; Joyce et al., 1983); reduced family stress (Joyce et al., 1983; Rimmerman, 1989); reduced isolation (Joyce et al., 1983); and the maintenance of the child in the community (Apolloni & Triest, 1983; Bristol & Schopler, 1983; Joyce et al., 1983). Second, lack of adequate child care can have social and economic consequences for the family. For example, as indicated previously, one member of the family (typically the mother) may be unable to accept employment (Knoll & Bedford, 1989).

Most states in the United States have some kinds of respite care services in place for parents (Knoll, 1990). Unfortunately, the structure and availability of these services frequently limit their helpfulness to families (Cohen, 1982; Ellison et al., 1992; Knoll & Bedford, 1989). The problem tends to be a lack of flexibility in the structure of programs and/or limits on the service (Cohen, 1982; Ellison et al., 1992; Knoll & Bedford, 1989). For example, families may be limited in the amount of time allotted for respite care or in their choice of respite care situations (e.g., out-of-home vs. in-home). Another problem frequently reported involves the limited training and skills of the persons providing respite care (Cohen, 1982; Upshur, 1982). Limited skills are particularly problematic when the child with a disability is medically fragile (Upshur, 1982).

Thus, at least in the United States, a number of improvements are needed to make respite care a service that is more useful and available to families. In a national survey of 2,800 parents of children with disabilities, Knoll and Bedford (1989) reported that parents want control over the services that affect their families. They also want a role in developing and reforming the system in ways that are more responsive to their needs. These views are consistent with a systems view of social support and the notion of empowerment.

Time and structure of program. A number of professionals (Brinker, 1992) have noted that the way in which programs are structured may not always be supportive to families. For example, Brinker (1992) notes that poor families from the inner city often may have to wait for the better part of the day for clinic appointments. If the same family has several children, limited transportation, and limited child care, the process of being seen in a clinic is not likely to be supportive; indeed, it may be quite stressful.

The time and structure of the program may interfere with the achievement of family-centered services in other ways as well. For example, most intervention programs operate during the day; relatively few have evening programs. Such a structure limits the participation of fathers and working mothers. A typical solution, particularly in home-based programs, is for early interventionists to visit the day care setting in which the children stay while their parents are working. While this is a way to see the child and more convenient for service providers, it is not necessarily particularly useful for the family.

Another issue in the delivery of services to infants and toddlers is the provision of year-round services. This difficulty is particularly prevalent in programs that were originally developed within a school-based model. In such programs, the early intervention program is on the same schedule as the other school-based programs. This results in a break of 2 to 3 months during the summer. For an infant who is initially identified prior to the summer break, this can result in a delay of 2 or 3 months before intervention begins. Service providers send a contradictory message to parents when they argue that early intervention is critical, and that the earlier the child receives services the better, while, at the same time, allowing an extensive period of time before beginning services. Such practices can also result in critical program disruptions for children who can ill afford such experiences.

Dealing with large numbers of service providers. In the course of receiving a full range of services, many parents encounter a large number of service providers. For example, it is not atypical for parents to interact with a physician, school administrator, teacher, physical therapist, occupational therapist, speech/language pathologist, and psychologist. It is not unreasonable to assume that the more complex the child's needs, the more likely the parent is to encounter increasing numbers of service providers. This may include multiple medical specialists, nursing care, and so on.

While, on the surface, access to the expertise of multiple service providers may appear to be supportive, there are reasons to question this assumption. First, parents report difficulties with the lack of privacy. In one study of parents of chronically ill children, parents reported substantial disruptions in privacy due to the sheer number of service providers who came into their homes (Thorp, 1987).

Second, service providers often contradict one another (Beckman & Boyes, 1993). Such contradictions are particularly problematic when service providers give conflicting information without helping the parent understand the basis for the conflict. For example, in a study of 21 mothers living with a disabled child between the ages of 3 months and 4 years who were participating in a parent support program, mothers were asked to identify the most difficult problem for them. The major factor that emerged was professional disagreement regarding the child's diagnosis (Segal, 1985). This problem can be illustrated by the story described by one family of a child with a fairly serious neurological disability. This family has, for job-related reasons, had to move several times. As a result, the child has been seen by a number of different neurologists. Not a single neurologist has given the same explanation for the child's disability. One reported that he needed neurological surgery immediately. Two weeks later, in the process of getting a second opinion, another neurologist told them that he not only did not need the surgery but that to do surgery could cause further neurological damage. This same family has reported receiving contradictory opinions on factors as diverse as when to remove the pacifier, whether the child needs vision services, and the most appropriate placement (Beckman & Boyes, 1993).

Beckman and Kohl (1993) have described a number of other potential difficulties that parents face when working with multiple service providers. These include limited contact with one or more of the providers, the attempt of one member of the team to dominate discussions regarding the services provided to the child, and professional turf issues. When such difficulties arise, parents may feel that they are caught in the middle and may spend much needed energy simply coping with the service providers. The source of such difficulties cannot be found in the children, the disability, or in the families. It is a source of stress that derives from the service system itself and the service providers within it. As service providers, it is critical that we find ways to eliminate these sources of stress for families so that we can create a system that is truly supportive.

Summary. Thus, even within the context of a service system that provides substantial resources for early intervention, there are many sources of stress for families. Many of these difficulties are specific to the structure of the system in the United States, while others are more universal phenomena.

The impact of the system is apparent in the United States in many other ways as well. For example, parents frequently report financial difficulties associated with obtaining and maintaining services for their children, even though a large number of services are provided at no cost. While many of these difficulties are linked directly to medical costs, there are many economic costs that are more hidden, such as the lost opportunity when one family member is unable to work, the costs of well-trained child care providers, and so forth. In addition, although federal provisions for Individual Education Plans (IEPs) and Individual Family Service Plans (IFSPs) represent a commitment to including families in their child's program decisions, there can sometimes be difficulties in the way such plans are developed and implemented (Beckman et al., 1993).

For the system to truly support families, it is critical that service providers ask themselves to what extent the policies and practices in their system reflect more attention to the administrative and personal needs of service providers than to the needs of families. The answer to this question is likely to provide important clues as to whether these exosystem factors function to truly support families.

2.3 Mesosystem - Encounters With Individual Service Providers

In applying an ecological framework as a way of viewing social support, the mesosystem refers to the relationships between various microsystems in which the family is involved. For purposes of this discussion, remarks will be confined to the relationships between individuals in the family and various members of the formal support system. While these relationships may frequently serve as sources of support for families, the positive nature of this relationship cannot always be assumed. Indeed, considerable evidence suggests that, in some cases, exchanges with individual service providers can become sources of stress as well. In a study of families of chronically ill children, 78% of the families reported difficulty in their relationships with service providers (Thorp, 1987). Upshur (1991) notes that while they do not always openly challenge service providers, families may frequently be unhappy about the way they were treated by service providers and/or disagree with their recommendations. Rather than openly challenging service providers, families may simply not implement recommendations and/or may seek other services. Creating a real partnership with parents demands that service providers understand the difficulties parents may experience in their exchanges with service providers. These exchanges may be stressful rather than supportive when service providers engage in one or more behaviors that convey negative messages to families. In this section, examples of such behaviors are identified.

Not listening. One factor that families frequently identify as stressful is when service providers fail to listen. For example, it is not uncommon for parents to cite circumstances in which they expressed concerns or provided a piece of information to service providers that was not acknowledged or taken into consideration (Segal, 1985). Failing to listen to the concerns expressed by families or to the information that they can provide can negatively influence perceived support. Seligman and Darling (1989) have emphasized the importance of empathetic listening and listening from the family members' point of view. Doing this effectively requires that service providers put aside their own biases and opinions. This is difficult if service providers are preoccupied with their own concerns, have hidden agendas, or are stressed because of the nature of the demands placed upon them.

Lack of respect. Another concern frequently expressed by families occurs when family members feel that they have not been treated with respect by service providers. In a recent qualitative study of families of infants who were low birthweight, Greig (1993) found that respect was a highly salient characteristic in determining which service providers were or were not helpful. For these families, respect was demonstrated when service providers recognized that the parent knew the child best, when there was honesty and trust in the relationship, and when service providers respected the family's right to information about the child.

Similarly, Moeller (1986) reports that when describing their relationship with service providers, parents most often view it in terms of the respect they received. She notes that this respect is reflected in the extent to which the service provider respects the dignity and integrity of the parental role and regards parent input about the child as unique and useful.

Attitudes. Still another area that requires examination is the attitude that service providers take toward parents. Some authors have argued that there is a tendency to focus on stereotypic terms that either place the locus of the problem on the parent (e.g., terms like depression, anger, guilt, denial), focus on the personality traits of parents, or interpret conflict with service providers in terms of evidence of problems in the individual parent or family. For example, saying that the parent is "in denial," "displacing their anger," and other terms that place the focus for the blame for the conflict on the parent (Lipsky, 1985; Seligman & Darling, 1989). These authors argue that these perspectives are often overgeneralized and overapplied. This overgeneralization often occurs to the extent that no matter what role the family assumes, there is potential for negative interpretation. For example, close family ties and willingness to assist may be interpreted as too intrusive or as discouraging efforts toward independence. When service providers make these kind of assumptions, it becomes a kind of a Catch-22 for families; whenever the family disagrees with or confronts service providers, their concerns can be dismissed as displaced anger, frustration, or denial (Lipsky, 1985; Seligman & Darling, 1989).

Professional insensitivity. Still another concern expressed by parents when dealing with service providers is related to the issue of insensitivity. While many of the issues described above constitute evidence of insensitivity, other concerns may be identified as well. These include the clearly obvious circumstances in which something derogatory is said or implied regarding the child or the disability, and circumstances in which difficult information (e.g., regarding a diagnosis) is given without warmth or compassion. However, it also includes the less obvious situations. For example, it is not uncommon to hear parents describe situations in which service providers promise to get back to parents quickly with information and fail to keep their promise; and situations in which service providers fail to think about the implications that a particular statement might have for the family member. Another form of insensitivity occurs when service providers fail to provide adequate information to parents. The literature is replete with studies indicating that honest information about the child is one of the major needs consistently expressed by parents (Bailey et al., 1992; Greig, 1993). It is a source of stress when parents are required to seek information repeatedly and when the information is not forthcoming. Greig (1993) reported that the perceived availability and quality of information that the parents in her study received was one of the major criteria by which they judged a service provider as supportive. The information families want seems to center fairly consistently on information about the child's condition, information about how to work with the child, and information about both current and future services and systems (Bailey et al., 1992; Gowen et al., 1993; Greig, 1993). However, Greig (1993) found that information was stressful when it was given in an insensitive manner, was uncoordinated or conflicting, or given in a way that parents did not understand. Moreover, Sokoly and Dokecki (1992) argue that when early interventionists fail to provide honest and adequate information to families or deny developmental concerns that do exist, they jeopardize subsequent communication with families.

Inadequate program. In an era when early intervention is shifting to increasingly family-centered approaches, it is easy to forget that one of the single greatest needs that parents have is for good, appropriate services for their child. In a study of families of children with autism, Bristol (1984) found that the top-ranked strategies that helped them best with coping involved direct services to the child. In another study, DeMyer and Goldberg (1983) asked parents of children in four different age groups (between 1-17 years) to identify family service needs. Parents of children in every age group ranked a good, year-long educational program among the top five service needs (depending on the age group, between 48% and 61% of the parents reported this as a need). In other words, it is sometimes easy to forget that parents want the direct services their child receives to be of high quality. Although this point may appear obvious, in my view, the tendency to view child-centered and family-centered programs as the opposite ends of the same continuum (Raver & Kilgo, 1991) is an unfortunate contrast. A truly ecological approach to families would view excellent child-centered services as an *integral part* of a family-centered perspective. A more appropriate contrast is between family-centered and professionally centered interventions. In other words, we have a responsibility to provide excellent, state-of-the-art services to children and families.

Summary. This review suggests that during the course of many routine exchanges with families, individual service providers have the capacity to substantially influence the extent to which the service system functions in a way that is supportive and empowering to families. When service providers behave in a manner that reflects an attitude of respect, when they provide honest information in a sensitive and caring manner, and when they refrain from making judgments about families, individual providers have the capacity to create a supportive context for intervention.

3 Conclusion

As early interventionists increasingly embrace a more "family-centered" philosophy, there is a corresponding need for changes in the strategies used to provide support. This movement represents a paradigm shift that is, in my view, overwhelmingly positive. Implicit within this shift is an emphasis on the role of social support and an expanded view of the role of early interventionists. But true implementation of this philosophy requires that researchers and service providers keep several key factors in mind.

First, although there is correlational evidence suggesting that social support may mediate stress and facilitate well-being, the evidence in that regard is not consistent across all forms of support. Specifically, while informal supports (e.g., support from family and friends) are associated with less stress and more well-being, that data concerned with formal support (e.g., the support received from service providers and agencies) is less consistent. There is a need to critically examine the formal mechanisms that are intended to provide support and services to families to determine whether they indeed function in the intended manner. Such an examination must extend beyond the family unit and into the meso-, exo-, and macrosystems. This information should serve as a basis for modifying our individual professional practice as well as the structure and functioning of our programs. Such information should also prompt advocacy around issues of macrolevel policies. The process should be one of separating intention from function and of modifying services so that there is a closer match between these two dimensions.

Second, there is a need to step beyond correlational studies of social support. As we are so eloquently reminded by Bell (1968) in his classic reinterpretation of the direction of effects, there are almost always two ways to interpret correlational data. An association between maternal stress and social support may as easily reflect the ability of a minimally stressed mother to access the support system as it does the actual mediation of stress.

Finally, like many other movements, family-centered intervention represents a shift in philosophy about best practice that has not been subjected to much empirical scrutiny. There is a need for researchers to document the effects of family-centered practice in order to better inform practice about the elements most likely to contribute to its success.

References

Apolloni, A., & Triest, G. (1983). Respite services in California: Status and recommendations for improvement. *Mental Retardation, 21,* 240-243.

Bailey, D. B., Blasco, P. M., & Simeonsson, R. J. (1992). Needs expressed by mothers and fathers of young children with disabilities. *American Journal of Mental Retardation, 97*(1), 1-10.

Beckman, P. J. (1983). Influence of selected child characteristics on stress in families of handicapped infants. *American Journal of Mental Deficiency, 88*(2), 150-156.

Beckman, P. J. (1991a). Comparison of mothers' and fathers' perceptions of the effect of young children with and without disabilities. *American Journal of Mental Retardation, 95*(5), 585-595.

Beckman, P. J. (1991b, June). *Institutional sources of stress for families of children with disabilities.* Keynote address presented at the Louisiana Conference on Early Intervention, Monroe, Louisiana.

Beckman, P. J., & Boyes, G. B. (1993). Introduction. In P. J. Beckman & G. B. Boyes (Eds.), *Deciphering the system: A guide for families of young children with disabilities* (pp. 1-6). Cambridge, MA: Brookline Books.

Beckman, P. J., Boyes, G. B., & Herres, A. (1993). The IEP and IFSP meetings. In P. J. Beckman & G. B. Boyes (Eds.), *Deciphering the system: A guide for families of young children with disabilities* (pp. 81-100). Cambridge, MA: Brookline Books.

Beckman, P. J., & Kohl, F. L. (1993). Working with multiple professionals. In P. J. Beckman & G. B. Boyes (Eds.), *Deciphering the system: A guide for families of young children with disabilities* (pp. 21-38). Cambridge, MA: Brookline Books.

Beckman, P. J., & Pokorni, J. L. (1988). A longitudinal study of families of preterm infants: Changes in stress and support over the first two years. *Journal of Special Education, 22,* 55-65.

Beckman, P. J., Pokorni, J. L., Maza, E. H., & Balzer-Martin, L. (1986). A longitudinal study of stress and support in families of preterm and full-term infants. *Journal of the Division for Early Childhood, 11*(1), 2-9.

Bell, R. Q. (1968). A reinterpretation of the direction of effects in studies of socialization. *Psychological Review, 75,* 81-95.

Breslau, N., & Davis, G. C. (1986). Chronic stress and major depression. *Archives of General Psychiatry, 43,* 309-314.

Brinker, R. P. (1992). A look back to the futures of children: Developing a shared vision of early intervention. In R. Levin (Ed.), *Comprehensive approaches to school reform: A resource for teachers.* Washington, DC: ERIC Clearinghouse on Teacher Education.

Brinker, R. P., Frazier, W., Lancelot, B., & Norman, J. (1989). Identifying infants from the inner city for early intervention. *Infants and Young Children, 2*(1), 49-58.

Bristol, M. M. (1979). *Maternal coping with autistic children: Adequacy of interpersonal support and effects of child characteristics.* Unpublished doctoral dissertation, University of North Carolina.

Bristol, M. M. (1984). Family resources and successful adaptation to autistic children. In E. Schopler & S. Mesibov (Eds.), *The effects of autism on the family* (pp. 289-310). New York: Plenum Press.

Bristol, M. M., & Schopler, E. (1983). Stress and coping in families of autistic adolescents. In E. Shopler & G. Mesibov (Eds.), *The effects of autism on the family* (pp. 251-258). New York: Plenum Press.

Bronfenbrenner, U. (1979). *The ecology of human development*. Cambridge, MA: Harvard University Press.

Chetwynd, J. (1985). Factors contributing to stress on mothers caring for an intellectually handicapped child. *British Journal of Social Work, 15*, 295-304.

Cohen, S. (1982). Supporting families through respite care. *Rehabilitation Literature, 43*, 7-10.

Crnic, K. A., Greenberg, M. T., Robinson, N. M., & Ragozin, A. S. (1984). Maternal stress and social support: Effects on the mother-infant relationship from birth to eighteen months. *American Journal of Orthopsychiatry, 54*(2), 224-235.

Crnic, K. A., Greenberg, M. T., & Slough, N. M. (1986). Early stress and social support influences on mothers' and high-risk infants' functioning in late infancy. *Infant Mental Health Journal, 7*(1), 19-33.

Deiner, P. L., & Whitehead, L. C. (1988). Levels of respite care as a family support system. *Topics in Early Childhood Special Education, 8*(2), 51-61.

DeMyer, M. K., & Goldberg, P. (1983). Family needs of the autistic adolescent. In E. Schopler & G. B. Mesibov (Eds.), *Autism in adolescents and adults* (pp. 225-250). New York: Plenum Press.

Dunst, C. J., Trivette, C. M., & Cross, A. H. (1986). Mediating influences of social support: Personal, family and child outcomes. *American Journal of Mental Deficiency, 90*(4), 403-417.

Dunst, C. J., Trivette, C. M., Hamby, C. M., & Pollock, B. (1990). Family systems correlates of the behavior of young children with handicaps. *Journal of Early Intervention, 14*(3), 204-218.

Dyson, L. L. (1991). Families of young children with handicaps: Parental stress and family functioning. *American Journal on Mental Retardation, 95*(6), 623-629.

Dyson, L., & Fewell, R. F. (1986). Stress and adaptation in parents of young handicapped and nonhandicapped children: A comparative study. *Journal of the Division for Early Childhood, 10*, 25-35.

Ellison, M. L., Bersani, H., Blaney, B., & Freud, E. (1992). Family empowerment: Four case studies. In V. J. Bradley, J. Knoll, & J. M. Agosta (Eds.), *Emerging issues in family support* (pp. 151-166). Washington, DC: Monograph of the American Association on Mental Retardation.

Flynt, S. W., Wood, T. A., & Scott (1992). Social support of mothers of children with mental retardation. *Mental Retardation, 30*(4), 233-236.

Frey, K. S., Greenberg, M. T., & Fewell, R. R. (1989). Stress and coping among parents of handicapped children: A multidimensional approach. *American Journal of Mental Retardation, 94*(3), 240-249.

Friedrich, W. N., & Friedrich, W. L. (1981). Psychosocial assets of parents of handicapped and nonhandicapped children. *American Journal of Mental Deficiency, 85*, 551-553.

Gallagher, J. J., Beckman, P., & Cross, A. H. (1983). Families of handicapped children: Sources of stress and its amelioration. *Exceptional Children, 50*, 10-19.

Gowen, J. W., Christy, D. S., & Sparling, J. (1993). Informational needs of parents of young children with special needs. *Journal of Early Intervention, 17*(2), 194-210.

Gowen, J. W., Johnson-Martin, N., Goldman, B. D., & Appelbaum, M. (1989). Feelings of depression and parenting competence of mothers of handicapped and nonhandicapped infants: A longitudinal study. *American Journal of Mental Retardation, 94*(3), 259-271.

Greig, D. L. (1993). *Extremely low birthweight infants (800 grams or less): Medical and developmental outcome at one to five years and social support needs of their mothers.* Unpublished doctoral dissertation, University of Maryland-College Park, College Park, MD.

Hanson, M. J., Lynch, E. W., & Wayman, K. I. (1990). Honoring the cultural diversity of families when gathering data. *Topics in Early Childhood Special Education, 10*(1), 112-131.

Harris, V. S., & McHale, S. M. (1989). Family life problems, daily caretaking activities, and the psychological well-being of mothers of mentally retarded children. *American Journal of Mental Retardation, 94*(3), 231-239.

Heinicke, C. M. (1984). Impact of prebirth parent personality and marital functioning on family development. *Developmental Psychology, 20*(6), 1044-1053.

Joyce, K., Singer, M., & Isralowitz, R. (1983). Impact of respite care on parents' perceptions of quality of life. *Mental Retardation, 21*(4), 153-156.

Kazak, A. E., & Marvin, R. S. (1984). Differences, difficulties and adaptation: Stress and social networks in families with a handicapped child. *Family Relations, 33*, 67-77.

Knoll, J. (1990). Current status of family support in the United States. *Family Support Bulletin, Summer*, 17-18.

Knoll, J., & Bedford, S. (1989). Respite services: A national survey of parents' experience. *Exceptional Parent, 19*, 34-37.

Kobe, F. H., Rojahn, J., & Schroeder, S. R. (1991). Predictors of urgency of out-of-home placement needs. *Mental Retardation, 29*(6), 323-328.

Krauss, M. W. (1986). Patterns and trends in public services to families with a mentally retarded member. In J. L. Gallagher & P. M. Vietze (Eds.), *Families of handicapped persons* (pp. 237-248). Baltimore, MD: Paul H. Brooks.

Lipsky, D. K. (1985). A parental perspective on stress and coping. *American Journal of Orthopsychiatry, 55*(4), 614-617.

Lynch, E. W., & Stein, R. C. (1987). Parent participation by ethnicity: A comparison of hispanic, black and anglo families. *Exceptional Children, 54*(2), 105-111.

Moeller, C. T. (1986). The effect of professionals on the family of a handicapped child. In R. R. Fewell & P. F. Vadasy (Eds.), *Families of handicapped children: Needs and supports across the life span.* Austin, TX: Pro-Ed.

Nihira, K., Meyers, E., & Mink, I. T. (1980). Home environment, family adjustment, and the development of mentally retarded children. *Applied Research in Mental Retardation, 1*, 5-24.

Palfrey, J. S., Singer, J. D., Walker, D. K., & Butler, J. A. (1987). Early identification of children's special needs: A study in five metropolitan communities. *Journal of Pediatrics, 111*, 651-659.

Peterson, P. (1984). Effects of moderator variables in reducing stress outcome in mothers of children with handicaps. *Journal of Psychosomatic Research, 28*(4), 337-344.

Raver, S. A. & Kilgo, J. (1991). Effective family-centered services: Supporting family choices and rights. *Infant Toddlers Intervention, I,* (9), 169-176.

Rimmerman, A. (1989). Provision of respite care of children with developmental disabilities: Changes in maternal coping and stress over time. *Mental Retardation,* *27*(2), 99-103.

Salisbury, C. C. (1987). Stresses of parents with young handicapped and nonhandicapped children. *Journal of the Division of Early Childhood, 11*(2), 154-160.

Salkever, D. (1985). Parental opportunity costs and other economic costs of children's disabling conditions. In N. Hobbs & J. M. Perrin (Eds.), *Issues in the care of children with chronic illness* (pp. 864-879). San Francisco: Jossey-Bass.

Sameroff, A. J., & Chandler, M. J. (1975). Reproductive risk and the continuum of caretaking casualty. In F. D. Horowitz (Ed.), *Review of child development research* (Vo. 4, pp. 189-244). Chicago, IL: University of Chicago Press.

Schorr, L. B. (1988). *Within our reach: Breaking the cycle of disadvantage.* New York: Anchor Books.

Segal, M. M. (1985). *An interview study with mothers of handicapped children to identify both positive and negative experiences that influence their ability to cope.* Paper presented at the Fourth Annual Conference of the National Center for Clinical Infant Programs, Washington, DC.

Seligman, M., & Darling, R. B. (1989). *Ordinary families, special children: A systems approach to childhood disability.* New York: The Guildford Press.

Sherman, B. R., & Cocozza, J. J. (1984). Stress in families of the developmentally disabled: A literature review of factors affecting the decision to seek out-of-home placements. *Family Relations, 33,* 95-103.

Smith, M. J., & Ryan, A. S. (1987). Chinese-American families of children with developmental disabilities: An exploratory study of reactions to service providers. *Mental Retardation, 25*(6), 345-350.

Sokoly, m.m. & Dokecki, P. R. (1992). Ethical perspectives on family-centered early intervention. *Infants and young children, 4* (4), 23-32,

Stagg, V., & Catron, T. (1986). Networks of social supports for parents of handicapped children. In R. R. Fewell & P. F. Vadasy (Eds.), *Families of handicapped children: Needs and supports across the life span* (pp. 279-296). Austin, Texas: Pro-ed.

Thorp, E. K. (1987). *Mothers coping with home care of severe chronic respiratory disabled children requiring medical technology assistance.* Unpublished doctoral dissertation, George Washington University, Washington, DC.

Upshur, C. C. (1982). Respite care for mentally retarded and other disabled populations: Program models and family needs. *Mental Retardation, 20*(1), 2-6.

Upshur, C. C. (1991). Families and the community service maze. In M. Seligman (Ed.), *The family with a handicapped child.* Boston, MA: Allyn & Bacon.

M. Brambring, H. Rauh, and A. Beelmann (Eds.). (1996). *Early childhood intervention: Theory, evaluation, and practice* (pp. 196-207). Berlin, New York: de Gruyter.

Family Expectations, Encounters, and Needs

Rune J. Simeonsson

1 Introduction

Family involvement in early intervention services is, in a formal sense, a relatively recent phenomenon. Informally, families have always been involved in one way or another in the activities provided for their at-risk or developmentally delayed child. As the early intervention enterprise has evolved, it can been seen as a serial progression of phases, each reflected by a corresponding perspective on the family's place in intervention (Simeonsson & Bailey, 1990).

In the initial establishment of early intervention services in the United States in the early 1970s, the focus was clearly, and singularly, on the individual child. The involvement of the family was essentially limited to that of the parental role. A second phase emerged fairly quickly in which the parent was assigned a role as teacher or co-teacher for their child, to a large extent coinciding with the popularity of the behavior modification movement. This role gave way to the official recognition of the family as both recipient and mediator of services, embodied in the passage of legislation (PL 99-457) and further clarified in the reauthorization of that law (IDEA). As this role found detailed expression in the specifics of the Individualized Family Service Plan (IFSP), the view of the family and its role was extended to encompass the provision of sources of support. At the present time, the approach to early intervention services is increasingly community-based, recognizing the importance of the ecocultural context (Gallimore et al., 1989).

These phases, reflecting the shifting focus of early intervention efforts from the child, to the parent, to the family, and to the community context, correspond to the progressive ecological frames of Bronfenbrenner (1977). His ecological perspective can be seen to have both contributed to these historical transitions and to be reflective of their expression. Furthermore, it is also likely that, to some extent, the progression from a focus on the child to the larger contexts of family, social group, and community is repeated in the family's own development. The interactive nature of these progressions over time determines and reflects the development of child and family as elaborated in Sameroff and Chandler's (1975) transactional model.

The extent to which developmental outcomes are favorable is very much a function of the valence of transactions.

The last decade or so has seen a substantial effort focused on the identification and exploration of situational and family factors that could enhance the planning of individualized interventions. Models and concepts that have been advanced to account for differential child and family outcomes have often focused on liabilities in the form of stress, inadequate resources, and other risk factors. There has also been a growing interest in identifying such family assets as resources, strengths, and other indices of resilience. Although, these approaches have contributed to the improvement of assessment and intervention planning in early intervention, they have largely had a practical focus. Systematic explorations couched in conceptual models have been less frequent. The contribution of the transactional model has been described by Sameroff and Fiese (1990) in broad terms of reeducation, remediation, and redefinition, but the nature of the transactions has not been detailed. Drawing on their model, it is clear that for the family and the child, developmental outcomes are a function of transactions with the environment. These transactions may be of a transient as well as more sustained nature. Furthermore, they can be positive, promoting development; or they can be negative, complicating or compromising adjustment.

Attempts to define the elements of such transactions would seem to be a timely activity in early intervention research, and this constitutes the focus of the present chapter. To this end, I shall examine important determiners of family involvement in early intervention, namely, family expectations and associated family concerns and needs.

In the search for conceptual models for early intervention, several contributions have been drawn from the field of family therapy. There has been some limited advocacy of therapeutic methods and strategies such as the clinical interview (Winton & Bailey, 1990). Of broader applicability, however, may be theories and concepts of family life. Relevant to an examination of family adaptation in this case may be Kempler's (1969, 1974, 1981) concept of the encounter as a distillation and representation of life experiences. Having derived his concepts from the Gestalt school of family therapy, Kempler asserts that "Experiences are the essential phenomena of existence. Experiences in which we interact with other people, called encounters, are the most powerful of all experiences for the development of skills which we can use to cope with future experiences" (1981, p. 7). Thus the encounter can be seen as a segment of a larger continuum of life experiences with an emphasis on the relationships they represent. "The encounters we have within our families, past and current, are the most significant in generating and influencing our capabilities" (1981,

p. 7). In the context of the individual's and the family's experiences, there are positive as well as negative encounters.

Dimension		**Expectation**	
		Transient	Enduring
Developmental		Child's mastery of walking skills	Child's social competence
Situational		Family's role in team evaluation of child	Community resources for respite care

Figure 1. Family expectations: Illustrative examples.

A good encounter is defined as one that is completed, one that leaves no sense of uneasiness, fear, or anxiety. Psychological distress and discomfort however, arise when encounters are not completed. These ". . . incomplete encounters - unfinished situations - are the source of psychological astigmata. Unfinished situations result in painful residues . . ." (Kempler, 1981, p. 31). The concept of encounters and the extent to which they are complete or incomplete seems particularly referant to a consideration of expectations, concerns, and needs in the life experiences of families of children with disabilities. The encounters families experience may involve expectations for child and family that are transient or enduring in terms of time and developmental or situational in nature (see Figure 1). The encounters may also encompass concerns or needs in a variety of domains (see Figure 2). When these expectations and needs are neither realized nor met, nor perhaps even acknowledged, the result is that the encounter is experienced as incomplete. In this regard, expectations have been posited to constitute significant elements of both primary and secondary appraisals in the family's attempt to cope with stress (Beresford, 1994). The birth or

	Need	
	Transient	**Enduring**
Dimension Information	Facts about child's medical condition	How to handle child's behavior
Support	Meeting with counselor	Finding time for self
Explaining to others	Knowing how to respond to questions from relatives	Knowing how to communicate nature of child's disabilities across time and setting
Community services	Locating dentist who will see child	Working with a parent group
Finances	Purchase of aid device	Child's ongoing chronic medical needs
Family functioning	Setting family priorities	Finding balance between individual and family activities

Figure 2. Family needs: Illustrative examples.

diagnosis of a child with a developmental disability, for example, is likely to be the first of many, and possibly the most significant, incomplete encounter for the family. The parents' expectation for a normally developing child is not realized, and the unfinished situation for many families is one of disappointment, anxiety, and grief. The personal nature of this encounter for a parent has been described poignantly by Reisz (1984) ". . . we knew the child who had arrived was not the one we had expected" (p. 36). Such incomplete encounters, encompassing the child's development, may be repeated time and again as the family's expectations for their child's mastery of developmental milestones do not match the reality of the child's achievement. Similarly, unfinished encounters may also involve child and family needs (Figure 3), which may be either of a developmental or more enduring nature, versus others, which are situational and transient. Illustrative of the former is the fact that while child evaluations may be a less frequent experience for the family, ". . . the questions raised in early months continue to be raised, as we try to assess the direction our lives are taking as a family" (Reisz, 1984, p. 51). In the situational contexts of daily life on the other hand, families may fail to get the answers they seek from professionals, may not get the professional support they expect (Wishart et al., 1993), have needs that are not adequately met by intervention services, and may feel that their concerns are not understood (Stallard & Lenton, 1992). These incomplete encounters, unrealized expectations, and unmet needs may be considerable in spite of frequent contact with services (Sloper & Turner, 1992).

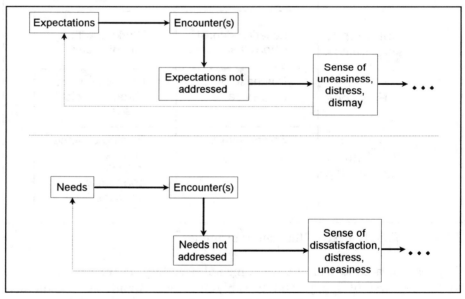

Figure 3. Incomplete encounters regarding family expectations and needs.

The implications of this framework for early intervention are that services should seek to foster the completion of families' encounters as shown in Figure 4. In Kempler's words, given the fact that a good encounter is a therapeutic encounter, a major goal of intervention ". . . should be to influence encounters so that each participant achieves greater, more consistent fulfillment" (Kempler, 1981, p. 30). The most essential step in this regard is first and foremost to acknowledge and seek the expectations and needs that families bring to the encounters in early intervention contexts. Some families may be assisted in resolving a specific unfinished encounter, whereas, for other families, it may involve the completion of a sequence of incomplete encounters experienced in contacts with support systems. To the extent that supportive interventions with families contribute to more satisfactorily completed encounters, the developmental progress of child and family can be facilitated.

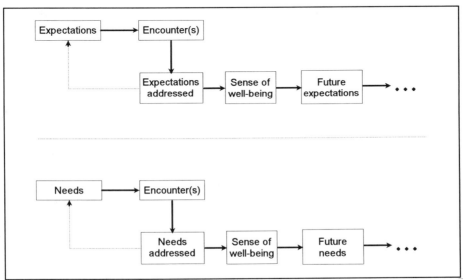

Figure 4. Completed encounters regarding family expectations and needs.

A productive way in which to apply Kempler's framework in the early intervention context is to examine aspects defining the nature of families' encounters. Aspects that can be identified in this regard are the expectations and needs that families bring to their encounter with helping professionals and the way these are experienced in their lives. In an interview study of Indian families with children who were mentally retarded, Narayan et al. (1993) found family expectations to fall into three main categories of treatment, education, training, and general information. In this and similar contexts, as shown previously in Figures 3 and 4, expectations serve as the reference or standard against which actual experiences are compared, whether they are developmental in nature (e.g., child's mastery of skills) or situational (e.g., diagnostic evaluation). A completed encounter is thus defined by congruence between expectation and reality. Thus, when

expectations and needs are addressed through information and supportive
interventions, encounters are experienced as completed. A lack of
congruence between expectation and reality, on the other hand, is
experienced as an incomplete, unfinished psychological situation. As
Worthington (1992) has noted, families of a child with special needs
experience stress over the loss of the "ideal" child they expected to have.
When parents feel that they are not listened to or their needs not addressed,
disappointment and distress are likely (Dunst et al., 1988; Thomas, 1991).
Such experiences constitute incomplete encounters.

Working within Kempler's frame of the encounter, it is important to
identify the expectations and needs that characterize families in order to
understand their role in family coping and adjustment. With such
information, interventions can be personalized to promote congruent
encounters with helping professionals, service systems, and the community.
To that end, involvement may take the form of providing opportunities in
which families share their   concerns and needs and express their
expectations for their child and themselves in their situation. Drawing on
findings from our own research and related studies, three questions serve as
the basis for examining family involvement within the context of the
assessment encounter: (a) What are the expectations of families as they
encounter the developmental assessment of their child? (b) To what extent
are such expectations congruent with those of professionals involved in child
assessment? (c) In what ways are expectations about involvement in child
assessment reflective of broader family expectations in the form of
perceived concerns and needs?

Multidisciplinary services, including the team evaluation of children,
provide a context in which the expectations of both families and
professionals play an important and reciprocal part. While the nature and
form of such evaluations have been detailed and the composition and roles
of the multidisciplinary team specified, little attention has been given to the
prerequisite to this activity, namely, the reciprocal expectations of families
and professionals. The traditional evaluation approach has been one in
which parents are asked to provide demographic information and factual
data about the history and nature of their child's condition. Minimal
exploration has been made of the fact that families bring significant
concerns and emotions to the evaluation encounter. It is likely that the
extent to which these expectations are addressed and met will significantly
determine subsequent encounters of the family with intervention systems
(Piper & Howlin, 1992).

It may be useful to consider family involvement as a continuum of roles
from a reactive role to an active, initiating role (Carnahan & Simeonsson,
1992). To promote family involvement, one useful approach would be to

survey expectations of parents about the developmental evaluation of their child. At least three key dimensions of their expectations might be important to assess: the form of evaluations, the content of evaluations, and their feelings about the evaluation process. Recognizing that any encounter is bidirectional, it is clear that the expectations of professionals also play a role. The congruence of expectations between client and counselor and its contribution to the working alliance have been seen as important factors in the related field of counseling (Al-Darmaki & Kivlighan, 1993). Documentation of expectations would seem to be a timely priority in early intervention.

These issues have been the focus of recently published studies as well as our own exploratory study in which we have surveyed the expectations and perceptions of families and professionals regarding the multidisciplinary evaluation of children (Simeonsson et al., 1995). The professionals who participated in the study were members of multidisciplinary teams staffing developmental evaluation centers in the state of North Carolina. Complementing their participation were parents whose children were seen for evaluations in these centers. While the surveys for professionals and parents covered similar content, there was not a one-to-one correspondence of survey items. Selected findings from this study and related research will be used to address the three questions posed in this chapter.

What are family expectations about the multidisciplinary evaluation of their children? First it is important to realize that these expectations may be quite variable for a number of reasons. A primary source of such variability comes from the referral itself: Does it reflect an informal suspicion or concern, a risk status, or a manifested condition? The source of the referral may also be a significant factor; self-referrals or those from a relative or friend may differ substantially from a referral made by a physician or other professional. Another source of variability of family expectations is cognitive and affective readiness to accept the child's referral. Some families may be quite accepting of the referral, whereas others may find it very difficult to deal with. The degree of acceptance, cognitively and emotionally, will be influenced by prior experience with professionals providing individual and team evaluations. Families for whom the evaluation is a novel experience are less likely to know what to expect than experienced parents, and coupled with their own concerns, they will feel anxious about the unknown. A final source of variability is attributable to individual differences among families in terms of educational level, social and cultural characteristics, prior experiences with human services, as well as personal style.

2   Expectations of Families

What the majority of new parents expected from the evaluation of their child was first and foremost, a description of their child's strengths and weaknesses and clear results. Related concerns pertaining to answers, diagnoses, and referrals were also central expectations for 60% to 80% of parents. As for the form of evaluation, more than 80% of the families expected professionals to acknowledge their expertise, but less than 40% expected to be asked personal questions.

In order to examine the congruence of family and professional expectations, the perceptions that professionals hold can also be defined. In general, professionals see parental expectations for child assessment in somewhat lower proportions than parents themselves do. The professional perceptions of parents were lower for the domains of diagnosis, clear purpose, clear results, referrals, and strengths and weaknessess. With regard to the form of assessment, 30% of the professionals endorsed the view that parents expected an acknowledgment of their expertise in regard to the current functioning of their child. In a related context, professionals did not see, as parents did, personal questions as a key aspect of information exchange. Professional perceptions about parental expectations of the assessment process itself ranged from 3% (assessment of family) to 79% (answers to questions) to what they felt was delivered: a diagnosis (18%) to complete confidentiality (92%). It is interesting to note that professionals generally see themselves as delivering more than parents expect.

3   Congruence of Family and Professionals Expectations

To what extent is there congruence of expectations about child evaluation and perceptions of the process between parents and professionals? When we compare these two participants in terms of what each sees as family expectations and priorities for evaluation, higher percentages were found for families on all but one domain. In this regard, it was interesting to note that professional attributions for family expectations were only higher for the domain of answers. On the other hand, their expectations about family concerns and priorities were substantially lower than those of families in the domain of child strengths and weaknesses and acknowledgment of parental expertise.

Turning to what each participant felt the professionals delivered, even though parents expect more from the evaluation process as noted, they also generally attributed higher levels of delivery to professionals than the professionals themselves did. Only in the area of receiving answers to questions did professionals assign a higher level than parents. In a comparison of attributed feelings, it is clear that professionals are likely to attribute more positive as well as more negative affect to parents than parents do. Finally, it may be informative to consider the extent to which the experience of evaluations confirmed the expectations of families and was a satisfactory encounter for them. The data indicated that the extent of congruence between expectations and experience was variable. Whereas the majority of families found the evaluation helpful, for a significant subgroup, there was substantial concern expressed that the multidisciplinary evaluation was less than satisfactory.

4   Expectations in the Context of Family Needs

Working within the metaphor of the encounter, these data suggest that, for many families, the evaluation experience was a complete and finished encounter, congruent with expectations. For others, however, expectations were probably not fully met, questions not adequately answered, and concerns not fully addressed. If this was the case, it was an incomplete encounter. A possible factor may have been a lack of congruence between what parents expected and the actual evaluation experience. The fact that the data do not represent specific pairings of parents and professionals in the same clinic prevents us from drawing definitive conclusions. However, some support for an assumption of incomplete encounters can be drawn from the perceptions of professionals about what should be changed about evaluations. While most professionals endorsed changes for the evaluation process, including greater family involvement, almost one third of the professionals indicated no need for change. Such a position among professionals is not likely to be congruent with parent expectations about involvement.

Support for this assumption may also be found in results of studies assessing family needs. The needs that families express can be seen as broader expectations reflecting what families expect in the form of supportive services. Across a number of studies using the Family Needs Survey (Halpern, 1994), a consistent finding has been the fact that information emerges as the highest need area. This has been true not only for families in the United States (Bailey et al., 1994), but has also been evident cross-culturally in findings from Sweden (Roll-Petterson & Granlund, 1993), Brazil (Halpern, 1993), and the People's Republic of China (Chen & Simeonsson, 1994). The disproportionate extent of unmet needs in the area of information has also been documented in other studies (Sloper & Turner, 1992). Furthermore, Stallard and Lenton (1992) conducted a consumer survey and found that families felt they received insufficient information about the child's condition (29%), the child's future (61%), help for the family (44%), and financial benefits (61%). Inadequate family support and a failure of professionals to understand their concerns were also identified as problems by 43% and 32% of families respectively. If expressed needs and expectations of families are complementary dimensions of anticipated encounters with professionals and service systems, congruence with actual experiences may well reflect the extent to which the encounter is completed. The goal of intervention may then parallel similar goals in related spheres of human services, namely, working alliances in psychotherapy (Al-Darmarki & Kivlighan, 1993).

5   Conclusion

This chapter has advocated for the systematic consideration and assessment of family expectations as a direct and productive way in which to promote the involvement of families in programs for their children with disabilities. The importance of such assessment is framed in the concept of the complete encounter (Kempler, 1981), defined in terms of congruence of expectations with experience. Within this frame, assessment of expectations can complement other ways in which families can be involved in personalizing and validating supportive interventions for their children and themselves.

References

Al-Darmaki, F., & Kivilghan, D. M., Jr. (1993). Congruence in client-counselor expectations for relationship and the working alliance. *Journal of Counsel Psychology, 40*(4), 379-384.

Bailey, D. B., Blasco, P., & Simeonsson, R. J. (1992). Needs expressed by mothers and fathers of young children with disabilities. *American Journal of Mental Retardation, 97*, 1-10.

Beresford, B. A. (1994). Resources and strategies: How parents cope with the care of a disabled child. *Journal of Child Psychology and Psychiatry, 35*(1), 171-209.

Bronfenbrenner, U. (1977). Toward an experimental ecology of human development. *American Psychologist, 32*, 513-531.

Carnahan, S., & Simeonsson, R. J. (1992). Family involvement in child assessment. *International Journal of Cognitive Education & Mediated Learning, 2*(3), 224-233.

Chen, J., & Simeonsson, R. J. (1994). Child disability and family needs in the People's Republic of China. *International Journal of Rehabilitation Research, 17*, 25-37.

Dunst, C. J., Leet, H. E., & Trivette, C. M. (1988). Family resources, personal well-being, and early intervention. *Journal of Special Education, 22*(1), 108-116.

Gallimore, R., Weisner, T., Kaufman, S., & Bernheimer, L. (1989). The social construction of ecocultural niches: Family accomodations of developmentally delayed children. *American Journal of Mental Retardation, 94*(3), 210-230.

Halpern, S. (1994). *Children with disabilities: A study of family needs in Pelotas, Brazil.* Unpublished master's thesis, University of North Carolina, Chapel Hill, NC.

Kempler, W. (1969). Family therapy of the future. *International Psychiatry Clinics, 6,* 135-158.

Kempler, W. (1974). *Principles of gestalt family therapy: A gestalt experimental handbook.* Sultlake City, UT: Deseret Press.

Kempler, W. (1981). *Experiential psychotherapy within families.* New York: Brunner Masel.

Narayan, J., Madhavan, T., & Prakasam, B. S. (1993). Factors influencing the expectations of parents for their mentally retarded children. *Journal of Intellectual Disability Research, 37,* 161-168.

Piper, E., & Howlin, P. (1992) Assessing and diagnosing disorders that are not evident at birth: Parental evaluations of intake procedures. *Child: Care, Health and Development, 18,* 35-55.

Reisz, E. D. (1984). *First years of a Down Syndrome Child.* Iowa City, IA: University of Iowa Publication.

Roll-Petterson, L., & Granlund, M. (1993). *Needs of Swedish families: Child characteristics and the role of the professional.* Stockholm: Stiftelsen ALA.

Sameroff, A. J., & Chandler, M. J. (1975). Reproductive risk and the continuum of caretaking casualty. In F. D. Horowitz, M. Hetherington, S. Scarr-Salapatek, & G. Siegel (Eds.), *Review of child development research* (Vol. 4, pp. 187-244). Chicago, IL: University of Chicago Press.

Sameroff, A. J., & Fiese, B. H. (1990). Transactional regulation and early intervention. In S. J. Meisels & J. P. Shonkoff (Eds.). *Handbook of early childhood intervention.* Campridge, England: University Press.

Simeonsson, R. J., & Bailey, D. B. (1990). Family dimensions in early intervention. In S. J. Meisels & J. P. Shonkoff (Eds.), *Handbook of Early Childhood Intervention.* Cambridge, England: University Press.

Simeonsson, R. J., Edmondson, R., Smith, T., Carnahan, S., & Bucy, J. (1995). Family involvement in multidisciplinary team evaluation: Parent and professional perspectives. *Child, Care, Health & Development, 21 (3),* 1-16.

Sloper, P., & Turner, S. (1992). Service needs of families of children with severe physical disability. *Child: Care, Health and Development, 18,* 259-282.

Stallard, P., & Lenton, S. (1992). How satisfied are parents of pre-school children who have special needs with the services they have received? A consumer survey. *Child: Care, Health and Development, 18,* 197-205.

Thomas, S. F. (1991). Three letters from parents. *Journal of Child and Adolescent Psychopharmacology, 1*(4), 299-303.

Wishart, J. G., Macleod, H. A., & Rowan, C. (1993). Parents' evaluations of pre-school services for children with Down syndrome in two Scottish regions. *Child: Care, Health and Development, 19,* 1-23.

Winton, P., & Bailey, D. B. (1990). Early intervention training related to family interviewing. *Topics in Early Childhood Special Education, 10*(1) 50-62.

Worthington, R. C. (1992). Families support networks: Help for families of children with special needs. *Family Medicine, 24*(1), 41-44.

M. Brambring, H. Rauh, and A. Beelmann (Eds.). (1996). *Early childhood intervention: Theory, evaluation, and practice* (pp. 208-218). Berlin, New York: de Gruyter.

Parenting Stress in Early Intervention

Klaus Sarimski

1   Introduction

Recent years have seen increased interest in studying the stress experienced by parents who have a child with disabilities. A variety of research designs and instruments have been applied. Initially, it was assumed that the presence of a child with disabilities in the family always resulted in high parental stress and family dysfunction. However, recent studies have abandoned this "pathological approach." They have suggested that parents of disabled children are able to regain their psychological well-being, and that these parents do not differ from others in their individually perceived stress. These studies have focused on variables that may affect the stress level in a family. By defining these variables, it has become possible to develop psychological interventions to meet the needs of the individual family. This approach may be called the "normality approach" (Mahoney et al., 1992).

Causes of parental stress include the greater amount of time needed for caregiving, individual difficulties in feeding or bathing, the demands of performing therapy at home, the parents' need for contact with a support group, and the lack of time available for leisure and regeneration. Other sources of stress are anxiety about the child's future and one's own parenting competence, loss of personal independence, and fear of social isolation. Although greater stress is a reality for many families, researchers and clinical staff agree that psychological distress and relationship problems cannot be seen in every family with a developmentally disabled child (Dyson, 1991; Gowen et al., 1989).

Factors that have an impact on reported stress level include the severity and type of disability the child has, his or her social maturity and communicative competence, or individual characteristics such as high irritability. However, parental and family resources are as important as child factors. Factors in this area that have been shown to mediate stress include the following: self-competence and perceived control, coping strategies, religious beliefs, spouse support, family structure, and economic resources. Another important factor is the presence of a supportive social network including family, friends, neighbors, and social services (Frey et al., 1989; McKinney & Peterson, 1987).

The following report discusses three of our own research projects in Munich. The purpose of these studies was to analyze some of the relationships mentioned above. We will report on three independent investigations that used separate samples.

The questions considered in the studies were the following: First, is there a difference in parenting stress level between mothers of young disabled children and a matched control group? What role do determinants such as child age, severity of disability, special caregiving problems, and demands of individual (physio-)therapy play (Sarimski, 1993)? Second, is there a relationship between perceived stress in parenting the disabled child and general self-confidence and attitudes toward childrearing? Is there a relationship between stress and special coping styles (Sarimski & Hoffmann, 1994)? Third, is there a relationship between these variables and stress perceived during an intensive treatment in early intervention, using physiotherapy as an example of this intensive treatment (Sarimski & Hoffmann, 1992)?

2 Parenting Stress and Special Demands

The sample for the first study contained 100 mothers. Sixty-seven of them had children with developmental disabilities; 33 mothers had normally developed children. The children ranged in age from 10 to 42 months. The first group was subdivided: 33 children had a mental and motor developmental disorder and received intensive physiotherapy (Vojta method, Vojta, 1981); 34 children were mentally handicapped without additional motor disorders. A variety of disabilities was represented within the sample. The groups were matched for child age and maternal educational level.

The primary instrument for this study was the Parenting Stress Index (PSI, Abidin, 1990). The PSI is designed to assess parent perceptions of stress within the parent-child system. It is composed of 101 items that are scored as a rating scale. Higher scores indicate greater levels of stress. The PSI contains two domains, one addressing child-related stress and the other parent-related stress. The child domain measures the mothers' perceptions on what the child contributes to the parent-child relationship. This includes child characteristics and behaviors. The following subdomains are assessed: adaptability, acceptability, demandingness, mood, distractability/hyperactivity, and child reinforcement for the parent.

Table 1. *Stress Perceived by Parents of Mentally Handicapped Children With/Without Movement Disorders and Normal Children*

	Group I (n = 33)	Group II (n = 34)	Group III (n = 33)	F (2, 97)
Child domain score	116.73[a] (18.81)	114.12[a] (17.43)	95.48[b] (19.97)	12.64***
Adaptability	28.73[a] (7.43)	27.50[a] (5.98)	23.65[b] (5.33)	5.36**
Acceptability	17.73[a] (4.82)	17.88[a] (4.02)	11.67[b] (3.20)	25.22***
Demandingness	26.30[a] (3.60)	24.26[a] (4.83)	18.52[b] (5.67)	23.62***
Mood	10.45 (4.12)	10.12 (3.50)	9.88 (3.84)	.19
Distractability/Hyperactivity	24.18 (4.19)	24.41 (5.05)	23.00 (3.77)	.99
Reinforces parent	9.61 (3.08)	9.85 (3.00)	9.48 (2.90)	.13
Parent domain score	128.58 (17.37)	126.91 (27.46)	120.36 (25.39)	1.10
Depression	17.88 (4.22)	18.79 (6.25)	17.85 (5.04)	.35
Attachment	11.85 (3.46)	12.50 (3.15)	12.82 (3.20)	.76
Restriction of role	21.64[a] (5.48)	19.76[b] (6.20)	17.39[c] (6.20)	4.18*
Sense of competence	33.88[a] (4.17)	33.09[a] (5.48)	30.03[b] (5.78)	5.06**
Social isolation	13.67 (5.64)	13.65 (4.24)	12.45 (4.40)	.69
Parent health	14.24 (4.09)	13.12 (4.79)	12.06 (3.49)	2.26
Total stress score	245.30[a] (33.06)	241.03[a] (42.02)	215.85[b] (42.47)	5.39**

Group I = mentally handicapped children with movement disorders.
Group II = mentally handicapped children without movement disorders.
Group III = normal children.
* $p < .05$.   ** $p < .01$.   *** $p < .001$.

Note. For significant F values, contrasts were computed with Scheffé tests. The same letters as indices on the means indicate nonsignificant individual comparisons; different letters indicate significant individual comparisons.

Table 2.   *Stress Perceived by Parents of Children With Low to Severe Mental Handicap (Means and Standard Deviations)*

	Normal	Mild MH	Moderate MH	Severe MH	F (3, 96)
	(n = 33)	(n = 15)	(n = 30)	(n = 22)	
Child domain score	95.49[a]	106.93[b]	112.97[b,c]	124.50[c]	12.17***
	(19.97)	(14.31)	(18.78)	(15.87)	
Adaptability	23.85[a]	24.13[a]	27.53[a,b]	31.59[b]	8.70***
	(5.33)	(5.07)	(6.52)	(6.41)	
Acceptability	11.67[a]	16.33[b]	18.03[b]	18.50[b]	18.01***
	(3.20)	(3.74)	(4.71)	(4.33)	
Demandingness	18.52[a]	24.60[b]	24.07[b]	27.36[b]	17.30***
	(5.67)	(3.40)	(4.89)	(3.46)	
Mood	9.88	8.67	10.63	10.77	.99
	(3.84)	(3.27)	(3.70)	(4.16)	
Distractability/Hyper-activity	23.00	23.87	23.33	25.91	2.26
	(3.77)	(5.46)	(4.67)	(3.57)	
Reinforces parent	9.49	8.67	9.70	10.36	.81
	(2.90)	(2.26)	(3.06)	(3.36)	
Parent domain score	120.36	127.40	124.27	132.68	1.24
	(25.39)	(17.74)	(27.22)	(19.27)	
Depression	17.85	17.87	18.47	18.50	.12
	(5.04)	(2.64)	(6.35)	(5.34)	
Attachment	12.82	12.53	11.80	12.45	.52
	(3.20)	(3.11)	(3.58)	(3.10)	
Restriction of role	17.39[a]	20.33[a,b]	19.47[a,b]	22.59[b]	3.45*
	(6.20)	(4.64)	(6.41)	(5.64)	
Sense of competence	30.03[a]	34.53[a,b]	32.77[b]	33.73[a,b]	3.65*
	(5.78)	(4.91)	(5.47)	(3.91)	
Social isolation	12.45	13.13	13.23	14.59	.88
	(4.40)	(3.42)	(3.94)	(6.80)	
Parent health	12.06[a]	12.80[a,b]	12.97[a,b]	15.33[b]	2.70*
	(3.49)	(3.82)	(4.27)	(4.89)	
Total stress score	215.85[a]	234.33[a,b]	237.24[a,b]	257.18[b]	5.09**
	(42.47)	(27.50)	(43.69)	(31.67)	

* $p < .05$.   ** $p < .01$.   *** $p < .001$.

Note. For significant F values, contrasts were computed with Scheffé tests. The same letters as indices on the means indicate nonsignificant individual comparisons; different letters indicate significant individual comparisons.

The parent domain assesses parent characteristics that are influenced by the parent-child relationship. Subdomains here include depression, attachment, restrictions of role, sense of competence, social isolation, relationship with spouse, and parent health.

After completing the PSI, maternal perceptions on feeding and sleeping behavior were obtained with a short 18-item questionnaire specially developed for the study.

Mothers of toddlers with disabilities reported significantly greater stress in the child domain, $F(2, 97) = 12.64$, $p < .01$, than the matched-age control group. No differences were found between samples in the parent domain of the PSI, $F(2, 97) = 1.10$, $p = .34$, with the exception of two scales: Mothers of toddlers with disabilities experienced greater restrictions of role and felt less confident in their maternal competence (see Table 1).

We found a wide range of individual differences. The amount of perceived stress depended in part on the severity of mental handicap, $F(3, 96) = 5.09$, $p < .01$ (see Table 2). Special caregiving problems such as feeding or sleeping disorders, or stress caused by intensive treatments seemed to be less important within this age group. There was no difference in the frequency of feeding and sleeping problems (i.e., 35%) between the high-stress and low-stress group. However, mothers with a high stress score in the child domain perceived these problems more often as a significant burden in their everyday lives.

3   Parenting Stress, Parental Attitudes, and Coping Style

On the basis of these data, we assumed (as other researchers before) that the large individual differences in reported stress seemed to depend on factors other than child characteristics such as the severity of the disorder and the amount of caregiving necessary. We tried to analyze data from a second sample in order to establish relationships between stress level and parental attitudes and coping style.

Seventy-five mothers of developmentally disabled children (mean age 34 months) participated in this study. All subjects were recruited from my regular psychological assessment and counseling contacts at the out-patient department of the *Kinderzentrum München*. Age was the only criterion for selection. Thirteen children had a mild general developmental disorder; 25, one of moderate degree; and 37 had a severe mental disability (DQ < 50). Forty percent were not yet able to walk independently, 20% had additional visual handicaps, and 7% had severe hearing impairments.

A battery of questionnaires was administered to the mothers. This included the following measures:

1. Infant Characteristics Questionnaire (Bates, 1979): This measure consists of 27 items for 1-year-olds (comparable to the mean mental age of the subjects) and assesses maternal perception of child difficulty, adaptability, persistence, and social orientation.

2. Einstellung von Müttern zu Kleinkindern (Engfer, 1984; Maternal attitudes toward toddlers): This scale was constructed for a longitudinal research project on social development. Scores are obtained for six subscales: parental enjoyment, rigidity, stress, frustration level, overprotection, depression.

3. Fragebogen zu Kompetenz- und Kontrollüberzeugungen (Krampen, 1991; Locus of control scale): This questionnaire is a 32-item self-report instrument assessing perceived competence and problem-solving ability as well as internal versus external locus of control (social dependency, fatalism).

4. Umgang mit Belastungssituationen in der frühen Mutter-Kind-Interaktion (Reicherts et al., 1989; Ways of coping in early mother-child interaction): This questionnaire was developed by a Swiss research group as a tool to assess the coping strategies that mothers use in ambiguous everyday mother-child interaction situations. The mothers are asked to imagine a stress event like nocturnal crying, refusal of body contact, or disinterest in maternal stimulation of play. The individually perceived emotional impact, locus of control over the course of event, and preferences among several coping strategies are rated on a 4-point scale.

Again, the results revealed a broad individual variation in maternal attitudes and perceptions of their special caregiving burdens. We divided the whole group into two subgroups according to the median maternal attitude scales stress score. Mothers reporting a high stress level perceived their children as more difficult and less socially adaptive on the temperament scales. They felt less enjoyment in parenting, felt frustrated and depressed more often, and described their attitudes as more rigid and overprotective than did the group reporting a low stress level (Table 3).

Mothers who rated their parenting stress as high displayed lower self-confidence on all four locus of control scales. They felt less competent in general problem-solving and less in control over the course of life events.

Table 3. *Temperament, Maternal Attitudes, and Perceived Control in Mothers With High Versus Low Parenting Stress*

	Low parenting stress ($n = 37$)		High parenting stress ($n = 38$)		t (73)
	M	*SD*	*M*	*SD*	
Difficulty	3.40	.65	4.24	1.09	***
Adaptability	3.08	1.16	3.42	1.10	ns
Persistence	4.35	1.73	4.85	1.37	ns
Social orientation	2.57	.86	3.03	.90	*
Child enjoyment	1.53	.38	1.71	.39	*
Rigidity	1.75	.32	1.99	.29	***
Frustration tolerance	1.62	.40	2.20	.43	***
Overprotection	1.64	.36	1.99	.43	***
Depression	1.62	.39	2.31	.65	***
Self-confidence	34.62	5.68	30.05	5.85	***
Internal control	31.38	5.38	28.68	3.93	*
Social external control	23.73	5.61	26.54	6.05	*
Fatality	22.76	6.15	26.76	6.87	**

* $p < .05$.   ** $p < .01$ *** $p < .001$

Table 4 shows the preferences among six coping strategies that the mothers described while imagining the three critical stress events. Their first preference was to search for a reason explaining negative or ambiguous child behavior. Cognitive reconstruction ("I think about it and decide that the behavior is not so bad/important") and palliative reactions were also highly preferred. Blaming oneself or the child and avoidance were less often chosen as coping strategies.

Correlational and regression analyses revealed that the ways of coping related significantly to parenting stress level. Mothers reporting a high stress level were less confident of self-regulation, felt more stressed by the critical event, felt they had less control over the situation, and showed a strong tendency to blame themselves or the other person.

These results exemplify the role that maternal cognitions and attributions play in mediating interactive stress. Blaming oneself, blaming the child, and having a low feeling of self-efficacy are related to high parenting stress. These maternal reactions, which include both cognitive and affective elements, may contribute to a vicious circle of interactive failures and maternal attitudes, selective perceptions, and anticipations. Unfortunately, we do not have much relevant data on cognitive determinants of parenting stress. Some researchers - especially those studying hyperactive children - suggest a system of "indiscriminative parenting," which is characterized by a lack of contingency in the relationship between what a child does and how the mother reponds.

Table 4.   *Coping Intentions and Coping Reactions Toward Three Critical Events in Early Mother-Child Interaction (n = 75)*

Coping intentions	M	SD
It is important for me ...		
to give my child what he/she needs	4.46	1.36
to remain calm	4.52	1.19
to follow my own needs	2.11	0.68
Coping reactions		
I don't think about it, distract myself, and don't let it bother me.	2.02	1.28
I calm my feelings (I encourage myself, relax, drink something, etc.).	4.08	1.84
I reflect carefully about it and how I can deal with it.	6.22	1.88
I blame my child inwardly.	1.47	1.38
I make it clear to myself: This situation is not so bad/important in comparison to other situations.	4.98	1.99
I blame myself.	2.06	1.22

Mothers experiencing a high level of parent-child interactive stress may focus their attention selectively on negative behaviors and overlook positive aspects of child behavior, inwardly accuse the child of having negative intentions, and tend to exert control over child behavior. They lose flexibility in problem-solving, feel more and more helpless in response to difficult child behavior, and attribute failures to personal incompetence. Finally, they act as though they were following a rigid internal script that is mediated by dysfunctional cognitions and contributes to an increase in interactive stress (Mash & Johnston, 1990).

4   Parent Stress and Early Intervention Treatments

Finally, I would like to present some data we obtained from a third study. The same instruments explained above were used. Forty-nine mothers of children with motor disorders participated in the study. The mean age of the children was 28 months. Sixty-five percent of the children had moderate or severe mental impairments as well. All children had received physiotherapy according to the Vojta method for more than 1 year. In this method of physiotherapy, a program of motor exercises is followed three to four times a day. The total amount of time required for treatment is 1 to 2 hours per day. The treatment is performed by the parents under the regular supervision of a therapist (Vojta, 1981).

During treatment, the child is stimulated in uncommon positions that are often not well accepted. Thus, oppositional behaviors, avoidance, and crying are frequent problems during treatment.

In order to analyze relationships between parental attitudes and coping strategies and the severity of individually perceived stress as a co-therapist, we asked the 49 mothers to imagine the treatment situation and the toddler's oppositional crying. The "Ways of coping in early mother-child interaction" questionnaire (see above) was adapted to this situation. Emotional impact, locus of control, and preferences among several coping strategies were rated by the mothers.

Again, the relationships of maternal attitudes, self-concept, and coping styles to perceived stress in treatment situations were analyzed. A correlational analysis revealed no significant relationship between stress and general childrearing attitudes. However, when the mothers had little confidence in their problem-solving abilities in general, tended to blame the other person or themselves, and made less effort to integrate treatment as one experience among other potentially less stressful child-raising experiences (cognitive reconstruction), they perceived stress to be higher. Stepwise regression was performed to predict the amount of stress experienced during treatment. Factors accounting for 73% of the variance in stress, $F = 10.71$, $p < .001$; $R^2 = .727$, were perceived control in everyday situations and specifically in treatment situations, cognitive reconstruction as a positive coping behavior, and the retrospective account of actual oppositional child behavior during treatment.

5   Conclusions

The findings from these studies appear to be highly compatible with theoretical coping models and with empirical investigations into the determinants contributing to parenting stress in families with disabled children. Mothers of toddlers with motor and mental diabilities experience a greater amount of interactional stress, but do not display signs of depression or psychological distress more frequently than parents of nondisabled children. The degree of mental impairment seems to be the most relevant factor contributing to parenting stress. Special demands made on parents by feeding and sleeping disorders or intensive treatments seem to pose less of a problem. There is a great range of individual differences in perceived stress: Mothers who report high levels of interactional stress in everyday situations and treatment situations generally feel less competent in problem-solving and tend to show dysfunctional coping reactions such as "self-blaming" and "blaming the child."

In my opinion, the results of these studies allow two recommendations for early intervention practice: The first is to provide psychological services individually tailored to parental needs instead of assuming that psychological and relationship problems in this population are a general fact. The second is to concentrate on those parents who report high levels of stress and to analyze maternal perceptions, attributions, and self-efficacy feelings as mediational factors in the context of interactive stress. Therefore, parent counseling should encourage parents to observe child behavior precisely, develop problem-solving ideas, and modify dysfunctional cognitions.

References

Abidin, R. (1990). *Parenting Stress Index*. Charlottesville, VA: Pediatric Psychology Press.

Bates, J. (1979). *Infant Characteristics Questionnaire* (ICQ). Bloomington, IN: Indiana University.

Dyson, L. (1991). Families of young children with handicaps: Parental stress and family functioning. *American Journal on Mental Retardation, 95*, 623-629.

Engfer, A. (1984). *Entwicklung punitiver Mutter-Kind-Interaktionen im sozioökologischen Kontext*. München: Institut für Psychologie.

Frey, K., Greenberg, M., & Fewell, R. (1989). Stress and coping among parents of handicapped children: A multidimensional approach. *American Journal on Mental Retardation, 94*, 240-249.

Gowen, J., Johnson-Martin, N., Goldman, B., & Applebaum, M. (1989). Feelings of depression and parenting competence of mothers of handicapped and non-handicapped infants: A longitudinal study. *American Journal on Mental Retardation, 94*, 259-271.

Krampen, G. (1991). *Fragebogen zu Kompetenz- und Kontrollüberzeugungen*. Göttingen: Hogrefe.

Mahoney, G., O'Sullivan, P., & Robinson, C. (1992). The family environments of children with disabilities: Diverse but not so different. *Topics in Early Childhood Special Education, 12*, 386-402.

Mash, E., & Johnston, C. (1990). Determinants of parenting stress: Illustrations from families of hyperactive children and families of physically abused children. *Journal of Clinical Child Psychology, 19*, 313-328.

McKinney, B., & Peterson, R. (1987). Predictors of stress in parents of developmentally disabled children. *Journal of Pediatric Psychology, 12*, 133-150.

218 Klaus Sarimski

Reicherts, M., Schedle, A., & Diethelm, K. (1989). *Zum Umgang mit Belastungssituationen in der frühen Mutter-Kind-Interaktion.* Fribourg: Universität.

Sarimski, K. (1993). Belastung von Eltern behinderter Kleinkinder. *Frühförderung interdisziplinär, 12,* 154-164.

Sarimski, K., & Hoffmann, I. (1992). Belastungsverarbeitung bei der Durchführung von Krankengymnastik durch die Eltern cerebralparetischer Kinder. *Kind und Entwicklung, 1,* 107-115.

Sarimski, K., & Hoffmann, I. (1994). Erziehung behinderter Kinder: Immer psychische Belastung und Überforderung? *Psychologie in Erziehung und Unterricht, 41,* 22-30.

Vojta, V. (1981). *Die zerebralen Bewegungsstörungen im Säuglingsalter. Frühdiagnose und Frühtherapie.* Stuttgart: Enke.

M. Brambring, H. Rauh, and A. Beelmann (Eds.). (1996). *Early childhood intervention: Theory, evaluation, and practice* (pp. 219-233). Berlin, New York: de Gruyter.

Family Dynamics and Development in Children at Risk

Gerhard Neuhäuser

1 Introduction

Over the last 20 years, early intervention has become an integral part of our health system. Whereas in the beginning, measures of immediate help for the child with developmental delay or handicap seemed to be most important, later on, there was increasing awareness of the needs parents and families have after experiencing the birth of an infant at risk for various reasons. This change in emphasis is also reflected by the titles of the symposia held and organized by our Association for Interdisciplinary Early Intervention in Germany: In 1991, we chose the title *Family-Oriented Early Intervention* to characterize the importance of all measures directed toward the child's environment.

Studies from different countries indicate that the development of "infants at risk" is influenced not only by abnormal conditions during pregnancy or by cerebral lesions from hypoxia and trauma during delivery but also by the psychosocial conditions arising from the situation in which the child has to live. This applies particularly to those infants and children with only minor handicapping conditions. There is much agreement today that a child's development is influenced by genetic or constitutional as well as by environmental or epigenetic factors, among which psychosocial conditions are most important. There are no simple relations, and development is not organized in a hierarchical manner. On the contrary, there is a continous interplay, and there are many complicated interrelations that shape the individual child. Negative exogenous circumstances, for example, may well enhance functional disabilities, whereas positive environmental influences may compensate partially, sometimes almost completely, for an impairment or developmental disability.

The close relationship and interdependence of somatic factors and psychosocial conditions is reflected by the findings of many follow-up studies (see Kalverboer et al., 1993) revealing that correlation coefficients for events during the prenatal and perinatal period become lower as development continues. Therefore, it is difficult to search for specific causal relationships, and it is almost impossible to analyze all the important factors of this multifactorial system. Results of different studies using various approaches have to be combined to gain further insight into this complexity. The aim of our study was to concentrate on parental feelings and family dynamics after the birth of an infant at risk for various reasons.

2   Design of the Giessen Prospective Study

In cooperation with our Department of Medical Psychology (Dieter Beckmann and colleagues), we decided to analyze some of the variables involved in family dynamics such as parental marital relations, psychosocial conditions of the extended family, social network, and life events following the birth of an infant at risk.

We followed premature and newborn infants who had been in intensive care for at least 2 weeks in our neonatal ward because of respiratory distress, seizures, infections, or other life-threatening conditions. We excluded children with known syndromes, such as Down's syndrome, and with major malformations, such as severe heart defect. We included all infants admitted during a given time ($n = 134$) whose parents agreed to cooperate and had no difficulty in using the German language ($n = 86$; see Table 1).

Table 1.   *Schedule of Follow-Up Study*

Methods	38 weeks $n = 97$	42 weeks $n = 97$	3 months $n = 75$	12 months $n = 68$	3 years $n = 63$	5 years $n = 51$
Social questionnaire	X			X	X	X
Family resources	X			X	X	X
Giessen Test		X		X	X	
Repertory Grid Test		X				
Optimality score	X					
Health and behavior			X	X	X	X
Neurological examination (Optimality score)	X	X	X	X	X	X
Neuropediatric examination				X	X	X
Bayley Scales				X		
Kramer Test					X	X
Therapeutic measures			X	X		X
EEG, Sono, CT	X	X	X	X		
Interview rating					X	X

Extensive data were gathered during the neonatal period concerning medical history (health of mother, pregnancy, and delivery; items sampled according to Prechtl's optimality concept) and clinical findings (neurological examinations at gestational age of 38 and 42 weeks respectively). In addition, social data were collected by structured interviews with both parents. The marital relationship of partners was assessed with the *Giessen-Test*, a reliable and valid method of obtaining information about feelings, concepts, and habits from both husband and wife (Beckmann et al., 1983); in some cases a Repertoy Grid Test (REP; Böker et al., 1984) was also administered. During the follow-up examinations at 3 months, 12 months, 3 years, and 5 years, the developmental progress of the children was documented by neurological examination quantified by optimality scores according to Stave and Ruvalo (1980) as well as Touwen (1982); assessment of intellectual functions and behavior on the Bayley Scales, Kramer Test, and Wechsler Test for Preschool Age (HAWIVA); and tests for coordinative abilities (Motoriktest für 3 - 6jährige, MOT). Special attention was given to the psychosocial situation as reflected in data obtained from an extensive semistructured interview with parents (or mother alone) when the children were 3 years old. The goal was to obtain comprehensive information about the coping process within the families, habits, and expectations. In addition, another Giessen-Test was given to assess changes in marital relations over time. We were interested in which social network parents could use, what life events had occurred, how parents judged their children's developmental progress, and what plans they had for the future.

The neurological findings were used as an independent variable. Quantified by the optimality concept (Prechtl, 1968, 1980), results of examinations at various ages could be compared. In addition, cross-sectional data could be used to validate the findings of the longitudinal study (in particular, optimality scores and results of neurological examination at age 3 years).

3 Results

3.1 Neuromotor Development of Infants at Risk

The results of neurological examinations during follow-up, assessed by different standardized methods, could be quantified using the optimality concept. Thus, comparison was possible over time. The data were processed by cluster analysis (Relocate Procedure from the Clustan Program; Wishart, 1984). After distribution of objects over the clusters, an agglomerativehierarchical procedure was followed to merge two clusters successively. In the first step, children were assigned to the best number of clusters. They were then relocated iteratively until the distribution suitable for the intended average distance was found. The clusters most similar were merged, and the procedure started again until a minimal number of clusters was reached. The children were relocated in a way that variable vectors between clusters had the greatest possible difference (Bäcker et al., 1992).

Data from 51 children could be used in the analysis because they were complete (29 boys, 22 girls). Neurological scores from six examinations were processed (Prechtl & Beintema, 1976, at 38 and 42 weeks gestational age; Stave and Ruvalo (1980) at 3 and 12 months; Touwen (1980, 1982) at 3 and 5 years respectively). Because the distribution was skewed to the right, scores had to be transformed. These transformed z values were entered into the cluster analysis (1 = first quartile, 2 = second and third quartile, 3 = fourth quartile). In this way, four types of developmental course could be differentiated (see Figure 1): Type 1 ($n = 17$) has a favorable development with some weakness around 3 months and 1 year. Type 2 ($n = 24$) obviously is less positive at the beginning, but shows improvement in optimality over time. Type 3 ($n = 11$) and Type 4 ($n = 9$) have an unfavorable course in common with differences at the beginning. Whereas Type 4 has low optimality scores constantly, Type 3 starts with good values that drop afterwards.

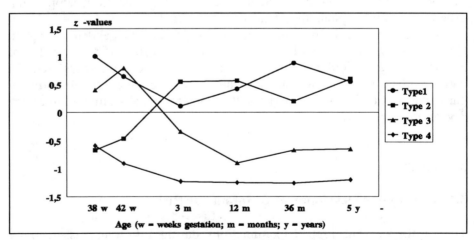

Figure 1. Different types of neurological development in children at risk Optimality scores.
Note. Cluster analysis (Wishart, 1984).

In some way, these results reflect the dynamics present in neuromotor development known to every clinician who follows children at risk, with cerebral palsy and mental retardation becoming apparent at the end of the first year. Discontinuities in developmental courses are represented by the curves of the four types identified. At the age of 3 months, there seems to be an important crossing point, again in agreement with clinical experiences in the diagnosis of abnormal motor development early in life.

Thirty-nine of the 51 children had Type 1 and 2 developmental courses. Thus, the majority show normal development. In 7 children, cerebral palsy was diagnosed (spastic diplegia in particular); in 5, mental retardation was present; all belonged to Type 4 (and 3).

The various types of neuromotor development did not show any differences in terms of social data, such as sex, parental age, income, housing, number of siblings, or employment of the father. Types 2 and 4 showed differences according to obstetrical optimality only.

3.2 Marital Relations of Parents and Child Development

Results of the Giessen-Test, which was given shortly after the child's birth and 1 and 3 years later, could be compared in detail in 29 couples (Beckmann, 1986, 1992). A special method of analysis was developed in which the results were entered into a diagram for comparison with data from other clinical groups and controls. Information on the self-concept of the husband and of the wife - how the husband saw his wife and how she judged him - were analyzed using five scales of variables such as social resonance, dominance, controlling, basic attitude, openness, and permeability. Various categories of couples could be identified, and 10 of these were ranked in a complementary and circular way. Comparing controls and problematic marriages, it became apparent which combinations were the most frequent and which changes obviously occurred over time.

The Giessen-Test was developed for use in different settings, for example, in evaluation of psychotherapeutic measures. It could be shown to be of help in analyzing marital relations. Extensive data are available from studies on different groups of patients (Beckmann et al., 1983). The method gives quantitative data, but also offers some insight into psychodynamic processes.

After the birth of an infant at risk, disturbed relationships could be seen concerning self-concept and alternative-concept in 30% of couples assessed with the Giessen-Test. One year later, this was true in almost half the couples when corresponding categories of test results were compared. In males, the number of roles "typical" for a disturbed marital relationship increased from 14% to 45%; in females, from 34% to 66%. The most frequent role of the husband after the child was born could be characterized as "self-realization with acknowledgement." On the other hand "fatalistic resignation" was seen more often in mothers. Thus, in the fathers, a tendency to withdraw in some sense from the family (Hunziker & Largo, 1986) and to be less involved than before became apparent, whereas the stress put on the mothers clearly increased over time. There is much variability concerning individual couples, of course. However, depressivity in mothers can be seen more often in children who develop less favorably or are retarded and handicapped.

If the development of an infant at risk turned out to be normal, marital conflicts obviously occurred less frequently. On the other hand, in parents of children with abnormal neurological findings, problems with relationship and concepts or roles were almost always observed, and they increased over the 3-year period of observation (data from the 5-year follow-up still have to be analyzed). Another finding was that reduced neurological optimality scores in the neonate correlated negatively with the role of "mother of a difficult child." It seemed that mothers were less resigned if abnormal development was present from birth, although, at the same time, they were more often left alone by their partners. Infants with abnormal neurological findings during the neonatal period turned out to have better developmental progress if the relationship between their parents was not impaired in any way and could be called normal in comparison with controls.

The results of the REP test (which was administered in some couples only) showed a high level of agreement with other findings (Böker et al., 1984). Alterations of social relationships in the families assessed could also be shown. However, we did not use the REP test further because it was time-consuming and results did not add a new dimension to our picture of child and family.

3.3 Family Dynamics and Child Development

In 54 families, it was possible to carry out a comprehensive follow-up study when the children were 3 years old (75% of the original sample). At this time, we were particularly interested in the social network of the family and their resources in terms of relatives and friends. Using a questionnaire similar to that used when the child was 1-year-old, economic conditions, life events, and psychosocial support from extended family or friends were assessed. In a semistructured interview during the follow-up examination of the child, performed by a trained psychologist, the following subjects and questions were among those addressed: How mother (and father) experienced their child's development, how affective relationship could be judged, if educational measures were oriented toward social norms, and how confident parents felt regarding their childrearing styles. The interviews were rated immediately afterwards by the psychologist together with a physician who had examined and tested the child. Data were processed with factor analysis, and eight factors (Sc1 to Sc8) could be extracted (see Table 2), together with additional variables (V1 to V3) concerning norm orientation, educational security, and parenting (see Table 3). Results of Scheffé's tests are given descriptively only, because clusters are dependent on factors. Therefore, z-transformed mean values, standard deviations, and F values are not given in detail (Meyer & Pauli, 1990).

Table 2. *Factor Analysis of Interview Ratings*

Factor		Factor loading
1	**Involvement of father - orientation toward him**	
	Father takes part in caring and education	.87
	Child plays often with father	.77
	Father is oriented toward child	.75
	Agreement between partners concerning education	.73
	Mother involves father in relationship with child	.70
	Child addresses father with problems	.63
		(Alpha = .86)
2	**Mother feels restricted by the child**	
	Mother feels her need restricted by child's activities	.78
	Self-supporting activities	.74
	Social behavior	.69
	Autonomous development	.61
	Feeding behavior	.59
	Motor activities	.13
	Sleeping behavior	.47
	Toilet training	.46
		(Alpha = .80)

(table continues)

Table 2.   *(continued)*

3	**Intentions and activities of child are acknowledged**	
	Mother oriented toward child	
	Child's intention and wishes in motor activities	.68
	Play facilities oriented to child's needs	-.62
	Mother accepts restriction by child's behavior	-.61
	Intention and wishes are acknowledged in toilet training	.59
	Mother oriented exclusively toward child	.51
	Intention and wishes are acknowledged in feeding behavior	.51
		(Alpha = .76)
4	**Parent-child relationship undetermined "laissez faire"**	
	Sleeping behavior according to child's wishes	-.81
	Intention and wishes are acknowledged in sleeping	.81
	Child all night in parents' bed	.67
	Education characterized as "laissez faire"	-.50
	For reinforcement, concessions never used	-.50
	For punishment, deprivation never used	-.43
	Never physical punishment	-.40
		(Alpha = .76)
5	**Affectionate needs of mother and child**	
	Mother and child often show affectionate behavior	.89
	Mother feels the child has affectionate needs	.79
	Affection is given because mother acknowledges child's needs	.64
	For reinforcement, affectionate behavior is used	.61
	Affection is oriented toward reinforcement	.59
		(Alpha = .84)
6	**Child self-determined**	
	Child plays often outdoors	.65
	Child looks for activities by him- or herself	-.62
	Child always plays with concentration	.50
	Child plays seldom with mother	-.53
	Child is able to verbalize needs	.47
		(Alpha = .68)

(table continues)

Table 2.   *(continued)*

7	**Autonomy of child is neglected**	
	Child is isolated because of overprotection	
	Intentions or wishes of child for autonomy not acknowleged	-.73
	Child seems to be isolated	.62
	Mother is overanxious	.49
	Intentions and wishes are not acknowledged in social behavior	.41
	Intentions and wishes are not acknowledged in autonomous activities	.40
	Mother anxious in regard to independent motor activities	.40
		(Alpha = .74)
8	**Childrearing style nonauthoritarian, verbally oriented**	
	Affectionate behavior oriented toward consolation	.71
	Punishment by verbal admonition	.66
	Reinforcement by verbal rewarding	.50
		(Alpha = .70)

Note. The factors explain 57.5% of variance. Percentage of variance per factor: 1 = 14.7%, 2 = 13.8%, 3 = 13.8%, 4 = 13.29%, 5 = 12.9%, 6 = 12.0%, 7 = 10.1%, 8 = 9.59%.

Table 3.   *Factors and Variables Used for Characterization of Family Types*

Comparing the child with other children generally important	(V1)
Childrearing style and management of educational problems definite	(V2)
Education generally overcontrolled	(V3)
Involvement of father, orientation toward father	(Sc1)
Mother feels restricted by the child	(Sc2)
Intention and activities of child acknowledged, mother oriented toward child	(Sc3)
Parent-child relationship undetermined, "laissez faire" education	(Sc4)
Affectionate needs in mother and child	(Sc5)
Child self-determined	(Sc6)
Autonomy of child neglected, child isolated because of overprotection	(Sc7)
Childrearing style verbally oriented	(Sc8)

Comparison with other families was for parents in general important or not; childrearing styles and management of educational problems were secure or not; education was generally overcontrolled or not; father was involved in decisions and gave directions or not; mother felt herself restricted by the child or not; intentions and activities of the child were respected or not; the mother's interest was mainly concerned with the child or not; the mother-child relationship did not set limits and could be characterized as "laissez-faire" or not; mother and child expressed wishes for more affection or not; the child was seen as self-determined or not; wishes for autonomy were neglected and the child was isolated because of overprotection or not; the educational style was oriented toward verbal instructions or not.

Further analysis of data with regard to these family types (Meyer & Pauli, 1990) showed no differences for socioeconomic situation, stressors, or specific life events as noticed in the interviews. However, differences became significant as far as social resources were concerned as well as possibilities of parents to have contact outside the family. Type I families especially showed what could be called an inward orientation, whereas Type III seemed to be fully integrated with regard to their social relationships.

Differences in family dynamics are obvious for these "types," and different behavior as well as interactions apparently influence the development of the child. Although it is impossible to draw any causal conclusions, some correlations should be regarded as important influences in shaping the individual child and his or her personality.

In 30 unselected families with 5-year-old children who were given the same type of questionnaire, interview, and analysis, the "types" mentioned could also be found: 13 families were regarded as "individualized" and engaged (Type III); there were 13 families similar to Type II that were characterized as "depressive" or insecure; and 9 families were called "authoritarian" or careless in this sample (Figure 2). When comparing motor development of children as assessed by neurological examination and the MOT test in these "normal" families, it could be shown to be less favorable in families called "depressive," obviously because they did not reinforce spontaneous activity and used more restrictive measures of education (Legner, 1993).

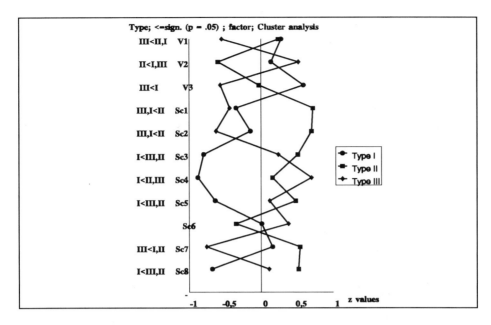

Figure 2. Profile of family "types."
   Note. Cluster analysis differentiated three "types" of families
   from interview data, characterized by specific variables and
   factors: Type I (n=19) = "authoritarian"; Type II (n=21) =
   "depressive"; Type III (n=19) = "individualized."

3.4 Consequences for Measures of Early Intervention

In 50 children in our sample, correlations between developmental progress
during the first year of life (assessed by neurological examination at
gestational age of 38 and 42 weeks and at 3 and 12 months respectively)
and their psychosocial situation (as reflected by an interview with the
parents when the child was 1-year-old) could be analyzed in detail (Böker
et al., 1984). In controlling for perinatal optimality, we tried to gain some
information about variables that could predict the developmental course of
a given child. The child's developmental status at 1 year was assessed with
the Bayley Mental Scale and Behavioral Record as well as the optimality
score from neurological examination (Stork, 1985). These results were
highly correlated ($r = .64$), which might be explained by similar variables,
because items concerned with motor behavior are important in both
methods: developmental test and neurological assessment.

The social variables analyzed consisted of economic conditions on the one hand, and of social resources on the other. The latter included factors such as time sharing between parents, contacts outside the family, or support from friends and relatives. Factor analysis of interview data resulted in classification of variables to these categories. Multiple regression then showed some significant correlations with developmental outcome: Less favorable developmental progress was seen if relatively old parents had lived together for only a short period of time; another less positive influence was seen if the mother intended to work or actually had a job, which, in turn, was often connected with more economic stress for the family. However, more refined analysis of data also revealed that the fact that a mother goes to work may have negative as well as positive consequences depending on other variables and on the child's condition or developmental progress (Pauli-Pott, 1989).

Apart from these psychosocial conditions, neurological optimality in the neonate was of minor prognostic significance. This was not true, however, in infants with a well-diagnosed handicap such as cerebral palsy or mental retardation. In clearly impaired infants, there was reduced optimality in the neonatal neurological examination, and findings at 3 and 12 months were similar. Thus the prognosis was possible soon after birth, and consequences for early intervention could be drawn at an early age. In addition, family dynamics have to be taken into account: Early intervention should be directed toward the special needs of families and parents. Awareness of the various types of family reactions and interactions may be important in this respect.

4 Discussion

The data of our follow-up study stress the clinical impression of different developmental courses in regard to neuromotor functions of infants at risk for pre- and perinatal complications (Touwen, 1993). In quantifying the results of neurological examinations by optimality scores, various developmental curves could be extracted by statistical methods in congruence with clinical experiences.

Comparing obstetrical and neonatal data according to their predictive value during the first years of life, only a few correlations could be shown, except for children with obvious developmental problems (Pauli-Pott & Neuhäuser, 1992). Therefore, definite conclusions are not always possible from an optimality score or from the neonatal neurological examination. This reflects the need for a continuous follow up in all and especially in at-risk children to assess for motor delay and signs of cerebral palsy or mental retardation as soon as possible.

The impact of social factors on motor and mental development could be shown by various approaches at different times during follow up. These results are in line with other authors, for example, with the Mannheim study in which a clear-cut separation of biological and social factors was possible (Laucht et al., 1992). We have been able to show that various family types are characterized by their educational habits and social relations among other variables. These types are found in the at-risk population but also in control families. Obviously they reflect some "traits" important for family dynamics and parent-child interaction as well as for social connections with extended family and friends.

In comparing neuromotor development of children with family types, some relations have been found. However, they should in no way be regarded as causal. In some way, the family climate may encourage children or restrict their motor behavior, in this way enhancing or impairing developmental processes (Pauli-Pott, 1989). Other studies have also shown that unfavorable psychosocial conditions may increase biological risks, whereas children with developmental disabilities may gain substantially from positive and rewarding interactions with parents and siblings.

The results in our at-risk population show that favorable environmental influences are found more often in children with normal or near normal development even after perinatal complications, and that less favorable family dynamics are seen more often in children with some kind of motor or mental impairment. Thus, there is a need to identify which families are to be helped and supported at an early stage in order to improve their interactions and family situation.

Starting from various approaches, it has been possible to obtain some indication of the importance of interactive-dynamic and psychosocial factors during early development in our clearly heterogeneous group of children. This holds especially true for infants at risk because of pre- and perinatal complications, if the developmental diagnosis cannot be given with a high degree of certainty, or if handicapping conditions are present. Obviously, interrelations are complex, and causal connections difficult to ascertain. However, because of the difficulty in dealing with a huge amount of data, we have restricted our interest to variables of family dynamics and interactions that seem significant for the psychosocial development of the child (Beckmann et al., 1989) and have major implications for all measures of early intervention. Family dynamics are to be considered if early intervention is organized to be successful and helpful for parents, child, and family. Although there is need for well-controlled studies (Lambert et al.,

1993), we have many experiences from practical work over the last 20 years that early intervention is successful and helpful; that the process of integration and normalization can be enhanced. It is essential not only to consider biological data but also to analyze in detail parental relations, parent-child interaction, family dynamics, and other psychosocial factors that influence a child's motor and mental development.

Measures necessary in a given situation have to be oriented toward these findings to provide the necessary help for individual children, their parents, and their families.

Note

The data from our follow-up study were analyzed in cooperation with A. Bäcker, D. Beckmann, A. Meyer, and U. Pauli-Pott.

References

Bäcker, A., Pauli-Pott, U., Beckmann, D., & Neuhäuser, G. (1992). Unterschiedliche neuromotorische Entwicklungsverläufe nach obstetrischen Komplikationen. *Kindheit & Entwicklung, 1*, 82-84.

Beckmann, D. (1986). Ehepaarbeziehung im Giessen-Test nach Geburt eines Risikokindes. *Psychotherapie und medizinische Psychologie, 36*, 159-166.

Beckmann, D. (1992). Ehepaarbeziehung im Giessen-Test drei Jahre nach Geburt eines Risikokindes. *Kindheit & Entwicklung, 1*, 85-91.

Beckmann, D., Brähler, E., & Richter, H. E. (1983). *Der Giessen-Test (GT). Ein Test für Individual- und Gruppendiagnostik. Handbuch* (3rd ed.). Bern: Huber.

Beckmann, D., Neuhäuser, G., & Pauli, U. (1989). Psychologische Determinanten neurologischer Symptome und neurologischer Syndrome bei Kleinkindern. In P. Jacobi (Ed.), *Psychologie in der Neurologie. Jahrbuch der medizinischen Psychologie* (Vol. 2, pp. 138-156). Berlin: Springer.

Böker, H., Gerlach, I., Beckmann, D., & Neuhäuser, G. (1984). Probleme der Eltern nach der Geburt eines Risikokindes. Psychologische Beziehungsdiagnostik und klinische Erfahrungen. In J. Scheer & E. Brähler (Eds.), *Beiträge zur medizinischen Psychologie* (pp. 157-164). Berlin: Springer.

Hunziker, U. A., & Largo, R. H. (1986). Betreuung von Risikokindern: Eltern-Kind-Beziehung im ersten Lebensjahr. *Monatsschrift für Kinderheilkunde, 134*, 246-252.

Kalverboer, A. L., Hopkins, B., & Geuze, R. (1993). *Motor development in early and later childhood: Longitudinal approaches.* Cambridge: Cambridge University Press.

Lambert, J. L., Piret, M., Scohy, Ch., & Lambert-Boite, F. (1993). Wirkungen der Früherziehung auf die Entwicklung der Kinder. Anwendung zweier Entwicklungsindices. *Vierteljahrsschrift für Heilpädagogik & Nachbargebiete, 62*, 29-40.

Laucht, M., Esser, G., Schmidt, M. H., Ihle, W., Löffler, W., Stöhr, R. M., Weindrich, D., & Weinel, H. (1993). "Risikokinder": Zur Bedeutung biologischer und psychosozialer Risiken für die kindliche Entwicklung in den beiden ersten Lebensjahren. *Praxis der Kinderpsychologie und Kinderpsychiatrie, 41*, 274-285.

Legner, A. M. (1993). *Die Beziehung familiärer Strukturen zum neuromotorischen und kognitiven Reifezustand gesundgeborener 5-jähriger Kinder.* Unpublished doctoral dissertation, University of Gießen.

Meyer, A., & Pauli, U. (1990). Entwicklungsverlauf und Familienklima bei Risikokindern. In I. Seiffge-Krenke (Ed.), *Krankheitsverarbeitung bei Kindern und Jugendlichen. Jahrbuch der medizinischen Psychologie* (Vol. 4, pp. 186-204). Berlin: Springer.

Pauli-Pott, U. (1989). *Motorische, kognitive und emotionale Entwicklung perinatal beeinträchtigter Kinder.* Unpublished doctoral dissertation, University of Gießen.

Pauli-Pott, U., & Neuhäuser, G. (1992). Entwicklungsprozesse nach perinatalen Komplikationen im ersten Lebensjahr. *Kindheit & Entwicklung, 1*, 77-81.

Prechtl, H. F. R. (1968). Neurological findings in newborn infants after pre- and paranatal complications. In J. H. P. Jonxis, H. K. A. Visser, & J. A. Troelstra (Eds.), *Aspects of prematurity and dysmaturity. Nutricia Symposium* (pp. 303-321). Leiden: Stenfert Kroese.

Prechtl, H. F. R. (1980). The optimality concept. *Early Human Development, 4*, 201-205.

Prechtl, H. F. R., & Beintema, D. J. (1976). *Die neurologische Untersuchung des reifen Neugeborenen.* Stuttgart: Thieme.

Stave, U., & Ruvalo, C. (1980). Neurological development in very-low-birthweight infants. Application of a standardized examination and Prechtl's optimality concept in routine evaluations. *Early Human Development, 4*, 229-241.

Stork, Ch. (1985). Zur Aussagekraft entwicklungsdiagnostischer Verfahren bei ehemals perinatal beeinträchtigten Kindern im Alter von 12 Monaten. *Klinische Pädiatrie, 197*, 458-466.

Touwen, B. C. L. (1982). *Die Untersuchung von Kindern mit geringen neurologischen Funktionsstörungen.* Stuttgart: Thieme.

Touwen, B. C. L. (1993). Longitudinal studies on motor development: Developmental neurological considerations. In A. L. Kalverboer, B. Hopkins, & R. Geuze (Eds.), *Motor development in early and later childhood: Longitudinal approaches* (pp. 15-34). Cambridge: Cambridge University Press.

Wishart, D. (1984). *Clustan* (3rd ed.). Stuttgart: Fischer.

M. Brambring, H. Rauh, and A. Beelmann (Eds.) (1996). *Early childhood intervention: Theory, evaluation, and practice.* (pp. 234-264). Berlin, New York: de Gruyter.

Social Support and Coping in Families of Children at Risk for Developmental Disabilities

Carol M. Trivette, Carl J. Dunst, and Deborah Hamby

1 Introduction

For the past 10 years, we have been engaged in a line of research examining the influences of social support on the adaptation of parents to the birth and rearing of a child with a developmental disability or a condition placing a child at risk for a developmental disability. Much of our work has been conducted at the Family, Infant and Preschool Program (FIPP), a family support and early intervention program located in Morganton, North Carolina, in the foothills of the Blue Ridge Mountains. This line of research was instigated in order to increase our understanding of the factors that influence parental responses and adaptation to the birth and rearing of a child at risk for poor developmental outcomes. The major focus of our research has been the study of variables that can be translated into intervention strategies that will produce positive effects and outcomes. The purpose of this chapter is to present a number of findings from several studies in which we have specifically examined the relationship between social support and parental well-being.

We began this line of research with a rather naive understanding of the relationship between social support and parental adaptation, and simplistic measures of social support. In our first study, social support was measured by availability of support and satisfaction with support (Dunst et al., 1986a). In each subsequent study, we attempted to refine our conceptual model and methodological techniques. Throughout this line of research, we have examined a number of outcome variables, including family functioning, parent-child interaction, and child development.

This chapter is divided into three sections: In the first section, we describe a social systems framework that has guided our research efforts. As part of the description of this model, we summarize research data from a series of studies that examine the relationships among intrafamily factors and external influences that affect parent functioning. In the second section, we summarize empirical findings from our own work that has involved the conduct of both cross-sectional and longitudinal studies. In the cross-sectional studies, we identify the social support variables most likely to influence parental well-being. From a prospective longitudinal study, we present results that examine whether the occurrence of a life event influences the maternal well-being in the predicted ways, and how maternal coping styles and multiple components of social support relate to maternal psychological well-being and both positive and negative affect. In the final section, we briefly reflect upon what we have learned from our research, and discuss what we believe are the next important unanswered questions.

2   A Social Systems Research Framework

The evolution of the social system model used to guide our research can be traced through a number of papers and reports, including Dunst (1982, 1983, 1985, 1986a, 1986b); Dunst and Trivette (1984, 1986, 1988a, 1988b); Dunst, Trivette, and Deal (1988); Trivette et al. (1986); and Trivette and Dunst (1992). The model draws heavily from several conceptual frameworks, including human ecology (Bronfenbrenner, 1979, 1986; Cochran & Brassard, 1979), social support theory (Cohen & Syme, 1985), and help-seeking theory (DePaulo et al., 1983). These three separate but complementary theoretical orientations indicate that ecological settings and social units, and persons and events within them, do not operate in isolation but influence each other both directly and indirectly, so that changes in one unit or subunit reverberate and impact upon members of other units.

Social support theory attempts to describe the properties of social units, the linkages among units, and how provision of support by network members promotes individual, family, and community well-being (Cohen & Syme, 1985). Social support refers to a "number of different aspects of social relationships" that have increasingly been found to have positive effects on various health outcomes (House & Kahn, 1985, p. 84). Human ecology emphasizes the interactions and accommodations between a developing person and his or her animate and inanimate environment, and how events in different ecological settings directly and indirectly affect the behavior of the person (Bronfenbrenner, 1979; Cochran & Brassard, 1979). For example, Bronfenbrenner (1979) argues "whether parents can perform effectively in the child-rearing roles within the family depends upon role demands, stresses, and *supports* emanating from other settings" (p. 7). Help-seeking theory examines the conditions that affect a decision to seek help, from whom help is sought, and the nature of help-seeking and help-giving exchanges (Dunst & Trivette, 1987, 1988c). Research on the relationship between help-seeking, help-giving, and social support has increasingly pointed to the importance of informal social networks as sources of help and assistance in response to both normative and nonnormative life events (see Wilcox & Birkel, 1983). Collectively, these three theoretical orientations provide a useful framework for studying how resources and support either directly or indirectly influence well-being.

2.1 Social Support Construct

The term social support tends to be operationalized differently depending upon the perspective of the researcher interested in the construct. There is, however, general consensus that the social support domain is multidimensional in nature, and that differing aspects of support have differential influences on individual and family functioning. Conceptually and operationally, the social support domain is comprised of distinct *components* and specific *dimensions* within components (Cohen et al., 1985; House & Kahn, 1985).

A number of conceptual frameworks have been proposed for specifying the components of support, their dimensional features, and the relationships among components (Barrera, 1986; Cohen et al., 1985; House & Kahn, 1985; Kahn et al., 1987; Tardy, 1985; Turner, 1983). An integration of available evidence suggests that the social support domain is comprised of five major components (relational support, structural support, constitutional support, functional support, and support satisfaction) and various dimensions within components. Table 1 lists a number of components within each social support dimension.

Relational support refers to the existence and quantity of social relationships, including marital and work status, number of persons in one's personal social network, and membership in such social organizations as a church. The existence of social relationships, as well as the breadth of these relationships, sets the occasion for supportive exchanges. Relational support is oftentimes described in terms of the persons, groups, and organizations that are important to individuals (Wills, 1985).

Structural support refers to a number of quantitative aspects of personal social networks, including physical proximity to social network members, duration and stability of relationships, frequency of contacts with network members, and reciprocity (give and take) in social relationships (see, especially, Hall & Wellman, 1985). The various dimensions of structural support are designed in ways that capture the specific features of social relationships that are thought to be crucial for interactions to be supportive in nature (Gottlieb, 1981).

Table 1.   *Examples of Dimensions for the Five Social Support Components*

Components	Examples of dimensions
Relational	Marital status Work status Network size Membership in social organizations
Structural	Network density Frequency of contacts Multiplexity Length of relationship Reciprocity Consistency Duration of ties
Constitutional	Indicated need Availability Congruence between need and resources
Functional	Source of support Type of support (e.g., emotional, informational) Quantity of support (e.g., utilization) Quality of support (e.g., willingness, dependability)
Satisfaction	Helpfulness Usefulness

Constitutional support refers to the indicated need for help and the congruence or match between needed support and the type of support offered or provided. The term constitutional is used to refer to resources that a person believes are basic and essential for maintaining or improving his or her health and well-being; hence, it reflects a highly personalized view of what is important and needed. The notion of constitutional support has evolved from our own work on explicating the nature of supportive exchanges, and has emerged as one of the most important determinants of positive influences on family functioning (Dunst & Leet, 1987; Dunst, Leet, & Trivette, 1988; Dunst & Trivette, 1988f). That is, the influences of social support seem to be greatest when resources are offered in response to an indicated need for support, and when the resources offered match what is specifically requested.

Functional support refers to the type, quantity, and quality of aid and assistance. Types of support include, but are not limited to, informational, emotional, material, and instrumental (e.g., child care) aid and assistance that is offered by others. Quantity of support refers to how much support is provided by network members. Quality of support refers to the manner in which support is requested from and provided by network members (e.g., willingness of relatives to provide child care in an emergency).

Support satisfaction refers to the extent to which aid and assistance is viewed as helpful and useful. During and at the completion of a social exchange, people generally evaluate subjectively the nature of the support provided by others. Unless a person is subjectively satisfied with the support he or she is provided, the influences of support are diminished considerably.

Figure 1 shows the potential connections among the different components of the social support domain. This conceptualization is derived, in part, from the work of Hall and Wellman (1985) and House and Kahn (1985), and has evolved from our own work on explicating the components of the social support construct (Dunst & Trivette, 1988b, 1988f, 1990). The existence or quantity of relational support is viewed as a necessary condition for and hence a partial determinant of: (a) defining needs (constitutional support), (b) the structural characteristics of one's social network, and (c) the types of help and assistance available from network members. Similarly, both the need for support and network structure may partially determine the particular types of support that are sought and offered. Finally, the types of support provided, and especially the relationship between constitutional and functional support, will in part determine the degree to which one finds the aid and assistance helpful, and thus the extent to which one is satisfied with the support.

There is a growing body of evidence indicating that social support directly and indirectly influences parent, family, and child behavior, including *personal and familial health* (Cobb & Kasl, 1977; Cohen & Syme, 1985; Embry, 1980; Gore, 1985; Kasl & Cobb, 1979; McCubbin et al., 1980; Mitchell & Trickett, 1980; Patterson & McCubbin, 1983), *parenting attitudes and behavior* (Colletta, 1981; Crnic et al., 1983; Crnic et al., 1984; Crnic et al., 1986; Crockenberg, 1981, 1985; Dunst, 1985; Dunst & Trivette, 1984, 1986, 1988b; Dunst et al., 1986a, 1986b; Dunst, Trivette, & Cross, 1988; Epstein, 1980; Hetherington et al., 1976, 1978; Wandersman & Unger, 1983; Wandersman et al., 1980; Weinraub & Wolf, 1983), *parental perceptions of child functioning* (Affleck et al., 1986; Dunst & Trivette, 1984; Dunst et al., 1986a, 1986b; Lazer & Darlington, 1982; Trivette & Dunst, 1987), and *child behavior and development* (Crnic et al., 1983; Crnic et al., 1984; Crnic et al., 1986; Crockenberg, 1981; Dunst, 1985; Dunst & Trivette, 1984; Dunst et al., 1986a, 1986b; Dunst, Trivette, & Cross, 1988; Trivette & Dunst, 1987).

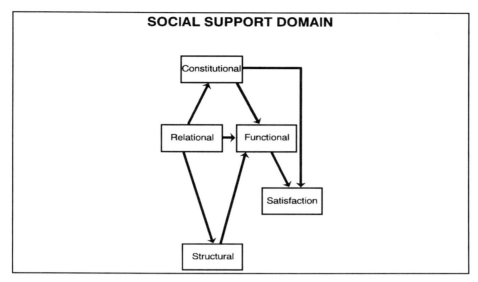

Figure 1. A conceptual framework for defining the major components of social support and their separate dimensions.

2.2 Intrapersonal Coping

The ways that individuals and families deal with and respond to different environmental events vary greatly. One factor that influences how individuals and families adapt to both normative and nonnormative life events has to do with the coping strategies that a person uses to respond or process the event or condition.

Coping is defined by Lazarus and Folkman (1984) as "the cognitive and behavioral efforts to manage external and/or internal demands that are appraised as taxing or exceeding the resources of the person" (p. 141). This definition of coping suggests that there are many possible responses or strategies that an individual may use in a situation, and that no particular strategy is better than any other. The value of any particular strategy depends on whether the strategy influences the well-being of the individual or family.

A number of taxonomies of coping strategies have been developed by researchers over the past decade (Antonovsky, 1979; Billings & Moos, 1981; Lazarus & Folkman, 1984; Pearlin & Schooler, 1978; Stone et al., 1988). Stone and Neale (1984) have developed eight categories of coping that are found in most lists of the coping strategies. These strategies include seeking social support from friends, families, and so forth; accepting the situation and feeling that nothing can be done about it; trying to see the problem from a different perspective; expressing emotions in response to the situation; seeking spiritual support; engaging in an activity in order to relax and take one's mind off the situation; and taking direct action to deal with the situation.

Much work has been done that examines the relationship between the use of coping strategies and a person's response to a particular situation or event. A number of studies have been descriptive in nature, simply trying to document the strategies employed to cope with a situation (Affleck et al., 1991; Folkman & Lazarus, 1980; Lazarus & Folkman, 1984; Rook et al., 1991; Stone & Neale, 1984; Thoits, 1991), while another area of research literature focuses on the relationships between various coping strategies and a number of outcomes, including psychological distress (Affleck et al., 1991; Rook et al., 1991; Thoits, 1991). For example, Affleck and his colleagues (1991) examined the influence of coping strategies on parental well-being and adaptation of mothers with infants in neonatal intensive care units. In this longitudinal work, they have shown that a number of coping strategies predict differences in both maternal well-being and the development of the children.

2.3 A Paradigmatic Framework

While we recognize the importance of social support and coping as factors affecting parent, family, and child functioning, we also fully recognize the influence of other extra- and intrafamily characteristics as explanatory, mediating, and moderating variables. Consequently, these factors have been examined as part of our research. This multiple determinant approach that we have taken may be stated in the following paradigmatic framework:

$$B = f(F, I, S, C, E)$$

in which B is an outcome or criterion measure (e.g., parent, family, or child functioning), and the relationship between B and the variables on the right side of the equation is of the form B varies as a function of F (parent and family characteristics), I (intrapersonal coping), S (social support), C (child characteristics), and E (environmental characteristics). Accordingly, one would expect to find *parental family characteristics* (parental age and education level, SES, income, etc.), *intrapersonal coping* (coping style), *social support* (relational, structural, functional, etc.), *child characteristics* (age, sex, level of functioning, etc.), and *environmental* factors (living arrangements, neighborhood characteristics, etc.) having both cumulative and interactive effects on behavior and development.

Figure 2 depicts the model we are currently using to assess the effects of several major categories of predictor variables on well-being and parent functioning. The social support domain and relationships among the five components of support are as described above (see Figure 1). Both parent and family characteristics, including intrapersonal coping, are considered partial determinants of support (Gore, 1985; Gottlieb, 1981; Heller et al., 1978; Holohan & Wilcox, 1978; Mitchell & Trickett, 1980). Parent and family characteristics are seen as mutually dependent, although parent characteristics are seen as exerting a greater influence on family characteristics rather than vice versa (Duncan et al., 1972; Sewell & Hauser, 1975). All three sets of variables (parent, family, and social support) are viewed as partial determinants of adaptation (Richman & Flaherty, 1985; Roskin, 1982; Shapiro, 1983; Tolsdorf, 1976) used in response to both normative (e.g., marriage) and nonnormative (e.g., birth of a child with a disability) life events (McCubbin et al., 1982; McGuire & Gottlieb, 1979). The combination of all five sets of variables directly and indirectly influence parent health and well-being (Cohen & Syme, 1985), as well as a number of aspects of behavior and development (Affleck et al., 1986; Colletta, 1981; Lazar & Darlington, 1982; Patterson & McCubbin, 1983).

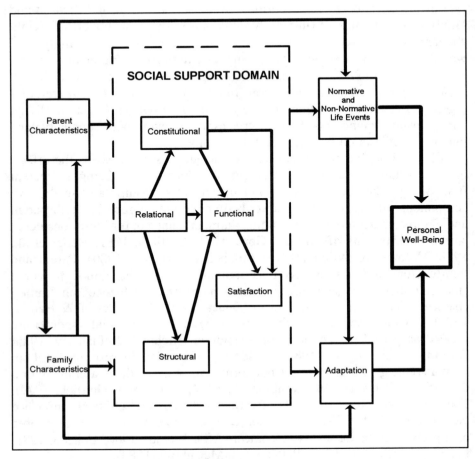

Figure 2. Conceptual framework for assessing the direct and indirect
influences of parent and family characteristics, social support,
and life events on personal health and well-being.

3   Empirical Evidence Supporting Our Social Systems Model

Two sets of results are presented in this section illustrating the relationship
between social support, coping, and personal well-being. The first set of
data is from eight cross-sectional studies demonstrating that social support
is highly related to well-being, and that the effects of support can lessen the
negative impact associated with the rearing of a child at risk for a poor

developmental outcome. The second set of data is from a prospective longitudinal study of pregnant women through which we are trying to disentangle the relationships between social support and coping and the occurrence of life events that we considered nonnormative (pregnancy-related complications, birth of a child with a developmental disability, poor socioeconomic conditions). The latter study specifically allowed us to assess whether social support and coping in fact buffered mothers from experiencing extremely negative responses to life events they deemed potentially harmful.

3.1 Cross-Sectional Evidence: Method

Subjects. The participants in the eight studies reported here were the families enrolled in FIPP, and included parents of preschoolers who were mentally retarded, physically disabled, or developmentally and environmentally at risk. Table 2 displays the means and standard deviations of the background characteristics for the families involved in these eight studies. The mothers and fathers were, on the average, 28 and 31 years of age, respectively. The average number of years of school completed was between 11 and 12 for both mothers and fathers. Their socioeconomic status scores (Hollingshead, 1975) were between 28 and 31, indicating that the majority of the families were predominantly from lower to middle SES backgrounds. The families' average gross monthly income was about $1,100. The average chronological age of the children was 34 months. The children's average Developmental Quotients (DQ) score was 64. Overall, the mean percentage of children with mental retardation was 44.6%; the mean percentage of children with physical disabilities was 31%; and the mean percentage of children who were considered at risk was 24.4%.

Procedure. Data were gathered from either or both a combination of self-report measures and in-home interviews. Indices of social support were obtained from a number of self-report rating scales and an extensive interview protocol with the subjects. Parental well-being was measured using several different self-report rating scales. Demographic information about the families, and diagnostic and developmental information about the children were also obtained.

The *social support* measures employed in the various studies included the Family Support Scale (FSS; Dunst et al., 1984), Maternal Social Support Index (MSI; Pascoe et al., 1981), Parent Role Scale (PRS; Gallagher et al., 1981), Psychosocial Kinship Network Inventory (PKI; Pattison et al., 1975), and Support Functions Scale (SFS; Dunst & Trivette, 1988e). Each of these

Table 2. *Means and Standard Deviations of Background Variables Across Eight Investigations*

Background characteristics	Study 1 (N = 51)		Study 2 (N = 132)		Study 3 (N = 106)		Study 4 (N = 40)		Study 5 (N = 65)		Study 6 (N = 84)		Study 7 (N = 35)		Study 8 (N = 45)	
	M	SD	M	SD	M	SD	M	SD	M	SD	M	SD	M	SD	M	SD
Mother's age	28.11	5.56	29.24	7.81	28.28	6.90	27.49	5.29	28.23	5.12	28.02	7.12	27.76	6.00	28.64	5.76
Father's age	30.86	6.92	32.55	7.49	32.20	8.07	31.02	6.62	30.85	5.56	32.26	8.17	31.19	8.13	---b	---b
Mother's education	12.18	2.03	11.77	2.61	12.30	2.54	11.95	2.57	12.14	2.68	12.11	2.63	11.64	2.05	12.49	2.55
Father's education	11.77	2.23	11.69	2.89	12.34	3.17	12.10	2.62	11.74	2.45	12.21	3.23	11.44	3.07	---b	---b
Socioeconomic status[a]	28.37	9.74	29.10	13.39	31.22	12.45	30.88	13.28	31.42	12.32	30.27	18.25	29.22	12.40	30.04	14.51
Gross monthly income	1,153	719	1,269	770	1,316	720	---b	---b	1,436	848	1,376	837	1,305	759	1,285	784
Child's age (in months)	27.05	13.55	36.07	13.25	39.26	21.72	27.47	16.67	40.71	13.44	31.81	19.51	29.46	17.42	38.42	18.36
Child's DQ	57.92	29.37	62.62	26.52	60.87	34.03	58.75	31.39	60.94	28.35	69.81	31.54	56.58	27.63	53.53	33.92

[a]Hollingshead, 1975.
[b]Not measured in this study.

scales measures one or more of the components of social support shown in Table 1 above, and indices derived from each scale were used as measures of a number of aspects of support from the respondent's spouse/mate, blood and marriage relatives, friends, church members, and so forth. The various indices used as measures of social support included the number of persons in the respondent's social network, the total number of persons who provided different types of support, ratings of willingness of network members to provide support, intrafamily support (role sharing), and ratings of the degree to which support was helpful and useful. Additionally, the independent contributions of maternal work status (working vs. not working outside the home) and/or marital status (married vs. not married) were also assessed in the majority of studies as indices of relational support.

The dependent measures assessing *psychological well-being* included several stress and well-being scales, including the Questionnaire on Resources and Stress, Emotional and Physical Health Subscale (QRS; Holroyd, 1974, 1985), the Psychological Well-Being Index (PWI; Bradburn & Caplovitz, 1965), and the Personal Well-Being Index (WBI; Trivette & Dunst, 1985). Global indices of well-being were used as measures of physical and emotional health. Each scale includes items that tapped the respondent's assessment of strains, feelings of depression, a sense of euphoria, physical energy level, and so forth that, taken together, form a basis for an overall measure of psychological well-being.

Methods of Analysis. The data from each study were analyzed by hierarchical regression analysis (Cohen & Cohen, 1983) by sets. This procedure yields information about the unique, nonshared variance accounted for in the dependent measure(s) by the individual independent variables, and thus aids in the substantive interpretation of the effects of these variables. The order of entry of the variables in the hierarchical regression analyses was as follows: parent characteristics, family characteristics, social support, child characteristics, and child diagnosis. The parent characteristic measures included mother's and father's ages (in years). The family characteristics were gross monthly income and socioeconomic status (Hollingshead, 1975). The child characteristic measures were child's age in months, Developmental Quotient (DQ), and diagnostic group (mental retardation, physically disabled, or developmentally at risk). Contrast coding (Cohen & Cohen, 1983) was used to render diagnostic group information into two orthogonal comparisons: mentally retarded versus physically disabled, and mentally retarded and physically disabled versus developmentally at risk.

3.2 Cross-Sectional Evidence: Results and Discussion

The results from the studies are shown in Table 3. In only 2 of the 12 analyses did any of the parent characteristics, and in only one of the analyses did family characteristics account for a significant amount of variance. Child age accounted for a significant amount of variance in only one analysis, and neither child DQ nor diagnosis accounted for a significant amount of variance *in any* of the analyses. In contrast, the average amount of variance accounted for by social support was 26% (*SD* = 13, Range = 10 to 60). In every analysis, social support accounted for a significant amount of variance in well-being, regardless of the well-being measure that was used as the dependent measure. In addition, the more components of support that were measured, generally the greater the variance accounted for in the well-being measure. This suggests that unidimensional measures of social support may fail to capture the impact that social support has on an individual's personal well-being.

Two important conclusions may be drawn from the results displayed in Table 3: One is that social support is an important moderator of personal well-being. Second, the data indicate that social support can "buffer" reactions to the rearing of a child with a disability. These findings call into question the assumption that the more intellectually impaired the child is, the more stress the child will create for the parents. Data from these eight studies simply do not support that belief. Unfortunately, because the studies were cross-sectional in design, causal statements cannot be made about the relationships we were able to detect. Additionally, because we did not include a coping measure in any of the studies, the impact of this apparently important intrapersonal characteristic was not discerned.

In order to better understand the influences social support, coping, and life events have on family and child functioning, we conducted a prospective, longitudinal study that addressed several methodological and procedural shortcomings of our cross-sectional research. This study was specifically designed to assess the extent to which a family's response to pregnancy- or birth-related life events was influenced by the nature of the mother's coping strategies and the mother's social support network. The methodology and results of this study are briefly described next.

3.3 Prospective, Longitudinal Evidence: Method

Subjects. The participants in this longitudinal study are mothers of infants and toddlers who were recruited during the second trimester of their

Table 3. Multiple Regression Coefficients and Increments (I) in R^2 for Several Personal Well-Being Measures Used in Eight Investigations

Study	Sample size	Dependent measure	Type of support	Parent characteristics (1)		Family characteristics (2)		Social support (3)		Child characteristics (4)		Child diagnosis (5)	
				R^2	I	R^2	I	R^2	I	R^2	I	R^2	I
Study 1	51	QRS Health	F,X	003	003	007	004	148	142**	149	001	161	012
Study 2	132	QRS Health	R,F,X	000	000	022	022	118**	096***	159***	041*	162**	003
Study 3	106	WBI Well-Being	S,F,X	016	016	016	000	133***	117***	159***	026	167**	008
Study 4	40	PWI Well-Being	R,S,F	029	029	230**	201***	518***	288***	521***	003	---ᵇ	
Study 4	40	QRS Health	R,S,F	019	019	072	053	289*	217*	331*	042	---	---
Study 5	65	QRS Health	R,F,X	109**	109**	137**	028	360***	223**	389***	029	399***	010
Study 5	65	PWI Well-Being	R,F,X	177***	177***	178**	001	385***	207**	402***	017	402***	000
Study 6	84	PWI Well-Being	R,X,F,X	045	045	067	022	281**	214**	286***	005	294***	008
Study 6	84	QRS Health	R,S,F,X	012	012	033	021	335***	302***	350***	015	351***	001
Study 7	35	QRS Health	R,S,F,X	000	000	091	091	467**	376***	505**	038	511**	006
Study 7	35	PWI Well-Being	R,S,F,X	028	028	051	023	650***	599***	664***	014	676***	012
Study 8	45	WBI Well-Being	R,S,C,F,X	013	013	013	000	317***	304***	332**	015	---	---

Notes. Decimal points have been omitted. The left-to-right progression of independent variables is the order in which they were entered into the regression analyses. QRS: Questionnaire on Resource and Stress Emotional and Physical Health Subscale; PWI: Psychological Well-Being Index, WBI: Personal Well-Being Index.

*$p < .01$. **$p < .005$. ***$p < .001$.

ᵃ R = Relational, S = Structural, C = Constitutional, F = Functional, and X = Satisfaction.

ᵇ Not measured in the particular study.

pregnancies and followed until their children were 2 years of age. Each mother participated in an interview and completed a number of self-report measures during the second and third trimesters of their pregnancies and at 1, 6, 12, 18, and 24 months postpartum.

Complete data are currently available on 244 families from pregnancy up to the 12-month assessment. At the first prenatal assessment, the mothers and fathers were, on the average, 25 and 28 years of age, respectively. The average number of years of school completed was 13 years for both mothers and fathers. Seventy-eight percent of the mothers were married, and 54% worked outside of the home. The average socioeconomic status score (Hollingshead, 1975) was 37. The families' average gross monthly income was $1,918.

The sample was divided into four groups of mothers--environmentally at risk, pregnancy-related complications, child-related complications, and a control group--based on the occurrence or nonoccurrence of a particular life event or life condition and the timing of the event. The environmentally at-risk group included mothers living under socioeconomic stress and teenage mothers. The pregnancy-related complications group included mothers who experienced some type of pregnancy-related risk or problem, or exposure to a dangerous chemical situation during the pregnancy over which they had no control. Although the mothers in this group experienced events that placed their children at risk for a poor developmental outcome, none of the children were found to be at risk following their births. The child-related complications group included children who had problems that manifested themselves during the first 6 months of life. This included children with low birth weights, physical anomalies, a diagnosed developmental disability (e.g., Down's syndrome, cerebral palsy), or other medically related problems. The control group was comprised of mothers who did not have any of the conditions described above. Table 4 shows the parental and family characteristics of the four groups. The differences in the background characteristics among the groups was expected because of the way in which the groups were constituted.

Procedure. The mothers completed both the Psychological Well-Being Index (Bradburn, 1969; Bradburn & Caplovitz, 1965) and the Personal Assessment of Social Support Scale (Dunst & Trivette, 1988d) as part of their participation in the study.

The Psychological Well-Being Index is a 10-item self-report rating scale measuring the emotional well-being of the respondent. This measure asks the respondent to indicate how often certain emotional states were experienced over the last week. The PWI includes five positively stated and five negatively stated emotional statements. The global measure of well-

Table 4. Descriptive Characteristics of the Groups of Subjects

Background characteristics	Environmental risk (N = 77)		Pregnancy-related complications (N = 24)		Child-related complications (N = 46)		Control (N = 97)		F Test
	Mean	SD	Mean	SD	Mean	SD	Mean	SD	
Mother's age	21.68	5.52	25.50	5.34	26.47	4.26	27.91	4.42	24.40***
Father's age	25.49	6.17	30.22	6.17	29.00	4.88	30.18	4.96	8.78***
Mother's education	10.97	1.91	13.29	1.78	13.63	2.20	14.68	1.96	51.26***
Father's education	11.00	1.41	13.27	2.65	13.69	2.17	14.80	2.22	35.97***
Socioeconomic status	23.85	6.04	36.91	11.61	39.45	12.29	45.67	10.50	71.64***
Gross monthly income	1,050	684	1,948	903	2,131	1,105	2,498	910	39.27***
	Percentage								χ^2
Race:									
White	87.0		91.7		95.7		97.9		16.67*
Mothers married	46.8		75.0		89.1		97.9		69.43***
Mothers working	27.3		54.2		63.0		70.1		33.74***
Child's sex:									
Male	49.4		50.0		54.3		51.5		0.31

$*p < .01.$ $**p < .001.$ $***p < .0001.$

being is the sum of all 10 items corrected for the response direction. The sum of the 5 positive items represents a measure of positive affect, whereas the sum of the 5 negative items represents a measure of negative affect.

The Personal Assessment of Social Support Scale assesses a number of components of the social support construct in a self-report format. The scale assesses the following dimensions of social support within the five major components described above: *relational* (network size), *constitutional* (adequacy of resources), *structural* (level of reciprocity), *functional* (level of dependability of the network), and *support satisfaction* (degree of satisfaction with the help received from network members). The sum of the ratings for each of these dimensions were used as the measures of social support.

The Personal Assessment of Coping Experiences Scale (Dunst, Trivette, Jodry, et al., 1988) was used to measure parents' coping styles. It is administered in an interview format. A respondent is first asked to sort 30 cards with possible life events into two groups: those events influenced by the birth and rearing of a child and those events or experiences that are not related or influenced. Next, the respondent is asked to sort the life-events cards that were influenced by the birth of a child into three piles: those that have been positively influenced by the event, those that have been negatively influenced by the event, and those both positively and negatively influenced by the event. The mother is then asked, for each event or experience, to indicate from a list of eight randomly ordered coping strategies which ones she used in response to the event. The coping methods from which she can choose are different for the positive and negative life events and are labeled proactive and reactive coping strategies. Proactive coping strategies are ones used to reflect upon, evoke, or prolong pleasurable or desirable life events; and reactive coping strategies are ones used in response to difficult or stressful life events. The measure of coping strategies that was used in these analyses is the difference between the number of proactive and reactive strategies that the mother used to cope with the events that occurred in her life.

Repeated measures analyses. A series of repeated measures ANOVAs were conducted to determine if there were predicted differences between the environmental risk and the control group, the pregnancy-related complications and the control group, and the child-related complications and the control group as a function of the occurrence and timing of the life events of interest. The hypothesized relationships that we tested are shown in Table 5.

Table 5. *Hypothesized Contrasts Between Groups*

	Environmental risk vs. Control	Pregnancy-related complications vs. Control	Child-related complications vs. Control
Prenatally	Yes	Yes	No
One month	Yes	No	No
Six months	Yes	No	Yes
Twelve months	Yes	No	Yes

We hypothesized that there would be differences on the well-being measure at each of the time periods for the environmental risk group versus the control group contrast. We expected the influences of these environmental factors to be so overwhelming that people who live under these conditions will, in spite of the coping strategies they use or the social support they have, experience depressed levels of well-being. Garbarino (1982) describes this phenomena as "environmental press," "the combined influence of forces working in a setting . . . shape the behavior and development of people in the setting" (p. 12). These forces in the lives of these mothers are tied to basic survival, and therefore have a powerful influence on the well-being of the mother regardless of other resources that are brought to bear on the situation.

We hypothesized that the pregnancy-related complications group would be different from the control group at the prenatal time period only. The events that were included in the pregnancy-related complications group were most salient at the prenatal period. Therefore, it was hypothesized that we would not find differences in the groups once the "event" or "stress" had passed.

We hypothesized that there would be differences for the child-related complications group versus the control group at 6 and 12 months. These mothers were not experiencing any problems prenatally; therefore, we did not expect an effect at the prenatal assessment. However, we did predict that the influences of the diagnoses of these children would manifest themselves at both 6 and 12 months.

Regression analyses. The prenatal measures of coping and support were used to predict well-being and affect outcomes prenatally and at 1, 6, and 12 months postpartum. The role that coping and social support played in buffering and lessening negative reactions to both normative and nonnormative life events has been well documented. Hierarchical multiple regression analyses by sets was used to test the mediating influences of coping and social support in response to the birth and rearing of a child with a poor developmental prognosis. The sets of independent variables were entered in the following order: coping strategies; relational, constitutional, structural, functional, and satisfaction with support; and group membership. Contrast coding (Cohen & Cohen, 1983) was used to render diagnostic group information into three orthogonal comparisons: pregnancy-related complications versus control, child-related complications versus control, and environmental risk versus control.

3.4 Prospective, Longitudinal Evidence: Results and Discussion

Repeated measures findings. Table 6 shows the results of the ANOVAs. The effects of living in a difficult environment are such that maternal well-being is depressed at all measurement occasions. These mothers are experiencing a chronic condition and not a one-time event; therefore we would expect that the influences of these situations would be present at each time period. We hypothesized differences between environmental risk and the contrast group at the prenatal, 1-month, 6-month, and 12-month assessment, and these were confirmed. These findings supported the notion that living in difficult conditions continues to have an influence on the mothers regardless of other events that are occurring.

The hypothesis that there would be a difference on the well-being measure between the pregnancy-related complications group and the control group at the prenatal assessment only was confirmed, suggesting that the "effects" of the stressor subsided once the prenatal events did not produce any problems for the child.

The results confirmed only one of our hypothesized predictions between the child-related complications group and the control groups: It had been predicted that we would find a difference between the two groups at both 6 and 12 months. The difference between the groups appeared only at the 12-month assessment. We had expected that being informed that your child had a developmental delay or was at risk for problems would manifest themselves at the 6-month as well as 12-month assessment. In fact, the effect does not appear until the 12-month assessment. It is unclear at this time exactly why the effect shows up later than expected at the 12-month assessment.

Regression analysis findings. Table 7 displays the results of the hierarchical regression analysis of the *global well-being* measure. Coping style accounted for a significant amount of the variance in the dependent

Table 6. Results of the ANOVAs at Each Time Period and the Orthogonal Contrast Analyses

Assessment period	Environ-mental risk (ER)		Pregnancy-related complications (PRC)		Child-related complications (CRC)		Control		Overall F value	Orthogonal contrasts		
										ER vs. Control	PRC vs. Control	CRC vs. Control
	M	SD	M	SD	M	SD	M	SD				
Prenatal	23.44	5.41	26.50	4.79	27.65	5.46	29.12	4.30	18.91***	55.22***	5.42**	2.64
One month	26.63	5.84	28.21	4.25	29.86	4.62	29.73	4.07	6.87***	17.14***	1.93	0.02
Six months	26.46	5.45	28.00	3.66	28.77	4.69	29.69	4.09	7.01***	20.46***	2.46	1.19
Twelve months	26.67	5.11	28.65	4.19	28.49	4.40	30.04	3.97	7.49***	22.42***	1.81	3.60*

*p < .06.   **p < .05.   ***p < .001

Table 7. Multiple Regression Coefficients (R^2) and Increments (I) in R^2 for the Analysis of Global Well-Being

	Measurement occasion							
	Prenatal		One month		Six months		Twelve months	
	R^2	I	R^2	I	R^2	I	R^2	I
Coping style	046****	046***	035***	035***	081****	081****	039***	039***
Social support:								
Relational	082****	036***	041**	006	090****	008	054***	014
Constitutional	103****	021*	069****	028*	102****	012	081****	026*
Structural	187****	084****	087****	018*	131****	029**	125****	045***
Functional	271****	084****	124****	037***	236****	105****	163****	038***
Satisfaction	272****	001	124****	000	237****	001	168****	005
Group contrasts:								
Environmental risk vs. Control	352****	080****	148****	024*	268****	031***	205****	037***
Child-related complications vs. Control	367****	015	179****	031***	277****	009	207****	001
Pregnancy-related complications vs. Control	367****	000	179****	000	278****	001	207****	000

Note. Decimal points have been omitted. All social support scales have been scored so that higher scores mean more support.
*$p < .05$. **$p < .01$. ***$p < .005$. ****$p < .001$.

measure at each of the time periods. Collectively, social support accounted for between 8% and 22% of the variance in well-being at the different time periods. Closer examination found that structural and functional support both made significant contributions to the variance in well-being at each of the time periods. In addition, relational support accounted for 4% of the variance at the prenatal assessment only, and constitutional support was a significant contributor to well-being at the prenatal, 1-month, and 12-month assessments.

The environmental risk versus the control group contrast accounted for a significant amount of variance at each of the time periods. The child-related complications versus control group contrast accounted for a significant amount of the variance at the 1-month assessment. The pregnancy-related complications versus control group contrast did not account for a significant amount of the variance at any of the time periods.

The relationships between the predictor variables and the *negative affect* measure are shown in Table 8. Coping style accounted for a significant amount of the variance in the negative affect measure only at the prenatal assessment. In contrast, constitutional, structural, and functional support accounted for an average of 16% of the variance at each of the four assessment occasions; with the social support measures, collectively, accounting for between 11% and 23% of the variance at the various time periods.

The results also indicated that the environmental risk versus control contrast made a significant contribution to the variance accounted for in negative affect at each of the measurement occasions. The influence of this variable on negative affect is most powerful at the prenatal assessment, and diminishes soon after the birth of the child, though it remains a significant contributor at each time period. The child-related complications versus control contrast was a significant contributor to the variance in negative affect at the prenatal and 1- month assessment.

The results of the multiple regression on the *positive affect* measure are shown in Table 9. As can be seen, the pattern of findings are quite different to those found for the negative affect analyses. Coping style was related significantly to the criterion measures at each of four assessment periods, accounting for between 3.6% and 6.5% of the variance at the different time periods. In contrast, the social support measures were found to account for a significant amount of the variance only at the prenatal assessment. Likewise, the group contrasts had a different pattern of influence on the positive affect measure compared to what was found in the previous analyses. The environmental risk versus the control group contrast accounted for 2.8% of the variance in positive affect only at the prenatal assessment.

Table 8. Multiple Regression Coefficients and Increments (I) in R² for the Analysis of Negative Affect Data

| | Measurement occasion | | | | | | | |
| | Prenatal | | One month | | Six months | | Twelve months | |
	R^2	I	R^2	I	R^2	I	R^2	I
Coping style	017*	017*	008	008	037***	037***	017*	017
Social support:								
Relational	037**	020*	015	007	039**	002	028*	011
Constitutional	099****	062****	066***	051****	088****	049****	099****	071****
Structural	170****	071****	090****	024*	123****	035****	154****	055****
Functional	254****	084****	122****	032**	217****	094****	202****	048****
Satisfaction	254****	000	124****	002	220****	003	204****	002
Group contrasts:								
Environmental risk vs. Control	346****	092****	177****	053****	280****	060****	259****	055****
Child-related complications vs. Control	367****	021**	215****	038***	292****	012	264****	005
Pregnancy-related complications vs. Control	367****	000	226****	011	294****	002	264****	000

Note. Decimal points have been omitted. All social support scales have been scored so that higher scores mean more support.
*p < .05. **p < .01. ***p < .005. ****p < .001.

Table 9 *Multiple Regression Coefficients and Increments (I) in R^2 for the Analysis of Positive Affect Data*

	Prenatal		One month		Six months		Twelve months	
	R^2	I	R^2	I	R^2	I	R^2	I
Coping style	059****	059****	044*****	044***	065*****	065*****	036***	036***
Social support:								
Relational	093*****	034***	046****	002	076*****	011	046**	010
Constitutional	094*****	001	048**	002	078*****	002	046*	000
Structural	144*****	050****	051*	003	084*****	006	060**	014
Functional	182*****	038****	068**	017	125*****	041***	071**	011
Satisfaction	185*****	003	069**	001	132*****	007	077**	006
Group contrasts:								
Environmental risk vs. Control	213*****	028**	081*	007	132*****	000	084**	007
Child-related complications vs. Control	217*****	004	082*	001	134*****	002	089*	002
Pregnancy-related complications vs. Control	217*****	000	074*	005	134*****	000	087**	003

Measurement occasion

Note. Decimal points have been omitted. All social support scales have been scored so that higher scores mean more support.
[a] At one month the Event Group contrasts entered the regression in the following order: Pregnancy-related complications vs. Control, Environmental risk vs. Control, and Child-related complications vs. Control.
[b] At 12 months, the Event Group contrasts entered the regression in the following order: Environmental risk vs. Control, Pregnancy-related complications vs. Control, and Child-related complications vs. Control.
$*p < .05.$ $**p < .01.$ $***p < .005.$ $****p < .001.$

Taken together, the results from the longitudinal study replicated what we have previously found in our cross-sectional studies. First, social support accounted for a significant amount of the variance in psychological well-being in each of the analyses. Second, measuring multiple dimensions of social support increased the amount of variance accounted for in the dependent measure. Third, the effects of the birth and rearing of a child with conditions placing him or her at risk for developmental delays were found to be lessened by the availability of social support.

In addition to replicating the findings from our cross-sectional research, the longitudinal study yielded some important new findings: First, we found differential relationships among the independent variables and psychological well-being when different dimensions of well-being were examined separately. Second, we found parental coping styles related to positive affect but not negative affect; whereas, social support was positively related to negative affect but somewhat less related to positive affect. Also, we found that the influence of environmental risk was especially powerful on a person's assessment of their negative affect regardless of the availability of social support.

4   General Conclusion

Collectively, the findings from both the cross-sectional and longitudinal studies demonstrate clearly the important role social support plays in helping mothers deal effectively with potentially stressful life events. More specifically, our work indicates that the effects of pregnancy, childrearing, and environmentally related life events are modified by the presence of social support, although it appears that the effects may be different depending on the type of event that occurs and the type of well-being that is measured.

In the past, much research attention has been paid to the differences in family and child outcomes among families whose children have different diagnoses. This line of research yields descriptive information about how groups of families differ on a number of dimensions, but provides no information about intergroup differences or external factors that influence the differences that are observed.

Over the years, we have moved beyond descriptive data, to the examination of factors that influence differences both between and within groups of families and children. The research presented in this chapter follows this line of thinking by examining the factors that influence maternal well-being. We have, in this same data set, a number of other family and child outcomes for which it will be important to use the same procedures within analyzing. This will allow us to determine whether there are similar or different patterns in the factors that influence various child and family outcome measures.

An important methodological feature of this study has been the measurement of both positive and negative aspects of health and well-being and their relationship between social support and coping. Well-being is a multidimensional construct, and to examine only the negative aspect of the construct seems, from our view, to provide only partial information about what a person is experiencing during a nonnormative life event. If we are going to understand the impact of an event on an individual or a family, it is important to examine the multiple dimensions of both the predictive and outcome constructs in order to gain full knowledge about the relationship between various predictor and outcome variables. The examination of both positive and negative coping strategies, positive and negative life events, as well as positive and negative well-being are but just a few of the constructs that can be used. Future research efforts should consider broadening the range of constructs that are considered important in understanding the functioning of children and families.

Note

Appreciation is extended to Pat Condrey and Norma Hunter for assistance in preparation of the manuscript.

References

Affleck, G., Tennen, H., Allen, D. A., & Gershman, K. (1986). Perceived social support and maternal adaptation during the transition from hospital to home care of high-risk infants. *Infant Mental Health Journal, 7,* 6-18.

Affleck, G., Tennen, H., & Rowe, J. (1991). *Infants in crisis: How parents cope with newborn intensive care and its aftermath.* New York: Springer.

Antonovsky, A. (1979). *Health, stress, and coping: New perspectives on mental and physical well-being.* San Francisco: Jossey-Bass.

Barrera, M., Jr. (1986). Distinctions between social support concepts, measures, and models. *American Journal of Community Psychology, 14,* 413-445.

Billings, A. G., & Moos, R. M. (1981). The role of coping responses and social resources in attenuating the stress of life events. *Journal of Behavioral Medicine, 4,* 139-157.

Bradburn, N. M. (1969). *The structure of psychological well-being.* Chicago, IL: Aldine.

Bradburn, N. M., & Caplovitz, D. (1965). *Reports on happiness.* Chicago, IL: Aldine.

Bronfenbrenner, U. (1979). *The ecology of human development: Experiments by nature and design*. Cambridge, MA: Harvard University Press.

Bronfenbrenner, U. (1986). Ecology of the family as a context for human development: Research perspectives. *Developmental Psychology, 22*, 723-742.

Cobb, S., & Kasl, S. (1977). *Termination: The consequences of job loss*. Cincinnati, OH: DHEW (NIOSH), Publication No. 77-224.

Cochran, M., & Brassard, J. (1979). Child development and personal social networks. *Child Development, 50*, 601-606.

Cohen, J., & Cohen, P. (1983). *Applied multiple regression correlation/analysis for the behavioral sciences* (2nd ed.). Hillsdale, NJ: Erlbaum.

Cohen, S., Meimelstein, R., Kamarck, T., & Hoberman, H. (1985). Measuring the functional components of social support. In I. G. Sarason & B. Sarason (Eds.), *Social support: Theory, research and application* (pp. 73-94). Dordrecht, The Netherlands: Martinus Nijhoff.

Cohen, S., & Syme, S. L. (Eds.). (1985). *Social support and health*. New York: Academic Press.

Colletta, N. (1981). Social support and the risk of maternal rejection by adolescent mothers. *Journal of Psychology, 109*, 191-197.

Crnic, A., Greenberg, M., Ragozin, A., Robinson, N., & Basham, R. (1983). Effects of stress and social support on mothers of premature and full-term infants. *Child Development, 54*, 209-217.

Crnic, K. A., Greenberg, M. T., Robinson, N. M., & Ragozin, A. S. (1984). Maternal stress and social support: Effects on the mother-infant relationship from birth to eighteen months. *American Journal of Orthopsychiatry, 54*, 224-235.

Crnic, K. A., Greenberg, M. T., & Slough, N. M. (1986). Early stress and social support influences on mothers' and high-risk infants' functioning in late infancy. *Infant Mental Health Journal, 7*, 19-48.

Crockenberg, S. B. (1981). Infant irritability, mother responsiveness and social influences on the security of infant-mother attachment. *Child Development, 52*, 857-865.

Crockenberg, S. B. (1985). Professional support and care of infants by adolescent mothers in England and the United States. *Journal of Pediatric Psychology, 10*, 413-428.

DePaulo, B., Nadler, A., & Fisher, J. (1983). *New directions in helping: Vol. 2. Help-seeking*. New York: Academic Press.

Duncan, O. D., Featherman, D. L., & Duncan, B. (1972). *Socioeconomic background and achievement*. New York: Seminar.

Dunst, C. J. (1982, November). *Social support, early intervention, and institutional avoidance*. Paper presented at the annual meeting of the Southeastern Association on Mental Deficiency, Louisville, KY.

Dunst, C. J. (1983). Emerging trends and advances in early intervention programs. *New Jersey Journal of School Psychology, 2*, 26-40.

Dunst, C. J. (1985). Rethinking early intervention. *Analysis and Intervention in Developmental Disabilities, 5*, 165-201.

Dunst, C. J. (1986a, October). *Helping relationships and enabling and empowering families*. Paper presented at the 11th Annual Regional Intervention Program Expansion Conference, Cleveland, OH.

Dunst, C. J. (1986b). Overview of the efficacy of early intervention programs. In L. Bickman & D. Weatherford (Eds.), *Evaluating early intervention programs for severely handicapped children and their families* (pp. 79-147). Austin, TX: PRO-ED.

Dunst, C. J., Jenkins, V., & Trivette, C. M. (1984). Family Support Scale: Reliability and validity. *Journal of Individual, Family and Community Wellness, 1*(4), 45-52.

Dunst, C. J., & Leet, H. E. (1987). Measuring the adequacy of resources in households with young children. *Child: Care, Health and Development, 13,* 111-125.

Dunst, C. J., Leet, H., & Trivette, C. M. (1988). Family resources, personal well-being, and early intervention. *Journal of Special Education, 22*(1), 108-116.

Dunst, C. J., & Trivette, C. M. (1984, August). *Differential influences of social support on mentally retarded children and their families.* Paper presented at the annual meeting of the American Psychological Association, Toronto, Canada.

Dunst, C. J., & Trivette, C. M. (1986). Looking beyond the parent-child dyad for the determinants of maternal styles of interaction. *Infant Mental Health Journal, 7,* 69-80.

Dunst, C. J., & Trivette, C. M. (1987). Enabling and empowering families: Conceptual and intervention issues. *School Psychology Review, 16*(4), 443-456.

Dunst, C. J., & Trivette, C. M. (1988a). Determinants of caregiver styles of interaction used with developmentally at-risk children. In K. Marfo (Ed.), *Parent-child interaction and developmental disabilities: Theory, research, and intervention.* New York: Praeger.

Dunst, C. J., & Trivette, C. M. (1988b). A family systems model of early intervention with handicapped and developmentally at-risk children. In D. Powell (Ed.), *Parent education as early childhood intervention: Emerging directions in theory, research, and practice* (pp. 131-180). Norwood, NJ: Ablex.

Dunst, C. J., & Trivette, C. M. (1988c). Helping, helplessness and harm. In J. Witt, S. Elliott, & F. Gresham (Eds.), *Handbook of behavior therapy in education* (pp. 343-376). New York: Plenum.

Dunst, C. J., & Trivette, C. M. (1988d). *Personal Assessment of Social Support Scale.* Unpublished scale, Center for Family Studies, Western Carolina Center, Morganton, NC.

Dunst, C. J., & Trivette, C. M. (1988e). Support Functions Scale: Reliability and validity. In C. J. Dunst, C. M. Trivette, & A. G. Deal (Eds.), *Enabling and empowering families: Principles and guidelines for practice.* Cambridge, MA: Brookline Books.

Dunst, C. J., & Trivette, C. M. (1988f). Toward experimental evaluation of the Family, Infant and Preschool Program. In H. Weiss & F. Jacobs (Eds.), *Evaluating family programs* (pp. 315-346). New York: Aldine de Gruyter.

Dunst, C. J., & Trivette, C. M. (1990). Assessment of social support in early intervention programs. In S. J. Meisels & J. P. Shonkoff (Eds.), *Handbook of early childhood intervention* (pp. 326-349). New York: Cambridge University Press.

Dunst, C. J., Trivette, C. M., & Cross, A. (1986a). Mediating influences of social support: Personal, family, and child outcomes. *American Journal of Mental Deficiency, 90,* 403-417.

Dunst, C. J., Trivette, C. M., & Cross, A. H. (1986b). Roles and support networks of mothers of handicapped children. In R. R. Fewell & P. F. Vadasy (Eds.), *Families of handicapped children: Needs and supports across the life span* (pp. 167-192). Austin, TX: Pro-Ed.

Dunst, C. J., Trivette, C. M., & Cross, A. (1988). Social support networks of Appalachian and non-Appalachian families with handicapped children. In S. E. Keefe (Ed.), *Mental health in Appalachia* (pp. 101-124). Lexington, KY: University of Kentucky Press.

Dunst, C. J., Trivette, C. M., & Deal, A. G. (1988). *Enabling and empowering families: Principles and guidelines for practice.* Cambridge, MA: Brookline Books.

Dunst, C. J., Trivette, C. M., Jodry, W., Morrow, J., & Hamer, A. W. (1988). *Personal Assessment of Coping Experiences Scale.* Unpublished scale, Center for Family Studies, Western Carolina Center, Morganton, NC.

Embry, L. (1980). Family support for handicapped preschool children at risk for abuse. *New Directions for Exceptional Children, 4,* 29-58.

Epstein, A. (1980). *Assessing the child development information needed by adolescent parents with very young children.* Final report of Grant OCD-90-C-1341. Washington, DC: Office of Child Development, Department of Health, Education and Welfare (ERIC Document Reproduction Service No. ED 183286).

Folkman, S., & Lazarus, R. (1980). An analysis of coping in a middle-aged community sample. *Journal of Health and Social Behavior, 21,* 219-239.

Gallagher, J. J., Cross, A. H., & Scharfman, W. (1981). *Parent Role Scale.* Unpublished scale, University of North Carolina, Frank Porter Graham Child Development Center, Chapel Hill, NC.

Garbarino, J. (1982). *Children and families in the social environment.* New York: Aldine.

Gore, S. (1985). Social support and styles of coping with stress. In S. Cohen & S. L. Syme (Eds.), *Social support and health* (pp. 263-278). New York: Academic Press.

Gottlieb, B. H. (1981). Social networks and social support in community mental health. In B. H. Gottlieb (Ed.), *Social networks and social support* (pp. 11-42). Beverly Hills, CA: Sage.

Hall, A., & Wellman, B. (1985). Social networks and social support. In S. Cohen & S. L. Syme (Eds.), *Social support and health* (pp. 23-42). New York: Academic Press.

Heller, W., Amaral, T., & Procidano, M. (1978). *The experimental study of social support: An approach to understanding the indigenous helper.* Paper presented at the 86th Meeting of the American Psychological Association, Toronto, Canada.

Hetherington, E., Cox, M., & Cox, R. (1976). Divorced fathers. *Family Coordinator, 25,* 427-428.

Hetherington, E., Cox, M., & Cox, R. (1978). The aftermath of divorce. In J. Stevens, & M. Mathews (Eds.), *Mother-child, father-child relations* (pp. 149-176). Washington, DC: National Association for the Education of Young Children.

Holohan, C. J., & Wilcox, B. L. (1978). Residential satisfaction and friendship formation in high and low rise student housing: An international analysis. *Journal of Educational Psychology, 70,* 237-241.

Hollingshead, A. B. (1975). *Four factor index of social status.* Unpublished manuscript, Yale University, Department of Sociology, New Haven, CT.

Holroyd, J. (1974). The Questionnaire on Resources and Stress: An instrument to measure family responses to a handicapped family member. *Journal of Community Psychology, 2,* 92-94.

Holroyd, J. (1985). *Questionnaire on Resources and Stress Manual.* Unpublished scale, University of California, Neuropsychiatric Institute, Department of Psychiatric and Behavioral Sciences, Los Angeles.

House, J. S., & Kahn, R. L. (1985). Measures and concepts of social support. In S. Cohen & S. L. Syme (Eds.), *Social support and health* (pp. 83-108). New York: Academic Press.

Kahn, R. H., Wethington, E., & Ingersoll-Dayton, B. (1987). Social support and social networks: Determinants, effects, and interactions. In R. P. Abeles (Ed.), *Life-span perspectives and social psychology* (pp. 139-165). Hillsdale, NJ: Erlbaum.

Kasl, S. V., & Cobb, S. (1979). Some mental health consequences of plant closing and job loss. In L. A. Ferman & J. P. Gordus (Eds.), *Mental health and the economy* (pp. 255-299). Kalamazoo, MI: W. E. Upjohn Institute.

Lazar, I., & Darlington, R. (1982). Lasting effects of early education. *Monographs of the Society for Research in Child Development, 47*(2-3, Serial No. 195).

Lazarus, R. S., & Folkman, S. (1984). *Stress, appraisal, and coping.* New York: Springer.

McCubbin, H., I., Cauble, A. E., & Patterson, J. M. (Eds.). (1982). *Family stress, coping, and social support.* Springfield, IL: Thomas.

McCubbin, H., Joy, C., Cauble, A. E., Comeau, J., Patterson, J., & Needle, R. (1980). Family stress and coping: A decade review. *Journal of Marriage and the Family, 42,* 855-871.

McGuire, J. C., & Gottlieb, B. H. (1979). Social support groups among new parents: An experimental study in primary prevention. *Journal of Clinical Child Psychology, 8,* 111-116.

Mitchell, R. E., & Trickett, E. J. (1980). Task force report: Social networks as mediators of social support. *Community Mental Health Journal, 16,* 27-44.

Pascoe, J. M., Loda, F. A., Jeffries, V., & Earp, J. (1981). The association between mothers' social support and provision of stimulation to their children. *Developmental and Behavioral Pediatrics, 2,* 15-19.

Patterson, J. M., & McCubbin, H. I. (1983). Chronic illness: Family stress and coping. In C. R. Figley & H. I. McCubbin (Eds.), *Stress and the family: Vol. II. Coping with catastrophe* (pp. 21-36). New York: Brunner-Mazel.

Pattison, E. M., DeFrancisco, D., Wood, P., Frazier, H., & Crowder, J. (1975). A psychosocial kinship model for family therapy. *American Journal of Psychiatry, 132,* 1246-1251.

Pearlin, L. I., & Schooler, C. (1978). The structure of coping. *Journal of Health and Social Behavior, 19,* 2-21.

Richman, J., & Flaherty, J. (1985). Coping and depression: The relative contribution of internal and external resources during a life cycle transition. *The Journal of Nervous and Mental Disease, 173,* 590-595.

Rook, K., Dooley, D., & Catalano, R. (1991). Age differences in workers' efforts to cope with economic distress. In J. Eckenrode (Ed.), *The social context of coping* (pp. 79-105). New York: Plenum.

Roskin, M. (1982). Coping with life changes--A preventive social work approach. *American Journal of Community Psychology, 10,* 331-340

Sewell, W. H., & Hauser, R. M. (1975). *Education, occupation, and earnings: Achievement in the early career.* New York: Academic Press.

Shapiro, J. (1983). Family reactions and coping strategies in response to the physically ill or handicapped child: A review. *Social Science Medicine, 17,* 913-931.

Stone, A., Helder, L., & Schneider, M. (1988). Coping with stressful events: Coping dimensions and issues. In L. Cohen (Ed.), *Life events and psychological functioning: Theoretical and methodological issues* (pp. 182-210). Newbury Park, CA: Sage.

Stone, A., & Neale, L. (1984). New measure of daily coping: Development and preliminary results. *Journal of Personality and Social Psychology, 46*, 892-906

Tardy, C. H. (1985). Social support measurement. *American Journal of Community Psychology, 13*, 187-202.

Thoits, P. A. (1991). Gender differences in coping with emotional distress. In J. Eckenrode (Ed.), *The social context of coping* (pp. 107-138). New York: Plenum Press.

Tolsdorf, C. C. (1976). Social networks, support, and coping: An exploratory study. *Family Process, 15*, 407-417.

Trivette, C. M., Deal, A., & Dunst, C. J. (1986). Family needs, sources of support, and professional roles: Critical elements of family systems assessment and intervention. *Diagnostique, 11*, 246-267.

Trivette, C. M., & Dunst, C. J. (1985). *Personal Well-Being Index.* Unpublished scale, Center for Family Studies, Western Carolina Center, Morganton, NC.

Trivette, C. M., & Dunst, C. J. (1987). Proactive influences of social support in families of handicapped children. In H. G. Lingren (Ed.), *Family strengths (Vols. 8-9): Pathways to well-being.* Lincoln, NE: University of Nebraska Press.

Trivette, C. M., & Dunst, C. J. (1992). Characteristics and influences of role division and social support among mothers of preschool children with disabilities. *Topics in Early Childhood Special Education, 12*(3), 367-385.

Turner, R. J. (1983). Direct, indirect, and moderating effects of social support on psychological distress and associated conditions. In H. B. Kaplan (Ed.), *Psychosocial stress: Trends in theory and research* (pp. 105-135). New York: Academic Press.

Wandersman, L., P., & Unger, D. G. (1983). *Interaction of infant difficulty and social support in adolescent mothers.* Paper presented at the biennial meeting of the Society for Research in Child Development, Detroit, MI.

Wandersman, L., Wandersman, A., & Kahn, S. (1980). Social support in the transition to parenthood. *Journal of Community Psychology, 8*, 332-342.

Weinraub, M., & Wolf, B. (1983). Effects of stress and social supports on mother-child interactions in single- and two-parent families. *Child Development, 54*, 1297-1311.

Wilcox, B. L., & Birkel, R. C. (1983). Social networks and the help-seeking process: A structural perspective. In A. Nadler, J. D. Fisher, & B. M. DePaulo (Eds.), *New directions in helping: Vol. 3. Applied perspectives on help-seeking and -receiving* (pp. 235-253). New York: Academic Press.

Wills, T. A. (1985). Supportive functions of interpersonal relationships. In S. Cohen & S. L. Syme (Eds.), *Social support and health* (pp. 61-82). Orlando, FL: Academic Press.

M. Brambring, H. Rauh, and A. Beelmann (Eds.). (1996). *Early childhood intervention: Theory, evaluation, and practice* (pp. 265-277). Berlin, New York: de Gruyter.

Preschool Integration or: Who is Afraid of Little Jessica?

Gisela Chatelanat

1 Introduction

Little Jessica exists: Today, she is a pretty 8-year-old girl with blond pigtails and a devastating smile, which makes it difficult for her parents and teachers to enforce family and classroom rules and to dampen her persistent enthusiasm for the use of four-letter words. Sturdy legs carry her safely down ski slopes in the winter and across the swimming pool in the summer. She likes reading little stories, making up the words she doesn't recognize yet. She writes short notes to her friends at school with a definite tendency to confuse ps and qs, bs and ds, which doesn't prevent her friends from understanding her messages. She prefers, as do many children, puzzles to maths, and working with a paint brush rather than with a dictionary. During her summer vacation, she attends camp with children of all ages and from all over the city; in the winter, she goes skiing with the school. Jessica has been attending this private school for 4 years now, from kindergarten to second grade. When we asked her this year to tell us something about her school and herself, this is what she said:

> My school, I adore. The children at my school, I love them. In the mornings, I like to go to school. All the teachers are super. I like to play on the computer with Cedric, my favorite friend. With him I also do painting. I do reading with Laurent. I like going to the library and checking out books. The books I like most are Peter Pan and Captain Hook. I draw and I learn numbers. I go to the swimming pool with Eric. I can swim very well. I know English and I know it well. I am good. Nearly everyone in the class knows more than I do. They are not stupid and I am not stupid either. School, sometimes, is hard. Writing attached words is hard. I like the big boys and girls at school, especially Joel. They are nice. Nobody is nasty at school, nobody bugs me. (Desbiolles, 1993, translated)

So, who, you may ask, would be afraid of little Jessica? And of course, the next question is "why?" The fact that Jessica was born with Down's Syndrome, known not to be contagious in any way, could not possibly be the answer.

But if nobody were afraid, how could it be that an incredible amount of time and energy were spent over the years, by a great number of people, in order to make Jessica's seemingly not very problematic integration into an ordinary school possible. Her parents, the state supervisor, the entire staff of the private school she attends, two special-education student teachers, psychologists and psychiatrists at the local diagnostic and therapy center, the speech pathologist, the physiotherapist, the members of a work team on integration at the local parent association, two university professors, and some other people I have forgotten or did not get to know, spent an extraordinary number of hours in meetings, on the telephone, writing letters and reports, visiting, counseling, proposing, rejecting, and questioning the adequacy of their own and other professionals' training, beliefs, competencies, and attitudes. This tremendous deployment of energy and money (of which very little was spent in direct interaction with Jessica or in preparing educational material and activities for her) conveys the impression that the mere idea of Jessica's participation in a regular school generated great anxiety.

If each preschool child, with or without a disability, mobilized only a fraction of the well-paid time of professionals and the equally valuable time of parents that Jessica mobilized, we would have to multiply the human and financial resources now allocated to preschool and elementary school education. Being the parents of one disabled preschooler would become a full-time job for two people and a full-time job for two teachers and two administrators. Disabled children would become afraid of themselves if they realized the investment believed to be necessary for what are, after all, only a few years of educational placement. They would become afraid for themselves if they could read or listen to what others anticipate will be their fate and impact on the friendly neighborhood of the kindergarten: that they will not progress, but regress; that they will be rejected by peers or teachers and suffer emotional damage; that they will retard the development of their peers without disabilities; that their parents will start to harbor unrealistic hopes about their developmental potential and might even be led to minimize or refuse to recognize their disability.

Most arguments against inclusion center on the individual child and his or her family and are professed and voiced in the belief that the child's and the family's best interest are in mind. I have heard the same arguments again and again over the years. Strangely enough, over the same period of time, I have met fewer and fewer people who are opposed to the principle of integration. Everyone seems to agree that it is a desirable situation for the disabled child to grow and learn together with children who have no disabilities. Yet it just happens that there are many special cases, many exceptions to this rule. I call it the "yes, but" attitude. In fact, most mentally disabled preschool children in Geneva seem to be exceptions.

It seems to me that at each attempt to integrate an individual disabled child into an ordinary preschool program, we activate defense mechanisms that concern a much larger issue than the adequate educational placement of an individual child. It is not Jessica who makes people afraid; I even believe that Jessica's disability and family situation have little to do with the reactions her inclusion provokes. Instead, the generous arguments about "the child's best interest and needs" are more often arguments regarding the best interest of our existing structures and old belief systems. And it is indeed possible and understandable that we are afraid when confronted with fundamental revisions of societal goals, of the functions and objectives of schools - regular and specialized - and of the roles of professionals and parents.

I am aware that there is nothing new about this analysis. Over the last 20 years, in all countries, eminent social scientists and professionals in the field of education have shown that integration of individuals with disabilities requires integrating different values and attitudes, different bodies of knowledge, different professional practices and training concepts, different budgets and administrative rules, new power structures and means of communication between all the people involved. But despite the impressive amount of work done to meet this challenge, it seems to me that we have not made significant progress, and that for one step forward we take, two new obstacles appear in front of us. My purpose here is not to present scientific arguments, data, or a review of the literature on the value or the limitations of integrated education. I would like us to think some more about the general "climate," the material, social, and emotional context in which, today, we pursue our efforts as parents, professionals, and citizens to optimize educational opportunities for all young children.

During my involvement with Jessica's preschool integration, I came to identify certain aspects of the integration process that I thought might account for what seemed to be unnecessary complications and misunderstandings. I would like to share my thoughts about these issues with you, in the hope that our experiences in Switzerland can contribute to a better understanding of the general situation and lead to some constructive action to get us out of what I consider, in my more pessimistic moods, to be a dead-end street.

One aspect that I believe needs more attention has to do with interpersonal communication. When I was asked to give a title to my paper, I immediately thought of something like: "Preschool integration," or "Not only children need to learn how to play together." Each time I help prepare the inclusion of a disabled child in a regular preschool setting, I am astounded indeed by the difficulties that all the actors in the integration process have in communicating openly, spontaneously, and effectively with each other. However, I believe that most of the people concerned, the professionals and the parents, are conscientious, well- meaning, and eager to offer the best education to the child they care for; they are sincere in their doubts, their wishes, or recommendations. So I ask myself: Why the unclear and often ambiguous demands, the evasive answers, the postponing of decisions and the last-minute decisions, the defensive reactions, the mounting tension, and finally everyone's impression to have won or lost a battle or to have laboriously negotiated an acceptable, but not wholly satisfactory compromise? This is when I perceive the high levels of anxiety underlying the entire process and try to uncover its origins.

I have come to the conclusion that each individual has legitimate reasons for wanting to maintain the status quo (i.e., separated special preschool) *and* desiring change at the same time (i.e., inclusion into the mainstream). This ambivalence introduces contradictions into the debates and negotiations that leave everyone confused, as much about their own position as about the positions of their discussion partners. Unfortunately, no one expresses freely the ambivalence of their own feelings and beliefs; no one deals with the contradictions underlying each position.

I propose here to take a look at the main actors involved in the integration process and some of their possible reasons to want simultaneously change and the status quo, to think about the possibilities of establishing clear communication, and, finally, to formulate some principles of action and interaction to restore a healthier climate to the debate and the realization of integrated preschool education.

Of course, my view is based mainly on concrete examples from Geneva or Switzerland, but I imagine that similar situations occur in other countries. I will also limit my comments to the integration of mentally disabled children, because their situation is more critical than that of children with other handicapping conditions.

2   Parents

In Switzerland, parent associations have been a decisive force in the development of expanded and improved services for children with disabilities. In Geneva, they have been responsible for creating and running special services, such as a home visiting program and a special kindergarten. The founding members of the parent association remember that, during this period, great progress was made in the early identification and diagnosis of handicapping conditions. New reeducation and rehabilitation methods became available, qualified professionals added new instruments for assessment and intervention to their repertoire each year, offering, at an early stage, expert care at home that took into account the cognitive, emotional, and behavioral problems of their disabled infant. The state and private organizations also provided adapted environments in special kindergarten and preschool classes that protected the children from hurtful experiences such as rejection by peers and adults or from the daily confrontations in a competitive world of inevitable difficulties and disappointments.

Parents were heard when they asked for services. However, today, they feel largely excluded from the decisions and the implementation of the educational and therapeutic process. Influenced by what happened in neighboring countries - particularly in Italy - they worry about the social isolation of their children from the mainstream and ask for more integrated education. Authorities and professionals, legitimately proud of the advances made in financing and providing more and more specialized services, tell parents to make up their minds: Hadn't they complained a few years back about inadequate education in regular settings? How could they now reject what they had asked for in the first place? The impression is conveyed to parents that they have to choose: the mainstream with little or no special intervention, or special settings with adequate care and education.

It is indeed frightening to think that the accomplishments for which parents have fought could now disappear or be diminished because integrated education cannot guarantee special services inside regular educational settings. And is it an acceptable risk to reject the protected environment for one's child, without being assured that the mainstream is prepared and willing to accept her?

In Geneva, a growing number of parents of mentally disabled children are now ready to take this risk. They have been encouraged by other groups of parents whose pressure has largely been responsible for the development of a system that has achieved, over the last 10 years, the successful inclusion of all visually impaired children without associated disabilities, as well as many hearing impaired children, into the regular preschool and school system of Geneva. A few years ago, parents of children with mental and emotional disabilities along with a small group of professionals formed "The Commission on Integration," which became an active study and pressure group with subcommissions working in special areas such as early intervention. At first, school officials, psychologists, special- education and regular teachers showed mild interest; later, the initiatives of the group frequently encountered passive resistance and, more recently, on certain occasions, even overt hostility. When ignored or confronted with an impossible choice (in this case, segregated education and adequate services or integrated education and insufficient special intervention), people become angry at those who ignore them or intimidate them and put them into a no-win situation. As a result, the members of this militant group now consider their achievements to be "victories," their actions formulated in terms of "strategies," and their leaders to be "up front, exposing themselves to the line of fire." In short, an entire combat vocabulary is applied to what ought to be a problem-solving task with complementary partners working to achieve a common goal.

I happen to agree with the parents' general concerns and with their taking the risk of asking for integrated preschool education without the guarantee that the regular education context is ready, meaning that it is willing, equipped, and trained, to deal adequately with this new challenge. After all, our regular education system also does not give any guarantees that it is always willing, equipped, and trained to deal adequately with normally developing children. I strongly believe that educational practices are best elaborated in the context in which they are supposed to be applied. No context will ever be entirely "ready" to receive an individual child; no child will ever be perfectly "ready" to join a new context. So my support goes to the parents, and I work on a regular basis with this group of parents. But I do worry about what it does to them to be ignored, misunderstood, or opposed; what it does to their priorities and their strategy when it comes to making themselves heard and to concretizing their ambitions. I wonder whether we have created a situation in which neither professionals nor parents are getting any closer to defining the best interest of groups of children and of individual children.

When Jessica's parents made the decision to withdraw her from the special kindergarten where she seemed unhappy and to be regressing rather than progressing, they did so against the advice of the special teacher, the physician, and the psychologist. In a way, they were saying: If she is unhappy and slow in progressing here, she might as well be this in a regular school. At least she'll get used to "real life," be with normally developing

children, and something "might rub off." Each of us would agree ,
is an insufficient individualized education project. Fortunately, hov
much more came out of this experience, although, from the start,
situation was left to chance. It took a year, and the refusal of regu.
teachers to work without special help, to get a special-education student
teacher to come into the classroom to assist the regular teacher in adapting
material and activities that helped Jessica participate in the program,
regulate her behavior, and actively develop her preacademic skills. It took
another year to include the teacher and the other children in the project and
attain her true social integration and not just her physical and sometimes
functional inclusion. Even today, Jessica's parents spend most of their
energy fighting for the continuation of her integrated education, for the
transfer of financial means from the special education budget to the regular
school, and for the rights of other disabled children to be integrated in the
regular school system. They have little time left on a daily basis to help
Jessica improve her academic and social skills or to meet with the teachers
and therapists in order to set new goals or evaluate progress. Outside the
small circle of people who helped them over the years to integrate and
maintain Jessica in the regular classroom, their relationship with
professionals is belligerent. They perceive them as potential enemies, which
often makes it difficult even for the professionals they trust to make
suggestions for changes and adjustments to Jessica's educational project.
They have become more involved in proving their point (that it was right
to abandon the special education circuit in order to join the mainstream)
than in giving support to Jessica and her teachers to make this experience
even better for everyone and to consolidate her achievements. I even suspect
that in fighting the professionals' reluctance to agree with their options, they
fight the doubts within themselves that inevitably haunt parents (as well as
professionals, for that matter) from time to time.

   Parents today want the best of two imperfect worlds: They want the
transfer of special-education resources into the mainstream. They know it
can be done, but they do not always see the complexity of the situation and
the many difficulties that have to be overcome - how can they? This is not
their job, the organization of the integration process is the task of
professionals -but it certainly will be much harder to overcome the obstacles
if we are working against each other rather than with each other.

3   Early Special-Education Teachers

Early interventionists know the complexities. For one thing, some of them remember the days when many people, even inside the field of education, believed that mentally disabled children could not learn much and were only to be pitied, ignored, or despised. They remember that they were considered as being something between a nun and a charity worker. Even today, people say to them: "We admire you so much . . . how can you work with those children every day, such patience!?" They hate the idea that the children they know and care for will be exposed to an often ignorant and intolerant social environment.

They also know how sensitive some of the children they work with are to unstructured situations, noise, the failure to accomplish a task, rough body contact, and unkind words. It is very difficult to believe that they would do just as well, if not better, in unprotected environments. Professionals have become so knowledgeable about the best conditions for learning, expressing feelings, and interacting that they think anything less than these good conditions will not do. They have reason to believe that they know what is in the child's best interest.

Special-education teachers feel wrongly accused of not being interested in the integration of disabled children. Is not the long range goal of social integration always mentioned as a main objective? Is not their work in the area of communication, self-help skills, and socioemotional development directly related to this final goal? They are preparing the children for their lives in the world of nondisabled people. The problem is to decide when they are ready. Not surprisingly, there are no clear-cut criteria on which to base this decision.

In addition, being specialists in early intervention, they know about the value of learning from one's peers, of the relative ease with which very young children approach and accept differences, and the relative tolerance regular teachers of very young children can show toward individual needs, because they are not yet subject to the pressure of having to adhere to a fixed academic program or to strict selection criteria and external standards of excellence.

One indication of their own doubts and ambivalent position is an argument professionals in early childhood education voice frequently: that the child could indeed go into a regular day-care center or kindergarten, but what about the continuity? What a disappointment if, later, they would have to leave and join the special education schools? This shows that most of them do see integrated placement as a positive experience and the return to special education as a reason for disappointment.

Each professional is also a citizen, a private person with a belief system. Today, this belief system includes the acceptance of differences, tolerance, and human rights. If they oppose an integrated education placement for a child, they find it difficult to reconcile these values with their professional position. I suspect sometimes that when they oppose the parents' wish for integration, they do it even more energetically when they need to silence an inner voice that points out the contradiction between their value system and their professional judgment.

When Jessica's parents returned to the local assessment center last year - mainly to tell the psychologist how well Jessica had developed in the integrated setting and invite her to observe Jessica in her classroom - the psychologist carried out another intelligence test and informed the parents that Jessica's IQ had not changed. Nor was any comment made about Jessica's greatly improved speech, her reading and writing skills, and her enthusiastic and well-formulated comments about her school. The psychologist maintained her opposition to this project and her belief that the parents did not have Jessica's best interest - here is the famous argument again! - in mind. Need I tell you that this visit has not done anything to change the parent's skepticism toward partnerships with professionals? Opponents met, each eager to prove something.

Other perhaps less noble, but still influential and legitimate arguments may determine special teachers' attitudes. Today teachers and therapists are recognized as valuable professionals and not as saints or as Lady Bountifuls. The recent development of interdisciplinary teams in special settings has brought them in close contact with other professionals and opened up new horizons for increasingly effective intervention strategies; transdisciplinarity gives them access to new competencies. Can you blame them for not wanting to exchange this situation with different, probably more difficult, working conditions? The sharing of influence and knowledge with regular teachers can appear less exciting and prestigious and more laborious. In a system of full inclusion, their status and working conditions (and even their salaries) have yet to be defined or guaranteed. It would be wrong to overlook, criticize, or dismiss these arguments.

The last element I would like to mention is what can be called institutional loyalty. If no strong political commitment is made in favor of integrated education; if the system, the employer of special-education teachers who hires special-education teachers, expresses great reluctance in this matter, then it is difficult for an individual teacher to personally defend a different position. Most people need to identify with the values and decisions made by the group they belong to. As long as the teachers and therapists working in special education centers are not presented with guidelines and a series of measures that can facilitate integrated education, they will not make advances in careful thinking and planning about this matter, and their support of some individual children's projects will not go beyond a short-lived, and often unsatisfactory "do-it-yourself" adventure.

4   Regular Kindergarten and Preschool Teachers

In the past, teachers received the message that they had failed students with special needs. A student who did not acquire the competencies and knowledge presented in the yearly curriculum reflected badly on the teacher's ability. Preschool and kindergarten became like a little kingdom in which teachers worked in splendid isolation. Educators were taught that "experts" were needed to understand and care for children who deviated from the norm; they were told to refer the problem child to a team of experts who more often than not recommended exclusion from the regular classroom. There were times when one wondered which child did not have special needs, and whether there were any children left who suited the regular classroom. (There is an interesting parallel evolution in the field of neonatology, when community maternity wards referred more and more cases to special care units, and, as a consequence, lost all experience, courage, and the means to deal with the slightest abnormality or crisis.

Separate bodies of knowledge emerged. Choices had to be made earlier and earlier in a child's life: languages or scientific training, university or vocational school? At age 10, parents and teachers had to decide on the future career of the child in their care. The selection process became an important issue, and, with it, competitivity increased. Now teachers are asked whether they are willing to spend more time with a disabled student, time in meetings, and collaborate closely with the same people who had told them not so long ago that it was not their job to teach those children. They are asked to change their working habits: individualized work, team teaching, tutoring systems. No special training is offered to them now; occasional optional workshops are all they can hope for. In addition, the integration of an increasing number of immigrant children (up to 19 nationalities in some classes) is gradually taking up their time and energy; they currently have other worries and are not necessarily eager to invest in another venture.

But most teachers also have the need to question their role and action in the classroom. Would some special-education practices not also be good practices for all children:- such as an individualized education project in which each child can develop according to his or her own schedule? Would it not be an interesting challenge to work together with a heterogeneous group of children and to have a colleague with whom to exchange, experiment, and elaborate new ways of teaching? In Geneva, the school not only has the mandate to teach but also to educate. Tolerance and acceptance of difference should be taught not only in the family but also in the classroom from an early age on when prejudices are not yet fixed and ingrained.

Jessica's second teacher voiced very serious doubts before accepting her in her class. "My job is to teach; the children in my class have to learn something; a mentally disabled child cannot follow the lessons and will not progress, and I will feel bad as a teacher." After only a few weeks, she noticed that even if Jessica could not follow the same program and make the same progress as the other children, she certainly learned and improved her skills and competencies every day. Now she finds Jessica's steady progress as rewarding and noteworthy as the results of her classmates. She is also excited about the social skills that they develop in interacting with Jessica: The first time Jessica recited a poem, the whole class spontaneously broke out into applause; frequently a child explains a lesson to Jessica, and they all insisted that Jessica join them for their ski camp, volunteering to help her in any way they could. Jessica also played a major role in integrating a new student whose initial reaction to his new school was to be aggressive and unpleasant toward his peers. Jessica's repeated demonstrations of affection and her efforts to make him join group activities proved to be effective and he has now taken on the role of her special mentor.

5   Politicians and Administrators

In Switzerland, we do not have any clear legislation that would enable parents to fight legally for their child's inclusion in the mainstream. Laws and regulations can be interpreted in many different ways. However, the financing of special treatments and educational measures is submitted to very precise and restrictive rules that leave very little freedom to administrators. The special education budget is a complicated combination of federal, cantonal, and community contributions, supplemented by private funds such as foundations and charitable organizations. This complicated system requires the specialists that they have become. They are not very eager to complicate matters further by trying to find the necessary agreements with the regular education budget.

In addition, politicians and administrators remember that the current situation in Switzerland, with its extended and generously financed special education system, has been possible because of a very favorable economic situation. They know how fragile goodwill and good intentions are, and that persons with disabilities are among the first to suffer from an economic recession. In Switzerland, the signs of a new frugality are already perceptible. Encouraging integrated education without having the guarantee that special education resources will be transferred to the ordinary preschool is a dangerous strategy in their opinion and according to their experience. Funding agencies could very well make integration an item on a hidden agenda in order to save money. Integrated preschool education appears to them as a gamble in which everyone takes great risks, the children, their parents, as well as the professionals.

Today in Geneva, I can see our apprehensions about organizing and forcing major changes, but also our understanding that changes are necessary: changes both in regard to our attitudes as citizens who want to influence the debate about which kind of society we want to live in and as professionals in the area of education - regular and special. In my opinion, the clash between fear and wish for change (both often present in the same individual) has created a tense and uncomfortable situation in Geneva with little room for an open discussion on the advantages and disadvantages of integrated education.

How can we change this situation? The first change to make is to urge people to express their opinions and feelings freely, even, or especially, if they are ambivalent and contain contradictory arguments. Each one of us, parent or professional, should be given a context in which he or she can feel allowed to have doubts, conflicting attitudes, and changing positions without taking the risk of receiving wholesale criticism of their value system or their competence.

The second change may seem a formal one, but strikes me as a chance to break a vicious circle in more fundamental ways: Each actor in the educational plan of an individual child should acquire the habit of saying: *I believe* these are the needs and priorities and the desirable short- and long-term goals as well as the means I propose to attain them, rather than insisting that one *knows* what is in the child's best interest. If people could formulate their views together in this way, many common concerns would emerge, and conflicts concerning the best ways to solve problems and achieve common goals would be circumscribed more differentially and manageably.

A third recommendation would be to merge as much as possible the training programs of special and regular teachers. Many special education methods and approaches are of great interest for all children; theoretical references of the same nature have to be taught to students in both fields;

a basis for common practices could be elaborated; and the future professionals would already learn to collaborate, help each other, and negotiate. This year, preparations are under way to integrate the training of primary education teachers, including preschool teachers, into the Department of Educational Science at the University of Geneva. The division of special education, of which I am part, will certainly recommend a largely common training concept for special and regular teachers.

The fourth recommendation concerns the hierarchical organization of the interdisciplinary team. I do not believe that all interdisciplinary teams ought to become transdisciplinary - this is another discussion altogether - but certainly by now we ought to be ready to coordinate and to communicate with each other about a child's needs and the priorities to be established. The anachronistic hierarchy of professions: physicians, psychologists, therapists, teachers, social workers, in that order, still gets in the way sometimes when priority choices have to be made for an individualized project. Obviously, the child's and the family's needs will determine whose imput is the most important and who should be the main contact for the parent and the child. For each family, the interdisciplinary team has to function in a different way. This demands flexibility, true respect for all professional competencies involved, and the ability to see one's own contribution to the child's and the family's well-being as relative to others' contributions, and sometimes even as dispensable.

If preschool integrated education is to become a priority concern of the 1990s, we really have to learn how to play together - families, children, and professionals. Playing together means elaborating and respecting common rules; creating, innovating, challenging, but also expressing our fears and doubts; allowing for mistakes; helping each other to overcome obstacles and resolve difficulties together. Above all, it means enjoying each other's company. With Jessica we could than say: We love our school.

References

Desbiolles, I. (1993). *L'Ecole? Mais moi j'y suis aussi.* Memoire de licence. Geneve: FAPSE, Université de Geneve.

Part Four

Planning and Evaluation
of Early Intervention

M. Brambring, H. Rauh, and A. Beelmann (Eds.). (1996). *Early childhood intervention: Theory, evaluation, and practice* (pp. 281-304). Berlin, New York: de Gruyter.

Recent Trends and Issues in Program Evaluation in Early Intervention

Robert Sheehan and Scott Snyder

1   Introduction

The most recent issue of the *Journal of Early Intervention* had as its lead article a discussion by Diane Bricker entitled "*A rose by any other name, or is it?*" (Bricker, 1993). We read that article and appreciated, as always, Diane's thoughts, and put the article aside concluding that it did not relate much to our work. After all, we are research methodologists, statisticians, and evaluation specialists. We have little to do with labeling our field, labeling our professionals, or labeling our children. We did recall how in 1989 the *Journal of Early Intervention*'s name was changed from the *Journal of the Division for Early Childhood*. We pursued this thought enough to go back and locate Sam Odom's editorial discussion (Odom, 1989) of why the Journal's name was changed and realized that the name change occurred as a way of recognizing the broadening of activity that occurs in our discipline. Once again, we put that thought aside thinking it had little relevance to our own work.

When preparing this chapter, we found our own discussions returning to Diane's article and Sam's editorial, and we concluded that these writings helped to crystallize the central point that we wished to make in this presentation. These writings helped us understand that in the decade of the 1990s, we are planning and conducting early intervention activities very differently than we did in earlier years. Consequently, we are evaluating the impact of our interventions very differently. It is our purpose in this chapter to discuss the changes we see in program evaluation as a result of changes that we see in early intervention.

We note as a preamble that program evaluation is a term distinct from child evaluation. We are sure that all of you at this conference would not confuse program evaluation - *the process of data collection for decision-making about a program* - with child evaluation - *the process of assessing a child's eligibility for early intervention*. We would not feel it necessary to mention this distinction if there were not one or two students every year who enroll in our graduate seminars in program evaluation thinking the course will teach them the finer points of diagnostic assessment.

2   Distinctions Between Program Evaluation and Basic Research

Before discussing our current strategies for evaluating intervention issues, we must provide a foundation for why the practice of program evaluation is tied so intrinsically to the practice of early intervention. We do so by making an important distinction between program evaluation and basic research. In 1978, one of us wrote an article that appeared in the Jossey-Bass Series: *New Directions in Program Evaluation* (Hodges & Sheehan, 1978). In that article, it was argued that the distinctions between program evaluation and basic research were largely cosmetic, and that basic research was equally able to answer applied questions of interest, whereas program evaluation was equally capable of generating new knowledge. Now, 15 years and many program evaluations later, we are less sure that this distinction is cosmetic. To the contrary, we are now convinced that the differences between program evaluation and basic research are real, they are important, and they play a positive role in shaping early intervention practice.

We acknowledge, at the outset, that there are important similarities between program evaluation and basic research. Both program evaluation and basic research require appropriate sampling, measurement, and design-and-analysis considerations. A good basic researcher has the same tools at hand as a good program evaluator.

Increasingly, however, we find ourselves writing and teaching our students about the important distinctions between program evaluation and basic research. These differences are summarized in Table 1.

These distinctions noted in Table 1 indicate that program evaluation is largely responsive rather than initiating. Program evaluation is driven by a need for information - a need for information that is based upon practice. As practice changes, program evaluation also changes. And early intervention practice is changing.

Table 1.   *Distinctions Between Program Evaluation and Basic Research*

Good program evaluation is:		Good basic research is:
1. Responsive to the data collection needs of administrators and staff.	vs.	1. Responsive to a need in a field or discipline for knowledge theories testing.
2. Best designed with full involvement of those to be affected by the evaluation.	vs.	2. Subjects of the study are rarely consulted in the design.
3. Contextually relevant.	vs.	3. Relatively unaffected by the context of any particular setting.
4. Concerned with collecting a minimal data set. If you cannot state how you would use data, you would not collect such data.	vs.	4. Concerned with collecting a maximum data set. If data might, at some point, be of interest, then collect such data.
5. Frequently modified midstream in response to partial data.	vs.	5. Typically fixed in design and data collection strategy from the start.
6. Reported back to constituents as soon as possible.	vs.	6. Reported back when the researcher is ready for professional critique and review of findings.
7. Greatly influenced by the actual format of reported results. Different formats are required for different audiences.	vs.	7. Written in a technical style that rarely varies across dissemination efforts.

3   Changes in Early Intervention Practice

How then, is early intervention practice changing? Early intervention practice is becoming:
1. More family-centered and more ecological.
2. More concerned with health care and health care settings.
3. More concerned with cost benefit.

Carl Dunst argues for a broad-based approach to early intervention that is family-centered and ecological rather than child-centered and separate from children's social and nonsocial environments (Dunst et al., 1993; Dunst et al., 1990). While the characteristics of a special needs child may be the precipitating cause for that child to be in an early intervention program, the child's entire family and social network actually become partners and recipients of the intervention process.

Consider Dunsts's (1993) recent argument that an early intervention program must identify *and measure* "multiple-risk factors" and intentionally support and evaluate "multiple-opportunity factors." An intervention program that is family-centered, working within a multiple-risk multiple-opportunity model, can be evaluated only by a multimethod, multivariable, multi-incident data collection design.

Recently, Carl Dunst and his colleagues (Dunst et al., 1990) presented data providing empirical support for the argument that changes in handicapped children's mental ages (measured as gain scores on the Bayley Scales of Infant Development, Bayley, 1969) were related to both children's behavioral characteristics and family systems variables. These findings led the authors to conclude that interventions should be aimed at providing support and resources to families as a way of reinforcing any direct efforts being made with developmentally disabled or delayed children. Any evaluation operating within such an early intervention program must document the family and social system side of such an intervention as well as the child's behavior and progress that is exhibited during the course of intervention.

Dunst and his colleagues have been leaders in developing instruments that capture the complexity of family and social systems variables. Such instruments include the *Family Resource Scale*, the *Family Support Scale*, and the *Family Needs Scale*. Most of these instruments are available from Brookline Books in Cambridge, MA (see Dunst et al., 1988, for a description of these forms).

The cornerstone of our early intervention efforts with infants and toddlers is a federally mandated Individualized Family Service Plan (IFSP). The IFSP must clearly meet family needs as well as children's needs (McGonigel et al., 1991). Meeting family needs is now an acceptable and mandated outcome of early intervention as well as a desirable process variable in early intervention. Don Bailey and his colleagues at the Frank Porter Graham Center have been leaders in developing instruments that capture family strengths and needs. For example, the *Family Needs Survey* (Bailey & Simeonsson, 1985) is a 35-item Likert scale that provides an opportunity for a family to assess their own needs. Additional family assessment tools are noted in Bailey and Simeonsson's 1988 text.

We also note that the family-centered nature of early intervention suggests a need for data collection procedures also to be family-centered. In 1988, the Association for the Care of Children's Health (McGonigel, 1988) convened a panel to address this concern and issued a number of principles and guidelines for funders, researchers, and families. The principles for researchers (including program evaluators) are listed in Table 2.

The principles suggested for these guidelines are very specific. For example, the principle calling for involvement of parents has guidelines on the nature, composition, and functioning of parent advisory committees. Note, these are parent committees advising on the research process, not advisory committees advising on the early intervention process. Researchers are also advised to ask themselves whether or not the potential value of a particular piece of research with families justifies its intrusiveness.

The increasing commitment of early intervention personnel to family-focused research certainly presents a worthwhile challenge to data collection activities occurring within those programs.

Table 2.   *Principles for Family Centered Research (for Researchers)*

---

1. Research on children with special health care needs or disabilities should be designed, conducted, and evaluated in collaboration with parents.
2. Researchers should acknowledge the diversity of families, respecting their culture, ethnicity, values, priorities, and coping styles.
3. The privacy and autonomy of families should be respected by researchers.
4. Research should include provisions for sharing with families complete and unbiased information about the purpose and use of the research and about the possible benefits of participation to the child and family and to other children and families.

Note.   Excerpted   from   *Guidelines For Family-Centered Research* (McGonigel, 1988) with permission.

How else is early intervention changing? If you were to ask persons working in early intervention today, you would likely find that they are all spending an increasing amount of time in hospitals and public health clinics.

The passage of the Individuals with Disabilities Act (IDEA, formerly P.L. 99-457) mandates that children with special health care needs are appropriate targets for early intervention. The fact that the IDEA mandates services to children with special health care needs is only one half of the reason why we spend so much time in health care settings. The other half of this reason is that children with any special needs are frequently a challenge to most health care professionals!

Like most Americans, I read the paper each day and pay careful attention to the changes underway in both Western and Eastern Europe. If we were to talk to colleagues from the former socialist countries of Bulgaria, Yugoslavia, Czechoslovakia, and the Soviet Union, we would hear even more clearly about the strong movement toward concern for special health care needs of children and the health care needs of all our special children. When the economic and political basis of our families is disrupted, health will most certainly deteriorate.

I do not even have to turn to Western and Eastern Europe for vivid demonstration of our increasing concern with health issues in early intervention programs. I now spend numerous days per month working with the Director and Staff of the Cleveland Health Department. Using Federal funds, we have been developing intervention methods to change the statistics noted in Table 3.

Our early intervention efforts in Cleveland (Healthy Family Healthy Start Project 1992-1997) are focusing on improved prenatal health care, improved job training, improved monitoring of immunizations, improvements in the health and nutritional status of families in targeted neighborhoods, and improved coordination of services between and among early intervention service agencies. Our efforts to intervene in these statistics are challenging our abilities to evaluate our own interventions. Within 3 years, we must document that our efforts have altered our infant mortality rates, our low birth weight rates, and our immunization rates. This assumes that we are able to establish reliable and valid benchmarks (or indicators) for each of our communities. Our evaluation efforts are becoming more like epidemiological studies than they are like highly controlled experimental studies.

Concurrent with our interest in health care, we have a growing concern in intervention programs about costs. At the time of preparing this chapter, America is engrossed in a national debate about Health Insurance reform. There is no doubt that for almost all Americans, health care reimbursement is what drives the delivery of health care services. If our children's health-related needs are not covered by some form of insurance or reimbursement, then our children will not receive the health-related early intervention services that we advocate.

Table 3.   *Statistics Driving Healthy Family Healthy Start Intervention Programs*

Health statistics about the nation

1. America ranks 22nd among industrialized countries in the number of babies who die in their first year. The national infant mortality rate is 8.9 deaths per 1,000 live births.
2. Low birth weight (less than 2,500 grams) leading to health and developmental complications is the leading cause of infant death. It is also the most preventable. The rate of babies born at low birth weight (7%) is at the highest levels (in 1993) observed since 1978. The rate of low birth weight births for Afro-American babies is twice the rate for white babies.
3. Nearly 20% of America's 738,200 pregnant women annually use one or more illegal substances at some point during their pregnancy.
4. Over 25% of all women giving birth in the US receive no prenatal health care. Among Afro-American women, 40% receive no prenatal health care.

Health statistics about the city in which I work

Cleveland is a large industrial city (500,000 residents) located in the north central part of America. It is part of what has been called the rust belt, because its industry has moved from heavy manufacturing to light manufacturing and public services in only three decades.

1. The Cleveland infant mortality rate is 16.8 infant deaths per 1,000 births (nearly twice the national average).
2. The Cleveland low birth weight rate is 12.1% (nearly 50% more than the national average). In several of our neighborhood communities, this figure rises to more than 20%.
3. Nearly 64% of Cleveland's children have not been immunized by age 2.

Note. Excerpted from City of Cleveland Department of Public Health Vital Statistics Report, 1991 & U.S. Department of Health & Human Services Fact Sheet, Healthy Start, May, 1992.

There is a movement in our country to establish a national guaranteed benefit program that would be available to all Americans, employed and unemployed. As currently structured, the plan proposed by President Clinton would cut off physical therapy, occupational therapy, and speech therapy for children with congenital disabilities. When a senior White House advisor (Ira Magaziner) was questioned about the omission of therapies for children with congenital abnormalities, he indicated that "the White House had looked at the possibility of providing such benefits but the way the actuaries scored it, it became extremely expensive." He further indicated that ". . . it's something we wish we could do, provide funding, and I'm just trying to be honest about what we have put together within the financial framework" (The Plain Dealer, October 1, 1993).

If the national health care plan has been developed omitting such therapies because of their expense, then a potential way of rebutting such a decision is to argue that early intervention including such therapies is cost-effective. In reacting to the omission of therapies, Dr. Greber, Director of St. Mary's Hospital for Children argued: "If a kid doesn't get therapy it's an obvious hindrance to the child's growth and potential." The President of the March of Dimes responded to the proposed health care plan by saying "Children with birth defects must have coverage for the services they need to prevent further disability and to help them function every day" (The Plain Dealer, October 1, 1993).

When dealing with politicians and administrators who wish to cut funding to save money, we are increasingly having to respond with data-based arguments that early intervention is cost-effective. This means that more than ever before, we must gather data describing the actual costs and projected savings of early intervention. To gather these data, we must think more like auditors, actuaries, and accountants without losing our perspectives as psychologists and educators.

Cost-benefit analyses dictate a much more complex approach to program evaluation. Consider Levin's (1989) argument with regard to programs for at-risk students:

> I have also suggested that cost-benefit analyses of educational investments for these students suggest large payoffs for society. The precise increase in spending that will be required depends upon the definition of the at-risk population, the goals of the programs, and the effectiveness of the interventions to reach these goals. (p. 58)

To support Levin's contention of the value of intervention programs, we must gather data on population definitions, program characteristics (including costs), and program impacts.

Almost 15 years ago, I was fortunate enough to work with Diane Bricker on a grant to develop a tracking and monitoring system that would be completed by parents as infants were developing into young children. I noticed 5 years ago that Diane was presenting the Infant Monitoring Project as a "Low Cost System Using Parents to Monitor the Development of At-Risk Children" (Bricker & Squires, 1989). Following Diane's example, and the example of Karl White and his colleagues at the University of Utah, we are beginning to present the costs of early intervention alongside the success of early intervention.

My point in raising these issues is not to initiate a debate here about the value of therapy for congenitally disabled children, nor to point out what type of intervention is most cost-effective, nor to argue for the cost-effectiveness of programs for at-risk children. Rather, it is to point out that early intervention decisions are likely to be made based upon availability of cost-effective evaluation data.

4   An Overview of Current Program Evaluation Practices

We (Snyder & Sheehan, 1993) have found it useful to categorize program evaluation practices into four categories by the types of decisions addressed by each evaluation. First, some program evaluations address front-end decisions. These are decisions that must be made prior to onset of an activity. Second, other program evaluations reflect program process. These decisions reflect a desire to change existing practice in the midst of that practice. Third, there are program evaluations that stress impact or outcome issues. Impact issues are typically the result of administrators needing to determine whether to continue, discontinue, or dramatically alter an early intervention program. Finally, and most recently, we have seen an increasing number of evaluations that we would describe as policy evaluations. Policy evaluations are an attempt to identify all relevant policies of two or more agencies (typically state and federal agencies) and identify areas of policy overlap, policy duplication, and policy discrepancy.

We have, at times, identified cost decisions as separate from the decisions already noted. We are beginning to realize that cost analysis is an important component of front-end evaluations, program-process evaluations, and impact studies. We have also argued elsewhere (Snyder & Sheehan, 1993) that ecological decisions are somewhat separate from the decisions already noted. Ecological decisions refer to a need to determine whether there is sufficient interface between an early intervention program and the community within which it operates. As we seek to match changing early interventions with changing program evaluations, we are now more inclined to argue that cost and ecological components should be included in most front-end evaluations, most program-process evaluations, most impact evaluations, and most policy evaluations.

4.1 Front-End Evaluations - What Are Recent Trends?

Front-end evaluations refer to evaluations that answer decisions about the need for intervention services, the likely impact of intervention services, and best ways to provide intervention services to an unserved or an underserved group. We are seeing a growing interest in front-end evaluations, an interest generated in part by the 1986 passage of Public Law 99-457, the Education of the Handicapped Act Amendments (this was later changed by P.L. 101-476 to the Individuals with Disabilities Act, or IDEA).

The first contribution of the IDEA was that each state was required to define the term "developmental delay." Under this Act, states were required to provide a definition for "at-risk" if they chose to serve the needs of at-risk children and their families. For several years we witnessed states conducting front-end evaluations seeking to determine how many children and families would be affected, statewide and regionally, by using certain definitions. For example, South Carolina could have identified a target population for early intervention ranging from 1,000 to 10,000 depending upon the particular definitions chosen (Sheehan, personal communication 1993). We saw similar statistics for the states of Indiana, Pennsylvania, and Colorado, and we are sure that they were available in all states providing early intervention services. Issues were addressed in determining definitions such as the numerical result of including or excluding certain congenital abnormalities (e.g., cleft palate) or including or excluding children of mentally retarded adults.

In South Carolina and Florida, we saw program eligibility definitions being formed based upon data gathered to determine the number and characteristics of children who might benefit from early interventions (Garwood & Sheehan, 1989; Mandolang, 1991; Sheehan, 1991, 1992). In other states, we saw decisions being made to initiate aggressive child find programs in regions in which the known child count did not correspond to an estimated percentage. Decision makers, therefore, were being informed by data gathered in a front-end program evaluation.

This same legislation (P.L. 99-457, later changed to P.L. 101-476) also caused states to have to report annually to the Federal Government on the number and age of served and unserved children. To date, funding for services to infants and toddlers through this legislation is based upon the proportion of each state's general population of children birth through 2 years of age. Under this approach, funding decisions are based upon a readily available statistic that comes from a State Census Office. States have expressed concern, however, that the day will soon come when funding levels will be determined by the actual number of served and unserved eligible children. When and if this occurs, front-end studies will become even more widespread, because they will directly affect allocations States will receive from the Federal Government.

We have also seen front-end studies (in the form of needs assessments) conducted for many years seeking to inform decisions about the delivery of staff development services to early intervention personnel. The most common method is to ask staff to rate their existing skill level on a number of dimensions and to make training decisions in light of the obtained ratings. This approach is very similar to needs assessment efforts evident in public schools (DeRoche, 1987) under the current effective schools movement.

We note that needs assessments in the staff development area are also used extensively in business and industry (Brinkerhoff, 1989), and that changes are underway in the manner in which businesses are conducting needs assessments. First, needs assessments are becoming increasingly more interactive and process-oriented, reflecting data gathered over several periods and typically in response to simulations rather than paper-and-pencil single administrations (Aquila et al., 1987). Second, needs assessments are increasingly becoming based upon data provided by a variety of sources. Consider the Supervisory Behavior Analysis (SBA) instrument developed by Ken Blanchard (undated). This scale is used by an employee and concurrently by an employee's subordinates and superiors. The intersection of these three points of view (self, below, and above) is considered the most viable point to begin training. With calls for privatization and public choice in our schools, we anticipate that our education practices will become much more like business and industry in the years to come.

Evaluability assessment is another type of front-end evaluation worth noting. Evaluability assessment involves an assessment, prior to conducting an evaluation, of the factors necessary to successfully evaluate a program. One outcome of an evaluability assessment may be a decision to delay an evaluation of a relatively new early intervention program until a later date. Alternatively, a decision might be made to conduct an evaluation, but to focus it in a certain way or to evaluate only one component of an early intervention program (i.e., the services to children and families component; or the screening and referral component).

In our work with agencies such as school districts and hospitals, we have, at times, advised that an evaluability assessment be considered as the first stage of an evaluation. During this first stage, documents are reviewed and staff are interviewed to determine the most likely decisions that could be affected by an evaluation. The outcome of the first stage is a decision to proceed or not proceed with an evaluation. If the recommendation is to proceed, the first stage report includes a complete evaluation plan with specific evaluation questions, instruments, and reporting requirements. Last year we conducted an evaluability assessment in a large community hospital and concluded that the politically volatile status of hospital administration-staff relations precluded any successful evaluation. The recommendation was to delay any evaluation activity for 6 months until there was a change in administration-staff relations or a change in the administration of the hospital.

We have heard it said that program evaluations are, too frequently, of little use, because they tend to either confirm existing practice or make unacceptable suggestions for change. Brinkerhoff examined many program evaluations of training programs (Brinkerhoff, 1989) and special education programs (Brinkerhoff et al., 1983) and concluded that they were a waste of time. We believe that more extensive use of evaluability assessments in early intervention programs would result in more productive evaluations.

4.2 Program-Process Evaluations - What Are Recent Trends?

Program-process evaluations reflect a desire to change existing practice in the midst of that practice. A major reason why an intervention program (or a state or regional office) might establish a process evaluation is to determine if the program is meeting compliance with internal and external standards. We suggested (Snyder & Sheehan, 1993) the following questions as appropriate for process evaluations:

1. To what extent are services congruent with the program's specific intervention model or curriculum?
2. To what extent is the program being administered in a manner congruent with a specified organizational management/supervision theory?

3. To what extent are program components carried out with prescribed procedures, on schedule, and with efficient use of resources?
4. To what extent are staff performing roles and responsibilities consistent with expectations?
5. What are the direct and indirect program expenditures incurred during a given period of time?
6. To what extent are program components carried out in a manner congruent with best practices?
7. To what extent are the clients for whom this program was developed actually receiving services?
8. What are the reasons for unexpected departures from pre-established expectations for 1 through 7 above? (p. 277)

We still see these as reasonable overall questions to include in any early intervention process evaluation.

We have worked the past year with the Ohio Department of Education in an endeavor that is occurring throughout the country: establishing statewide standards and monitoring systems for early intervention programs operating in public school programs. This work reaffirms our belief that administrators want decisions to be based on program process data. Decisions include granting or renewing licenses for programs; identifying areas of compliance and incompliance in program operation; and identifying programs that are meeting standards of excellence. During the course of this work we have designed the data systems described in Table 4.

These systems have been used for the past 8 months and are currently undergoing revision. The systems were designed by working closely with state officials to identify each of their decision-making needs and then ensure that data collection systems exist to meet each need. An excerpt from one of these monitoring systems is included in Figure 1.

Table 4.   *Data Systems Included in Statewide Early Childhood Monitoring Project*

1. *Early Intervention Program Monitoring System Form*
   A system to determine if an early intervention program is in compliance with state standards.
2. *Early Intervention Program Resources Form*
   A system to record information about persons, organizations, or documents that might assist an early intervention coordinator.
3. *Early Intervention Program Key Contact Directory*
   A system to record names, addresses, and contact information about early childhood service providers in a region.
4. *Early Intervention Program Contact Log*
   A system to record information about the contacts (phone, mail, in person) that an early childhood coordinator might have.
5. *Early Intervention Program Monthly Activities Report*
   A system to record information about the activities of an early intervention coordinator during each month.
6. *Early Intervention Program Profile/Needs Assessment*
   A system to record characteristics of an early intervention program and assess program needs.
7. *Early Intervention Program Training TA Contract Form*
   A system to record training and technical assistance contracts.
8. *Early Intervention Program Consultant Reaction Form (On Site)*
   A system to evaluate activities of a consultant.
9. *Early Intervention Program Workshop Reaction Form*
   A system to evaluate a workshop.
10. *Early Intervention Program Site Visit Scheduling System*
    A system to schedule and record information about monitoring visits.

Regional Consultant_____   Field Representative_____   Date Observation

License Status: ___New   ___Provisional (6 Month)   ___Provisional (1 Year) ___2 Year
District Name _____   District (IRN) _____
County _____   Building/Site Name _____
Onsite type: ___Scheduled   ___Unscheduled

Compliance Summary

Rules		Compliance		Date
3301-37-02	Program	Yes	No	_____
3301-37-03	Staff	Yes	No	_____
3301-37-04	Policies & Procedures	Yes	No	_____
3301-37-05	Child Information	Yes	No	_____
3301-37-06	Facilities	Yes	No	_____
3301-37-07	Equipment & Supplies	Yes	No	_____
3301-37-08	Evaluation	Yes	No	_____
3301-37-09	School Food	Yes	No	_____
3301-37-10	Diapering	Yes	No	_____
3301-37-11	Mgmt. Communicable Disease	Yes	No	_____

Compliance Detail Record
301-37 PRESCHOOL CHECKLIST
3301-37-02 Program

1.	Evidence of developed philosophy and goals. DOCUMENTATION: Written philosophy and goals on file which give direction to program.	Y N I NA
2.	Evidence of developed plan which describes activities, learning environment, and other age appropriate approaches to meet developmental needs of child. DOCUMENTATION: Written plan on file.	Y N I NA
3.	Evidence of developed parent involvement program which is given to parent of each child enrolled. DOCUMENTATION: Written plan on file which includes how parents access inspection reports.	Y N I NA
4.	Evidence of two conferences held each year. DOCUMENTATION: Written documentation that conferences will be scheduled .	Y N I NA
5.	Evidence of balance of quiet and active play throughout program. DOCUMENTATION: Written plan on file detailing quiet and active play; actual observation of program .	Y N I NA
6.	Evidence of nap for program five hours or more. DOCUMENTATION: Schedule on file which indicates nap.	Y N I NA

Note. This form continued through all state regulations with appropriate coding of legislative and policy references.

Figure 1.   Excerpts from Early Intervention Program Monitoring System Form.

In addition to our work at the State level, we have also developed a number of process evaluation systems for local early intervention programs. Figure 2 represents an excerpt of a computerized data collection system that includes the titles of all forms relevant to an early intervention program.

```
            >>> ADD/EDIT DATA <<<
            AVAILABLE SELECTIONS

 1.   REFERRAL INFORMATION AND ADDING A NEW CHILD            R1
 2.   REGISTRATION FORM                                      R2
 3.   SCREENING RESULTS                                      SR1
 4.   FAMILY INFORMATION                                     FI1
 5.   BIRTH AND MEDICAL HISTORY                              BM1
 6.   FEE AND CONTACT SHEET/ENROLLED CHILDREN                FC1
 7.   DISCHARGE SUMMARY (DISCHARGE A CHILD)                  DS1
 8.   MONITORING RESULTS/DEVEL. MONITORING CHILDREN          MR1
 9.   DEVELOPMENTAL PROGRESS                                 DP1
10.   CORE INFORMATION FOUND ON MORE THAN ONE FORM           CI1
11.   CASE MANAGER TIME/MANAGEMENT                           TM1
12.   CASE MANAGER CONSULTATION AND EVALUATION UNITS         CE1
      RETURN TO PREVIOUS MENU
```

Figure 2. Excerpt from a local early intervention program data system.

As the titles of these forms suggest, local early intervention programs are interested in gathering data that record a child's and family's activity from screening to discharge. Local programs also need data describing the activity of staff throughout the day. The decision makers in these programs need such information to be recorded just once within a system, and then have the system update all necessary fields on all forms when information in that field changes.

Local decision makers are also very much in need of reports that can generate an unduplicated count of children served by an intervention program. Figure 3 represents an excerpt of a computerized data collection system that generates a number of reports based upon data entered in the data collection forms names in Figure 2.

Developing program-process evaluations is not particularly exciting evaluation work. An enormous amount of time and energy is directed toward creating forms and computerized systems that are user-friendly and distract only minimally from the process of providing early intervention services. The outcome of such systems is typically of greatest relevance for the single program that is the subject of the evaluation. It is extremely difficult to publish the results of program-process evaluations, and program

```
┌─────────────────────────────────────────────────────────────────────────┐
│                          >>>  REPORTS  <<<                                 │
│                         AVAILABLE SELECTIONS                               │
│                                                                           │
│    1.   MONTHLY SERVICE REPORT                                  REPORT1   │
│    2.   MONTHLY UNITS OF DIRECT SERVICE TO FAMILIES            REPORT2   │
│    3.   MONTHLY PROGRAM STATISTICS                             REPORT3   │
│    4.   UNDUPLICATED COUNT OF ENROLLED CHILDREN               REPORT4   │
│    5.   REFERRAL INFORMATION ON CHILDREN                      REPORT5   │
│    6.   DIRECTOR'S MONTHLY REPORT ON ENROLLED CHILDREN        REPORT6   │
│         RETURN TO PREVIOUS MENU                                           │
└─────────────────────────────────────────────────────────────────────────┘
```

Figure 3. Excerpt of available reports from an early intervention program data system.

evaluators' greatest satisfaction is to be found in providing useful information without creating a cumbersome bureaucracy. Decision makers are keenly aware that we are in an information society. These administrators are demanding process data collection systems that are simple to use, immediate in their response, and helpful. Our job is to respond to these requests.

4.3 Impact Evaluations - What Are Recent Trends?

Impact evaluations *should be* the result of administrators needing (and wanting) to determine whether to continue, discontinue, or dramatically alter an early intervention program. We note that these *should be* the reasons for impact evaluations, but, in our experience, they are too frequently not the reasons for impact evaluations. We have found that program administrators who ask for impact evaluations are frequently doing so with no clear decisions in mind but rather an earnest desire to evaluate something in their program. To help clarify such a situation, as part of planning for an impact evaluation we will frequently ask: "*What decision will you make if the evaluation is all quite positive?*" We also ask "*What decision will you make if the evaluation results are quite negative?*" We are then typically told that if the results are positive, present practice will continue. We are also typically told there is no real reason to expect that results will be negative, so no thought has been given to that possibility. Alternatively, we have been told that current funding and staffing patterns will not change, therefore any decision-making options in those areas are not possible.

The point that we are making is that administrators in early intervention programs are typically not prepared to modify existing practices, even when they have asked for an impact evaluation study. The administrators will typically ask for an impact study to provide justification for current practice - to demonstrate that current practice is working rather than to truly evaluate with an open mind about program changes. One day, the following quote was found attached to our door: "*Sure, We will listen to your suggestions for change . . . . Quick, kill him while his back is turned*" (Anonymous and Undated, for a reason). This quote does typify the difficult circumstances under which impact evaluations are sometimes conducted. To support this argument, consider the title of Kleinfeld and McDiarmid's (1986) article: *Living to tell the tale: Researching politically controversial topics and communicating the findings.* These authors argue that to successfully conduct research in politically controversial areas one should:

1. Identify the decision makers.
2. Gain the confidence of stakeholders by personally asking for their advice.
3. Set up a steering committee.
4. Frame the research questions in nonthreatening ways.
5. Design research from the outset with human credibility, not only scientific credibility, in mind.
6. Design research from the outset with a dissemination strategy, not only the research report, in mind.
7. Communicate preliminary research personally to stakeholders.
8. Use your steering committee to disseminate findings and make policy recommendations.
9. Use a mixture of media to get the message out.
10. Communicate findings in small pieces.
11. Write for the right audience.
12. Say it again, Sam (send your message out again and again in different forms).

These suggestions are as relevant for impact evaluations as they for any other type of program evaluation in early intervention settings.

Yet another factor limiting the utility of impact evaluations is that they are quite hard to do well. Numerous reviews (Dunst & Rheingrover, 1981; Shonkoff et al., 1988; Simeonsson et al., 1982; Snyder & Sheehan, 1985) have documented the inadequacies of the large volume of published efficacy research. Most published efficacy studies fail to control for even the most basic methodological concerns - comparability of comparison groups, the effects of testing and maturation, documentation of treatment fidelity, and so forth.

Many authors have pointed to yet another complicating factor in designing our outcome studies: limitations of our outcome measures. The validity of most standardized tests for measuring children's progress is undocumented, if not questionable. The utility of most standardized tests for children with motor or sensory problems is an enormous problem. The limited range of developmental performance captured by most standardized tests is in direct conflict with the wide range of developmental targets identified by early intervention programs. Shonkoff et al. (1988) advise us that we must "plan more complex evaluations that seek to explore the specific influences of early intervention services within the ecology of child and family life" (p. 87). A single standardized test simply does not work with this complex evaluation approach.

Given each of these concerns, what can we say are the recent trends in conducting outcome studies? First, as noted, we try to avoid conducting outcome studies when there is no clear purpose for such studies to occur, or when studies of another type (i.e., front-end studies or program-process studies) are likely to contribute more to decision making.

Second, when outcome studies are, in fact, appropriate, we build sufficient time into designing outcome studies to achieve consensus (from all stakeholders) on the intended impacts of the program. Stating that an intended impact is for all children to progress at their optimum rate is not enough. Some strategy must also be suggested for determining how to calculate children's optimum rate. For some children (i.e., many at-risk children), our intended goal is to prevent decline in developmental progress. For other children (i.e., developmentally delayed children), our intended goal is to arrest and reverse a declining developmental rate. For yet other children (i.e., terminally ill children with progressive neurological disorder), we may have as our goal a reduction or a delay in the likely decline of developmental performance.

Stating that a program is designed to enhance family functioning is not enough. Is this a goal for all families? What about families whose functioning levels are quite strong? What is meant by "enhance?" What is meant by "family functioning?" What is meant by "family?"

Where do we turn when we are trying to build consensus about our intended outcomes? We turn to our increasingly sophisticated and articulated model of intervention. Does our intervention model have a theoretical base? Does it have a practical base? What assumptions are implied or stated in our model? What implications do these assumptions have for achieving consensus on our outcomes?

Consider Carl Dunst's recent article (Dunst et al., 1990). His intervention model reflects a social systems perspective. The data collected included:

1. *Child Outcome Variables.* Children's mental age expressed as developmental gain score over a 12-month period (Bayley Scales; Bayley, 1969).
2. *Child Behavior Variables.* Children's behavior characteristics (Carolina Record Infant Behavior; determined *a priori* as four dimensions: cognitive style, social responsiveness, temperament, negative affect).
3. *Family Social Status Variables.* Mother's education, family's socioeconomic status, and family gross monthly income.
4. *Family Social Support Variables.* Family Support Scale, Maternal Social Support Index.
5. *Family Well-Being Variable.* Questionnaire on Resources and Stress.

The findings from these data provided overall support for the intervention model, as children's developmental gains were seen to be related largely to family's positive well-being indicators and, to a lesser extent, to negative aspects of family's social support variables. Children's gains were seen to be related to the intervention program's theoretical bases, thus confirming the direction of the program.

In this research, a hierarchical multiple regression design was employed with theory dictating the order of variable entry rather than correlational strength. This is an unusual approach and worth noting. All too often we conduct research with numerous variables and then assume that the order in which these variables should be entered into an equation is to be dictated by a computer or by a correlation matrix. If we are serious in our impact studies, we will accept Shonkoff's views and Dunst's practice that for our knowledge base to advance, our outcome studies "must be conducted within a theoretical framework that is more consistent with the philosophy of current service organization and delivery" (Shonkoff et al., 1988, p. 87).

If outcome studies are to be successful, they must be guided by the theoretical design of early interventions, and they must also be guided by true decision-making needs of early intervention professionals. Perhaps nothing is as offensive to clinicians as watching the time and effort that goes into conducting an outcome study and then perceiving no discernible results from it.

We have recently begun to develop procedures that can be used in outcome evaluations to examine impact of intervention efforts on entire communities. To evaluate the effect of our work in Healthy Family Healthy

Start, we are having to pull data from a variety of existing sources: census data, immunization reports, lead poisoning and screening reports, infant mortality reports, crime statistics, student attendance, and public health center activity reports. These data are being aggregated to create a geographic composite of need and strength on a city block by city block basis. To integrate these data into coherent units, we are using a system called Geographic Information Systems (GIS). GIS is a rapidly growing technology and approach to combining, managing, analyzing, and displaying otherwise disparate data bases and phenomena that share spaces in the real world. This approach combines data-base and graphics technology to provide indices of community activity on any subset of city streets in the country. We hope that use of this technology helps us to reflect and capture some of our intervention impacts.

4.4 Policy Evaluations - What Are Recent Trends?

Policy evaluations are an attempt to identify all relevant policies of two or more agencies (typically state and federal agencies) serving early intervention children and to identify areas of policy overlap, policy duplication, and policy discrepancy. We have seen a growing interest in policy evaluations, largely in response to the requirement mandated in P.L. 99-457 that states must create a statewide, comprehensive, coordinated, multidisciplinary, interagency program of early intervention services for handicapped infants and toddlers and their families (Garwood & Sheehan, 1989). The use of so many words in one sentence should not obscure the simple meaning implied by this law: States with fragmented service delivery systems must undergo systems change and emerge with a unified system of early intervention.

What type of data are necessary to effect a systems change at the State level? Thus far, we have been referring largely to data reflecting the policies and practices of individual early intervention programs. While such data might help improve or ensure program quality, they will be of little use in changing an entire statewide system. The statewide system mandated by P.L. 99-457 requires, in part:

1. A comprehensive system of personnel development.
2. A single line of responsibility within a state.
3. Identification and coordination of all available early intervention resources.
4. Procedures for resolving intra- and interagency disputes.

Each of these requirements almost ensures that extensive policy evaluations must be conducted.

Conducting a thorough policy analysis requires that all regulations, policies, resources, and services being provided by agencies be scrutinized thoroughly. As an example, we point to a statewide policy evaluation by Bogan and LaParo (1991), but we emphasize that almost every state has conducted such an evaluation.

In Louisiana, Bogan and LaParo conducted a scrutiny of state agencies beginning with P.L. 99-456 statutory and regulatory language, Louisiana Act 377 (the State's implementing legislation for P.L. 99-457, Part H), and various Louisiana SICC (State Interagency Coordinating Council) policy documents. This document review was following by development and completion of a 10-page survey for each agency and a series of interviews to follow up on the survey (Bogan & LaParo, 1991). The result of this effort was a series of recommendations designed to reduce contradiction of terminology and regulation, to enhance coordination and communication, and to reduce the red tape confronting children and families in need of early intervention services.

5   Conclusions

To conclude, we return to our beginning point: Good program evaluations take their lead from decisions that must be made about early intervention programs. As early intervention programs change, the design and conduct of program evaluations must also change.

Early intervention efforts are changing. They are becoming more complex, more family-centered, and more ecologically valid. They are also becoming more concerned with health-related issues and with issues related to cost-effectiveness.

Front-end evaluations, evaluations that address the needs for early intervention services, are increasing in number, scope, and importance. Program-process evaluations are still quite important in early intervention settings, especially as a vehicle for statewide or regional monitoring. Impact evaluations, though often misused, are still occurring frequently, and require a significant amount of planning and insight to ensure valid and usable results. Policy evaluations are also increasing in number and scope, as early intervention agencies attempt to change the systems within which early intervention services are delivered.

The challenge to all these types of evaluations is to plan evaluations in response to needed data. The determining factor in identifying needed data is to identify decisions that must be made with regard to early intervention and then plan evaluations accordingly.

References

Aquila, F., Tracy, S., & Sheehan, R. (1987). Hiring winners. *Journal of the Ohio School Boards Association, 31(5)*, 20-22.

Bailey, D., Simeonnson, R. (1985) *Family Needs Survey Form.* Chapel Hill, NC: H. Frank Porter Graham Child Development Center, University of North Carolina at Chapel Hill.

Bailey, D., & Simeonnson, R. (1988). *Family assessment in early intervention.* Columbus, OH: Merrill Publishing Company.

Bailey, N. (1969). *Bailey Scales of Infant Development.* New York: Psychological Corporation.

Blanchard, K. (undated). *Supervisory behavior analysis.* Blanchard Training and Development Inc., Escondido, CA.

Bogan, E., & LaParo, K. (1991). *Louisiana Early Intervention Policy Analysis Project.* Louisiana State University Medical Center, School of Applied Health Professions, New Orleans, LA.

Bricker, D. (1993). A rose by any other name, or is it? *Journal of Early Intervention, 17(2)*, 89-96.

Bricker, D., & Squires, J. (1989). Low cost system using parents to monitor the development of at-risk students. *Journal of Early Intervention, 13*(1), 50-60.

Brinkerhoff, R. (1989). Using evaluation to transform thinking. In R. Brinkeroff (Ed.), *Evaluating training programs in business and industry. New directions for program evaluation series.* Nick L. Smith (Editor-in-Chief), *44* (Winter), 5-20.

Brinkerhoff, R., Brethower, D., Hluchyj, T., & Nowakowski, J. (1983). *Program evaluation: A practitioners guide for trainers and educators.* Boston, MA: Kluwer-Nijhoff.

DeRoche, E. (1987). *An administrator's guide for evaluating programs and personnel.* Boston MA: Allyn and Bacon.

Dunst, C. (1993). Implications of risk and opportunity factors for assessment and intervention practices. *Topics in Early Childhood Special Education, 13*(2), 143-153.

Dunst, C. J., Johanson, C., Trivette, C. M., & Hamby, D. (1991). Family-oriented early intervention policies and practices: Family-centered or not? *Exceptional Children, 58*, 115-126.

Dunst, C., Trivette, C., & Deal, A. (1988). *Enabling and empowering families: Principles and guidelines for practice.* Cambridge, MA: Brookline Books.

Dunst, C. J., Trivette, C. M., Hamby, D., & Pollock, B. (1990). Family systems correlates of the behavior of young children with handicaps. *Journal of Early Intervention, 14*(3), 204-218.

Dunst, C., & Rheingrover, R. (1981). An analysis of the efficacy of infant intervention programs with organically handicapped children. *Evaluation and Program Planning, 4*, 287-323.

Garwood, S. , & Sheehan, R. (1989). *Designing a comprehensive early intervention system: The challenge of Public Law 99-457.* Austin, TX: Pro-Ed. Publishers.

Hodges, W., & Sheehan, R. (1978). Evaluation: Strategies for generating knowledge. In C. C. Rentz & R. Rentz (Eds.), *New directions in program evaluation* (pp. 81-93). San Francisco: Jossey-Bass.

Kleinfeld, J., & McDiarmid, G. (1986). Living to tell the tale: Researching politically controversial topics and communicating the findings. *Educational Evaluation and Policy Analysis, 8*(4), 393-401.

Levin, H. (1989). Financing the education of at-risk students. *Educational Evaluation and Policy Analysis, 11*(1), 47-60.

Mandolang, N., (1991). *Florida's Cost/Implementation Study for Public Law 99-457, Part H, Infants and Toddlers Phase II Findings: Prevalence/Utilization Study.* Florida Department of Education, Bureau of Education for Exceptional Students and the Florida Interagency Coordinating Council for Infants and Toddlers, Tallahassee, FL.

McGonigel, M. (1988). *Guidelines for family-centered research.* Washington, DC: Association for the Care of Children's Health.

McGonigel, M. J., Kaufmann, R., & Johnson, B. (1991). A family-centered process for the individualized family service plan. *Journal of Early Intervention, 15*(1), 46-56.

Odom, S. (1989). Editorial. *Journal of Early Intervention, 13*(1), 3-5.

Sheehan, R. (1991). *Report of the unduplicated count project - 1990 data.* Submitted to Department of Health & Environmental Control, Columbia, SC.

Sheehan, R. (1992) *Report of the unduplicated count project - 1991 data.* Submitted to Department of Health & Environmental Control, Columbia, SC.

Sheehan, R. (1993). Personal communication with officials of the South Carolina Department of Health & Environmental Control.

Shonkoff, J., Hauser-Cram, P., Krauss, W., & Upshur, C. (1988). Early intervention efficacy research: What have we learned and where do we go from here?. *Topics in Early Childhood Special Education, 80*(1), 81-93.

Simeonnson, R., Cooper, D., & Scheiner, A. (1982). A review and analysis of the effectiveness of early intervention programs. *Pediatrics, 69*, 635-641.

Snyder, S., & Sheehan, R. (1985). Integrating research in early childhood special education: The use of meta-analysis. *Diagnostique, 9*(1), 9-15.

Snyder, S., & Sheehan, R., (1993). Program evaluation in early Intervention. In W. Brown, S. K. Thurman, & L. Pearl (Eds.), *Family-centered early intervention with infants and toddlers* (pp. 269-302). Baltimore, MD: Paul Brooks.

M. Brambring, H. Rauh, and A. Beelmann (Eds.). (1996). *Early childhood intervention: Theory, evaluation, and practice* (pp. 305-334). Berlin, New York: de Gruyter.

Using Assessment Outcomes for Intervention Planning: A Necessary Relationship

Diane Bricker

1 Introduction

In the United States, the initiation of intervention programs for young children with disabilities occurred in the early 1970s, and, in the ensuing two and half decades, many significant changes have occurred in the field of early intervention. The important lessons learned during these 25 years have permitted the development of conceptual positions and guiding principles that dictate present policy and shape best practice. Some of the important and influential positions and principles include:

1. Family members and other caregivers should be included as partners in assessment, intervention, and evaluation.
2. Specialized training is required for personnel who work with infants and young children and their families.
3. Children with disabilities should be placed in community-based integrated settings.
4. Intervention approaches that rely on naturalistic approaches are meaningful to young children and therefore are effective.
5. Intervention programs should be driven by conceptually sound principles that link assessment, intervention, and evaluation.
6. The development of relevant, useful, and functional Individual Family Service Plans (IFSPs) is dependent upon the use of appropriate assessment procedures.
7. Interdisciplinary and interagency collaboration is fundamental to comprehensive and effective intervention for young children and their families.

Other lessons have been learned, but those listed above appear to be some of the more critical concepts that are currently being integrated into the guidelines that govern the structure and content of the field. These lessons reflect the important conceptual progress that has occurred in early intervention programs; however, progress toward full implementation of these best practice concepts by direct service personnel is less robust. Although today in the United States, more children and families are receiving services and the quality of the services has improved, application of state-of-the-art practice described in the literature and promoted at professional conferences has not kept pace. In fact, the little empirical data that have been collected on locally operated programs not associated with research and training efforts directed by higher education find that state-of-the-art practice is not being used or employed (Bagnato et al., 1989; Bricker & Campbell, 1980; Brown 1991; Gallagher, 1993; Lynch et al., 1991).

In spite of the obvious progress made in the field of early intervention, it is troubling to note the continuing discrepancy between what experts argue is best practice and what occurs daily in community-based early intervention programs. Observations of and conversations with interventionists lead me to speculate that there are several likely explanations for this best practice discrepancy. First, it appears that many interventionists indicate that they do engage in best practice when, in fact, they do not. For example, interventionists often indicate that their program promotes genuine involvement of family members as partners, when, actually program staff do little to encourage caregiver initiative and participation. It is not clear whether interventionists recognize such discrepancies. One is not likely to change if one believes he or she is engaged in best practice already. Second, some interventionists do not know or understand what is best practice. Many interventionists may be unaware of the importance many experts assign to the linking of assessment, intervention, and evaluation efforts. A third reason discrepancies may occur is that administrative structures and regulations can conflict with the use of best practice. For example, many programs operate with a policy that dictates the development of a child's IFSP prior to entry into the intervention program. Most experts would not see this as best practice. These three reasons probably combine in multiple ways to hinder progress toward implementation of best practice.

This paper addresses what I believe to be one important discrepancy between what a number of experts believe is best practice - choosing assessment measures and strategies that yield the necessary information to formulate comprehensive, appropriate, and meaningful IFSPs and intervention plans (Bagnato et al., 1989; Bricker, 1989; Bricker & Cripe, 1992; Hutinger, 1988; Shinn & Good, in press) - and what is generally occurring in the field. The formulation of appropriate and useful IFSPs and intervention plans that can be used to direct intervention efforts of early intervention personnel and family members requires the collection of accurate, complete, and meaningful assessment findings. The development of intervention plans based on incomplete and inaccurate assessment findings will probably lead to the formulation of shoddy plans, which will, in turn, produce less than optimal outcomes for children and families.

To build a bridge, architects and engineers conduct functional assessments to generate the information needed to develop an appropriate and useful blueprint. This process entails careful examination of the physical environment and variables that may impinge on the location of choice. Using this critical information, an extensive set of blueprints is developed that attempts to account for all critical factors that may affect construction of the bridge. Once completed, the blueprint or plan is used to guide the construction of the bridge. Professionals associated with building the bridge would not or should not consider undertaking such a project if the plan were incomplete or based on inaccurate findings. As construction moves forward and problems are encountered or changes found necessary, the blueprint is adjusted. No one would support or expect professionals to build a bridge without first conducting a proper assessment of the terrain and other factors that impact the construction or safety of the bridge. Further, one would expect all subcontractors to be familiar with the blueprint and follow its specifications. Finally, if a subcontractor determines that a change is in order, that change would be integrated into the blueprint and shared with all subcontractors who might be affected by the change.

The development of an IFSP and intervention plan for a child and family can be compared to the development of a blueprint for a bridge. Best practice dictates that a comprehensive and appropriate assessment be conducted. This assessment should yield relevant information about the child's current status and family expectations and goals. Further, the assessment should yield the necessary information to build a functional plan to guide future intervention efforts. The development of the plan should include all parties who have a stake in the intervention efforts and outcomes, including family members and professionals. Finally, the plan should be used to guide daily intervention efforts. When change is required, the plan should be examined by all relevant parties who should then collaborate to make the necessary modifications.

The field of early intervention is making progress toward the development of systems that strongly support the use of appropriate assessment tools and procedures that produce information for the development of relevant and functional IFSPs; however, many programs still persist in the use of assessment approaches that yield incomplete and inaccurate outcomes or outcomes that cannot be used directly to formulate sound IFSPs and intervention plans. The pupose of this chapter is to discuss the barriers to the development of systems in which functional assessments are used to develop appropriate and useful IFSPs, which, in turn, are used to guide intervention planning and efforts. Pointing out problems is of questionable value unless accompanied by potentially useful solutions; therefore, the major portion of this chapter will describe a systems approach to early intervention that was specifically formulated to link a functional assessment to IFSP development and intervention planning efforts.

2   Functional IFSPs and Intervention Plans: Overview

Before discussing the barriers to the development of functional intervention plans, it may be useful to define what is meant by "functional" IFSPs and intervention plans. In this chapter, the IFSP refers to a written document that states the long-range goals and short-term objectives for the child and, when appropriate, family outcomes. In addition, IFSPs generally contain the following information: timelines for meeting the goals or outcomes, resources necessary, and the responsible agent (Johnson et al., 1989). An intervention plan refers to a written document that is an expansion of a child's IFSP. The purpose of the intervention plan is to provide detail on how to reach the targeted IFSP outcomes or goals. The level of detail provided is dependent upon the problems of the child, the experience of the interventionists, as well as other factors (e.g., personnel resources, need for coordination). It is possible that some interventionists can develop effective intervention activities directly from the IFSP; however, most program staff require more detailed information on which strategies and activities might be used and when and how to use them to reach intervention targets. The format used to provide this information can be flexible and should suit the needs of the program staff and family members.

To be functional, IFSPs and intervention plans for children must meet several important criteria. First, functional IFSPs and intervention plans contain objectives (content) and intervention strategies and activities that will improve the child's independent functioning and responsiveness to environmental demands. For example, learning to communicate one's food/drink needs when a child is hungry or thirsty clearly can enhance independence and is likely to improve the child's ability to respond when hungry or thirsty. Learning to name pictures of food is less likely to foster independence or responsiveness.

A second criterion requires that functional IFSPs and intervention plans contain objectives and activities that are perceived as meaningful by the child and family. That is, the target objective will assist children in developing daily living and play skills that they find useful and interesting. For example, learning to throw a ball so one can participate in games with other children is likely to be more meaningful than learning to walk on a balance beam. Rotating one's wrist to open a door to go outside is likely to be more meaningful than rotating one's wrist to stack rings.

Functional IFSPs and intervention plans also do not target objectives that are either so specific that they are unimportant or so broad that they are useless. This balance between too narrow or too broad is the third criterion for a functional intervention plan. A too specific objective might be having the child place small blocks in a cup; a more functional objective might require that the child be able to place a variety of small objects into containers such as pieces of food in a bowl, soap in a soap dish, or socks in a dresser drawer. An objective that is too broad might include improving the child's social skills; a more functional objective might target the development of taking turns, reciprocal responding, and initiation of play sequences.

Although there are other important requirements, discussed later in this chapter, for the development of appropriate and useful IFSPs and intervention plans, the three criteria described above are essential parameters of functional intervention plans.

2.1 Barriers to the Development of Functional IFSPs and Intervention Plans.

The barriers to implementation of an approach that uses appropriate and relevant assessment procedures to develop a functional intervention plan composed of meaningful and appropriate goals and objectives closely parallel those barriers to best practice described above and include: interventionists who do not appreciate or do not know how to implement such an approach; and administrative regulations that promote barriers to the approach.

Lack of Understanding or Appreciation for Functional IFSPs and Intervention Plans. Many interventionists have been trained in traditional models in which standardized tests are routinely used to assess children and families upon entry into a program. These interventionists have used tests such as the Revised Gesell and Armatruda Developmental and Neurologic Examination (Knobloch et al., 1980) for the purposes of developing an IFSP. These are the same interventionists who probably do *not* use or refer to their IFSP (blueprint), because it does not contain relevant goals and objectives and therefore does not provide assistance in the development of daily intervention efforts. These interventionists either are unfamiliar with measurement procedures that will provide more relevant information or choose not to use such instruments.

If one does not use a procedure or instrument that yields relevant information for the development of a useful IFSP and subsequent intervention plan, then it becomes extremely difficult, if not impossible, to write an IFSP that targets relevant goals for children and outcomes for families. The Bayley Scales of Infant Development (Bayley, 1969, 1993) were developed, as were most standardized, norm-referenced tests, to discriminate between children who can do certain activities or have certain knowledge and those who do not (Salvia & Ysseldyke, 1981). That is, items that the majority of 4-year-old children can perform successfully become 4-year-old test items. Further, items are chosen that can be presented and scored reliably; items are not chosen for their potential value as intervention goals or objectives (Bricker, 1989). Therefore, norm-referenced tests were/are developed to sort children into groups that can pass items at certain developmental levels compared to children who cannot pass those items. Norm-referenced, standardized tests do not provide adequate information to develop appropriate and useful IFSP goals and outcomes and therefore yield planning documents that are of questionable use.

When faced with a poorly developed, off-target IFSP, interventionists generally disregard the document as a blueprint for designing intervention goals and activities and adopt another strategy. Many interventionists rely on a variety of curricular documents and materials. Interventionists pore over these materials in search of goals and objectives that appear relevant and useful; they also search for activities that may assist children in the development of important skills. Unfortunately, such an approach has two fundamental problems: First, because a careful, functional assessment of the child's repertoire does not drive the selection of goals, those selected may or may not be appropriate and/or useful for the child. Children may spend time involved in activities that do not lend themselves to enhancing and expanding their repertoires. Second, this approach is likely to result in a "mishmash" of targets and activities that are neither coordinated nor planned sequentially. With no overall coordination or planning, a variety of critical skills or elements necessary to build toward an independent, functional repertoire may be overlooked or missed.

Administrative Barriers to Functional IFSPs and Intervention Planning. Again, conversations with interventionists throughout the United States suggest that best practice is often hindered because of administrative rules and regulations or by perceived limitations of administrative procedures. For example, many states have developed a system in which a predetermined diagnostic and evaluation team assesses a child and family, writes an IFSP, and sends the child and the IFSP on to a program. There are several problems with this approach. First, these teams often employ a standardized, norm-referenced test, because a primary interest is in determining the child's eligibility for services. Most states (Gallagher, 1993) require that eligibility be determined by a child's percent of delay or standard deviation from the mean, which requires the use of a norm-referenced test. Unfortunately, information used to establish the child's eligibility is the same information used to develop the IFSP.

A second problem is the manner in which the child is assessed. Usually children and family members are expected to come to a center where the child is asked to participate in a variety of assessment activities. The setting, the people, and often the activities are unfamiliar to the child. The validity of the assessment outcomes for the development of an IFSP and the subsequent intervention plan are extremely questionable. The child may be considerably more competent than he or she demonstrates under such conditions. Consequently the goals and objectives on the IFSP may be inappropriate, and teachers and children may be spending time focused on activities that will not lead to the enhancement of the child's repertoire.

Third, the professionals who will be working with the child are often not present on the diagnostic and evaluation team. Thus, the interventionist is not included in the IFSP development. The team is often unfamiliar with the physical setting of the program, the nature of the other children, and adult resources in the environment with the likely result being the development of an IFSP that has little relevance to the child, the setting, or the interventionist.

Finally, many parents and family members require time and patience to develop the necessary confidence to contribute to a child's assessment and IFSP development. When asked for input, many parents defer to professionals. Interventionists in the child's program often have the opportunity over time to build trust and confidence of family members so they can become contributing members in the development of IFSPs and subsequent intervention plans.

Given these serious drawbacks, it seems odd that federal and state regulations have established procedures that are driven primarily by the need to complete the IFSP within a specified time frame. The quality and usefulness and the participation of interventionists and family members become secondary. Such regulations produce results that, I believe, are contrary to best practice in the field today.

2.2 An Alternative Approach to Developing Functional IFSPs and Intervention Plans.

The first step to adopting an approach that is designed to produce functional IFSPs and intervention plans is to realize that such systems exist (Bricker, 1989). These systems are predicated on the use of assessment tools or procedures that yield appropriate and comprehensive outcomes that are directly applicable to the development of relevant and useful IFSPs and intervention plans. Many interventionists, diagnostic and evaluation team members, program coordinators, and administrators in the field of early intervention do not appear to appreciate the need to establish a firm relationship between the processes of program assessment, intervention, and evaluation.

The lack of continuity found between assessment, intervention, and evaluation program components may occur because of the nature of the assessment tools used and/or the procedures used to conduct the assessment. Attempting to use outcomes from norm-referenced tests or trying to implement an IFSP developed by a diagnostic and evaluation team unfamiliar with the child or the receiving program does little to promote a direct link between assessment, intervention, and evaluation. Systems that rely on assessment tools and procedures that yield intervention-relevant findings do much to promote a strong and reciprocal relationship between assessment and intervention program components.

A conceptual appreciation for systems that relate assessment outcomes directly to functional IFSPs and intervention plan development needs to be accompanied by the necessary tools and procedures that permit efficient and effective application of the approach. The remainder of this chapter describes one such approach with an emphasis on its application.

3   Functional IFSPs and Intervention Plans: The Model

3.1 Necessary Components

An effective intervention program requires the development of functional IFSPs and intervention plans that serve to keep program staff and caregivers focused on appropriate and meaningful intervention activities. The development of functional IFSPs and intervention plans is based on a system that employs assessment procedures designed to yield the necessary information on children and families to develop these documents. Such systems require a direct link between program components such as assessment and IFSP development, as shown in Figure 1. Variations of this simple model have been described elsewhere by a number of writers (Bagnato et al., 1989; Bricker, 1989, 1993; Hutinger, 1988).

The present model is composed of five components: (a) assessment; (b) IFSP development; (c) intervention planning; (d) intervention activities; and (e) evaluation. Each component is linked to the next one in a linear fashion, and all five components are regulated or influenced by the program's philosophy. Program philosophy refers to the pervasive climate and guiding principles that drive the program; for example, a commitment by staff to family involvement in assessment and intervention activities, professional team collaboration to develop and implement intervention plans, or a developmental perspective of children's growth might all be guiding principles for a state-of-the-art program. The model shown in Figure 1 illustrates the direct relationship between assessment and IFSP development, which, in turn, drives the formulation of intervention plans that then provide the structure for intervention activities. The evaluation component provides on-going and direct feedback as to the success of the intervention activities, intervention planning, and progress toward IFSP goals and outcomes.

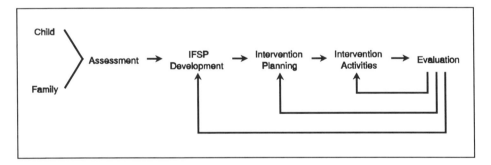

Figure 1. Model directly linking program components
          (IFSP = Individual Family Service Plan).

3.2 Curriculum-Based Assessment: The Necessary Tool

A linked system in which assessment outcomes are used directly to develop functional IFSPs and intervention plans requires the use of assessment tools and procedures that yield relevant information. Norm-referenced, standardized tests are unsatisfactory for this purpose for several reasons that have been discussed in detail elsewhere (Bricker & Littman, 1982;

Garwood, 1982; Johnson, 1982; Sheehan, 1982). The general category of assessment most useful for developing functional IFSPs and intervention plans is the type of criterion-referenced tests referred to as curriculum-based assessment (CBA) or preferably a curriculum-based assessment/evaluation test. CBAs have been defined as: "A direct application of criterion-referenced assessment strategy to instructional content. Assessment and curricular content are coordinated to address the same skills and abilities" (Notari et al., 1990, pp. 162-163). The explicit design of CBAs provides a direct and on-going link between an assessment and intervention (curriculum). A number of CBAs have been developed for use with infants and young children who are at risk and disabled. Notari et al. (1990) reviewed 10 of these CBAs, examining features such as number of items, test organization, adaptions, administration time, data collection method, scoring options, type of outcome, standardization, and psychometric data.

Although these CBAs vary across these features, each is able to provide interventionists and caregivers with more useful information that is directly applicable to the development of functional IFSPs, intervention plans, and intervention activities than are screening tests, norm-referenced tests, or even other criterion-referenced tests that do not have accompanying curricula materials.

3.3 The Assessment, Evaluation, and Programming System

Of the CBAs available for use with infants and young children, the Assessment, Evaluation, and Programming System (AEPS) particularly emphasizes the use of its test outcomes to develop functional IFSPs and intervention plans (Bricker, 1993). As Bricker and Cripe (1992) point out, the AEPS Test has several features that promote the link between assessment and intervention.

First, the AEPS Test targets functional skills - skills thought to be essential for infants and young children to manage themselves independently and to cope with environmental demands. Each item is potentially an appropriate intervention target. *Second*, the AEPS Test is comprehensive, covering the major areas of development: fine-motor, gross-motor, cognitive, adaptive, social-communication, and social. *Third*, the recommended method of obtaining information using the AEPS Test is through observation of children while they participate in daily activities. *Fourth*, the AEPS Test permits the user to adapt or modify item presentation and/or item criterion to accommodate children with motor or sensory impairments. *Fifth*, items on the AEPS Test are written to be generic response classes rather than singular, specific responses. *Sixth*, parallel assessment/evaluation measures are available for use by family members to help insure involvement in developing the IFSPs and intervention plans. *Seventh*, the AEPS Test contains a set of associated IFSP goals and objectives that can be modified by interventionists and caregivers for individual children.

The organization of the AEPS Curriculum parallels the AEPS Test, so the user can move between documents with ease (Cripe et al., 1993). The AEPS Curriculum contains a series of intervention activities that are potentially useful to assist children in acquiring each targeted goal or objective. For example, if a child is unable to use five action words appropriately - an AEPS Test item in the social-communication domain - and that item is chosen as an IFSP goal, the interventionist can refer to the AEPS Curriculum to find a list of concurrent goals and objectives, a set of activity-based teaching suggestions, suggested environmental arrangements, and teaching considerations that may be useful when working on this target with the child.

The AEPS Test has been studied extensively (Bailey & Bricker, 1986; Bricker et al., 1990; Cripe, 1990; Notari & Bricker, 1990). Congruent validity ($N = 155$), test stability ($N = 155$), interrater agreement ($N = 122$), and test-retest reliability ($N = 58$) have all been examined and found to be acceptable to good (Bricker et al., 1990). In addition, the utility of the AEPS Test has been addressed by asking test users in the field a series of questions. These data indicate that the respondents generally found the content of the test appropriate and useful for developing IFSPs and intervention plans. Seventy-eight percent of the respondents ($N = 23$) indicated that the goals and objectives of the AEPS Test covered the most important behaviors to be targeted for the children they served as well as saved them time in writing IFSPs.

A well-controlled study examined the usefulness of the AEPS Test for developing IFSP/IEPs (Notari & Bricker, 1990). Forty-eight interventionists developed IFSP/IEPs; those that used the AEPS Test wrote significantly better goals and objectives than did the control subjects who did not use the AEPS Test.

A study conducted by Cripe (1990) examined the effectiveness of the AEPS family measures when developing IFSPs. Following treatment, which included training on the AEPS materials, interventionists ($N = 30$) wrote significantly better IFSPs and included significantly more family outcomes on their IFPSs.

The data collected on the AEPS Test and particularly the Notari and Bricker (1990) and Cripe (1990) studies suggest that the AEPS Test and family involvement materials do enhance interventionists' capacity to write more functional IFSPs, which should, in turn, assist in the development of functional intervention plans.

4   Application of the Model

4.1 An Overview

Application of the model shown in Figure 1, which links assessment, IFSP development, intervention planning, intervention activities, and evaluation, is dependent upon the use of a measurement tool or system that yields comprehensive, accurate, and meaningful data for IFSP development and intervention planning. In the following sections, a general overview of the model's application and a specific example of its application are described.

As indicated earlier, the use of a model that directly links program components is dependent upon the availability of an assessment tool and procedures that provide the necessary and relevant information to develop functional IFSPs and intervention plans.

Three features of the AEPS Test make the link between assessment and intervention direct and relevant. First, the AEPS Test is comprehensive and covers all developmental areas for which one is likely to program (i.e., fine-motor, gross-motor, adaptive, cognitive, social-communication, and social). Second, as far as possible, each domain is composed of items that are arranged hierarchically from simple to increasingly complex, which is helpful in determining the sequence of skills to be taught. Third, items on the AEPS Test measure functional skills and are thus all potentially relevant intervention targets.

The importance of family participation in a child's intervention program, particularly for the infant and young child, cannot be overemphasized; therefore, it is important to use an IFSP process that generates meaningful caregiver participation. A strategy for enhancing active family participation in the IFSP process is to provide information to help them select relevant goals and objectives for their child. The AEPS Family Report can be used in conjunction with the AEPS Test for this purpose.

The first step in developing an IFSP from the AEPS Test, AEPS Family Report (Bricker, 1993), and AEPS Family Interest Survey (Cripe & Bricker, 1993) assessments is summarization of the results. Items taken from the AEPS Test and AEPS Family Report can be used by interventionists and family members as a basis for developing IFSP long-range goals and short-term objectives. The caregivers and interventionists can review the results from each developmental domain. By using this procedure, goals and objectives selected for inclusion on the child's IFSP are taken directly from the child's programmatic assessments (i.e., AEPS Test and Family Report). This procedure provides a direct tie with assessment and a common base for the selection of IFSP goals by caregivers and interventionists.

Once the goals and their associated objectives are selected, the next step is for program staff and caregivers to prioritize the goals. Caregivers and interventionists should select only the highest priorities as intervention targets. Our experience suggests that interventionists often select more goals than they and caregivers can comfortably address. Three to four well-selected goals that target important response classes or skills is sufficient and generally manageable by program staff.

The next step is to develop intervention plans for the selected priority goals. These plans should specify the intervention settings, type of training activities, child progress procedures, and decision rules to be used when deciding if change to the intervention plan or activities is in order. For example, if child progress data indicate no progress toward a specific goal after 2 weeks of intervention, different intervention activities may be in order.

Once intervention plans are designed, intervention activities can be initiated. The final step is the conduct of systematic evaluation procedures to determine progress toward priority IFSP goals and family outcomes. As shown previously in Figure 1, evaluation results are used to provide systematic feedback on the success of the intervention activities and intervention plans as well as to monitor progress toward IFSP goals and to offer guidance for modification as necessary.

4.2 An Example

Assessment. To begin, Jane, a 1-year-old child with Down's syndrome, was assessed using the AEPS Test. Her performance across settings, people, and events was observed, and items were scored by the program interventionists. For purposes of this example, only results from the social-communication domain will be used, and are shown on the AEPS Test protocol in Figure 2.

Social-Communication Domain

S =	Scoring Key	Q =	Qualifying Notes
2 =	Pass consistently	A =	Assistance provided
1 =	Inconsistent	B =	Behavior interfered
	performance	R =	Reported assessment
0 =	Does not pass	M =	Modification/adaptation
		D =	Direct test

Name: _____JANE_____

Test Period: _FIRST_

Test Date: _9_ / _93_ / ___ / ___ / ___

Examiner: _Mrs. Jones_

	IEP	S	Q	S	Q	S	Q	S	Q
A. Prelinguistic communicative interactions									
1. Turns and looks toward person speaking		2							
1.1 Turns and looks toward object and person speaking		2							
1.2 Turns and looks toward noise-producing object		2							
2. Follows gaze to establish joint attention		2							
2.1 Follows pointing gesture to establish joint attention		2							
2.2 Looks toward object		2							
3. Engages in vocal exchanges by babbling		2							
3.1 Engages in vocal exchanges by cooing		2							
B. Transition to words									
1. Gains person's attention and refers to object, person, or event		0							
1.1 Responds with vocalization and gesture to simple questions		0							
1.2 Points to object, person, or event		1							
1.3 Gestures and/or vocalizes to greet others		2							
1.4 Uses gestures and/or vocalizations to protest actions or reject objects/people		2							
2. Uses consistent word approximations		0							
2.1 Uses consistent consonant-vowel combinations		0							
2.2 Uses nonspecific consonant-vowel combination and/or jargon		0							

(continued)

__A*EPS*_____   Social-Communication Domain
_____

A raw score can be computed for the domain by adding all the 2 and 1 scores entered in
the S column for a specific test period. To determine the total percent score divide the total
score by the total score possible.

RESULTS

Test Date	*9/93*	_____	_____	_____
Total Score Possible	84	84	84	84
Total Score	*21*	_____	_____	_____
Total Percent Score	*25*	_____	_____	_____

Figure 2. Strand A an B of the AEPS Test Social-Communication Domain
Protocol completed on Jane by interventionist.

Jane met the criteria for all items in Strand A. In Strand B, she met the
criteria for two of the simplest items but did not meet criteria for the other
objectives nor the associated goals. According to the interventionists'
scoring of the social-communication domain, Jane was unable to meet the
criteria for all other items in this domain. Jane's parents completed the
AEPS Family Report as they observed their child at home. The parents'
findings shown in Figure 3 are similar to the interventionists' AEPS Test
results.

IFSP development. The AEPS Test and Family Report assessment
information provided Jane's parents and interventionists with an adequate
picture of the infant's present status (i.e., what she can currently do) and
what the next developmental targets should probably be (i.e., IFSP goals).

AEPS _____

Social-Communication Domain

1. Does your child turn to look at someone who is
   talking nearby? For example, when playing near you,
   your child looks at you when you speak. (A1)

2. Does your child turn to look in the same direction that
   you are looking? For example, when playing together
   you turn and look out the window and your child turns
   and looks out the window. (A2)

3. Does your child make at least two vocal exchanges
   with others by babbling? For example, you say "Hi
   baby," and your child says, "ba-ba." You then say,
   "What?" and your child says, "ba-ba-ba." (A3)

4. Does your child get your attention and then point to
   an object, person, or event? For example, he or she
   pulls on your arm and then points to a ball, or looks at
   you and then looks at a cat. (B1)

5. Does your child use at least 10 consistent word
   approximations to name objects, people, or events. (A
   word approximation is a sound that resembles the
   word or is part of the word.) For example, your child
   sees a dog and says, "gog," or says, "ju" when asking
   for juice. (B2)

Y = Yes; S = Sometimes; N = Not Yet.

Priority Goals: _Helping Jane learn to get adult's_
attention and then point to what she wants.

Figure 3. Position of Social-Communication Domain on AEPS Family
Report Protocol completed by Jane's parents.

For the social-communication domain, Jane's parents selected the goal:
Gains person's attention and refers to an object, person, and/or event, and
its associated objective: Points to an object, person, and/or event (Social-
Communication Domain, Strand B, Goal 1 and Objective 1.2). Table 1
shows the relationship between the selected AEPS Test items and their
wording as the IFSP goal and associated objective.

Table 1.   *Correspondence between AEPS Test item and IFSP goal and objective statements.*

AEPS Test Goal and Objectives		IFSP Goal and Objective Statements
Goal 1	Gains person's attention and refers to an object, person, and/or event	The child will gain a person's attention (e.g., look at, reach for, touch, vocalize) and then point to an object, person, and/or event (e.g., pull on a person's arm, then point out the window).
Objective 1.1	Responds with a vocalization and gesture to simple questions	The child will respond to simple questions with a vocalization and gesture (e.g., person asks, "Where's Mommy?" and child points to mother and says, "Ma-ma.").
Objective 1.2	Points to an object, person, and/or event	The child will point to an object, person, and/or event.
Objective 1.3	Gestures and/or vocalizes to greet others	The child will wave and/or vocalize when greeting and leaving others.
Objective 1.4	Uses gestures and/or vocalizations to protest actions and/or reject objects or people	The child will use gestures and/or vocalizations to protest actions and/or reject objects or people.

Taken from the AEPS Measurement for Birth to Three Years (Bricker, 1993).

Intervention plans. The next step is to develop an intervention plan for Jane focused on the selected IFSP goals and their associated objective. For each selected priority goal and its associated objective, in our example a social-communication goal, an intervention plan should be developed and written. An intervention plan can follow a number of formats but should contain the following information: (a) identification of information such as child's name and interventionist; (b) dates for initiation of training and expected completion; (c) intervention domain; (d) types of settings in which intervention may occur; (e) specification of goal and associated objective if appropriate; (f) specification of more discrete intervention targets if necessary (particularly appropriate for children with severe disabilities), called developmental programming steps; (g) specification of child progress evaluation procedures; and (h) decision rules to be used.

The intervention plan that is developed for each goal and its associated objectives provides caregivers and interventionists with a framework and guidance for choosing and directing intervention activities. A sample functional intervention plan addressing Jane's social-communication goal and its associated objective is contained in Figure 4. As shown in Figure 4, intervention plans contain more detail and specification than an IFSP document.

Child:_____*JANE*_____ Interventionist: *Mrs. Jones*_____

Initiated: *9/93*____ Expected Completion: *12/94*____

Domain: FM   GM   Adap   Cog   SC   Soc

Type of Setting: ____ Group __*x*__ Individual _____ Home

Strand B

  Goal 1:   Gains person's attention and refers to an object, person, and/or
                event

  Objective 1.2: Points (10-12 times per day) to objects, persons, and/or events
                across settings for 10 consecutive days

Developmental Programming Steps:

        Confirmation function: The adult says: "There's the ball." The child
        points to the ball.

        Comment/reply function: The adult asks, "What happened?" The child
        points to spilled milk.

        Information function: The adult asks, "Where's your teddy?" The child
        points to the teddy bear.

        Request function: The child points to the bottle. The adult asks, "Do
        you want your bottle?"

        Attention function: The child points to a sibling jumping in a
        swimming pool. The adult says, "There's Billy."

        Question function: The child points to a new stuffed animal. The adult
        says, "What's that?"

        Comment/describe function: The child points to a truck. The adult
        says, "That's a truck."

Child Progress Procedures: During free play, three times per week, frequency
                             of pointing will be recorded.

Decision Rule: If frequency of pointing does not double within 3
                             weeks, review teaching procedures and number of
                             opportunities provided to practice the skill.

Figure 4. Functional intervention plan for Jane's priority social-communication goal. Taken from AEPS Measurement Birth to Three Years (Bricker, 1993).

Intervention activities. Using the intervention plan as a guide, Jane's parents and interventionists can design an array of daily activities to address the child's targeted goals and objectives. This process is greatly facilitated when using a CBA tool such as the AEPS. The intervention activities described in the AEPS Curriculum (Cripe et al., 1993) correspond directly to the AEPS Test items, making it straightforward to relate intervention activities for Jane directly to her selected goals and objectives. For each AEPS Test item (goal and objectives), the AEPS Curriculum contains an associated section that describes the importance of the targeted skills, lists preceding and concurrent objectives, and provides a series of suggested intervention activities. The AEPS Curriculum pages associated with Jane's selected social-communication goal are shown in the Appendix.

   Evaluation. Once intervention has begun, it is essential for Jane's interventionists, and hopefully her parents as well, to monitor her progress toward the selected IFSP goals and objectives. Without systematic documentation of change, interventionists and caregivers cannot determine the effects of their intervention efforts. It is important to conduct both quarterly and weekly evaluations.

   Quarterly evaluations. Readministration of the AEPS Test and Family Report at 3- to 4-month intervals can provide an important record of Jane's progress toward her selected IFSP goals. Results from quarterly evaluations can be displayed on the summary graphs included with the AEPS Test protocols and shown in Figure 5 or on the AEPS Child Progress Record shown in Figure 6.

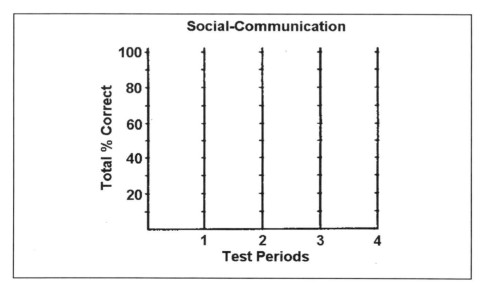

Figure 5.   AEPS test summary graph.

Social Communication Domain

Strand A: Prelinguistic communicative interactions

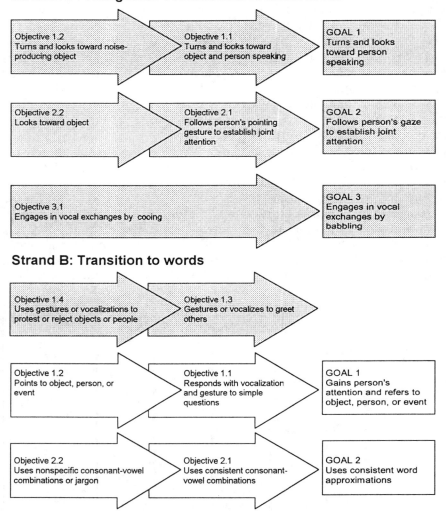

Strand B: Transition to words

Figure 6. Position of AEPS Child Progress Record Social-Communication Domain completed for Jane. Shaded arrows indicate child has met criterion for that objective or goal.

Weekly monitoring. Given adequate staff or caregiver time, the use of observational systems to collect weekly child progress data is also recommended. Continuing with the example, progress toward Jane's selected social-communication goal, "Points to an object, person and/or event" can be monitored by conducting weekly probes at her center-based program and at home if her parents are willing (as shown in Figure 7).

For example, Jane shifts to a new activity center at school, toys and objects can be placed out of her reach. This simple procedure requires that she point to obtain a desired toy or object. The interventionist can conduct these brief probes frequently by observing Jane's behavior, noting her response, and prompting a point if necessary. These data can be plotted on a graph. Using this or a similar procedure can alert parents and interventionists to when Jane has met the established criteria for a particular goal or objective. Once the criterion is met, training should begin on the next objective or goal. If, according to specified decision rules, progress is nonexistent, extremely slow, or variable, some form of change is likely to be in order.

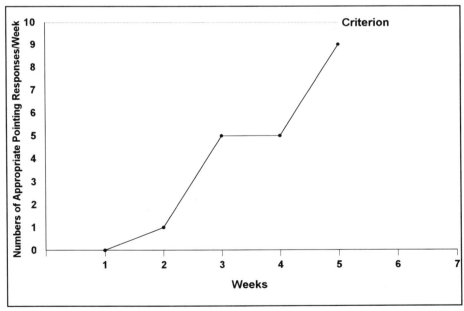

Figure 7.   Number of appropriate pointing responses by Jane collected during weekly probes.

5 Summary

Quality intervention services require the systematic and direct linking of assessment, intervention, and evaluation processes. The material contained in this chapter has provided a rationale, conceptual model, and set of practical procedures for the development of functional IFSPs and intervention plans that should assist greatly in the delivery of quality services to infants and young children who are at risk or disabled and their families.

For a field such as early intervention to improve, two important factors should be at work. First, there must be clear vision or visions by leaders and experts as to what constitutes improvement for the field. Without such vision, even if time shows it to be flawed, it seems unlikely that there can or will be concerted efforts to move in a new direction or change current policy or practice. Second, specification, often at a concrete level, of how to actualize a desired change is necessary. For many, a conceptual model or framework is of limited use unless accompanied by a set of clear practices that help people see how the approach can be applied.

This chapter has described my vision for the improvement of intervention services to infants and young children. Accompanying this vision is a set of relatively specific procedures for its application. The use of this approach, in which the assessment/evaluation tool is pivotal to the development of functional IFSPs and intervention plans, has much to recommend it over alternative approaches; however, the collection of future data will, without doubt, show us the flaws in this approach and suggest new and better alternatives. The future will offer many challenges and we can meet them best by using our current state-of-the-art knowledge and practice as the foundation for the formulation of new and better visions and practice.

References

Bagnato, S., Neisworth, J., & Munson, S. (1989). *Linking developmental assessment and early intervention curricula-based prescriptions.* Rockville, MD: Aspen Publications.

Bailey, E., & Bricker, D. (1986). A psychometric study of a criterion-referenced assessment instrument designed for infants and young children. *Journal of the Division for Early Childhood, 10*(2), 124-134.

Bayley, N. (1969). *Bayley scales of infant development.* New York: The Psychological Corporation.

Bayley, N. (1993). *Bayley scales of infant development II.* San Antonio, TX: The Psychological Corporation.

Bricker, D. (1989). *Early intervention for at-risk and handicapped infants*. Palo Alto, CA: VORT Corp.

Bricker, D. (Ed.). (1993). *Assessment, Evaluation, and Programming System (AEPS) for Infants and Children*. Baltimore, MD: Paul Brookes.

Bricker, D., Bailey, E., & Slentz, K. (1990). Reliability, validity, and utility of the Evaluation and Programming System: For Infants and Young Children (EPS-I). *Journal of Early Intervention, 14*(2), 147-160.

Bricker, W., & Campbell, R. (1980). Interdisciplinary assessment and programming for multihandicapped students. In W. Sailor, B. Wilcox, & L. Brown (Eds.), *Methods of instructions for severely handicapped students* (pp. 3-45). Baltimore, MD: Paul Brookes.

Bricker, D., & Cripe, J. (1992). *An activity-based approach to early intervention*. Baltimore, MD: Paul Brookes.

Bricker, D., & Littman, D. (1982). Intervention and evaluation: The inseparable mix. *Topics in Early Childhood Special Education, 1*, 23-33.

Brown, C. (1991). IFSP implementation in the fourth year of P.L. 99-457: The year of the paradox. *Topics in Early Childhood Special Education, 11*(3), 1-18.

Cripe, J. (1990). *Evaluating the effectiveness of training procedures in a linked system approach to individual family service plan development*. Unpublished doctoral dissertation. University of Oregon, Center on Human Development, Eugene, OR.

Cripe, J., & Bricker, D. (1993). *AEPS Family Interest Survey*. Baltimore, MD: Paul Brookes.

Cripe, J., Slentz, K., & Bricker, D. (Eds.). (1993). *Assessment, Evaluation, and Programming System (AEPS) Curriculum for Birth to Three Years*. Baltimore, MD: Paul Brookes.

Gallagher, J. (1993). *The study of federal policy implementation: Infants/toddlers with disabilities and their families, a synthesis of results*. Carolina Policy Studies Program, University of North Carolina, Chapel Hill, NC.

Garwood, G. (1982). Early childhood intervention: Is it time to change outcome variables? *Topics in Early Childhood Special Education, 1*, IX-XI.

Hutinger, P. (1988). Linking screening, identification, and assessment with curriculum. In J. Jordon, J. Gallagher, P. Hutinger, & M. Karnes (Eds.), *Early childhood special education: Birth to three*. Reston, VA: Council for Exceptional Children.

Johnson, N. (1982). Assessment paradigms and atypical infants: An interventionist's perspective. In D. Bricker (Ed.), *Intervention with at-risk and handicapped infants* (pp. 63-76). Baltimore, MD: University Park Press.

Johnson, B., McGonigel, M., & Kaufmann, R. (1989). *Guidelines and recommended practices for the individualized family service plan*. Bethesda, MD: National Early Childhood Technical Assistance System (NEC*TAS) and Association for the Care of Children's Health (ACCH).

Knobloch, H., Stevens, F., & Malone, A. (1980). *Manual of developmental diagnosis: The administration and interpretation of the revised Gesell and Armatruda developmental and neurologic examination*. Hagerstown, MD: Harper & Row.

Lynch, E., Jackson, J., Mendoza, J., & English, K. (1991). The merging of best practices and state policy in the IFSP process in California. *Topics in Early Childhood Special Education, 11*(3), 32-53.

Notari, A., & Bricker, D. (1990). The utility of a curriculum-based assessment instrument in the development of individualized education plans for infants and young children. *Journal of Early Intervention, 14*(2), 117-132.

Notari, A., Slentz, K., & Bricker, D. (1990). Assessment-curriculum systems of early childhood/special education. In R. Brown & D. Mitchell (Eds.), *Early intervention for disabled and at-risk infants*. London: Croom-Helm.

Salvia, J., & Ysseldyke, J. (1981). *Assessment in special and remedial education*. Boston, MA: Houghton Mifflin.

Sheehan, R. (1982). Infant assessment: A review and identification of emergent trends. In D. Bricker (Ed.), *Intervention with at-risk and handicapped infants*. Baltimore, MD: University Park Press.

Shinn, M., & Good, R. (1993). CBA: An assessment of its current status and prognosis for its future. In: I. Kramer (Ed.), *Curriculum-based measurement* (pp. 139-178). Lincoln, NE: Buros Institute of Mental Measurements

Appendix

AEPS Curriculum Sections Corresponding to Jane's Selected Social-Communication Goal and Objective. Taken from AEPS Curriculum Birth to Three Years (Cripe, Slentz, & Bricker, 1993).

Strand B

Transition to Words

GOAL 1   **Gains person's attention and refers to an object, person, and/or event**

DEVELOPMENTAL PROGRAMMING STEPS

No standard developmental sequence appears to exist for the development of these pragmatic skills. Careful observation of the child will help determine the child's current skill level. Begin programming at the child's level of interest.

PS1.0a The child gains a person's attention.

PS1.0b The child establishes joint reference to an object, person, or event.

IMPORTANCE OF SKILL

Prior to comprehension and production of words, most children vocalize or gesture for a variety of communicative functions. Vocalizations and gestures are called prelinguistic communication signals because they precede symbolic language. It is important to establish a relationship between a vocalization or gesture from the child and some response from the environment. From this relationship, the child learns that communication signals serve a variety of functions and allow the child to gain a person's attention and refer to an object, person, or event. Eventually, vocalizations and gestures are shaped into more conventional language forms (i.e., first words).

PRECEDING OBJECTIVE

SC B:1.2   Points to an object, person, and/or event

CONCURRENT GOALS AND OBJECTIVES

FM A:2.3   Reaches toward and touches object with each hand
FM B:2.0   Assembles toy and/or object that require(s) putting pieces together
GM C:1.0   Walks avoiding obstacles
Adap A:3.0 Drinks from cup and/or glass
Adap A:4.0 Eats with fork and/or spoon
Adap B:1.0 Initiates toileting
Cog B:3.0   Maintains search for object that is not in its usual location
Cog C:2.0   Reproduces part of interactive game and/or action in order to continue
Cog D:1.0   Imitates motor action that is not commonly used
SC A:2.0   Follows person's gaze to establish joint attention
SC A:3.0   Engages in vocal exchanges by babbling
Soc A: 3.0 Initiates and maintains communicative exchange with familiar adult

TEACHING SUGGESTIONS

Activity-Based

- Encourage the child to draw your attention to objects and events by responding to the child and continuing the interaction.
- As events occur throughout the day, pretend not to notice immediately, giving the child an opportunity to direct your attention. For example, let the phone ring an extra ring or two, or use a kitchen timer, alarm clock, or doorbell to initiate a response.
- Use gestures with your words. For example, say, "Bye-bye," and wave or say, "Do you want up?" and hold out your hands. These frequent models are easily imitated by the child.
- Respond to the child's vocalizations and gestures in a variety of settings so that the child learns to gain attention in many situations. Watch for the child to indicate interest at the store, in the car, or at playtime with familiar and unfamiliar people. Respond consistently.

If your data indicate the child is not making progress toward the goal, provide additional structure within the suggested activities by incorporating the following environmental arrangements:

Environmental Arrangements

- Arrange the play area so that desired toys are visible to the child but just out of reach. Wait for the child to use a vocalization or a gesture to gain your attention and refer to a desired toy. Then give the toy to the child.
- Show the child a noise-producing object such as a musical toy. Activate the toy and observe the child's response. If the child uses a vocalization or gesture, give the toy to the child. Wait for the child to use a vocalization or gesture to gain your attention and refer to the object, then reactivate the toy and give it to the child.
- When the child is consistently focusing on objects, people, or events of interest, refrain from offering the desired material until the child uses a gesture or vocalization to gain your attention and refers to the object, person, or event of interest. For example, when giving a snack to peers or siblings, wait until the child uses a vocalization or gesture to gain your attention and refers to the food or the other child eating. Then give the child the desired snack.
- The child may not attempt to gain your attention if you are too far away. Check for an optimal distance, then vary the distance after the child responds consistently.

If this goal is particularly difficult for a child, it may be necessary, within activities, to use an instructional sequence.

Instructional Sequence

- Model gaining a person's attention to refer to an object. For example, say, "Ginny, would you like a cracker?"
- Systematically introduce the use of time delay and visual cues. For instance, during snack time, show the child a desired snack, establish eye contact, and give an expectant look. Wait for the child to vocalize or use a gesture to refer to the desired food, then give it to the child.
- Gestures are easy to model. Any looking, vocalizing, or motor gesture that can be shaped into a communicative signal should be encouraged and reinforced. Cues should be consistent and redundant, and all opportunities should be capitalized.
- Show the child an interesting toy placed just out of reach and provide a verbal cue, "Show me what you want." Once the child is consistently vocalizing or gesturing to refer to the object, vary the distance between the object and the child.
- When playing with the child, provide verbal and physical cues. For example, say, "Show me what you want." Then point to or move the desired toy closer to the child. Gently guide the child's hand toward the toy.

Combining or pairing different levels of instructions may be helpful when beginning to teach a new and difficult skill. Fade to less intrusive instructions as soon as possible to encourage more independent performance.

TEACHING CONSIDERATIONS.

1. The child's vocalizations need not approximate actual words.
2. Socially appropriate gestures and vocalizations should be modeled and encouraged to facilitate the child's acquisition of conventional and acceptable attention-getting behaviors.
3. A child with a visual impairment may orient his or her body toward the adult rather than look at the adult's face. Adaptations of conventional gestures may be necessary.
4. If the child has a restricted range of motion, the adult should stand in a position other than where the child is visually focused, but still within the child's field of vision. Adaptations of conventional gestures may be necessary.
5. A child with a hearing impairment may be acquiring an augmentative or alternative communication system such as a picture or sign system. Consult a qualified specialist for teaching techniques.

Objective 1.2 **Points to an object, person, and/or event**

DEVELOPMENTAL PROGRAMMING STEPS

No standard developmental sequence appears to exist for the development of prelinguistic or social-communicative signals. Careful observation of the child will help detemine the function of early communicative vocalizations and gestures. Begin programming at the child's level of interest.

PS1.2a Confirmation function: For example, the adult says, "There's the ball." The child points to the ball.

PS1.2b Comment/reply function: For example, the adult asks, "What happened?" The child points to spilled milk.

PS1.2c Information function: For example, the adult asks, "Where's your teddy?" The child points to the teddy bear.

PS1.2d Request function: For example, the child points to a bottle. The adult asks, "Do you want your bottle?"

PS1.2e Attention function: For example, the child points to a sibling jumping in a swimming pool. The adult says, "There's Billy."

PS1.2f Question function: For example, the child points to a new stuffed animal. The adult says, "What's that?"

PS1.2g Comment/describe function: For example, the child points to a truck. The adult says, "That's a truck."

IMPORTANCE OF SKILL

Communication signals serve a variety of functions and the child learns of the relationship between a vocalization or gesture and a response from the environment. This skill is an important step toward successful communication. For example, the child points to a desired object and the adult gives the object to the child to play with. Eventually vocalizations and gestures are shaped into more conventional language forms (first words).

PRECEDING GOAL

SC A:1.0   Turns and looks toward person speaking

CONCURRENT GOALS AND OBJECTIVES

FM A:2.3   Reaches toward and touches object with each hand
FM B:2.0   Assembles toy and/or object that require(s) putting pieces together
GM C:1.0   Walks avoiding obstacles
Adap A:3.0   Drinks from cup and/or glass
Adap A;4.0   Eats with fork and/or spoon
Adap B:1.0   Initiates toileting
Cog B:3.0   Maintains search for object that is not in its usual location
Cog C:2.0   Reproduces part of interactive game and/or action in order to continue game and/or action
Cog D:1.0   Imitates motor action that is not commonly used
SC A:2.0   Follows person's gaze to establish joint attention
SC A:3.0   Engages in vocal exchanges by babbling
Soc A:3.0   Initiates and maintains communicative exchange with familiar adult

TEACHING SUGGESTIONS

Activity-Based

- While bathing, name body parts and ask the child to point to them. When the child touches a body part, say, "That's right! That's your foot." Repeat with different body parts.
- If the child is reaching for or pointing to a favorite toy, label it, talk about it, and give it to the child to play with.
- While reading a book, name the pictures that the child points to. Take turns pointing to favorite pictures and add new ones.
- During trips to new places, watch the child's gaze, name the objects and events the child looks at, and model pointing.

Environmental Arrangements

- Play "This Little Piggy Went to Market" and point to the child's toes. Then ask the child to point to your toes as you say the rhyme.
- During snack, give the child a small piece of cracker (or any favorite food). Put the next piece just out of the child's reach and ask, "Where's the cracker?" Wait for the child to reach for or point to the cracker and then give it to the child to eat.
- To encourage the child who does not point, offer two items (preferred and nonpreferred). Give the child the nonpreferred item while you hold the preferred item and wait for a gesture.
- Hold two objects, one a bright-colored or musical toy and the other a plain toy. Ask the child, "What do you want?" Wait for the child to reach for or point to the desired toy, then give it to the child.
- Use songs and finger plays that incorporate use of pointing.

Instructional Sequence

- Model pointing to an object or person and comment.
- Systematically introduce the use of time delay and visual cues. For instance, during snack time, show the child a desired snack, establish eye contact, and give an expectant look. Wait for the child to use a gesture to refer to the desired food, then give it to the child.
- Pointing is easy to model. Be consistent about requiring a response before reinforcing the child in all contexts. Cues should be consistent and redundant and all opportunities should be used.
- While looking at books, verbally instruct the child to find certain items in pictures. Encourage a single-finger pointing response.
- Show the child common objects around the house and hold them within the child's reach. Name them one at a time and ask the child, "Where's the ball?" Gently guide the child's hand toward the object. Repeat with different objects.
- While the child is bathing, name and touch the child's body parts. The child may relate to body parts more easily than objects at this stage of development. Ask the child to point to his or her own foot. If the child does not respond, gently guide the child's hand to the foot. Repeat with different body parts.

TEACHING CONSIDERATIONS

1. Respond to the child's vocalizations and gestures in a variety of settings so that the child learns to respond in many situations.
2. A child with a visual impairment may orient his or her body toward the adult rather than look at the adult's face. Adaptations of conventional gestures may be necessary.
3. If the child has a severe visual impairment, use another sensory modality, such as sound, smell, or touch, to direct the child's attention to an object, person, or event. Encourage the child to use the modality independently.
4. If the child has a restricted range of motion, the adult should stand in a position other than where the child is visually focused, but still within the child's field of vision. Adaptions of conventional gestures may be necessary.
5. A child with a hearing impairment may be acquiring an augmentative or alternative communication system such as a picture or sign system. Consult a qualified specialist for teaching techniques.

M. Brambring, H. Rauh, and A. Beelmann (Eds.). (1996). *Early childhood intervention: Theory, evaluation, and practice* (pp. 335-348). Berlin, New York: de Gruyter.

How to Detect Effects? Power and Clinical Significance in Early Intervention Research

Kenneth J. Ottenbacher

1   Introduction

Twelve years ago, Simeonsson et al. (1982) published an article in *Pediatrics* titled "A review and analysis of the effectiveness of early intervention". The authors suggested that evidence was accumulating that early intervention produced positive results. They noted, however, that many questions remained unanswered. These questions included: How does early intervention work? For whom is it most effective? Are certain programs better for certain children? Who should be enrolled? When? For how long?

In the past 20 years, many research investigations have attempted to address these questions (cf. Bronfenbrenner, 1975; Odom, 1988). Numerous primary studies have been reported, and the results of these investigations synthesized in several quantitative reviews or meta-analyses of early intervention research (Casto & Mastropieri, 1986; Casto & White, 1985; Ottenbacher & Peterson, 1985; White & Casto, 1984; White et al., 1984). These studies have contributed substantial knowledge regarding the efficacy of early intervention, but they have not answered all of the questions posed by Simeonsson et al. (1982).

Based on the progress made in early intervention research during the past two decades, Dunst (1986) and others (e.g., Meisel, 1985) have argued that we should move beyond asking the question "does early intervention work?" and focus our empirical efforts on "what dimensions of early intervention are related to changes in different outcome measures?" and "how much variance does early intervention account for beyond that attributed to other formal or informal treatments?" (Dunst, 1986, p .80). To answer these questions will require well-designed examinations of early intervention that are sensitive to specific treatment effects.

A lack of sensitivity and weak experimental design are frequently identified concerns in the early intervention research literature (Dunst, 1986; Dunst & Rheingrover, 1981; Dunst et al., 1989; Guralnick & Bennet,

1987; Halpern, 1984). In a comprehensive examination of the methodology of 49 studies on the effectiveness of early intervention programs for children with biological impairment, Dunst and Rheingrover (1981) concluded that "flaws in the experimental designs make most of the studies uninterpretable from a scientific point of view." Along similar lines, Halpern (1984) reviewed existing early intervention studies and concluded that limitations in measurement, research design, and statistical analysis have obscured some positive effects.

An important methodological factor that may obscure positive intervention effects in some early intervention studies is low statistical power. Inadequate statistical power is considered a form of statistical conclusion invalidity by Cook and Campbell (1979). They define statistical conclusion invalidity as the inappropriate use or interpretation of statistical tests. The presence of statistical conclusion invalidity can reduce the sensitivity of experimental and quantitative manipulations and affect the ability of an experimental trial to reveal covariation among variables.

1.1 Implications of Low Statistical Power in Early Intervention Research

The power of a study is defined as its ability to detect a phenomenon of specified magnitude, given the existence of that phenomenon (Cohen, 1988; Oakes, 1986). Power is the complement of the miss rate (beta or type II error) and can be readily calculated for a variety of statistics (Cohen, 1988). For example, when studies are concerned with mean differences due to treatment, the power can be calculated, provided that the effect size, the within group variability, the required type I error probability (usually .05), and the sample size are specified. These components of power have recently been described and defined in the early intervention literature (Ottenbacher, 1989, 1992). The larger the treatment impact (effect size), the higher its probability of detection as statistically significant, given that other factors such as sample size and alpha level (type I error rate) remain constant. Power is inversely related to noneffect variability within the study. Factors such as uncontrolled sources of random error, subject heterogeneity, and error of measurement decrease power (Lipsey, 1990).

A field in which low research power exists is empirically inefficient and unable to detect new effects of small magnitude that might be the basis for eventually developing effective therapeutic interventions. Or worse, investigations with low power may not detect intervention effects that may have educational or clinical significance. Power values also bear upon other issues of research interpretation that appear to be understood less commonly (Oakes, 1986). These issues have not received detailed attention in the early intervention literature, although they are very relevant to the development of empirical and statistical consensus regarding the effectiveness of early intervention.

The ubiquitous concern with producing statistical significance and control of type I errors in the education and behavioral science research literature (Bakan, 1966; Oakes, 1986) is clear evidence that investigators wish to maintain a research literature with a low frequency of false alarms. It is perhaps not as widely appreciated that control of alpha in hypothesis testing is not the only factor that determines the actual proportion of false alarms in the literature. As Oakes (1986) has eloquently reviewed, the proportion of false alarms in the literature will depend on factors other than the type I error rate selected for the statistical procedure. Two key factors are: (a) the prior probability that we are conducting a study on a hypothesis with an effect of the stipulated magnitude or greater; and (b) the power of the study. The effects of these factors on the number of type I errors in the research literature are described below.

Table 1. *Hypothetical Outcomes of 1,000 Studies With Average Power of .50, Type I Error Set at .05, and a 30% Incidence of "True" Effects*

	True state of null hypothesis	
Researcher's conclusion	H_o **true**	H_a **true**
Accept H_o	665	150
Reject H_o	35	150
Total	700	300

Proportion of type I errors = (35/185 x 100) = 18.9%.

Consider a hypothetical early intervention literature comprising 1,000 studies (Table 1). We might (generously?) assume that, based on current theories, clinical experience, and the guidance of previous research, we are able to select hypotheses that contain a true effect of an anticipated magnitude 30% of the time. Thus, we do not face an equiprobable choice among hundreds of alternatives, many of which may be ineffective. That situation would give a minuscule prior probability of success. Rather, we assume some a priori ability to filter from prior empirical experience and theory. We thus progress, before even starting an experiment, from a very small probability of success to a sizable 30% chance of selecting a treatment that produces the desired effect. Let us further assume that despite fears occasionally voiced, the early intervention literature is no worse than that of related fields. For example, in the behavioral sciences (Brewer, 1972; Chase & Chase, 1976; Cohen, 1962; Orme & Combs-Orme, 1986), average power is around .50 or 50% for detecting what Cohen (1988) has defined as a medium-sized effect. Let us finally assume that alpha is scrupulously controlled in all studies to be only 5% ($p < .05$). What is the proportion of type I errors or false alarms in this hypothetical literature? The data from Table 1 shows that, under these circumstances, 35 of the 1,000 studies would be false claims that an effect exists and 150 would be accurate claims that an effect exists. Thus the proportion of false alarms in this literature would be 18.9% (35/185 x 100), not 5%. Stated more generally, if α is the stipulated probability for type I error, $1 - \beta$ is the power; and if $p(H_o)$ is the proportion of null hypotheses in the population of hypotheses, then $p(FA)$, the actual proportion of erroneous claims that an effect was detected (false alarms), is:

$$p(FA) = [\alpha p(H_o)] \div [(1 - \beta) (1 - p(H_o)) + \alpha p(H_o)] \qquad (1)$$

This equation, or reworking of Table 1, can readily demonstrate the effect of varying the power on the actual proportion of false alarms. For example, if we increase power to .80, a value sometimes suggested as a reasonable compromise (Oakes, 1986), $p(FA)$ is reduced from 18.9% to 12.7%. This is still not the desired or sometimes imagined 5%, but does represent a large (30%) reduction in the proportion of false alarms in the literature. What if we were as stringent about controlling the type II error as we typically are about the type I error? If $1 - \beta$ is .95, then $p(FA)$ becomes 10.9%. Clearly then, the power of a study ought to be of concern if we are interested in keeping the proportion of false alarms in the literature low.

The probability of false alarms in the literature might be reduced substantially if our blind selection of hypotheses to test, based on prior information, for example, practical experience, theory, or prior research, was particularly good. If our "blind luck" was such that we had an even chance of selecting a hypothesis that contains an effect of "medium" size according to Cohen's criteria ($p(H_o) = .50$), then $p(FA)$ is 19.2% when the power is as low as .21 and alpha is the usual .05. Low power, such as .21, in fact, has been reported as characteristic of the early intervention literature (Ottenbacher, 1989). With such low power, our blind luck would need to be very good.

Algebraic manipulation of Equation (1) to solve for $p(H_o)$ yields the following expression:

$$p(H_o) = [p(FA) (1 - \beta)] \div [\alpha - p(FA) (\alpha - (1 - \beta))] \qquad (2)$$

Equation (2) indicates that if we wish $p(FA)$, the proportion of false alarms in the literature, to remain at only .05 when power is .21 and alpha is set at .05, then $p(H_o)$ would need to be as low as 25%. That is, our "blind" chance would need to be good enough to permit selection of intervention effects that are of Cohen's (1988) medium effect size ($d = 0.50$) on virtually four out of five studies. We might question whether our theoretical development, existing research, and clinical experience are that accurate in guiding us toward new hypotheses to test (LeLaurin & Wolery, 1992).

The practical and theoretical interpretation of statistical hypotheses indicates that a consideration of power is necessary in any analysis of the status of a body of literature, particularly if that literature is characterized by a lack of consensus. First, low power implies by definition an increase in type II errors ($\beta = 1$ - power). Second, as demonstrated above (Lipsey, 1990), low power also contributes to the accumulation of type I errors in the published literature, a conclusion that deserves wider appreciation. The influence of power on the false alarm rate is mediated by the prior probability that a true effect has been selected for testing; another theoretical conclusion that deserves wider appreciation. Furthermore, given the stage of theory development in early intervention (LeLaurin & Wolery, 1992), it does not seem unreasonable to hypothesize that the prior probability factor introduces significant additional risk of the accumulation of false alarms in early intervention research. These arguments converge to indicate that low power in hypothesis tests will affect the incidence of both false alarms and misses in the literature. An increase in both types of error will produce a research literature with contradictory findings, and these will, in turn, contribute to empirical, statistical, and theoretical confusion. As Lipsey (1990) has accurately observed, "statistical comparisons that lack power make for treatment effectiveness research that cannot accomplish its central purpose - to determine the effectiveness of treatment" (p. 21).

The full implications of power and type II errors on the interpretation of early intervention research cannot be assessed without current knowledge of the level of statistical power in the published literature. To determine the current power levels in the research literature, 30 early intervention studies were examined. The purpose of the study was to find representative power values for early intervention research and investigate the relationship between power, sample size, effect size, and alpha level.

2   Methods

Thirty studies from the recent early intervention literature were examined. The 30 studies were obtained from the following journals: *Journal of Early Intervention, Journal of Developmental and Behavioral Pediatrics, Developmental Medicine and Child Neurology*, and *Research in Developmental Disabilities*. To be included in the analysis, a study had to meet the following criteria: (a) intervention began prior to 3 years of age; (b) the majority of children included in the program had one or more disabilities; (c) the program contained a quantitative evaluation of performance; (d) outcome measures included some type of functional or behavioral assessment (studies that used only physiological measures such as heart-rate or respiration were not included); and (e) the study contained adequate statistical and descriptive information about the sample and results. Studies were selected by two research assistants with graduate level training in research design and statistical methods. Each journal was reviewed beginning with the last issue of 1992 and working back until a total of eight studies meeting the above criteria were identified ($N = 32$). Studies included in the analysis were published from 1988 through 1992.
     Data from each of the studies concerning type of research design, sample size, statistical test, and statistical outcome were transcribed to a coding form and used in subsequent analysis. The coding was performed by two trained raters with experience in data reduction and coding. Two original studies were eliminated because of disagreements between the two raters over coding of the type of research designs. The elimination of these two studies left 30 investigations that were included in the analysis. Reliabilities were determined for all items coded from the 30 studies. Reliability values ranged from Kappa's of .77 to .86, and intraclass correlation coefficients (ICC) values of .86 to 1.00.

2.1 Determination of Power

Power coefficients were obtained for each statistical test of a hypothesis associated with a dependent variable included in the 30 early intervention studies. Power values were obtained from tables provided by Cohen (1988). The power for each statistical test to detect a "small," "medium," and "large" treatment effect was read directly from the appropriate table in Cohen's text or calculated by interpolation between tabled values. Cohen's guidelines were used to label treatment effects as small, medium, or large.

These guidelines were developed as "conventional frames of reference" to make judgments concerning the impact of independent variables in various fields. Cohen notes that what may be considered a small effect in one area may have important practical (clinical or educational) implications in another field. Given this caveat, Cohen's guidelines have proven useful in establishing basic information for interpreting treatment effects when additional information is not available. For two group comparisons, characteristic of the 30 studies included in this review, Cohen provides the d index as a measure of effect size. A small d index ranges from 0.20 to 0.50, a medium d index from 0.50 to 0.80, and a large d index is defined as a value equal to or greater than 0.80. A d index of 0.30 means that 3/10 of a standard deviation separates the average subjects in the two groups/conditions being compared.

To complete the power analysis of the early intervention studies, some additional parameters were defined. First, the .05 alpha level was assumed for all statistical tests when determining power levels. A two-tailed (nondirectional) version of the null hypothesis was also assumed for all statistical tests. Adopting this convention may have produced underestimates of power in some cases. However, the assumption of a two-tailed test eliminated the more serious problem of inflated significance levels and power in nonpredicted directions.

3   Results

There were a total of 143 statistical hypothesis tests of various dependent measures included in the 30 early intervention studies. The average early intervention study included 4.76 statistical tests ($SD = 3.71$). This is slightly fewer dependent measures than reported in the clinical research literature (Pocock et al., 1987).

Power is determined by a combination of factors including the alpha level, effect size, and sample size. It is often suggested or implied that sample size is the easiest factor to manipulate in improving power (Kraemer & Thiemann, 1987). Table 2 contains sample size information for the 30 early intervention studies. Each sample size is indicated by a combination of stem and leaf following procedures suggested by Tukey (1977). The stem and leaf table provides all the information contained in a traditional bar graph, but also shows the actual values for all sample sizes. The stem and leaf table also includes additional descriptive and summary statistics related to the sample values included in the early intervention studies.

Table 2.   *Stem and Leaf Table for Sample Size for 30 Clinical Trials Included in the Analysis*

Stem	Leaf					
0	8					
1	1	3	4	9		
2	0	0	2	2	4	
3	0	0	3	6	7	8
4	0	2				
5	3					
6	2	4				
7	1					
8	3	6				
9	1					
10	1	3				
11						
12						
13	2					
14	0					
15	2					

Mean	52.90	Max	152
Median	37.50	Min	8
SD	40.00	Q_1	21
N	30	Q_3	71

Results of the power analysis for small, medium, and large effect sizes are presented in Table 3. The table presents cumulative frequencies and summary statistics for various power ranges assuming either small, medium, or large effect size. The power coefficients included in Table 3 are based on the 143 individual hypothesis tests included in the 30 early intervention investigations.

Inspection of Table 3 reveals that the median power of the 143 hypothesis tests to detect a small treatment effect as defined by Cohen ($d = 0.20$) was .09. The median power to detect medium and large treatment effects present in the target population was .33 and .69 respectively. Another way to interpret the results is to estimate the probability of committing a type II error for the range of effect sizes examined. The probability of committing a type II error (beta) was .91 or 91% if the population treatment effect was in the range Cohen considers small (i.e., d index = 0.20). The miss rates (beta) for medium and large effect sizes were 67% and 31% respectively. These results suggest that even when the population treatment effect is in the range Cohen considers large, the probability of committing a type II error is substantial, approximately 30%.

Table 3. *Summary Statistics for Power to Detect Small, Medium, and Large Population Effect Sizes Using Individual Statistical Tests as the Unit of Analysis*

	Small effects	Medium effects	Large effects*
N	143	143	143
Maximum	.37	.92	.99
Minimum	.05	.10	.32
Median	.09	.33	.69
Mean	.14	.43	.77
SD	.09	.29	.48

*All effects (small, medium, and large) based on criteria developed by Cohen (1988).

4 Discussion

Examination of the 30 early intervention studies revealed that investigators had a poor chance of correctly rejecting the null hypothesis unless the effect produced by the intervention was very large. The argument could be made that much of the effectiveness research in early intervention will be concerned with small and medium effect sizes due to the lack of rigorous experimental control in natural and educational settings, the heterogeneous nature of the target population, and the insensitivity of many measuring instruments. The median power values to detect small and medium effect sizes in the 30 trials reviewed were .09 and .33 respectively. The median power for all 143 reviewed hypothesis tests was .37, suggesting that the probable type II error rate for the reviewed literature was very high (β = .63). Thus, the results suggest a high incidence of type II error in the early intervention literature.

A traditional method for setting a desirable power for an efficacy study is to use the formula: power = 1 - 4(α). If the .05 level is selected for a study, then power is established at 1 - 4(.05) or .80. Using this criterion, none of the statistical evaluations included in the 30 investigations evidenced sufficient power to detect a small effect. The percentages of studies with adequate power (> .80) to detect medium and large effect sizes were 24% and 46% respectively.

4.1 Implications

Several investigations have identified and described the negative impact that studies of low power can have on a developing research literature (Fagley, 1985; Freiman et al., 1978; Lipsey, 1990; Ottenbacher, 1989; Ottenbacher & Barrett, 1989). First, low power decreases the probability of rejecting the null hypothesis, and thus increases the likelihood of committing a type II error. Second, inadequate power may increase the probability of committing a type I error; this interpretation derives from the Bayesian statistical concept of conditional alpha probability (Overall, 1969) and was illustrated previously (see Table 1). A third negative consequence of low power concerns the interpretation of statistically nonsignificant findings. When a researcher reports a failure to reject the null hypothesis, the various methodological factors and design features contributing to the obtained outcome (i.e., small sample size, measurement error, sample heterogeneity, etc.) should be considered carefully, particularly when power is low.

All of these factors associated with low power contribute to the conflict that appears in the early intervention literature, although this may not be recognized. As Oakes has commented in a general vein, control of alpha at $p < .05$ is sometimes (erroneously) imagined to mean that the probability of replication is 95%. In fact, power also determines the probability of replication as does the prior probability of null and nonnull hypotheses. It is instructive to consider quantitatively the influence of these factors on probability of replication.

What is the probability that a second study, identical to the first, will replicate the original findings? If a null hypothesis is being tested and alpha is .05, then the probability that H_o will be accepted twice in succession when using conventional statistical methods will be $.95^2$, that is, .9025. The probability that it will be falsely rejected twice is $.05^2$, that is, .025. Thus, the overall probability of replication is .93. If, however, we are dealing with a genuine effect (H_a true), power becomes a critical factor. Assuming a power of .33, the median power found in the sample of early intervention literature to detect a medium effect size (see Table 3), we obtain p (replication) $= .33^2 + (1 - .33)^2 = .557$. These figures are even more dismal if we consider that, in this last example, the majority of the replications represent confirmations of a false impression. In fact, $(1 - .33)^2 \div [.33^2 + (1 - .33)^2] = .804$, or 80% of the replications strengthen a false impression.

The overall probability of replication in a given field will further depend on the proportion of times we have selected to work with what are in actuality null or nonnull hypotheses, in other words, the a priori probability of H_a. If we assume $p(H_a) = .30$, based on the example in Table 1, $\alpha = .05$, and a power of .33 to detect a medium effect size as reported in the previous section (see Table 3), then the overall probability of replication is: p(replication) $= .7[.05^2 + (1 - .05)^2] + .3[.33^2 + (1 - .33)^2] = .974$.

Of course, we probably prefer to imagine that our theories, observation, and prior research are valuable guides, so that we are led to conduct research on situations in which the effect does exist more often than 30% of the time. If we reverse the above example so that $p(H_a) = .70$ and $p(H_o) = .30$, we obtain p(replication) $= .736$, a lower value. The apparently paradoxical and (painfully) amusing conclusion is that the more often we are well guided by theory and prior observation, but conduct a low-power study, the more we decrease the probability of replication! Thus, a literature with low power is not only committing a passive error, but can actually contribute to statistical confusion. Of course, if theories and prior observations lead to testing what are true null hypotheses, the practice of setting alpha at .05 will allow a high probability of replication, as shown above. Our best chance of replication appears to be when we discover nothing.

Rosenthal (1990) has provided an excellent example of the confusion that can result when statistical power is ignored in considering the results of replication studies. Assume that two investigations have been conducted. The first, Study A, produces statistically significant results. A second study is conducted using the same research design, same independent variable, and same dependent variable, but with one important difference - a smaller sample size. The results of the second study (B) are not statistically significant, and the conclusion is a failure to replicate, that is, confusing results. A closer look at the actual statistical outcomes reveals the following.

Study A: $t(78) = 2.21, p < .05$
Study B: $t(18) = 1.06$, n.s.

If a d index is computed for these two investigations using the formula presented by Rosenthal (1990) and others (Friedman, 1968; Hedges & Olkin, 1985), $d = 2t/\sqrt{df}$, we find that the effect size ($d = 0.50$) is identical for both studies. The discrepancy between the statistical significance test results and the effect size results is obviously due to the smaller sample size ($N = 20$) and subsequently lower power for Study B. The power to reject the null hypothesis at $p < .05$ (two-tailed) is .18 for Study B. The probability of a type II error is .82 or 82%.

Cohen (1988) defines an effect size as the degree to which a null hypothesis is false. In this example, the degree to which the null hypothesis is false is identical in both Study A and B. The agreement or consistency of treatment impact across trials is obscured when the focus is primarily on the results of statistical significance testing. In such cases, low power leads to statistical confusion. As Lipsey et al. (1985) accurately note, "research with low statistical power has the potential for falsely branding a program as a failure when, in fact, the problem is the inability of the research to detect an effect, not the inability of the program to produce one" (p. 26).

4.2 Conclusion

One consequence of a failure to replicate a previous investigation is a proliferation of studies developed around hypothesized "explanations" for the discrepancies observed in the literature. These explanations are usually based on theories or conjecture related to the original independent variable. Rarely is the mundane hypothesis of mere sampling variation and/or low statistical power considered as the preferred explanation and the inspiration for a more powerful replication study to settle the issue. Disagreements in the literature are more commonly used as springboards for variants of the original studies. As noted by Lindsay and Ehrenberg (1993), exact replication is rare. Even rarer is replication with a more powerful design. Thus, the consequence of low power is a contradictory research literature, apparently dynamic, but failing to resolve uncertainties - failing to establish consensus.

The responsible early intervention researcher must be concerned with power. A concern with power, however, cannot end with its calculation. Since ability to detect treatment effects ought to be optimized, the responsible scientist must also be concerned with all factors that determine effect size. These factors include not only parameters controlled by research circumstances and method, such as sample size, sensitivity of measuring instruments, sample heterogeneity, and design characteristics (blocking, repeated measures, etc.), but also parameters influenced by the goals set for the study, such as the effect size to be detected. Several excellent resources exist to assist the researcher in understanding and improving statistical power in applied investigations (Cohen, 1988; Lipsey, 1990). An appreciation of statistical power will help ensure that future early intervention research will be reported accurately and interpreted correctly.

References

Bakan, D. (1966). The test of significance in psychological research. *Psychological Bulletin, 66*, 423-437.

Brewer, J. K. (1972). On the power of statistical tests in the American Educational Research Journal. *American Educational Research Journal, 9*, 391-40.

Bronfenbrenner, U. (1975). Is early intervention effective? In B. Z. Friedlander, G. M. Sterritt, & G. E. Kirk (Eds.), *Exceptional infant* (Vol. 3, pp. 449-475). New York: Brunner/Mazel.

Casto, G., & Mastropieri, M. A. (1986). The efficacy of early intervention programs: A meta-analysis. *Exceptional Children, 52*, 417-424.

Casto, G., & White, K. R. (1985). The efficacy of early intervention programs with environmentally at-risk infants. *Journal of Children in Contemporary Society, 17*, 37-50.

Chase, L., & Chase, R. B. (1976). A statistical power analysis of applied psychological research. *Journal of Applied Psychology, 61*, 234-237.

Cohen, J. (1962). The statistical power of abnormal-social psychological research. A review. *Journal of Abnormal and Social Psychology, 65*, 145-153.

Cohen, J. (1988). *Statistical power analysis for the behavioral sciences* (2nd ed.). Hillsdale, NJ: Erlbaum.

Cook, T. D., & Campbell, D. T. (1979). *Quasi experimentation. Design & analysis issues for field settings.* Chicago, IL: Rand McNally.

Dunst, C. J. (1986). Overview of the efficacy of early intervention programs. In L. Bickman & D. L. Weatherford (Eds.), *Evaluating early intervention programs for severely handicapped children and their families* (pp. 79-148). Austin, TX: PRO-ED.

Dunst, C. J., & Rheingrover, R. M. (1981). An analysis of the efficacy of infant intervention programs with organically handicapped children. *Evaluation and Program Planning, 4*, 287-323.

Dunst, C. J., Snyder, S. W., & Mankiner, M. (1989). Efficacy of early intervention. In M. C. Wang, M. C. Reynolds, & H. J. Walberg (Eds.), *Handbook of special education: Research and practice: Vol. 3, Low incidence conditions* (pp. 259-294). New York: Pergamon Press.

Fagley, N. S. (1985). Applied statistical power analysis and the interpretation of nonsignificant results of research consumers. *Journal of Counseling Psychology, 32*, 391-396.

Freiman, J., Chalmers, T., Smith, H., & Kuebler, R. (1978). The importance of beta, the type II error and sample size in the design and interpretation of the randomized trial. *New England Journal of Medicine, 299*, 690-694.

Friedman, H. (1968). Magnitude of experimental effect and a table for its rapid estimation. *Psychological Bulletin, 70*, 245-251.

Guralnick, M. J., & Bennet, F. C. (1987). Early intervention for at-risk and handicapped children: Current and future perspectives. In M. J. Guralnick & F. C. Bennet (Eds.), *The effectiveness of early intervention for at-risk and handicapped children* (pp. 365-382). New York: Academic Press.

Halpern, D. (1984). Lack of effects for home-based early intervention? Some possible explanations. *American Journal of Orthopsychiatry, 54*, 33-42.

Hedges, L. V., & Olkin, I. (1985). *Statistical methods for meta-analysis*. Orlando, FL: Academic Press.

Kraemer, H. C., & Thiemann, S. (1987). *How many subjects: Statistical power analysis in research*. Beverly Hills, CA: Sage.

LeLaurin, K., & Wolery, M. (1992). Research standards in early intervention: Defining, describing, and measuring the independent variable. *Journal of Early Intervention, 16*, 275-287.

Lindsay, R. M., & Ehrenberg, A. S. C. (1993). The design of replicated studies. *The American Statistician, 47*, 217-228.

Lipsey, M. W. (1990). *Design sensitivity: Statistical power for experimental research*. Newbury Park, CA: Sage.

Lipsey, M. W., Crosse, S., Pankle, J., & Stobart, G. (1985). Evaluation: The state of the art and the sorry state of the science. *New Direction for Program Evaluation, 27*, 7-28.

Meisel, S. J. (1985). The efficacy of early intervention: Why are we still asking this question. *Topics in Early Childhood Special Education, 5*(2), 1-12.

Oakes, M. (1986). *Statistical inference: A commentary for the social and behavioral sciences*. New York: Wiley.

Odom, S. L. (1988). Research in early childhood special education. In S. L. Odom & M. B. Karnes (Eds.), *Early intervention for infants and children with handicaps: An empirical base* (pp. 1-21). Baltimore, MD: Brookes.

Orme, J., & Combs-Orme, T. (1986). Statistical power and type II errors in social work research. *Social Work Research Abstracts, Fall*, 3-10.

Ottenbacher, K. J. (1989). Statistical conclusion validity of early intervention research with handicapped children. *Exceptional Children, 55*, 534-540.

Ottenbacher, K. J. (1992). Practical significance in early intervention research: From affect to empirical effect. *Journal of Early Intervention, 16*, 181-193.

Ottenbacher, K. J., & Barrett, K. A. (1989). Statistical conclusion validity of rehabilitation research. *American Journal of Physical Medicine and Rehabilitation, 69*, 102-107.

Ottenbacher, K. J., & Petersen, P. (1985). The efficacy of early intervention programs for children with organic impairment. *Evaluation and Program Planning, 8*, 135-146.

Overall, J. E. (1969). Classical statistical hypothesis testing within the context of Bayesian theory. *Psychological Bulletin, 71*, 285-292.

Pocock, S. J., Hughes, M. D., & Lee, R. J. (1987). Statistical problems in the reporting of clinical trials: A survey of three medical journals. *New England Journal of Medicine, 317*, 426-432.

Rosenthal, R. (1990). Replication in behavioral research. In J. W. Neulep (Ed.), *Handbook of replication research in the behavioral and social sciences* (pp. 1-30). Newbury Park, CA: Sage.

Simeonsson, R. J., Cooper, D. H., & Scheiner, A. P. (1982). A review and analysis of the effectiveness of early intervention programs. *Pediatrics, 69*, 635-641.

Tukey, J. W. (1977). *Exploratory data analysis*. Reading, MA: Addison-Wesley.

White, K. R., & Casto, G. (1984). An integrative review of early intervention efficacy studies with at risk children: Implications for the handicapped. *Analysis and Intervention in Developmental Disabilities, 5*, 177-201.

White, K. R., Mastropieri, M., & Casto, G. (1984). An analysis of special education early childhood projects approved by the Joint Dissemination Review Panel. *Journal of the Division of Early Childhood, 9*, 11-26.

M. Brambring, H. Rauh, & A. Beelmann (Eds.). (1996). *Early childhood intervention: Theory, evaluation, and practice.* (pp. 349-375). Berlin, New York: de Gruyter.

Meta-Analyses of Early Intervention:
A Methodological and Content-Related Evaluation

Andreas Beelmann

1 Introduction

The last 20 years have seen a dramatic increase in research designed to integrate scientific knowledge. Particularly in the field of program evaluation, meta-analysis has become an technique that is often used to combine results from different studies on the same topic. Although the concept of meta-analysis has changed over the years (see Cooper & Hedges, 1994a), it can be defined generally as a term covering a number of conceptual and statistical methods used to summarize findings from different primary studies in a quantitative and most comprehensive, systematic, and unbiased way. The core of this process is the calculation of some unified effect-size parameter (Cohen, 1988) that makes it possible to compare and integrate the results from different studies based on different outcome criteria.

Since the classic work of Smith and Glass (1977; Smith et al., 1980) on psychotherapy evaluation, a number of meta-analyses have become available on a wide range of different topics dealing with psychological and educational treatments (see Lipsey & Wilson, 1993). Several meta-analyses have also been published in the field of early intervention, and their outcomes have been subject to more controversial discussions than those found in many other fields of research. For example, on the basis of their meta-analytical results, Casto and Mastropieri (1986a) have questioned some widely accepted assumptions on early intervention efficacy (such as "earlier is better"). These provocative statements were followed by hard conceptional and methodological criticism (Dunst & Snyder, 1986; Strain & Smith, 1986), and were countered by a likewise harsh reply (Casto & Mastropieri, 1986b, c). The aim of this paper is to clarify some points of this discussion through a critical evaluation of methodological and content-related considerations in meta-analyses on early intervention.

2   Overview of Meta-Analyses on Early Intervention

If one wants to carry out an evaluation of the available meta-analyses on early intervention, it is initially necessary to ascertain which studies should be considered. This particularly calls for a more precise definition of which interventions can be viewed as early intervention. With reference to recent work (e.g., Dunst, this volume; Shonkoff & Meisels, 1990), this evaluation will be based on a very broad concept of early intervention: It is defined as all psychological, educational, special educational, and medical forms of intervention that are directed toward the prevention and intervention of developmental delays or problems in normal, disabled, disadvantaged, and at-risk children up to the age of 6 years. These programs do not necessarily need to be restricted to the children, but can also include, to a varying extent, parents and persons within the social setting. Selected were meta-analyses on early intervention that were published up to 1993 with the major feature that they use effect-size parameters to integrate the findings of various treatment effectiveness studies. The only meta-analyses excluded were those on drug treatments and diets.

   To identify appropriate studies, the first step was to search relevant databanks (PsychLIT, ERIC, medline) with the keywords *meta-analysis* and *early intervention* (as well as comparable terms such as *early childhood intervention* or *early childhood special education*). In addition, previously identified meta-analyses, relevant primary studies, and qualitative reviews (e.g., Dunst et al., 1989; Guralnick, 1991; Guralnick & Bennett, 1987; Farran, 1990) served as data sources. Finally, Lipsey and Wilson's (1993) review of meta-analyses on psychological and educational intervention was inspected. With the help of these strategies and on the basis of the above-mentioned selection criteria, a total of 25 published meta-analyses were identified for the period from 1983 to 1993 (see Table 1)[*].

   Most meta-analyses (15 articles) are studies issuing from the work carried out at the Early Intervention Research Institute at Utah State University (see Casto et al., 1983; Casto & White, 1987). It is therefore hardly surprising that some individual publications show large overlaps in the information presented [e.g., 22 with 3 and 23] or even partially or almost completely duplicated publications [e.g., 4 and 23; or 12 and 14]. However, the information given in these publications always differed in some way, and, for this reason, they were treated separately in this

---

[*] When individual meta-analyses are not discussed in detail, they will be cited in brackets with the identification numbers in Table 1 in order to save space and improve transparency.

evaluation. The contents of the 25 articles can be separated into four large groups: The first contains one work [22] on the *general effectiveness* of early intervention programs. A second large group (10 studies) addresses *specific populations* [3, 4, 5, 8, 9, 13, 15, 16, 18, 23, 24]. The third group of meta-analyses (8 studies) addresses mainly *specific types of early intervention* [1, 7, 10, 11, 12, 14, 17, 21]. Finally, the fourth group contains analyses of *specific treatment parameters*, such as treatment intensity [6] and parent involvement [2, 25] or certification of intervenor [20]. One study [19] is only a demonstration project without content-related research questions.

It should be noted that there are four integrations of single-case studies [8, 15, 16, 17], which is an otherwise neglected field of integrative research (Wilson & Rachman, 1983). It should also be noted that some analyses have integrated studies on older children or even adults [1, 10]. However, such primary studies with older populations were in the minority, and so these works were retained in the analysis. On the other side, several meta-analyses of some typical forms of early intervention were dropped from the analysis, because the majority of primary studies were mainly with older children (e.g., on psycholinguistic training programs, Kavale, 1981; and perceptual motor training, Kavale & Mattson, 1983). In addition, general meta-analyses of psychotherapeutic methods with children and adolescents (e.g., Baer & Nietzel, 1991; Beelmann et al., 1994; Casey & Berman, 1985; Weisz et al., 1987), which also contain results on preschool children, were excluded because of the wide age range.

3   Methodological Evaluation of Meta-Analyses on Early Intervention

In their quantitative, systematic techniques, meta-analyses have, from very early on, enjoyed the reputation of being broadly free from objectivity and reliability problems. Criticism was directed more against the rationale of the procedure (e.g., Eysenck, 1978), or could be traced back to problems in the primary studies. It was only with the consolidation of the procedure at the beginning of the 1980s that methods of meta-analysis also became subject to criticism (e.g., Jackson, 1980). One consequence of this discussion was the systematic further development of this technique (see Cooper & Hedges, 1994b). Two main developments should be noted here:

continued on page 356

Table 1. *Summary of Early Intervention Meta-Analyses*

Identification number and Study	Treatment or treatment variable	Population (age at entry)	Outcomes
1 Arnold et al. (1986)[a]	Language interventions	Mentally retarded (mostly up to 72 months; see Notes)	All outcomes
2 Casto & Lewis (1984)[a]	Effects of parent involvement	Disadvantaged[b] (up to 66 months)	All outcomes
3 Casto & Mastropieri (1986a)[a]	EIPs	Handicapped (up to 66 months)	All outcomes
4 Casto & White (1985)[a]	EIPs	Environmentally at-risk infants and preschoolers (up to 66 months)	All outcomes
5 Goldring & Presbrey (1986)	EIPs	Disadvantaged (up to 60 months)	All follow-up outcomes
6 Innocenti & White (1993)[a]	Effects of treatment intensity	Disadvantaged; handicapped; at-risk (up to 66 months)	All outcomes
7 Lewis & Vosburgh (1988)	Kindergarten programs	Normal (about 60 months)	All outcomes
8 Mastropieri & Scruggs (1985-86)[a]	Behavioral interventions	Handicapped; socially withdrawn (up to 66 months)	All outcomes
9 Mastropieri et al. (1985)[a]	EIPs	Behaviorally disordered (up to 66 months; $M = 52.3$)	All outcomes
10 Ottenbacher et al. (1986)	Neurodevelopmental treatments	Handicapped; at-risk ($M = 71.0$ months; see Notes)	Developmental outcomes
11 Ottenbacher et al. (1987)	Tactile stimulation	Normal; at-risk; handicapped ($M = 15.9$ months)	Developmental outcomes
12 Ottenbacher & Petersen (1984)	Vestibular stimulation	Normal; pediatric population (mostly infants and toddlers; see Notes)	Developmental outcomes
13 Ottenbacher & Petersen (1985a)	EIPs	Organically impaired (up to 36 months)	All outcomes

N of Primary Studies (Year-Range)	N of ES	Mean ES (d index)/ Main result	Notes
30 (1950-1984)	87	0.59	Contains studies with older children; population selected by mental age
NR (1937-1983)	NR	No additional effect of parent involvement	Results are also presented in White & Casto (1985); Casto & White (1985); White (1985-1986)
74 (1937-1984)	215	0.68	Results are also presented in White (1985-1986)
69[c] (1937-1983)	415[c]	0.63[c]	Results are also presented in White & Casto (1985); Casto & Lewis (1984); White (1985-1986)
8 (1973-1977)	30	0.24 (0.25)[d]	Study selection restricted to Darlington et al. (1980)
155 (+ 20)[e] (1937-1984) (up to 1990)[f]	NR	No general effect of treatment intensity	
65 (1963-1983)	388	0.41	
18 (1964-1984)	19	NR	Integration of single-subject research
15 (1969-1979)	44	0.80	
9 (1963-1982)	35	0.31	Contains studies with older children (up to 14 years)
19 (1965-1981)	103	0.58	
14 (1964-1982)	31	0.71	Contains studies with older children (up to 14 years); the dataset is also contained in Ottenbacher & Petersen (1985b)
38 (M = 1976)	118	0.97	Study selection restricted to Dunst & Rheingrover (1981)

table continues

Table 1.   (*continued*)

Identification number and Study	Treatment or treatment variable	Population (age at entry)	Outcomes
14 Ottenbacher & Petersen (1985b)	Vestibular stimulation	Normal; pediatric population (mostly infants and toddlers; see Notes)	All outcomes
15 Scruggs et al. (1986)[a]	Behavioral treatments	Behavioral disordered (up to 66 months)	All outcomes
16 Scruggs et al. (1988a)[a]	Language interventions	Language disordered or delayed (up to 66 months)	All outcomes
17 Scruggs et al. (1988b)[a]	Physical/motor and nutritive treatments	Handicapped (up to 66 months)	All outcomes
18 Shonkoff & Hauser-Cram (1987)	EIPs	Handicapped; disabled (up to 36 months)	All outcomes
19 Snyder & Sheehan (1983)	EIPs	NR	All outcomes
20 Tingey-Michaelis (1985)[a]	Effects of certification of intervenors	Handicapped; disadvantaged (up to 66 months)	All outcomes
21 Turley (1985)	Information-based treatments for mothers	Mothers with normal newborns (up to 2 months)	Outcomes on mother-child interaction
22 White (1985-86)[a]	EIPs	Disadvantaged; handicapped; at-risk (up to 66 months)	All outcomes
23 White & Casto (1985)[a]	EIPs	Disadvantaged; at-risk (up to 66 months)	All outcomes
24 White et al. (1984)[a]	Projects in the JDRP	Handicapped (mostly up to 72 months; see Notes)	All outcomes
25 White et al. (1992)[a]	Effects of parent involvement	Disadvantaged; handicapped; at-risk (up to 66 months)	All outcomes

EIPs = Early intervention programs. JDRP = Joint Dissemination Review Panel. *ES* = Effect-size (*d* index). NR = Not reported. [a] Studies from Early Intervention Research Institute at Utah State University. [b] Some results with handicapped children are also presented. [c] All immediately post-test results. [d] Mean study effect size in parentheses. [e] Number of alternative treatment studies in parentheses. [f] Only for alternative treatment studies.

N of Primary Studies (Year-Range)	N of ES	Mean ES (d index)/ Main result	Notes
18 (1964-1984)	41	0.78	Contains studies with older children (up to 16 years); contains the dataset from Ottenbacher & Petersen (1984)
16 (1966-1981)	43	PND = 79.0%[g]	Integration of single-subject research
20 (1968-1986)	128	PND = 83.3%[gh]	Integration of single- subject research
14 (1967-1986)	42	NR	Integration of single- subject research
31	91	0.62	Subset of Casto & Mastropieri (1986a)
8 (1981)	182	0.48 (0.74)[d]	Only a demonstration meta-analysis
NR (1937-1983)	635	Certification is slightly better	
20 (1970-1981)	181	0.44	
326 (1937-1984)	2,266	≈0.70[i]	Summary of Casto, White, & Taylor (1983); see also Casto & Mastropieri (1986a), White & Casto (1985)
NR (1937-1983)	751	0.42	Results are also presented in Casto & Lewis (1983; Casto & White (1985); White (1985-86)
27 (21)[j] (1975-1983)	18[k]	0.96	Some studies contain older population (up to 8 years)
236 (+ 31)[d] (1937-1984) (up to 1991)[e]	881	No additional effect of parent involvement	

[g] PND-Index = Percent of nonoverlapping data points (see Scruggs et al., 1987). [h] Only direct treatment effects (without generalization and maintainance effects). [i] Only results from immediate posttest; only separate graphical display for disadvantaged and handicapped children. [j] Number of projects in parentheses. [k] Effect-size calculation was not possible in some cases.

1. It has been shown that the meta-analytical integration process contains subjective decisions just like the narrative review (Abrami et al., 1988; Wanous et al., 1989). These involve, for example, the type of literature search, the implementation of selection criteria, the type of coding, the calculation of effect sizes, and so forth. Subjective decisions may well be responsible for the fact that different meta-analyses on the same topic and even using the same data pool have produced contradictory outcomes (Beelmann, 1991; Bullock & Svyantek, 1985). For example, Beelmann (1991) studied the influence of different methods of mean effect-size calculation. Overall, he found marked differences between the different meta-analytical variants (mean d range from 0.37 to 0.76), although they were based on the same datapool. These and other results (e.g., Bullock & Svyantek, 1985) show that it seems advisable to not just rely on the outcomes of a single meta-analysis (McCohany, 1990), but to perform replication studies in order to validate findings. Among other things, such replications are dependent on the quality of documentation of the meta-analytical methods applied.

2. A great number of papers have been published on conceptual and statistical problems of meta-analysis. Two of these works should be mentioned: First, the work of Hedges and colleagues (see Hedges & Olkin, 1985) that has concentrated on methods for a closer study of effect-size variance. In particular, homogeneity analyses, which permit a more exact analysis of the variability of effect sizes between and within aggregated studies, are now one of the standard instruments in meta-analysis. Second, the research group centered on Hunter and Schmidt (1990) has pointed out that even larger differences in effect sizes between studies are due to methodological artifacts (such as sampling error, poor reliability of measurement instruments, etc.). These authors consistently recommend that calculated effect sizes should be corrected for these artifacts, which requires at least the weighting of effect sizes with the sample sizes of the primary studies.

Against the background of these developments, it seems advisable to perform meta-analysis very carefully and to take account of conceptual and methodological standards. For the purpose of this analysis, I have selected three evaluation criteria: (a) descriptive quality, (b) quality of literature search, and (c) validity of effect-size calculation (for a more comprehensive list, see Beelmann & Bliesener, 1994; Bryant, 1986; Matt & Cook, 1994). Table 2 presents an overview of these criteria. Each aspect (with the exception of effect-size weighting by sample size and independence of effect sizes) has been coded on a 3-point scale (high, moderate, low; see Table 2).

Table 2. *Definition and Coding of Selected Quality Criteria for Meta-Analyses*

Quality criteria	Definiton	Coding
Descriptive quality	Extent and precision of presentation of meta-analytic methods (e.g., definition of relevant constructs, literature search, description of codings, etc.)	*High*: All stages of integrating results presented in detail; replication possible without additional information *Moderate*: Transparent methods; complete replication not possible without additional information (e.g., correspondence with authors, additional literature) *Low*: Nontransparent presentation of methods
Quality of literature search	Extent and breath of literature search (e.g., multiple strategies, multiple databases)	*High*: Using multiple strategies (e.g., computer search, manual search in abstracts and journals, primary study analysis) and multiple databases (e.g., published and unpublished work) *Moderate*: Using at least two strategies *Low*: Using only one strategy
Validity of *ES* calculation		
- Databases	Number of studies	*High*: over 100; *Moderate*: 30 to 100; *Low*: less than 30
- Independence of *ES*	Unit of analysis (single effect-sizes vs. study effect sizes)	Yes/no
- *ES* weighting by sample size	Using weighting procedures	Yes/no
- Analysis of and/or corrections by methodological artifacts	Analysis of methodological moderators (e.g. design, validity rating); Using of correction procedures	*High*: moderator analysis with statistical tests or effect-size corrections; *Moderate*: only descriptive moderator analysis; *Low*: no moderator analysis
- Analysis of *ES* variance	Quality of subgroup analysis	*High*: Using homogeneity tests; *Moderate*: Using other statistical analyses (e.g., *t* tests, analysis of variance); *Low*: purely descriptive

ES = Effect size.

These ratings are self-explanatory. For example, descriptive quality is rated as high if there is a detailed explanation of meta-analytical methods and a full replication of the study is possible without additional information; as moderate, if methods are transparent, but replication would require writing to the authors or additional literature; and as low, if methods are not transparent at all.

A glance at the findings on *descriptive quality* (see Table 3) shows that all meta-analyses on early intervention receive at least an intermediate rating. In nearly all cases, the moderate quality has to do with the lack of exact references on the aggregated primary studies ($n = 12$). This type of presentation, which certainly also has something to do with the publishing practices of scientific journals, nonetheless makes it difficult for the reader to obtain a clear view of the methods used, it reduces transparency, and it makes it harder to make comparisons across meta-analyses. Nonetheless, the descriptive validity of the studies can be regarded to be generally positive. This also applies to the *quality of literature search*. A total of fifteen analyses (60%) performed comprehensive literature searches with the help of multiple search strategies and took account of both published and unpublished work. Only 4 of the 25 articles indicate a restricted literature search; and 3 of these [5, 13, 18] are reanalyses of other reviews and thus refer to the literature searches of other authors.

Table 3.   *Quality Ratings of Early Intervention Meta-Analyses*

Quality criteria	Rating and number of meta-analyses		
	High	**Moderate**	**Low**
Descriptive quality	12	13	0
Quality of literature search	15	6	4[a]
Validity of *ES* calculation			
- Databases[b]	3	5	13
- Analysis of and/or corrections by methodological artifacts	5	14	6
- Analysis of *ES* variance[c]	0	12	13

$N = 25$ meta-analyses. *ES* = effect-size. [a] Three of these analyses refer to the database of a previously published meta-analysis or qualitative review. As a result, the quality of literature search is probably underestimated. [b] In four cases, reports on databases are completely lacking. [c] Please note that the four single-case study integrations could not be given a high-quality rating, because, up to now, comparable methods are not available.

Turning to the third criterion, the *validity of the effect-size calculation*, we can see that the analyses were generally based on a small number of primary studies; in most cases, less than 30. As a result, most used individual effect sizes rather than study effect sizes as a unit of analysis ("Glassian meta-analysis," see Bangert-Drowns, 1986). This means that each study is entered according to the number of measurements performed, and this naturally leads to a drastic increase of the effect sizes. However, this also means that the statistical dependence between the integrated effect sizes is large. Only 2 of the 25 analyses permit a calculation of a study effect size [5, 19] or independent subgroup analyses. Furthermore, no study uses methods of weighting effect sizes by the sample sizes of the primary studies.

The meta-analyses seem to be slightly better in terms of the analysis of *methodological artifacts*. Fourteen studies show at least one descriptive comparison according to different features (global validity ratings, design features, etc.); five additionally perform comprehensive inferential analyses [10, 11, 13, 14, 16]. No examination of methodological moderators can be found in six studies [5, 7, 8, 15, 21, 24]. Corrections for effect sizes, as proposed by Hunter and Schmidt (1990), were carried out in none of the articles examined. However, it has to be taken into account that this meta-analytic procedure has been developed and applied particularly within correlative studies, and most of the available meta-analyses were carried out or published parallel to these methodological developments. This may well explain why no content-related moderator analyses following the model of Hedges and Olkin (1985) were carried out in any of the 25 articles. Homogeneity analyses based on the mean total effect size are found only in the work of Goldring and Presbrey and Ottenbacher and colleagues [5, 10, 11, 13]. Otherwise, the subgroup analyses of content moderators are restricted to traditional inferential procedures [*t* tests, *U* tests, etc., see 7, 8, 12, 15, 16, 18, 21], which show serious shortcomings compared to the homogeneity test (see Shadish, 1992), or purely descriptive comparisons [1, 2, 3, 4, 6, 9, 14, 17, 19, 20, 22, 23, 24, 25].

In sum, it can be ascertained initially that - measured in terms of the descriptive quality and the quality of literature search - the quality of the early intervention meta-analyses is intermediate to good. Problems arise particularly with regard to the validity of the effect sizes calculated. It is particularly critical that generally only a relatively small number of studies were aggregated, effect sizes were not weighted according to the sample sizes of the primary studies, results were summarized almost exclusively on the basis of individual effects (and are thus statistically dependent), and, finally, the majority of all subgroup analyses were purely descriptive. I shall return to the implications of these findings later.

4   Content-Related Evaluation of Early Intervention Meta-Analyses

Before presenting some findings on the contents of early intervention meta-analyses, I shall give a brief overview on the potentials of meta-analyses in the evaluation of intervention programs (see, also, Beelmann & Bliesener, 1994; Cook, 1991; Cook et al., 1992). Table 4 presents three typical goals of literature reviews and possible potentials and advantages of meta-analysis.

Table 4.   *Potential of Meta-Analysis in the Field of Program Evaluation*

Review goals	Potentials of meta-analysis
Description of a research field	- Delivering a quick, comprehensive view of a research field - Describing of a broad range of study features based on a great number of studies
Description of a causal relationship	- Specifying strength of effects based on a great number of studies - Delivering information about the general effectiveness of a program, especially in comparison to alternative programs - Improved ways of determining and correcting methodological weaknesses in primary studies (improved internal validity) - Improved ways of generalizing to different treatments, persons, settings, and times (improved external validity)
Development and testing of theories (explanation of phenomena; process evaluation)	- Generating new research hypotheses/ questions based on a comprehensive overview of research standard - Testing hypotheses never tested in primary studies - Improved ways of analyzing moderator variables - Use of effect sizes for subsequent methods of causal analyses (e.g., path analysis)

4.1 Description of a Field of Research

There can be no question that meta-analysis has provided a heuristic for a comprehensive presentation of a research field or of individual research issues. The description of general features of research activity such as the volume of research, culture-specific differentiations, research groups involved, or the historical course of research activity, as well as more specific descriptive dimensions such as the type of outcome criteria, methodological quality of the primary studies, up to the pointing out of special gaps in research, has to be viewed as a major precondition for more directed and thus better research in the future. However, in the descriptive analysis of a field of research, there is, in principle, no genuine advantage for meta-analysis. Nonetheless, it takes a major role within overviews, because it permits integrative analyses of large sets of studies. Traditional reviews, in contrast, are primarily interested in content-related and theoretical implications, for which the analysis of a larger number of primary studies seems to be inappropriate when not impossible (see Cook et al., 1992).

Which descriptive statements can be made on the basis of the meta-analyses carried out on early intervention? Several major features of the aggregated primary studies can already be deduced from Table 1 (e.g., year of publication, age range of population, etc.). However, beyond these descriptions, in general, a rather reserved documentation of primary studies can be ascertained. For example, more or less comprehensive lists of the individual primary studies and their specific features (treatment, populations, etc.) can be found in only seven meta-analyses [5, 6, 9, 15, 16, 24, 25]. Analyses of the type and occurrence of various forms of parent involvement, as in White et al. (1992), remain an exception. Therefore, in nearly all cases, descriptive features of the primary studies can only be filtered out of subcategorizations in the presentation of the results. Nonetheless, five relatively sound statements can be derived:

1. Almost all articles confirm a lack of methodologically convincing studies. This can be concluded not only from analyses on the impact of the general methodological quality of the primary studies on effect sizes [e.g., 1, 2, 3, 4, 22, 23] but also from the analysis of individual methodological features of the studies such as type of design or blind assessment [e.g., 10, 13, 24].

2. Despite a large number of primary studies [over 300 up to 1983, see 22], specific hypotheses on differential patterns of effects cannot be confirmed with sufficient validity. For example, the articles that have studied differential patterns of effects are generally confronted with the

problem that insufficient primary studies are available for computing differential effects [see, e.g., the analyses on specific forms of treatment: 10, 11, 12, 14]. Only one meta-analysis [1] followed up an issue that took account of a combination of treatment and problem group. Evaluations that take simultaneous account of the dimensions of treatment and population features as well as treatment goals (see Guralnick, 1991, 1993) are not present in any of the 25 meta-analyses. There is also a lack of direct comparison studies that compare different forms or different levels of early intervention with each other [see, e.g., 6, 22, 23, 25].

3. The main outcome variable is the children´s IQ or cognitive performance [approximately 40% of all dependent variables, see 22]. Only general developmental parameters (DQ), language, motor, or physiological measures were also measured sufficiently frequently. Additional childhood and, in particular, family variables, as found in [21], are rarely reported in detail [see 3, 5, 7, 10, 11, 12, 13, 14, 15, 17, 18, 22, 23, 24, 25].

4. Comprehensive longitudinal studies with large follow-up intervals are rare [see 3, 4, 5, 6, 8, 16, 22, 23, 24, 25].

5. Up to the present, there are more studies on socially disadvantaged children than disabled children [compare 3 and 18 with 4; see, also, 22, 23].

Despite these findings, it can be stated in summary that the present meta-analyses have exploited their descriptive potential only in part. This is particularly the case when it is considered that a number of excellent qualitative reviews are available from which the descriptions mentioned above could also have been taken (see, in particular, Dunst et al., 1989; but also, Bricker et al., 1984; Bronfenbrenner, 1975; Dunst, 1986; Dunst & Rheingrover, 1981; Farran, 1990; Guralnick & Bennett, 1987; Simeonsson et al., 1982). In part, the neglect of the descriptive potential may be due to the inadequate documentation level in the primary studies themselves. Nonetheless, in these cases, a detailed quantitative evaluation of these inadequacies (e.g., on the inadequate reporting of sample features) would have been desirable.

4.2 Description of Causal Relationships

Historically, the quantitative specification of causal effects can be viewed as the starting point of meta-analytical literature integrations. The advantage of meta-analysis is that the *direction and strength* of relationships can be specified on the basis of a large number of studies. In this context, Cook (1991) has specified further advantages of meta-analysis on the basis of the validity concept of Cook and Campbell (1979). Accordingly, the *statistical validity* is increased by the aggregation of highly reliable mean differences and the accompanying increase in statistical power. The *internal validity* is improved by the great numbers of primary studies that perhaps lead to a reciprocal balancing out of methodological artifacts, and offer the possibility of detecting and correcting effectiveness according to systematic bias. *Construct validity* increases because a series of different operationalizations is available, making it possible to analyze the generalizability of the results to different forms of treatment and their effects. Finally, there are greater opportunities than in primary studies and qualitative reviews to systematically test the generalizability of the findings through heterogeneous replications in different target groups, different settings, and at different points in time, and thus increase *external validity*. According to Cook (1991), limits to the generalization of causal relationships result only when (a) a low number of primary studies is integrated and systematic distortions are also present, (b) results are unclear (high outcome variance), and (c) negative effects (side effects) are ignored.

A look at the general effects in the 25 articles on early intervention analyzed here shows that effect sizes of approximately one half to three quarters of a standard deviation are obtained across all integrations (see Table 1). This result can be interpreted as a medium effectiveness in the sense of Cohen´s (1988) terminology; it is relevant in both educational and clinical terms (Tallmadge, 1977); and it is in line with many findings from psychological and educational intervention research (see Lipsey & Wilson, 1993).

Alongside specifying effect sizes, the meta-analyses also contribute to the validation of this outcome. This applies particularly to questions of *statistical validity*. Ottenbacher (1989, this volume) has shown impressively that problems with statistical power play an important role in studies on the effectiveness of early intervention for disabled children. This applies particularly to studies of types of handicap with low incidence rates (see, e.g., Beelmann, 1994). By aggregating studies with low sample sizes, this problem can be reduced to a large extent. However, one remaining criticism is that no study performed an integration that took the sample sizes of the primary studies into account, although this would have led to a more precise estimation of parameters.

Specific contributions can also be found for the area of *internal validity*. One of the clearest results of meta-analyses on early intervention is that the effect sizes vary to a large extent with the validity of the studies, regardless of whether this is based on general estimations of methodological quality or on the impact of individual methodological features [see 1, 2, 3, 4, 6, 10, 11, 13, 16, 20, 22, 23, 24, 25]. Poor methodological quality in intervention studies has also been a complaint in many qualitative reviews (e.g., Dunst et al., 1989; Dunst & Rheingrover, 1981; Simeonsson et al., 1982), although these have tended to point more to a general unreliability of results. However, in the meta-analyses, studies with greater threats to internal validity generally produce higher effect parameters [see, e.g., 3, 13, 22]. For example, Casto and Mastropieri (1986a) have shown that the mean effectiveness of studies sinks by more than one third (from $d = 0.68$ to $d = 0.40$) when only qualitatively "good" studies are analyzed (the problem of estimating methodological quality will not be dealt with here, see Bliesener, 1994). In their analysis of tactile stimulation, Ottenbacher et al. (1987) have shown that type of assignment (from pre-existing groups to random) systematically reduces mean effectiveness (from $d = 0.93$ to $d = 0.42$). In Ottenbacher and Petersen (1985a), the mean effect sizes of pre-experimental designs dropped in true experimental designs (from $d = 1.20$ to $d = 0.46$). Such methodological distortions can be traced back to publication bias (see Rosenthal, 1979): "Poor" studies are published only when particularly positive effects are reported. However, the relationship between effect sizes and the methodological quality of the studies is not always inverted. For example, Weiss and Weisz (1990) have shown that methodologically demanding studies tended to produce higher effect sizes in their analysis of psychotherapeutic procedures for children and adolescents. However, systematic effects of methodological features should have particularly serious effects when the number of aggregated studies is low, the variance in effect sizes is particularly large, and a random balancing out of methodo- logical distortions cannot be anticipated, that is, particularly in the analysis of differential issues. I consider that differential findings from the meta- analyses on early intervention have to be interpreted particularly carefully for these reasons. Nonetheless, it is still a positive contribution - compared to qualitative reviews - that the results of meta-analysis clearly reveal that the methodological distortions that are present tend to lead to an over- estimation of the effectiveness of early intervention.

With regard to *construct validity*, it first has to be noted that there is hardly any other form of intervention that shows such a broad range of different treatments. Early neuromotor therapy, preschool education for socially disadvantaged children, speech therapy for mentally retarded children, as well as social training programs for children with behavior disorders can all be regarded as early intervention in the broadest sense (see above). This heterogeneity is also the reason why many authors have rejected the question of the general effectiveness of early intervention as being of little use (e.g., Meisels, 1985). In line with Guralnick (1991, 1993), at least three dimensions have to be considered when questioning effectiveness: features of the intervention, characteristics of the target population, and the treatment goal. As we have seen when looking at internal validity, the contributions of meta-analysis to the validation of such differential questions are very limited. On the other hand, one can argue that a contribution to construct validation can be found on the side of the *independent variable*, in that none of the forms of early intervention studied have proved to be ineffective. This statement is not just a precondition for the study of differential relationships, but is also of great value in its impact on the legitimation pressure exerted by policymakers (particularly as a result of the changes in social law in the USA in the 1980s; see, also, Kavale & Glass, 1984). However, general effectiveness -with only very few exceptions (e.g., Ferry, 1981; Halpern, 1984) - is also confirmed in many qualitative reviews (e.g., White et al., 1985-1986), which greatly reduces the specific contributions of the meta-analyses studied here. However, one specifically meta-analytic outcome is the studies on the impact of experimenters [i.e., blind assessment, see 10, 11, 13]. These studies have shown a systematic decline in estimated effectiveness with informed researchers in the sense of anticipation effects or judgment errors. This can be traced back at least partially to specific validity problems in the assessment of disabled children (see, e.g., Brambring & Tröster, 1994; Hupp & Kaiser, 1986). This brings us to questions regarding construct validation on the side of *dependent variables*. The problems arising from measuring outcomes predominantly in terms of the children's general and cognitive development, a practice which was continued at least into the mid-1980s, have been mentioned already. A look at the systematic contrasts of the effect sizes obtained in different areas of judgment reveals that the effects are highly comparable [see, e.g., 3, 13, 18], and this in no way applies to all forms of psychological and educational intervention (see, e.g., Beelmann et al., 1994).

Finally, I shall turn to *external validity* and questions on the generalizability of findings across persons, settings, and time. As in construct validity, meta-analyses on early intervention also provide only indirect conclusions here: There are no signs that early intervention has no effects in individual groups or in certain settings. However, no mentionable differences can be determined between different groups of clients and settings, apart from the relatively favorable outcome for biologically and organically disabled children compared to the socially disadvantaged [see 3, 13, 18, 23]. In contrast, analyses on the persistence of effects generally show relatively low long-term effects or a drastic decline in effect sizes over time [see 4, 5, 16, 22, 23]. These results partially contradict findings from qualitative reviews (e.g., Bronfenbrenner, 1975; Dunst et al., 1989) that have revealed at least a few long-term effects, although these were not consistent. However, these findings must be interpreted against the background that the level of knowledge on long-term effects is exceptionally sparse and insufficiently confirmed empirically, particularly for disabled children.

In summary, we can state that the potentials with regard to an improved validation of a causal relationship could be exploited to only a limited extent in the present meta-analyses on early intervention. Their content-related contributions can either also be derived from the available qualitative reviews or they are restricted - particularly because of a low number of studies and the systematic effects of methodological variables on the results - to very general statements. These include (a) a general total effect of approximately one half to three quarters of a standard deviation, and (b) a systematically negative relationship between methodological quality and effect size.

4.3 Contributions to Formulating and Testing Theories

Up to now, meta-analytical studies have been directed, above all, toward the determination of mean effect sizes (Cook et al., 1992). However, particularly at the advanced stage of evaluation, we want to know how changes are achieved and which processes are involved. The question regarding how changes occur calls for explanations of the corresponding phenomena and thus, finally, theories. Comprehensive process evaluations remain a relative rarity in research on intervention in the social sciences, despite strong calls for them over the last decade. However, this should not make us forget the potentials of meta-analysis for formulating or testing theories. Important steps in *theory formulation*, such as working out new research issues (see Eagly & Wood, 1994) or generating new, directed research hypotheses, are broadly possible even today, as well as an improved *testing of theories* by tests on additional hypotheses that have not yet been tested in primary studies (Cooper, 1991). On the other hand, the use of meta-analytic results for theory formulation also has its limits (Cooper & Hedges, 1994c). First, studies differ on more than one feature (they are also not available in a randomized form, see Shadish & Sweeney, 1991); second, as Wachter and Straf (1990) have argued, data cannot be used simultaneously for both formulating and testing theories.

According to Cook et al. (1992), meta-analysis can contribute to improving the explanation of relationships in three ways, namely through (a) the specification of contingencies, that is, the analysis of potential moderator variables and/or of treatment and effect components; (b) the identification of factors that account for variance, that is, by explaining the variance between studies and predicting effect sizes in simple or multivariate regression models; and, finally, (c) explicating mediating processes by processing meta-analytical findings in subsequent statistical procedures of causal analysis (e.g., path analysis, structural models, see, e.g., Shadish & Sweeney, 1991).

A glance at the meta-analyses studied in this chapter shows that we are restricted to the first possibility, the analysis of moderator variables through subgroup analyses. However, subgroup analyses are particularly useful when larger samples of studies are available. Results can specify global effects, for example, through closer studies of the impact of personal characteristics on effectiveness; analyses of individual treatment components; impact of various dosages or implementation modalities; and so forth.

Now how do the published meta-analyses on early intervention shape up with regard to these possibilities? As mentioned above, subgroup analyses on content-related moderators could be found in almost every article. From the multitude of individual findings, four, relatively reliable results will be emphasized (see, also, Beauchamp, 1989):

1. Inconsistent or nonsignificant findings were obtained when the variables *age at start* [1, 3, 4, 10, 11, 12, 16, 19, 22, 23]; *extent of parent involvement* [2, 3, 4, 7, 18, 22, 23]; and *treatment intensity* [3, 6, 10, 11, 12, 14, 25] were studied (see Table 5 for a summary of these results). These findings have been subject to controversial discussion in the literature because of their practice- and policy-related implications. Also, they contradict findings from almost every qualitative review (see White et al., 1985-1986) and even some outcomes from other meta-analysis [e.g., significant findings on parent involvement in 18]. One reason for these contradictory findings may well be the relatively high unreliability particularly of differential effect sizes, which are generally based on a very small database. For example, in order to study the impact of the intensity of treatment, Innocenti and White (1993) have classified the number of hours of treatment per week into no less than seven subcategories, and they also differentiated according to study quality (high, medium, low) and problem group (disabled, disadvantaged, medically at risk), thus creating a 7 x 3 x 3 ANOVA problem. Despite the strong reasons for striving toward a differentiated perspective, the results show that the database is simply not sufficient for a reliable estimation of effect sizes in such studies. Hence, in this analysis, only one effect size was based on more than 10 studies, 28 out of 63 (44.4%) could not be computed at all, and a further 22 (34.9%) were based on the results of a maximum of two studies (see Innocenti & White, 1993, p. 38, Table 1). However, these findings do not mean that the results of the meta-analyses were totally meaningless. It is far more the case that

they encourage us to study differential patterns of findings on a micro-process level and not be held back by our previous assumptions.

Table 5.   *Meta-Analytical Results on Potential Moderator Variables*

Relation to effectiveness	Moderator variables and number of meta-analyses		
	Age at start (*n*=14)	Extent of parent involvement (*n*=8)	Treatment intensity (*n*=8)
(++)	0	1	2
(+)	1	0	2
(o)	7	7	4
(-)	2	0	0
(--)	4	0	0

n = Number of meta-analyses addressing this question (*N* = 25). (++) = generally positive relationship; (+) = fairly positive, or positive in some domains; (o) = no systematic relationship; (-) = fairly negative, or negative in some domains; (--) = generally negative relationship.

2. Somewhat more positive findings seem to be gained when the level of structuring in early intervention is raised, for example, through the availability of comprehensive intervention manuals [3, 4, 7, 18, 19]. This finding can also be confirmed for the generalization and durability of changes: Programs that do not emphasize such issues (which is often labeled the "train and hope mentality") produce relatively poor outcomes [16]. In addition, certification of intervenors shows a slightly positive influence on outcome [20, 23]. In sum, these findings suggest that a well-planned treatment implementation leads to stronger effects, and finally implies that we need (a) more data on treatment implementation (see, e.g., Beelmann, 1994) and (b) more theory-driven early intervention (see, e.g., the activity-based approach, Bricker & Cripe, 1992).

3. There are relatively low differences between home-based and center-based early interventions [2, 16, 18, 23]. These findings need to be tempered by the fact that little attention has been paid to parent or family variables. Further comparisons with more comprehensive outcome assessment are needed here in order to produce sounder statements.

4. As already mentioned, generally, no great differences can be found between various subpopulations. Probably the only exception is the slightly

higher effect sizes for biologically or organically impaired children confirmed in several meta-analyses [e.g., 3, 13, 18]. However, insufficient attention is paid to the interaction between programs, subpopulations, and aims of intervention (Guralnick, 1991, 1993).

Taken together, the contribution of the currently available meta-analyses on early intervention to the description and explanation of specific effects and processes and therefore to the development and testing of theories has been only tentative. Three reasons are responsible for this: First, the quality of moderator analyses is low, because they generally remain only descriptive. Second, the reliability and validity of many differential effect sizes is low, because the underlying number of studies is low. Third and most importantly, methodological variables, such as the estimated validity of the primary studies, exhibit almost consistently negative relationships to the effect sizes. Hence, the only contribution of the meta-analyses is that their results question several intuitively logical relationships such as "earlier is better" or "more intensive is better." If these findings contribute to increased research in the near future in the sense of a second generation of treatment outcome effectiveness research (see, e.g., Fewell, this volume; Rauh et al., 1988; White & Boyce, 1993), their heuristic function should in no way be underestimated.

5   Conclusions

This chapter has made it clear that the meta-analyses on early intervention show some methodological and content-related weaknesses. However, this statement has to be tempered in view of the further developments in meta-analysis that have occurred only over the last few years. Nonetheless, the present evaluation of meta-analyses on early intervention has to be based on current standards and knowledge. This is not to say that the newest meta-analytical techniques are now problem-free. The choice of selection criteria, dealing with different study qualities, and missing data in the primary studies, as well as the interpretation of effect sizes are topics that seem to avoid any final objective judgment. The perfect meta-analysis is, like the perfect primary study, a fiction. However, on the basis of present-day standards - in order to contradict a frequently cited prejudice - meta-analyses can be "better" than the primary studies on which they are based. For example, unlike primary studies, it is possible to study the impact of the methodological quality of the primary studies and perform a corresponding correction of effect sizes. From this perspective, even qualitatively low-level studies can contribute to expanding knowledge, although this should not be understood as an invitation to use poor methods.

Nonetheless, a precondition for the responsible application of meta-analytical techniques is - as self-evident as this may sound - the presence of a larger number of primary studies, and this need increases with the heterogeneity of the research questions. In my opinion, it is exactly here that the greatest problem is to be found in the early intervention meta-analyses. Nowadays, there is no doubt that the evaluation of early intervention concerns, above all, the judgment of differential relationships (which programs for which population under which circumstances). Yet these meta-analyses reveal that there are clearly not enough studies on these relationships. Without a sufficient database, conclusions from meta-analysis are easily unreliable and inapplicable. Meta-analysis should finally not mean to torture data long enough until it confesses! The task for evaluation research is thus not to perform further meta-analyses but to encourage new, high-quality primary research.

References

Abrami, P., Cohen, P. A., & d'Apollonia, S. (1988). Implementation problems in meta-analysis. *Review of Educational Research, 58*, 151-179.

Arnold, K. S., Myette, B. M., & Casto, G. (1986). Relationships of language intervention efficacy to certain subject characteristics in mentally retarded preschool children: A meta-analysis. *Education and Training of the Mentally Retarded, 21*, 108-116.

Baer, R. A., & Nietzel, M. T. (1991). Cognitive and behavioral treatment of impulsivity in children. A meta-analytic review of the outcome literature. *Journal of Clinical Child Psychology, 20*, 400-412.

Bangert-Drowns, R. L. (1986). Review of developments in meta-analytic method. *Psychological Bulletin, 99*, 388-399.

Beauchamp, K. D. F. (1989). Meta-analysis in early childhood special education research. *Journal of Early Intervention, 13*, 374-380.

Beelmann, A. (1991). *Zur methodenbedingten Ergebnisvariation bei Meta-Analysen: Ein Erfahrungsbericht am Beispiel der Evaluation sozialer Kompetenztrainings bei Kindern.* University of Bielefeld, Special research unit on prevention and intervention in childhood and adolescence, Preprint No. 59.

Beelmann, A. (1994). *Evaluation der Frühförderung entwicklungsgefährdeter Kinder. Formative und summative Analysen eines Interventionsprojektes zur Frühförderung und Familienbetreuung blinder Klein- und Vorschulkinder.* Doctorantal dissertation, University of Bielefeld, Faculty of Psychology and Sport Science.

Beelmann, A., & Bliesener, T. (1994). Aktuelle Probleme und Strategien der Metaanalyse. *Psychologische Rundschau, 45*, 211-233.

Beelmann, A., Pfingsten, U., & Lösel, F. (1994). The effects of training social competence in children: A meta-analysis of recent evaluation studies. *Journal of Clinical Child Psychology, 23,* 260-271.

Bliesener, T. (1994). *Der Einfluß der Forschungsqualität auf das Forschungsergebnis: Zur Evaluation der Validierung biographischer Daten in der Eignungsdiagnostik.* Postdoctoral thesis, University of Erlangen-Nuremberg, Faculty of Philosophy.

Brambring, M., & Tröster, H. (1994). The validity problem and the instruction problem in the assessment of cognitive development in blind infants and preschoolers. *Journal of Visual Impairment and Blindness, 88,* 9-18.

Bricker, D., Bailey, E., & Bruder, M. B. (1984). The efficacy of early intervention and the handicapped infant: A wise or wasted resource. In M. Wolraich & D. K. Routh (Eds.), *Advances in developmental and behavioral pediatrics* (Vol. 5, pp. 373-423). Greenwich, CT, JAI Press.

Bricker, D., & Cripe, J. (1992). *An activity based approach to early intervention.* Baltimore, MD: Paul Brookes.

Bronfenbrenner, U. (1975). Is early intervention effective? In M. Guttentag & E. L. Struening (Eds.), *Handbook of evaluation research* (Vol. 2, pp. 519-603). Beverly Hills, CA: Sage.

Bryant, F. B. (1986). Improving the quality of research synthesis in program evaluation. *Policy Studies Review, 5,* 709-721.

Bullock, R. J., & Svyantek, D. J. (1985). Analyzing meta-analysis: Potential problems, an unsuccessful replication, and evaluation criteria. *Journal of Applied Psychology, 70,* 108-115.

Casey, R. J., & Berman, J. S. (1985). The outcome of psychotherapy with children. *Psychological Bulletin, 98,* 388-400.

Casto, G., & Lewis, A. C. (1984). Parent involvement in infant and preschool programs. *Journal of the Division for Early Childhood, 9,* 49-56.

Casto, G., & Mastropieri, M. A. (1986a). The efficacy of early intervention programs: A meta-analysis. *Exceptional Children, 52,* 417-424.

Casto, G., & Mastropieri, M. A. (1986b). Strain and Smith do protest too much: A response. *Exceptional Children, 53,* 266-268.

Casto, G., & Mastropieri, M. A. (1986c). Much ado about nothing: A reply to Dunst and Snyder. *Exceptional Children, 53,* 277-279.

Casto, G., & White, K. (1985). The efficacy of early intervention programs with environmentally at-risk infants. *Journal of Children in Contemporary Society, 17,* 37-50.

Casto, G., & White, K. R. (1987). *Final report of the Early Intervention Research Institute (1982-1987).* Logan, UT: Utah State University.

Casto, G., White, K. R., & Taylor, C. (1983). *Final report of the Early Intervention Reserach Institue (1982-1983).* Logan, UT: Utat State University.

Cohen, J. (1988). *Statistical power analysis for the behavioral science* (2nd ed.). New York: Academic Press.

Cook, T. D. (1991). Meta-analysis: Its potential for causal description and causal explanation within program evaluation. In G. Albrecht & H. U. Otto (Eds.), *Social prevention and the social sciences* (pp. 245-285). Berlin: de Gruyter.

Cook, T. D., & Campbell, D. T. (1979). *Quasi-experimentation. Design & analysis issues for field settings.* Boston, MA: Houghton Mifflin.

Cook, T. D., Cooper, H. M., Cordray, D. S., Hartman, H., Hedges, L. V., Light, T. A., & Mosteller, F. (1992). *Meta-analysis for explanation: A casebook.* New York: Russell Sage Foundation.

Cooper, H. M. (1991). An introduction to meta-analysis and the integrative research review. In G. Albrecht & H. U. Otto (Eds.), *Social prevention and the social sciences* (pp. 287-304). Berlin: de Gruyter.

Cooper, H. M., & Hedges, L. V. (1994a). Research synthesis as a scientific enterprise. In H. M. Cooper & L. V. Hedges (Eds.), *Handbook of research synthesis* (pp. 3-14). New York: Russell Sage Foundation.

Cooper, H. M., & Hedges, L. V. (Eds.). (1994b). *Handbook of research synthesis.* New York: Russell Sage Foundation.

Cooper, H. M., & Hedges, L. V. (1994c). Potentials and limitations of research synthesis. In H. M. Cooper & L. V. Hedges (Eds.), *Handbook of research synthesis* (pp. 521-529). New York: Russell Sage Foundation.

Darlington, R. B., Royce, J. M., Snipper, A. S., Murray, H. W., & Lazar, I. (1980). Preschool programs and later school competence of children from low-income families. *Science, 208,* 202-204.

Dunst, C. J. (1986). Overview of the efficacy of early intervention programs. In L. Bickman & D. L. Weatherford (Eds.), *Evaluating early intervention programs for severely handicapped children and their families* (pp. 79-147). Austin, TX: pro-ed.

Dunst, C. J., & Rheingrover, R. M. (1981). An analysis of the efficacy of infant intervention programs with organically handicapped children. *Evaluation and Program Planning, 4,* 287-323.

Dunst, C. J., & Snyder, S. W. (1986). A critique of the Utah State University early intervention meta-analysis research. *Exceptional Children, 53,* 269-276.

Dunst, C. J., Snyder, S. W., & Mankinen, M. (1989). Efficacy of early intervention. In M. C. Wang, M. C. Reynolds, & H. J. Walberg (Eds.), *Handbook of special education. Vol. 3: Low incidence conditions* (pp. 259-294). Oxford: Pergamon Press.

Eagly, E. A., & Wood, W. (1994). Using research synthesis to plan future research. In H. M. Cooper & L. V. Hedges (Eds.), *Handbook of research synthesis* (pp. 485-500). New York: Russell Sage Foundation.

Eysenck, H. J. (1978). An exercise in mega-silliness. *American Psychologist, 33,* 517.

Farran, D. C. (1990). Effects of intervention with disadvantaged and disabled children: A decade review. In S. L. Meisels & J. P. Shonkoff (Eds.), *Handbook of early childhood intervention* (pp. 501-539). Cambridge: Cambridge University Press.

Ferry, P. C. (1981). On growing new neurons: Are early intervention programs effective. *Pediatrics, 67,* 38-41.

Goldring, E. B., & Presbrey, L. S. (1986). Evaluating preschool programs: A meta-analytic approach. *Educational Evaluation and Policy Analysis, 8,* 179-188.

Guralnick, M. J. (1991). The next decade of research on the effectiveness of early intervention. *Exceptional Children, 58,* 174-183.

Guralnick, M. J. (1993). Second generation research on the effectiveness of early intervention. *Early Education and Development, 4,* 366-378.

Guralnick, M. J., & Bennett, F. C. (Eds.).(1987). *The effectiveness of early intervention for at-risk and handicapped children.* Orlando, FL: Academic Press.

Halpern, R. (1984). Lack of effects for home-based early intervention? Some possible explanations. *American Journal of Orthopsychiatry, 54,* 33-42.

Hedges, L. V., & Olkin, I. (1985). *Statistical methods for meta-analysis.* New York: Academic Press.

Hupp, S. C., & Kaiser, A. P. (1986). Evaluating educational programs for severely handicapped preschoolers. In L. Bickman & D. L. Weatherford (Eds.), *Evaluating early intervention programs for severely handicapped children and their families* (pp. 233-261). Austin, TX: pro-ed.

Hunter, J. E., & Schmidt, F. L. (1990). *Methods of meta-analysis.* Newbury Park, CA: Sage.

Innocenti, M. S., & White, K. R. (1993). Are more intensive early intervention programs more effective? A review of the literature. *Exceptionality, 4,* 31-50.

Jackson, G. (1980). Methods for integrative review. *Review of Educational Research, 50,* 438-460.

Lewis, R. J., & Vosburgh, W. T. (1988). Effectiveness of kindergarten intervention programs. A meta-analysis. *School Psychology International, 9,* 265-275.

Lipsey, M. W., & Wilson, D. B. (1993). The efficacy of psychological, educational, and behavioral treatment. Confirmation from meta-analysis. *American Psychologist, 48,* 1181-1209.

Kavale, K. (1981). Functions of the Illinois Test of Psycholinguistic Abilities (ITPA): Are they trainable?. *Exeptional Children, 47,* 496-510.

Kavale, K. A., & Glass, G. V. (1984). Meta-analysis and policy decisions in special education. In B. K. Keogh (Ed.), *Advances in special education. Vol. 4: Documenting program impact* (pp. 195-247). Greenwich, CT: Jai Press.

Kavale, K., & Mattson, P. D. (1983). "One jumped off the balance beam": Meta-analysis of perceptual-motor training. *Journal of Learning Disabilities, 16,* 165-173.

Mastropieri, M. A., & Scruggs, T. E. (1985-1986). Early intervention for socially withdrawn children. *Journal of Special Education, 19,* 429-441.

Mastropieri, M. A., Scruggs, T. E., & Casto, G. (1985). Early intervention for behaviorally disordered children: An integrative review. In R. B. Rutherford (Ed.), *Severe behavior disorders of children and youth* (Vol.8, pp. 27-35). Reston, VA: Council for Children with Behavior Disorders.

Matt, G. E., & Cook, T. D. (1994). Threats to the validity of research syntheses. In H. M. Cooper & L. V. Hedges (Eds.), *Handbook of research synthesis* (pp. 503-520). New York: Russell Sage Foundation.

McCohany, N. (1990). Can reliance be placed on a single meta-analysis? *Australian and New Zealand Journal of Psychiatry, 24,* 405-415.

Meisels, S. J. (1985). The efficacy of early intervention: Why we are still asking the same question? *Topics in Early Childhood Special Education, 5,* 1-11.

Ottenbacher, K. J. (1989). Statistical conclusion validity of early intervention research with handicapped children. *Exceptional Children, 55,* 534-540.

Ottenbacher, K. J., Biocca, Z., DeCremer, G., Gevelinger, M., Jedlovec, K. B., & Johnson, M. B. (1986). Quantitative analysis of the effectiveness of pediatric therapy. Emphasis on the neurodevelopmental treatment approach. *Physical Therapy, 66,* 1095-1101.

Ottenbacher, K. J., Muller, L., Brandt, D., Heintzelman, A., Hojem, P., & Sharpe, P. (1987). The effectiveness of tactile stimulation as a form of early intervention: A quantitative evaluation. *Developmental and Behavioral Pediatrics, 8,* 68-76.

Ottenbacher, K. J., & Petersen, P. (1984). The efficacy of vestibular stimulation as a form of specific sensory enrichment. *Clinical Pediatrics, 23,* 428-432.

Ottenbacher, K. J., & Petersen, P. (1985a). The efficacy of early intervention programs for children with organic impairment: A quantitative review. *Evaluation and Program Planning, 8,* 135-146.

Ottenbacher, K. J., & Petersen, P. (1985b). A meta-analysis of applied vestibular stimulation research. *Physical and Occupational Therapy in Pediatrics, 5,* 119-134.

Rauh, V. A., Achenbach, T. M., Nurcombe, B., Howell, C. T., & Teti, D. M. (1988). Minimizing adverse effects of low birthweight.: Four-year results of an early intervention program. *Child Development, 59,* 544-553.

Rosenthal, R. (1979). The "file drawer problem" and tolerance for null results. *Psychological Bulletin, 86,* 638-641.

Scruggs, T. E., Mastropieri, M. A., & Casto, G. (1987). The quantitative synthesis of single-subject research: Methodology and validation. *Remedial and Special Education, 8,* 24-33.

Scruggs, T. E., Mastropieri, M. A., Cook, S. B., & Escobar, C. (1986). Early intervention for children with conduct disorders: A quantitative synthesis of single-subject research. *Behavioral Disorders, 11,* 260-271.

Scruggs, T. E., Mastropieri, M. A., Forness, S. R., & Kavale, K. A. (1988). Early language intervention: A quantitative synthesis of single-subject research. *Journal of Special Education, 22,* 259-283.

Scruggs, T. E., Mastropieri, M. A., & McEwen, I. (1988). Early intervention for developmental functioning: A quantitative synthesis of single-subject research. *Journal of the Division for Early Childhood, 12,* 359-367.

Shadish, W. R. (1992). Do family and marital psychotherapy change what people do? A meta-analysis of behavioral outcomes. In T. D. Cook, H. M. Cooper, D. S. Cordray, H. Hartman, L. V. Hedges, T. A. Light, & F. Mosteller (Eds.), *Meta-analysis for explanation: A casebook* (pp. 129-208). New York: Russel Sage Foundation.

Shadish, W., & Sweeney, R. B. (1991). Mediators and moderators in meta-analysis: There's a reason we don't let Dodo Birds tell us which psychotherapies should have prizes. *Journal of Consulting and Clinical Psychology, 59,* 883-893.

Shonkoff, J. P., & Hauser-Cram, P. (1987). Early intervention for disabled infants and their families: A quantitative analysis. *Pediatrics, 80,* 650-658.

Shonkoff, J. P., & Meisels, S. J. (1990). Early childhood intervention: The evolution of a concept. In S. L. Meisels & J. P. Shonkoff (Eds.), *Handbook of early childhood intervention* (pp. 3-31). Cambridge: Cambridge University Press.

Simeonsson, R. J., Cooper, D. H., & Scheiner, A. P. (1982). A review and analysis of the effectiveness of early intervention programs. *Pediatrics, 69,* 635-641.

Smith, M. L., & Glass, G. V. (1977). Meta-analysis of psychotherapy outcome studies. *American Psychologist, 32,* 752-760.

Smith, M. L., Glass, G. V., & Miller, T.I. (1980). *The benefits of psychotherapy.* Baltimore, MD: John Hopkins University Press.

Snyder, S., & Sheehan, R. (1983). Integrating research in early childhood special education: The use of meta-analysis. *Diagnostique, 9,* 12-25.

Strain, P. S., & Smith, B. J. (1986). A counter-interpretation of early intervention effects: A response to Casto and Mastropieri. *Exceptional Children, 53,* 260-265.

Tallmadge, G. K. (1977). *Ideabook: The Joint Dissemination Review Panel.* Washington, DC: U. S. Office of Education.

Tingey-Michaelis, C. (1985). Early intervention. Is certification necessary? *Teacher Education and Special Education, 8,* 91-97.

Turley, M. A. (1985). A meta-analysis of informing mothers concerning the sensory and perceptual capabilities of their infants: The effects on maternal-infant interaction. *Maternal-Child Nursing Journal, 14,* 183-197.

Wachter, K. W., & Straf, M. L. (Eds.).(1990). *The future of meta-analysis.* New York: Russell Sage Foundation.

Wanous, J. P., Sullivan, S. E., & Malinak, J. (1989). The role of judgment calls in meta-analysis. *Journal of Applied Psychology, 74,* 259-264.

Weiss, B., & Weisz, J. R. (1990). The impact of methodological factors on child psychotherapy outcome research: A meta-analysis for researchers. *Journal of Abnormal Child Psychology, 18,* 639-670.

Weisz, J. R., Weiss, B., Alike, M. D., & Klotz, M. L. (1987). Effectiveness of psychotherapy with children and adolescents: A meta-analysis for clinicians. *Journal of Consulting and Clinical Psychology, 55,* 542-549.

White, K. R. (1985-1986). Efficacy of early intervention. *Journal of Special Education, 19,* 401-416.

White, K. R., & Boyce, G. C. (Eds.).(1993). Special issue: Comparative evaluations of early intervention alternatives. *Early Education and Development, 4,* 221-378.

White, K. R., Bush, D. W., & Casto, G. C. (1985-1986). Learning from reviews of early intervention. *The Journal of Special Education, 19,* 417-428.

White, K., & Casto, G. (1985). An integrative review of early intervention efficacy studies with at-risk children: Implications for the handicapped. *Analysis and Intervention in Developmental Disabilities, 5,* 7-31.

White, K. R., Mastropieri, M., & Casto, G. (1984). An analysis of special education early childhood projects approved by the Joint Dissemination Review Panel. *Journal of the Division for Early Childhood, 9,* 11-26.

White, K. R., Taylor, M. J., & Moss, V. D. (1992). Does research support claims about the benefits of involving parents in early intervention programs? *Review of Educational Research, 62,* 91-125.

Wilson, G. T., & Rachman, S. J. (1983). Meta-analysis and the evaluation of psychotherapy outcome: Limitations and liabilities. *Journal of Consulting and Clinical Psychology, 51,* 54-64.

M. Brambring, H. Rauh, & A. Beelmann (Eds.). (1996). *Early childhood intervention: Theory, evaluation, and practice.* (pp. 376-390). Berlin, New York: de Gruyter.

Supportive Organizational Variables in Early Intervention Centers: Empirical Results and Recommendations

Franz Peterander and Otto Speck

1 Introduction

For the last 20 years, Bavaria has had a dense regional network of early intervention centers that care for 0- to 6-year-old children with various developmental disorders. The children are supported by an interdisciplinary team of specialists, partly within the family unit and partly on an outpatient basis.

The entire early intervention process is integrated into organizational structures within the centers, which, to a great extent, have an influence on the educational and therapeutic process. Whereas in past years, many studies have investigated various methods of early intervention and individual methods for supporting children's development, the structure and dynamics within the early intervention organization have not been studied, in particular, questions dealing with personnel and organizational development. As a result, important issues related to the quality of early intervention work have been neglected almost completely until recently (Peterander & Speck, 1993). In particular, questions dealing with the area of organization and management, as well as questions on the evaluation of one's own work, have hardly been discussed at all in the social services field (Grawe, 1992; Wöhrle, 1992), despite the fact that experiences from other institutions have shown that these variables are of utmost importance for the success of individual intervention as well as for early intervention as a whole.

Especially with regard to today's visible trend in early intervention toward individualized, complex developmental concepts (Speck, 1983), the specialists' support through leadership, the early intervention team, or the entire organization has gained increasing significance. The quality of early intervention work depends on the specialists' ability, as far as is possible, to make available the organizational conditions that support their work. These conditions can provide the specialists with important resources such as motivation, knowledge, professional competence, or willingness to become personally involved (Schuler, 1993; Weinert, 1987), and these resources can improve early intervention work. Although, in the social services, "organization" may often be considered to be a kind of "bureaucracy," in many cases, it is precisely this sort of opportunity for structuring one's own work that increases the specialists' efficiency in the centers. This aspect, in view of forseeable limited financial resources and as a result of various legal alterations in the area of early intervention and the integration of children with disabilities, will become the object of even more concern in the future.

In the light of this altered situation, the early intervention system should be willing to explore new territory in order to maintain its leading position in the support of handicapped children and their families.

2   Research Objectives

The tasks and goals of our research in the area of early intervention concentrate more than ever on the question of organization and evaluation of the centers. A preliminary empirical study examined the following areas:

1. The actual conditions in the early intervention centers were examined with regard to content and structure, and with regard to all the problems as well as opportunities for working with children and their families.

2. The organizational conditions controlling the type and quality of work at the early intervention centers and the specialists' personal situations, as well as the interaction between these two variables, were studied in order to bring about a positive change in the quality of diagnosis and the therapeutic process.

3. In addition, an attempt was made to create a basis for the development of a self-evaluation for early intervention and other institutions.

Three subject areas composed the primary object of our research:

1. We recorded and analyzed the composition and impact of different occupational groups in the early intervention team, the concrete working conditions and the specialists' specific professional situations, the quality of leadership and direction of the interdisciplinary teams, and the content and effects of team meetings and public work.

2. Emphasis was placed on the description of child disorders; the children's family situation; form and content of the educational, psychological, and medical support of children; the personal and vocational

situation of the specialists in the various vocational groups, their specific areas of activity, as well as the type and extent of further inservice training acquired.

3. We examined the extent and quality of the specialists' cooperation with other partners. This mainly dealt with a significant aspect of early intervention: cooperation with parents of the children in therapy, as well as cooperation with physicians and therapists outside the center.

3 Method

We gave two different questionnaires containing questions on 20 different areas of early intervention work to the specialists and directors at nearly 100 early intervention centers in Bavaria. In order to make the study as representative as possible, a two-part 90-page survey, specially created for early intervention, was sent to the centers. Participation in the study was voluntary. Over 600 surveys were completed and returned to us anonymously, permitting differentiated analyses of the eight vocational groups' situations in the early intervention centers. In a second study, another survey was given to the parents of children at the early intervention centers, asking about their situation and experiences at the center (Peterander & Speck, 1993). Over 1,000 parents participated in this study.

4 Results

4.1 Supportive Organizational Conditions at the Centers

From the wide range of results attained in our study, we shall concentrate on the supportive organizational conditions at the center, because we view them as being very important for improving the quality of early intervention, and because they are very closely related to other positive variables. The analyses of the institution not only revealed that the specialists' work is constantly embedded in a more or less permanent institutional framework, but also that organizational conditions have an enormous impact on the way things are done at the centers. This applies not only to the specialized aspect of early intervention work but also to the motivational and emotional condition of the specialists, which, in the end, affects the outcome of their work. For this reason, the question of productive and counterproductive conditions plays a key role in the organization of early intervention work, since our knowledge of this can enable further development of organizational factors on an empirical basis. This is why we would like to elaborate on three important variables of productivity in this report. However, we shall initially report which eight occupational groups are active in early intervention.

Nearly half of the early intervention personnel at the centers are pedagogically trained specialists, such as educational personnel, special education personnel, and social workers (Table 1). The other half is divided up among six specialized vocational groups from the fields of medicine, psychology, and education. Within the team, the most frequently represented personnel from these areas are physical therapists; the least frequently represented, physicians.

Table 1.   *Proportion of Various Occupational Groups in the Early Intervention System*

Occupational groups	Percent
Physician	2.1
Occupational therapist	5.6
Speech therapist	6.3
Psychologist	7.9
Special education teacher	9.2
Physiotherapist	10.2
Social worker	12.0
Special education personnel	14.0
Education personnel	17.0

4.2 Supportive Organizational Variables

Correlational and regression analyses revealed that 25 individual variables were good indicators of the specialists' positive cooperation at the center and also indicated the specialists' satisfaction with their work. The most important productive conditions at the early intervention centers are shown in Table 2.

Table 2. *Supportive Institutional and Personal Variables in Early Intervention*

Positive atmosphere among colleagues
Positive team leadership
Satisfaction with the quality of team meetings
Influence on decisions about personnel and organization
Free choice in further training
Flexible working schedules
Substantial support in psychological and social matters
Short waiting lists for intake of children
Longer duration of team meetings
Team's helpful knowledge and supportive work
Satisfaction with the quality of public work
Specialists' positive emotional conditions
Professional stability
Behavior directed by a clear picture of one's profession
Fair amount of experience in one's profession

We shall now present more detail on three of these positive variables.

Positive atmosphere among colleagues. The first positive variable is how often the specialists view cooperation with their colleagues as a positive experience, and which items describe the variable "Positive atmosphere among colleagues."

Table 3. *Positive Atmosphere Among Colleagues*

No.	Item	Percent[a]
	With my colleagues ...	
36	I can also discuss personal matters	42.8
14	Mistakes are admitted openly	51.3
7	We are able to express criticism to one another	58.0
4	We often say nice things to each other	62.6
24	We often have fun together	62.8
15	We give each other encouragement in difficult situations	72.8
37	We are in agreement about early intervention topics	78.9
8	I feel understood	78.9
34	Cooperative work with various vocational groups proves to be positive	81.1
29	Duties are carried out with care	84.4
1	Different opinions are accepted	87.7
11	I feel recognized	90.0
21	Arrangements agreed to are kept	93.7

[a] Percentage of respondents who agreed to a great extent or completely.

Table 3 shows what percentage of specialists reported that the 13 aspects describing "Positive atmosphere among colleagues" applied "to a great extent" or "fully" to their colleagues. Ninety percent of the specialists indicated that their colleagues follow through with arrangements agreed upon (Item 21), that they feel they receive recognition from their colleagues (Item 11), that different opinions are accepted (Item 1), and that duties are carried out with care (Item 29). On the other hand, only about one half of the specialists indicated that mistakes can be admitted to openly within the team (Item 14) and that criticism can be expressed openly (Item 7). In addition to the frequency analyses, we also computed correlations between "Positive atmosphere among colleagues" and other institutional and personal variables of early intervention (see Table 4).

Table 4.   *Correlations Between "Positive Atmosphere Among Colleagues" and Institutional and Personal Variables of Early Intervention*

Variable	*r*
Positive leadership	.69***
Early intervention center is psychologically well equipped	.46***
Early intervention center is well-organized	.39***
Satisfaction with content of team meetings	.59***
Supervision at team meetings	.49***
Further training at team meetings	.41***
Length of team meetings	.36***
Strength for early intervention work through colleagues' support	.52***
Influence of specialists in decisions about personnel and work	.37***
Specialists' positive mental conditions	.31***

*** $p < .001$.

The correlations indicated that a positive atmosphere among colleagues had a highly significant correlation with the team director's competence as a leader, the psychological support of early intervention work at the center, as well as the way and extent to which specialists are able to influence the early intervention work and how it is carried out. At the same time, positive reciprocity was also taking place on the structuring of content at team meetings. In view of the complex relations and interactions, it does not seem very promising to want to make inprovements only in individual variables of a positive atmosphere among colleagues. The establishment of positive relations among specialists will only be possible when, in conjunction with the center's management and on the basis of a solid professional foundation, mutual respect for the individual and his or her work is shown, and when favorable emotional conditions are created for specialists. These are all important requirements for a positive atmosphere among colleagues.

Positive leadership. Another important supportive variable is the director's "positive leadership" in the center. The frequency analyses painted a very diversified picture (see Table 5): More than 70% of the specialists considered that their performance is recognized by the team leader (Item 24), that important decisions are made together in the team (Item 20), and that they can count on their leader in difficult situations (Item 8). On the other hand, many specialists were very critical of the directors. Only about 30% of them reported that their director introduces new ideas into their work (Item 22), that they are constantly motivated by their director (Item 35), and that the team director sets an example for them (Item 26). These results reveal that the specialists at many centers feel emotionally supported by their director, but that they receive distinctly less concrete support of a professional nature.

Table 5. *Specialists' Evaluation of Team Leader's Personal Qualities and Behavior (Positive Leadership)*

No.	Item	Percent[a]
	In my work ...	
22	The team leader introduces many ideas	23.8
35	I am always motivated in my work by the team leader	32.9
26	The team leader sets an example for all	34.3
11	The team leader makes clear decisions	50.0
17	The team leader knows how to coordinate and organize early intervention work in a logical way	62.0
8	I can count on my team leader in difficult situations	70.7
20	Together with our team leader, we make important decisions	75.5
24	My performance is recognized by our team leader	77.8

[a] Percentage of respondents who agreed to a great extent or completely.

The directors' behavior within the team, the way they set goals to coordinate tasks, to motivate colleagues through discussions, to create opportunities for further vocational training, and to structure interdisciplinary discussions within the team in a creative way could be described as primary leadership duties. This means - above all with regard to the management of social institutions - emphasizing social interaction processes, social influence, and social perception (Greif, 1983; von Rosenstiel et al., 1991). In this way, the team directors adopt a moderating function in the organization of early developmental work at these centers. If one assumes that, in this connection, the director's behavior takes on a decisive quality that influences and determines other conditions in the center as an independent variable, then the director's significant position in early intervention becomes extremely evident.

Even simple correlations showed that productive conditions and the director's specialized competence and leadership ability are very closely related to one another (see Table 6).

Table 6. *Correlations Between "Positive Leadership" and Institutional and Personal Variables of Early Intervention*

Variable	r
Positive atmosphere among colleagues	.69***
Early intervention center is well-organized	.48***
Satisfaction with the quality of public work	.35***
Positive cooperation with other institutions	.34***
Improvement of early intervention through another organizational structure	-.47***
Length of waiting time for intake of children	-.47***
Satisfaction with the quality of team meetings	.58***
Further training at team meetings	.51***
Supervision at team meetings	.45***
Duration of team meetings	.36***

*** $p < .001$.

It is not just the atmosphere among colleagues and the quality of teamwork and public work that profit from positive leadership. Further inservice training within the center is also more likely with "good" leadership, as well as cooperation with other centers, which has a better chance of turning out positive. Surprisingly, good leadership also has a positive effect on the waiting time for the intake of children into the early intervention centers. In other words, in centers with good leadership, waiting times are shorter. In view of the significance of supportive variables, special attention must of course be paid to the area of qualification and further training for centers' directors in light of the significance of positive variables. Most importantly,

it is a matter of conveying necessary leadership competencies that enable
the director of the team to create positive conditions for the organization
and content of early interventional work.

Structuring of team meetings. The third factor used in describing
supportive conditions at the centers is the structure of the team meetings,
which usually take place on a weekly basis. The subject areas listed in
Table 7 describe aspects of positive cooperation with respect to content
during team meetings.

Table 7.   *Frequencies and Importance of Topics at Team Meetings*

No.	Item	Frequency[a]	Importance[b]
7	Team members' supervision of one another	11.4	64.8
5	Discussion of research results for the diagnosis and therapy of individual children	12.0	59.1
2	Drawing up plans for therapy	13.4	56.2
3	Individual specialists' demonstration of work procedures and behavior	14.0	56.1
6	Specialists' reports about further inservice training sessions attended	18.4	76.7
4	Discussions about specialists' feelings and burdens	30.1	78.0
8	Coordination of individual educational and therapeutic measures	47.1	81.6
1	Presentation and discussion of cases	56.5	93.6

[a] Question: Which topics are dealt with the team meetings? (Percentage of respondents
who answered often or very often). [b] Question: In your opinion, which topics do you
think should be a priority? (Percentage of respondents who rated the item as important
or very important).

On the whole, the results of the analysis of the team meeting were not very
satisfying. Only 15% of the specialists reported reciprocal supervision
within the team (Item 7), discussion of research results (Item 5),
cooperative making of therapy plans (Item 2), or further inservice training
sessions attended (Item 6). On the other hand, approximately one half of the
specialists reported that cases are presented and discussed (Item 1), which,
in our opinion, in view of the significance of this item, does not actually
take place very often. In general, a great discrepancy could be found
between reality and the specialists' wishes for emphasis on certain
important topics at the meetings. Between 80% and 90% of the specialists
would like to see the presentations and discussions of cases (Item 1), the
coordination of individual educational/therapeutic measures (Item 8), and

discussions about feelings and burdens given much higher priority in team meetings (Item 4). It was a little surprising how highly the variable "Structuring of team meetings" was assessed as being productive for the quality of work in early intervention centers. Table 8 shows how far "Satisfaction with structuring of content in team meetings" was related to other positive variables.

Table 8. *Correlations Between "Satisfaction With the Quality of Team Meetings" and Institutional and Personal Variables of Early Intervention*

Variable	r
Positive atmosphere among colleagues	.59***
Positive leadership	.58***
Early intervention center is well-organized	.43***
Satisfaction with the quality of public work	.32***
Further training at team meetings	.60***
Supervision at team meetings	.52***
Influence of specialists on decisions about personnel and work	.49***
Satisfaction with salary	.35***
Insufficient involvement of specialists	-.38***

*** $p < .001$.

It was particularly those meetings that were used as an opportunity for further training and, at the same time, for supervision of one's own early intervention activities that led to greater satisfaction in the specialists. Work done at team meetings whose content was of quality, was often related very closely to "Positive atmosphere among colleagues" (discussed above), positive "Leadership behavior," as well as the specialists' ability to take part in the structuring and organizing of their own early intervention work.

These results emphasize the significance of structuring the team meetings with regard to content, and establish a requirement for the improvement of quality in early intervention in general.

4.3 Improvements

The following two tables show the exact way in which specialists picture the improvement of such organizational and content-oriented conditions in their work and which of these aspects seem especially important to the parents of the disabled children (see Table 9).

Table 9.   *Possibilities for Improving Early Intervention Work as Assessed by Specialists*

No.	Item	Percent[a]
	My work conditions could be improved by ...	
11	A more exact knowledge of the living conditions of the individual families	32.1
9	Better furnishing of the institute with materials	38.2
8	Closer supervision of one's intervention work	45.5
4	Improving the personnel situation in the intervention center	49.4
5	More intensive parental cooperation	53.9
10	Increased opportunities for reflection on one's work in team setting	65.9
12	Further inservice training on a regular basis	66.0
1	More time for each case	72.8

[a] Percentage of respondents who agreed to a great extent or completely.

Specialists. According to nearly 70% of the specialists, the quality of the early intervention work could best be improved if they were to have more time to spend on each individual case (Item 1), if regular sessions for further inservice training were to be available (Item 12), and if they were to have the opportunity within the team to reflect on their individual early intervention activities (Item 10).

Therefore, they declared themselves in favor of improving their own professional competence through regular qualification measures, as well as improved team communication and interaction, which, in turn, addresses the significance of the supportive variables "Positive atmosphere among colleagues," "Leadership," and "Team meetings."

More than one half of the specialists saw another possibility for the improvement of early intervention work in more intensive parent involvement (Item 5).

Parents. With regard to more intensive parent involvement, a high level of agreement was found among the specialists and the parents of children in the early intervention system. The results of the above-mentioned questionnaire given to over 1,000 parents of disabled children, which we carried out in the extension of our "Organizational Study," showed the strength of the parents' desire to work in close cooperation with the early intervention specialists (Table 10).

Table 10. *Importance of Aspects of Early Intervention as Assessed by Mothers*

No.	Item	Percent[a]
	When working with intervention specialists ...	
19	I'd like the specialists just to support my child's development and not include the parents so much	6.0
23	I'd like to be able to discuss my private concerns with the specialists	11.2
26	I'd like it if the specialists had more time for personal discussions	23.2
6	I'd like it if the specialists would inform me thoroughly about their specialized knowledge on the subject	29.2
7	I'd like to be able to discuss with specialists my feelings toward my child	36.0
11	I'd like it if the specialists could provide some books about how to better support my child's development	42.3
8	I'd like the specialists to explain to me the cause of my child's problem	52.4
21	I'd like to take part regularly in my child's therapy sessions	58.5
28	I'd like to exercise with my child on my own	61.1
13	I'd like the specialists to teach me how to support my child's development so that I could continue with it at home	67.9
1	I'd like the specialists to give me help and encouragement in dealing with my child	72.3
4	I'd like the specialists to inform and advice me about my child's possibilities for development	72.9
12	I'd like the specialists to have comprehensive professional knowledge	81.1

$n = 984$. [a] Percentage of mothers who rated the items as very or most important.

Apart from the importance of the specialists' comprehensive professional knowledge (Item 12), two thirds of the parents placed great importance on being taught how to support their childrens' development so that they could continue this on their own at home (Item 13), being able to do exercises on their own with their children (Item 28), and being able to take part in the early intervention sessions on a regular basis (Item 21). Consistently, only 5% of the parents considered that specialists should promote the development of their child by themselves and that the parents should be included less in this activity (Item 19). These evaluations on the part of the parents coincided with the specialists' desires for improving their professional competencies as well as their desires for more intensive parental participation in the centers.

5   Conclusion

The analysis of supportive conditions in the organization of early intervention has brought to light important aspects of this field that have been discussed very little until now. We have been able to show in what way and to what extent the quality of the specialists' work is influenced by the institutional conditions under which this work normally takes place. If these conditions are productive and supportive, then the available resources can be employed to the benefit of parents and children. Doubtless, the question is raised about supportive conditions, especially regarding the close cooperation of many occupational groups in the early intervention team, all with differing points of view and priorities. It is precisely in such a complex situation that productive working conditions are necessary to support the specialists professionally and to enhance their competence. In our opinion, there can be no doubt that early intervention must turn more to the areas of organizational and personal development in the next few years if all possibilities for the improvement of early intervention work are to be exhausted.

The objective of our analysis was not only to provide results for the stimulation of conceptional development in early intervention, but also to create the basis for a data-based evaluation of social institutions on an organizational level. Evaluation research in this context is understood to be an attempt to ask, with the aid of quality criteria, to what extent the early intervention centers are able to meet the standards expected of them (Peterander et al., 1993). The highlight of such an evaluation is not so much to measure the effectiveness of individual early intervention programs or measures, but rather to examine the characteristics of quality in such institutions. It is known from individual research projects, field studies, and practical reports that the presentation of certain quality characteristics in the institutions has a long-term positive effect on the parents' and childrens' developmental concept and proves to be effective. An evaluation of social institutions in this sense naturally proves to be especially difficult for many reasons (Wottawa & Thierau, 1990). One of the main reasons is probably the fact that, even today, no clear quality criteria exist. In view of this, the assessment of the individual evaluations and statements about their organization and activities made by the specialists and team leaders at the institutions, as well as the parents' assessments of the work performed at early intervention centers, provides an important source of data and a foundation for the evaluation of the institutions.

A further step in the direction of a systematic evaluation for this purpose may be the development and accessibility of computer-aided evaluation (Franke & Kühlmann, 1989) and feedback systems for social institutions. This will be made possible by a computer-based system, the so-called *Münchner Analyse- und Lernprogramm* (MAL), which was developed within the framework of our research project. This program is able to provide diversified feedback to individual specialists as well as to all early intervention centers.

When necessary, various subjects can be taken up in this way within the team, and the specific situation can be discussed on the basis of comparative data. And, if necessary, alteration processes can be implemented. Finally, interaction processes can be prompted to take into account the specialists' influence through the situation, as well as the specialists' influence on the conditions at the institution. In coming years, we will be experimenting with this kind of self-evaluation of the centers with the aim of further developing the specialists' work in their own institutions, in order to develop this kind of highly individualized system of feedback for the early intervention centers as well as for other social institutions.

Note

Funds for this project were granted by the Bundesministerium für Bildung und Wissenschaft and the Bayerisches Staatsministerium für Unterricht und Kultus.

References

Franke, J., & Kühlmann, T. M. (1989). Organisationsdiagnostik. In S. Greif, H. Holling, & N. Nicholson (Eds.), *Arbeits- und Organisationspsychologie - Internationales Handbuch in Schlüsselbegriffen.* München: Psychologie Verlags Union.

Grawe, K. (1992). Psychotherapieforschung zu Beginn der neunziger Jahre. *Psychologische Rundschau, 43*, 132-162.

Greif, S. (1983). *Konzepte der Organisationspsychologie.* Bern: Huber.

Peterander, F., & Speck, O. (1993). *Strukturelle und inhaltliche Bedingungen der Frühförderung.* Research report. München: Ludwig-Maximilans-Universität.

Peterander, F., & Speck, O. (1993). *Eltern in der Frühförderung.* Unpublished questionnaire. München: Ludwig-Maximilans-Universität.

Peterander, F., Opp, G., & Speck, O. (1993). Analyzing structure and content of early intervention in Bavaria, Germany: Implications for education of young children with special needs. *Learning Disabilities Research & Practice, 8,* 52-57.

Rosenstiel, L. von, Regnet, E., & Domsch, M. (Eds.).(1991). *Führung von Mitarbeitern. Handbuch für erfolgreiches Personalmanagement.* Stuttgart: Schäffer.

Schuler, H. (Ed.).(1993). *Organisationspsychologie.* Bern: Huber.

Speck, O. (1983). Ganzheitlichkeit und Methoden in der Frühförderung. *Frühförderung interdisziplinär, 2,* 97-101.

Weinert, A. B. (1987). *Lehrbuch der Organisationspsychologie* (2nd ed.). München: Psychologie Verlags Union.

Wöhrle, A. (1992). *Jugendhilfe und Management.* München: Steinbauer und Rau.

Wottawa, H., & Thierau, H. (1990). *Evaluation.* Bern: Huber.

Part Five

Practice of Early Intervention

M. Brambring, H. Rauh, and A. Beelmann (Eds.). (1996). *Early childhood intervention: Theory, evaluation, and practice* (pp. 393-402). Berlin, New York: de Gruyter.

Early Intervention for Low-Birthweight, Premature Infants: Findings From the Infant Health and Development Program

Rebecca R. Fewell

1 Introduction

It is well known that low-birthweight (LBW) infants are at increased risk for developmental delay during the early years, including lower scores on tests of cognition (Drillien, 1964; McBurney & Eaves, 1986; McCormick, 1985) and behavioral functioning (Crnic et al., 1983; Landry et al., 1990; Minde et al., 1989) and, later, performance on tests of academic achievement (Caputo et al., 1979; Dunn, 1986; Grunau, 1986; Nickel et al., 1982). Few studies prior to 1985 explored the use of intensive early intervention with LBW children. In 1985, a large number of American researchers collaborated in the design and implementation of a multisite study to test the efficacy of educational and family support services in addition to pediatric follow up for LBW children (Infant Health and Development Program [IHDP], 1990). Subsequent to the release of the major findings of this study, researchers continue to report results from some of the ancillary investigations. This chapter provides an overview of the IHDP, presents a summary of the major study findings, reviews some of the more recent findings, and suggests implications from the collection of studies.

2 Infant Health and Development Program Study

The IHDP was an eight-site randomized clinical trial designed to investigate the efficacy of an early intervention program aimed at improving the health and development of low-birthweight, premature infants. The eight participating sites were: University of Arkansas for Medical Sciences; Albert Einstein College of Medicine; Harvard Medical School; University of Miami School of Medicine; University of Pennsylvania School of Medicine; University of Texas Health Science Center at Dallas; University of Washington School of Medicine; and Yale University School of Medicine.

During the enrollment period, 4,551 births were screened for consideration. Subjects enrolled were 985 infants, stratified by site and weight (one-third from the heavier weight group, 2,000-2,500 grams; and two-thirds from the lighter weight group, <2,000 grams), then randomly assigned, one-third to intervention and two-thirds to follow-up group. Approximately 135 infants were enrolled according to this distribution at each site. The major reason for exclusion from the study was that the home was outside of the catchment area.

The IHDP offered six program services. Three services, health surveillance, developmental assessments, and referral services, were offered to both groups throughout the study. Health surveillance was provided when children were at preset ages. Each child continued to have his or her own primary physician outside of the program. Developmental assessments were provided periodically for research purposes, and referral services for medical or family problems were provided as needed.

The intervention group received three additional services. Home visitors provided health and developmental information and family support, and they implemented a curriculum of cognitive, linguistic, and social development for the children and problem-solving for the parents. The home-visit component consisted of weekly visits during the first year, then biweekly visits thereafter.

At the age of 12 months, children enrolled in a second component, the child development centers (CDCs), and continued at these sites until the age of 36 months. The CDCs can best be described as a combination nursery school and high-quality child care center. CDC staff continued to implement the curriculum conjointly with the home visitors. Each CDC had a teaching staff ratio of 1:3 in the first year and 1:4 in the second year. The programs were open 5 days a week, 8 hours each day, providing full day care for those who needed it. Transportation was provided for all requesting this service.

The third component of the intervention program was that of parent groups. These groups began when the children were 12 months and met bimonthly to address parent needs and concerns and to inform them on health, safety, and childrearing.

The major question for this study was "Do the intervention and follow-up groups differ in the three major areas of *cognitive development, behavioral competence*, and *health status*?" All major outcomes were investigated at 36 months. There were significant differences in effect sizes between the two weight groups, therefore, results were presented separately for the two groups for the three primary outcomes.

2.1 Cognitive Development Outcomes

The mean IQ scores on the Stanford-Binet Intelligence Scale, Form L-M, 3rd edition (Terman & Merrill, 1973) were significantly higher for intervention children than for the follow-up children. The effect in the heavier intervention versus the heavier follow-up groups was 13.2 IQ points ($ES = .83$, $p < .001$), and in the lighter intervention versus lighter follow-up groups, 6.6 IQ points ($ES = .41$, $p <. 001$). Controlling for site and initial status variables, the adjusted odds for having IQ scores less than 70, that is, in the mental retardation range, were 2.7 times greater in the follow-up group (95% confidence interval, 1.6 to 4.8) than for children in the intervention group.

A few other findings related to cognitive outcomes are relevant to the focus of early intervention for children with special needs. When IQ scores were grouped <70, <85, <90, and <100, there was a larger percentage of follow-up than intervention children in each group. The analyses revealed a significant interaction between birthweight and the effect of the intervention. The intervention was more effective for heavier than lighter weight infants. Upon examination of three birthweight groups, there was a larger proportion of follow-up than intervention group children with low IQ scores. In the group of infants <1,500g with IQs in the <70 range, this difference was negligible.

In addition, the investigators found an interaction between birthweight and the effect of the intervention on the mental scale of the Bayley Scales of Infant Development (Bayley, 1969) at 24 months, but no effect at 12 months. There were no differences in the Bayley motor scale at 12 or 24 months.

When the Binet scores were examined by site, wide variability was found in the follow-up and the intervention groups. The follow-up group scores ranged from a mean of 68.0 at the University of Miami School of Medicine to a mean of 96.7 at Harvard Medical School. The means between intervention and follow-up groups varied from 14.3 at the University of Arkansas for Medical Sciences to 0.4 at Harvard. The intervention group scores were significantly higher than the follow-up group scores at seven sites. It was concluded (IDHP, 1990):

> We speculate that the nonsignificant results at one site, Harvard University, may be related to the sociodemographic characteristics of the site, such as the large proportion of college-educated mothers, as well as the relative abundance of community resources compared with the other sites. (p. 3040)

2.2 Behavioral Competence Outcomes

The Child Behavior Checklist for Ages 2 to 3 years (Achenbach et al., 1987) was used to measure the primary outcome of behavioral competence. The average score on this scale was significantly lower for the intervention group than the follow-up group, with higher scores indicating more reported behavior problems ($ES = -.18$, $p = .006$). Although the difference in scores between the two groups was small, the odds of having a score above 63, the at-risk cutoff score for clinically significant behavior problems, were 1.8 times greater in the follow-up than in the intervention group. The multiple regression analysis indicated significant main effects on several initial status variables. Higher scores were associated with some sites, with being black or hispanic, with being male, and with lower maternal age and education level.

2.3 Health Status Outcomes

Health status was viewed along three dimensions: (a) morbidity, or the presence or absence of health conditions; (b) functional status, or limitations in activities of daily living caused by health-related problems; and (c) maternal perception of the child's health. The researchers used six procedures to measure health status. These six measures are described in detail in the major IHDP paper (IHDP, 1990). Only the Mother's Report: Morbidity Index produced a significant treatment effect. This index is a summary, over the 3-year period, of the number of hospitalizations, outpatient surgeries, injuries not resulting in hospitalization or outpatient surgery, and different illnesses and conditions. Mothers reported higher morbidity scores for lighter born children in the intervention group than for the lighter born children in the follow-up group ($ES = .29$, $p < .001$). No significant difference was found in the heavier groups. Further analysis of the Index indicated that the difference was accounted for by an increase in the number of minor illnesses reported such as colds and diarrhea. In fact, there were no serious infectious epidemics or accidents at any site during the 2-year period (IHDP, 1990). One feasible explanation for this finding could be linked to both the weight group and the recall of mothers. It is possible that lighter born infants are more susceptible to minor illnesses. The mothers of infants sent to the CDCs each day had established daily routines, often including work for themselves. When infants are ill, routines are amiss and child care must be arranged. Perhaps this occurred more often with lighter infants, and these mothers had better recall of the number of times they had to make exceptions to their routines.

3   Subsequent Studies From IHDP

Following the 1990 publication of the major findings of the IHDP, researchers continue to report findings from the very rich archive of data available to them. Reported here are the major findings of selected studies on topics of interest to researchers and practitioners.

3.1 Maternal Education and Child Outcome

Brooks-Gunn et al. (1992) examined the effectiveness of IHDP in enhancing the intellectual outcomes for children from different ethnic backgrounds and born to mothers with different levels of education. They found children whose mothers had a high school education or less benefited from the intervention regardless of ethnicity. The authors indicated they found similar results using the Bayley Mental Scale at 24 months as the outcome. In contrast, white children whose mothers had attended college did not exhibit significantly higher IQ scores at 3 years. When the authors also examined birthweight in addition to ethnicity and mother's education, one significant group interaction was found: Among white mothers with some college, the lighter children were less influenced by the intervention than were the heavier children. The authors speculated that this finding may reflect the fact that the follow-up mothers may have provided their infants with a stimulating environment that maximized their intellectual abilities.

3.2 Maternal Intelligence and Child Outcome

Ramey and Ramey (1992) examined the impact of maternal verbal intelligence on child outcome. Using mothers' Peabody Picture Vocabulary Test scores, the researchers divided mothers into four groups (maternal IQ >100, 86-100, 70-85, and <70) and plotted the IQs (Bayley and Binet) of children at 12, 24, and 36 months for both the intervention and the follow-up groups. Infants at greatest risk for functioning in the borderline or mentally retarded category by 36 months had mothers with scores below 70. According to the researchers, by 36 months of age, 47% of the follow-up children had IQ scores less than 75. In contrast, only 23% of intervention group infants had scores of less than 75. Clearly, these findings support the use of the IHDP model for children born to mothers who score in the retarded or borderline range.

3.3 Intensity of Delivery and Child Outcome

For persons concerned with the spiraling costs of early intervention services, questions of intensity and of service models of the intervention are of interest. IHDP used two models, home and center, but these were not contrasted. Rather, in Years 2 and 3, both models were used for all intervention children. In addition, this study had only one model for service intensity, with all children receiving 5 days of intervention per week, thus we cannot examine two levels of intensity.

However, intensity of curriculum delivery was examined by Sparling et al. (1991) and produced very informative findings. These researchers investigated the relationship between the rate at which activities from the curriculum were delivered and IQ at 36 months. The number of activities delivered in the CDC and the home added significantly to the variance in predicting the IQ outcome at 36 months. When children received an average of 2.3 activities per visit for home intervention and 6.5 activities per CDC day, the results indicated a 13-IQ-point advantage for lighter children and a 6-point advantage for the heavier children. Because of differences in findings by weight group, the researchers concluded that for the intervention program planner, a minimum of 5 activity episodes, but with 10 more desired, per CDC day, might be the minimum for the lighter weight children. However, for heavier weight babies, the number of activities for each day might be a matter of teacher preference.

3.4 Intensity of Family Participation and Child Outcome

Intensity of service delivery and child outcome was also examined by means of the Family Participation Index (FPI). Participation rates were summed scores of three intervention modalities: the number of home visits; attendance at parent group meetings; and days attended at the child development centers. Ramey et al. (1992) used multiple regression analysis to examine the relationship between the degree of family participation in the IHDP and the child's intelligence at age 3. The researchers found that families with higher participation rates had children with higher IQs at age 3.

3.5 Mother-Child Interaction and Child Social Competence

The effects of the intervention program on mother-child interaction were examined at 30 months of age in 683 subjects. Spiker et al. (1993) coded videotapes of three types of mother-child interactions: 8 minutes of free-play, a clean-up period, and three different problem-solving tasks. The researchers reported small significant positive effects: The intervention mothers had higher ratings on quality of assistance; intervention children had higher ratings on persistence and enthusiasm and on an overall rating of competence and involvement, and lower ratings on percentage of time off-task. In addition, dyads from the intervention group were viewed as more synchronous. The results of this study mitigate the concerns that group care for young children potentially disrupts mother-child relationships or has adverse effects on young children's social behavior.

3.6 Intervention Effects and Child Social Competence

Other researchers have completed further studies of the impact of the intervention program on children's social competence. During the IHDP study, three researchers, Hogan, Scott, and Bauer (1992) developed a scale to examine social competence in the children. This scale, the Adaptive Social Behavior Inventory (ASBI), reflects social competence as multifaceted and separate from behavior problems. The resulting scale included 30 items and three subscales, *Express, Comply*, and *Disrupt*. The Express and Comply subscales, when grouped, form a Prosocial Composite Scale. Data from the ASBI has been a source for a number of important findings about the social competence of the children in the intervention group.

Hogan and Scott (1993) designated four groups of intervention subjects based on median splits of responses on the Express and Disrupt subscales of the ASBI. The groups were named on the basis of attributes of their behavioral characteristics. The "Laid-Backs" were low on Express and low on Disrupt; the "Inepts" were low on Express but high on Disrupt; the "Stars" were high on Express and low on Disrupt, and the "Wild Things" were high on Express and high on Disrupt. According to the researchers, the Stars and Wild Things were from homes that were more verbal and affectionate at 12 months than the homes of the members of the other two groups. They examined scores from these groups on the modalities of the Family Participation Index (FPI) and found no group differences for home-visiting or parent-meeting components, but significant differences in school attendance. The Stars and Wild Things attended the CDC significantly more frequently than did the other two groups.

3.7 Participation and Social Behavior

More recently, Liepack (1993) investigated the relationship between the FPI and prosocial behavior at age 3 years. Prosocial behavior was measured on the Prosocial Composite Scale of the ASBI with the effects of initial status variables controlled. Liepack used the FPI quite differently from the way in which it was used by Ramey and his colleagues. Liepack converted the modality scores of the FPI to z scores in order to give each of the modalities of the FPI equal weight in the Index. When the z scores were used, no significant relationship was found between the FPI and the Prosocial outcome. When the effects of participation on individual ASBI scales were examined, only the Express subscale resulted in a significant relationship to participation. Further analysis of the FPI modalities revealed that only the attendance at the CDCs was a significant predictor for the Express scores. Liepack's analysis is important, because it provides positive support for daily attendance in the CDC programs. Moreover, it specifically reveals "that increasing activity in the intervention program has a significant relation with increasing the outgoing social and emotionally expressive qualities in the children" (p. 36). These results do raise questions about the positive contributions of home visits and parent group meetings as contributors to a participation index that was found to be related to prosocial behavior. This does not indicate that these contributions are not important, rather it questions their contribution to the prosocial behavioral outcomes of children.

4   Implications and Conclusions

The results of the major IHDP study provide strong evidence that a comprehensive, high-quality program of early intervention can reduce, by age 3, the number of LBW premature infants at risk for developmental disabilities (IHDP, 1990). When viewed in conjunction with some of the more recently published findings, it appears that some subgroups of LBW children benefit more than others. Of particular importance are findings that indicate children born to mothers who are undereducated or who score in the retarded or borderline range on tests of verbal intelligence demonstrate cognitive gains when they participate in high-quality early intervention programs. Findings from IHDP studies also inform us on two important program variables: The intensity of the delivery of curricula content and attendance at the child development centers are related to child outcomes. The rich archival data base of the IHDP will produce many more findings, some of which will be published in a two-volume book to be released in the near future (see Gross et al., in press).

These comprehensive, well-designed studies have the potential to shape policy at governmental and programmatic levels. Decision makers are beginning to use these findings to rethink present policies and practices. With new, mandated entitlement programs to serve increasing numbers of children and familiy members, yet finite resources, it is tempting to generalize these findings to all children with risk conditions. We must exercise caution: We do not know the long-term outcome of this intensive program of early intervention, nor do we know the effectiveness of this program with other populations. The challenge for present and future researchers is to draw upon the strengths of this model and these findings and investigate the impact of service parameters on children with other serious risk conditions (e.g., mental retardation, emotional disorders, physical disabilities, prenatal exposure to substance abuse, etc.). The IHDP results purvey knowledge, direction, and encouragement. Our responsibility is to continue these investigations in response to the critical needs of our times.

References

Achenbach, T. M., Edelbrock, C. S., & Howell, C. T. (1987). Empirically based assessment of the behavior/emotional problems of 2- and 3-year-old children. *Journal of Abnormal Child Psychology, 15*, 629-650.

Bayley, N. (1969). *Bayley Scales of Infant Development.* New York: The Psychological Corp.

Brooks-Gunn, J., Gross, R. T., Kraemer, H. C., Spiker, D., & Shapiro, S. (1992). Enhancing the cognitive outcomes of low birth weight, premature infants: For whom is the intervention most effective? *Pediatrics, 89*, 1209-1214.

Caputo, D. V., Goldstein, K. M., & Taub, H. B. (1979). The development of prematurely born children through middle childhood. In T. M. Field, A. M. Sostek, S. Goldberg, & H. H. Shuman (Eds.), *Infants born at risk: Behavior and development* (pp. 219-232). New York: Spectrum.

Crnic, K. A., Ragozin, A. S., Greenberg, M. T., Robinson, N. M., & Basham, R. B. (1983). Social interaction and developmental competence of preterm and full-term infants during the first year of life. *Child Development, 54*, 1199-1210.

Drillien, C. M. (1964). *The growth and development of the prematurely born infant.* Edinburgh, Scotland: E & S. Livingstone.

Dunn, H. G. (Ed.). (1986). *Sequelae of low birthweight: The Vancouver study.* Philadelphia, PA: Lippincott.

Gross, R. T., Spiker, D., & Haynes, C. (Eds.). (in press). *The Infant Health and Development Program.* Palo Alto, CA: Stanford University Press.

Grunau, R. V. E. (1986). Educational achievement. In H. G. Dunn (Ed.), *Sequelae of low birthweight: The Vancouver study.* Philadelphia, PA: Lippincott.

Hogan, A., & Scott, K. (1993, March). *Predicting and promoting social competence in high risk children: Recent results from IHDP.* Paper presented at the meeting of the Society for Research on Child Development, New Orleans, Louisiana.

Hogan, A., Scott, K., & Bauer, C. (1992). The Adaptive Social Behavior Inventory (ASBI): A new assessment of social competence in high risk three-year-olds. *Journal of Psychoeducational Assessment, 10,* 230-239.

Infant Health and Development Program (1990). Enhancing the outcomes of low birthweight, premature infants: A multisite randomized trial. *Journal of the American Medical Association, 263,* 3035-3042.

Landry, S. H., Chapieski, M. L., Richardson, M. A., Palmer, J., & Hall, S. (1990). The social competence of children born prematurely: Effects of medical complications and parent behaviors. *Child Development, 61,* 1605-1616.

Liepack, S. A. (1993). *The impact of family participation in The Infant Health and Development Program on three-year olds' adaptive social behavior.* Unpublished master's thesis, University of Miami, FL.

McBurney, A. K., & Eaves, L. C. (1986). Evolution of developmental and psychological test scores. In H. G. Dunn (Ed.), *Sequelae of low birthweight: The Vancouver study* (pp. 54-67). Philadelphia, PA: Lippincott.

McCormick, M. C. (1985). The contribution of low birth weight to infant mortality and childhood morbidity. *New England Journal of Medicine, 312,* 82-90.

Minde, K., Goldberg, S., Perrotta, M., Washington, J., Lojkasek, M., Corter, C., & Parker, K. (1989). Continuities and discontinuities in the development of 64 very small premature infants to 4 years of age. *Journal of Child Psychology and Psychiatry, 30,* 391-404.

Nickel, R. E., Bennett, F. C., & Lamson, F. N. (1982). School performance of children with birthweights of 1000 g or less. *American Journal of Diseases in Children, 136,* 105-110.

Ramey, C. T., Bryant, D. M., Wasik, B. H., Sparling, J. J., Fendt, K. H., & LaVange, L. M. (1992). Infant Health and Development Program for low birth weight, premature infants: Program elements, family participation, and child intelligence. *Pediatrics, 3,* 454-465.

Ramey, C. T., & Ramey, S. L. (1992). Effective early intervention. *Mental Retardation, 30,* 337-345.

Sparling, J., Lewis, I., Ramey, C. T., Wasik, B. H., Bryant, D. M., & LaVange, L. M. (1991). Partners: A curriculum to help premature, low birthweight infants get off to a good start. *Topics in Early Childhood Special Education, 11*(1), 36-55.

Spiker, D., Ferguson, J., & Brooks-Gunn, J. (1993). Enhancing maternal interactive behavior and child social competence in low birth weight, premature infants. *Child Development, 64,* 754-768.

Terman, L. M., & Merrill, M. A. (1973). *Stanford-Binet Intelligence Scale: Manual for the Third Revision, Form L-M.* Boston, MA: Houghton Mifflin.

M. Brambring, H. Rauh, and A. Beelmann (Eds.). (1996). *Early childhood intervention: Theory, evaluation, and practice* (pp. 403-418). Berlin, New York: de Gruyter.

Enhancing Communication in Early Childhood

Yvette M. Dijkxhoorn, I. A. van Berckelaer-Onnes, and D. van der Ploeg

1 Introduction: Communication, Autism, and Mental Retardation

From the very first moment of life, a baby communicates continuously with his or her environment. Most children have the capacity for communication and the various communicative skills develop spontaneously. However, not all children are gifted with these capacities. In particular, autistic children experience serious problems in communication. In this paper, we shall first consider the social and communicative development of children with autism and mental retardation. Then we shall describe the early intervention method used in our research project. Finally, some of the results of this method will be reported.

We all take it for granted that we can communicate. Unfortunately not everyone is able to do so. In particular, children with autism experience severe problems in communication and social interaction. The characteristic impairments of autism include the early expressive and receptive capacities that form the basis of social development. The early deficits of these children limit their access to social and communicative experiences, especially when they are also mentally retarded. In total, 75% of the autistic population suffers a combination of the two syndromes. However, awareness of others in young autistic children and their communicative behavior can be increased by means of stimulation.

Before describing and evaluating a program for the social and communicative development of mentally retarded autistic children, we shall first consider the concepts autism and mental retardation. In Kanner's (1943) original article on infantile autism, he mentioned "the failure to use language for the purpose of communication" as one of the core features of the syndrome. Since then, impaired communication is described as one of the most striking features in every paper on autism. Nowadays, autism is considered to be a neuropsychiatric syndrome (Schopler & Rutter, 1987; Van Berckelaer-Onnes & Van Engeland, 1986). In the Diagnostic and Statistical Manual of Mental Disorders (DSM-III-R; American Psychiatric Association, 1987, pp. 38-39), impairment of communication and social behavior play a decisive role in the classification of autism. The description of the autistic disorder (category: pervasive developmental disorders) is:

> Qualitative impairment of reciprocal social interaction.
> Impairment of communication and imaginative activity.
> Markedly restricted repertoire of activities and interests.
> Generally, the disorder becomes manifest before the age of 36 months.

Autistic children exhibit a characteristic pattern of deficits in their cognitive functioning (Howlin & Rutter, 1987). The most striking of these cognitive deficits is the first step needed to obtain information: perception. Several research findings on the perception of autistic children indicate that their sensory channels are intact: They do hear, feel, and see, but they find it very difficult to select and incorporate the different stimuli. They seem unable to connect new impressions with past experiences. Apparently, stimuli are not particularly salient or meaningful for them. Their perception of meaningful information is impaired. It is obvious that this has a major impact on the development of their communicative capabilities. Children learn to communicate by imitating others and by developing the concept that their actions will evoke reactions in others.

Kanner's first publication on autism was based on the clinical observation of 11 autistic boys with normal intelligence, but now we know that 75% to 80% of the autistic population shows some degree of mental retardation (Rutter, 1987).

The DSM III-R describes mental retardation as follows (American Psychiatric Association, 1987, pp. 31-32):

> Significantly subaverage general intellectual functioning (an IQ of 70 or less).
> Concurrent deficits or impairments of adaptive functioning.
> Onset before the age of 18.

Mentally retarded children exhibit a general cognitive deficit. Mentally retarded autistic children exhibit both general and specific (due to the autism) cognitive deficits.

Children with autism and mental retardation suffer two disorders. This combination has consequences for the treatment of these children. The TEACCH-program (Treatment and Education of Autistic and related Communication handicapped Children) from North Carolina was one of the first to acknowledge this fact. Autistic children were offered strict programs in structured classrooms, and parents were used as co-therapists to facilitate generalization to the home situation (Schopler & Reichler, 1971). Another important view on treatment is offered by Rutter (1986). He described three therapeutic strategies:

Stimulation of general development (communication, social development, etc.).

Reduction of specific behavioral problems (rigidity, stereotypy, etc.).

Elimination of nonspecific behavioral problems (sleeping and eating problems, etc.).

For the treatment and teaching of autistic children, the main concept is "structure" in time, in space, and in situation.

2   Early Communication Development

Social development and communication development are closely related. In this paper, "communication" refers to the transmission of information by any means, not just through a system of symbols. It covers the range of purposeful behavior used, with varying degrees of intentionality, to bring about changes in the immediate physical environment and/or to structure social exchanges (Schuler & Prizant, 1987).

Autistic children do not develop normal communicative skills. Both their verbal and their nonverbal communicative skills are severely impaired, probably from a very early age. Coupe and Goldbart (1988, pp. 105-120) described the levels of early communication, roughly following Piaget's stages of sensory-motor development. This schedule permits an assessment of the level of early communication.

Level 1 (0-3 months). *Preintentional: Reflexive Level.* The first movements of babies are reflexes (sucking, grasping, etc.). Babies do not act intentionally, but their parents react as if they do. If a father places his finger in his daughter's hand, she will grasp it and the parent will believe that there is contact.

Level 2 (2-6 months). *Preintentional: Reactive Level.* Baby's reflexes are starting to look more like a (nonintentional) reaction to the environment: They are now able to turn their head toward the sound of a human voice.

Level 3 (from 6 months on). *Preintentional: Proactive Level.* The signals the child is sending are becoming increasingly "understandable" for the parents. Parents are able to distinguish forms of crying (hunger, pain). The child starts to abstract a meaning from the reaction of the adults.

Level 4 (from 8 months on). *Intentional: Primitive Level.* The child now intentionally tries to seek contact and provoke a reaction (e.g., dropping a toy and looking at a parent). Comprehension of nonverbal communication increases rapidly.

Level 5 (from 9/10 months). *Intentional: Conventional Level.* Infants begin to use gestures, such as waving "goodbye," pointing, and so forth. They also start to use sounds that are meaningful to others. The child now understands linguistically.

Level 6 (12 months). *Intentional: Referential Level.* At their own level, infants are now able to communicate, using the same references we all use. The basis for further communication and reciprocity is laid.

People with mental retardation pass through, at their own pace, roughly the same stages. However, children with autism do not. Parents of these children feel they miss reciprocal contact from the beginning. The development of eye contact and smiling (during the first two stages) is late; autistic children generally do not smile at their mothers, but they do smile, for example, at a shadow on the ceiling. An action of the parents does not provoke a predictable reaction. During the next stages of development, the unpredictability of the reactions becomes only worse. Autistic children do not react to friendly voices; do not stop crying when they are picked up. This has a marked influence on parents' responses: It makes them very insecure. When normally developing children start to undertake more intentional actions, the autistic child is not able to do so. They have a primitive notion of what they do and do not want, but their signals are difficult to understand.

The step to the conventional level is a huge one for an autistic child. They are unable to connect actions (e.g., gestures and vocalization). They "ask for" what they want (usually food) by pointing at it or just taking it, but there is very little interaction.

Normal children begin to talk around the age of 1 year, while autistic children are far from being able to use speech at 12 months (Van Berckelaer-Onnes & Kuiper, 1990). About 50% of the autistic population does not speak at all, and this percentage is significantly higher for the mentally retarded autistic population.

3   A Research Project: Homogeneous versus Heterogeneous Treatment

One of the research projects of the State University of Leiden (Department of Special Education and Child Care) on children with severe developmental disorders focuses on measuring the effects of treatment of autistic children in homogeneous and heterogeneous settings. There is, as yet, no agreement (at least in the Netherlands) on the question whether autistic children should live and/or be treated in groups consisting only of other autistic children. Some say the child will not benefit socially from a homogeneous group. On the other hand, they must not disturb the heterogeneous group. In a highly structured situation, with specifically trained childrearers/teachers, behavioral problems can be handled more easily and development can be stimulated more. For these reasons, a few institutions decided to form "auti-groups." One of the first experiments was evaluated by the State University of Leiden, and, since then, more have followed. On the basis of our experience with homogeneous groups, we believe that children benefit enormously from placement for a specific period in a homogeneous group. Treatment in a homogeneous group should, however, prepare the child for placement in a heterogeneous group (Van Berckelaer-Onnes, Van der Ploeg, & Hiel, 1993).

More research is now in progress on homogeneous and heterogeneous groups. Measuring the effect of treatment programs is an important step toward establishing a theory on the particular subject. Some participating institutions have auti-groups; others, which do not have such groups, function as controls for this research project. The explanatory model is shown in Figure 1.

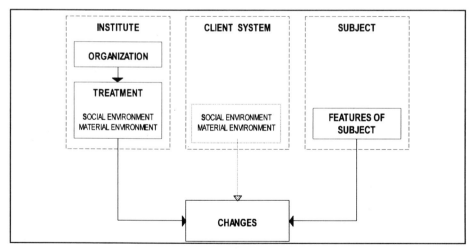

Figure 1.   The explanatory model.

The instruments used on the individual level are the Psycho-Educational Profile (PEP; Schopler & Reichler, Dutch version 1982) and the Handicaps, Behaviour and Skills Schedule (HBS) (Wing & Gould, 1978, 1982). The first one is administered within a very structured situation (1:1), and yields a score on several areas of development (motor skills, perception, verbal cognition, etc.). The HBS is administered to parents and provides information about daily living skills in particular. The HBS is based on the Vineland Adaptive Behavior Scales (Doll, 1965), so it is possible to calculate a social age equivalent. This schedule also provides an overview of deviant behavior. We have chosen these instruments because they were specially developed for the target group. More research on these instruments is also one of the goals of our research project.

Information on the treatment programs is provided by the participating institutions. We have access to daily reports on the children. Clinical observations are a very important part of this research project.

Enhancing communication is one of the most important aspects of treating autistic children. The communication program, presented in the next section, is used in one of the participating day-care centers for mentally retarded children. In this paper, we will describe the evaluation of seven children who followed this program. Evaluations took place twice a year over a 3-year period (1991 to 1993). For the four children who entered the program in 1991, six scores are available; others entered the group at a later date.

4   Developing an Early Intervention Program

When we talk about early intervention for autistic children we must realize that the diagnosis "autism" is seldom established before the age of 3 years. Before one is able to develop a curriculum to enhance communication, careful assessment of the developmental level and especially the level (and means) of communication is essential.

A vast amount of research on language training for autistic children has been performed since the mid-1960s (Howlin, 1989). Later attention was directed mainly toward augmentative forms of communication, for example, sign language, bliss symbols, pictures, and communication boards. The results of research on these augmentative forms were, however, not conclusive. Konstantareas (1987) has argued for a combination of speech and signs.

In 1980, Fay and Schuler published an important book on emerging language in autistic children. They emphasized the importance of natural teaching. Communication should be stimulated within the daily life situation. However, training should take place within the structured context of predictable routines.

We would like to describe a communication program used in a day-care center for mentally retarded autistic children. This institution has two homogeneous groups (auti-groups) containing eight mentally retarded autistic children. The group used here as an example contained four children and two caretakers who first took a special course on working with autistic children. The children were both autistic and severely mentally retarded. They did not speak. The method used is based on several other programs (e.g., TEACCH). The classroom is highly structured. Structure in space is established by fencing in a "free-time" area.

This area contains a trampoline, a cassette-player, and the favorite toys of each child. Every child has his or her own communication board that establishes structure in time. Every event of the day is shown on the board by means of photographs (e.g., the toilet, a group of swimmers, a picture of the gym teacher). For one boy (who cannot comprehend photographs), the events of the day are depicted by means of objects (e.g., diapers, swimming trunks, ball). When in interaction with the child, a photograph or object is always accompanied by spoken words and sometimes gestures. The goal is that the children will connect the photographs with the spoken words, so that eventually the photographs will no longer be needed. Some children react better to words, others to gestures or pictures. Every attempt of a child to undertake active communication is praised.

Before an activity starts, the child is asked to go to the board and turn the picture. Children who find it difficult to generalize take the picture with them to the activity. One of the activities that recurs every day is "working." On a one-to-one basis, every child sits at his or her own table and works with developmental materials for half an hour.

This system is used during the day. Everyone who enters the group and works with the children (physiotherapist, psychologist, speech therapist, physician, music therapist) applies the same communication system.

According to the schedule of early communication of Coupe and Goldbart (1987), skills are enhanced as follows:

Reflexive and reactive level. The reflexes of mentally retarded autistic children are intact, but they do not react predictably to sounds or people. Integrating stimuli and evoking reaction to stimuli are the most important goals at this stage. Their attention is caught by sounds that they like, for example, musical instruments, songs, or knocks. When they do not react, their heads are turned toward the sound, so they can see it. Extreme reactions of fear to sounds are diminished by explaining what the sound is and comforting the child. Calm music is used during periods of rest and free play.

Another way to stimulate reactions is through sensopathical play, accompanied by soft music and light. Contact is made through rocking, hugging, or rough-and-tumble play. This method is also used when a child seems to be really uncomfortable and is crying a lot for no apparent reason. At this stage, establishing eye contact can be tried, but a child must never be obliged to do this. The child has to think that it would be nice to have (physical) contact with another person.

Proactive level. At this stage, we try to find out what stimuli provoke a reaction. Reactions can be evoked through little games (e.g., tickling and romping games). Musical instruments, toys, and also, for example, turning on a tap together can play an important role in establishing reactions and a notion of action-reaction. Every attempt by an autistic child to imitate should be praised.

Primitive level. Autistic children do not seek contact by themselves. Contact can be evoked through little games (e.g., "peek-a-boo" and hide and seek), participating in the child's stereotype play, and introducing small variations. By stopping and starting play with the favorite toy, the child is stimulated to "ask" for another time by pointing or touching. At this point, a system is introduced to tell the child when an activity is finished and thus when it is time to clean up. Very useful in this respect is the alarm clock; to avoid the stress of taking away a favorite toy, a specific time for playing with this toy is entered on the board. When the alarm goes off, the toy is taken away. Children react very positively to this system.

Another task at this level is starting to imitate noises and gestures. Singing seems to be a good way to evoke sounds and gestures. For example, sing a song and leave out certain sounds. The transition can be made from concrete objects (e.g., a cookie) to a picture of these objects (or gestures). In this way, a child can "ask" for something that is not within sight. Pointing and eye contact are also established at this stage. Pointing evolves from touching the object and then enlarging the distance. A good moment to practice this is during lunch; let children choose what they want on their sandwich. At first the child will look at the object and not at the person who is supposed to carry out the action.

Conventional level. Gestures are taught to the children by making them together. In particular, gestures made while singing songs are often remembered. You actually have to teach autistic children how to point by taking their index finger and pointing it for them. Pointing to objects farther away is forced by putting their favorite toy on a shelf. To get children to ask for help, hide some raisins in a jar that they cannot open. You have to find objects that motivate the child to react. When the child is able to communicate, the concept of choosing can be introduced. Autistic children have the tendency to choose the same things all the time. This routine has to be broken. Every choice a child makes is rewarded. This is very important in establishing social timing.

At this stage, speech therapists also start their program. If a child has the ability to speak, talking should always be combined with pictures or gestures to make sure that language is functional. Special games to imitate sounds are tried. Whenever a child is asked something, a photograph or picture symbolizing the action is shown. Every action by the child is vocalized.

Referential level. The referential level is hardly ever reached by autistic children. They are not able to understand abstract concepts such as "wait a minute," "tomorrow," and so forth. However, by means of the board, the child can experience these concepts. Autistic children find it very difficult to generalize. Their understanding of language is often restricted to a certain context. They have to learn that the means of communication used in the classroom can also be used in other situations. Some children have a booklet of pictures that they take home. Considerable time is spent teaching the parents how to use the alternative communication system.

5   Outcomes

Since the beginning of the project 3 years ago, seven children have followed the special program. Four of them (Numbers 501 to 504) started in 1991, and the other three entered at later stages. Both quantitative and qualitative results are available. We will start by describing the children and presenting a qualitative analysis of their communicative skills.

Number 501. This boy started in the auti-group at the age of 8 years. He was able to understand some frequently used words. He could also say some words, although his articulation was very poor, which made it difficult to understand him. He imitated gestures, and sometimes used them to facilitate speaking. He only communicated to satisfy his needs (food, rough-and-tumble play). His communicative skills were on the verge of becoming intentional. After 1 year in the auti-group, he went to another auti-group that offered individual attention as well as the possibility of integration.

At present, he is able to understand tasks like "go find your shoes and coat." He can say words to indicate what he wants and uses names for people. He supports his words (because his articulation is still very poor) with gestures or pictures. There is a growing tendency to seek contact with other people; although the contact is usually physical, he also sometimes wants to ask or show something. He can play little games with rules. Today his communicative skills have reached the level of other mentally handicapped children of about the same developmental age. He will be placed in a heterogeneous group in the day-care center.

Number 502. This boy started in the auti-group at the age of 6 years. His understanding of language was very poor. His parents tried to raise him to be bilingual (English/Dutch). According to his parents, he had spoken some words when he was 2-years-old. If he wanted something, he took one of his parents with him to get it (instrumental). He would only communicate to get what he wanted, especially missing parts of toys. There was hardly ever any interaction with other children. He did not react to a lot of sounds (doorbell, telephone). Most of the time, he seemed to be totally aloof. His level of communication was mainly preintentional.

Because it was believed that two languages would only complicate his understanding of language, the parents were asked to use mainly Dutch. After 3 years in the auti-group, he can understand simple tasks. Words without context are very difficult for him to understand. He makes some noises, from which his mood can be deduced. He is able to choose through photographs. He still cannot point; he points by using the finger of another person. He tries to interact with other children, but cannot play by their rules; he can become very sad when this happens. He really enjoys rough-and-tumble play. He is much more aware of his environment than 3 years ago. Communication has become much more intentional.

Number 503. This boy started in the auti-group at the age of 5 years. He understood some words that recurred often. He made a lot of sounds with no meaning. He expressed his moods with his entire body (tension, happiness, etc.). He was not able to make any gestures by himself. There was a special interaction with his mother, but hardly any with other people. His communication level was preintentional.

Today, after 3 years in the auti-group, he can understand more words and also reacts to verbal warnings. He says "mama" (but not only to his mother) and "yes" and "no." He does not use gestures or pictures. He interacts with others on a physical level (is attracted to their hair, for example). His communication is becoming more intentional but remains focused on his needs. Because of the severe behavioral problems of this child, he has now been placed in an institution for mentally retarded children.

Number 504. This girl entered the auti-group at the age of 7 years. She was not able to understand any language. She reacted to routines, for example, showing her a diaper meant it was time to change. She made hardly any sounds except to shout when in pain. She only interacted with her parents to get what she wanted. She did not react to her environment at all. She exhibited severe resistance to change. Communication was on the preintentional level.

After 3 years in the auti-group, she is now able to understand simple instructions (bring to the table, etc.). She makes some noises that help you to understand her mood. She still cries without sound. She can choose through photographs, but does not use gestures. She is now able to make clear what she wants by pointing, taking people to the object she wants, and so forth. Her resistance to change can be controlled through explaining to her by means of photographs what is going to happen. There is hardly any interaction with other children, but she seems to enjoy watching other people. She enjoys physical contact now. Communication is intentional, but limited to her needs.

Number 505. This boy started in the auti-group, with the specific goal of eventual integration, 2 years ago at the age of 5. He had been raised to be bilingual (Turkish and Dutch). He was a boy with severe behavioral problems, which were partly caused by a lack of communicative skills. His understanding of language was reasonable. He could perform simple verbal tasks. He spoke a few words, some in Turkish and some in Dutch. His interaction with people was based purely on satisfying his own needs. He provoked a reaction from most people, but it was always a negative reaction; for example, he made his baby sister cry, because he liked the sound. Most of his communication was intentional.

After almost 2 years in the group, his behavior is now manageable, but unfortunately only within the structured surroundings of the group. His communicative skills have improved considerably, but during speech training, it became increasingly clear that he had a specific speech problem. He can pronounce every letter, but is not able to integrate them to form a word. Using signs, he can make sentences up to five words long. His understanding of Dutch is in accordance with his level; his ability to speak Turkish is much less now. His mother speaks mostly Dutch with him; his father, Turkish. He is increasingly able to understand jokes. His communicative skills are very intentional and sometimes reach the referential level, but they remain focused on his own interests. He can play games with other children, but adult supervision is necessary.

This child has the ability to learn how to read and write and should go to a school for very difficult learners. His behavioral problems are still very severe, and therefore he needs a highly structured environment.

Number 506. This girl entered the auti-group almost 2 years ago at the age of 10 years. Her understanding of language was very poor. Her parents sometimes thought that she understood a lot, but she rarely reacted to language. She would just take what she wanted without really asking for it. She could say "cookie." Interaction with other children was always negative (hitting, kicking, etc.). She could be interested in another person because of a sparkling earring or because they had food. The level of communication was preintentional.

Now she reacts better to spoken words. You can ask her to get her shoes, for example. She has started to use more words, especially to indicate songs she wants you to sing and food she wants. Sometimes she uses new words only for a given period of time and then they disappear again. Her interaction with other children is still very poor and always negative. A lot of children are scared of her. Her communication with adults is mainly intentional, to help her satisfy her physical needs.

Number 516. This boy entered the auti-group 1 year ago at the age of 4 years. At first, he only attended in the mornings. He understood a few words. He had spoken a few words in the past, but, by the time he entered the group, he did not talk. He was able to interact with older children and adults but not with children his own age or younger. As a rule he was very passive. Communication was preintentional.

After 1 year in the auti-group, he has started to talk again. He uses words together with gestures in a communicational way (ask for help, a cookie, etc.). If you ask him, he will repeat the words you say. His understanding of language is also much better. You can give him simple verbal instructions now. He thoroughly enjoys watching other children, but is not really able to join in their games. He will go to an adult to seek comfort, for example. Communication has become intentional and he is much more focused on people.

Social age equivalents (SA) and developmental ages according to the PEP are shown in Table 1.

All children made considerable progress, both in their more general development, as indicated by the PEP, and their social development, as indicated by the HBS. The differences between social age and developmental age are due to personal differences and are not specific for autism (Van Berckelaer & Van Duyn, 1993). It appears that the children who are more severely retarded (502, 503, 504, 506) have more or less reached their ceiling as far as their general cognitive functioning is concerned, but can still be trained in the more practical skills. They seem unable to make the cognitive step from the sensomotoric to the preoperational stage.

Table 1.   *Social Ages (SA) and Developmental Ages (PEP) in Years*

Subject		1991 I[1]	1991 II	1992 I	1992 II	1993 I	1993 II	Progress[2]
501	SA	1.97	3.30	4.00	3.70	4.30	4.60	2.63
	PEP	2.63	2.50	2.75	2.90	3.02	3.02	.39
502	SA	1.85	2.30	2.60	2.80	3.00	2.70	.85
	PEP	2.08	2.08	2.38	2.38	2.42	2.46	.38
503	SA	1.79	2.40	2.40	2.50	2.10	2.40	.61
	PEP	2.00	2.17	2.25	2.50	2.28	2.25	.25
504	SA	1.59	1.53	1.77	2.20	2.40	2.20	.61
	PEP	1.86	2.10	2.21	2.30	2.25	2.30	.44
505	SA	-	3.50	3.30	3.60	4.70	*	1.20
	PEP	-	2.72	3.10	3.29	3.38	-	.66
506	SA	-	-	1.53	1.97	1.97	2.05	.52
	PEP	-	-	1.88	2.21	2.30	2.30	.42
516	SA	-	-	-	2.20	2.90	2.70	.50
	PEP	-	-	-	2.30	2.72	2.83	.53

[1] I = first semester of the year, II = second semester of the year.
[2] progress = last score - first score.

On the verbal items of the PEP, almost all children scored 0; only two children scored one point (501, 505). Two items of the HBS concern the understanding of language and the ability to speak. The results of these items are shown in Tables 2 and 3. The age equivalents are indications; therefore, it is not possible to calculate a "progress score."

All children have made progress in their understanding of language. The age equivalents for the "understanding of language" are roughly on the same level as their total social age. The scores for "ability to speak," however, are much lower. These scores are, except for the one boy with a specific problem, not much higher than the scores for ability "to use sign language." The expressive language of these children is much more severely impaired than their receptive language.

Table 2.   *"Understanding of Language" Scores (1st row) and Age Equivalents (AE) from the HBS in Years*

Subject	1991 I[1]	1991 II	1992 I	1992 II	1993 I	1993 II
501	3 (1.25-2.0)	4 (2.0-2.5)	5 (2.5)	6 (3.0)	4 (2.5)	6 (3.0)
502	2 (1.0-1.25)	2 (1.0-1.25)	3 (1.25-2.0)	3 (1.25-2.00)	4 (2.5)	4 (2.5)
503	2 (1.0-1.25)	3 (1.25-2.0)	4 (2.5)	4 (2.5)	4 (2.5)	4 (2.5)
504	1 (0)	1 (0)	2 (1.0-1.25)	2 (1.0-1.25)	4 (2.5)	4 (2.5)
505	- -	4 (2.5)	6 (3.0)	6 (3.0)	7 (3.0)	* -
506	- -	- -	3 (1.25-2.0)	2 (1.0-1.25)	3 (1.25-2.0)	4 (2.5)
516	- -	- -	- -	3 (1.25-2.0)	3 (1.25-2.0)	4 (2.5)

[1] I = first semester of the year; II = second semester of the year.

Table 3.   *"Speaking ability" Scores (1st row) and Age Equivalent (AE) in Years from the HBS.*

Subject	1991 I[1]	1991 II	1992 I	1992 II	1993 I	1993 II
501	3 (1.33)	2 (.75)	4 (1.67)	2 (.75)	4 (1.67)	4 (1.67)
502	1 (.25)	2 (.75)	1 (.25)	2 (.75)	2 (.75)	2 (.75)
503	2 (.75)	2 (.75)	2 (.75)	2 (.75)	3 (1.33)	2 (.75)
504	0 -	0 -	0 -	0 -	0 -	1 (.25)
505 (speech)	- -	2 (.75)	3 (1.33)	3 (1.33)	4 (1.67)	* -
505 (sign)	- -	5 (2.0)	4 (1.67)	4 (1.67)	5 (2.0)	- -
506	- -	- -	2 (.75)	3 (1.33)	4 (1.67)	3 (1.33)
516	- -	- -	- -	2 (.75)	2 (.75)	4 (1.67)

[1] I = first semester of the year; II = second semester of the year.

6 Discussion

Although this research is only based on a small sample, it shows clearly that early communication skills can be enhanced, even in severely retarded autistic children. The improvement that can be accomplished is, however, dependent on the severity of the mental handicap. It is clear that early intervention is important in autistic children, but that does not mean that this program should not be used with older persons.

The special auti-groups are better equipped to handle the often difficult behaviors and to stimulate the development of mentally handicapped autistic children. But these very intensive programs are expensive, and only a limited number of treatment places is available. More research has to be done to establish criteria for placement in these groups. The level of communication skills and the possibility of improving them should be an important criterion, because improving communication means improving the quality of life of these children.

Note

We particularly wish to thank the people at the day-care center for mentally retarded children *De Springplank*, Haarlem, the Netherlands.

References

American Psychiatric Association (1987). *Diagnostic and statistical manual of mental disorders* (3rd ed.). Washington: Author.

Berckelaer-Onnes, I. A. van (1980). *Vroegkinderlijk autisme een opvoedingsprobleem.* Amsterdam/Lisse: Swets & Zeitlinger.

Berckelaer-Onnes, I. A. van (1988). Autisme en zwakzinnigheid. N.V.A. *Engagement 5.*

Berckelaer-Onnes, I. A. van, & Duijn, G. van (1993). A comparison between the Handicaps and Behaviour and Skills Schedule and the Psycho-Educational Profile. *Journal of Autism and Developmental Disorders 23*(2), 263-272.

Brinton, B., Fujiki, M., & Erickson, J. E. (1985). Establishing a functional manual sign in an autistic child. *Australian Journal of Human Communication Disorders 13*(10), 117-126.

Cohen, D. J., & Donellan, A. M. (Eds.). (1987). *Handbook of autism and pervasive developmental disorders.* New York: Wiley.

Coupe, J., & Goldbart, J. (1987). *Communication before speech.* Kent: Croom Helm Ltd.

Crain, W. C. (1985). *Theories of development: Concepts and applications.* New York: Prentice Hall.

Doll, E. (1965). *Vineland Social Maturity Scale*. Circle Pines, MN: American Guidance Service.

Fay, W. H., & Schuler, A. L. (1980). *Emerging language in autistic children*. London: Arnold.

Gillberg, C. (Ed.). (1989). *Diagnosis and treatment of autism: Proceedings of the state-of-the-art conference on autism*. New York: Plenum Press.

Howlin, P. (1989). Changing approaches to communication training with autistic children. *British Journal of Disorders of Communication 24*, 151-168.

Howlin, P., & Rutter, M. (Eds.). (1987). *Treatment of autistic children*. Chichester: Wiley.

Kanner, L. (1943). Engagement special (1989), N.V.A. *Engagement 4*.

Konstantareas, M. M. (1985). Review of evidence on the relevance of sign language in the early communication training of autistic children. *Australian Journal of Human Communication Disorders 13*(2), 77-96.

Lemmens, D., Haarhuis, A., & Koning, S. (1991). *Begrijpen en begrepen worden*; totale communicatie met verstandelijk gehandicapte autistische kinderen. Utrecht: Fiat-Wdt.

Neale, J. M., & Liebert, R. M. (1986). *Science and behavior; An introduction to methods of research* (3rd ed.). Prentice Hall.

Rutter, M., & Schopler, E. (Eds.). (1978). *Autism: A reappraisal of concepts and treatment*. London: Plenum Press.

Schopler, E., & Reichler, G. B. (Eds.). (1985). *Communication problems in autism*. New York: Plenum Press.

Schuler, A. (1985). Selecting augmentative communication systems on the basis of current communicative means and functions. *Australian Journal of Human Communication Disorders 13*(2), 99-115.

Sparrow, S. S., Balla, D. A., & Cicchetti, D. V. (1984). *Vineland Adaptive Behavior Scales*. Circle Pines, MN: American Guidance Service.

Wing, L., & Gould, J. (1982). *Schaal voor Handicaps en Sociale Vaardigheden*, Medical Research Council, London. Nederlandse vertaling (1983) Leiden.

M. Brambring, H. Rauh, and A. Beelmann (Eds.). (1996). *Early childhood intervention: Theory, evaluation, and practice* (pp. 419-435). Berlin, New York: de Gruyter.

Early Intervention With Blind Children: Main Findings of the Bielefeld Longitudinal Study

Michael Brambring

1 Introduction

Even today, we have little scientific knowledge about the impact of congenital blindness on early development. This is because of low incidence rates, the resulting problem of access to samples, and the use of inadequate assessment procedures (Ferrell, 1986; Warren, 1984, 1989). In particular, there is a lack of longitudinal analyses that could provide information on the sequence of development and on interactions in development. Up to now, only two longitudinal studies have been carried out in the United States, and these are now almost 20, respectively 40, years old (Fraiberg, 1977; Norris et al., 1957). Because of their age, these studies cannot be related to more recent findings in developmental psychology such as the idea of transactional processes in childhood development (Sameroff & Fiese, 1990).

In the United States, there are comprehensive manuals for early intervention in the visually impaired and for counseling their parents, for example, the "Oregon Project" (Anderson et al., 1991), "Reach Out and Teach" (Ferrell, 1985), "Early Focus" (Poground et al., 1992), or "First Steps" (Blind Children's Center, 1993). In Germany, there are only two rather outdated manuals (Arbeitsgemeinschaft Früherziehung, 1976, 1981). Both the American and German manuals are based mainly on theoretical considerations or, at best, on expert's judgments. There has generally been no empirical evaluation by collecting developmental data on blind children or collecting ratings from their families (Behl et al., 1993; Olson, 1987).

The Bielefeld Project on Early Intervention and Family Counseling for Blind Infants and Preschoolers is a longitudinal research project designed to provide empirical data on some of these basic and applied issues. It is directed toward the following goals:

1. To collect the widest possible range of longitudinal and cross-sectional data on visually impaired infants and preschoolers (*developmental aspect*).

2. To assess the childrearing situation and the childrearing practices of parents of visually impaired children and to relate these to characteristics of the children's development (*childrearing aspect*).
3. To develop specific observation, test, and questionnaire procedures to permit a more detailed and blindness-specific assessment of children's and family characteristics (*assessment aspect*).
4. To implement appropriate early developmental interventions for blind children and to provide childrearing and emotional support to their parents (*intervention aspect*).
5. To empirically test the acceptance and effectiveness of the interventions provided (*evaluation aspect*).

This article presents some selected findings in order to provide an overview of the research carried out by the Bielefeld Project.

2   Method

2.1 Conception of the Bielefeld Project

The core of the Bielefeld Project is the longitudinal study of a group of 10 congenitally blind children and their families. The families are being visited at regular intervals over a period of approximately 5 years. These visits have been used to try out exercises to promote development together with the parents and to discuss the parents' childrearing and emotional problems. From the end of the first year of life up to the end of the third year of life, 2- to 3-hour early intervention visits were carried out every 14 days. Since the fourth year, 3- to 4-hour interventions have been performed only every 4 weeks (Brambring, 1993a).

The early interventions are based on a family-centered model, that is, all interventions should be given in a form that the parents can adopt in everyday life. Early intervention for the child and counseling for the parents are viewed as equally desirable goals of the Project.

Following the method of participant observation, checklists are being used to collect comprehensive longitudinal data on the development of the blind children and maternal behavior after each home visit. The intervention exercises proposed during each visit as well as the contents of parent counseling are being protocolled on structured checklists and analyzed for the formative evaluation. For the summative evaluation, the developmental level of the children is being assessed at set intervals with the Bielefeld Developmental Test.

Alongside the Bielefeld Project group, further groups of blind and visually impaired children have been assessed for evaluation purposes and in order to access large samples. These samples provide cross-sectional data on characteristics of blind children and their families that are being used as control data in the summative evaluation.

2.2 Samples

Bielefeld Project group. Between the end of 1989 and the beginning of 1990, 10 families with congenitally blind children were recruited for the Bielefeld Project. All children were either completely blind or possessed at most light perception. At the time of recruitment, none of them exhibited any neurological evidence of brain damage in a pediatric examination of reflexes and posture. At this time, the children were aged between 8.0 and 16.5 months (corrected for prematurity) or between 9.5 and 19.0 months (uncorrected). Five were full-term (diagnosis: anophthalmos, microphthalmos, cortical blindness, Leber's amaurosis, and persisting primary hyperplastic vitreous bodies). The other five were preterm (diagnosis: retinopathy of prematurity, ROP, Stages IV or V). In this subgroup, mean duration of pregnancy was 27.2 weeks (with a range of 26 to 29 weeks), and mean birthweight was 878 grams (range: 650 to 1,015 grams). Five of the children were girls and five were boys. All families were German-speaking and came from a cross-section of socioeconomic classes.

Control or evaluation groups. For the summative evaluation, that is, comparisons of developmental data between Project children and controls, separate groups, each containing 10 congenitally blind children, were tested with the Bielefeld Developmental Test for Blind Infants and Preschoolers at the ages of 12, 15, 18, 24, 30, 36, and 48 months. These children were receiving assistance from other early intervention centers for blind and visually impaired children. For temporal and organizational reasons, data were gathered from controls before the beginning of the intervention with the Project group. Criteria for inclusion in the control group were (a) complete blindness (at most, light perception); (b) no additional neurological impairments; and (c) by the age of 36 months, they had to be able to walk at least a few steps by themselves and speak two-word phrases. The goal of these selection criteria was to assess so-called simply impaired blind children.

Comparison samples. To extend the data base, developmental data were obtained from approximately 250 blind, partially sighted, and sighted children in a parent survey. Parents' reports could be used to classify the children not only according to their visual impairment (blind, partially sighted) but also according to additional impairments (simply and multiply handicapped).

3   Assessment Instruments (Assessment Aspect)

Special instruments were developed for the longitudinal and cross-sectional assessment of characteristics of the children and their families, because the available instruments were considered to be methodologically invalid (Brambring, 1989; Brambring & Tröster, 1994; Ferrell, 1986). The design of previous instruments was related too closely to developmental tests for sighted children, and either simply dropped or modified items that can only be solved with vision. Our procedures, in contrast, focused on areas of development that emphasize the specific problems of blind children such as orientation and mobility or daily living skills.

   A total of seven different instruments were developed to assess characteristics of the children and their families. Four were used for the continuous protocols after each home visit, that is, they were applied in the sense of participant observation. The remaining three instruments were a developmental test and two questionnaires given to the Project group and controls at set ages. All instruments were designed for preschool-age children. Table 1 presents an overview and a brief description of the procedures used in the Bielefeld Project.

Table 1.   *Participant-Observation Procedures for Early Intervention and Tests/Questionnaires for Comparative Studies and Evaluation*

Participant-observation procedures

1   Criterion-oriented observation scales for childhood development
    (motor system, cognition, language, socioemotional development,
    orientation and mobility, daily living skills)

2   Qualitative and quantitative assessment of special aspects of
    development
    (preferences, refusals, and anxieties; assessment of residual vision;
    stereotypies; language peculiarities; play behavior; temperament)

3   Behavior-oriented observation scales for maternal behavior
    (emotionality, responsivity, directivity, childrearing stimulations)

4   Qualitative and quantitative assessment of implemented early
    intervention
    (temporal duration and contents of developmental intervention,
    temporal duration and contents of counseling talks)

Tests and questionnaires

5   Developmental test for blind infants and preschoolers
    (basic neuromotor skills, cognition, language, socioemotional
    development, orientation and mobility, daily living skills)

6   Parent questionnaire on characteristics of childhood development in
    visually impaired and sighted children
    (sleep behavior, daily living skills, toilet training, play behavior,
    stereotypies, social behavior)

7   Questionnaire on the childrearing situation of parents of visually
    impaired children
    (childrearing problems, early intervention needs, personal and
    family problem areas)

4   Developmental Aspect (Longitudinal Study)

4.1 Analysis of Developmental Trajectories

The longitudinal study was designed to gain a continuous assessment of the developmental progress of the blind children. There were clear differences in the course of development between pre- and full-term children in the Bielefeld Project group.

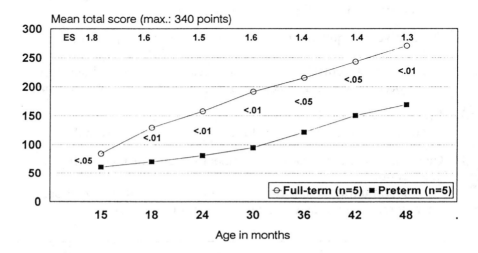

Figure 1.   Longitudinal comparison of total scores on the Bielefeld Developmental Test for pre- and full-term children (for means and standard deviations, see Table 4: Longitudinal group). Mann-Whitney U test.
ES = effect size $((M/FT - M/PT)/SD_{pooled})$

Figure 1 shows the expected progress in development with increasing age. However, the developmental performance of preterm blind children was significantly below that of the full-term blind children at all age levels (Mann-Whitney U tests, $p < .05$). A bivariate analysis of variance for dependent measures revealed significant main effects of age, $F(5, 40) = 42.0$, $p < .01$, and birth status (pre- vs. full-term), $F(1, 8) = 13.7$, $p < .01$. However, there was no significant interaction, $F(5, 40) = 1.20$, $p > .10$, that is, there was no statistical evidence that initial developmental differences between pre- and full-term blind children either increased or decreased.

The effect sizes (ES) for birth status in our sample of blind children, which varied between 1.3 and 1.8 standard deviations depending on age, were much higher than the differences between pre- (less than 1,500 g) and full-term children with normal vision reported in the literature (an average of 0.5 standard deviations; see Aylward et al., 1989). This indicated that prematurity may represent a far greater risk to development in blind children than in sighted children (Hecker, 1994). However, we still do not know whether these differences are due to as yet undiagnosed brain damage or to additional problems of information processing in the preterm children.

4.2 Analysis of Sequences of Development

The longitudinal design for our study allowed us to examine whether blind and sighted children follow the same sequences of development. Table 2 presents the example of the age at which blind (pre- and full-term) and sighted children learn to walk and crawl (Brambring, 1992). The data on blind children were collected through participant observation during the home visits.

Table 2.   *Age for the Acquisition of Selected Motor Skills in Blind and Sighted Children*

Motor skill	Full-term blind (*n* = 5)	Preterm blind (*n* = 5)	Sighted (Bayley, 1969)
Pulls to stand on furniture	12.0 (10.5-13.5)	18.0 (13.0-22.0)	8.6 (6.0-12.0)
Walks held by two hands	12.0 (11.0-12.5)	13.0 (12.0-18.0)	8.8 (6.0-12.0)
Walks along furniture	13.5 (12.5-15.5)	18.5 (15.5-22.5)	9.6 (8.4-11.7)
Walks 3 steps alone	15.5 (13.5-18.0)	26.5 (23.0-41.0)	11.7 (9.0-17.0)
Walks 10 steps alone	17.5 (15.5-20.0)	30.0 (24.0-41.0)	13.6 (12.3-16.0)
Crawls in a coordinated way	19.0 (14.0-23.5)	22.5 (19.5-27.5)	9.7 (12.3-16.0)

Note. Age (in months) at which 50% of the children mastered the task. Second line: Age span (Bayley: 5% to 95%; Project: 0% to 100%).

Blind children exhibited marked developmental delays in the acquisition of gross-motor skills compared to norms for sighted peers. These differences were particularly strong in preterm blind children. Such findings indicate the particular importance of vision for the initiation and acquisition of locomotor skills (Tröster et al., 1994).

The full-term blind children exhibited one major shift in the sequence of the development of crawling and walking: On average, they exhibited coordinated crawling only 3.5 months *after* their first steps, whereas sighted children crawled in a coordinated way 2.0 months *before* their first steps. Does this suggest that vision is more important for the acquisition of crawling than for learning how to walk, and that it is necessary to assume a blindness-specific shift in the developmental sequence of motor skills - at least for full-term blind children? If it is assumed that the level of neurological maturity for crawling and walking takes a comparable sequence in blind and sighted children - although with strong delays in the preterm blind - the difference could well be due to a practice effect rather than a blindness effect.

Sighted children are stimulated to crawl by interesting, visible objects and persons as soon as they are mature enough to do this, and this occurs before walking. Blind children lack this stimulation, naturally for both crawling and walking. However, the parents of blind children start to practice walking movements when they assume that their child is old enough (at the end of the first year of life). Naturally, they want to have a "normal" child. At this age, they practice walking very intensively, but they do not, or only rarely, practice crawling, because this is not so easy to do with children. These "exercises" seem to have been successful with the full-term blind children, because they were mature enough to learn how to walk. This is why there is a switch in the developmental sequence in these children. In the preterm children, parents soon abandon these exercises because of their children's strong developmental delays, so that these children once more exhibit the usual sequence when their maturity permits.

4.3 Analysis of Interactions in Development

Longitudinal studies permit an analysis of interactions in development, that is, whether there is a close temporal--and, therefore, potentially causal--link between the acquisition of two skills from different developmental areas. In blind children, such a link has been proposed between "reaching for sound objects" and "walking" or "crawling." According to Fraiberg (1977) and Bigelow (1992), blind children only become motivated to engage in independent locomotion when they have "recognized" that they are able to reach for sound objects that they cannot touch. Fraiberg (1977) has reported that 10 of the children she observed started to crawl shortly after they had managed for the first time to grasp a sound object (Stage 4 of object permanence in Piaget's classification). Bigelow (1992) has reported similar findings.

To replicate these findings, we compared the ages at which the 10 Project children acquired the skills "reaches toward a known sound object without having touched it first," "crawls in a coordinated way," and "walks three steps." Although all children reached toward sound objects before they walked or crawled for the first time, the mean amount of time between the acquisition of reaching for sound objects and walking was 4.0 months in full-term blind children and even 19.0 months in the preterm children. The mean time interval before coordinated crawling was 8.0 months for full-term and 13.5 months for preterm blind children. In view of these time differences, the causal and temporal link between the acquisition of object permanence ("reaches toward sound objects") and locomotor performance (crawling or walking) could not be confirmed.

5   Childrearing Aspect

5.1 Longitudinal Observation of Maternal Behavior

Maternal behavior was rated on detailed observation scales after each home visit. Continuous observation permitted an assessment of not only changes in maternal behavior over the course of the early intervention but also the relation between maternal behavior and the child's behavior.

There were only slight changes in the ratings of maternal behavior across the first 50 home visits. In other words, either maternal behavior proved to be very constant, or it was judged as such by the raters.

Further analyses studied whether relations could be found between maternal behavior and characteristics of the child's development. Correlations at various ages were moderate, but they all tended in the same direction. For each of the four scales, they were about .30, but did not differ statistically from zero. These weak correlations were probably confounded by variables such as the influence of the father or the child's own biological contribution.

As could be expected, positive maternal emotionality toward the child, high responsivity, and good childrearing stimulations tended to have a favorable impact on the child's development. It was somewhat surprising to see that the directivity scale took the same direction, that is, children with a directive, controlling mother performed better on the Bielefeld Developmental Test.

5.2 Childrearing Situation of the Parents

Fifty-two families with blind 2- to 6-year-olds reported their childrearing and personal situation on a questionnaire assessing the childrearing situation of the parents of blind children (Brambring et al., 1990). One section of the questionnaire asked them to report "serious" childrearing problems, that is, problems that their child had had over a longer period of time, and regarding which parents had wanted or sought professional help.

Approximately three quarters of all parents reported that they had experienced such serious childrearing problems. Unexpectedly, it was not blindness-specific problem areas such as motor skills or daily living skills that they named most frequently, but their children's social and emotional difficulties. Fear of loud noises, animals, and new materials, as well as interaction problems such as dealing with other children and adults or fixation on the mother were the childrearing problems mentioned most frequently by the parents of blind children.

One possible interpretation of this finding is that although all parents are assisted by early intervention centers for the blind, insufficient attention is paid to blind children's socioemotional difficulties compared to the "typical" areas of blindness. Another interpretation is that such areas are less accessible to intervention than blindness-specific problems such as orientation and mobility or daily living skills.

6   Intervention and Evaluation Aspect

The intervention exercises performed in the Project were subjected to formative and summative empirical evaluation.

6.1 Formative Evaluation

In order to describe and evaluate the main themes of the early intervention - child and family aspects - the type of intervention for the child and the content of parent counseling were protocolled after every home visit.
Table 3 presents the evaluation of these protocols up to the end of the third year of life, that is, for the first 2 years of early intervention (see Beelmann, 1994).

Table 3.   *Relative Proportion of Total Home Visit Spent on Early Intervention and on Counseling Parents up to 36 Months*

Content	Percentage of total time		
	M	**SD**	**Range**
Early intervention			
Orientation	13.3	(6.5)	3.7 - 27.6
Fine-motor	12.8	(4.8)	8.1 - 22.9
Gross-motor	11.7	(2.9)	6.5 - 14.7
Cognitive development	5.0	(3.0)	1.1 - 10.0
Training residual vision	4.9	(3.6)	0.0 - 12.2
Other	4.4	(1.9)	2.0 - 7.6
TOTAL	52.0	(10.4)	36.2 - 72.1
Parent counseling			
Developmental aspects	15.0	(5.5)	7.2 - 23.6
Emotional problems	7.4	(3.3)	3.5 - 12.4
Medical aspects	5.5	(2.0)	3.1 - 8.2
Legal aspects	5.0	(1.5)	2.7 - 7.0
Other	4.2	(1.8)	0.0 - 5.9
TOTAL	37.1	(8.3)	22.8 - 46.6
Private talks	10.9	(5.5)	4.6 - 18.8

Note. Reports based on 10 Project families and 334 early intervention sessions. Mean length of sessions: 179 minutes ($SD = 23.1$).

Promoting the child's development and counseling the parents received approximately equal attention in line with the conception of the Bielefeld Project. Parent counseling concentrated on general and specific questions regarding development such as the child's age-appropriate progress. Counseling on emotional topics such as the consequence of blindness or reactions to the blind child in the social environment was also very frequent.

Turning to the early intervention measures for the child, exercises focused on orientation (searching behavior, localization and navigation, measures to facilitate the learning of spatial relationships) and on fine- and gross-motor exercises (manual and daily living skills, posture and balance, self-initiated locomotion). Residual vision trainings were less frequent, because only a few of the children possessed light perception. The

promotion of cognition and, even more strongly, language and social
behavior (other), either received less time between the end of the first and
the end of the third year of life or were less accessible to a systematic early
intervention.

6.2 Summative Evaluation

To test the effectiveness of the early intervention, the Project children's
developmental test scores were compared with the scores of blind children
in the care of other early intervention centers at fixed ages (see Table 4;
Brambring, 1993b).

Table 4.   *Comparison of Total Scores on the Bielefeld Developmental
Test for Blind Infants and Preschoolers in Project Children
(Longitudinal Group) and Controls (Cross-Sectional Groups)
at Various Ages*

Age in months	Cross-sectional groups			Longitudinal group			p	ES
	M	*SD*	*n*	*M*	*SD*	*n*		
Full-term children								
15	89.2	(32.1)	5	84.8	(13.0)	5	.75	-0.19
18	103.2	(38.5)	5	129.4	(25.3)	5	.34	0.78
24	113.5	(64.8)	6	157.8	(40.3)	5	.36	0.78
30	130.8	(46.8)	10	191.4	(43.0)	5	.03	1.14
36	187.3	(41.1)	8	215.4	(50.6)	5	.46	0.62
42	225.9	(49.4)	10	243.2	(56.6)	5	.54	0.34
48	290.0	(49.1)	6	270.6	(50.7)	5	.41	-0.40
Preterm children								
15	57.0	(18.0)	4	61.0	(13.8)	5	.62	0.26
18	68.0	(17.0)	6	70.8	(16.1)	5	.71	0.18
24	101.2	(35.2)	6	81.6	(15.3)	5	.36	-0.68
30	108.0	(36.2)	4	95.0	(16.2)	5	.46	-0.50
36	136.6	(25.0)	5	121.8	(50.0)	5	.25	-0.39
42	222.7	(70.1)	3	150.6	(42.1)	5	.10	-1.17
48	248.8	(43.8)	4	169.4	(62.4)	5	.09	-1.19

Note. Maximum score: 340 points.
ES = effect size [$(M_{long} - M_{cross})/ SD_{pooled}$]. Mann-Whitney *U* tests.

There were positive effects sizes for the full-term blind children from the ages of 18 to 42 months. At 30 months, this difference was statistically significant.

The preterm Project children showed negative effect sizes compared to controls from the age of 24 months onward. The strongly negative effect sizes at 42 and 48 months were due to a selection effect. When selecting controls at the beginning of the project, the ability to walk and speak two-word phrases at 36 months was used as an additional criterion alongside no confirmed brain damage. However, as four of the five preterm Project children failed to meet this criterion at 36 months, the match was unsuccessful. This was supported by the fact that the test scores of the only preterm Project child who met the selection criteria were higher than the mean test scores of controls at 36, 42, and 48 months (Brambring, 1993b).

The lack of a difference in test scores up to 36 months is not so easy to interpret, because it can be assumed that controls and Project children were matched. One explanation could be that it is very difficult to confirm any positive intervention effect in preterm children because of their generally very slow progress in development. However, it is also possible that the type of early intervention these children received in the Bielefeld Project hardly differed from that provided to controls at other intervention centers.

In the full-term children, an increasingly positive intervention effect can be seen up to 30 months. On closer inspection, the differences prove to be due to better performance on the blindness-specific scales *Orientation and Mobility* (M = 48.2 vs. M = 31.0, ES = 0.99, U = 6.0, z = -2.3, p < .02) and *Daily living skills* (M = 42.4 vs. M = 25.2, ES = 1.16, U = 11.0, z = 1.7, p < .10). It is not possible to ascertain which specific elements of the early intervention in the Bielefeld Project led to this positive effect. Nonetheless, more global differences in the type of early intervention carried out at Bielefeld can be named: (a) more intensive family counseling; (b) good knowledge of developmental psychology in the team; (c) close interlinking of diagnosis and intervention (criterion-oriented intervention); and (d) strong structuring and individualization of early intervention exercises.

The decline in effect sizes among the full-term children after 36 months was also due to an unsuccessful match between Project children and controls as in the preterms. Two of the five full-term Project children did not conclusively meet the selection criteria for the control group.

Alongside the developmental data, the summative evaluation also used parent reports to test whether Project children and controls differed in the number of stereotypies they exhibited (Tröster et al., 1991a, 1991b). As the factor *birth status* had hardly any impact on this variable (Hecker, in prep.), results were aggregated for pre- and full-term children (see Table 5).

Table 5.   *Comparison of the Number of Different Stereotypies Occurring Every Day in Project Children (Longitudinal Group) and Controls (Cross-Sectional groups) at Various Ages*

Age in months	Cross-sectional groups			Longitudinal group			p	ES
	M	*SD*	*n*	*M*	*SD*	*n*		
12/15	4.4	(2.9)	19	3.3	(2.8)	9	.28	0.38
18	4.7	(2.3)	9	2.7	(2.5)	9	.10	0.78
24	3.1	(2.4)	21	2.0	(1.5)	10	.24	0.53
30	3.7	(2.2)	15	2.9	(2.0)	9	.45	0.39
36	2.8	(2.5)	13	2.4	(1.6)	9	.91	0.19
42	3.4	(2.0)	10	1.7	(1.6)	10	.05	0.87
48	2.6	(1.5)	8	1.4	(1.3)	8	.06	0.88

Note. ES = effect size [$(M_{long} - M_{cross})/ SD_{pooled}$]. *t* tests.

The project children exhibited fewer stereotypies than controls. This difference was significant in the older children (at 42 months and a strong trend at 48 months). This positive intervention effect was probably due to the fact that alternative behaviors such as development-appropriate play were demonstrated to the Project parents at a very early age. The origins and functions of stereotypies in the development of the congenitally blind were outlined, and, in individual cases, principles of behavior modification were even explained and demonstrated.

7   Conclusions and Outlook

This overview has tried to illustrate some of the major findings of the Bielefeld Project on Early Intervention and Family Counseling for Blind Infants and Preschoolers. The Project has collected a vast amount of data for the longitudinal analysis of characteristics of children and their families. From a methodological perspective, the multiple measurements (1st to 3rd year of life: every 14 days; 4th year onward: every 4 weeks) mean that a large aggregate of data are available. However, the fact that they are based on a sample of only 10 congenitally blind children calls for caution in generalization.

Regarding the Project's goals, we have obtained satisfactory answers to some of our research questions, for example, we now possess more precise and more differentiated knowledge about blindness-specific development, and we have obtained more information on appropriate intervention for the congenitally blind. On the other hand, the Project has raised new research issues, such as what kind of early intervention could have led to a positive effect in the preterm blind children as well.

Further publications will present individual aspects of the research project in detail.

Note

The research project *Early Intervention and Family Counseling for Blind Infants and Preschoolers* is part of the Special Research Unit on *Prevention and Intervention in Childhood and Adolescence*, financed by the German Research Association (DFG).

References

Anderson, S., Boignon, S., & Davis, K. (1991). *The Oregon project for visually impaired and blind preschool children. Skill inventory and manual.* Medford, OR: Jackson Educational Services District.

Arbeitsgemeinschaft Früherziehung (1976). *Anregungen für die Förderung sehgeschädigter Kinder im Früh- und Elementarbereich (0-6 Jahre).* Hannover: Verein zur Förderung der Blindenbildung.

Arbeitsgemeinschaft Früherziehung (1981). *Mediative Frühförderung Würzburg.* Hannover: Verein zur Förderung der Blindenbildung.

Aylward, G. P., Pfeiffer, S. I., Wright, A., & Verhulst, S. J. (1989). Outcome studies of low birth weight published in the last decade: A metaanalysis. *The Journal of Pediatrics, 115*, 515-520.

Bayley, N. (1969). *Manual for the Bayley Scales of Infant Development.* New York: Psychological Corporation.

Beelmann, A. (1994). *Evaluation der Frühförderung entwicklungsgefährdeter Kinder: Formative und summative Analysen eines Interventionsprojektes für blinde Klein- und Vorschulkinder.* Unpublished doctoral dissertation, University of Bielefeld.

Behl, D. S., White, K. R., & Escobar, A. E. (1993). New Orleans early intervention study of children with visual impairments. *Early Education and Development, 4*, 256-274.

Bigelow, A. E. (1992). Locomotion and search behavior in blind infants. *Infant Behavior and Development, 15*, 179-189.

Blind Children's Center (1993). *First steps. A handbook for teaching young children who are visually impaired.* Los Angeles: Blind Children's Center.

Brambring, M. (1989). Methodological and conceptual issues in the construction of a developmental test for blind infants and preschoolers. In M. Brambring, F. Lösel, & H. Skowronek (Eds.), *Children at risk: Assessment, longitudinal research, and intervention* (pp. 136-154). Berlin: de Gruyter.

Brambring; M. (1992). Development of blind children: A longitudinal study. In International Council for Education of the Visually Handicapped (Ed.), *Conference Proceedings 9th Quinquennial & Early Childhood* (pp. 217-218). Bangkok: ICEVH.

Brambring, M. (1993a). *"Lehrstunden" eines blinden Kindes: Entwicklung und Frühförderung in den ersten Lebensjahren.* München: Ernst Reinhardt.

Brambring, M. (1993b). *The effectiveness of early intervention with blind children.* Bielefeld: 10th International Symposium.

Brambring, M., Hauptmeier, M., & Hecker, W. (1990). *Erziehungssituation und Bedürfnisse von Eltern blinder Klein- und Vorschulkinder.* Bielefeld: Universität Bielefeld, SFB 227, Preprint Nr. 30.

Brambring, M., & Tröster, H. (1994). The validity problem and the instruction problem in the assessment of cognitive development in blind infants and preschoolers. *Journal of Visual Impairment and Blindness, 88*, 9-18.

Ferrell, K. A. (1985). *Reach out and teach. Materials for parents of visually handicapped and multihandicapped young children.* New York: American Foundation for the Blind.

Ferrell, K. A. (1986). Infancy and early childhood. In G. T. Scholl (Ed.), *Foundations of education for blind and visually handicapped children and youth: Theory and practice* (pp. 119-136). New York: American Foundation for the Blind.

Fraiberg, S. (1977). *Insights from the blind. Comparative studies of blind and sighted infants.* New York: New American Library; Meridian Book.

Hecker, W. (1994). *Blind und zu früh geboren: Ein doppeltes Risiko für die Entwicklung?* Bielefeld: Universität Bielefeld, SFB 227, Preprint Nr. 81.

Norris, M., Spaulding, P. J., & Brodie, F. H. (1957). *Blindness in children.* Chicago, IL: University of Chicago Press.

Olson, M. (1987). Early intervention for children with visual impairments. In M. J. Guralnick & F. C. Bennett (Eds.), *The effectiveness of early intervention for at-risk and handicapped children* (pp. 297-324). Orlando, FL: Academic Press.

Poground, R. L., Fazzi, D. L., & Lampert, J. S. (1992). *Early Focus. Working with young blind and visually impaired children and their families.* New York: American Foundation for the Blind.

Sameroff, A. J., & Fiese, B. A. (1990). Transactional regulation and early intervention. In S. J. Meisels & J. P. Shonkoff (Eds.), *Handbook of early childhood intervention* (pp. 119-149). Cambridge: Cambridge University Press.

Tröster, H., Brambring, M., & Beelmann, A. (1991a). Stereotype Bewegungs- und Verhaltensmuster bei blinden Klein- und Vorschulkindern: Prävalenz und situative

Auslösebedingungen. *Zeitschrift für Entwicklungspsychologie und Pädagogische Psychologie, 23*, 66-89.

Tröster, H., Brambring, M., & Beelmann, A. (1991b). The age dependence of stereotyped behaviors in blind infants and preschoolers. *Child: Care, Health and Development, 17*, 137-157.

Tröster, H., Hecker, W., & Brambring, M. (1994). *Die motorische Entwicklung blinder Kinder. Ergebnisse der Bielefelder Längsschnittuntersuchung.* Universität Bielefeld, SFB 227, Preprint Nr. 80.

Warren, D. H. (1984). *Blindness and early childhood development.* New York: American Foundation for the Blind.

Warren, D. H. (1989). Implications of visual impairments for child development. In M. C. Wang, M. C. Reynolds, & H. J. Walberg (Eds.), *Handbook of special education, research and practice: Vol. 3. Low incidence conditions* (pp. 155-172). Oxford: Pergamon Press.

M. Brambring, H. Rauh, and A. Beelmann (Eds.). (1996). *Early childhood intervention:*
Theory, evaluation, and practice. (pp. 436-456). Berlin, New York: de Gruyter.

Promoting Peer-Related Social Competence of Young Children With Disabilities

Samuel L. Odom and Scott R. McConnell

1   Introduction

The formation of social relationships with peers during the preschool years
is one organizing theme for the development of young children. Participation in these peer groups represents a departure from the adult-child social
experiences that are the predominant aspect of the infant's social world. In
peer-group social interactions, children venture into a world in which social
interactions are more co-equal in nature and require skills that differ from
interaction with adults. Although children surely use social skills (e.g.,
reciprocity or turn-taking) that they literally "learned at their mother's knee,"
in their social interaction with peers, children learn qualitatively different
social skills. Such skills are necessary for forming positive relationships
with peers in their current and future social settings. These skills are
characterized by their effectiveness in reaching social goals and their appropriateness for the social context (Guralnick, 1992; Odom, McConnell, &
McEvoy, 1992), and they are the essence of peer-related social competence.

Unfortunately, for many young children with disabilities, the development of peer-related social competence follows a different developmental
path than for typically developing young children. Young children with
disabilities may lack the basic skills necessary for participation in successful
social exchanges with peers, or their participation in such exchanges does
not result in extended positive interactions that may be the foundation for
positive social relationships (Guralnick & Groom, 1988; Guralnick &
Weinhouse, 1984; Kopp et al., 1992). Concern about the acquisition of
necessary social skills and the formation of positive peer relationships has
lead professionals to emphasize the development of peer-related social
competence as a central dimension within early childhood intervention
programs (Guralnick, 1992; Strain, 1990).

Central to the understanding of peer-related social competence in early
childhood is the establishment of a definition for such a construct and an
approach to assessing it. The first purpose of this paper will be to describe
an approach to the assessment of social competence of young children with

disabilities. A study examining the use of this assessment approach will be presented. The second purpose of this paper is to describe briefly a range of approaches that might be used to promote social competence of young children with disabilities. A study that examined the differential treatment effects of the more intensive approaches will also be described. Finally, the implication of these findings for early childhood intervention will be examined.

2   Assessment of Peer-related Social Competence

Researchers and practitioners have employed a variety of approaches in both defining social competence and its assessment. Odom and McConnell (1985) characterized these approaches as "all-inclusive" (in which all competent performance of young children is included; Zigler & Trickett, 1978), "behavioral" (in which only discrete social behaviors of young children are included; Strain, 1983), and "cognitive" (in which sociocognitive skills of children were included; Guralnick, 1992). Although each of these approaches contribute to the understanding of children's social functioning, the approaches are generally unidimensional in nature and may underrepresent the actual interpersonal social functioning of children. Hops (1983) and McFall (1982) have proposed that social competence is not reflected solely by the social behaviors of children or sociocognitive processes that underlie those behaviors, but rather by judgments of children's participation in social interchanges. Odom and McConnell (1992) extended this "performance-based" definition of social competence to young children with disabilities. They defined performance-based social competence as the *interpersonal social performance of children with other children or adults as judged by significant social agents in the child's environment.*

A performance-based approach to social competence implies that single measures of children's social participation provide only a limited view of social performance. Only through a multimethod assessment approach that draws upon multiple social agents (i.e., peers, observers, teachers, parents) within the child's environment may one gain a comprehensive picture of a child's success or lack of success in interactions. Each source of information would provide both common information as well as information that represents the judge's unique perspective (Odom, McConnell, & McEvoy, 1992).

3 An Examination of a Performance-Based Assessment of Peer-Related Social Competence

A performance-based assessment approach shares many of the advantages suggested by individuals interested in measurement of social competence and assessment of young children in general. It would draw upon multiple methods (Gresham, 1986) and contexts that extend across settings (Neisworth, 1993). In addition, information is drawn primarily from natural social contexts within a child's life rather than analogue, standardized, hypothetical settings (Neisworth & Bagnato, in press). Such an assessment approach is also very compatible with assessment methodology that follows developmentally appropriate practice guidelines (Bredekamp, 1987; Guralnick, 1993). However, to date, few studies have examined the use of a performance-based approach to the assessment of peer-related social competence. The purpose of the first study described in this paper is to examine such an approach when used with young children with disabilities. A multimethod, performance-based assessment of social competence was conducted with young children with and without disabilities. A principal components analysis was conducted to examine the interrelationship across methods. Performance differences between young children with and without disabilities were examined.

3.1 Method

Two hundred and twenty-two preschool-aged children participated in this study. Their demographic characteristics appear in Table 1. One hundred and seventy-three children had a disabling condition that met either Tennessee or Minnesota criteria for participation in special education. The disabling condition was documented by a rating scale that yielded a judgment of developmental delay; the information for completing this rating scale was obtained from the children's school records. All children with disabilities were enrolled in preschool special education classes, most of which did not include children who were typically developing. All children without disabilities were enrolled in typical child care centers.

Table 1. *Demographic Characteristics of Children*

	Children with disabilities	Children without disabilities	Total
% female	31.3	57.1	37.9
% minority	24.3	--	--
Mean age (months)	62.5	60.5	62.1
Age range (months)	24-105	41-78	24-105
Judgment of developmental delay			
At-risk	15.5%	--	
Borderline	28.2%	--	
Mild	34.5%	--	
Moderate	14.8%	--	
Severe	7.0%	--	

A range of assesment information was collected for each child. These assessment measures appear in Table 2.

Table 2. *Measures of the Performance-Based Assessment of Social Competence (PASC).*

Peer Sociometric
    Average rating, picture roster-and-rating
Teacher Rating
    Total Score, California Preschool Scale of Social Competency
Observer Rating of Quality of Social Behavior
    Total Score, Observer Impressions Scale
Observational Assessment of Social Behavior
    Percent of time in social interaction
    Total frequency of interactions
    Mean length of interactions
    Rate of subject initiations and responses to peer initiations
    Rate of peer initiations to subject & responses to subject initiations
    Sociability Ratio (subject initiations: peer initiations)

A picture roster and rating sociometric assessment was collected from classmates of all children (Asher et al., 1979). Teachers completed the *California Preschool Social Competency Scale* (Levine et al., 1969), a rating scale of social competence and adaptive behavior. Direct observation information was collected on the children's social interaction using an interval sampling system (McConnell & Odom, 1990).

Six 5-minute samples were collected during free-play sessions on different days. This observational assessment yielded information on time in interaction, frequency of interaction, length of interaction, rate of subject initiations and responses, rate of peer initiations and responses, and sociability ratio. After each observation, observers also completed the Observer Impressions Scale (OIS). This 16-item scale was designed to assess the quality of the interactions in which the child participated.

3.2 Results

A primary purpose of this study was to examine the degree to which the different sources of information within this multimeasure, performance-based assessment provided common information about social competence (i.e., shared variance), and also the extent to which separate or unique information was provided by the different sources. A principal components analysis was conducted to analyze this relationship. This analysis yielded four principal components with eigenvalues above 1.0. The principal components and component loadings for each variable appear in Table 3.

Table 3. *Principal Components (PC) Analysis of PASC*

Measure	PC 1	PC 2	PC 3	PC 4
Peer sociometric	-.052	.080	-.282	.949
Teacher rating	.330	.007	.491	.154
Observer impression	.845	.127	.066	.002
Percent social	.908	.126	.200	.105
Total interactions	.949	-.047	-.183	.033
Mean length of interaction	.239	.314	.780	.146
Subject initiation	.844	.330	-.224	-.096
Peer initiation	.748	-.568	-.054	-.068
Subject response	.774	-.501	-.189	-.040
Peer response	.866	.311	-.209	.001
Sociability ratio	.016	.861	-.196	-.189
% of variance	47.5	15.1	10.4	9.2

The first principal component accounted for 47.5% of the variance, with eight of the component loadings on this variable above .30. The peer sociometric measure was the single primary source of information that did not load on this component. Three other principal components also had variables loading .30, with these factors appearing to represent variance associated with initiations and interactions, teacher ratings and length of interaction, and peer sociometrics, respectively.

To examine the criterion-related validity of this assessment, an analysis of variance was used to compare difference in the component scores (identified as Performance-Based Assessment of Social Competence or PASC scores) for the groups of children with disabilities and typically developing children. The results of this analysis appears in Table 4.

Table 4. *Analysis of Variance of PASC Scores*

PASC scores	Children with disabilities		Children without disabilities		F (1,181)
	M	(SD)	M	(SD)	
PASC 1	-.19	(0.95)	.63	(0.89)	25.58[***]
PASC 2	.00	(1.03)	-.01	(0.92)	.00
PASC 3	-.17	(0.97)	.54	(0.93)	17.98[***]
PASC 4	.06	(1.08)	-.19	(0.64)	2.00

[***] $p < .001$

The PASC scores for the first component (the primary PASC variable) and the third component (teacher ratings and length of interaction) were significantly different for the two groups of children.

Table 5 presents a correlational matrix of the four component scores and four demographic variables. Significant correlations did not occur for age, gender, or race. However, significant correlations did occur for level of developmental delay and both PASC 1 and PASC 3 scores.

Table 5. *Correlation Matrix of PASC Scores and Demographic Variables*

Demographic variables	PASC scores			
	PASC 1	PASC 2	PASC 3	PASC 4
Age	.08	.07	-.10	.07
Gender	.05	-.01	.09	.12
Judgment of developmental delay	-.37[**]	-.04	-.34[**]	.11
Race (majority/nonmajority)	-.08	.11	.03	.10

[**] $p < .01$

3.3 Discussion

This study suggests that the use of multiple measures may generate a performance-based assessment of peer-related social competence that incorporates information from multiple sources in the child's social environments. This assessment approach can provide a common metric across sources as well as information about the contribution of individual sources. This common metric, which was called the PASC score, successfully differentiates between social performance of young children with and without disabilities, as does a secondary PASC component score related to length of interaction and teacher ratings.

Two of the measures included in this analysis do not load highly on the primary PASC scores. The peer sociometrics do not load at all on this central measure, and teacher-rating scores load at a somewhat lower rate. We and others (Odom & Fewell, 1988) have had concerns about the reliability of the peer ratings assessments. In the current study, it appears to us that some of the young children with disabilities may not have understood the assessment task, although training was provided. Also, for the specific teacher-rating measure employed, only about half of the items relate directly to social competence, with the others being related to adaptive behavior. Use of a scale that was more centrally related to social performance may have generated different results. Certainly, the examination of the utility of both peer ratings and teacher ratings would be directions for future research. Also, in the study, information from parents is not included. Parents may have a unique perspective on their child's social performance in settings outside of the classroom. This information could contribute substantially to our understanding of children's social competence.

The utility of the PASC analysis of peer-related social competence lies primarily in the theoretical and research domains. This PASC approach could be used to examine the ongoing development of social competence across the age range, and would yield a more accurate analysis than any single measure. In such a program of research, an ongoing examination of children's social competence could yield information on the continuity and discontinuity of children's development of peer-related social competence as well as an examination of factors that inhibit or promote social competence. Practically, a PASC assessment could be used as a standard against which to establish the concurrent validity of individual assessment instruments that might be used by practitioners. For example, the OIS loads highly on the primary PASC component, yet it is less costly in time, and is an approach that teachers could easily learn to use in assessing young children with disabilities. Although it would yield less comprehensive information about children's social competence, its correlation with the PASC1 component would provide support for its validity.

4 Strategies for Promoting Peer-Related Social Competence

As noted above, promoting peer-related social competence is a central concern for many early childhood intervention programs in the United States. Since the early 1970s, researchers have examined a range of treatment strategies that are designed to increase the social participation of children in positive interactions with their peers (McEvoy et al., 1992) and the generalization of those social interaction skills across settings (Brown & Odom, 1994). Such intervention programs have been designed for young children with general developmental delays (McEvoy et al., 1992), children with communication impairments (Goldstein & Gallagher, 1992), children with hearing impairments (Antia & Kreimeyer, 1992), and children with visual impairments (Skellenger et al., 1992). The purpose of this portion of the paper is to describe a conceptual framework for planning interventions for young children with disabilities who are enrolled in inclusive programs that contain children without disabilities, as well as to describe a study of differential treatment effects of the most intensive intervention approaches.

4.1 Conceptual Framework for Interventions

Strategies or intervention approaches that might promote the peer-related social competence of young children with disabilities may be organized conceptually according to the intensity of the intervention (degree to which it focuses directly on a specific child) and the amount of time that is required to conduct the intervention. Figure 1 presents a framework for conceptualizing this relationship and the types of approaches that might fall

444   Samuel L. Odom and Scott R. McConnell

along this range (from Odom & Brown, 1993). As the intensity of
intervention increases, the amount of consultant or teacher time to run an
intervention also increases. Each of the levels of this hierarchy is discussed
below.

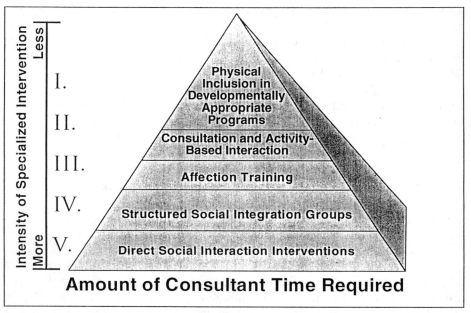

Figure 1. Intensity of intervention and amount of consultant time
(From Odom & Brown, 1993).

Physical inclusion in a developmentally appropriate program. The first
level of treatment would be the simple inclusion of children with disabilities
in high-quality child care programs for young children without disabilities.
The notion is that such inclusion would naturally provide a socially
responsive peer group, and participation in such a peer group would provide
natural opportunities for learning age-appropriate social interaction skills.
For most typically developing children and some children with disabilities
(especially those with social and play skills that will allow them to
participate in social interactions), this type of experience may well be
sufficient. However, for many children with disabilities in socially integrated
settings, patterns of interaction that typically develop suggest that co-equal
interaction opportunities may not exist for these children or exist at a less
frequent level than occurs for typically developing children (Guralick &
Groom, 1988; Odom & McEvoy, 1988).

Consultation and activity-based intervention. For children with disabilities, early childhood educators and early childhood special educators may collaborate to create a program that could support the development of social competence as well as development in other areas (Peck et al., 1989). In such collaborative arrangements, the early childhood special educator often serves as a consultant, with the early childhood educator planning and arranging activities in the preschool setting. In such settings, an activity-based intervention approach (Bricker & Cripe, 1992) might be employed in combination with consultation with an early childhood special educator to arrange activity and the classroom environment in a way to support the development of social skills. For example, the early childhood educator may arrange the materials during an art activity to increase the opportunities that children may have to share materials, which is an important prosocial skill, and provide needed assistance when it does not occur. Hundert and Hopkins (1992) have documented the generalized effects of classwide collaborative planning on the social behavior of young children with disabilities.

Affection training/group socialization activities. A third level of intensity might be represented by affection training activities. Twardosz et al. (1983), McEvoy et al. (1988), and Brown et al. (1988) have designed and evaluated a set of activities for promoting prosocial participation among children with and without disabilities. These activities adapt songs and games that typically occur in US early childhood education settings so that they include positive social or affectionate dimensions. For example, a typical teacher command in the "Simon Says" game might be "Simon says, take a giant step." In the affection training activities, the command would be changed to "Simon says, hug Jonathan" (a child with developmental delays). The researchers noted above have all documented the effectiveness of this strategy in promoting positive social interaction among children with and without disabilities. Such a strategy could easily fit into the routine of a typical preschool day.

Structured social integration groups. A fourth level of intensity that teachers might employ is the formation of structured social integration groups. The teacher might choose to introduce this level of intensity if, after using strategies at the previous level, a child or children with disabilities are not becoming engaged in social settings. In structured play groups, the teacher organizes a play activity that contains specific roles that encourage social interaction (i.e., activities change daily), arranges the social play activity in a specific space in the room, and chooses children with and without disabilities who will play in the activity for a short time period each day (5-10 minutes). In this activity, children who are very positive and socially responsive are grouped with children with disabilities who do not actively engage in social interactions. Odom et al. (1988) have designed a set of curriculum procedures and play activities that represent this structured play activity approach, and Jenkins et al. (1989) have documented the positive effects of this intervention on language and social competence.

Direct social interaction interventions. A last level of intensity that teachers may choose is called direct social interaction intervention. Direct interventions may include social skills lessons for children with disabilities (McConnell et al., 1990), social skills lessons for typically developing peers who will then attempt to support the behavior of children with disabilities (Odom & Watts, 1991), teacher prompting and reinforcement (Kohler et al., 1990), and procedures for fading teacher prompts (Odom et al., 1992). A large research literature documents the effects of such techniques (for a review, see Odom & Brown, 1993), although examination of their implementation in the typical inclusive settings has been limited (but see Hundert et al., 1993).

5 Differential Treatment Effects of the More Intensive Intervention

Although the literature documents a range of effects of the more intensive interventions noted above, little is know about the relative effects of these intervention approaches. The purpose of the study described below is to determine the relative effects of four social interaction intervention strategies on the social competence of young children with disabilities.

5.1 Method

Eighty-eight children with disabilities participated in this study. These children were enrolled in 10 special education classrooms in Nashville, TN and 12 comparable classrooms in the Minneapolis-St. Paul, MN area. Children were between 3- and 5-years-old and exhibited mild to moderate developmental delays. Specific disabling conditions included mental retardation, behavior disorders, communication disorders, health impairments, and hearing impairments.

Because random assignment of individual students to conditions was not possible, at least two classrooms at each site were randomly assigned to one of five conditions. These conditions were Contrast (C) in which teachers followed their typical routine without prescribed interventions; Environmental Arrangement (EA) in which teachers planned and implemented structured play groups; Child-Specific (CS) in which teachers conducted social skills lessons for children with disabilities, prompted target children to interact, and faded prompts; Peer-Mediated (PM) in which teachers conducted social skills lessons for peers that taught them ways to engage the children with disabilities, prompted the peers, and faded the prompts; and Comprehensive (CM) in which all of these program features were included in the intervention. The program features and intervention conditions appear in Figure 2.

Conditions	Structured play	Social skills lessons for		Prompting/ prompt fading for	
		peers	targets	peers	targets
Contrast					
Environmental arrangement	X				
Child specific	X		X		X
Peer-mediated	X	X		X	
Comprehensive	X	X	X	X	X

Figure 2. Program features of conditions.

Teachers in the four treatment conditions implemented standardized intervention packages for a 55- to 60-day period. Each treatment package included typically developing peers from kindergarten classes in the school building. Teacher implementation of the treatments was assessed weekly with an observational instrument, the Observer Rating of Implementation, as well as a direct observation measure of children's social interaction and teacher prompts. Research staff met weekly with teachers to review data collected on implementation and to plan the intervention activities for the next week.

Dependent measures were collected following the performance-based assessment of social competence (PASC) conceptual model described previously, with the exception that summary data generated by the individual measures rather than factor scores were analyzed in this study. The individual dependent measures consisted of a direct observational measure, the Observer Impression Scale (OIS; which was completed after each observation), the California Preschool Social Competence Scale (CPSCS), and the peer-rating assessment. The direct observation measure (Neimeyer & McEvoy, 1988) in this study differed from the one used in the previous PASC study in that it was an event-recording system and was collected with hand-held computers (rather than paper and pencil). Although it generated the same information as the previously described assessment, frequency of interactions and percent time spent in interactions were the two variables included in this analysis.

The entire battery of PASC measures was collected in the fall of the school year (PRE). At that assessment period, the direct observation data (six 5-minute samples) were collected during free-play periods containing only peers with disabilities from the special education classrooms in which the subjects were enrolled. During the spring of the year, after the treatment packages were implemented, three 5-minute observations were collected again in free-play consisting of classmates with disabilities (POST-D) and also in structured play groups consisting of peers with and without disabilities who had participated in the interventions (POST-N). The OIS was completed after each observational sample. In the spring of the year, the teachers also completed the CPSCS, and the peer rating assessments were conducted (POST). Last, in the fall of the next year, each measure of the PASC was readministered in the next educational placement for the children (FOLLOWUP). Three 5-minute samples of observational data were collected in free play settings with peers (with disabilities) in the classrooms (FOLLOWUP), and associated OISs were completed. Again, the CPSCS and peer rating measures were administered.

5.2 Results

To examine the effects of each condition on the children across time and the differential magnitudes of effects, the analysis followed a stepwise progression (MANOVA --> Factorial Repeated Measures ANOVA for each variable --> Repeated Measures ANOVA for each Treatment --> Effect Size Analysis). First, a 5 (treatments) X 4 (PRE, POST-N, POST-D, FOLLO-WUP) repeated measures MANOVA was conducted for the observational variables (frequency of interaction, time in interaction, and OIS). A 5 (treatments) X 3 (PRE, POST, FOLLOWUP) repeated measures MANOVA was conducted for the rating scale information (CPSCS total scores and mean peer rating score). For the observational measures, significant effects occurred for time, $F(2, 89) = 278$, $p < .001$, and time by treatment, $F(8, 89) = 1.79$, $p < .02$. For the rating measures, significant effects occurred for treatment, $F(4, 88) = 3.05$, $p < .003$, time, $F(2, 88) = 2.87$, $p < .005$, and time by treatment, $F(8, 88) = 700$, $p < .001$.

Given the significant time by treatment interaction, further analyses were conducted to determine the nature of the treatment differences for each variable. For the individual observational variables, 5 (Treatment) by 4

(Time) ANOVAs were conducted. For the frequency of interaction variable, significant effects were found for time, $F(3, 234) = 18.53$, $p < .001$, and time X condition interaction, $F(12, 234) = 2.08$, $p < .02$. Significant effects were not found for the percent time in interaction variable. Repeated measures ANOVAs were then conducted for each condition (for the frequency of interaction variable). Significant effects were not found for the C or the CM conditions, but were found for each of the other treatment conditions. For the EA condition, $F(3, 42) = 8.88$, $p < .001$, the post hoc analyses revealed that both the POST-D and POST-N differed from the PRE condition, and the POST-N was significantly higher than the FOLLOWUP (for this and subsequent post hoc analyses, the Fischer LSD analysis at the .05 level of significance was used). For the CS condition, $F(3, 54) = 9.25$, $p < .001$, the POST-N was significantly higher than the PRE, FOLLOWUP, and the POST-D. For the PM condition, $F(3, 51) = 5.15$, $p < .03$), the POST-N was greater than the PRE. These post hoc differences are identified by superscripts in Table 6.

Few significant changes across time occurred for the percentage of time engaged in social interaction. The 5 x 4 repeated measures ANOVA yielded a significant main effect only for time, $F(3, 234) = 700$, $p < .001$. Given that a time X condition effect was not found, further analyses were not conducted.

For the OIS, a significant main effect occurred for time, $F(3, 231) = 20.77$, $p < .001$, and a marginally significant effect occurred for the time X treatment interaction, $F(12, 231) = 1.57$, $p < .10$. Follow-up ANOVAs for individual treatment conditions revealed a significant effect for time for the C condition, $F(3, 45) = 3.21$, $p < .04$, although post hoc analyses did not distinguish differences among conditions. No significant effects occurred for the EA condition. For the CS condition, significant effects occurred, $F(3, 54) = 12.33$, $p < .001$, with post hoc analyses revealing higher OIS scores for the POST-N, POST-D, and FOLLOWUP than for the PRE condition. For the PM condition, $F(3, 43) = 6.54$, $p < .001$, POST-N and FOLLOWUP scores were higher than the PRE scores. Last, for the CM condition, $F(3, 51) = 4.55$, $p < .007$, FOLLOWUP OIS scores were significantly higher than PRE scores.

Rating measures. Similar analyses were conducted for the rating measures, with the exception that only three points in time, PRE, POST, and FOLLOWUP, were included. For the CPSCS, a significant effect for time, $F(2, 156) = 20.83$, $p < .001$, and a marginal effect for treatment X time interaction, $F(8, 156) = 1.79$, $p < .054$, were found.

Table 6. *Effect Sizes for Experimental Conditions Across Dependent Variables*

Condition	Frequency			Observer Impression Scale			California Preschool Social Competence Scale		Peer Rating	
	P-N	P-D	FUP	P-N	P-D	FUP	P	FUP	P	FUP
Control	.54	.71	.71	1.03	1.11	1.20	.38	.17	.74	.38
Enviormental Arrangement	1.36[1,2]	.98[1]	.12	.39	.69	.46	.39	.50[1]	.95[1]	.82[1]
Child Specific	1.86[1,2,3]	.69	.75	1.65[1]	1.14[1]	.92[1]	.50[1]	.82[1]	-.24	-.36
Peer-Mediated	1.11[1]	.29	.95	1.64[1]	.60	1.61[1]	1.38[1]	.87[1]	.40	.78
Combined	1.32	-.04	.06	1.13	.98	1.56[1]	.30	.67[1]	-.68[1,2]	.02[3]

Note. The effect sizes reflect the magnitude of changes across assessment periods; the superscripts the significant differences between mean scores detected by post hoc analyses ($p < .05$). P-N = POST-N; P-D = POST-D; FUP = FOLLOWUP; P = POST (see text). [1] Significantly different from the PRE. [2] Significantly different from the FOLLOWUP. [3] Significantly different from the POST-D.

In subsequent repeated measures ANOVAs, the C condition did not generate a significant time effect. For both the EA, $F(2, 28) = 5.48$, $p < .01$, and the CM, $F(2, 36) = 5.56$, $p < .007$, conditions, FOLLOWUP scores were higher than PRE scores, but differences between PRE and POST did not occur. For both CS, $F(2, 28) = 10.01$, $p < .001$, and PM, $F(2, 36) = 8.86$, $p < .001$, the POST and FOLLOWUP scores were greater than PRE scores.

Last, the five X three repeated measures ANOVA for the mean peer rating scores yielded a marginally significant main effect for time, $F(2, 152) = 2.90$, $p < .06$, and a significant interaction effect for time X condition, $F(8, 152) = 3.28$, $p < .002$. When repeated measures ANOVAs were conducted for each condition, significant effects were not found for the C, CS, and PM conditions. For the EA condition, $F(2, 26) = 6.02$, $p < .007$, post hoc analyses revealed that both the POST and FOLLOWUP mean peer ratings were significantly higher than the PRE mean ratings. For the CM condition, $F(2, 34) = 4.80$, $p < .015$, the POST mean ratings were significantly lower than the PRE, and the FOLLOWUP was significantly higher than the POST.

The analyses above were designed to reflect differential changes across time, but they do not allow a comparison of the magnitude of the changes that occur across time. To portray magnitude, effect sizes were computed for PRE to POST-N, PRE to POST-D, and PRE to FOLLOWUP for the observational measures and PRE to POST and PRE to FOLLOWUP for the rating measures. These effect sizes were computed using the formula POST or FOLLOWUP mean scores - PRE mean scores/standard deviation of the PRE scores. This was analogous to the strategy proposed by Glass et al. (1981) for computing effect sizes for differences between mean scores for groups (we were interested in the difference in changes across time that occurred for groups). These effect sizes are found in Table 6. Effect sizes were not computed for percentage of time in interaction because a significant time X treatment effect was not found in the previous analysis.

For the frequency and OIS observational measures, effect sizes tended to be higher for the POST-N observations, perhaps reflecting the presence of typically developing children in those groups. At POST-D, the EA condition generated the greatest effect size. At FOLLOWUP the next year, only the PM condition yielded an effect size substantially greater than the C condition. For the OIS measure, effect sizes at POST-N in the PM and CS groups were substantially larger than other conditions (by at least 0.60 SD), while, in the POST-D assessment, treatment effect sizes were similar to or smaller than for the C. However, in the FOLLOWUP observations, effect sizes of the PM and CM groups were substantially larger than the C group (by about 0.40 SD).

The rating measures yielded interesting and somewhat contrasting results. For the CPSCS, the effect size at POST for the PM intervention was substantially larger than any of the other conditions (nearly 1 *SD* larger than the control group). At FOLLOWUP, the effect sizes for the CS, PM, and CM conditions were substantially higher (by at least 0.6 *SD*) than the C condition. In contrast, for the mean peer rating measure at POST, effect sizes for the C and EA conditions were substantially higher than the other treatment conditions, while at FOLLOWUP, effect sizes for the EA and PM conditions were substantially above other conditions. Last, the negative effect size for the CM condition at POST reflected the lower mean peer rating scores after the treatment; the effect size at FOLLOWUP indicates that the peer rating scores the next year were similar to the PRE scores (suggesting that the decline in peer ratings did not maintain into the next classroom setting).

5.3 Discussion

Several general but tentative conclusions can be drawn from this study. First, it appears that two of the more direct social interaction interventions (CS and PM) and to some extent the EA intervention have the most immediate effect on the frequency of children's social behavior, the quality of that behavior, and the teachers' ratings of children's social competence. Interestingly, the peer ratings are affected only by the EA condition, a finding that deserves much greater study in the future. Also, at posttest, the CM condition appear to have a negative effect on peer acceptance.

It is important to note that pretest to posttest effects for frequency of interaction and the OIS are seen primarily in the posttest setting with typically developing children. Two variables may have contributed to this difference: First, it could be that in the special education classrooms in which the children had access only to peers with disabilities, the peer group was not socially responsive (i.e., they may not have provided a social context in which skills practiced in the interventions could be used). In the play groups with typically developing peers, such a receptive social context may have existed. Secondly, the environmental arrangements of the play groups differed, with the observations with children with disabilities occurring in the free-play settings, and the observations with typically developing peers occurring in structured play settings. This latter setting difference alone could also increase the probability that differences would occur.

The follow-up data, collected in different classes the next year, and in some cases with different teachers, indicate that the more direct interventions (CS, PM, CM) appear to have ongoing effects on the quality of the interactions and the ratings by teachers. Interestingly, the single effect on peer ratings at follow up occurred for the EA intervention. This may suggest that different intervention procedures may have differential effects on long-term outcomes. Specifically, EA seems to affect social acceptance by peers, a concern if one is interested in establishing peer relationships. However, the more direct interventions appear to affect the quality of social participation with peers and the teachers' ratings of social competence.

Last, from our analysis at posttest, it appears that the CM intervention is less effective than the other direct interventions (CS or PM). On some measures, changes across time are worse than those for children in the C condition. This is surprising in that this intervention appeared to be more intense than any of the other interventions. However, at FOLLOWUP, quality of the children's interactions in this intervention appears to be at least as positively affected as the children in the CS and PM condition and more so than the children in the EA and C conditions. This same trend appears to be true for the teacher rating scores. Clearly, further investigations are needed to determine the actual interactions that occur during these interventions and their subsequent outcomes.

6   Conclusions

In conclusion, the two studies in this paper reported on the development of a multimethod, performance-based assessment of peer-related social competence and its use in examining treatment strategies for young children with disabilities. Such an approach could well serve as a composite measure of peer-related social competence in research. Also, as seen in the second study, the use of multiple methods allows a view of different dimensions of social competence that may be affected by different intervention approaches or strategies.

In the second part of this paper, a range of intervention strategies were identified and a process from moving from less intense to more intensive interventions was suggested. Also, an examination of the relative effects of these interventions suggested that the more direct intervention may have immediate effects on children's social behavior as long as factors that are supportive of peer interaction are occurring (e.g., a socially responsive peer group and structured play). This study also suggested that the effects on quality of social interaction and teacher ratings may maintain across follow-up settings, and also that a less intense, but structured intervention approach may well have long-term effects on the development of peer acceptance and perhaps peer social relationships.

454   Samuel L. Odom and Scott R. McConnell

Note

The analyses described in both of the studies in this paper and the results should be viewed as tentative. Both studies have been submitted for publication in a peer-reviewed journal. The analyses could conceivably change (as could the results) based upon the recommendations of the reviewers and editors.

References

Antia, S. D., & Kreimeyer, K. H. (1992). Social competence intervention for young children with hearing impairments. In S. Odom, S. McConnell, & M. McEvoy (Eds.), *Social competence of young children with disabilities: Issues and strategies for intervention* (pp. 135-164). Baltimore, MD: Paul Brookes.

Asher, S. R., Singleton, L. C., Tinsley, B. R., & Hymel, S. (1979). A reliable sociometric measure for preschool children. *Developmental Psychology, 15*, 443-444.

Bredekamp, S. (Ed.). (1987). *Developmentally appropriate practice in early childhood programs serving children from birth through age 8*. Washington, DC: National Association for the Education of Young Children.

Bricker, D., & Cripe, J. J. (1992). *An activity-based approach to early intervention.* Baltimore, MD: Paul H. Brookes.

Brown, W. H., Ragland, E. U., & Fox, J. J. (1988). Effects of group socialization procedures on the social interactions of preschool children. *Research in Developmental Disabilities, 9*, 359-376.

Brown, W. H., & Odom, S. L. (1994). Strategies and tactics for promoting generalization and maintenance of young children's social behavior. *Research in Developmental Disabilities, 15*, 99-118.

Glass, G. V., McGaw, B., & Smith, M. L. (1981). *Meta-analysis in social research.* Beverly Hills, CA: Sage.

Goldstein, H., & Gallagher, T. M. (1992). Strategies for promoting the social-communicative competence of young children with specific language impairment. In S. Odom, S. McConnell, & M. McEvoy (Eds.), *Social competence of young children with disabilities: Issues and strategies for intervention* (pp. 189-214). Baltimore, MD: Paul Brookes.

Gresham, F. M. (1986). Conceptual issues in the assessment of social competence in children. In P. Strain, M. Guralnick, & H. Walker (Eds.), *Children's social behavior: Development, assessment, and modification* (pp. 143-179). New York: Academic Press.

Guralnick, M. J. (1990). Social competence and early intervention. *Journal of Early Intervention, 14*, 3-14.

Guralnick, M. J. (1992). A hierarchical model for understanding children's peer-related social competence. In S. Odom, S. McConnell, & M. McEvoy (Eds.), *Social competence of young children with disabilities: Issues and strategies for intervention* (pp. 37-65). Baltimore, MD: Paul Brookes.

Guralnick, M. J. (1993). Developmentally appropriate practice in the assessment and intervention of children's peer relations. *Topics in Early Childhood Special Education, 13*, 344-371.

Guralnick, M. J., & Groom, J. M. (1988). Friendships of preschool children in mainstreamed playgroups. *Developmental Psychology*, *24*, 595-604.

Guralnick, M. J., & Weinhouse, E. M. (1984). Peer-related social interactions of developmentally delayed young children: Development and characteristics. *Developmental Psychology*, *20*, 815-827.

Hops, H. (1983). Children's social competence and 1: Current research practices and future directions. *Behavior Therapy*, *14*, 3-18.

Hundert, J., & Hopkins, B. (1992). Training supervisors in a collaborative team approach to promote peer interaction of children with disabilities in integrated settings. *Journal of Applied Behavior Analysis*, *25*, 385-400.

Hundert, J., Mahoney, W. J., & Hopkins, B. (1993). The relationship between the peer interaction of children with disabilities in integrated preschools and resource and classroom teacher behaviors. *Topics in Early Childhood Special Education*, *13*, 328-343.

Jenkins, J. R., Odom, S. L., & Speltz, M. L. (1989). Effects of social integration on preschool children with handicaps. *Exceptional Children*, *55*, 420-428.

Kohler, F. W., Strain, P. S., Maretsky, S., & DeCasare, L. (1990). Promoting positive and supportive interactions between preschoolers: An analysis of group-oriented contingencies. *Journal of Early Intervention*, *14*, 327-341.

Kopp, C. B., Baker, B. L., & Brown, K. W. (1992). Social skills and their correlates: Preschoolers with developmental delays. *American Journal on Mental Retardation*, *96*, 357-366.

Levine, S., Elzey, F. F., & Lewis, M. (1969). *California preschool social competency scale*. Palo Alto, CA: Consulting Psychologist Press.

McConnell, S. R., & Odom, S. L. (1990). *Observer impressions scale*. Unpublished manuscript. Nashville, TN: Vanderbilt/Minnesota Social Interaction Project.

McConnell, S. R., Sisson, L. A., Cort, C. A, & Strain, P. S. (1991). Effects of social skills training and contingency management on reciprocal interaction of preschool children with behavioral handicaps. *Journal of Special Education*, *24*, 473- 495.

McEvoy, M. A., Nordquist, V. M., Twardosz, S., Heckaman, K. A., Wehby, J. H., & Denny, R. K. (1988). Promoting autistic children's peer interaction in an integrated setting using affection activities. *Journal of Applied Behavior Analysis*, *21*, 193-200.

McEvoy, M. A., Odom, S. L., & McConnell, S. R. (1992). Strategies for promoting peer social competence of young children with disabilities. In S. Odom, S. McConnell, & M. McEvoy (Eds.), *Social competence of young children with disabilities: Issues and strategies for intervention* (pp. 113-134). Baltimore, MD: Paul Brookes.

McFall, R. M. (1982). A reformulation of the concept of social skill. *Behavioral Assessment*, *4*, 1-33.

Neimeyer, J. A., & McEvoy, M. A. (1990). *Observational assessment of reciprocal social interaction: A training manual*. Unpublished observer training manual. Nashville, TN: Vanderbilt/Minnesota Social Interaction Project.

Neisworth, J. T. (1993). Assessment. In DEC Recommended Practices Task Force (Ed.), *DEC Recommended Practices: Indicators of quality in programs for infants and young children with special needs and their families* (pp. 11-18). Reston, VA: Council for Exceptional Children.

Neisworth, J. T., & Bagnato, S. J. (in press). Assessment for early intervention: Emerging themes and practices. In S. Odom & M. McLean (Eds.), *Early childhood special education/early intervention: Recommended practices*. Austin, TX: PRO-ED.

Odom, S. L., Bender, M., Stein, M., Doran, L., Houden, P., McInnes, M., Gilbert, M., DeKlyen, M., Speltz, M., & Jenkins, J. (1988). *Integrated preschool curriculum.* Seattle, WA: University of Washington Press.

Odom, S. L., & Brown, W. H. (1993). Social interaction skills interventions for young children with disabilities in integrated settings. In C. Peck, S. Odom, & D. Bricker (Eds.), *Integrating young children with disabilities into community programs* (pp. 39-64). Baltimore, MD: Paul Brookes.

Odom, S. L., Chandler, L. K., Ostrosky, M., McConnell, S. R., & Reaney, S. (1992). Fading teacher prompts from peer-initiation interventions for young children with disabilities. *Journal of Applied Behavior Analysis, 25,* 307-315.

Odom, S. L., & Fewell, R. F. (1988). *Peer rating assessment of an integrated preschool class: Stability and concurrent validity of the measure.* Unpublished manuscript.

Odom, S. L., & McConnell, S. R. (1985). A performanced-based conceptualization of social competence of handicapped preschool children: Implications for assessment. *Topics in Early Childhood Special Education, 4*(4), 1-19.

Odom, S. L., & McConnell, S. R. (1992). Improving social competence: An applied behavior analysis perspective. *Journal of Applied Behavior Analysis, 25,* 239-244.

Odom, S. L., McConnell, S. R., & McEvoy, M. A. (1992). Peer-related social competence and its significance for young children with disabilities. In S. Odom, S. McConnell, & M. McEvoy (Eds.), *Social competence of young children with disabilities: Issues and strategies for intervention* (pp. 3-36). Baltimore, MD: Paul Brookes.

Odom, S. L., & McEvoy, M. A. (1988). Integration of young children with handicaps and normally developing children. In S. Odom & M. Karnes (Eds.), *Early intervention for infants and children with disabilities: An empirical base* (pp. 241-267), Baltimore, MD: Paul Brookes.

Odom, S. L., & Watts, E. (1991). Reducing teacher prompts in peer-initiation interventions through visual feedback and correspondence training. *Journal of Special Education, 25,* 26-43.

Peck, C. A., Killen, C. C., & Baumgart, D. (1989). Increasing implementation of special education instruction in mainstreamed preschools: Direct and generalized effects of nondirective consulation. *Journal of Applied Behavior Analysis, 22,* 197- 210.

Skellenger, A. C., Hill, M., & Hill, E. (1992). The social functioning of children with visual impairments. In S. Odom, S. McConnell, & M. McEvoy (Eds.), *Social competence of young children with disabilities: Issues and strategies for intervention* (pp. 165-188). Baltimore, MD: Paul Brookes.

Strain, P. S. (1983). Identification of social skill curriculum targets for severely handicapped children in mainstreamed preschools. *Applied Research in Mental Retardation, 4,* 369-382.

Strain, P. S. (1990). LRE for preschool children with handicaps: What we know, what we should be doing. *Journal of Early Intervention, 14,* 291-296.

Twardosz, S., Nordquist, V. M., Simon, R., & Botkin, D. (1983). The effects of group affection activities on the interaction of socially isolated children. *Analysis and Intervention in Developmental Disabilities, 3,* 311-338.

Zigler, E., & Trickett, P. K. (1978). IQ, social competence, and evaluation of early childhood intervention programs. *American Psychologist, 33,* 789-798.

M. Brambring, H. Rauh, and A. Beelmann (Eds.). (1996). *Early childhood intervention: Theory, evaluation, and practice* (pp. 457-472). Berlin, New York: de Gruyter.

Reduced Complexity of Input: A Basic Principle of Early Intervention in Information-Processing Problems?

Udo B. Brack

I. Introduction

Psychological therapy of deviant behavior in children has a long history. A traditional model is concerned with treatment of symptoms by solving the supposed original conflicts. A later model considers symptoms to be the result of learning processes - in problem behavior and in normal behavior. Therefore, therapy is the attempt to initiate new learning processes (see Figure 1).

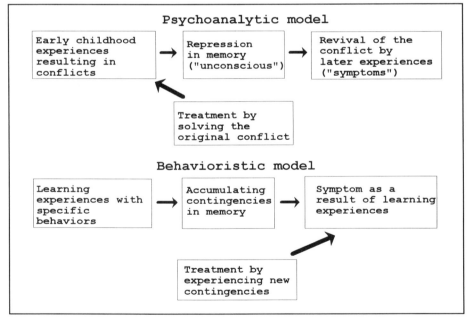

Figure 1.   Two models for the treatment of problem behavior.

Both models were developed originally for behavioral problems, that is, for undesired behavior resulting from critical episodes in the life of the individual. The development of the second model had important consequences: About 30 years ago, some therapists tried to apply it to a completely different problem, that is, to the treatment of developmental retardations. The cause of these retardations are not specific experiences of conflict, but deficits in the maturation of the brain, brain lesions, or even deprivation.

In the field of behavioral disturbances, one distinguishes between conduct disorders and personality disorders. Within developmental retardations, the World Health Organization differentiates between impairment, disability, and handicap (see Table 1).

Table 1.   *Rough Classification of Behavior Disorders and Developmental Retardations*

Disturbed behavior

Conduct disorders   ⟶   Aggressiveness

Personality disorders   ⟶   Anxiety, depression

Developmental retardation

Impairment	Disability	Handicap
Cerebral palsy	Coordination problems	Mobility problems
Language impairment	Dysphasia	Communication problems
Mental deficiency	General intellectual limitations	School achievment problems

Impairment is the organic basis of retardation; disability is the deficit in achieving the specific requirements in everyday life; and handicap is the resulting social consequence, mainly a lack of social integration.

The learning model for treating behavior disorders proved to be effective in training retarded developmental areas as well. There are numerous publications on effective training of language, perceptual discrimination, concept formation, logical reasoning, and so forth.

The most important method used in these trainings is operant conditioning. Typical examples are the various language training programs published over the last 25 years. In these programs, children are confronted with verbal stimuli and, if they react correctly, they are reinforced by food or praise. If the response is wrong, the child is given a verbal prompt. Correct reactions to the prompt are also reinforced (see Figure 2).

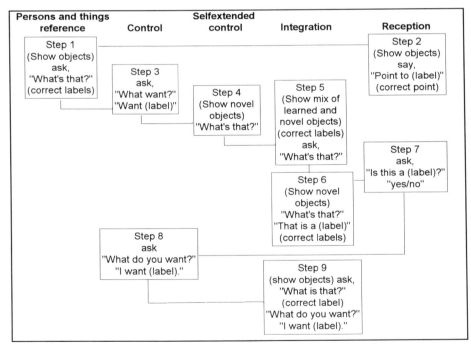

Figure 2.   An excerpt from a traditional language training program (taken from Guess et al., 1976).

Step by step, the structure of demands becomes more complicated. Hence, the child is learning by a shaping procedure, the rationale of which is derived from operant learning and differential reinforcement (see Table 2).

Table 2.   *Part of a Shaping Procedure Within the Main Steps of a Language Training Program (taken from Guess et al., 1976)*

Train to criterion, items:
      1 and 2 (e.g., ball and cup)
      3 and 4
      1, 2, 3, and 4
      Administer skill test (if criterion is reached, proceed to Step 2)
      5 and 6
      7 and 8
      5, 6, 7, and 8
      Administer skill test (if criterion is reached, proceed to Step 2)
      9 and 10
      11 and 12
      9, 10, 11, and 12
      Administer skill test (if criterion is reached, proceed to Step 2)
      13 and 14
      15 and 16
      13, 14, 15, and 16
      Administer skill test (if criterion is reached, proceed to Step 2)

Programming for generalization: Upon completion of the step, a list of trained objects should be given to the student's parents, parent surrogates, teacher(s), etc. Every few days, these individuals should present the same objects to the student and ask, "What's that?" New (nontrained) objects and body parts should be added gradually to the list if the student maintains an acceptable level of performance (above 80%) in labeling the already learned objects. A record of the student's performance should, of course, be kept for review.

Note. If the student fails to reach criterion on the final skill test, you have the option of discontinuing training on this step, and moving the student on to Step 2 or continuing to train randomly chosen sets of four objects to criterion, while also continuing to administer the skill test until the student reaches criterion. This decision depends on whatever reasons you may have for concluding that failure to reach criterion will not prevent progress in Step 2.

But differential reinforcement originally refers to a very restricted mechanism: Reinforcement or punishment (in the Skinnerian meaning) influences only the frequency of behavior. Precisely, it is only behavior that already exists that is made more frequent or infrequent. The basic principle of shaping in this model, strictly speaking, does not create new behavior. Only the natural range of behavior is used to restrict reinforcement to a part of that range and thus to shift behavior in a certain direction. An example: A pigeon is reinforced by food for pressing a key. Now the experimenter can decide to reinforce only responses with the foot and not with the bill, then responses with the left foot only, then responses with the left foot after a response with the right foot, and so forth. Thus, very complex patterns of behavior can be established, but the quality of behavior is not really enhanced. On the other hand, in training programs for retarded children, the task is not to make behavior that is already available more frequent, but to produce more complex classes of behavior. Nevertheless, many of the shaping programs mentioned have proved to be very effective in realizing that aim.

According to the Skinnerian tradition, behavior therapists have attributed that effectiveness mainly to the application of reinforcers. But a lot of experimental results since about 1970 question this argument. Astonishingly, these results have had almost no impact on treatment research in developmental retardation. Therefore, I shall cite two of these investigations published more than 15 years ago:

In the context of the "stimulus overselectivity" phenomenon, Laura Schreibman (1975) published an article entitled "Effects of within-stimulus and extra-stimulus prompting on discrimination learning in autistic children." She trained six autistic children to discriminate two pairs of visual and two pairs of auditory stimuli with only very small differences between the items of each pair. The external prompt consisted of a cue with the index finger in the visual and a buzzer signal in the auditory discrimination. The internal prompt was a sophisticated shaping procedure starting with a very simple discrimination and continuing in extremely small steps (see Figure 3).

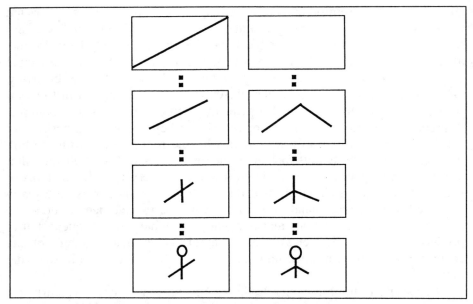

Figure 3.   Four of 15 steps in a visual discrimination training (taken from
                Schreibman, 1975).

In the visual case, training the discrimination of two complex patterns began
with a white card with a wide black diagonal line versus an empty white
card; in other words, the discrimination was simplified by reducing
redundant information to a minimum and stressing the characteristics of the
difference. The main results of the experiment were:

1. Two thirds of the 24 discriminations (6 children, 4 discriminations)
    were not learned without prompting.
2. Discriminations not learned in 60 trials were not learned in 200
    trials either.
3. The internal prompting was much more effective than the external
    one.
4. The external prompting in many cases reduced or even destroyed
    discriminations that had been established already.
5. These results hold for both sensory modalities.

This experiment shows that autistic children with marked perceptual
disabilities could learn the differences between stimuli, not primarily by
reinforcement, but by a sophisticated arrangement of stimulus presentation.

In other words, the irrelevant information was removed, the relevant one was emphasized strongly, and then the irrelevant information was faded in progressively.

To support these findings, Schreibman (1975) carried out an additional experiment with one child who had not learned an auditory discrimination task without prompting. The child first was given external cues but did not learn the discrimination in spite of an enormous number of trials. With internal cues, the child then learned the discrimination very quickly. After that, when external cues were given additionally, the child again unlearned the discrimintion. Finally, the external cue was given while the discriminative stimuli were faded in gradually. After that procedure, the discrimination was established again even when the external cue was removed.

This additional experiment shows that it is not the external cue by itself that interferes with learning, but that the crucial variable for the acquisition of the discrimination is the connection of learning with a gradual increase of the information to be processed by the child or, to put it briefly, the reduced complexity of input.

In 1977, Mary Louise Willbrand published an investigation on a very different topic but on the same problem, namely on "Psycholinguistic theory and therapy for initiating two-word utterances." She worked with dysphasic children, that is, children with severe language retardations but normal nonverbal intelligence. She wrote:

> When children do not exhibit interfering or neurological sensory deficits and when children seem to have been exposed to normal language stimulation the concern is why these children have not demonstrated normal linguistic acquisition. The theoretical assumption was that certain children may be unable to process the vast amount of primary linguistic data that most children cope with. Therefore, the primary data needed to be simplified for these children. (p. 39)

Willbrand (1977) worked on the basis of the so-called pivot grammar: In early language development at the stage of beginning two-word utterances, the words children use can be divided into two classes: a class of many, relatively seldomly used words, the "x-words," and a class of few but very often used words, the "pivots." Children combine these classes to two-word utterances in the form of "pivot + x-word" or "x-word + pivot." The author cites as examples for pivot plus x-word: "see boy," "see sock," "see hot;" and as examples for x-word plus pivot: "boot off," "light off," "show off."

The subjects were 10 children aged between 3 and 4 1/2 years with marked isolated language retardations. They used only a restricted number of single-word utterances. In 45-minute sessions, the therapist played with the children using language that consisted only of pivot structures, for example, "see baby," "see rope," "see ball," "see cookie," "see juice."

Only one pivot like "see" was used until it had been uttered 10 times by the child. Then a second pivot was introduced, and so forth.

The children were praised for all two-word utterances but otherwise no carefully directed operant conditioning was carried out. In other words, the main treatment method consisted of presenting a language with highly reduced content information. Additionally, the adult did not give any demands or questions; he or she used only pivotal constructions and interspersed intervals of silence. In this way, not only the complexity of the verbal input structure but also the number and variety of the adult's utterances were reduced dramatically.

The treatment was very successful. In 7 to 18 sessions, all children progressed to a lot of two-word utterances. Willbrand (1977) stated: "The children created novel utterances and used them spontaneously . . . . All of these children progressed into more advanced stages of language development" (p. 44).

From investigations like that of Schreibman (1975) and Willbrand (1977), we concluded that early developmental retardation that later manifests itself in mental retardation or specific learning disabilities can be described as a deficit of information processing; and that a possible form of treatment is a strong reduction of complexity of input followed by a gradual increase of that complexity.

In an earlier investigation (Brack, 1977), we had already found some interesting data on stimulus processing in retarded children. In a language training program using verbal stimuli and reinforcement of verbal imitation, we applied three levels of stimulus presentation and three levels of reinforcement (see Table 3).

Table 3.   *Effects of Different Types of Stimulus Presentation and Reinforcement on Verbal Limitation*

	Normal children			Retarded children		
Presentation	**A**	**B**	**C**	**A**	**B**	**C**
Mean number of imitations	88.3	93.9[1]	109.2[1]	93.3[1]	107.8[1,2]	117.8[2]
Reinforcement	**I**	**II**	**III**	**I**	**II**	**III**
Mean number of imitations	96.1	95.4[1]	100.0[1]	102.8	108.4	107.2

Note. Presentation: A = independent of attention; B = full attention; C = full attention plus picture. Reinforcement: I = no reinforcement; II = social reinforcement; III = social plus food reinforcement. Analysis of variance, Newman-Keuls Test on differences between pairs of means. Conditions with the same indices are significant $p < .01$ (taken from Brack, 1977).

The presentation of the stimuli, two-word sentences, occurred independently of the attention of the child (I), with the adult waiting until the child was fully attentive (II), and with full attention of the child plus presentation of a picture corresponding to the two-word sentence (III). Reinforcement of correct imitations of the sentence consisted of no reinforcement (A), social reinforcement, that is, a short praise (B), and social plus food reinforcement (C).

To our surprise, we found that within the variable of *reinforcement* there was no difference between no reinforcement and social reinforcement in the normal children; but these children showed a significant increase of imitation with social plus food reinforcement. On the other hand, we could not find the often mentioned dependency on reinforcement and specifically on food reinforcement in retarded children: There was no significant difference between the three types of behavior consequences in these children, the factor "reinforcement" was not at all significant in the analysis of variance; only social reinforcement produced even more (nonsignificant) imitations than social plus food reinforcement!

A similarly important difference holds for the factor of *presentation*. In normal children, there was only a significant effect from full attention to full attention plus additional picture. For the retarded children, however, not only the progress from full attention to full attention plus picture, but also the progress from chance attention to full attention was highly significant.

Thus, we could suppose that retarded children profit less from adequate reinforcement than from a skillful arrangement of the stimuli, that is, the structure of the information to be processed. To test the truth of that conclusion, we carried out some other experiments (see Brack, 1994).

The first investigation was very similar to that of Willbrand (1977). Shortly after (and without knowledge of) the publication of her paper, we also trained children with pivot structures. But we primarily worked with generally mentally retarded children (7 out of 10); only 3 of our children were dysphasic like those of Willbrand's experiment.

First, we transcribed the spontaneous utterances of the children during 45 minutes of play with a reference person. The resulting pivots were used in the following 20 treatment sessions of 45 minutes each. In these sessions, the adult played with the child and spoke in two-word sentences only. These consisted of the individual pivots of the child and one additional word suitable to the toys and pictures at hand. After each of these sentences, the adult introduced an interval of silence lasting at least 10 seconds. After 20 sessions of that treatment, the spontaneous utterances in a free-play situation were recorded once more.

Additionally, the spontaneous language of three of the children was analyzed 2 weeks before treatment to compare the progress without treatment during this interval of time with the progress during a treatment phase of 2 weeks. The *number* of spontaneous utterances during 45 minutes showed considerable intra- and interindividual variation. But there was no statistically significant difference between the means before and after treatment.

The variable we mainly were interested in was the effect of treatment on the *percentage of two-word utterances*. The average increased from 6.5% to 21.8%, which was significant on the .005 level. The progress of the three children controlled during waiting time was clearly smaller (see Table 4).

Table 4.   *Pivot Training*

Child	I	II
1	18.7	40.4
2	0.0	15.9
3	6.3	10.0
4	16.4	45.8
5	0.0	26.0
6	12.0	36.3
7	3.1	10.1
8	8.7	31.4
9	0.0	0.0
10	0.0	2.4
M	6.5	21.8*
SD	7.2	16.3

Note. Percentage of two-word utterances (I) = immediately before treatment; (II) = immediately after treatment. Treatment: 20 sessions of 45 minutes each within 2 weeks; * = $p < .005$; Wilcoxon Signed-Ranks Test.

This means that after twenty 45-minute sessions, that is, in 15 hours, the percentage of two-word utterances was three times the amount before treatment. Evidently the children had profited from the reduced complexity (and perhaps reduced quantity, too) of the language presented to them. It has to be stressed that they did not have to do any training and that neither demands nor reinforcers were given to them. Just the simplification of the input enabled the children to take the information necessary for creating the syntactic structure of two-word sentences.

If we look at the results the question arises whether the specific *pivot pattern* was the active variable or simply the fact that the adult spoke in *two-word sentences* only. Therefore we carried out another experiment that unfortunately failed. The reasons were that we wanted to compare two different pivot trainings and one training with arbitrary two-word sentences within the same children and thus enter too many variables into the experiment; and that the training evidently was too short with ten 30-minute sessions, that is, 5 hours in total; and mainly that we examined children with different types of language retardation, including socially deprived children (see Table 5).

Table 5.   *Overall Effects of Three Types of Reduced Complexity of Input*

		Mean length of utterance		Number of utterances		Number of 2-word sentences		Number of different 1-word sentences		Number of different 2-word sentences	
		b	a	b	a	b	a	b	a	b	a
Experim. group	M	1.14	1.29	123.0	189.7	13.5	19.7	24.0	30.0	5.3	10.5
(n = 6)	SD	.11	.27	115.5	164.2	14.4	18.5	31.7	21.8	6.2	12.2
Control group	M	1.09	1.08	55.5	103.0	1.0	7.5	14.2	21.7	1.0	3.0
(n = 6)	SD	.11	.04	64.7	97.1	1.5	12.8	11.5	16.4	1.5	6.0

Note. 10 sessions of 30 minutes each (b = before, a = after).

Though, in contrast to the control group, the mean length of utterance (MLU), measured in morphemes, increased in the experimental group by about 12% (from 1.14 to 1.29), we had enormous variations. One child, for example, reduced the number of two-word sentences from 30 to 0 (and simultaneously the number of *different* two-word sentences from 15 to 0), but increased the number of different one-word utterances (which might be a first step toward increasing the variety of communication). Other children, on the other hand, showed the expected effects, increasing the total number of two-word sentences and the number of different one-word and two-word sentences.

But we found some progress in the control group, too, because two of the children increased the two-word utterances without treatment from 0 to 14 and from 4 to 31. The other controls remained on their original level.

What we learned from this experiment is that it is evidently necessary to optimize the standardization of treatment conditions for retarded children, to exclude socially deprived children who supposedly profit from every type of stimulation, to make the different sessions similarly interesting for the child, and to carry out enough sessions to allow the treatment variables to produce an effect.

Therefore, in our next experiment, we separated the treatment variables and intensified the training. That could be realized only by a reduction in the number of children examined in the different groups. We matched three groups of four children each to test the clinical relevance of differently structured and simplified presentations of verbal stimulation on the language of retarded children.

Only children who were language-retarded on the basis of a general developmental retardation, evidently caused by a mostly perinatal brain lesion, were selected for the investigation. Children with a clear history of social deprivation and children not producing at least 10 single-word utterances were excluded. Before and after treatment, 45 minutes of spontaneous language in a play situation with a reference person were recorded. The children were carefully matched for the groups by "mean length of utterance" (MLU), age, and "relative language developmental level" (RLDL); the last measure was computed by the formula: (MLU x 100): age in months.

Three conditions of stimulation were compared, which were given in 15 sessions of 45 minutes each (see Table b). The first condition was a traditional behavior therapeutic imitation training (IT) with steps like imitating single words, using these words for naming objects, imitating two-word utterances, and using them for describing pictures. Clearly defined criteria determined the transition from one step to the next one. The second condition was "reduced input" (RI). The therapist, playing with the child, uttered only single words each followed by an interval of silence lasting at least 10 seconds. After the child had produced 20 different single-word utterances, the therapist switched to the presentation of two-word sentences. The third condition was a "pivot training" (PT). Here, too, the therapist first used single words and, after the child had produced 20 different single-word utterances, two-word sentences. In contrast to the second condition, the single words of the therapist were pivots used by the child, starting with the most frequent one. Similarly, the two-word sentences of the therapist consisted of the most frequent pivot of the child combined with an arbitrary word. After children had produced this pivot word 10 times by themselves, the second most frequent pivot was used, and so forth. The effects of treatment on "mean length of utterance" (MLU), "relative language developmental level" (RLDL), number of all utterances, and number of different utterances were measured (see Table 6).

Table 6.   *Comparison of Treatment Effects in Three Measures of Language Complexity and One Measure of Language Quantity*

	Mean length of utterance		Relative language develop- mental level		Number of all utterances		Number of different utterances	
	b	a	b	a	b	a	b	a
Imitation training (n = 4)	1.18 $p < .10$	1.28	2.36 p ---	2.51	73.8 p ---	103.8	22.3 p ---	34.0
Reduced input (n = 4)	1.16 $p < .10$	1.34	2.87 $p < .10$	3.32	93.3 p ---	103.0	27.0 p ---	48.5
Pivot training	1.08 $p < .05$	1.36	2.27 p ---	2.83	86.3 $p < .10$	157.8	15.3 $p < .05$	53.5
Total group	1.14 $p < .005$	1.33	2.50 $p < .005$	2.89	87.8 p ---	118.2	21.5 $p < .005$	45.3

Note. Welch Test and Wilcoxon Signed-Ranks Test (b = before, a = after).

As expected, the overall effect (total group) was highly significant in the three measures of complexity but not in the measure of quantity. When computing the effects within the groups, we had the problem of very small group sizes. But the trends are clearly recognizable: Language training was very effective. The two methods (reduced input and pivot training) using reduced complexity of input, mainly the pivot training (imitation training), seem to be superior to the traditional behavior therapeutic training in the measures of complexity.

Two of the children were available for a continuation of the experiment to test the effects of each respective other treatment technique. One child who was given the behavior therapeutic training in the experiment was then confronted with the reduced input method. The other child, having had the pivot training in the experiment, was then first exposed to the behavior therapeutic training and afterwards to the reduced input method. The trend was the same as in the original experiment: In the relevant variables, the techniques using reduced complexity of input again seemed to be superior to the imitation training.

Finally, we wanted to test whether the principle of reduced complexity of input is successful in other areas of disabilities too. In the past we had treated many children with spelling problems. We saw that teachers at school and mothers during homework gave many extra-stimulus prompts to the children, that is, they confronted them with much irrelevant information by blaming them for mistakes, admonishing them to be attentive, and so forth.

Therefore, we applied a method of reduced complexity of input with seven children with spelling problems as follows: The adult sat in front of the child and dictated a continuous text *word by word* in 15 sessions with 100 words per session. One session required about 15 minutes. If the word was written by the child correctly, the therapist put a coin into a glass as reinforcement and feedback. If the child wrote the word incorrectly, the therapist said "wrong" *in the moment of the formation of the mistake*. In this case, the child had been trained to stop and to try to write the word once more. If the word was now written correctly, the child was given a short praise. If the word was incorrect again, the therapist immediately spelled the word letter by letter. Then the next word was presented and so forth. Except for the dictated words, the occasional short praise (like "mmh"), and sometimes "wrong," the adult did not speak one word to the child during the whole session.

To test the effect of the treatment in a realistic way, we used a continuous text by one author and standardized it by dictating it to five students who showed no spelling problems but were somewhat younger and one grade lower than the subjects in the experiment. This gave us comparable levels of orthography. We compared the number of mistakes in the first two with those in the last two sessions in the experimental and in the control group (see Table 7).

Table 7.   *Results of Training Spelling by Reduced Complexity of Input*

	First 2 sessions (1 + 2)	Last 2 sessions (9 + 10)
Control group (*n* = 7)	56 (25+31)	66 (28+38)
Experimental group (*n* = 7)	49 (23+26)	31 (16+15)

Note. The differences in mistakes in the first and the last two sessions (with 100 words written in each session) between the groups is significant on the .05 level (Chi^2-Test).

To teach spelling by reduced complexity of input seemed to be very effective: Compared with controls, the children in the experimental group reduced the number of mistakes to about half of the expected amount. This result was obtained in only 15 sessions of about 15 minutes each, that is, in less than 4 hours of training.

   Summarizing the results, we consider that treatment of developmentally retarded children taking into consideration the aspect of reduced complexity of input, that is, presenting information adapted to the processing capacity of the retarded child, is a promising procedure.

References

Brack, U. B. (1977). *Spracherwerb und Imitationslernen.* Weinheim: Beltz.

Brack, U. B. (1994). *Überselektive Wahrnehmung bei retardierten Kindern. Befunde zu einer klinischen Fragestellung.* Manuscript submitted for publication.

Guess, D., Sailor, W., Keogh, B., & Baer, D. M. (1976). Language development program for severely handicapped children. In N. G. Haring & L. J. Brown (Eds.), *Teaching the severely handicapped* (Vol. I, pp. 301-324). New York: Grune & Stratton.

Schreibman, L. (1975). Effects of within-stimulus and extra-stimulus prompting on discrimination learning in autistic children. *Journal of Applied Behavior Analysis, 8,* 91-112.

Willbrand, M. L. (1977). Psycholinguistic theory and therapy for imitating two-word utterances. *British Journal of Disorders of Communication, 12,* 37-46.

M. Brambring, H. Rauh, and A. Beelmann (Eds.). (1996). *Early childhood intervention: Theory, evaluation, and practice* (pp. 473-487). Berlin, New York: de Gruyter.

Early Childhood Intervention Through Play

Rolf Oerter

1 A Dilemma: Play and Learning

Most attempts to enhance child development occur through one or the other form of play. Play is used as a situation that seems meaningful to the child/infant and provides fun. So play seems to be the ideal medium for intervention in early childhood. One should, however, bear in mind that the child does not play in order to learn but plays without any purpose outside of play. This is already true for the first kind of play, the mastery play in early infancy. Although the child obviously improves since the motor skills he or she is engaged in mastery play, enjoying the one-sided assimilation (Piaget, 1969). In later years, it is often observed that children play at a lower cognitive level than in other tasks (Tolicic, 1963). For this reason, Piaget considered play to be different from the equilibrium processes in intellectual development. He describes play by the domination of the assimilation process. So we can claim that the child does not play in order to learn something or to develop further. Rather, the child pretends to develop: For example, he or she pretends to be a strong powerful adult, a superman, or an attractive woman. Learning through play thus seems to be more or less a by-product rather than the main outcome of play.

On the other hand, adults especially in intervention programs, utilize well-defined plans and schedules for learning through play. Play is used intentionally as an instrument for learning. This seems to be a contradiction. As soon as a child becomes aware that play is a learning situation, the frame of play disappears. How, then, can play be used for intervention? What are the conditions for successful intervention through play?

2 Starting From Play: Another Perspective

I shall attempt to present a perspective in which we start from play and its typical characteristics. This also means that we have to understand play better, and that we have to start from a theory of play. In the following, I shall adopt an action-theoretical approach, because it seems especially fruitful for intervention procedures.

I shall try to answer questions like: What is the structure of play? In which pathways does play work? How can we utilize play for intervention? I shall begin with three main criteria of play: (a) self-reinforcing effects of play behavior (intrinsic motivation); (b) the frame of play: change of reality-reference; and (c) repetition and rituals.

2.1 Self-Reinforcement

In play, action itself is reinforcing. As long as the child is attracted by the play situation, no other additional motivation such as achievement or affiliation motivation is necessary. Actually, other motivational components are often involved, especially in social play, but they are not a necessary condition for play. The self-reinforcing quality of play is in many cases an experience of flow (Csikszentmihalyi, 1975).

2.2 The Frame of Play

Since Bateson's description of play as the construction of a frame in which action is put as something else, play is understood as a frame in which another reality is constructed (Bateson, 1972; Bretherton, 1984; Leslie, 1987). The change of reality is assumed to occur not only in symbolic play or role play. Even a simple sensorimotor play changes the reality reference: For example, a Piagetian task of object permanence becomes a funny social interaction in which the child quickly removes hidden objects and observes the adult's reaction (a situation I experienced with my grandson).

2.3 Repetition and Rituals

The third criterion results partially from the self-reinforcing power of play and partially from the change of reality reference. Self-reinforcement of play action also means that the tendency to repeat the action increases. Repetition itself, on the other hand, is a reinforcer if the child interprets action as play. Rituals in repetitive actions give them a clearer profile, a good "Gestalt," and simultaneously make them outstanding events. In this respect, rituals in play resemble those of religion and manners and customs. Furthermore, rituals and repetitions are governed by rules that are attractive in play, whereas they are often rejected outside of play. Although rules are found in every kind of play, they receive their most articulated form in games.

3   Some Consequences for Intervention

The criteria described above can be used to derive some preliminary consequences for intervention. First, as long as the child remains in play, repetition is nearly unlimited and only restricted by fatigue, which, of course, is a substantial factor for some cases of disability. If the child abandons repetition, the specific form of play is finished, and the child may move to another play or to another kind of activity. Second, the frame of play can be maintained best if there is a theme of play (topic) that determines the single actions of the child. If the child invents a message "this is play" or "we are going to play" (to pretend), or if the child agrees to such a message proposed by another person, it is easier for him or her to maintain action and action repetition. Third, the completion of action is a crucial goal to be aimed at. I shall demonstrate this last aspect with three examples.

3.1 Completion of Action

In mastery play in early infancy, the infant repeats a complete action several times. The character of play is maintained only if each of these actions is really finished before the next action starts, because the effect of an action is also a stimulus for the next one, or, to put it in a less behavioristic way, the course of an action with its beginning, progress, and end is the experience the child wants to repeat. Another example for the necessity of completing an action is the so-called activation circle first mentioned by Heckhausen (1963-1964). Some interactive play is characterized by a gradual increase in arousal up to a peak followed by a sudden drop. Of course, this enjoying circle of arousal only occurs if the whole action is completed. A third example is the handling of objects. Building a tower with blocks, moving a car to a toy garage, or using a hammer are actions that should be completed in an appropriate way. The aspect of action completion is, as we shall see later, an important guideline for intervention with handicapped children.

3.2 Reality Transformation and Rituals

As already mentioned, reality transformation is crucial for play, and it is assumed to occur in every kind of play. The most common case is symbolic play or pretend play. In the second year of life, parents usually introduce play interaction in which some kind of "as-if" transformation is provided. It is important to realize that this occurs mostly when the child does not yet understand what the adult's pretending means. So he or she might look very surprised when confronted with a doll or a toy animal that seems to speak or to feel. On the other hand, all observations of infants show that a self-centered transformation of reality occurs very early (Belsky & Most, 1981; McCune-Nicolich & Carroll, 1981; Piaget, 1969). As Elkonin (1980) has shown, children are able to engage in differentiated and complex action within the frame of a play theme, since they can always orient the action toward this frame (theme, subject). This is in accordance with the theory of pretend play presented by Harris and Kavenaugh (1993), claiming that children give objects a new label within the play frame and remove this label again after play is finished. From this research, we can draw one important conclusion for intervention with infants: It is easier for the child to perform a sequence of actions within a whole frame (e.g., script) than to train each action separately and unconnectedly. Of course, at the beginning, the sequence of action must be short and the frame must be a simple one. Examples of play themes are: cooking, dining, making a visit, organizing a party. The question is whether handicapped children are able to understand a play frame proposed by a social partner. We know that mentally retarded children have greater difficulties in engaging in symbolic play. Therefore, the play frame should be scaffolded by visible objects like dolls, clothes, and tools belonging to the play action. In the special case of handicapped children, a high degree of realism of objects is necessary.

With regard to rituals, both the adult partner and the child should perform language, gestures, and movements in an exaggerated way in order to give the sequence a good profile. This is already done by parents of normally developing children, and children like this kind of performance especially when it is accompanied by emotional arousal up to a peak.

4   Common Object Relationships

Most play, especially with handicapped children, can be described as shared actions that are directed toward a common object. In the simplest case, the object is a material object like a toy. But in every play situation, the play theme (subject) is the more important, common "object." A general formula for a shared object relation in play as elsewhere is

$$P1 \rightarrow O \leftarrow P2.$$

Two or more persons are directing their actions toward a common "object." In play, there are many objects that support a common object relationship, such as a seesaw, a carousel, a play house, and, of course, role play. Material objects stimulate a common object relation if they offer action possibilities that coordinate two or more persons, as is the case in the above- mentioned seesaw or carousel. Other objects like a toy car often prevent common relationship because they elicit conflicts as a result of every participant wanting to have the object and manipulate it for him- or herself. Thus, the selection of objects is very important for starting and maintaining play with common object relationships. In parallel play, children avoid conflict by each handling a separate object but often producing the same action with the object. So in intervention, the transition from solitary play to social play often may use parallel play as a kind of interaction that already provides some understanding of the common object relation.

4.1 An Action Grammar

With handicapped children, it seems useful to analyze forms of shared object-related play. Figure 1 presents some descriptions of simple shared relationships that form a sort of "action grammar." Five shared object relations are selected: verbal comments on an action, asking for help, asking for an action, showing the partner one's own action (look what I am doing), and to trick (feint) the other. All these examples were observed in infant play during the second year of life.

   One of the purposes of such an "action grammar" is to get a clearer diagnosis of disturbance of action. In case of disturbance of social interaction, we can analyze where the problem should be allocated. So in our example "asking for help" in which a child wants assistance in handling an object, one can analyze whether the adult understands what the child (P1) wants (arrow from P1 to P2) or whether the adult fails to assist in a better handling of the object (arrow from P2 to O or to the arrow P1 ---> O). Finally, P2 may assist before P1 asks for help (no arrow between P1 and P2). All that was said so far about action completion, reality transformation, and repetition as well as rituals becomes more important in the system of common object relationship. Actually, meaningful intervention can be realized only within this system. Both partners have to engage in actions that are related through the same object (theme, contents).

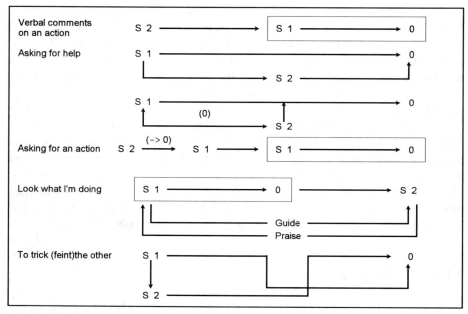

Figure 1. The common object relationship of simple actions.

4.2 Three Forms of Disturbance

More generally, three types of disturbance of the common object relationship exist:

The actions toward the object are not well tuned. In motor play, for example, the movements may not be tuned appropriately to the object, like tipping a seesaw, rolling a ball, or turning a carousel. Another example is that the child does not perform the complementary action within the shared object relation, for example, getting a block necessary for the construction of a building or playing a complementary role in a role play.

Different definition (understanding) of the "object." The mother may treat the doll appropriately, but the child may use it as a hammer. The mother may construct a tower with blocks, but the child may prefer to move the blocks in a row like a train. We videotaped the interaction between a mother and her 18-month-old daughter handling a plastic box that could be opened. The mother offered many action alternatives for handling the object, but not the one the child wanted. Finally, the mother incidentally opened the box and the child could realize her own intention of putting something into the box.

Uncomplete and holistic action. Sometimes the child does not make a distinction between object and partner. In other cases, actions and objects are unseparated.

> *Example:* We observed a play scene between a mother and her 3-year-old daughter in which they pretended to fly and to look outside the plane. The child interpreted the mother as the plane and simultaneously as a partner in the plane, whereas the mother was pretending to be a passenger in the plane showing the child the scenery outside. The child was sitting between her mother's legs, putting them around herself and demonstrating that she wanted to ensure that she was in the plane, which she pretended to be her mother. This behavior was a key for the relation between mother and child, the latter being too strongly attached to the mother.

4.3 Zone of Proximal Development

The common object relationship is also the basis for providing the zone of proximal development through play. In play interaction, the more competent partner is able to enhance development in many ways. According to Vygotski (1978, p. 86) the zone of proximal development can be understood as "the distance between the actual developmental level as determined by independent problem-solving and the level of potential development under adult guidance or in collaboration with more capable peers." Beyond the possibilities already mentioned, new skills and schemes or scripts can be trained. The adult partner introduces, for example, a new script of role play and teaches the role to be taken by the child. After a while, roles are switched, and the child learns the complementary role. Because action sequences in everyday life as well as in play are ordered according to scripts, a child does not learn specific concrete actions but more general schemes of action sequences that can be adapted to a concrete scene negotiated in a common play. More generally, within the zone of proximal development, a broad variety of skills can be fostered through play. Especially social communication skills, social cognition, and conflict resolution can be trained in a natural way within play.

5. Theoretical Extensions: Three Levels of Action in Play

Following Leont'ev's (1977) [german spelling: Leontjev, cf. references] division of activity into three levels, it is useful to distinguish between play activity, play action, and play operation. So far we have discussed play action, that is, the overt goal-directed action of the child and the adult partner in play. Play theory as it is used here assumes, however, one level above and one level below this overt action. The upper level is usually called activity (in German *Tätigkeit*).

5.1 The Level of Activity: The Meaning of Play

This level is related to the motive of play, for example, to the question why the child plays at all. Freud (1920) und Erikson (1978) have claimed that play enables the child to master the situation and to add an active counterpart to passive experience (Freud, 1932, p. 202). Play governed by the principle of pleasure handles negative or traumatic experience in a satisfying way. Vygotski (1980) also assumes that the child realizes wishes in play that cannot be fulfilled in reality outside of play. Those wishes, however, are more generalized affects, for example, the wish to be big and strong. Even Piaget (1969), whose work on play is often reported incompletely, understands play as unbalanced assimilation. In contrast to intelligence, in which equilibrium is constructed at increasingly higher levels, play activity is the defense against the world of adults and of the general reality that disturbs "the world of the I" (Piaget, 1969, p. 216). In nearly all our observations of children's play, we have found those one-sided assimilations or, to put it another way, vicarious wish fulfilment lying behind the play action.

In summary, activity mediates as subjective meaning for the child's (a) heightened self-experience and thus self-enhancement, and (b) mastery of reality.

5.2 Operations

The lowest levels in play (as in other forms of action) are operations that consist of already automatized and mastered skills. They are used in play action in order to reach a goal, to fulfill an intention, and to complete an action. Play action as well as other actions can be performed only if a sufficient number of operations are available that allow the child to realize the action. The performance of a sensorimotor play, for instance, demands a series of coordinated movements that have already been acquired and automatized. Building houses or towers with blocks is possible only if the child posseses some knowledge about physical laws and is able to use the necessary sensorimotor coordination. Finally, shared object relations demand in most cases verbal communication. Therefore, language must be acquired as a set of operations to a certain degree.

Figure 2 presents an overview of the three characteristics and the three levels of play.

Three characteristics
        self-reinforcing property of play:
           intrinsic motivation, flow
        Repetition, rituals:
           no boredom, low effort, salience
        Reality transformation:
           change toward an invented
           frame of reference
           egocentric, in social play
           serving common interests

Levels of action in play
        Motive and meaning of play; non conscious
        Two functions related to each other
           a) Self-enhancement
           b) Mastery of reality
        Action: Overt, goal-directed, and
                  object-related; conscious
        Operation: Automatized skills, low effort,
                  no memory space; non conscious

Figure 2.   Characteristics and levels of action in play.

5.3 Enhancement of Operations

As already emphasized by Robby Case (1984), the training of automatized cognitive processes is very important for mentally handicapped children. Case argues that the working memory of retarded children is overloaded, and its functioning can be improved through training automatized cognitive processes that do not need space in working memory. As a general rule, more processes have to be automatized with retarded than with normal children, because the working memory of retarded children is impaired. In a similar vein, motor and sensory operations are needed as skills. However, the training of operations of automatized skills places a double burden on handicapped children, because they need (a) a higher amount of automatized skills and (b) more repetitions for the acquisition of operations. Play could be an excellent medium for training those operations if we manage to maintain a play frame in which actions can be repeated as often as necessary. To tell it once more, this is only possible if a kind of reality transformation is provided in play.

In many cases of training operations, the intervention program is planned according to a logic of information processes. In any domain, this kind of orientation leads to a system of processes or skills to be trained. Play-oriented intervention would proceed the other way around: It would start with play themes and play objects relevant for infants and/or preschoolers. These themes offer a broad variety of actions that need skills, scripts, and verbal competencies. The variety of play corresponds to the variety of reality that surrounds the child, including the reality presented by television and other media. Even special deficits could be covered in normal play activity if we use the component of repetition and ritual extensively. The advantage of this kind of orientation is that the child is engaged in meaningful activity. This aspect has to be treated next.

5.4 The Level of Activity in Intervention

At first glance, it seems that the level of activity is not of major importance with handicapped children. Especially at the early age of infancy, it seems unlikely that such children try to cope with traumatic experience and/or socialization pressure through play. The importance of the activity level becomes clearer when we realize the meaning of play as postulated by Freud, Vygotski, Piaget, as well as others up to two points (see, also, Table 2): (a) the function of play as a medium of increased self-awareness and heightened self-experience and (b) play activity as a way of mastering reality. Play as a source of pleasure is connected with the first aspect, providing positive emotions and, as a consequence, self-enhancing properties. It is clear that this component is in any case important for handicapped children, since they can overcome restrictions of self-experience in everyday life. The self-concept of those children is often not as highly developed as with normal children. Furthermore, the lack of opportunity to receive positive self-awareness may lead to lower self-esteem from a very early age. Play in the meaning defined above would be an excellent instrument to mediate new kinds of self-experience including feedback on one's own abilities and skills. Thus, providing play activity may be the main source for establishing a positive self-concept. Two examples might illustrate this.

One is taken from the case study of a blind infant reported by Brambring (1993). At the age of 13;6 months, a blind infant explores her environment by turning around and grasping objects behind her. She then follows a rolling board moved by her father. These performances were reported as being a remarkable progress. What the infant gains from these successful actions at the activity level is a self-enhancing experience consisting of a new kind of control over her own body and over the environment.

The second example concerns an infant videotaped by chance. A blind infant was sitting near her mother who left her in frustration after failing to stimulate some shared action. The therapist approached and sat down near the infant, getting into communication with her. The child relaxed and began to softly kick the legs of the therapist, who kicked back. So a sort of interactive play developed. This play is, beyond fun and social contact, an experience of self-enhancement for the infant and a contribution to a positive self-concept in a world that is strange and frightening for the child (Franz Peterander, oral report).

The second aspect of play activity, mastering reality, is also an important component of infant's play. With normally developing children (Oerter, 1993), we could show that even 18-month-old infants express their needs and wishes in play.

Example: An infant plays with the experimenter bathing a doll. He uses the receiver of a toy telephone as a shower head, but is very reluctant to hold it over the doll. After some repetitions, the experimenter persuades the child to pretend to take a shower himself. The child hesitates, then holds the shower head only very briefly over himself. After that, he repeats the pretended action several times showing more security and joy.

The mother of the child informed us that the boy did not like to be washed and showered. His attempt to master the situation in play was obvious and visible at an early time of development.

Another example is a 21-month-old infant pretending to have a telephone call with his mother. The boy pretends to be the father at work telling the mother that he will come home only very late this evening. The mother pretends to be very sad about this news and asks: "So I'll only see you tomorrow morning?" The infant answers: "Yes," showing also an expression of sorrow.

In this scene, the child tries to cope with the situation that the father often comes home very late when the child has already gone to sleep.

Pretending to be the father himself provides more control over the situation, because now the child himself can determine his arrival. But, even then, he expresses his negative feelings about the situation.

Now the question arises whether handicapped children also can express their problems through play. If we look at children with sensory and motor handicaps, this is certainly the case. Many of these children develop quite well mentally but experience a high degree of traumatic events. The main experience is that the world around them is not constructed for their capabilities (i.e., action possibilities). Unlike normal children, the affordances (Gibson, 1982) of the environment are very restricted, and, in many respects, the child is not able to realize his or her intention. Furthermore, the socialization pressure of the environment is much higher than with normal children, because learning is more difficult and frustrating for handicapped children. Consequently, we have to assume that these children have a high need to reduce this stressful experience. A main method for mastering the situation could be play activity. In play, children with sensory and motor handicaps can express their needs, change their reality into a wishful situation, and look for vicarious solutions. Although such solutions are illusionary, and also mediate only an illusionary control of the situation, the child gets relief from the imbalance accentuating processes of assimilation. Especially for these children, play at the activity level could offer a way of reaching or maintaining psychological hygiene. Since play activity is mostly embedded in a common object relationship as described above, it occurs in an atmosphere of warmth and appropriate feedback. The perspective of play activity changes the view of intervention. If we give way to the play intentions of the child, we shall often find actions that do not seem to be very appropriate or useful for enhancing development. We have to take the standpoint that play in the first place probably serves other motives than enhancement of development. Fostering development is probably only a by-product (Smith, 1982; Vandenberg, 1986). As long as we view general psychological health as more important than the fostering of specific functions, we have to look at the level of play activity and the fulfilment of wishes lying behind overt play action.

What about mentally retarded children? Developmental research shows that they have difficulties in engaging in symbolic play or even in role play. As mentioned earlier, play activity goes beyond pretend play and is viewed theoretically as a leading power in every play. So if we start intervention with mentally retarded children through play in infancy, we can encourage forms of play that do not need representation in the complicated way that is necessary for pretend play. On the other hand, pretend play is a key for higher mental activities and should therefore be activated in any case. I have already described how pretend play usually is introduced to the child. The mother or care person suggests some play with a doll or a toy animal, thus providing a model for the child. In most cases, the care person starts with this kind of play at a time when the child is unable to understand what is meant by pretending. Papousek (1991), for example, found out that mothers nearly always introduce pretending to 10-month-old infants regularly. Therefore, the normally developing infant experiences a similar situation as the retarded child who is introduced to pretend play by a model. Since mentally retarded infants have much greater difficulties in activating representations and still more difficulties in representing a transformed reality, play intervention should focus on the introduction of pretend play much more than with normal children. Unfortunately, in most cases the opposite is true: Mentally retarded children are not encouraged to engage in pretend play.

6   Summary and Conclusions

Figure 3 presents an overview of the main theoretical aspects discussed above and the consequences for intervention in infancy.

 If one starts from a theory of play based on an action approach, one fact should be considered important for intervention through play: Intervention can only operate directly at the level of overt action. The influence of intervention upon other levels of play is only indirect. It works via repetition and acceleration toward the establishment of automatized operations and via reality transformation and rituals toward the activity level.

 Finally, I shall sketch two golden rules as recommendations for intervention through play.

 The first recommendation is to start with the infant's object relation. As already described, overt action can be seen as a person-object relationship. Within this context, the term "object" means (a) a material object (e.g., a toy spoon), (b) this object embedded in the situational context (e.g., a toy spoon near a plate), and (c) the play theme (topic) for this object (e.g., pretending to eat soup). If one is close to the infant's object reference, intervention can follow the pathways the infant prefers, but still introduce aspects of enhancement of development such as object permanence, naming objects, scripts of handling objects, and so forth. This procedure also leads to the reduction of complexity in a natural and ecologically valid way.

The second recommendation follows from the first one: The infant's object relation should be transformed into a shared object relationship. Or, even

Self-reinforcing properties of play:
      Maintenance of activity
Repetition:
      Training without effort
Reality transformation:
      Maintenance of play and hence its reinforcing function and
      facilitating effect of training
Overt action:
      Completion of action
      Stimulation of shared object relations
Operation:
      Training of skills
      Automatization of action
Activity:
      Balancing the stressful experience of restricted
      action possibilities, high socialization pressure,
      and frustration

Note: Intervention can only work at the (conscious) level of action. The impact upon the
         two other levels acts indirectly via action(e.g., toward operations through repetition;
         toward activity through reality transformation).

Figure 3.   Intervention through play: An overview.

better: The object relationship in play should be established in advance as a shared object relationship. This shared relationship forms a system in which the infant and the adult person or peers are involved.

In a basic way, this is what Kempler (1969; see Simeonsson, this volume) has called a *complete encounter*. A complete encounter is not a perfect state of harmony and goodness of fit, but rather a dynamic system in which both or more partners negotiate and try to maintain play, enjoying the increase and decrease of shared emotional arousal.

References

Bateson, G. (1972). A theory of play and phantasy. In G. Bateson (Ed.), *Steps to an ecology of mind* (pp. 177-193). Aylesbury, England: Chandler.

Belsky, J., & Most, R. K. (1981). From exploration to play: A cross-sectional study of infant free play behavior. *Developmental Psychology, 17*, 630-639.

Brambring, M. (1993). *"Lehrstunden" eines blinden Kindes. Entwicklung und Frühförderung in den ersten Lebensjahren.* München: Ernst Reinhardt Verlag.

Bretherton, I. (1984). Representing the social world in symbolic play . In I. Bretherton (Ed.), *Symbolic play* (pp. 3-41). London: Academic Press

Case, R. (1984). The process of stage transition: A neo-Piagetian view. In R. J. Sternberg (Ed.), *Mechanisms of cognitive development* (pp. 19-44). San Francisco: Freeman.

Csikszentmihalyi, M. (1975). *Beyond boredom and anxiety.* San Francisco: Jossey-Bass.

Elkonin, D. (1980). *Psychologie des Spiels.* Köln: Pahl-Rugenstein.

Erikson, E. H. (1978). *Kinderspiel und politische Phantasie.* Frankfurt:.

Freud, S. (1920). *Jenseits des Lustprinzips.* (Vol. Ges. Werke, 13). London: Hogarth.

Freud, S. (1932). *Concerning the sexuality of woman* (Vol. 1). In Psychoanalytic Quarterly (Ed.).

Gibson, J. J. (1982). *Wahrnehmung und Umwelt.* München: Urban & Schwarzenberg.

Harris, P. L., & Kavanaugh, R. D. (1993). Young children's understanding of pretense. *Monographs of the Society for Research in Child Development, 58*(1).

Heckhausen, H. (1963-1964). Entwurf einer Psychologie des Spiels. *Psychologische Forschung, 27*, 225-243.

Leontjev, A. N. (1977). *Tätigkeit, Bewußtsein, Persönlichkeit.* Stuttgart: Klett. [English spelling: Leont'ev]

Leslie, A. M. (1987). Pretense and representation: The origins of "Theory of Mind." *Psychological Review, 94*(4), 412-426.

McCune-Nicolich, L., & Carroll, S. (1981). Development of symbolic play. Implications for the language specialist. *Topics in Language Disorders, ?*, 1-15.

Oerter, R. (1993). Kinderspiel. In M. Markefka & B. Nauck (Eds.), *Handbuch der Kindheitsforschung* (pp. 377-388). Neuwied: Luchterhand.

Oerter, R. (1993). *Psychologie des Spiels. Ein handlungstheoretischer Ansatz.* München: Quintessenz.

Papousek, M. (1991). *Vorsprachliche Kommunikation zwischen Mutter und Kind als Wegbereiter der Sprachentwicklung.* Unpublished postdoctoral dissertation, University of Munich, Germany.

Piaget, J. (1969). *Nachahmung, Spiel und Traum.* Stuttgart: Klett.

Smith, P. K. (1982). Does play matter? Functional and evolutionary aspects of animal and human play. *The Behavioral and Brain Sciences, 5*, 139-184.

Tolicic, I. (1963). Die wechselseitige Beziehung zwischen Spielverhalten und geistiger Entwicklung von Kindern. *Schule und Psychologie, 10*, 225-233.

Vandenberg, B. (1986). Play, myth and hope. In R. van der Kooij & J. Hellendoorn (Eds.), *Play, play therapy, play research* (pp. 77-87). Berwyn, IL: Swets North America. Lisse: Swets & Zeitlinger.

Vygotski, L. S. (1978). *Mind in society: The development of higher psychological processes.* Cambridge, MA: Harvard University Press.

Vygotski, L. S. (1980). Das Spiel und seine Rolle in der menschlichen Entwicklung. In D. Elkonin (Ed.), *Psychologie des Spiels.* Köln: Pahl-Rugenstein. (Original work published 1933)

M. Brambring, H. Rauh, and A. Beelmann (Eds.). (1996). *Early childhood intervention: Theory, evaluation, and practice* (pp. 488-503). Berlin, New York: de Gruyter.

Preparing Early Intervention Professionals for the 21st Century

Don Bailey

1 Introduction

As early intervention programs for young children with disabilities have expanded in recent years, increased attention has been directed toward the preparation of early intervention professionals (Bailey, 1989). A high-quality program can be achieved only when the adults responsible for the program have the skills necessary to plan and implement an individualized, developmentally appropriate, and effective set of services for each child and family. In recognition of this fact, several major efforts have been initiated in the United States. For example, the Division for Early Childhood of the Council for Exceptional Children has published a set of competencies that should be expected of all early childhood special educators (McCollum et al., 1989). Other professional organizations, such as the American Speech and Hearing Association (ASHA, 1989), have also published statements regarding recommended competencies. Stimulated by extensive federal funding and the demands of federal legislation, a large number of special education departments now have special tracks for preparing early childhood special educators, and nearly every state has established a teaching certificate especially designed for work with children under 6 years of age who have disabilities. Although it is now typical for most states to have several colleges and universities with early childhood special education training programs, a focus on young children is rarely seen in other disciplines, with the most likely exceptions being speech and hearing sciences and school psychology.

These efforts have largely been effective in improving the supply of qualified special education professionals, although shortages still exist in the allied health professions. Unlike 10 years ago, when many professionals working in early intervention at best had a degree in mental retardation or some other categorical area, the majority of special education professionals today have or are working on a more appropriate early childhood certificate. Despite these advances, however, it is the thesis of this paper that most training programs are not designed to prepare professionals in education and other key disciplines to accommodate to the changing demands of early intervention reflected in major philosophical shifts in our field. To illustrate this point, I describe three themes that characterize contemporary movements in early intervention. Data and examples illustrating the shortcomings of traditional training programs are provided. I conclude with a number of suggestions for revamping personnel preparation efforts so that professionals will be more adequately prepared for work in the 21st century.

2   Trends in Early Intervention

As with any new field, early intervention today finds itself in the middle of a changing ecology. New laws, emerging philosophical ideas, the escalation of low birthweight and premature children, the rapid rise of children affected by AIDS and maternal substance abuse, advocacy movements, and research findings all contribute to ongoing discussions about the nature, intent, and focus of early intervention. Most of these debates represent a complex interaction of values, practical considerations, and empirical research. Although they vary in nature and complexity, these debates inevitably have important implications for personnel preparation.

Examples of changing perspectives on what constitutes quality in an early intervention program are abundant. However three key areas are central to professional practice and provide a substantial challenge for traditional ways of preparing personnel: (a) the movement toward family-centered services; (b) the integration of children with disabilities into programs serving normally developing children; and (c) the provision of specialized services in an integrated and developmentally appropriate fashion.

2.1 The Movement to Family-Centered Services

One of the most significant shifts in early intervention over the past decade has been the change in views about parent-professional relationships. Although early intervention programs have always felt a close alliance with families, the nature of that relationship has changed over the years. Initially parents were viewed as teachers of their children. Thus the primary role of professionals vis-a-vis parents was to "educate" parents as to the proper way of teaching or perhaps even providing therapeutic activities for their children. The parent's role was to learn from the professional and to faithfully carry out instructional and therapeutic activities at home. In recent years, this view of the parent-professional relationship has been replaced by a "family-centered" philosophy (Bailey, 1987; Dunst, 1985; Dunst, Trivette & Deal, 1988). Based in part on data, in part on advocacy movements, and in part on legislation, this perspective argues that family support is one of the most fundamentally important goals of early intervention. However, family support is redefined as a process by which professionals seek to (a) learn about and respond to each family's resources, priorities, and concerns; (b) identify and support the roles that families want to play in the decision-making process; and (c) provide comprehensive child and family services in a coordinated fashion. The ultimate goal is to help families achieve their goals and to feel competent as parents and decision makers.

To what extent are professionals being prepared to fill this important role? Unfortunately, data from a number of sources suggest that such training is inadequate. A set of national surveys of more than 500 college and university training programs in the 10 different disciplines found that, with the exception of nursing, social work, and early childhood special education, the typical student receives little training in working with families (Bailey, Simeonsson, Yoder, & Huntington, 1990). For example, the typical student in occupational or physical therapy was reported to receive only 3 to 6 clock hours of classroom-based instruction on information about families. Even in early childhood special education, where the average master's degree student receives nearly 50 hours of classroom instruction on families, we found that students received few practical opportunities to work with families during their clinical internships (Bailey, Palsha, & Huntington, 1990). Two major reasons cited were the need to focus more directly on child-related skills, as well as the reluctance of community programs to allow students to work with families in any significant ways. These findings have been replicated in more detailed studies of training programs within individual states (e.g., Hanson & Lovett, 1992).

The results of this limited focus on training to work with families is evident in several studies of practicing professionals. Bailey et al. (1991), for example, found that although therapists and special education teachers valued work with families, they felt more skilled in working with children and expressed many concerns about the movement to family-centered practices. Bailey et al. (1992), in a study of early intervention professionals in four states, found that the professionals reported significant discrepancies between typical and desired practices in working with families, a finding also reported in other hospital-based and early intervention settings (e.g., Brown & Ritchie, 1990; Mahoney & O'Sullivan, 1990; Rushton, 1990).

Data from these studies point to the first key challenge for personnel preparation programs that have traditionally prepared professionals to work with children. How can they include all of the information and practical experiences needed to work effectively with children with complex disabilities and also provide substantive training in the competencies needed to work with families? This challenge expands as professionals must work with an array of families that are highly diverse with respect to culture, race, income, personal resources, support systems, age, and cognitive abilities.

2.2 Integrating Children With Disabilities Into Programs Serving Typically Developing Children

A second challenge for personnel preparation programs is the movement to integrate children with disabilities into programs serving typically developing children. This movement is not a new one, tracing its roots back to the normalization and deinstitutionalization movement in the 1960s (Wolfensberger, 1972). In the 25 or so years since that time, we have witnessed a gradually increasing tendency in the US toward integration, variously referred to as mainstreaming or the currently popular term "inclusion." The rationale for inclusion is based in part on an explicit value of normalized experiences. Legislation in the US has continued to emphasize placement of school-age children in the "least restrictive environment," and, for infants, placement is recommended in community programs in which the child would ordinarily participate if she or he did not have a disability. Research continues to show that children with a wide array of disabilities can be integrated successfully if provided proper support, and a recent review of comparative studies provides clear evidence that mainstreaming settings are superior to segregated settings in promoting social skills and play behavior (Buysse & Bailey, 1993).

If taken to its full extent, mainstreaming will mean dramatically different roles for early childhood special educators and therapists. Many already are being called upon to serve as consultants to regular early childhood programs rather than teach in their own program or provide therapy in a clinic (Coleman et al., 1991). This consultant role will likely involve a range of activities, including working with teachers and parents to identify the most appropriate mainstreamed setting, providing advice and support for regular early childhood educators and paraprofessionals who are not familiar with disabilities, and occasionally providing special individualized or group activities to supplement the regular center activities or to provide a model for the early childhood teacher. In another scenario, the early intervention specialist may work directly as a teacher, therapist, or director in an integrated program. This would undoubtedly require work and care for normally developing children as well as children with disabilities.

In either scenario, it is unlikely that current personnel preparation programs are adequately preparing teachers for inclusion. In schools of education, for example, early childhood and early childhood special education traditionally have operated separate and independent programs. Students preparing to work with normally developing children rarely receive information or experience related to disability. Likewise, students in early childhood special education usually learn comparatively little about normal child development or about designing and operating a "typical" child care program. Students in allied health professions spend most of their practice time in clinics or hospitals, rarely seeing typical child care settings. Furthermore, almost all training programs are so preoccupied with preparing students for their own special teaching or therapy roles that little if any attention is paid to the expertise required to be a good consultant. Buysse and Wesley (in press) suggest that the merger of consultant and service provider roles in the context of integrated settings is likely to result in role conflicts, role overload, and role ambiguity. Training programs will need to help students develop a professional identify that is consistent with this expanding range of professional roles and must teach the skills needed to fill these roles successfully.

2.3 Providing Integrated Services

A third arena challenging traditional personnel preparation is the need to provide services in a coordinated, integrated, and interdisciplinary fashion, a challenge that is evident at multiple levels (Bailey, 1992). At the community level, it is clear that numerous agencies and programs have responsibility for serving children and families. Effective work at this level of a child's ecology requires a knowledge of these agencies and the services they provide, awareness of eligibility criteria, and the ability to coordinate and negotiate among various programs.

At the program level, early intervention professionals must work with specialists from multiple disciplines to design and implement a comprehensive and individualized program of services. This requires not only the ability to work with other adults and to negotiate roles and relationships but also an understanding of the philosophical models and working assumptions that form the basis for the prevailing assessment strategies and treatment models for each profession.

At the child level, professionals must provide a coherent set of integrated services that is consistent with the way the infant, toddler, or preschooler makes sense of his or her environment. It has been suggested that traditional models of providing special education and therapy, in which the professional works individually with the child away from peers and out of the context of play activities, tend to segment the child's experiences in an artificial fashion not likely to produce generalized learning (e.g., Giangreco et al., 1989). It is argued that an approach more appropriate to the young child's development is one in which special education and therapeutic activities are integrated more naturally into ongoing activities and routines. However, a recent study by McWilliam and Bailey (in press) found variability in the extent to which early intervention team members endorsed integrated practices. Early childhood special educators were most likely to endorse integrated options for treatment, whereas physical therapists were significantly more likely to endorse more traditional models.

Each of these roles -- community coordination, interdisciplinary collaboration, and integrated treatment -- requires training and experiences that are not typically included in personnel preparation programs (Bailey, Simeonsson, Yoder, & Huntington, 1990). Rather, students focus almost exclusively on the treatment of the child, using the techniques and equipment of a particular discipline, defining the problem from the individual discipline's perspective, being supervised only by licensed specialists from within that discipline, and providing individual interventions justified on the basis of the need for highly specialized treatments unencumbered by the trappings and confusion of the daily routine in a child care program.

3   Some Future Directions in Personnel Preparation

As may be evident from the above discussion, it is this author's opinion that traditional personnel preparation programs are organized in ways that are inconsistent with the most basic and important trends within early intervention. This statement is especially true of training programs in the allied health professions: occupational therapy, physical therapy, and speech and language pathology. Furthermore, I would like to argue that this problem will not be solved by the mere addition of new coursework or the revision of old coursework. Rather, it will require a fundamental restructuring of training programs so that their organizational framework is consistent with the values, research, and applied knowledge in early intervention. In the remainder of this paper, I take the liberty of suggesting four strategies by which this goal might be achieved.

3.1 Building a Philosophical Value Base in Training

The changes in our field described above reflect the value-based nature of early intervention activities. The very existence of early intervention is, of course, based on the assumption that every individual has value and worth as a human being. Although data are being examined constantly to determine the effects of early intervention, it is often justified as a basic human right that has evolved from our sociocultural value systems. For example, Dokecki (1983) argued that intervention is justified by the right of individuals and families to achieve their potential. A logical extension of this argument suggests that specific models or frameworks within which early intervention is conducted also emanate from strongly held values. Although data exist to support family-centered practices, mainstreaming, and integrated service delivery, in reality, each is firmly grounded in strong beliefs about what is morally or ethically right. For example, the family-centered movement argues that families have the right to exert strong influence in determining the nature and extent of services provided for their child, that families deserve support because of the unique challenges of rearing a child with a disability, and that early intervention practices should enable and empower families (Dunst et al., 1988). The mainstreaming movement argues that children have a right to live life as normally as possible, to associate with normally developing peers, to participate in normal environments, and to be fully included in the lives of their families. The integrated services movement values professional collaboration, coordinated service delivery, and the provision of specialized services in a fashion that is as normal as possible.

Recognizing the value basis of the fundamental shifts in early intervention practice bears several implications for personnel preparation. *First*, we must recognize the important roles that values play in shaping practices and we must help students and professionals discriminate knowledge based on empirical research, knowledge based on the "accumulated wisdom of practice," and knowledge based on moral or ethical principles (Shulman, 1986, p. 11). A critical part of this process is for students to examine their own strongly held values and determine the extent to which those values are consistent with those held by families and other professionals. *Second*, students must come to realize that some values are universally held, whereas others are specific to individual families or cultures. Professionals cannot assume that a particular value is endorsed by an individual family, thus emphasizing the importance of developing an individualized understanding of each family's resources, priorities, and concerns. Furthermore, professionals cannot assume that families will endorse the same values held by professionals. For example, Harry (1992) suggests that culture and cultural values can result in conflicts between professionals and parents over the meanings of disability, concepts of family structure and identity, parenting style, communication styles, views of appropriate professional roles, and ultimately over the basic goals of early intervention. *Third*, students need a framework for understanding and responding to situations in which their values differ from those held by parents or other professionals. For example, Kaiser and Hemmeter (1989), drawing on a framework proposed by Dokecki (1983), suggest that intervention practices should be judged on the extent to which they (a) enhance community participation by children with disabilities and their families, (b) strengthen the family, (c) enable parents to do their jobs well, (d) benefit both the child and the family, and (e) protect child and family rights. *Finally*, students must realize the counterproductive effects of trying to impose a set of values on a family. As Aponte (1985) suggests, the parent-professional relationship is a constant negotiation of values. However, ultimately, the professional must accept that, with the exception of cases of abuse or neglect, families have a right to the values they hold.

I realize that the insertion of values into a training program has its pitfalls. Values continue to emerge and be refined over time. The prevailing values and philosophies of the 1990s are different from those of the 1970s. Some professionals, especially those in the allied health professions, are less likely to endorse the values embedded in family-centered care, inclusion, and integrated service delivery (Bailey et al., 1991; Johns & Harvey, 1993; McWilliam & Bailey, in press), resulting in fundamental discrepancies between the value base and goals of professionals from different disciplines, all of whom work in early intervention. Values can often clash with research, especially if data are lacking to support a particular value orientation. Furthermore, if we assume that parents have a right to their own value system, then we must also ask ourselves if students and professionals have the right to hold and express their own values, even if they differ from the prevailing zeitgeist. Despite these dangers, a discussion of values is unavoidable, because values form the basis of so much of what we have come to define as early intervention. By explicitly acknowledging this fact and discussing relevant principles, guidelines, and strategies, professionals can be better prepared to handle the conflicts that inevitably will occur.

3.2 An Infusion Model for Underlying Principles

In test construction, *internal consistency* refers to the extent to which the items on a given measure all assess the same construct. In personnel preparation, internal consistency refers to the extent to which the training program reinforces certain basic messages throughout the coursework and experiences provided. Internal consistency is essential, because it serves to reinforce key concepts and shows students how those concepts can be applied across a variety of professional activities. It is especially important in the case of principles, such as those discussed in this paper, that are assumed to be fundamental and that permeate virtually every professional endeavor.

Our experience suggests that information related to families, inclusion, and integrated services often receives inadequate attention in most training programs, with the likely exception of early childhood special education. When it is provided, the information is likely to be compartmentalized and isolated. For example, students may take a course on working with families, but it is offered at the end of the program after the "essential" coursework is completed. Family-centered principles are not integrated into other coursework, and students rarely have opportunities to interact with families in a significant and ongoing fashion. Or students may have a module on the importance of a team and some information about team process, yet the assessment course describes only the assessment procedures conducted by the student's own discipline. The result of isolated and fragmented presentation of concepts is that students quite likely fail to grasp the extent to which these concepts lie at the heart of effective practice. More fundamentally, they quite likely will graduate with a sense of professional identity that does not incorporate those concepts or, in many cases, may actually conflict with those concepts. For example, in our own interdisciplinary course on working with families, we have had many students tell us that the principles and practices regarding family empowerment and decision-making authority emphasized in the course differ from the professional-as-expert model generally advocated within their particular department.

Our surveys of preservice training programs found that most colleges and universities were not able to establish new courses to address the topics of families, inclusion, and integrated services. Although we feel that a focused course can provide important information, an alternative approach is an infusion model in which this information is embedded throughout existing courses. Thus, faculty from our institute developed guidelines for infusing information about family-centered practices in speech language pathology (Crais, 1991), occupational therapy (Hanft et al., 1992), and physical therapy (Sparling, 1992). For example, Crais' (1992) curriculum is based on infusing family-centered principles into the child diagnostics course. Several modules related to families and the child assessment process were developed, and key principles related to the inclusion of families in this process were embedded throughout the course. Such a model ensures that students receive a consistent message across multiple courses and settings regarding the importance of a family-centered support model.

3.3 Promoting Interdisciplinary Training

Despite the fact that early intervention legislation in the United States requires that personnel preparation systems include interdisciplinary training, the typical student in almost every discipline related to early intervention spends most of his or her higher education experience interacting with faculty, fellow students, and practitioners who share similar clinical and educational experiences, focus on similar problems, and to some extent hold similar values. Not only is training in interdisciplinary processes limited, but students rarely have opportunities to interact with students and professionals from other disciplines or to read journals or books published in other disciplines. In some respects, this isolated training is appropriate. Students must gain the specialized expertise offered by their discipline, and they must develop a personal and professional identity that is consistent with the norms, practices, and ethics within that discipline. An exclusive focus on within-discipline training, however, comes at a high cost when professionals are expected to interact with each other in a truly interdisciplinary fashion.

A continuum of options exists for enhancing interdisciplinary preparation. At the level of minimum exposure, students may read about other disciplines or have a faculty member provide a lecture about the interdisciplinary process and the primary roles, training, and assumptions of other disciplines. Faculty or practitioners from other disciplines could provide guest lectures and students could see videotapes reflecting typical practices and procedures of other disciplines. Students usually are allowed to take one or two elective courses during their required period of study, and sometimes they will choose to take a course in another department or program. These options provide an important set of basic information for students and should be encouraged. However, they are likely to be insufficient for interdisciplinary practice. Furthermore, because the information is often isolated and decontextualized, students fail to realize that team functioning is an integral part of professional practice. Isolated training also deprives students of opportunities to develop collegial support from peers who view disability from a variety of perspectives (Fenichel & Eggbeer, 1991). At least three options should be considered for expanding interdisciplinary support for students.

The first such option is to offer an interdisciplinary course that is likely to draw students from multiple disciplines. Although it is possible that such a course could have the interdisciplinary team as its primary focus, this could be of limited success if the interdisciplinary process is studied as an isolated phenomenon. We have had success offering an interdisciplinary graduate course on working with families (Winton, 1991). Typically, the course has drawn students from six to eight disciplines. The focus on working with families provides a natural context for understanding how different professions approach families, discussing the implications of different perspectives, and developing more of a shared view of appropriate family practices. Factors that have made the course a success include (a) involving faculty from each discipline in initial course development; (b) using parents as co-teachers and consultants in the class; (c) focusing on applied issues in service delivery; (d) allowing extensive time for discussion of issues; (e) establishing a requirement or strong recommendations for students to elect to take the course; and (f) working with other departments to schedule the course at a time that does not conflict with required courses or clinical experiences. The initial development of the course was completed by an interdisciplinary faculty through a grant supporting a research institute on personnel preparation. Once the course was developed and implemented for several semesters, it became a standard part of a master's degree program in early intervention offered by the university's school of education and a birth-to-three master's program in speech and hearing sciences with a continuing commitment to broad-based inclusion of students from other disciplines. Similar courses could be developed in areas such as consultation or assessment.

A second strategy focuses on the clinical or practicum experiences required of each student (Rowan et al., 1990). Traditionally, these have focused almost exclusively on the specialized preparation of students for their own discipline, with supervision limited to a professional with disciplinary licensure or certification. Although this practice will undoubtedly continue of necessity, it is critical that students have opportunities to work in interdisciplinary settings prior to graduation. Only in such an environment can the prospective professional get "hands-on" experience related to interdisciplinary processes and see how an experienced professional from his or her own discipline functions in such a context.

A third and more radical strategy involves coordinating training programs for the purpose of establishing a new track or, at the greatest extreme, combining programs to create a new single effort. Coordination of training programs is being explored at several US colleges and universities. Typically, this involves establishing an early intervention track for students in several disciplines. Each discipline is responsible for teaching critical disciplinary content to their own students, but several courses form a common core taken by all students in the track, regardless of discipline. These programs have received initial funding through grants from the U.S. Department of Education. This is a relatively recent phenomenon, so it will be interesting to see if such collaboration becomes institutionalized in the absence of federal funding.

In addition, some effort is being invested in the possible merger of regular early childhood education and early childhood special education (Miller, 1992; Stayton & Miller, 1993). Stimulated primarily by the inclusion movement, this merger is based on the assumption that within the next decade, most early childhood settings will be integrated, serving children with and without disabilities. Also, some states such as North Carolina have replaced existing teaching certificates with a combined certificate for both regular and special early childhood education. Obviously this is a major step that requires universities to make a formal commitment to integrated training. Although some concern could be raised that such a move weakens both disciplines, obvious benefits could apply to all children.

3.4 Developing Problem-Solving Skills Through Case Studies

The complex situations described above point to the need for training that extends beyond knowledge acquisition and skill application. Professionals frequently find themselves in positions in which they "confront particular situations or problems, whether theoretical, practical, or moral, where principles collide and no simple solution is possible" (Shulman, 1986, p. 13). These situations require strategic decision-making skills, skills that are not typically learned through didactic instruction in the classroom. Unfortunately, the didactic classroom instruction and specialized clinical training that characterize much of our higher education experiences are likely to be insufficient preparation for these situations. What is needed is a real or simulated context in which students have the opportunity to explore the costs and benefits of decision-making options, with the benefit of feedback from others.

The case method of instruction offers one strategy by which students can be prepared more adequately to deal with complex situations such as when parents and professionals disagree over the best course of action. Case method instruction is a discussion-oriented procedure that emphasizes decision-making and problem-solving, use of real-life situations, and active student participation in the learning process (McWilliam, 1992; McWilliam & Bailey, 1993). Widely used in schools of business, law, and medicine, the case method approach assumes that professional knowledge must be embedded within the context of problem-solving and decision-making. Case discussion encompasses the majority of classroom discussion. Realistic cases are selected, ones that are detailed, thought-provoking, and require decision-making. The effectiveness of the discussion depends upon the competence of the discussion leader, who uses questions to guide the discussion, but allows the participants to carry it. The leader may play a variety of roles, but must encourage the participants to become actively involved in the discussion, prompt consideration of a variety of options, and, at times, challenge participants.

Case method strategies have not been used widely in early intervention training programs, but have the real benefit of helping students see how principles and guidelines can be applied in the world of work. Especially in the areas of working with families, inclusion, and integrated services, they can provide situations in which students can explore options for services in a relatively safe fashion. Some students feel some initial frustration with the case method because it does not meet traditional expectations for what constitutes classroom instruction. The method means that students must be prepared and must participate actively in the class discussion, exposing not only their knowledge about a given situation but also their feelings about the participants and their values and expectations regarding the problem being discussed. Case studies are especially important in interdisciplinary contexts, because they provide concrete situations in which students apply their own disciplinary perspectives but also have the opportunity to see how students from other disciplines would approach the situation.

4 Summary

Although many efforts are currently under way to improve personnel preparation programs, three fundamental movements within early intervention -- family centered services, inclusion, and integrated services -- challenge current programs and prompt a reflection about the nature and purpose of both early intervention and professional preparation. Each movement bears significant implications for professional practice, and if implemented to the fullest, each would result in major changes in the way professionals go about their work. To some extent, each represents a rethinking of the ultimate goals of early intervention. Because of the inherent value structure underlying each of these movements, I have argued here that significant changes are warranted in training programs if the goals embedded within each of these movements are to be realized: making explicit the value base underlying early intervention, infusing key concepts throughout the training experience, promoting interdisciplinary training, and engaging students in frequent problem-solving activities. In the short term, inservice education activities are needed to help practicing professionals incorporate family-centered services, inclusion, and integrated services into their work. If these practices are to become institutionalized over the long term, however, preservice programs must take steps to insure that students develop a professional identity that is consistent with the philosophical value base that underlies early intervention today.

Note

I would like to express my appreciation to Virginia Buysse, Robin McWilliam, and Pam Winton, who provided feedback on an earlier version of this manuscript.

References

Aponte, H. (1985). The negotiation of values in therapy. *Family Process, 24*, 323-338.
ASHA Committee on Language Subcommittee on Speech-Language Pathology Service Delivery with Infants and Toddlers (1989). Communication-based services for infants, toddlers, and their families. *ASHA, 31*, 32-34.
Bailey, D. B. (1987). Collaborative goal-setting with families: Resolving differences in values and priorities for service. *Topics in Early Childhood Special Education, 7*(2), 59-71.
Bailey, D. B. (1989). Issues and directions in preparing professionals to work with young handicapped children and their families. In J. J. Gallagher, P. L. Trohanis, & R. M. Clifford (Eds.), *Policy implementation and P.L. 99-457* (pp. 97-132). Baltimore, MD: Paul H. Brookes.
Bailey, D. B. (1992). The ecology of early intervention. In D. B Bailey & M. Wolery (Eds.), *Teaching infants and preschoolers with disabilities* (2nd ed.) (pp. 63-94). Columbus, OH: MacMillan.
Bailey, D. B., Buysse, V., Edmondson, R., & Smith, T. (1992). Creating family-centered services in early intervention: Perceptions of professionals in four states. *Exceptional Children, 58*, 298-309.

Bailey, D. B., Palsha, S. A., & Huntington, G. S. (1990). Preservice preparation of special educators to work with infants and their families: Current status and training needs. *Journal of Early Intervention, 14*, 43-54.

Bailey, D. B., Palsha, S. A., & Simeonsson, R. J. (1991). Professional skills, concerns and perceived importance of work with families in early intervention. *Exceptional Children, 58*, 156-165.

Bailey, D. B., Simeonsson, R. J., Yoder, D. E., & Huntington, G. S. (1990). Preparing professionals to serve infants and toddlers with handicaps and their families: An integrative analysis across eight disciplines. *Exceptional Children, 57*, 26-35.

Brown, J., & Ritchie, J. A. (1990). Nurses' perceptions of parent and nurse roles in caring for hospitalized children. *Children's Health Care, 19*, 28-36.

Buysse, V., & Bailey, D. B. (1993). Behavioral and developmental outcomes in young children with disabilities in integrated and segregated settings: A review of comparative studies. *Journal of Special Education, 26*, 434-461.

Buysse, V., & Wesley, P. (in press). The identity crisis in early childhood special education: A call for professional role clarification. *Topics in Early Childhood Special Education*.

Coleman, P. P., Buysse, V., Scalise-Smith, D. L., & Schulte, A. C. (1991). Consultation: Applications to early intervention. *Infants and Young Children, 4*(2), 41-46.

Crais, E. (1991). *A practical guide to embedding family-centered content into existing speech-language pathology coursework*. Chapel Hill, NC: Frank Porter Graham Child Development Center, University of North Carolina at Chapel Hill.

Dokecki, P. R. (1983). The place of values in the world of psychology and public policy. *Peabody Journal of Education, 60*(3), 108-125.

Dunst, C. J. (1985). Rethinking early intervention. *Analysis and Intervention in Developmental Disabilities, 5*, 165-201.

Dunst, C. J., Trivette, C. M., & Deal, A. G. (1988). *Enabling and empowering families: Principles and guidelines for practice*. Cambridge, MA: Brookline Books.

Fenichel, E. S., & Eggbeer, L. (1991). Preparing practitioners to work with infants, toddlers, and their families: Four elements of training. *Infants and Young Children, 4*(2), 56-62.

Grangreco, M.F., York, F., & Rainforth, B. (1989). Providing related services to learners with severe handicaps in educational settings: Pursuing the least restrictive option. *Pediatric Physical Therapy, 1*, 55-63.

Hanft, B., Humphry, R., Cahill, M., & Swenson-Miller, K. (1992). *Working with families: A curriculum guide for pediatric occupational therapists*. Chapel Hill, NC: Frank Porter Graham Child Development Center, University of North Carolina at Chapel Hill.

Hanson, M. J., & Lovett, D. (1992). Personnel preparation for early interventionists: A cross-disciplinary survey. *Journal of Early Intervention, 16*, 123-135.

Harry, B. (1992). Developing cultural self-awareness: The first step in values clarification for early interventionists. *Topics in Early Childhood Special Education, 12*(3), 333-350.

Johns, N., & Harvey, C. (1993). Training for work with parents: Strategies for engaging practitioners who are uninterested or resistant. *Infants and Young Children, 5*(4), 52-57.

Kaiser, A. P., & Hemmeter, M. L. (1989). Value-based approaches to family intervention. *Topics in Early Childhood Special Education, 8*(4), 72-86.

Mahoney, G., & O'Sullivan, P. (1990). Early intervention practices with families of children with handicaps. *Mental Retardation, 28*, 169-176.

McCollum, J., McLean, M., McCartan, K., & Kaiser, C. (1989). Recommendations for certification of early childhood special educators. *Journal of Early Intervention, 13*, 195-211.

McWilliam, P. J. (1992). The case method of instruction: Teaching application and problem-solving skills to early interventionists. *Journal of Early Intervention, 16*, 360-373.

McWilliam, P. J., & Bailey, D. B. (Eds.). (1993). *Working together with families and children: Case studies in early intervention.* Baltimore, MA: Paul H. Brookes.

McWilliam, R. A., & Bailey, D. B. (in press). Predictors of service delivery models in center-based early intervention. *Exceptional Children.*

Miller, P. S. (1992). Early childhood intervention and education: The urgency of professional unification. *Topics in Early Childhood Special Education, 11*(4) 39-52.

Rowan, L. E., Thorp, E. K., & McCollum. J. A. (1990). An interdisciplinary practicum to foster infant-family and teaching competencies in speech-language pathologists. *Infants and Young Children, 3*(2), 58-66.

Rushton, C. H. (1990). Family-centered care in the critical care setting: Myth or reality? *Children's Health Care, 19*(2), 68-77.

Shulman, L. S. (1986). Those who understand: Knowledge growth in teaching. *Educational Researcher, 15*(2), 4-14.

Sparling, J. (1992). *A practical guide to embedding family-centered content into existing physical therapy coursework.* Chapel Hill, NC: Frank Porter Graham Child Development Center, University of North Carolina at Chapel Hill.

Stayton, V. D., & Miller, P. S. (1993). Combining general and special early childhood education standards in personnel preparation programs: Experiences from two states. *Topics in Early Childhood Special Education, 13*, 372-387.

Winton, P. J. (1991). *Working with families in early intervention: Interdisciplinary perspectives.* Chapel Hill, NC: Frank Porter Graham Child Development Center, University of North Carolina at Chapel Hill.

Wolfensberger, W. (1972). *The principle of normalization in human services.* Toronto: National Institute on Mental Retardation.

Subject Index

The index is compiled according to content terms rather than individual words. It only includes terms that are covered by at least a few sentences in the text. As a result of this categorization according to content, the exact term in the index may be represented by a synonym in the text, for example, "integration" in the index and "mainstreaming" in the text.

The index has been compiled both alphabetically and in content clusters. The alphabetical index also gives cross-references to the clustered index. Here are some examples:

(1) action-theoretical approach (in) play* *472-474, 477-478* means that the term "action-theoretical approach" is listed with further terms under the heading "play" (marked with an asterisk) in the clustered index.

(2) assessment issues* (and) intervention methods* *297-326* means that the two headings are linked together. Further terms are entered under both headings in the clustered index.

In the clustered index, headings are listed alphabetically. Each heading is accompanied by related terms or cross-references to other headings.

Alphabetical Subject Index

action-theoretical approach (in) play*
  472-474, 477-478
assessment issues* (and) intervention
  methods* *297-326*
assessment methods* (and) developmentally retarded* children *151-152*
assessment methods* (and) social competence* *429-433*
age dependence (in) developmental outcome* *95- 98*
autistic children* (in) children* *395-
  410*
autistic children* (and) intervention
  methods* *397-402*

barriers (in) intervention methods*
  301-303
basic research (in) program-process
  evaluation* *274-275*

behavior therapy* (and) intervention
  methods* *449-464*
biological (pre-, perinatal) factors (in)
  risk factors* *93-95, 147, 149-150,
  211-212*

characteristics of play (in) play* *465-
  466, 468, 477-478*
characteristics of child (in) family*
  200-204, 232-251
characteristics of families (in) family*
  *168, 189, 195, 200, 204-207, 215-
  224, 226, 232-251, 389-390, 419-420*
cerebral palsy (in) children* *93, 98*
communication problems (in) autistic
  children* *395-397*
community-based programs (in) trends*
  (USA) *188, 297, 483-484*
components (in) social network* *168,
  228-230*

Clustered Subject Index

Prevention and Intervention in Childhood and Adolescence

WALTER DE GRUYTER · BERLIN · NEW YORK
Genthiner Strasse 13, D-10785 Berlin, Tel. (030)26005-161, Fax: (030) 26005-222
200 Saw Mill River Road, Hawthorne, N. Y. 10532, Tel. (914)747-0110, Fax (914)747-1326

Prevention and Intervention in Childhood and Adolescence

Vol. 13
Meeus, Wim/de Goede, Martijn/Kox, Willem/Hurrelmann, Klaus (Editors)
Adolescence, Careers, and Culture
Interdisciplinary, Longitudinal, and Cross-Cultural Studies
1993. 24 × 17 cm. 428 pages. **Cloth.** ISBN 3-11-013679-1

Vol. 12
Otto, Hans-Uwe/Flösser, Gaby (Editors)
How to Organize Prevention
Political, Organizational, and Professional Challenges
to Social Services
1992. 24 × 17 cm. XVI, 424 pages. **Cloth.** ISBN 3-11-013536-1

Vol. 11
Albrecht, Günter/Otto, Hans-Uwe (Editors)
Social Prevention and the Social Sciences
Theoretical Controversies, Research Problems,
and Evaluation Strategies
In cooperation with Karin Böllert and Susanne Karstedt-Henke
1991. 24 × 17 cm. XII, 638 pages. **Cloth.** ISBN 3-11-012387-8

Vol. 10
Otto, Hans-Uwe
Sozialarbeit zwischen Routine und Innovation
Professionelles Handeln in Sozialadministrationen
In cooperation with Karin Böllert, Horst Brönstrup, Gaby Flösser,
Gabriele Hard, Ann Wellinger
1991. 24 × 17 cm. IX, 204 pages. **Cloth.** ISBN 3-11-012285-5

WALTER DE GRUYTER · BERLIN · NEW YORK
Genthiner Strasse 13,   D-10785 Berlin,   Tel. (030)26005-161,   Fax: (030) 26005-222
200 Saw Mill River Road, Hawthorne, N.Y. 10532, Tel. (914)747-0110, Fax (914)747-1326